PRAISE FOR
NEVER-ENDING PRESENT

"Reading this was so painful, and yet there are great, funny stories in here. The more you knew Downie, the greater impact this story has. It's not a normal read. It's an amazing read."

—Terry David Mulligan, *Mulligan Stew*

"I think it's important for storytellers to tell stories about storytellers. This book is so personal, so meaningful, so beautiful, written with passion and commitment. Narrating the audiobook was particularly emotional; I had to stop myself from crying many times. The Hip have done a masterful job telling us their story, and it's deeply important for their friends and fans to do the same. It's one of the ways we celebrate."

—George Stroumboulopoulos, *The Strombo Show*,
Audible audiobook narrator

"This excellent book will turn a hipster into a Hip fan as the author skilfully reveals true artists who were rightfully rewarded for their talent and vision."

—Moe Berg, lead singer of The Pursuit of Happiness

"With both a critic's rigour and a fan's fervour, it's a book fully worthy of its beloved subjects' unique place in the Canadian firmament."

—*Montreal Gazette*

"Barclay combines his admiration of the band with his knowledge of the music industry to make a clever, touching and very informative book that may well be the definitive work on an important piece of Canadian pop culture." —*Publishers Weekly*, starred review

"Barclay's writing about [the final tour] is transcendental. His account of watching the final performance in the band's hometown is emotionally devastating." —*Quill & Quire*

"An immensely pleasurable read, full of info and lyrical insight I had never seen before. This is a monumental, definitive chronicle of the band."

—Stephen Dame, HipMuseum.com

"A treasure trove of information that will help in appreciating the beautiful music and lyrical genius of one of Canada's best-kept secrets."

—*Weekly Standard*

"*The Never-Ending Present* climaxes with that exclamation mark, that night in August 2016 . . . It helps to explain why an event that had every reason to seem sad and funereal instead ended up indeed feeling like 'a national celebration.'" —*Literary Review of Canada*

"The definitive Tragically Hip bible . . . Barclay weaves together reportage and interviews with the band and their family members, friends and contemporaries to demystify the Hip's transcendent reputation as the sound of a nation." —*Toronto Life*

The
NEVER-ENDING PRESENT

the Story of
GORD
DOWNIE
and **THE**
TRAGICALLY
HIP

Michael Barclay

Library and Archives Canada
Cataloguing in Publication

Barclay, Michael, 1971 , author
The never-ending present : the story of Gord
Downie and the Tragically Hip / Michael Barclay.

Issued in print and electronic formats.
ISBN 978-1-77041-469-3 (softcover)
ISBN 978-1-77041-436-5 (hardcover)
ISBN 978-1-77305-207-6 (PDF)
ISBN 978-1-77305-206-9 (EPUB)

1. Tragically Hip (Musical group).
2. Downie, Gordon, 1964–2017.
3. Rock musicians—Canada—Biography.
I. Title.

ML421.T765B23 2019   782.42166092'2
                            C2018-905300-3

Editor for the press: Michael Holmes
Cover design: David A. Gee
Cover images: ZUMA Press, Inc./Alamy
Author photo: Liz Sullivan

The publication of *The Never-Ending Present* has been generously supported by the Canada Council for the Arts which last year invested $153 million to bring the arts to Canadians throughout the country and is funded in part by the Government of Canada. *Nous remercions le Conseil des arts du Canada de son soutien. L'an dernier, le Conseil a investi 153 millions de dollars pour mettre de l'art dans la vie des Canadiennes et des Canadiens de tout le pays. Ce livre est financé en partie par le gouvernement du Canada.* We acknowledge the support of the Ontario Arts Council (OAC), an agency of the Government of Ontario, which last year funded 1,737 individual artists and 1,095 organizations in 223 communities across Ontario for a total of $52.1 million. We also acknowledge the contribution of the Government of Ontario through the Ontario Book Publishing Tax Credit, and through Ontario Creates for the marketing of this book.

PRINTED AND BOUND IN CANADA BY FRIESENS   5 4 3 2 1

Dedicated to all the parents, spouses, siblings, children, teachers and loved ones who enable creative people to do the work they have to do. We are all richer for having you in our lives.

Half of this book is a chronological history of the Tragically Hip's career, which ended in 2017 with the death of Gord Downie. Those chapters are written in the past tense.

The other half, appearing between the chronological chapters, extrapolates on various themes throughout the band's 32-year career, quoting the band's peers and other observers speaking in 2016–17. Those chapters are situated in the present tense.

The *Secret Path* chapter, about the work Gord Downie considered to be the most important of his life, spans the years 2012–17, overlapping with four other chapters set in that time frame.

All chapters are written in a way that they can be read in isolation: you are invited to dip into *The Never-Ending Present* in whatever order you like.

PREFACE

OVERHEARD BACKSTAGE AT a Tragically Hip show in the 2000s: *"Don't you go write a book about us!"*

In the 2012 film *Bobcaygeon*, an uberfan named Wesley Crawford gestures to an empty spot on his bookshelf—stacked mostly with tomes about the Rolling Stones—and says, "The Hip have to make a book. There is no book on the Tragically Hip, other than Gord Downie's poetry. I need to put a book in that spot." Wesley, here is your book.

The main reason why there has been no book about the Tragically Hip is because the band didn't want one. A book ossifies its subject matter, providing a punctuation mark—namely a period—that implies whatever comes after its publication is less important than what preceded it. The Hip never viewed their career this way. They were always about the next album, the next tour. Don't look back, Bob Dylan would say. Do your impression of the never-ending present, Gord Downie would say.

"It is probably a good thing that little is written about writers and artists in Canada while they are alive," wrote novelist Hugh MacLennan in 1954, eulogizing his late wife, Dorothy Duncan, a writer. "This peculiar

Canadian attitude is fundamentally healthy, for it leaves them free to do their work and to tell and paint the truth as they see it. But it is a bad thing for the country that they are almost never written about at all, not even after they are dead, for it is only through its creative ones that a nation acquires a personality and the right to stand in history."

The members of the Tragically Hip are intensely private people who prefer to control their own narrative. They always hated talking to the press. They did not like most things written about them, or even covers of their songs. Downie in particular didn't like revealing what was behind the curtain, or even taking a peek for himself; during a 2012 CBC Radio interview, he dismissed the wildly popular autobiography of one of his rock'n'roll heroes, Keith Richards, for blowing the mystique. They read their reviews; they held some grudges. They were invited to participate in this project; they declined. Understandable: 2017 was an intensely emotional time for everyone in the Hip camp, although guitarist Rob Baker did give several interviews during that calendar year. "Anyone can write whatever they want to write," he told the *Toronto Sun* on October 17, 2017. "That's fine with me. It's just not our story as we would tell it. I have no interest in a chronological history of the band or talking about who influenced us and what our influence on others might be. It's irrelevant . . . Never let the truth get in the way of a good story." Two months later, the band declined a request to review a fact-checking document for this book.

The few times the Hip allowed themselves to be documented in film—1992's *Full Fledged Vanity*, 1993's *Heksenketel*, 2012's *Bobcaygeon*—featured precious little live footage and next to no valuable interviews. *Heksenketel* spent more time talking to the band's bus driver and the stage crew than it did the band members themselves. *Bobcaygeon* was primarily a documentary about some of the Hip's biggest fans, not the story of the Hip. Thankfully, 2005's *That Night in Toronto* was a valuable live document, and 2017's brilliant *Long Time Running* showed the band members at their most forthcoming and vulnerable. None of those films told the story fully and completely.

The story of the Tragically Hip does not belong only to the band. As was abundantly evident in the summer of 2016, the story of the Tragically Hip is the story of Canadian music: the people who make it, the people who make it happen, and the fans who celebrate it every day. Maybe it's even the story of Canadian culture itself, from Northrop Frye to Drake, from Jacques Cartier to Justin Trudeau, and everything in between.

The story of the Tragically Hip does not belong to one person, either. Despite the prominence of Gord Downie's name in the subtitle, this is a book about the Tragically Hip. They never once billed themselves as Gord Downie and the Tragically Hip, even if that's the way they were consistently portrayed in the media, even if fans have tattoos of Downie's face but not Gord Sinclair's. Celebrity culture always focuses on the singer. To the chagrin of most musicians who don't front a band, that will never change. Some singers replace their entire band, keep the name and have few fans notice. This was not a group of sidemen, however. This was a democratic band who made all decisions together—granted, some of those decisions were driven by Downie, who possessed the strong will and stubbornness found in all leaders. It was that charisma and strength that defined the final two years of his life, when Downie decided to shine a light on a dark corner of Canadian history with his *Secret Path* project. In doing so, he prompted a reckoning among white Canadians about their country's shameful treatment of Indigenous people. For that and for his courage in battling brain cancer in a very public way, Downie became more famous than he'd ever been; even Canadians who never even cared for the Tragically Hip were now very aware of who the singer was and what he stood for. But why did we care about this man in the first place? The story of Gord Downie is by no means confined to 2016–17, even if that's how he will now be remembered.

In *Long Time Running*, Rob Baker says, of the band's historical relationship with their singer, "We always knew there was a big danger that the focus would become Gord, Gord, Gord. In a weird way, it came to pass with this [final] tour because it was unavoidable. Because of the situation, the focus was very much on Gord. That trumps the democracy." In both 2016 and 2017, it was Gord Downie, not the Tragically Hip, who was chosen as "Newsmaker of the Year" by Canadian Press.

Gord Downie put out his first solo record in 2001, a decision that did not go over well in the Hip camp. He put out six solo records in all, which is part of the reason why you will read more about Downie in this book than the other members. But after dragging them all into an open relationship, he was firm in his decision that their bond was "until death do us part." In 2010, a *Calgary Journal* writer asked him straight up: "What's keeping you with the Tragically Hip? Why not go on your own completely?" Downie's simple response: "Because I love them."

CHAPTER ONE

IN A BIG COUNTRY
BRAND NEW RENAISSANCE

*"Song is not desire, not wooing any favour
that can still be attained; song is existence."*

RAINER MARIA RILKE, "SONNET TO ORPHEUS, 3," 1921

*"Give me the making of the songs of a nation,
and I care not who makes its laws."*

ANDREW FLETCHER OF SALTOUN, 1703

IN THE BEGINNING, in the period known as Dreamtime, giants roamed the Earth, singing as they travelled far and wide, calling out the names of animals, plants, topography—"singing the world into existence." As they walked, they left words and musical notes in their footprints. These songs were then passed down through generations of human descendants. This was not mere music; this was cartography. If you knew the song, you knew where you were going. You knew how far you'd travelled by where you were in the song.

This is the creation myth of Australia's Indigenous people, a myth known outside the country via *Songlines*, a 1987 book by British travel writer Bruce Chatwin, which was enthusiastically passed around the Tragically Hip's camp in the early '90s. It's easy to see why.

"Aboriginals could not believe the country existed until they could see and sing it," wrote Chatwin. "Just as, in the Dreamtime, the country had not existed until the Ancestors sang it.

"So the land," Chatwin asked his Australian guide, "must first exist as a concept in the mind? Then it must be sung? Only then can it be said to exist?"

"True," responded the guide.

"In other words, 'to exist' is 'to be perceived'?"

"Yes."

———

Let's shake the beaver off our back. Let's get the Canadian thing out of the way right off the top. Because there is a lot more to the Tragically Hip than their passports.

The Tragically Hip are often spoken of as "Canada's band." As if there are no others. As if there were no other before. As if there will never be another. Only that last statement is definitively true, if only because there is no monoculture in popular music or in any other sphere of the splintered public imagination.

English Canada is often invisible to itself, particularly in our popular songs. For years, some considered Ian Tyson's "Four Strong Winds" an alternate national anthem because it was the only explicitly Canadian song in the popular lexicon. This is the country that didn't get around to making "O Canada" the official national anthem until 1980: 100 years after the song was written, 113 years after Confederation. Let it never be said that Canadians are a decisive people. And let it never be forgotten that the song's composer, Calixa Lavallée, fled the country as a young man to find work in America, fought as a Union soldier in the Civil War, married a Massachusetts woman, advocated that the U.S. annex Canada and died an American citizen. So there's that.

Then there's Margaret Atwood, never known to mince words, who canonized the Canadian cultural mindset in her epochal 1972 book *Survival*. Her thesis cast an inescapable shadow over Canadian literature for the next 30 years, when new voices began redefining the canon. Positing the story of a Canadian writer in the 1960s, she wrote:

> *If he was lucky enough to acquire an American or English publisher he might get some attention from the Canadian literati and thus from a more widespread audience; but in order to do that he would have to squeeze his work into shapes that were not his, prune off anything "they" might not understand, disguise himself as a fake American or Englishman. At this point he either gave up in disgust . . . and left the country and headed for*

one of the "centres of culture"—London, New York or Paris—or stayed
and tried to follow his own vision as best he might, knowing that he could
expect, at the very best, publication in a slender edition of 500 copies for
poetry and a couple of thousand for novels; at the worst, total oblivion.

For the longest time, the fate of Canadian musicians was not much different.

Many Canadians see this dilemma as unique to this country, caught between our colonial mother and our bullying big brother to the south. Yet in the 1921 novel *The Age of Innocence*, set in Manhattan's aristocratic social scene, Edith Wharton's characters are so enamoured with what they perceive as superior British and/or European culture that they look askance on anything produced in their backyard—*and these characters lived in New York City*! Likewise, in *Last Train to Memphis*, Peter Guralnick's biography of Elvis Presley, the author tells the story of how Memphis DJs were reluctant to play Presley's early singles—because they didn't think anybody local could be any good. It's a joke as old as the Bible—specifically, John 1:46: "Nazareth?!" exclaims Nathaneal, soon to be one of the first disciples, upon hearing about the new messiah making the scene. "Can anything good come from Nazareth?"

In the late 1960s, a furious Stompin' Tom Connors decided to single-handedly write a new Canadian songbook and he spent the rest of his career doing that—and only that. The CBC hired Gordon Lightfoot to write "Canadian Railroad Trilogy"—because of course they did. The Guess Who had a No. 1 smash hit with "American Woman," which is Canadian only by negation—not unlike the Tragically Hip's "Last American Exit." Joni Mitchell, Neil Young and Leonard Cohen would all occasionally nod to their native land; Bruce Cockburn did so much more often. Rush might do so only to title an instrumental ("YYZ," "Danforth and Pape"). Bryan Adams, never.

At the time the Tragically Hip released their debut EP in 1987, 20 years after the country's centennial celebrations, Canada was barely an *imaginary* presence in popular song—because precious few could be bothered to imagine it. It was time to sing this country back into existence.

The Tragically Hip were by no means alone in doing so. Andrew Cash and Charlie Angus wanted their early '80s band L'Etranger to be to Toronto's punk and new wave scene what the Clash was to England, connecting local concerns to international struggles. The Rheostatics discovered Stompin' Tom and Neil Young and started singing about hockey players and the "Canadian Dream." Spirit of the West wrote about the Expo '86 evictions and Indigenous rights, inspired by the political pop songs of the Smiths and Billy Bragg. The dawn of hip-hop in Canada, a genre as loyal to regional peculiarities as folk music, meant that Maestro Fresh Wes, Michie Mee and Dream Warriors were all identifiably Canadian when all other Top 40 pop music was not. Even Blue Rodeo didn't start specifically situating their songs in Canada until their third album, in 1990.

Fully Completely, released in 1992, is the Tragically Hip's most commercially successful album. Perhaps that was inevitable. It's their third album, and Canadians had fervently embraced the first two and flocked to the live shows: 1992 may well have been the point when they were destined to reach critical mass. It could be a coincidence—but likely not—that it's also the album where Gord Downie's writing was most explicitly Canadian.

In 1992, Canadians were engaged in a constitutional referendum. They were gearing up for a federal election that would decimate the ruling political party. Quebec separatism was again on the rise. Four years earlier, a federal election was fought on the issue of a free-trade deal with the United States; a continental deal was on the horizon. The Oka Crisis of 1990 kick-started a new awareness of Indigenous issues. Clearcuts in Clayoquot Sound were sparking massive civil disobedience. The Cold War was over. Canada was unusually interesting for a while there. Into all of that came *Fully Completely*.

"We hit the Canadian music scene at a good time, when the winds of change are blowing," said Downie in 1990, right after the Tragically Hip won a Juno for Most Promising Band. "Ten years ago we probably wouldn't have gotten away with doing what we do."

Despite endless comparisons to R.E.M. and the Rolling Stones, the Tragically Hip most resembled their immediate peers. Listen to "Another Midnight" from 1989's *Up to Here*, and, other than Downie's unmistakable voice, it's interchangeable with anything by 54.40, Skydiggers, Crash Vegas, Blue Rodeo or, later, Sarah Harmer's Weeping Tile. It's a Canadian sound.

"We were maturing as a nation, and the Hip was a huge part of that," said the Rheostatics' Dave Bidini, whose song "Saskatchewan" Downie cited as pivotal in the Tragically Hip's own approach to writing. "Gord would tell you that it was a collective, combined effort. There would have been a lot of people in the sea. But there was this wave that surged, and the Hip were in a canoe at the top of that, riding the crest."

"There was an amazing concurrence of circumstances that led to a bunch of bands starting to reflect their own lives," said Blue Rodeo's Jim Cuddy, of the Hip's ascent. For a long time in Canadian culture, "Anything we took was co-opted, and anything we created was secondary. I think [Blue Rodeo and the Tragically Hip] were lucky that we came in at a time when Canadian audiences, whether they knew it or not, were sick of that. From the get-go, the Hip really reflected their own background. When audiences saw the Hip for the first time, they thought, even subconsciously: 'Finally, our own band.'"

Because *Fully Completely* was so Canadian in its content and so massively popular in its home and native land, that led—of course—to musings about why it didn't move similar numbers in the U.S. There were myriad reasons why that didn't happen—most involving luck, timing and record company support—but Downie's lyrics being "too Canadian" was never one of them. American music fans might be myopic, but they're not the complete xenophobes they're made out to be. Midnight Oil wasn't too Australian. The Smiths weren't too British. Björk wasn't too Icelandic— and then there's Sigur Rós, who are a whole other kettle of fermented fish. Hell, think of all the random one-hit wonders from around the world: was Falco too German? Psy too Korean?

"I don't see *Fully Completely* as 'too Canadian,'" said Bruce Dickinson, the American A&R executive who signed the Tragically Hip in 1988. "I see it as a fresh viewpoint on reality. Its uniqueness separates it from other albums of its time."

Dickinson also thought Canadians routinely underestimate Americans' knowledge of Canadian culture. "On a personal level, I knew who Hugh MacLennan was," he said. "I had read Robertson Davies. Most of my high school and college friends had read Leonard Cohen's *Beautiful Losers*. The Band was successful in the U.S. The Hip have a certain level of darkness like those artists. In the U.S., *Fully Completely* sold where it was heard, and mostly that is where airplay from Canadian radio came across the border to American cars and homes. Case closed. The Hip's music can work in the U.S."

And it did. Not just in border towns like Buffalo and Detroit, but in Texas and Arizona. *Fully Completely* sold almost 100,000 copies in the U.S.— not a blockbuster by any stretch, but not insignificant, either. The reason the Tragically Hip toured the U.S. extensively during their entire career *was because they could*: they have hundreds of thousands of American fans, they played large and lovely theatres everywhere and—most important —their audiences there kept growing. But because Canadians never saw the Tragically Hip on *The Tonight Show* or in *Rolling Stone*, we liked to assume that they were our little secret, serving the paradoxically smug insecurity that persists in being a national character trait. "Sometimes," said Dickinson, the American A&R rep, "I've wondered if thoughts like that are a manifestation of unjustified, excessively debilitating self-consciousness or—worse—some feeling of unworthiness. What a crock."

The *Fully Completely* song "Courage" was dedicated to Hugh MacLennan, a brilliant writer of the 1940s and '50s whose novels, set in Canada, were internationally acclaimed. In a 1952 essay, he wrote, "If you drop a stone into the ocean, the impact is as great as if you drop it into a farmer's pond. The difference is that the ocean doesn't seem to care. It swallows the stone and rolls on. But the pond, if the stone is large enough, breaks into waves and ripples that cover its surface and are audible in every cranny along its banks." The Tragically Hip's waves and ripples were more than audible; they were a roaring flood into the idea of Canada.

Keyboardist Chris Brown toured with the Hip in 2000, when it struck him that when the band played in a town like Moncton, "It's not the cover story in the entertainment section—it's the cover of *the entire paper*. It's this cultural event and this whole identity-branding on this national level, which the band was aware of carrying. It's not like they asked for it or wore Canadian flags, but they displayed a sense of ownership of that." Sportscaster Dave Hodge said, "We adopted them more than they applied for adoption. I don't see any real concerted effort on their part to be a Canadian band other than, sure, some of the subject matter. They never said, 'Let's be the Canadian band.' It just happened that way. If I were them, I'd prefer it that way."

One fan told the *Kingston Whig-Standard* in 1995 that the Hip are "like a Molson Canadian beer commercial. They're a real Canadian hard rock kind of band." How blatantly Canadian were the Tragically Hip, though, really? It's not like they ever performed with an enormous Maple Leaf flag and a beaver logo as a backdrop—like the Guess Who did. Or with a giant replica of the CN Tower as part of their stage design—like Drake did. (Granted, the modest Kingston skyline is not as striking.) Downie might have introduced "So Hard Done By" to a Montreal audience by dedicating

*Book doesn't start w/ Downie's child hood?

it to Mordecai Richler, or occasionally arrived onstage and said, for no discernible reason, things like, "Hello and welcome. My name is Maurice Duplessis," as he did on the stage of Vancouver's Thunderbird Stadium on Canada Day, 1992. And there was always a Tragically Hip gig somewhere on Canada Day.

This was all a red (and white) herring: American and international references outnumber Canadian ones in Tragically Hip songs. (Go ahead, count 'em.) Downie never threw darts at a map of Canada for song ideas, nor did he seek to set *Heritage Minutes* to music. His subject matter was always broader than he was given credit for, but it's easier for armchair academics to latch onto songs about hockey and a "late-breaking story on the CBC"; those images were low-hanging fruit in the dense forest of Downie's imagination.

Downie is not a writer like Stompin' Tom, an artist for whom provincialism in the face of a colonial mindset was the entire point of his oeuvre. "When I mention Halifax or Edmonton in a song, I know that beers get cracked," said songwriter and Downie-disciple Joel Plaskett. "Gord's writing goes all over the place. It's rich, and you can dig deeper than what most people associate with it."

The Hip's fans were happy to literally wrap themselves in the flag. It's detailed in a biting Spirit of the West song called "Our Ambassador," about encountering such fans while touring with the Hip in the U.S. At a 2000 show at Massey Hall, the *Toronto Star* reported that "one young woman in the front row of the balcony stripped down to a bra that had a red Maple Leaf planted on the middle of each cup."

Downie was somewhat amused by all this, but insisted, "I'm not a nationalist. I started using Canadian references not just for their own sake, but because I wanted to pick up my birthright, which is this massive country full of stories." One of Downie's heroes was the poet Al Purdy, who once wrote, "There are few things I find more irritating about my own country than this so-called 'search for identity,' an identity I've never doubted having in the first place."

Dropping a few proper nouns in a song seems trivial—and it is. It's easy enough to do. There was absolutely zero reason, other than an awkward rhyme, for Downie's decision to set one of the Hip's songs in Bobcaygeon, despite the fact that there is an entire feature film dedicated to the "significance" of the band's gig there in 2011. ("A *Heritage Moment* equivalent of Roger Waters playing *The Wall* in Berlin," claimed *Maclean's*.) But proper nouns also provide signposts: signs that can seem exotic even to citizens of the same country; signs that can tweak interest in local geography and history and culture; signs that can, in fact, sing a country into existence—especially a country rendered invisible when most of its cultural icons are readily absorbed into its southern neighbour.

It wasn't that Downie elevated Canadian geography and mythology to the level of the mystical; it's that almost no one else did. This country has dozens of Gord Downies, all of whom tell Canadian stories in vivid detail, all of whom critically examine the notion of Canada itself—but none of those come close to having the broad appeal that Downie enjoyed. The only massively popular performer to do so in Downie's wake is Drake, although his lyrics suggest he's never seen Canada beyond the Greater Toronto Area.

By 2009, Downie was tired of being Captain Canada. "There's an adherence to motifs," he said. "An artist gets a couple of motifs that are easily repeatable, and people usually see if you're meeting that motif. 'They're popular because they have Canadian references'—that really scratches the itch for the patriots and nationalists in this country. But I would want no part of that. I want no part in propagating or galvanizing or burnishing some of the stupid mythology in this country. That we're this clean, pristine place, that we know [what's] best for the world, that there's nothing anyone can teach us—these types of things I want no part of, and I don't know anybody who would.

Not as good as we act like we are.

"So these things I write about I try to think are the real Canada, the Canada I know. If it *is* a thing, it's an abstract, obviously, but I wouldn't do it if I thought I was just propping up old, stupid mythology." The man who helped sing this country into existence was content to say, simply, "I think people like to hear their town mentioned, or their touchstone, or anything they can relate to."

———

Rock'n'roll was still a vital force in the 1980s and 1990s. It had been around long enough that a new band, particularly one steeped in traditions of previous generations, could have broad appeal to both baby boomers and their children. The Tragically Hip started out covering garage rock from the '60s British Invasion, so their multi-generational appeal was there from day one. When Progressive Conservative pollster Allan Gregg first signed the Hip to his music management company, Downie told the *Toronto Star* in 1990 that "he was probably thinking, 'Ah, demographics! This will appeal to yuppies.'" That the Hip appealed to multiple generations and strata of society was central to their success.

The raw, no-frills sound of the Hip's first three releases stood apart from the L.A. metal and glossy production that sucked the life out of even the best rock'n'roll bands in the 1980s (see: the Replacements). In its infancy, the Hip's music was built to win over disinterested bar patrons in Great Lakes beach towns. That made it instantly palatable to the classic rock crowd once radio signed on. Crowds got exponentially bigger between 1989 and 1992; all Hip albums released in that time would become three of only 25 Canadian records to ever sell more than a million copies domestically—six of those are by Céline Dion.

"Their brew is a totally distinct recipe," said Joel Plaskett. "What more can you ask for than when you drop the needle on something and you can instantly say, 'Oh, that's the Tragically Hip.' Even though their records are produced differently, you never think, 'Oh, it could be something else.'" The evolution from 1989's *Up to Here* to 2016's *Man Machine Poem* is remarkable. "The brilliance of the band and their legacy," said Dave Bidini, "is that they were able to transform what everybody thought of them into something nobody thought of them. That's beautiful."

The problem—if it is in fact a problem—is that the Tragically Hip were always square, at a time when rock music was being blown wide open. They were a Cornelius Krieghoff painting surrounded by Picassos and Pollocks. The Hip didn't fit in with the Seattle scene or the fractured indie underground, which was pulled in about 10 different directions at once, from the Breeders to the Beastie Boys to Sebadoh to Stereolab and everything in between. As mainstream rock got more aggressive, hip-hop was more of a cultural force, and popular music began its slide back into segregation. An immensely popular artist could now be completely unknown to half the population. For rock fans, the Tragically Hip were nowhere near as daring as Sonic Youth or Pavement or Beck—or even Neil Young in the early 1990s. Instead, they were last year's model. That's why the 1996 cross-genre pop hit "Ahead by a Century"—placed in high rotation on rock, pop and easy-listening stations—was essential to securing their legacy, and why it was the one song sung and quoted most often on the final tour in 2016.

The Hip were reluctant rock stars, suspicious of celebrity. They found it funny, more than anything—especially in 1995 when Kato Kaelin, a prosecution witness in the O.J. Simpson trial that year, showed up backstage in L.A. Filled with the delusion of cable-news celebrity, he stood outside the band's dressing room door, yelling, "I'm Kato Kaelin! I'm Kato Kaelin! I love the Tragically Hip! Don't they know who I am?!" That summer, on the band's Another Roadside Attraction tour, the Hip issued all-access backstage passes with Kaelin's face on them, which allowed peers and family to sit in the "Posers' Gallery," bleachers on the side of the stage. "Don't you know who I am?" read the text underneath his face.

"A lot of bands have their eyes on a different prize than we do," Rob Baker told *Maclean's* in 2000. "Our goal has always been to have a long career. Big hit singles and being on the covers of lots of magazines can work against you. People get tired of your mug and they get tired of hearing the same few songs. Our fans tend to be people who have been with us for a long time."

There were few decisions in the Tragically Hip's career over which they did not have direct control. Early in their career, they had the benefit of a wealthy benefactor, Allan Gregg, which insulated them from compromises to which other bands were routinely subjected. But they certainly weren't afraid of telling Gregg or anyone else to take a hike. "Most of the decisions you've seen made about that band, they are personally involved," said Dave Levinson, who worked for the Hip's management in the mid-2000s. "It's not just: 'Let the management handle it, let the record company handle it.' They protect their image, they protect the things they stand for and believe in. Which is why their integrity is unquestioned, all these years later."

The entire band valued their privacy, but Downie even more so: perhaps because of the adulation directed his way, but also because of the way he was raised. "I think I take my nana's approach," he said. "She said, 'I wouldn't go to the lobby of my building to see Frank Sinatra.'" In a 1991 profile of the Hip, a reporter from the *Kingston Whig-Standard* visited all the band members' families. The Downie residence was the only one where the Hip's gold record was nowhere to be seen; the elder Downies couldn't remember the name of his high school punk band, the Slinks. "When you have five children, it's hard to remember all the details," said his father, Edgar. "Gordie doesn't like to be the centre of attention," added Lorna, his mother.

That's an odd thing to hear about one of the most riveting performers in rock'n'roll history. In the 1980s in Ontario, there was no shortage of great frontmen: Frankie Venom of Teenage Head, Dave Robinson of UIC, Andy Maize of the Skydiggers, Dave Wall of the Bourbon Tabernacle

Choir. Downie had something different, something that seemed to chemically alter the physical space the band inhabited. Anyone who caught the Tragically Hip in 1985, playing covers at a roadhouse in Renfrew, Ontario, could tell you that. As could anyone who watched Downie command 40,000 people at outdoor appearances during the 1990s, singing songs that were summer soundtracks for an entire generation. Video clips don't do justice to the energy in the room generated by a performer who communicated more with a flick of the finger than anyone else's high kicks.

"Songs are only half-finished when they're recorded," said Downie. "You have to perform them to finish them. That's what's going on every night. The stage is the underlying question, at which you're just throwing solution after solution after solution. I've read that I have goofy stage antics and that I have rants. I do know that I'm planning on a beginning, middle and end. I'm cognizant of composition. Onstage, it all makes sense. In terms of music and dance—I love dance as an expressive form, being able to express yourself in that way."

It is Downie's words that truly set the Tragically Hip apart from every other band. His lyrics are tapestries of imagery, allusions and narratives that blur the personal, the historical and the fantastical. He sits beside Bob Dylan and post-*Graceland* Paul Simon for keeping it surreal. With Gord Downie, there are more layers to peel back than there are with his contemporaries Michael Stipe of R.E.M. or Stephen Malkmus of Pavement. Downie said he learned from, among others, Gordon Lightfoot. "As a ten-year-old kid listening to 'Sundown,' it sounded like a secret, from [the singer] to me," he said. "It blew my mind to know that a song could be so mysterious and sound so dangerous—it's a dangerous song. I think about [Lightfoot's] austerity and economy every time I put pen to paper."

Fans were enchanted by the task of building that mystery, coming up with wildly variant interpretations of Downie's lyrics. They also loved to sing them at the top of their lungs. "Standing side-stage, it was mind-blowing some nights," said Ian Blurton, whose band Change of Heart was a frequent opening act in the mid-'90s. "The sound of the crowd was so loud. I can't imagine trying to compete with 20,000 people singing every lyric back to me." Neither could backing vocalist Kate Fenner, who toured with the Hip in 2000. "The first time we played an arena," she said, "as we walked to the stage in Vancouver, the house lights went down and the sound of the crowd came up through my in-ear monitors. I jumped up and yelled, 'WHAT THE FUCK WAS THAT?!' 'That's the crowd.' 'Oh.'"

"I can't think of very many people who work as hard at songcraft as Gord does," said Steve Berlin, the saxophone player in Los Lobos who produced two Hip albums in the late '90s. "It was life or death: every syllable was important. He had—oh God, it looked like a phonebook, a binder that was literally bursting with ideas. I've worked with a lot of songwriters who, when they're stuck, they'll cobble through other ideas they have. But for Gord, it wasn't about just plugging in something he hadn't used before; everything had to be perfect."

Downie's commitment to his own writing meant he was a voracious reader of others. He's one of the rare songwriters who can claim a deep relationship with poetry. Since 2007, poet Damian Rogers has co-curated an annual confluence of writers and musicians in Toronto called the Basement Revue, in which Downie once participated; she knows both literary and musical worlds intimately. "I'm familiar with the generosity of Gord and the Tragically Hip in the world of underground music; if they love a band, they do everything they can to make that band comfortable [as an opening act], with genuine love and enthusiasm," she said. "I see that same spirit in Gord's relationship to poetry. I can't think of anyone else of our generation who is so deeply engaged in this country's poetry. Not just that he's read by poets, which he is, but also, he reads them. I can't overstate how unusual that is."

——

One unusual thread emerges from decades of press clippings and interviews about the Tragically Hip: there are no press reports of drug busts in Saskatoon, or of affairs with fellow musicians, or cocaine binges with Dan Aykroyd. No, this is a band that does the dishes.

Shortly after the Hip signed a management contract in 1986 with Allan Gregg and Jake Gold, Gregg invited the band over to his house for burgers and beer and was completely shocked by their behaviour. "As if scripted," he said, "the five of them stood up in unison, cleared off all the plates, walked over to the sink and started washing them. Rock'n'rollers are supposed to dip their cigarette butts in the plates and throw them against the wall, but they are just very, very fine young men." The same scenario took place in the office of their hometown newspaper three years later. In a 2017 interview for this book, Downie's good friend Mark Mattson chose dishwashing as a metaphor for the band's work ethic. "No matter what party you were at, no matter where you were, no matter who you were with, Gord was always the guy doing the dishes. Always! 'No, no, let me do the dishes. I'm doing the dishes.' It was always about the work. Everyone in that band is hard working, but Gord might be the epitome of hard work."

All but Downie were scions of the Kingston elite—sons of doctors, deans, judges and popular teachers. They found it as odd as anyone that they were drawn to punk music. "We summon a sense of rage, but it is rage about the music, more than anything," Downie told the *Toronto Star* in 1990. "Let's face it, when you are born to a middle-class family and raised in white-bread Kingston, Ontario, it tends to stack the deck against that kind of intensity. It involves imagination. That's where these songs come from.

"I was watching Ken Dryden's *Home Game* [CBC-TV series] on hockey," Downie continued, "and I agree with him that the best players come from small towns, usually from the middle or lower-middle class. We had no interest in becoming the big band in Toronto, which seemed to be the thing to do." Though they had a monthly gig at a dive bar in a nowhere Toronto neighbourhood, they gigged in every roadhouse in eastern and southern Ontario. "The situation of facing a different audience every night," said Downie, "that forces you to dig into your reserves, and you discover that you can thrive on intensity when it's good or survive on humour when it's not."

Guitarist Rob Baker and bassist Gord Sinclair never moved away from Kingston. Rhythm guitarist Paul Langlois spent some time in Toronto before moving back. Drummer Johnny Fay bounced back and forth between the two. Gord Downie left for the Big Smoke as soon as the band got big and never really came back. He loved Toronto. But the band itself was always Kingston, through and through. In 1991, Sinclair told the *Whig-Standard*, "We'd never be like Poison, who now say they're from Hollywood when they're from Mechanicsburg, Pennsylvania. We were playing in Pittsburgh once, and they came on TV in a restaurant where we were eating. The waitress told us she went to high school with the drummer and that everyone there hates them now for saying they're from somewhere else." That same year, some Kingstonians were outraged when the Hip were nominated in various categories at the Toronto Music Awards: Best Toronto Group, Best Toronto Bassist, etc. How dare Toronto claim the biggest thing to come out of Kingston since federal cabinet minister Flora MacDonald?

The Hip's popularity rubbed off on other Kingston acts, like Weeping Tile, but not always in the most welcome ways. Mike O'Neill of the bass-and-drums duo the Inbreds recalled meeting people after shows on tour: "They'd say, 'Where you guys from?' 'Kingston.' 'Oh yeah, you guys sound like the Hip.' 'What the fuck are you talking about? What part of us sounds like the Hip?' When we lived in Kingston, the Hip were already gone. I never saw them. When we got the call for us to play with them, that was like God calling. Total burning bush."

Kingston is a fascinating town. It's one of the oldest in Canada. It's alleged that ice hockey was born there (naturally, this is highly disputed). It was a major military centre in the War of 1812. It was the capital of the province of Canada in 1841. Queen's University opened the next year. The country's first prime minister, Sir John A. Macdonald, is from Kingston. Bryan Adams was born there, though as a military kid he grew up elsewhere. The high school where the members of the Tragically Hip met, Kingston Collegiate Vocational Institute, dates back to 1792. Its halls are haunted with history: centuries of faded photographs follow you as you stroll from one end to the other. It's exactly the kind of school where one would see "pictures of our parents' prime ministers."

[handwritten in left margin: I drive past here to get grocery Colby went here]

KCVI instilled in the Hip a simple lesson that shaped their entire career. "KCVI is one of those schools, particularly back then, that really drew from a wide variety," said Rob Baker. "You had the rich kids and you also had the people who lived in what we called the inner city, so there's a real cross-section of kids. There were different entrances. If you were from one social set, you walked in the Earl Street entrance, whereas the rich kids tended to use the Frontenac Street entrance, and the real outsiders used the Alfred Street entrance. I don't know why, but we were able to transcend those divisions and use whatever door we liked and hang out with whichever group we liked. At the university, it was the same thing. Those barriers all seemed artificial." On the night of the Hip's final show in 2016, Downie echoed this point: "Everyone is invited. Everyone is involved."

[handwritten in left margin: My school was similar → not based on class though]

As the Hip's popularity increased, hometown shows became rarer. After 1995, they refused to play the decrepit, acoustically challenged Memorial Centre, which was finally superseded in 2008 by the new K-Rock Centre— of course, it was the Hip who inaugurated the new venue. In between, there were only tiny, secret shows before a tour, with two exceptions. One was the 2004 Across the Causeway festival. The other was in 1999, when they made a surprise appearance at the Kingston Blues Fest. After headliner Duke Robillard cancelled with two days' notice, organizers asked local blues fan Dan Aykroyd to lend a hand, so he called the Tragically Hip.

[handwritten at bottom: I don't like how it shifts ↩ the timeline, confusing]

They played in front of 14,000 people who paid five dollars for a festival wristband.

Outside of Kingston, the Tragically Hip always felt like outsiders. They didn't sound like the mainstream: a February 1988 ad for Sam the Record Man shows the Hip's self-titled EP alongside INXS, Debbie Gibson, Elton John, New Order, Def Leppard and Images in Vogue. Later that year, playing the Toronto Music Awards at Massey Hall, the band didn't mingle with the other acts; they stuck to their dressing room like the shy small-town guys they were. When the band won the Entertainer of the Year Juno in 1991, Rob Baker opened their acceptance speech by saying, "We feel like Carrie on prom night."

"They were guests at the party that was this rising scene" in the late '80s, said Bidini. "They're great party guests, because they're good guys and easy to be around. But they were kind of in their own van for a long time."

A very long time, in fact: 32 years, or 30 once Paul Langlois joined in 1986. To maintain the same lineup for that long—and at that level of success—is phenomenally rare, practically unheard of in the history of rock'n'roll. How did they do it? "I've often said we're like a five-way marriage without sex," said Rob Baker in 2004, only partially joking. "Like any marriage, after 20 years, we don't talk to each other at all. We've survived by a total lack of communication. There's an intuitive thing, there's a little raising of eyebrows. There's an occasional snort or guffaw that happens, but outside of that, most of the communication is pretty intuitive. We don't sit down and analyze, we don't spend any time looking backwards. It's all about what's happening today, six months from now."

Part of the Hip's appeal was that they were recognizable. "When you went to see a show, you knew who they were," said Dave Hodge. "Each guy is interesting in his own right: interesting to look at, to talk to, interesting parents, interesting wives. To know them in 1995 is to know them in 2005 and 2015." Hugh Larkin is a superfan who met the band "20 or 30 times," by his estimation: first by hanging out by their bus behind a venue and eventually through backstage passes. "When I'd get invited to the meet-and-greets, they were super friendly," he says. "I saw when people had illness or difficulties and they'd contacted the management, and the band would always welcome this person who needed a little boost or a hug or whatever."

"All the guys knew that you can't treat some of your fans better than other fans," said sportscaster Mark Hebscher. "I remember situations after a show where there were some pretty big names waiting in line to talk to

Gord—the other guys, too, but Gord especially—and the Hip guys would never say to someone, 'Excuse me, I have to go because person X is here.' They'd always finish the conversation with the person, look them in the eye and when they felt it was the right time, they'd move on. They'd never say, 'Oh my God, there's Mark Messier!'"

If political candidates are expected to be "someone you'd have a beer with," the Hip had that down right to the denim—and the hockey jerseys. The Hip and hockey are intertwined, in ways that could only ever happen in Canada. Producer Steven Drake, from Vancouver band the Odds, recalls working with the Hip at their studio outside Kingston, where the band had cleared a spot for an ice rink on the adjacent Great Lake. "It was 11:30 at night, no moon, clear sky, stars above, skating on Lake Ontario with Gord Downie, passing the puck. I will never have a more Canadian night than that."

The Tragically Hip were Canadian in the way that internationally successful homebodies Gordon Lightfoot, Anne Murray and Bryan Adams were Canadian (Rush will always have that kimono period to answer for). "I always thought that if there was a Canadian sound, it would be the troubadour who walks onstage, and they're the same people they are onstage as they are offstage," said Baker. "I always got that sense from Neil Young and Joni Mitchell. Then there was this whole period in the '80s that we kind of reacted to, all these bands who seemed really desperate to make it in the States. We really reacted against that. We thought: no, you sing about what you know and try to be yourself. Be real, genuine."

"We're basically fairly dull and regular and ordinary," Downie once told MuchMusic, "in the hope that we may be violent and original in our work."

—— 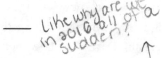 Like why are we in 2016 all of a sudden?

On that unforgettable summer night in Kingston, on August 20, 2016, the set list dipped back to the Tragically Hip's first hit single, "Blow at High Dough." It's the one that opens with the line about a movie being shot in the singer's hometown. His movie, our hometowns: Gord Downie's lyrics imbued Canada's music scene with mystery and magic. The band behind him helped bring his screenplay to life, transforming what might have been an art-house hit into a summer blockbuster, with lasting images ingrained in the collective consciousness of their homeland.

CHAPTER TWO

I CAN ONLY GIVE
YOU EVERYTHING
1984—88: BEGINNINGS

*"We like the same books and we like the same sounds /
There's a reason that I love this town"*

JOEL PLASKETT, "LOVE THIS TOWN"

GORD DOWNIE WAS often asked when he realized the Tragically Hip were a success. His answer was always the same: "When I first walked out of Robbie's basement."

Anyone who saw them in Kingston from 1984 to 1988 will tell you that. They were the talk of the town, the band to see. They were already a minor supergroup in the small-stakes world of Kingston cover bands, if the names the Slinks, the Rodents or the Filters meant anything to you at the time, or if you happened to notice the hot-shit high school drummer and the elder beatnik saxophonist from B.C. around town. Together, they became the Tragically Hip. Two years later, a new guitarist was in, the saxophone player was out, and those five graduates of Kingston Vocational Collegiate Institute would stay together for another 30 years.

"One thing we did know: we were a collective, even though there was nothing to split up and no spoils to speak of," said Downie. "There was a philosophy that we were going to do this together. Everyone was in it and no one could get out of it."

Their first gig was in November 1984, at the Kingston Artists Association on the Queen's University campus. It was a white room with a rented PA. It was the kind of gig you put on yourself because no bar will book you yet. The chemistry they discovered in Rob Baker's basement quickly caught on around town. At Clark Hall Pub on the Queen's campus, with the stage eight inches off the ground, bodies pressed against the edge showered in sweat from Gord Downie's mane. At the tiny Terrapin Tavern, above a bar in a haunted alley. At Dollar Bill's in the back of the Prince George Hotel, where the teenage Downie and his friend Hugh Dillon had snuck in to see gigs by John Lee Hooker and Muddy Waters's guitarist, Luther "Guitar Junior" Johnson. At Alfie's, the underground Queen's pub where the stairwell to the entrance would have long lines snaking up to the street every time the Hip played. At the Lakeview Manor, the daytime strip bar that became a live music hub at night, attracting every level of Kingston society.

By the time the Hip signed with a Toronto management team in 1986, no Kingstonian was surprised to see them pack bars in the Big Smoke. What happened after that, however, no one could have seen coming.

————

Rob Baker and Gord Sinclair met in 1964, on Churchill Crescent in Kingston. Gord Sinclair could barely speak; he was not yet two years old. Rob Baker was two-and-a-half. They played in the sandbox. In a few years' time, they truly bonded over hockey—of course. Music came later.

Rob Baker's mother, Mary, was the 1947 United States Figure Skating Dance Champion. She met Philip Baker, a Toronto law student driving a taxi to pay for tuition, at the Toronto Skating Club. They were married in 1952. Son Matthew and daughter Vicky preceded Rob, who was born on April 12, 1962. Philip was a figure skater himself and judged competitions for most of his life. More important, he became the longest-serving provincial judge in Ontario: he started the year Rob was born and retired at age 70 in 1996. Philip was known as the "Sleeping Judge," because he often sat in court with his eyes closed. It was a habit from his childhood: his own father, Lt.-Col. Edwin Baker, was blinded in the First World War and served as the first managing director of the Canadian Institute for the Blind, from 1920 to 1962. Rob said his dad "grew up in a house where the lights were always out and they listened to the radio with their eyes closed." Philip would tell his son, "You can tell if someone is lying by listening to their voice. If you watch them, you don't always know." Mark Mattson, a law student at Queen's whose family had a cottage on nearby Wolfe Island, remembered the senior Baker as "an amazing man—a tough, good man. Kingston was a one-judge town back then, so everybody charged with a crime went in front of Justice Baker. You're talking about a town where there are six prisons. I don't know if there was a more influential guy in town. You might be the mayor for four years at a time here and there, but a judge is forever." Both Philip and Mary were fans of big-band leaders Glenn Miller and Guy Lombardo, but neither were musical. "We're just beginning to appreciate the Beatles," they told the *Kingston Whig-Standard* in 1991.

Part of what attracted them to the Sinclair family across the street was music. Duncan Sinclair, who became dean of the medical school at Queen's University, once played sax in a big band three nights a week, for seven dollars a night. His wife, Leona, played piano. Every December 23, the Sinclair family would host a "Night Before the Night Before Christmas" singalong party; all neighbours were invited. They had two sons: Robert Gordon, a.k.a. Gord, born November 18, 1963, and younger brother, Colin. Young Gord was extremely musical, learning to play bagpipes in the Rob Roy Pipe Band and later fife with the Fort Henry Guard. He studied piano and recorder and played saxophone in high school. It was his neighbour who pulled him into rock'n'roll.

Rob Baker's sister, Vicki, let Rob listen to her Bob Dylan and Sly Stone records when he was five years old. Soon he was jumping around with a tennis racquet playing air guitar to Led Zeppelin and Alice Cooper. As a teenager, he went to any big rock shows he could: Santana, Peter Frampton, April Wine, Heart, even Rush on their very first tour, with original drummer John Rutsey. Baker and Sinclair would obsess over the soundtrack to *Woodstock*, especially the Jimi Hendrix tracks. By the time Baker discovered the Rolling Stones at age 12—specifically Mick Taylor's solo on 1974's "Dance Little Sister"—he put away the tennis racquet and picked up a guitar. "Taylor just has this seamless, fluid way of just floating these beautiful lines over, and that's really what drove me," Baker later told *Canadian Musician*. "That fluid sound is something I was always really attracted to." A friend sold him an unplayable hunk of junk for $30. Baker struggled with it for a year before his dad felt sorry for him and bought him a new acoustic guitar—which can be heard on "Boots or Hearts" and other Tragically Hip songs. A year after that, when he was 14, his parents were impressed enough to cave in to his request for a Fender Stratocaster, identical to Robbie Robertson's ("Robbie was like God," said Baker). Baker also persuaded Sinclair to buy a bass guitar and start a band with him. Sinclair studied records by Free, John Mayall's Bluesbreakers—featuring a pre–Fleetwood Mac John McVie—and Donald "Duck" Dunn's work with Booker T and the MGs.

Drummer Rick McCreary, guitarist/keyboardist Andrew Grenville and vocalist John Estabrooke soon signed on. By 1980, Rick and the Rodents were the kings of KCVI. "We played high school dances, public school dances, sweet 16 parties, any gig we could get an opportunity to play," said Baker. They played covers of the Stones, the Kinks, the Who, the Clash, the Jam and the Sex Pistols. One of their biggest fans was two grades behind them. His name was Gord Downie.

———

Gordon Edgar Downie was born on February 6, 1964, in Amherstview, Ontario, just slightly west of Kingston, to Lorna and Edgar, a travelling salesman—cutlery and lingerie, mostly. "My dad was a bra salesman," said Gord, who was the fourth of five children (older siblings Charlyn, Mike and Paula, and younger brother Patrick). Gord was the first in his family to be born in the Kingston area; the Downies relocated there from Oakville when Edgar decided to go into real estate, in search of a more stable life for his growing family. In summers, Gord fished in Lake Ontario nearly every day, sometimes even tying skipping rope to a pitchfork to try and spear carp. In the winters, as one did in small-town Canada in the 1970s, Gord played hockey; his team, the Ernestown Raceway Auto Parts Bantams, won the provincial B championship when he was 13, with Downie in net. But his interest in the sport waned once the family moved to Kingston in 1980, next to the Queen's Faculty Club on King St. W., across from Breakwater Park. The pier there would be named after him, 37 years later.

Downie started classes at KCVI in grade 11. His fashion sense stood out right away: a jean jacket accessorized with a silk scarf—low-brow and high-brow right from the beginning. One of Downie's first friends in Kingston was Paul Langlois, whose parents, Terry and Adrien "Tic" Langlois, were both teachers; Adrien was KCVI's gym teacher and football coach. Langlois, born August 23, 1964, grew up with three sisters: Michelle, Monique and Susanne. He resisted the call of football until grade 13, when he played linebacker on the defence. He was a big music fan, but had yet to take guitar seriously. He entered the picture later.

One night, in the fall of 1980, Downie went to a house party at Grant Ethier's house. Ethier was a drummer whose band didn't have a singer. Downie knew all the words to "The End" by the Doors, which he performed that night. "I just wanted in," he said. "Nothing was going to stop me. Up until that time, I don't remember ever having had that singularity of purpose. I was going to be in that band. I wanted to sing—even if I couldn't."

"That band" Downie had to be in was called the Slinks, featuring Grant Ethier on drums, Andrew Frontini on bass, Steve Holy on guitar and Joe Pater on harmonica, guitar and keyboards. The first Slinks gig with Downie was at the Kingston Yacht Club, in the fall of 1981. "We weren't really a punk band," said Downie, "because we did more esoteric material as well." Lou Reed's "Sweet Jane" often opened the set. Other songs in the Slinks' repertoire at one time or another: "Midnight Rambler" by the Stones, "Roadhouse Blues" by the Doors, "London Calling" and "Brand New Cadillac" by the Clash. Some deep cuts, too: "Lucy Potato" by Teenage Head, "Messing with the Kid" by Junior Wells, "Watch That Man" by David Bowie, "Consolation Prizes" by the Stooges. By far the oddest song in their set was "Super Freak" by Rick James. Naturally, the Slinks looked up to the Rodents. "They were revered," said Downie. "Robbie walked the halls and people definitely knew who he was. It was an amazing thing."

The Slinks broke up near the end of high school, after a gig at a Polish hall. Downie claims he was kicked out, because the rest of the Slinks had played one ignominious gig without him—the previous summer, while he was hitch-hiking to Nova Scotia with Paul Langlois—at which they got another singer who delivered a pornographic version of Rod Stewart's "Hot Legs" in front of a country music crowd in a public park. The performance ended abruptly when someone literally pulled the plug. "As great as that one show was," recalled Joe Pater, "I'm pretty sure we didn't break up the Slinks to do it. But who knows, maybe we were stupid enough to kick Gord out of the band." Guitarist Steve Holy went on to a life in music, playing jazz in Vancouver. Grant Ethier joined 13 Engines, fronted by songwriter John Critchley, and made some of the finest Canadian rock records of the late '80s and early '90s.

The Rodents' Rob Baker was a fan of the Slinks. "We thought: 'We're a really good band, but we don't have a really good front man. We got to get that guy in our band.'" That happened soon enough, though not in the Rodents. It was Finny McConnell who brought Baker and Downie together. McConnell played in yet another KCVI band, Pressure Drop, and was smitten with Downie's star wattage. "From the moment I saw him play in the KCVI gym, I thought, 'Okay, this guy's going to be a rock star,'" he said. "He's got the moves like Iggy Pop, and he's got the swagger of Mick Jagger. He's a great front man and entertainer, and I wanted to play some music with him." A new band, with McConnell, Downie, drummer Mauro Sepe and bassist Kelly Campbell, was called the Filters. They played together a short while in the spring of 1983 until McConnell embarked on a brief jaunt overseas with old classmate Hugh Dillon. When McConnell returned in the spring of 1984, he wanted to restart the Filters. Downie agreed, on one condition: he wanted Baker in the band.

The Filters played classic rock covers around eastern Ontario—Cornwall, Brockville, Belleville—three or four nights a week in 1984. "We played the worst gigs," said McConnell. Kingston soundman Larry Stafford sometimes travelled with the band. He recalled one particularly dour gig, where afterwards, "I went up to the room just to see how everybody was, and they were all sitting on the floor. In the room was a mattress and a rope attached to the wall for a fire escape, and they were just sitting there, and Gord Downie looked at me and said, 'So, is this as good as it gets?'" Baker was similarly restless. The band's schedule was eating into his time to study at Queen's, where he was doing an art degree; Downie was just about to enrol in English and film.

Baker and Downie decided to start a new band where the sole objectives were to play for beer and have fun. Baker pulled Sinclair back into the fold. There was a drummer, too, but he missed the first three rehearsals. Downie remembered a really good drummer who was still in junior high back when he'd played the Neil Peart role in a Rush tribute band called Anthem, with some future members of the Slinks. They called him over. His name was Johnny Fay.

Fay's parents knew the Bakers. Years before, Dr. John Fay and his wife, Loretta, emigrated from England and arrived in Kingston just before the end of a calendar year; they soon met the Bakers, who invited them to what the Fays would later say was the best New Year's Eve party they'd ever been to. Born on July 7, 1966, young John Philip marched to his own beat and was soon using knitting needles to bang on anything he could find. His parents finally put him in drum lessons at age 10; they were tired of hearing him play the same beat all the time, on a snare borrowed from a brother's friend. The Fays—who had two other boys, Mark and

Paul—matched Johnny dollar for dollar to save up for his first kit. But his teacher, Chris McCann, had a $1,800 kit that Johnny coveted, so at 14 he took a job as a dishwasher at Olympic Harbour to save up for a similar one without his parents' help. "He had seen other people get everything handed to them [by their parents] and they didn't appreciate it as much," said McCann. "I was really impressed with that."

Fay was a big Stewart Copeland fan—maybe too big. "I had live Police tapes," Fay recalled. "I could play his part from an Australian show, another part from a London show in 1982, or from a show from France. I had all these cassettes of him, and I played them so much that the polarity on the tapes switched. It got to the point where my teacher told me [the Copeland obsession] was really killing my playing." In the break between grade 10 and 11, Fay's mother asked him what he was going to do that summer. "I told her I was just going to hang out and do nothing; she told me that wasn't going to happen. She packed me up and took me down to the Berklee College of Music [in Boston]; they have a great summer program down there. That's when I started getting focused because I was playing drums every day for three months. I never really expected to get into a rock band, because when I was practising, I was playing a lot of jazz. When I got home, my mom told me I should play with other people since I'd been doing all this practising." Fay had an audition at McGill, where the professor told him to give up—which, of course, fuelled his fire. That's when he got the call from Baker, Sinclair and Downie to try out for their new band. He was in grade 11.

The new band's name was chosen at the last minute, before the first gig in November 1984. They were almost called the Bedspring Symphony, after a Rolling Stones bootleg. The new name was taken from a skit on *Elephant Parts*, a 1981 late-night comedy special by the Monkees' Mike Nesmith. "There's one skit in there that is sort [of] like a TV plea: 'Send some money to the Foundation for the Tragically Hip,'" said Downie. The skit aired as a pre-taped segment of *Saturday Night Live* that same year. The phrase "tragically hip" also surfaces in the Elvis Costello song "Town Cryer," from 1982's *Imperial Bedroom*.

That first set list was mostly covers. But in each of the three sets, the Hip played three original tunes. They knew they were not going to be a cover band forever. Writing largely fell to Sinclair, a history student who once wrote an essay about Gordon Lightfoot's "Black Day in July." As Baker put it in the band's first-ever interview, in the *Queen's Journal*, "Gord Sinclair writes the basic songs, I arrange it and Gord Downie forgets it." Shortly afterwards, they added a fifth member: saxophonist Davis Manning, a beatnik from B.C. who was in his mid-30s. He worked at Bubba's Pizzeria and was dating a friend of the band. If the rest of the band were young punks, Manning brought both a hippie vibe and a connection to the R&B material they were covering. He brought years of experience to a band of neophytes and strongly encouraged them to develop more original material. "He was the coolest guy," remembered Jennie Punter, who was the entertainment editor at the *Queen's Journal* in 1985. "Women really liked him. He was a gentleman. You kind of knew he was just passing through, though." More than one Kingstonian later likened Manning to the character Joey "the Lips" Fagan in the book and film *The Commitments*.

"People were going nuts for a cover band, which seemed crazily disproportionate to me at the time," said Punter. "Then you see them and you go, 'Oh, okay.' I wasn't necessarily a big fan. I was really into punk and the super cool music of the day, like Sonic Youth. But I loved seeing the Hip play as much as anyone else. I felt strongly that they were going to be famous."

"I couldn't even tell if they wanted to be famous," said Steve Jordan, who was a teenage DJ at Kingston Top 40 station CKLC and later became its music director. "Most Kingston bands would talk about girls and fame and maybe a record deal—these guys just wanted to be awesome, and play, and deliver. Everything that happened to them afterwards came from that stance."

———

"No one was playing original music in clubs," recalled Gord Sinclair. "It was totally frowned upon. There was this one club we used to play in Sarnia where the [manager] made you write out your set list and the [names of the] original artists, just to prevent people from playing original tunes. That was where music was at back then. In Kingston, it was a tribute to Genesis one week and a tribute to the Stones the next." Steve Jordan remembered seeing a CCR cover band, Green River: "They'd come out with Vietnam paint and wearing battle fatigues. They'd come through the crowd with machine guns before getting onstage and playing this Vietnam War soundtrack stuff. I'd actually see the Hip guys at these shows; Gord in particular thought they were great."

The only Kingston band to make waves out of town at that time were the Blushing Brides, a Stones cover band formed in 1979. At their height, they played 250 shows a year all over central Canada and the Eastern Seaboard. A Boston newspaper headline called them "Stones clones," which apparently inspired the term "clone band." "They were really good, as cover bands go," said Jordan. "Then RCA signed them and they put out an album of originals, with a cover of [CCR's] 'Fortunate Son.'"

The Hip, of course, also played a lot of Stones covers—but not ones you would recognize. "I was a Stones fan," said Jordan, "but probably only songs from [the '60s compilation] *Hot Rocks*. I didn't know what 'Down Home Girl' was, that it was a Stones cover of Alvin Robinson. It just sounded really cool."

"If you look at the first three or four Rolling Stones albums, around '64 to '66, the Hip played every song on those albums that was a cover," said Jeffrey Barrett, who saw every Hip show he could in their first four years of existence. "Suzie Q" by Dale Hawkins. "King Bee" by Muddy Waters. Don Covay's "Mercy Mercy." Marvin Gaye's "Hitch Hike." Bobby Troup's "Route 66." "Same arrangements, sped up by 50 per cent, and they'd burn through these in two-and-a-half minutes," said Barrett. "At the time, Davis Manning basically played all the solos. Bobby didn't seem comfortable playing any kind of heavy-duty solo."

The best-known Jagger/Richards song in the Hip's repertoire was probably "2000 Light Years from Home," into which they would weave a bit of the Doors' "L.A. Woman" and Jimi Hendrix's "Third Stone from the Sun." Even though the only Doors song they would cover in full was "Roadhouse Blues," more than a few people saw a lot of Jim Morrison in Gord Downie. Rob Baker recalled, "A guy came up to us in London and said, 'I can guarantee you $1,500 a week as a Doors cover band.' And we kind of laughed about it, because we didn't even have a keyboard in the band."

"Sinclair and Bobby were the real music heads," said Jennie Punter, "the kind of guys who would usually be DJing at a house party or saying, 'Here's something by a band you think you know, so check this out.'" The Hip covered "Bedrock Twitch Twitch," as performed by a character called Rock Roll on an episode of *The Flintstones*. They introduced the Monkees' "I'm a Believer" by saying, "This is a song by Neil Diamond"—who wrote it before his own solo career took off. They did the Monkees' "Mary Mary" years before it was sampled by Run-DMC. ("Mary, Mary, where are you going with that swaddling baby in your arms?" Downie asked at one gig.) They were doing Roy Head's "Treat Her Right" before George Thorogood got to it in 1988 and before it appeared in the film *The Commitments*. They did songs by '60s British garage band the Pretty Things. "If you were 18 in 1985, you didn't listen to the Pretty Things from 1968—nobody did," said Jeffrey Barrett. "I had a bunch of box sets by the Yardbirds, and the Hip must have played 10 songs they picked out of the Yardbirds' catalogue." Davis Manning was likely responsible for some of the deepest cuts, like one song by Mickey Most and the Gear, a British obscurity from the early '60s. "There's no way Bobby or Gord had that in their record collection," figured Barrett.

There were more obvious nods, too. Van Morrison and Them's "Gloria" and "I Can Only Give You Everything." Sam the Sham's frat-house favourite "Wooly Bully." Otis Redding's "These Arms of Mine," sometimes performed as a duet with local blues singer Georgette Fry. "Who Do You Love," which had been a Canadian favourite ever since Ronnie Hawkins ruled the roost at roadhouses across Ontario in the '50s, when he would swing from the rafters and belt out Bo Diddley tunes like that one.

"We specifically shied away from songs that people would know," said Sinclair, "because it was easier for us to learn the gist of a song. Most of them were one-four-five [blues] progressions anyway. Gord would learn the first verse, and then we'd jam the rest and try to make it our own." That's how "New Orleans Is Sinking" was eventually sprung from "Baby Please Don't Go," the blues standard covered by Van Morrison's Them. "They'd play 50 songs over three sets in a night," said Jeffrey Barrett, "and I guarantee Gord faked his way through the lyrics of at least five of them. He'd just be making stuff up."

Other than the tribute bands, a lot of acts relied heavily on covers just to pad out their sets. "Playing covers was what you needed to do to entertain the audience," said Kris Abbott, a guitarist who moved to Kingston from nearby Perth in 1978 when she was 18, with the express intent of joining a band. She played in two cover bands, the Web and Too Cold to Hold, before moving to Toronto and joining the Pursuit of Happiness. "These places had live music every single day, all night, so you needed to know a lot of material. Everybody did do original music; they slipped it in. Gradually the people would like the originals more and more." Early Hip songs included "Baby Blue Blood," "Psychedelic Ramblings of Rich Kids," "Heart Attack Love," "Reformed Baptist Blues," "(I'm an) Alternative Guy," and an unusually jazzy ballad, "If She's Seventeen." "Highway Girl" and "Evelyn," later heard on the debut EP, were also early originals.

When the Hip played at Alfie's, only students came to see them—partially because the pub wasn't allowed to advertise off-campus. "People would always be talking about it the next day," said Jennie Punter. "How long the lineup was and if they got in, what [the band] played, how Gord would have to change his clothes four times because his shirt would be drenched. Gord had something that so many electrifying performers have, where he is for everybody and for no one. People would love to see what he was going to do: not in an Iggy Pop way or a punk rock way, but a performance artist. He would be spitting non sequiturs and then would break character and be right on the level, like he was drinking beer with you and it was all good. It wasn't an act he planned out; it was coming from a real place. That was all there at the beginning."

They soon moved downtown. "After the buzz started, every restaurant, every club, every bar—it didn't matter what it was, they wanted to have them in there," said Jeffrey Barrett. "Half of these places had never had live music before, and they never have since. At the Copper Penny family restaurant, they played in the front window, amps stacked on top of amps, no monitors. People would be eating dinner and suddenly this band shows up and plugs in. Then at nine o'clock, 45 totally psychotic people would show up and start slammin' down beers and want to get right in front of the band. Students were wedged between tables where people were trying to finish their dinner." The Hip played parties at a warehouse that had freight elevators leading to a loft with a stage set up in the middle of the room; organizer Mark Mattson would buy 100 cases of beer and charge $10 for admission and all you can drink. They often played the 40-capacity Terrapin Tavern, a short-lived venue above the Toucan Pub, which also hosted early gigs by Blue Rodeo and k.d. lang. "One of the most memorable shows I've ever seen was the night the Hip closed the Terrapin," said Jordan. The date was January 31, 1986. "It was a Beatles-at-the-Cavern-Club kind of thing. The limestone walls were sweating. You could not move, and you did not want to leave."

———

The Hip found a true home at the Lakeview Manor, a club in Portsmouth Village, west of downtown, with an incredibly tacky paint job, featuring yellow, orange, purple and white stripes in a V formation. It first opened in 1870. At one point in the 1970s, the sign over the front door welcomed "ladies and escorts." By the mid-'80s, it was a strip club during the day. Strippers and musicians shared the same dressing rooms. The strippers' stage, extending into the middle of the room, would be pushed under the band stage at night.

"The Lakeview was a hub," said Kris Abbott. "It was a large place, where one room had dancers and music, and other rooms where you hung out and ate pub food or played pool. People even brought kids in there—not in the dancer area, obviously. There was no demographic. It was just a place people went."

"The audience was a true spectrum," said Steve Jordan. "Ex-cons, bikers, poets, artists, dropouts, conservatives, lefties—it was pretty much the only place I've ever seen all those people come together and not hate each other." Gord Sinclair met his first wife, Chris, at the Manor, where she was a waitress. The Hip's friend, driver and occasional lighting tech Fraser Armstrong also met his wife there; she too was a waitress, who once dumped a tray of drinks on his head.

The bands played at night; the strippers worked during the day—mostly. "It was not unusual to have to stop your set because a dancer was going to do her thing," said Abbott. "You didn't just play one show, you played four 45-minute sets. Your first set might start at the end of the dancers' day. There were lots of times the dancers would still be doing a routine on the rug and you couldn't open the back door, because it would be too cold [for them]—so you'd wait for them to finish before loading in your gear." That didn't scare the band's parents away, though Dr. Fay had to be convinced not to show up in a jacket and tie.

"There weren't a lot of local bands who could fill the Lakeview," said Jordan. Acts like David Wilcox, 54.40, Toronto, Doug and the Slugs and Colin James would make their Kingston stop at the 500-capacity venue, as would the Northern Pikes, who wrote a song about the Lakeview called "Place That's Insane." The Hip's local competition was slim. "There were a couple of bands based out of Queen's that were sort of trying to do the same thing we were doing," said Gord Sinclair. "We felt that we were in direct competition. One group in particular would do a Them song while we were doing another Them song. They were always a couple of months behind us."

The Raging Groovies were a somewhat Smiths-sounding combo fronted by Gavin Tighe, who later became a lawyer for Toronto mayor Rob Ford. Guyana KoolAid, managed by Steve Jordan, wisely changed their name to the Pariahs; bassist Scott Megginson's father was a judge who served beside Justice Baker when the number of judges in town doubled. The two judges' sons met at the courthouse one day when they both showed up to borrow their dads' cars. "What else is a judge's boy to do but to play in a rock'n'roll band?" Megginson joked to the *Whig-Standard*. Gord Sinclair co-produced the Pariahs' 1992 debut EP.

The Hip were making a full-time living as musicians by just playing in Kingston. "There was a time when they oversaturated," said Steve Jordan, "and had to get scarce for a while." Rob Baker was the band's booking agent for the first 18 months. "I didn't like lifting gear," he said, "so I didn't like playing too many gigs. We each had to make $50, all the beer we could drink and all expenses covered—which is a lot more than bands make [in 2017], by the way."

On their very first overnight trip—a two-night stand in Renfrew, Ontario— the engine fell out of the van that Gord Sinclair's mother had helped purchase. The local mechanic told them he could get them a new engine by Thursday. "But *this is* Thursday!" the band protested. "Next Thursday," he deadpanned. "That type of stuff makes you a band," said Downie. "It's those failures and how you handle them. Because there are many of them."

The band-of-brothers mentality was there early on. "It was like when people sometimes talk about twins who almost have a secret way of communicating," said Jennie Punter. "Like any band of guys, they have in-jokes—they like you enough that they're letting you in on this. But there was something deeper than that. They were very protective of each other, in a way that wasn't necessarily overt, but you really felt like it was this mysterious thing—like they knew something you didn't." Like 99 per cent of rock bands in 1986, "it was very much a guy world—you knew there would never be a girl in that band," said Punter, "but they were not bad boys. I never got hit on; it wasn't a lecherous scene. I'm sure they had their fun, but a lot of those guys settled down very early on."

There were some big shows on the Queen's campus, including one on October 18, 1985, opening for Teenage Head at Fleming's Field; the Hip played two sets at the Manor that same night, featuring "three stylish female dancers," according to the *Queen's Journal*. They also played the Jock Harty Arena with other local bands, including Guyana KoolAid.

One July 1985 set at the Copper Penny II restaurant—a venue co-owned by friend and future Hip manager Bernie Breen—was recorded as a demo for a radio contest; the audio surfaced on YouTube in 2017. On it, along with a rare glimpse of what they were like with Manning on saxophone, one gets a taste of Downie's stage banter at the time. Introducing the band, he says, "Of course, fresh out of prison, Mr. Bobby Baker on guitar . . . We're here for one more night and that's it. Then it's on to the Seattle Kingdome, Houston Astrodome, Toronto ConnDome—we might never be back! We're the Tragically Hip! We drink Molson Canadian and lots of it! Egg salad sandwiches for lunch! Our favourite colour is green! Favourite pastime is pulling the hair out of baby dolls! We sleep on the floor! We'll see you tomorrow night. 'I'm not your stepping stone . . .'"

What you also hear on that Copper Penny tape is an incredible R&B band, unrecognizable to any fans of what the Tragically Hip became. "When Davis was in the band, you *danced*," said Steve Jordan; Paul Langlois was usually right at the front dancing beside him. "You could only get close to the band if you danced. If you just wanted to stand and gawk, you had to go to the back of the room."

In the spring of 1986, Johnny Fay graduated from high school. Immediately after writing his last exam, his brother picked him up and drove him to Toronto to play a show at the Horseshoe Tavern. "I ended my high school career and started my professional career in the same day," he said. The band was now ready to get busier. The momentum permanently derailed any postsecondary plans for the son of a professor of medicine. Luckily, the Fays were fine with that. "Who are we to say what he should do?" Dr. Fay told the *Whig-Standard*. "It's obvious to me that it's hard work. It's not an idle life, and being idle is one thing I couldn't abide."

Davis Manning didn't want to stick around. He quit in April 1986. "He'd been there, done it all," said Baker. "He knew how it should be done, and we were out there making all the rookie mistakes we had to make." Manning's parting words to the Tragically Hip were, "I can't put my life in the hands of a bunch of dumb college fucks."

Baker saw Manning's departure as a good time to get a second guitarist to bolster the rhythm section. "We were the name band in Kingston, and we could have picked a hot guitar player. But if we started picking hot musicians, the rest of us would be out! So we got someone who was a friend who could learn how to play guitar." They didn't have to look very far. Downie and Sinclair turned to one of their roommates at 585 Brock Street, Paul Langlois. He was driving a cab and had been contemplating moving to Nashville to try his luck as a songwriter. He was the Tragically Hip's number one fan. "He knew how to play four chords on the guitar;

he was writing songs; and we thought, he's a great guy, he's a friend, it's a guitar—it's not that hard, anyone can learn it," said Baker. "I was shocked he wasn't in the band already," said Jordan.

After KCVI, Langlois had headed to Carleton University in Ottawa for its journalism program. He left after one year; his marks were fine, but he was starting to play more guitar. He returned to Kingston and moved in with his high school buddies. Joining the Hip was a dream come true—for his parents as well. "When the band called to ask Paul to come jam with them, I was more excited than when he got accepted into Carleton," said his mother, Terry. "I think Paul might have thought we would be disappointed when he dropped out of Carleton because we had expectations for him. But all we've ever wanted is for him to be happy."

The band was getting itchy to make a change and start regularly playing outside of Kingston. They weren't sure how to do it. "We didn't have a lot of experience, coming from Kingston," said Downie. "There was nobody running record labels out of their basement at the time. I think we went to anybody and everybody at some point. Sinclair and I put together a list of 300 songs once, to get a booking agent at the Blaise Agency. The guy there said, 'Next time, could you guys bring me a list of 40?'"

———

Allan Gregg was often described as a "political rock star." That's because his polling firm, Decima Research, was largely credited with helping Brian Mulroney's Progressive Conservatives form two majority governments in 1984 and 1988. He was also president of the Festival of Festivals (now known as the Toronto International Film Festival). Gregg was often seen interviewed on television, a scruffy-looking guy in a suit who happened to wear an earring—not a typical conservative look at the time, which endeared him to TV producers. He looked like a rock'n'roller deep in the establishment, which he was. In August 1986, he heard the Tragically Hip for the first time.

Gregg grew up in Edmonton as a huge music fan, but not a musician. "My ambition far outstripped my talent," he said. In university, he managed a local blues band. Upon graduation, he and a friend became concert promoters. They brought Led Zeppelin to the Edmonton Gardens in May 1969, on that band's second North American tour. The band was paid $1,750, and Gregg's management client, the Angus Park Blues Band, opened the show. "It was very successful, and we thought it was easy," he said. He and his business partner travelled to Toronto to talk to promoters there and get some tips. They were introduced to a guy who claimed to be managing a newly reformed Yardbirds, who had split in 1968 (guitarist Jimmy Page started Led Zeppelin shortly afterwards). "I loved the Yardbirds," said Gregg, "and I'd heard stories that they were reforming. So we booked them in Edmonton. As the show got closer, we weren't getting the kind of free promotion you normally get from the radio. Finally, we got this telex saying, 'Warning: Dee and the Yeomen, a Toronto band, are touring as the Yardbirds.' There were a whole bunch of these fake bands: fake Animals, fake Zombies, who were out touring. We let the show go on, but refused to pay them the back half of their fee. That was the end of my promoting career."

Gregg set his sights on academia instead. But he was drawn to conservative politics and in 1979 found himself the national campaign secretary for Progressive Conservative leader Joe Clark, who managed to temporarily interrupt Pierre Trudeau's 15-year run as prime minister. Gregg was 25 at the time. He then started Decima Research and became heavily involved in Brian Mulroney's 1984 campaign. But music was still on his mind. In January 1986, Gregg was trying to help an old Edmonton friend who performed under the name Peter Panter. Gregg gave Panter money to make demos with Randy Bachman and to make a video. He brought him to Toronto for an industry showcase at the Diamond Club and enlisted the help of a mustachio-and-mulletted young manager he'd met a month earlier at a Christmas party for *Music Express* magazine. His name was Jake Gold.

Jake Gold was born in New Jersey but his family moved to northwest Toronto when he was two. In high school, he sang in cover bands. "I was a decent singer, not a great performer," he recalled. "I liked the scene. I sang Neil Young, Led Zeppelin, Peter Gabriel. Anything that was cool." After high school, he joined a cover band's road crew, doing lights. In 1979, he went to L.A. to visit a girl; he ended up staying and getting a job selling office supplies on the phone, and later worked as a technical director at a theatre. When he returned to Toronto in 1981, it was because an old high school friend wanted him to road manage and do lights for his band, Hot Tip. That band soon morphed into the Purple Hearts, which landed a song in rotation on Toronto new wave radio station CFNY. Gold then started a partnership with Dave Kirby, who managed the Tenants; that band had a Top 40 single with "Sheriff." Gold's client New Regime landed an RCA deal and modest radio play. When Gregg called Gold to ask for a favour on the Peter Panter gig, Gold put his technical background to work.

"Jake got everything: sound, lights, crew," said Gregg. "The production values were stunning. All the labels came out, but no one was interested. I said to Jake, 'How much do I owe you for this?' He said, 'Nothing. This is a great opportunity.'" Gold was looking to get out of his arrangement with Dave Kirby. Gregg saw a potentially complementary relationship and made Gold an offer to start something together, with Gregg sticking to strategy and marketing and Gold doing the day-to-day. "Jake is far more aggressive," Gregg told the CBC-TV business program *Venture* in 1989. "I won't even deal with things like the club owner and the promoters. A major part of dealing with them is beating them up. Jake is very good at that—and seems to enjoy it from time to time." As of January 31, 1986, the company was called Jacob J. Gold and Associates, renamed the Management Trust in 1988. It was funded by Allan Gregg. "I put up the sweat," said Gold. "Allan put up the money."

One of Gregg's many Progressive Conservative connections was Hugh Segal, who had been a senior aide to longtime Ontario premier Bill Davis. (Segal later ran for the federal leadership in 1998 and was appointed a senator in 2005.) Segal's wife, Donna, had family in the Kingston area; her brother was a young landscape architect named Fraser Armstrong, who was hanging out with the Tragically Hip on the road a lot—maybe too much. Donna wanted to make sure her brother wasn't wasting his life with a bunch of deadbeats. As a favour to his wife, Segal agreed to courier a demo cassette from Armstrong to Allan Gregg.

On a Friday in August 1986, Gregg was meeting with a radio promoter and waiting for a third person to arrive. While they were waiting, Gregg decided to play some of the demo tapes piling up on his desk. One was a four-track recording by the Tragically Hip. He was immediately smitten. "It was really, really rough," he said, "but both of us looked at each other and said, 'Holy mackerel, is this ever raw and dynamic, a really exciting sound.'" That Sunday, Gregg played the tape for Gold while they were driving to a Blue Jays game. Gold booked a showcase gig for the Hip that same week at Larry's Hideaway; it was an opening slot for a Rolling Stones cover band called Hot Lips. "Literally 30 seconds into the first set," said Gregg, "we looked at each other and just said, 'Wow.' It was Gord. He was just so charismatic and unusual. The energy was unbelievable. The band were such great rhythm players."

"Here was [an audience] predisposed to hearing the Rolling Stones," said Gold. "Except the Hip came out and did originals and maybe one or two covers. Had it been opening for anybody else, [they] might not have got the same reaction—although maybe [they] would, because of how good they were. But this was an easy fit. There were 200 people there, sitting down; it was a cabaret set-up, all tables in the front. By the end of the set, all the people sitting at the tables gave them a standing O." All parties agreed to sign a management contract immediately. Then they all went to celebrate at the Pilot Tavern in Yorkville.

When still booking themselves, the Hip had landed a weeknight gig at the Horseshoe Tavern on Toronto's Queen Street West strip back in May 1986, but their forays into the heart of the city's music scene were few and far between. Gold and Gregg set about changing that immediately. They booked the Hip into a regular gig at the Hotel Isabella, on Sherbourne Street south of Bloor Street, nowhere near any live music strip. It was the middle Wednesday of every month. They booked a bus to bring in fans from Kingston, to make sure the place was packed. After six months, they didn't need the bus; there were lineups out the door. Gold and Gregg would invite various industry people to see the band. "We purposely chose not to try to get them signed," said Gold. "We treated everyone at those shows as a social thing: 'Let's go have dinner, come check out our new clients.'"

The Hotel Isabella was "a real fucking dump," said Gregg. "The stage was so small that Robbie had to stand on the dance floor. Gord would hang from the pipes, which were exposed. People would come and say, 'How the fuck did this happen? And why have I never heard of this band before?'"

But that was only once a month. The rest of the province beckoned. Gregg put a down payment on a van they named the Lisa Marie, after Elvis Presley's daughter. "I tried to get them an agent, but I couldn't," said Gold. He knew most of the bookers on the circuit, so he started doing it himself. These weren't one-off gigs; as was the norm then, a working band might be booked for a week in one small-town bar, or three days in a row. The set list changed back to being mostly covers, about 70:30, by Gold's estimation: "We would submit our song list, and we would never say they had originals. You'd say 'Stones B-side' or whatever."

When the Hip would return to Kingston, suddenly they were playing far more recognizable songs than Steve Jordan had ever seen them do, like "Honky Tonk Women" and "Like a Rolling Stone." "I remember thinking, 'This is weird,'" said Jordan. "That was a mercilessly short time. Nothing against [their] versions, but what they were doing before felt a bit subversive. To play around Ontario, they had to play some stuff that the locals knew." Gord Sinclair admitted, "That was a bit of a blow to our ego."

Sometimes they got paid, sometimes they didn't. "We played at the Whippletree Shanty in Calabogie, Ontario," Downie recalled. The venue is still there, down the road from the Redneck Bistro. "Halfway through our first set of five, the owner comes up and stands in front of the five patrons there and tells us, 'I'M NOT PAYING YOU.' Sinclair puts his bass down and says, 'Keep playing!'—because he was smart enough to know that we might breach the non-existent contact [if we left the stage]. He goes off and haggles the guy and hangs him upside down. Then he comes back, picks up his bass and continues to play. We got paid half."

At one early gig at Bannister's in Hamilton, the few people in the bar quickly vacated after a waitress from the strip club downstairs came up to announce that the Jell-O wrestling was about to begin. Even the bartender left. The band played their set anyway, considering it a rehearsal. At least they didn't get fired, which they did in Brockville when a bar owner thought the erratic Downie was on drugs.

The Hip fared considerably better in London, which they considered a sister city to Kingston: the University of Western Ontario, like Queen's, is part of what could be called Canada's Ivy League, prestigious schools of choice for the country's smartest and/or wealthiest. Both London and Kingston are equidistant from Toronto in opposite directions. "It's sort of a secondary market to Toronto," said Baker. "We thought it was important to play those places instead of concentrating on the big city. We considered London our home away from home. We had friends there who lived in a place on Charles Street; we called it the Charles Mansion. It's since burned down. We'd all sleep on the floor and on couches." London is also where Gord Downie met his future wife, Laura Usher of Toronto, who was attending Western.

The Tragically Hip were booked on the same circuit that Daniel Lanois would have played with various bands 10 years earlier, that Levon and the Hawks would have played 10 years before that: Grand Bend, Sarnia, Port Dover, Cornwall, North Bay, Peterborough, Brockville—anywhere that would have them—and plenty of campus pubs and venues like the Shady Lady Disco in Renfrew. They ate a lot of what they called "Scottish food," a.k.a. McDonald's.

Often tagging along in 1987 was 16-year-old Sarah Harmer, a young music fan whose older sisters Barbara and Mary were close friends of the band at Queen's. With ambitions to be a songwriter herself, the young Harmer was thrilled to witness the Hip up close everywhere from Kingston to Kincardine. The Hip would often stay at the Harmer household in Burlington, outside Hamilton, when they had a gig nearby. "One night when I was 17 or so, the Hip were playing in Hamilton," she recalled. "I hadn't gone to the show because I'd been at the Twilight Zone in Toronto with my friends dancing all night. I have this incredibly vivid memory of pulling up my parents' driveway and seeing the band's van. It was dawn. I knew they were staying there after the gig; my parents were away. There were all these soaking clothes next to the pool, and I just assumed someone fell into the pool. So I hung all the clothes on the line. Later that day, I realized they were Gord's totally gross, sweat-drenched stage clothes."

Downie had fond memories of the youngest Harmer's nascent musical talent. "I remember going to the Harmer farmhouse and sitting around the pool, and Sarah had a guitar," he said. "Maybe I knew four chords, but she knew five. After doing 600 gigs that week, I would sing with her in a ragged voice, and she had the voice of a bird. I sensed she had this look on her face like, 'Jesus, if you can do it, I certainly can.'"

———

After a year on the road in Ontario, it was time to make a real recording. Jake Gold played hockey in a musicians' league that included Ken Greer, the guitarist in Tom Cochrane's Red Rider (who, oddly enough, had just lost a drummer named Rob Baker). Greer mentioned that he was starting to branch into production. Gold thought it would be a perfect fit. The band agreed, excited to work with someone whose work they admired. The recording cost $5,000, all in. Other than a lot of reverb typical to the era, the Greer sessions were largely the sound of a well-seasoned live band playing in the studio. The intention was just to make a demo, something to fuel their first national tour.

For the only time in the Hip's career, songs are credited to individual songwriters. The best ones all belong exclusively to Gord Sinclair: "Small Town Bringdown," "Last American Exit," "Evelyn" (the latter based on the 1971 Clint Eastwood film *Play Misty for Me*). Baker and Downie are a team on three more songs: "Killing Time," "I'm a Werewolf, Baby" and "Highway Girl," the latter being the only song from the EP to appear on the

2005 compilation *Yer Favourites*, the tracklist for which was crowd-sourced from fan votes. One track recorded for the EP, "Get Back Again," was a live favourite for a couple of years but never placed on a record.

The EP bridges the gap between the garage-rock R&B band heard on early live tapes and the muscular rockers that would appear on 1989's *Up to Here*. The "baby blue" EP—as the band calls it, referring to the album design—sounds very much like other North American roots rock albums from 1987, such as Los Lobos (*By the Light of the Moon*), the BoDeans (*Love & Hope & Sex & Dreams*), Steve Earle (*Exit o*), and Canadian peers 54.40 (self-titled), the Northern Pikes (*Big Blue Sky*) and Andrew Cash (*Time and Place*). Though it had obvious merit, very little on the EP suggested the power of the live show.

The EP was ready in the fall of 1987. Gold and Gregg pitched it to all the labels. No one responded. Steve Jordan wasn't surprised. He was now music director at CKLC. "I told every single label about this band, prior to Jake coming on board," he said. "No one cared. It really took someone like Jake and Allan to say, 'No, we're excited about this. This is the future.' Jake and Allan saw what we all saw in Kingston, which is that this band should be huge. The difference is that they weren't all 'Kingston' about it; they wouldn't say, 'You know what? It's okay if it stays our little secret.' They were relentless."

The one person who finally agreed to bite was Jim Fotheringham at RCA, who had signed another of Gold's clients, New Regime, a band that was consciously trying to be Top 40. Gold and Gregg didn't want the Hip to sign a deal yet—they wanted to license the EP to a major for one year in hopes that it would generate enough buzz to get a better deal for the debut. They asked for and got a non-recoupable $25,000 to be put into marketing. They also requested that the EP be serviced to only seven key commercial radio stations, and otherwise focus on campus stations. Gregg says the label was taken aback. "Well, what if CHED in Edmonton complains?" RCA asked. "Let them complain," Gregg responded. "A: they aren't going to play it. B: if they do complain, then we've got someone interested who wouldn't be otherwise." Sure enough, the other commercial stations started calling once they saw it getting airplay on Q107 in Toronto and FM96 in London, among others.

One RCA rep claimed to understand the undersell, saying in the *Kingston Whig-Standard*, "This record can't compete in the international market because the production values aren't good enough. But the songs are strong." He then added, in somewhat of a contradiction, "You don't want them getting too crafted, or that would destroy what they are."

RCA wanted to release the EP in January 1988, a time of year when it's easier for new artists to get media attention; most major releases come out in the fall and spring. The Tragically Hip didn't see any reason to wait—especially in their hometown. They wanted it out before Christmastime. RCA balked, for some reason Gregg found to be "complete horseshit and bureaucratic. I said, 'Forget that. Sell us 2,000 records right now. I'll put them in the trunk of my car.' I drove to Kingston, where there were only six record stores. We took Gord [Downie] around with us. We'd go to some mall and say, 'This is Gord Downie, he's with a local band called the Tragically Hip. This is their new record, and we're hoping you'll take some on consignment.' The guy in the store would look at the record, look at Gord and say, 'Oh, yeah, you're the goaltender!'" As always in Canadian culture, hockey supersedes the arts.

The album release show was held on December 11, 1987, at the Lakeview Manor, of course. They also debuted the video for "Small Town Bringdown" that night, which had been shot earlier at the same venue. The album immediately went to No. 1 in the Kingston market. When it was released in the rest of Canada on January 15, 1988, Gold and Gregg put out a press release that read: "On December 31, in every market in North America, the No. 1 record was U2 and the No. 2 record was John Mellencamp. Except in Kingston, Ontario, where those two artists were No. 2 and No. 3. No. 1 was the Tragically Hip." "Now we had a story," said Gregg. "We put them on the road and sold 11,000 copies."

MuchMusic started playing the video, and commercial radio continued to climb aboard. The band was taken aback at the immediate response. "I was pretty surprised, to be honest," said Downie. "And I think it created this impostor syndrome, this fear of fraudulence that took, like, 10 years to eradicate. I couldn't catch up with it for a long time. I was waiting at any moment for the door to burst open and someone to say, 'You didn't make this happen.'"

The Tragically Hip, like good young men, went west. "For the most part, it was really fun," said Sinclair, who told a tale familiar to every young musician who has ever made a similar trek. "It was just the five of us and our sound engineer in a van, driving across the country, smoking pot, drinking beer, eating McDonald's and playing three sets a night. There were some really lame gigs, no doubt—five people, 10 people, no people—but it made us a great band. All that time spent together in the van, learning how to deflate disputes before they started happening, learning how to respect each other's space, learning to write songs together."

The tenor of the tour was set at the first gig, which was in Winnipeg—a 24-hour drive from Kingston. The Hip had been booked for three nights at the Diamond Club, a glitzy Top 40 bar where the booker was eager to snag this hotly tipped Ontario band, and another three-night stint later in the week at another bar owned by the same person. The band's first night in town, a Monday, coincided with a John Mellencamp concert that had been sold out for months. Just about every rock fan in Winnipeg was at the Mellencamp show that night, said Winnipeg music writer John Kendle. Meanwhile, he said, "The Diamond Club's manager had been horrified by the band's first set, their bum's eye for clothes and by Downie's performance, which included singing one tune while lying on his back." The band was fired after their first set. "He said he didn't know that he'd hired a punk band," said Downie. "All of a sudden, we had a week blown out, like a massive torpedo midship. We thought, 'Wow, this is going to be rough.'"

The band consulted the musicians' union—who were involved because the Friday show was to be broadcast on the radio—and weighed their options. They were also turfed out of the hotel accommodation that came with the gigs. Word spread through Winnipeg's music community, who found the band a place to stay and a gig for the weekend, at a place called Cornerboys, owned by former boxer Donny Lalonde, which Kendle described as being more of a rec room than a bar. "Pretty soon we'd made up five nights, just piecemeal," said Downie. Kendle wrote a column in that Friday's paper about the ordeal, and the Cornerboys gigs were packed, as was a return visit on their way back east.

The rest of the tour was equally full of extremities. The plan was to shoot a video for "Last American Exit" at a club in the West Edmonton Mall called Dancin' Shoes; only 10 people showed up. "That's why there are no long shots of the band: there was nobody there," said Sinclair. But the shows at the Town Pump in Vancouver "blew the roof off," said Gregg, who described the show as "a pool of lava, moving as one single mass." He was standing beside Flea of the Red Hot Chili Peppers, who turned to Gregg and said, "Where the fuck did these guys come from?"

On the first jaunt out east, the Hip played six nights in Halifax and six nights in the adjacent city of Dartmouth. One of those gigs was in a Mexican restaurant, at a point in the tour when band funds were low.

"On day three, we pooled our money together and didn't have enough to buy a can of Coke," said Baker. "We were living on coffee and free pop and nacho chips from the restaurant. Then we found our soundman doing rails [of cocaine] off his bedside table. That's the rock'n'roll life—we found out where all the money was going."

"Like any rock band going across the country, everything was brand new and everything was possible," Downie told Kendle in 2005. "Every whiff of interest or approval distilled itself into confidence, and anything that wasn't confidence was just well-disguised insecurity. We also had a very self-deprecating sense of humour, collectively, so we turned all those kinds of sad-sack stories into tales of triumph. I don't think you can do that if you have an ounce of ambition or aspiration beyond just having fun. You're just blown away by the fact you're actually doing this. You're putting another load of gas in the tank to take you farther away from home on a mission that is totally undefined and potentially endless, perhaps resulting in death or disfigurement—emotionally speaking, spiritually speaking and philosophically speaking."

CHAPTER THREE

EVERYBODY KNOWS
THE WORDS
UNDER THE COVERS

"I can't imagine why anyone would want to stifle their own creativity by playing only one other band's material, ours or anyone else's. If it meant that an original band couldn't get a gig because the local Hip cover band drew more people and sold more beer, that would indeed be tragic."

GORD SINCLAIR, NOVEMBER 5, 1996

ROCK'N'ROLL IS FOLK MUSIC. It started that way and remains that way. Songs that are easy to play when you're first learning an instrument. Songs shared and played by teenagers in their basement and by their parents on the weekend. Songs performed live in local pubs, where everyone's head perks up in recognition. Songs by artists who might not ever come to your hometown, or if they do you might not be able to get or afford tickets. Songs that deserve to be heard and sung and celebrated in an act of communion.

Everybody has seen a cover band, a group that doesn't perform original material. We've all been to high school talent shows, weddings, office parties or suburban pubs, where cover bands are the norm. We sing. We dance. We drink. We have fun. For musicians, cover bands are where you start out—and, more than likely, where you end up, no matter what happens in between.

Cover bands play a central role in the musical ecosystem, yet they're the subject of derision from all critics, from some fans and from the lucky few musicians who became successful: "What, you couldn't make it playing your own tunes?" Never mind the fact that pipe dream is only possible for 0.001 per cent of the world's working musicians. What are the rest supposed to do, pawn their instruments?

"There are musicians who don't like me because I'm in a tribute band," says guitarist Joe Foley of the Hip Show in Vancouver. "They think I sold out. But I'm 54 years old. I can't play original music for $10 and a beer ticket anymore. I'm too old for that shit. No one is going to buy my music at this stage anyway. You gotta be 20 years old and be willing to be bent over, basically."

The Beatles built their reputation in Liverpool and Hamburg as a cover band; their first two albums were almost half covers. Bob Dylan's first album consisted only of two original songs, one of which was written about—and blatantly apes—his idol, Woody Guthrie. The Rolling Stones' debut has but one Jagger/Richards composition. With the exception of Smokey Robinson and Marvin Gaye, few Motown artists penned their own material. So right there, most of the 1960s' most revolutionary artists started out as derivative knock-offs. Yet in their wake, rock bands for generations to come were expected to arrive out of the gate with an arsenal of original songs.

The Tragically Hip started out as a cover band. They did play originals at their first show, and were always developing more, but for the first three years of their existence the vast majority of their set was comprised of '60s covers, mostly of R&B songs in turn covered by the Rolling Stones or the Yardbirds. Once the Hip put out their debut album, it would be another 17 years before they played anything but their own songs, and that was solely on the 2006 tour, where each night would close with a different cover.

What's weird is that a mere 14 months after *Up to Here* was released in 1989, a band calling itself Almost Hip, from Kitchener, Ontario, played its first show. Only 18 Hip songs had ever been released commercially; Almost Hip's set list was predictable. By 1992, other Hip acts started sprouting up across the country, including one in the band's own backyard: Road Apples. By 1995, Road Apples were playing 200 gigs a year, some in venues like the North Oshawa Arena, with dry ice, a big light show and even two 12-foot screens on either side of the stage—a technological innovation the Hip themselves wouldn't adopt until about a decade later. Meanwhile, Road Apples were always sure to tell audiences that they doubled as an original band called Vagabond Groove, and they would slip some originals into their Hip set. "The whole purpose of Road Apples was to be musicians, to play full-time so we can only get tighter," singer Mike Compeau told

Toronto Life in 1995, "to not have to get a day job and to get our Vagabond Groove name known."

Todd Sharman, of the Ontario band Wheat Kings, has a story similar to other Hip imitators. In the early '90s, he and the Wheat Kings' drummer were in an original band. "We did that for many years, and it was an uphill battle," he says. "Then that band broke up, so he and I started a Tom Petty tribute. We stuck in some other music just to spice it up." Hip tunes in particular went over extremely well: "People started freaking out." Those people included two different booking agents who happened to call Sharman in the same 24-hour period, to tell him he'd make a lot of money if he did an all-Hip act. It was 1994, arguably the zenith of the band's popularity, and so Wheat Kings were born. In the '90s, they played about 80 gigs a year for about $1,500 a night, mostly in Ontario and Quebec. They travelled to both coasts as well. They once played a Canada Day show in Ottawa in front of 5,000 people.

Canada Day shows are manna from heaven for Hip acts. Many of them play several in the same day, at various municipal events and then a club show at night. Joe Foley of the Hip Show remembers headlining a large outdoor venue in Vernon, British Columbia, on July 1, 2015: "It was off the hook. We came onstage and felt like rock stars. If we never play another show, that's okay—that's how good this show was. The audience was pushed against the crowd barrier like a Who concert in the '80s."

Foley has actually worked for the Tragically Hip before. He's a customer service rep for a lighting company, so he's worked on West Coast shows of theirs since 1991. Todd Sharman met the Hip once, via an old high school friend who became the Hip's lighting director for 10 years; the Hip went to the friend's wedding. Singer Dan Hilts of Ottawa's Little Bones tribute band once met Gord Sinclair in an airport. Sinclair, always the most affable and polite member of an affable and polite band, thanked him for playing their songs.

In 1996, Sinclair said, "I don't really have a problem with bands covering our material at all. If it's done in moderation, it can be flattering. However, I've never been a fan of the tribute band genre at all, let alone those who pin themselves down to doing exclusively Hip material." Years later, Rob Baker's side project with the Odds' Craig Northey, Strippers Union, released a song mocking tribute bands called "Everybody Knows the Words." None of that should be surprising; no one enjoys seeing themselves imitated, musicians or otherwise.

Obviously, many Hip fans don't take issue with the cover acts—after all, someone is keeping these bands in business. But superfan Hugh Larkin could never bring himself to do it. "No interest," says the Michigan firefighter. "I'd just be so critical: 'Gord doesn't do that. Rob doesn't play like that. That doesn't sound like Johnny Fay.' I almost feel like I'd be cheating on the guys." Oddly enough, some audiences prefer the carbon copy. One Buffalo man had never heard the Tragically Hip before he stumbled into a Practically Hip gig; he told the *Toronto Star*, "When I hear the original songs, they don't sound right to me."

There's a fine line between tribute bands and cover bands. Cover bands may or may not focus on one band's material; early Hip, for example, covered all kinds of acts from a certain time and genre. Most cover bands simply play an artist's greatest-hits record live, either to get gigs or just out of sheer love; if you're in a Joy Division cover band, you're not doing it for the money. Some cover bands deliver a twist, like the all-female bands Sheezer, Hervana or Vag Halen. Punk band Junior Battles do covers of Drake songs in a band they call Thirst Behaviour; they play every August long weekend during OVO Fest in Toronto.

Tribute bands, on the other hand, not only stick to the repertoire of one artist, but they dress the role as well. The "mock star" will imitate the vocal tics and physical mannerisms of the actual rock star. This likely began with the 1977 stage production of *Beatlemania*, which eventually made it to Broadway. It's also evident in the numerous Kiss tributes that perform with pyrotechnics and makeup, or the ABBA tributes complete with horrific pantsuits. Then there's the Musical Box from Quebec, a painstakingly faithful tribute to Peter Gabriel–era Genesis, to which the original group allowed access to visuals from their early theatrical performances to facilitate faithful recreations; Phil Collins and Steve Hackett have even joined them onstage. In the case of the Beatles, ABBA and early Genesis, none of those artists had any desire to play those songs together ever again (all the Beatles were still alive when *Beatlemania* debuted); the tribute acts bring the music to life instead of letting it ossify on old recordings.

The Tragically Hip being the no-frills band they were—until 2016, there would never be any need to dress up to be in a Hip tribute band—most imitators stick to the music, without worrying about Gord Downie's wardrobe or stage movements. "We could try to dress the part," says Todd Sharman of Wheat Kings, "but there's nothing I could do to myself short of plastic surgery to make myself look like Gord Downie. We just want to play the music and be honest with it." Likewise, Jeremy Hoyle of Strictly Hip in Buffalo, likely the most commercially successful Hip band, clarifies, "We're not a Hip impersonator band. We're about the music presentation. We do note-for-note shows. Other bands have a guy who tries to look like Gord and dances around like Gord. That works for some people, but that's not what we do. We really want to be respectful to the music, and accurate."

Vancouver's Joe Foley thinks his band, the Hip Show, does both. "We're as real as it gets, right down to the clothing," says the guitarist, who has maintained the length of his hair to be the same as Rob Baker's. "We don't really hold back. If you're going to do it, do it right. People see the authenticity if they see my rhythm guitarist with a '75 Les Paul deluxe cherry sunburst [guitar], because Paul [Langlois] plays one of those. And I'm not going to go up there and wear jeans and a T-shirt and stand on the wrong side of the stage and then tell people I'm Rob Baker. Audiences are getting a psychological fix as well as the auditory. I wish we could dye our bassist's hair; it's as white as the driven snow. But I know it burns his scalp, so we don't.

"It's really easy to cheat," Foley continued. "I hear this all the time: 'Hey, check out our Hip tribute.' First, don't call it a tribute, because you look like a bunch of accountants. Second of all, what? Where's that guitar tone coming from? It's not like anything on any of the albums. The minimum I can do a show with is five guitars, because of all the open tunings [Baker uses]. When we're playing close to home, I'll bring eight." He owns 31.

Until 2016, keeping up with the Hip was not much of a concern for most Hip acts. Set lists still draw predominantly from the first three albums. "The songs we play every single night stop after [2000's] *Music @ Work*," says Strictly Hip's Jeremy Hoyle. "I love a lot of the new stuff," says Wheat Kings' Todd Sharman. He's a big fan of 2016's *Man Machine Poem*. "Maybe because I'm not playing it!" he continues. "We'd always pick up some stuff from the new albums, but it seemed to fall on deaf ears. As the gigs began to diminish in the 2000s, we figured we should play to our strengths and get the audience on our side. People definitely want the hits and don't get it when we do the mid-tempo, darker songs—even though a lot of those songs are bloody awesome. But when people just want to hear 'Courage' and 'Blow at High Dough,' I can't blame them."

It's hard to imagine any Hip band to be as effective evangelists as Strictly Hip, in Buffalo. The band started in St. Catharines in 1994; Hoyle joined a year later. In 1999, he moved the band to Buffalo, where he saw an untapped market. He hit the jackpot, getting four or five gigs a week wherever Canadian radio crossed Lake Ontario. Strictly Hip landed two residencies in Buffalo: every Thursday at a big suburban club and every Sunday downtown. The Sunday gig lasted eight years. "Sunday being such a weird night," says Hoyle, "it became the thing to do in Buffalo. If there were celebrities in town—football players, anybody like that—they would come to our gig. Consequently, it became a social thing that was beyond the music. That's what my mission has always been: spreading the message of my favourite band. That's why I came to Buffalo. It's like that Hip song ['Pigeon Camera'], 'It grew up into something we could no longer contain.'" In 2010, Strictly Hip won the inaugural Buffalo Music Awards Hall of Achievement Award; they'd already racked up eight Best Tribute Band awards prior to that.

Author talks about himself → 1st person POV

————

Disclosure: I've spent a brief time in two professional cover bands. One was more enjoyable than the other, but it was that other one that was more eye-opening.

Naturally, my first high school rock band played only covers: Jerry Lee Lewis, Tom Petty, Prince. In my 20s, I was playing in original bands who toured from coast to coast, had (extremely limited) CBC airplay and, in the early '90s at least, sometimes played three or four nights a week. Not one musician in any of those original groups ever pocketed a cent. It all went back into the band: rehearsal space, gas, recording, CD manufacturing, etc. All those bands eventually drifted apart for various reasons; each was a money pit.

In my 30s, I joined a bunch of musicians who banded together to play covers from the '50s to the present day, for an annual campus radio fundraiser in my small university town. It was not as rewarding as playing original songs, but it was both a lot more fun and more challenging musically. Soon that band started getting offers to play weddings and parties. It was a great social reason to keep my musical chops up.

I'd only ever seen one tribute act in my life. It was a tribute to Rod Stewart, whose appeal outside of "Maggie Mae" baffles me. One summer night in the early '90s, I stumbled into a gig in Coboconk, Ontario, because some friends decided we had to see the Miss Pattie House bikini contest in the Kawartha Lakes. The bar was too full. We somehow ended up in a barn with a guy who'd styled his hair like mid-'80s Stewart, wore *Risky Business* Ray-Bans, kicked soccer balls into the audience and butchered Tom Waits's "Downtown Train," which would have made me angry were it not so comical.

Years later, I got a call from an old kindergarten friend to see if I wanted a gig. We hadn't played together since we did piano duets of "Heart and Soul" as kids. He was now a professional keyboardist who gigged regularly with Classic Albums Live, a Toronto promoter that does for rock music what symphonies do for the classical canon: faithfully stage well-loved works, featuring every instrument heard on the original recording. When they do Pink Floyd's *The Wall*, for example, they always employ an actual children's choir. They don't do dress-up—this is just about the music, man. The company routinely plays Massey Hall and Roy Thomson Hall in Toronto, as well as theatres across North America. It provides a lot of steady work for some great players. (The only Canadian albums in their repertoire are 2112 and *The Last Waltz*.)

Because my friend runs in that world, he also gets calls from other cover bands or tribute acts to do fill-in gigs. This time, it was a Bob Seger tribute band whose pianist was recovering from surgery; they were also looking for someone who could play both organ and saxophone—which I do. The gig paid well; I'd even be paid for rehearsals. Was I interested? Sure! I get to play with my oldest friend in the world, make some dough and, hey, how hard can Bob Seger songs be?

It was the most humbling musical experience of my life.

I know and like about 10 Seger songs, max. This was a 30-song set, with lots of deep cuts I'd never heard. Physically, the singer was a dead ringer, but he lacked the same range as Seger in his prime—which meant we had to transpose all the songs several semitones down (apparently Seger himself does this in his old age), which adds extra layers of transposition when you're playing a saxophone. And if I were to play the opening notes of "Turn the Page" in the key and range we were doing it, I sounded like a bleating goat. I warned the bandleader about all of this ahead of time. "It'll be fine," he said. "Keep practising." He was cordially desperate.

I soon learned we were not interpreting the oeuvre of Bob Seger; we were replicating it. So if his *Live Bullet* version of "Bo Diddley" had a 64-bar guitar solo, that's exactly how long we had to play it, despite the drummer's (and my own) frequent inability to count that far. "Can't we just wrap it up or extend it depending on how it's feeling?" I asked, naively. Nope: 64 bars. Any song we played from that live album was also preceded by the same spoken intro heard on the record.

I was way out of my element, a complete fraud and a snob. I'm not sure which is worse. The rest of the band were fantastic, including the young jazzbo they hired as a last-minute ringer to replace me on sax, leaving me stranded on the organ. The gig, held at a large banquet hall in a Whitby industrial park, drew several hundred people who paid $50 a ticket. They came to hear the songs they loved in high school, songs that soundtracked lonely nights, lucky nights, house parties, road trips, weddings. Seger rarely tours Canada anymore: where would these people ever dance to a live band playing all their favourite songs of his? Should they be confined to their recorded versions? Related question: should a play be retired after its first run, never to be performed by different actors?

All these thoughts came rushing back in a wave of empathy when I went to see three Tragically Hip cover bands in the spring and summer of 2017.

———

"I! Come from Rex-dale!" That's how the singer changes the chorus of "Grace, Too," the first song at the first Hip cover gig I see, in deep Etobicoke, in west Toronto. The bar is full. Some are there for a birthday party. Some are there because they're there every Friday. Some are decked out in Hip paraphernalia. The band is still sound checking when I arrive after nine p.m. The first person I chat up is a guy in his 60s standing alone at the bar. He tells me he's a regular. I ask if he was here to see the Hip cover band. "Oh, is that what it is tonight? Christ, no." You're not a Hip fan? "The most overrated band ever. Guy has a terrible voice. I mean, it's sad what happened, of course . . ." On the other side of me is a Botox doctor with a gold chain and trophy wife. In front of me, an orthopaedic surgeon runs into a hockey buddy from 20 years ago, who is somehow convinced that Meryl Streep is going to play his mother in an adaptation of his self-published memoir. A group of twentysomethings gather close to the stage. Lots of people are wearing hockey jerseys. I don't know if this is a Hip thing or just an Etobicoke thing. Probably both.

Two women are the first on the dance floor: one is 25, one is maybe 50. They don't look like mother and daughter. A few songs in, the band plays "Bobcaygeon," from 1998, which is the most recent Hip song I end up hearing all night. Couples in their 60s come on the floor to slow dance. They stay there for the next song, R.E.M.'s "The One I Love," the least romantic song imaginable. Why is a Hip band playing R.E.M.? It makes at least some audience members edgy; they start yelling, "Hip! Hip! Hip!" The band follows up with "Fiddler's Green," clearly getting the slower material out of the way in the first set of three. And then it's . . . "Laid" by James?! Clearly, this band is not out to impress the hardcore Hip heads; they're just entertainers aiming to please a lay audience, a band whose set list happens to lean heavily on one artist. Nonetheless, in the bathroom during the set break, my urinal mate tells me, "I'm not even a big Hip fan. I like these guys better!" Back in the bar, the PA is playing Bob Seger's "Rock'n'Roll Never Forgets." I shudder.

The second set begins with "Blow at High Dough." The crowd eats it up. As they should: it sounds incredible, as this song always does, in any context. It's also very hard to fuck up. But I'm starting to be impressed by this band, even if they are—obviously—a simulacrum devoid of the chemistry the real band possesses. This could be a lot worse, I think. Watching the crowd reaction to even "Trickle Down," a deep cut on *Up to Here*, starts to warm my heart. It's not like the Hip themselves trotted out this song often in the last 25 years. *Up to Here* sold more than a million copies in a nation of 33 million people; we know every song on it intimately.

But then it starts to get weird. A Sublime cover, really? Followed by AC/DC's "TNT"? This is getting more tangential by the minute. Nothing, however, tops "Courage," which—and this is actually quite musically impressive, if nothing else—somehow segues into Bob Marley's "Three Little Birds." Then, without missing a beat, they somehow morph that into the Beatles' "Help"—and then right back into "Courage." None of those songs have anything in common, musically: tempo, genre, chord structure. It's ballsy, but baffling. Is there a thematic thread here related to Gord Downie's current condition? Is every little thing going to be all right? I'm sure I'm the only person in the bar even thinking about this. Then there's another '90s cover, one I don't recognize. And then: "Night Moves" by Bob Seger. He haunts me still. I leave. I'm not sure how much Hip would even be in the third set.

The next Hip band I see is at a food fair northeast of Toronto. The carefully curated culinary selections on offer are six food trucks serving nothing but burgers and fries. The craft beer booths push their sour and hoppy beer; the lager sells out early. It's an unseasonably chilly summer night; there are only about 300 people when the Hip band goes on, which dwindles to about 100 by the end.

This is one of the oldest Hip cover bands in existence, so my expectations are high. They, too, open with "Grace, Too." But their third song is "Opiated," the last track on *Up to Here* and the one song from that album I did not expect to hear; later, they do the equally unlikely "Last of the Unplucked Gems." They follow that with "In a World Possessed by the Human Mind," one of only two songs they play released after 2000 ("Yer Not the Ocean" being the other). This is definitely a band for Hip heads. And yet: they're just okay. The first band I saw was better—despite, or maybe because of, the fact that the Hip is not the only trick in their book. This band makes a couple of mistakes. They don't bother trying to play the upside-down beat that kicks off "Little Bones." They're not capable of capturing the trance of "Don't Wake Daddy."

Not that anyone here really seems to care. Nor do I. I enjoy watching the gaggle of 10-year-old girls dancing to "Boots or Hearts" while a 14-year-old in an AC/DC shirt sings along. It's adorable to see the 70-year-old woman maintain her position in a lawn chair while rocking out vigorously to "Nautical Disaster" as the singer inserts the reference to Jane Siberry's "Temple" that Downie does on *Live Between Us*. I laugh when the lady in the non-vintage Platinum Blonde T-shirt takes a selfie with friends in front of the stage during "Locked in the Trunk of a Car" while kids with light sabres dance all around them. I love seeing the father of four dance to "Bobcaygeon" while holding an ice cream cone in one hand and his youngest in his other arm, while one of his other kids has passed out in a sleeping bag beside him—he's hardcore.

I could be cynical about all this. I'll have a lot more fun if I'm not.

The last Hip cover band I see is playing the midway stage at the Canadian National Exhibition on the Friday of Labour Day weekend in Toronto—29 years to the day after the Hip themselves played this exact same gig, on the exact stage. I had almost gone to see this act earlier in the summer, opening for Sloan at a county fair northwest of the city. Clearly, these guys get the plum gigs.

Unlike the other bands, the singer here bears at least a slight resemblance to Gord Downie: he's tall and bald and is a natty dresser. He imitates some of Downie's stage gestures—which, to me, is weird, but I totally get why a crowd would want to see that. He's intriguing enough that it actually transcends mere mimicry; he has a fascinating face and looks like he may well have studied clowning in drama school (yes, that's a thing). More likely, he's simply learned a lot of lessons from watching Downie over the years. He once told an interviewer he considers himself "the Gordiest Gord in all the land." I won't argue.

It's a gorgeous, if slightly chilly evening. As always at the CNE, the people of Toronto look beautiful: multi-generational, multicultural, the full swath of the city. The crowd in the beer garden is sparse and disinterested when the band starts their first set with "Fifty Mission Cap," just as the Hip did at their final show. But the few twentysomethings crowded around the stage are psyched. So is the fiftysomething biker wearing a *Sons of Anarchy* T-shirt, who's standing at a table near the front with a woman and an oversized Minion doll; he's the only other person I see stay for all three sets. The other constant is a large turd-emoji doll abandoned on a table near the front, which the band is forced to stare at the entire time. Other than the fact they play every song about 10 bpm slower than the Hip would, they're a tight band—obviously, if they play these songs every single weekend of the year, which their website indicates they do. They even have a recorded loon call to intro "Wheat Kings."

But one has to wonder how much the singer connects with the lyrics, or even knows about Hip history. Introducing "Fiddler's Green," he dedicates it to "all those out there who are in love. Who here is randy? Do you even know what randy means? It means excitable!" The song he's introducing is about a dead five-year-old boy.

Ah, well, we live to survive our paradoxes, don't we?

Like the first band's, this set list doesn't venture beyond 2000, although the singer slips some of 2004's "Gus" into "Grace, Too." They avoid some obvious singles from *Phantom Power* and play "Vapour Trails" instead. They dip back to "Highway Girl," leaving out the double-suicide rant (thankfully) and instead slide in a bit of "Bang a Gong," which makes perfect musical sense. In a real nod to the geeks, they open the third set with "Get Back Again," an unreleased *Up to Here*–era track heard only on bootlegs.

Despite the number of people listening—in the beer garden, strolling the midway, above in the gondola—there is little engagement beyond a few obvious diehards. Most are looky-loos, passers-by, weary and/or thirsty travellers. It's the CNE, after all: a Tragically Hip tribute band is just another relic of Canadian history that's part of the scenery here, along with military bands and agricultural fairs and sand sculptures and Top 40 blasting from the midway rides. Halfway through the third set, I bump into an associate producer of the soon-to-be-released Hip film *Long Time Running*. He's there with a Parisian friend, to whom he wanted to show off peak Canadiana. He figures a Hip cover band at the CNE is his best bet. I can't say he's wrong.

I didn't want to name any of the three Hip acts I saw. I don't think it's fair to review one night out of hundreds, for posterity in this book. They're all from southern Ontario, but these could be any of the dozens of Hip cover bands that have existed in Canada for almost 30 years. And as Todd Sharman told *Toronto Life* in 1995, "It kills me when people compare one Tragically Hip cover band to another. Who cares if you're better than a band that doesn't even play its own songs? Who the fuck cares? At the end of the day, there's no glory in it."

In 2017, Sharman also had other fish to fry. His Bee Gees act was doing really well. In fact, he was touring with it in Fort Wayne, Indiana, the night of the Tragically Hip's final show, giving him an excuse to turn down several offers for Wheat Kings gigs that night, offers that made him extremely uncomfortable. He got back to his hotel in time to watch the last half-hour online.

———

In 2016, after Gord Downie revealed his new stage attire on the first night of the *Man Machine Poem* tour, the Hip Show singer Matt Mattson had a bespoke silver "space suit" made and bought a hat with feathers to match. That same year, other Hip acts took to wearing the *Jaws* T-shirt Downie wore onstage for his last shows. Some even added the two-socks-as-scarf Downie wore around his neck, which some fans assumed was hiding a scar from his surgeries. (It was actually to keep his vocal cords warm.)

In a year when all Hip fans were bracing themselves for bad news, that onstage reminder seemed morbid, like wearing a death mask. Todd Sharman's daughter bought him a *Jaws* shirt that year. "I won't ever wear it onstage," says the Wheat Kings front man. "I contemplated it. Then I thought, 'No, I'll just frame that shirt with the poster I bought at the Toronto show and my ticket.' Because that's Gord's thing. I've never been the kind of guy to dress up and try to be someone else anyway. People would just say, 'That's Todd in a *Jaws* shirt.'"

By 2016, Strictly Hip gigs had dwindled to a mere three a week. That changed with Downie's diagnosis. "Consider that I've been doing this since *Day for Night* came out [in 1994]," Jeremy Hoyle said in May 2017, "the interest level has never been like it is in the last year." Joe Foley of Vancouver's Hip Show agrees. "Now that the Hip are not playing anymore, all the fans are looking for a place to happen. Before, we'd play pubs that would be three-quarters full; now there are lineups out the door, and most of them are raging Tragically Hip fans."

In January and February 2017, Strictly Hip booked six weekly shows at a 500-capacity club in Buffalo, each week dedicated to one of the first six Hip albums. All sold out except one. Hoyle himself, who works at the venue as a sound tech, was shocked. "The club had never done that for any artist, even national artists," he says. "Strictly Hip normally play there four times a year. We'd have big nights, but never like that." It didn't stop there. They then did a "Hipstory" night, playing songs from all 13 records. On June 30, 2017, Strictly Hip drew 8,000 people to an outdoor show with the Buffalo Philharmonic, for whom seven Hip songs had been arranged orchestrally. Hoyle sought and received blessing from the Hip's management.

Despite that success, Hoyle says, "It worries me that people will think we're opportunists or something. We're very careful about it, and I think people understand. Some people study a particular author or poet. I just devoted myself musically to the Tragically Hip. This is what I do for a living."

That got a little weird(er) in 2016, when these bands found themselves imitating a man who was dying in front of all of us. Weirdest of all was the news that Darren Sawchuk, the singer in Winnipeg Hip act 59 Divide, was also facing a terminal cancer diagnosis. He had a front-row ticket to the Hip's show in his hometown and told the CBC he was hoping to be called up to sing harmony on "Wheat Kings." That didn't happen. He died less than a year later, in March 2017; Sawchuk was one year younger than Downie.

Todd Sharman's wife woke him up with the news of Downie's diagnosis on May 24, 2016. The Wheat Kings' singer was shaken. He had a huge lump in his throat all day. Then the phone started ringing. "I had agents saying, 'Oh, you gotta get a plan of attack here to really cash in on this.' I was like, 'You know what? I don't even like what you're saying and I don't care to cash in on someone else's bad fortune.' That's just sleazy, and I'd rather not play, if that's the thinking. I'm still going to perform, but—I don't know, it's wrong. The guys in the band felt the same way, unless it's a charity event or a positive thing and it's not just something to line my pockets—or someone else's."

Many Hip acts—including Sawchuk's, and some of the six or seven new ones formed in 2016—did play cancer benefits that year. The Practically Hip played one on the night of the final concert, performing before the CBC broadcast for emergency-service workers in Mississauga, Ontario, with proceeds from the $30 ticket price going to the Gord Downie Fund for Brain Cancer Research at Sunnybrook Hospital. Others played gigs just to celebrate the final tour; Wheat Kings played a tailgate party outside the venue the Hip played in London, Ontario.

The Hip Show were hired to play a backyard party in Vancouver the night of the last show. "It was very well organized, beautiful setting; there were about 200 people there," said Foley. A stage was built and professional lights and audio brought in. The broadcast was over by eight p.m. Pacific time; the Hip Show played until 11. "We played for about as long as they did," says Foley. "We had people standing in front of us bawling their eyes out while we were playing, grown men weeping during 'Long Time Running.' We were emotionally charged in every direction as well. My wife and daughter were there, and we were all crying while watching the concert. It was one of those magical nights you can't repeat."

And yet many Hip acts will try and do exactly that, for decades to come.

CHAPTER FOUR

ON THE VERGE

1989–91: *UP TO HERE, ROAD APPLES*

"By walking I found out where I was going"

IRVING LAYTON, "THERE WERE NO SIGNS"

IT BEGAN WITH a mic drop. Not an intentional one, not done for dramatic effect. It was a blunder in front of Toronto's music industry elite, onstage, in perhaps Canada's most hallowed hall. It landed the Tragically Hip a major American record deal.

The band were playing the Toronto Music Awards on Remembrance Day, 1988, held at Massey Hall and promoted by rock station Q107. Metal queen Lee Aaron and fiery blues guitarist Jeff Healey were on the bill, among others.

"It was such a weird night," said Downie. "Geddy Lee and all these great Toronto people gathered around, and here we are from Kingston and nobody wants to know us. We're not gregarious, we don't go around 'pressing flesh,' so we just tucked away in our broom closet / dressing room all day with all the beer we could want. We ended up a bit . . . you know."

The Hip, like the other acts, had two songs to make their case. During the second song, Gord Downie swung the mic stand over his head: it fell into three pieces as the mic's screen came off and the mic itself somehow became unplugged. Rather than fumble and try to cover up the mistake, he turned it into part of the act, throwing himself to the ground and enacting a sperm-and-egg routine in which the cable swam back to the microphone. The rest of the band exchanged wary glances but never missed a beat. As he usually did, Downie started improvising vocally as he re-entered the mix.

Among the audience were a reviewer from Britain's *New Musical Express*—in town to profile Mary Margaret O'Hara—as well as an A&R rep from EMI Canada and Bruce Dickinson, an A&R rep from MCA in New York, who had flown up just for this gig. He was sitting beside Jake Gold to his right and Allan Gregg two seats down. Both looked totally dejected when the mic mishap happened.

When the Hip finished, Dickinson turned to Gold and said, "I love them. They can play. Big personality. I love their presence and their presence of mind. I want to sign your band." The managers' demeanour changed instantly. Dickinson continued, "I just want to take them to lunch tomorrow to make sure their heads are screwed on right."

Gregg, the Progressive Conservative pollster—whose party, in 10 days' time, was about to win an election fought on a free-trade deal with the U.S.—leapt in front of Gold into the row of seats in front and gushed to Dickinson, "Oh, their heads are screwed on all right. These are great guys, really together, really smart."

Gold added, "You have to come see them at the Horseshoe tomorrow." He'd pulled favours to squeeze the Hip onto a bill there, in the event that Dickinson wasn't immediately smitten by a two-song performance.

"Can't. I'm flying back to New York tomorrow after lunch."

"Change your flight," insisted Gold. The American acquiesced.

———

Allan Gregg and Jake Gold had been angling to get the Tragically Hip a record deal for most of 1988. Their RCA licensing deal for the EP would expire at the end of the year. The A&R guy who'd made that deal, Jim Fotheringham, was no longer there. The new guy, David Bendeth, came with the unfortunate nickname "David Band Death." (That faded in the next three years, after he signed Cowboy Junkies, Crash Test Dummies and Prairie Oyster.) Bendeth saw the Hip as similar to Blue Rodeo, who had finally broke through to radio with "Try." He wanted to market the Hip as an alt-country act. Gold and Gregg weren't having that. They kept looking.

They knew they had some interest from EMI, who found out about the band back in December 1987 when Ken Greer, who was signed to the label as Tom Cochrane's guitarist, casually mentioned that a record he produced was about to come out. "Uh, what record?" asked the EMI employee. Soon enough, Gregg and Gold got a call from the label, wanting to see the Hip. Their next gig was at the Scarborough campus of the University of Toronto, the night before the Kingston EP release show. Suitably impressed, the label said that if the one-year deal with RCA didn't pan out, to give them a call.

In 1988, Deane Cameron became president of Capitol/EMI Canada, after years as an A&R rep; he'd signed Glass Tiger. He started his career in music as the drummer in Tom Cochrane's very first band. In 1988, he also coaxed the contrarian Stompin' Tom Connors out of retirement and signed him to a new deal. Cameron's Canadiana fetish was obvious to anyone who walked into his office: he kept a taxidermied beaver there. He and A&R rep Tim Trombley were interested in the Hip and gave them some money to make a demo. And another. And another. "Like a lot of these guys," said Gregg, "they wanted to polish the apple. We were getting frustrated by the delay." EMI was surprised that Gregg and Gold wanted to put up half the money for the demos themselves in exchange for the right to shop the demos to other people, granting EMI matching rights if another deal emerged. Gold and Gregg didn't want to get locked into something unless a label was fully on board, on both sides of the border. They wanted to make sure Americans had a chance to see the band.

Every fall from 1980 to 2015, the *College Music Journal* (CMJ), a trade publication for campus radio stations, held a conference and "music marathon" in New York City, predating Austin's South by Southwest by seven years. Hundreds of groups would play five-band bills during one weekend in Manhattan, while radio programmers, managers and labels scouted the next big thing. It cost money to play it, and even more to get a track placed on a sampler CD distributed to all attendees in advance of the conference. In 1988, Gold and Gregg asked EMI if they wanted to split the $5,000 cost— which also covered hotel, transportation, an ad in the program and a clip on the video reel—and invite their U.S. counterparts to the one a.m. showcase at a midtown club called the Big Kahuna. The label declined. Gold and Gregg went ahead without them.

Bruce Dickinson had not yet started his new job as head of A&R at MCA Records. The day after he signed his contract, he was at home making breakfast and put on the CMJ sampler that had just arrived. "Over the noise of the eggs in the frying pan, I heard this voice," he recalled. "I stopped, went down to my living room, picked up the sleeve and it said: Tragically Hip, 'Small Town Bringdown.' Gord Downie's voice made an immediate impression. It cut through all the noise."

Dickinson had been in the record business since the late '70s, shepherding the careers of the Psychedelic Furs, Men at Work, Midnight Oil and others. In 1988, he was lured away from his position at Chrysalis by MCA. During his job interview with MCA CEO Al Teller, Dickinson was asked to speak frankly about the label's roster. "With Al, I knew you could only be honest, no bullshit," said Dickinson. "So I said, 'Well, you may not want to hear this, but here are some concrete examples of what you're doing wrong with a couple of your rock bands.' They had this band, Transvision Vamp. They were trying to promote them as a rock band, and they had this full-page, full-colour ad. 'That's nice, you're spending money—but take a look at the boots on this band's feet. You have them all lying on the floor, and the soles of their boots are facing the camera, and those boots have never hit the pavement. There isn't a single mark on the soles of those boots. How rock'n'roll is that?!' Al Teller looked at me and said, 'I'm willing to offer you a job *right now*.'"

A few weeks later, after hearing the sampler, Dickinson called Teller to say he was pretty sure he'd found his first band for MCA and that he might need to go to Toronto. Teller gave him carte blanche, even though Dickinson had yet to step foot inside the MCA offices.

Dickinson then called the number on the back of the sampler. It was Gold. "Hi, my name is Bruce Dickinson and I'm just about to start at MCA. I'd like to see your band, the Tragically Hip."

Silence on the other end of the line. Uncharacteristic for Gold.

Finally, Gold responded, "Well, we, uh, we do have a show coming up this Saturday night . . ."

"Great, I'll be there."

"Well, er, um . . ."

"Jake, you do want me to see your band, don't you?"

"Well, yes, it's just that it's an industry gig."

"I've been to industry gigs before."

"It's at Massey Hall."

"Oh, great, I love Massey Hall! No problem."

"Well, they're only doing two songs."

"What's the big deal? I'll be there."

Gold picked him up at the airport that Friday and drove him to Gregg's office. On the way there, he popped a Hip demo in the cassette player. Until that point, Dickinson had heard only "Small Town Bringdown." The tape started with "Blow at High Dough" and had most of the songs that would appear on *Up to Here*. "Jake was trying to chat me up, and I'm not saying a word," said Dickinson. "I'm just trying to hear the tape, and Jake is Mr. Talk. By the time we got to Allan's office, I'd heard half a dozen songs at least: they were all different, and they were all great. Most demo tapes start with a song like 'Blow at High Dough' and then have a half-dozen songs that leave no impression at all. But every song on this tape had something going for it."

At the Horseshoe show after Massey Hall, every A&R rep in Canada tried to angle their way into the dressing room. Johnny Fay told them to get lost. Dickinson recalled the drummer saying, "The only reason you guys are here is because some guy from New York offered us a deal last night. You guys can forget it. You had your chance for a year." Dickinson added that during his own time at Chrysalis/EMI, he was a liaison between the American and Canadian branches when the Hip were recording demos for EMI. "I'd been to Canada several times," he said of that time. "EMI Canada took me to see bands. They played me things. Everybody but the Tragically Hip."

EMI Canada eventually presented an offer that was "every bit as good an EMI deal as I've ever seen," said Gold, "except they didn't have the U.S. guys on board. Which, in hindsight, why wouldn't they just have said they did? And if nothing happens, nothing happens. But by virtue of having access to the U.S. market, the MCA deal was better. We wanted an American label."

At the Horseshoe show, Gord Sinclair mentioned to Dickinson that the band really liked the way Tom Petty's recent records sounded, as well as the just-released Traveling Wilburys album, featuring Petty. Knowing the Hip were also big Stones fans, Dickinson knew just the producer who could capture what he'd just witnessed live, and he shared the name with Sinclair.

"Don who?" Sinclair asked.

Don Smith was not a name producer in 1988. Primarily an engineer, the only records on which he had a production credit were by the Welsh metal band Budgie and American rock band the Call, as well as a 10,000 Maniacs B-side. Smith was primarily an engineer, a studio role even more misunderstood or ignored by music fans than that of a producer.

If a music producer is akin to a film director—with musicians the actors and songwriters the screenwriters—then the engineer is the cinematographer. The engineer is responsible for the fine details of the big picture: the sonic nature of the record. Their role is to execute the vision of the producer and the artist. Needless to say, great producers don't work with sub-standard engineers, which can render their work invisible. By 1988, Don Smith's footprint was anything but invisible, even if his name was. In 1982, he worked on Bob Seger's *The Distance* and Tom Petty and the Heartbreakers' *Long After Dark*. Subsequent albums with Petty followed, as did work with Stevie Nicks, Bob Dylan, Lone Justice and Eurythmics ("Would I Lie to You," "Sisters Are Doing It For Themselves"). He also assisted with the first Traveling Wilburys album, and "Crying," the duet between Roy Orbison and k.d. lang. He engineered one track on U2's *Rattle and Hum*. And Smith engineered and mixed *Talk Is Cheap*, the first-ever solo album by Keith Richards, released the month before Dickinson met the Tragically Hip.

At the mention of Richards, the Hip did not need much convincing. Nor were there any objections to Dickinson's suggestion that they record their debut album, *Up to Here*, at Ardent Studios in Memphis. The budget: $175,000. Smith told Allan Gregg that he'd been looking for "a real band you could just bring in and turn on the tape."

Ardent is one of the great American recording studios, founded in the mid-'60s at the height of Stax Records' influence; many of that label's classic records, including Isaac Hayes's *Hot Buttered Soul*, were made there. In the '70s, it was where *Led Zeppelin III* was mixed, and it was home for Alex Chilton and Big Star. ZZ Top made almost every one of their records there, including 1983's *Eliminator*. By the time the Hip showed up in January 1989, so had the Replacements (*Pleased to Meet Me*), Steve Earle (*Copperhead Road*) and R.E.M. (*Green*). It was a teenage dream come true: recording a major-label debut in Elvis Presley's hometown, in a studio where some of their favourite albums were born, with a producer who had just worked with Keith Richards. Memphis in 1989 was not glamorous, however. Tommy Stinson of the Replacements described it as "this weird ghost town where rock'n'roll had come from."

During the recording process, the Hip had a club gig booked in town, opening for a hard rock band from L.A. called Little Caesar, who were signed to Geffen Records. "Tremendous hype," recalled Dickinson. "They'd grown up listening to Skynyrd records. They weren't terrible; the singer had a presence, but the rest of the band had no charisma and they had no songs. It was really interesting to watch the guys from Little Caesar watch the Tragically Hip. They were, in a word, crestfallen."

The Hip spent a total of five-and-a-half weeks in Memphis, starting in January 1989, eating at Rendezvous Ribs and cutting take after take while the beer cans collected on every available surface in the studio. "We had stamina," said Downie. "We'd do a hundred takes in a row because we'd played those songs 300 nights in a row. The voice I'm using on *Up to Here* is my voice from the stage. It's the voice of a host, saying, 'Welcome.'"

The opening track was also the first single: "Blow at High Dough." It begins with a bass riff from Gord Sinclair, who at that point was still the Hip's principal songwriter. Gord Downie's lyrics paint a picture of the time a film crew invaded his hometown—clearly a once in a lifetime event, long before Canada became a popular and economical place for U.S. studios to shoot films. The plot has something to do with an Elvis impersonator performing at the local speedway. Hollywood versus the hayseeds; the big time and the small potatoes. And then, before our ears, with a suspended stop and one ringing power chord—a moment filled with the tension of a cliff diver right before he makes impact—this bar band from a tiny Ontario city transforms into stadium-worthy status alongside AC/DC. By the time Downie tells us he can "get behind anything," just before the entire band comes crashing in, many Canadians knew they'd found their new favourite band.

As Dickinson had discovered on the *Up to Here* demos, the wellspring of songs didn't dry up after that opening bombshell. The band went to Memphis with 14 songs and wrote four more while down there. The track-list was whittled down to 11. As the cliché goes, it was all killer, no filler: a top-notch rock'n'roll barn-burner from top to bottom. "New Orleans Is Sinking" was the second single, becoming the Hip's signature song and a beloved live staple, even after 12 more albums of original material. Kingston DJ Steve Jordan distinctly remembered being at the Lakeview Manor show where the Hip first played "New Orleans." "My jaw dropped," he said. "This was suddenly more exciting than it ever was." Based on an uncharacteristically flashy guitar riff by Rob Baker, influenced heavily by the blues staple "Baby Please Don't Go (Down to New Orleans)" and the Guess Who's "Shaking All Over," the song's inspiration came from what clearly sounds like a psychedelic trip Downie took with some friends to the Crescent City in 1984. Though set in America, it carries a classic Canadian theme of overcoming elemental destruction—in this case, water. The narrator is also clearly a tourist, a northerner out of his element in a seemingly lawless Southern town.

Many of the songs were written together, though "She Didn't Know" and "When the Weight Comes Down" were sole Langlois compositions. "Boots and Hearts" was Sinclair; Downie once introduced it live by saying, "This song is about a podiatrist who meets a young college co-ed, and she kills him with his own devices."

In his own lyrics, Downie is at a crossroads between his more abstract self ("New Orleans Is Sinking," "Trickle Down") and a narrative songwriter in the Lightfoot mode ("Blow at High Dough," "Opiated"). The latter is most evident in "38 Years Old," an entirely fictional story that references the biggest prison break in Canadian history, which took place at Millhaven Correctional Institute, one of eight federal prisons once located in the Kingston area (there are now six). In July 1972, when Downie was eight years old, 14 inmates—most of whom were serving at least 10 years for armed robbery—escaped through a hole in a fence during a softball game. Seven were caught within the first few days, some within hours. The others, however, remained at large for more than a month; one was eventually caught in Vancouver. The Downie family lived 10 miles away from the prison, in Amherstview. "It had this huge, spooky effect on our community—everyone was locking their doors," recalled Downie. "For me, it was pretty exciting at the time, the biggest thing ever to happen where nothing ever happens. The song extends that idea into fantasy, wondering what you'd do if a member of your family actually came home from jail before they were supposed to. What would you do? Offer him a coffee?"

Downie's version of the story shifts some numbers around: 12 men in '73, not 14 in '72. (Because "maximum security" rhymes with 73—sort of.) His story is about a virginal 18-year-old convicted of killing the man who raped his sister; 20 years later, he breaks out of prison and knocks on his younger brother's window. Unfortunately, for a song written in the first person by the younger brother in the story, Downie references an "older brother Mike"—which he himself has, as well as two sisters. For years, the Downie family was plagued by fans who thought the song was autobiographical. As a result, it was left off set lists for years, although it is a fan favourite.

Considering that *Up to Here* boasts such a muscular, masculine sound, there are two other songs on here about avenging crimes against women, these ones from the female perspective: "She Didn't Know" and "I'll Believe in You." Not many, if any, all-male bands dared to go there in their lyrics, to address male violence on women. Conversely, not many, if any, dudes in the audience picked up on this fact. Of the line in "38 Years Old" about the sister getting raped, one fan recalled standing on a table at a university bar, bellowing out the words with exuberance, not even really understanding what the song was about or why doing so might make anyone feel uncomfortable.

Up to Here portrays small-town life, with its struggles, limitations, dreams of escape and—much like a Kids in the Hall skit that aired two months after the album's release—lots of guys named Dave. The Hip may have shared some musical similarities with John Cougar Mellencamp, but their take on small-town life was considerably different than the parochial one heard on his 1985 single "Small Town." Intensely proud of their hometown, they were also not blind to its dark side.

Shortly before the album's release, the Hip made a decision that would bind them together for almost 30 years: all songs would be credited to the Tragically Hip, with royalties split five ways. Songwriting teams like John Lennon and Paul McCartney or Greg Keelor and Jim Cuddy had agreed to co-credit all songs they wrote for their respective groups, even if one partner made no contribution at all to a specific song. But the practice was rare for groups—R.E.M. being a notable exception. The rationale was that if any one band member's song was chosen as a single and became a massive hit, that person wouldn't be driving to gigs in a limo while everyone else was on public transit arguing about who wrote the bridge. "These are the things that kill bands," said Baker. "We thought if we're going to do anything in terms of a career, we should eliminate those problems right away." This was a lot to swallow for Gord Sinclair, who had written two-thirds of the songs at that point, both music and lyrics. But he took one for the team. Downie agreed to the deal on one condition: that he write all the lyrics from then on in. The music might become more democratic, but a benevolent dictator was soon to be on the mic.

———

Up to Here was released on August 8, 1989. It was an immediate hit. It went gold after Christmas and platinum by March, on the strength of "New Orleans Is Sinking." It sounded like nothing else on the radio. It was raw and fresh enough to appeal to young audiences, with plenty of nods to the rock'n'roll of a previous era. In a decade when rock records almost never sounded like five people playing live in a room, *Up to Here* stood out immediately.

"It sounds like there's an amplifier in the room when you put the record on," said Baker. "Even if you think the band stinks, you'd have to say it's a great-sounding record. It just leaps out at you." If Don Smith took the Hip gig because he wanted to be a producer, *Up to Here* mostly proved that he was an expert engineer at capturing electricity in the room. "He's not a wild creator in the studio like a Todd Rundgren," said Baker. "He's more of a craftsman. He worked strictly on how to get a certain sound captured the best way on tape and had nothing to do with the creative aspect."

That said, the difference between *Up to Here* and demos of the same material, recorded in Toronto with Chris Wardman, is staggering: the arrangements are much more dynamic and powerful, making a good live band sound even better on record. Yet there was one song Smith couldn't fix: Gord Sinclair's "Get Back Again," a live staple at the time. They'd tried it with Wardman and had high hopes. "I remember really concentrating and thinking, 'This is really good,'" said Baker. "I looked up and caught Gord Sinclair's eye and he was looking at me and I could tell this was it, we were hitting it out of the park here. At the end of the track, [Wardman] said, 'That was fantastic, perfect, I loved it. Now do it one more time, because we didn't have tape rolling.' We did it again and it wasn't as good." It didn't work in Memphis, either, although bootleg versions of the track have made it a favourite among hardcore fans.

Both "Blow at High Dough" and "New Orleans Is Sinking" were No. 1 songs on Canadian radio. Mainstream rock stations were on board right away. Even Top 40 stations signed on, which came as a relief to CKLC's Steve Jordan in Kingston, who was the first music director to put the Hip into Top 40 rotation, back in 1987, when he "had to fight to get them on the radio," he recalled of the EP. "Think of how many times you can hear 'Nothing's Gonna Stop Us Now' by Starship and multiply that by 100—that's how many times we played that song. Or 'I've Had the Time of My Life' from *Dirty Dancing*. Those were huge hits in 1987. Bruce Hornsby. Phil Collins until you're blue in the face. That was the kind of landscape we were in." Nevertheless, in 1989, Jordan programmed the acoustic blues stomper "Boots or Hearts" in CKLC rotation and it went to No. 1. "I knew I could play it during the day," he said. "We had played 'Small Town Bringdown' and 'Highway Girl' in the nighttime and charted both of them in the top 10. But *Up to Here*, sound-wise, was *whoa*.

"With few exceptions, mainstream CanCon was kind of terrible," Jordan continued. "There were a lot of what we called 'turntable hits' back in the day that filled CanCon requirements, but no one cared about these bands. Obviously there were exceptions, and some artists in between, like Luba, who had tons of airplay and was likeable but never a massive star. I'm sure people didn't even know the Tragically Hip were Canadian. Blue Rodeo had a bit of that, too, and Sarah McLachlan. Those were probably the big three. And 54.40, Northern Pikes and Grapes of Wrath. All those bands were great, but they were not like the Hip."

"*Up to Here* came out the summer before I arrived at Queen's," recalled Dave Ullrich, who played drums in a new Kingston duo called the Inbreds. "Almost every time I'd go to the Toucan, they would play that record in its entirety. There was something in the air. Something was bubbling up. This was more than just another MuchMusic band."

Crowd response was getting rabid. Colin Cripps, whose band Crash Vegas had just released its debut album, went to see the Hip in his native Hamilton in early 1990. "It was in the east end," he recalled. "Terrible venue, beside a Triple A rink. The buzz was big, but they were only playing to 600 people or so. All the elements were there: there was an electricity in the room, and Gord was fantastic as a front man. The crowd was about 90 per cent male, Friday night in the east end, knucklehead crowd: you could feel the electricity rising. I grew up in Hamilton, so I knew this wasn't going to end well. I stayed until the last song before the encore, and I thought, 'I gotta get out of here.' I left. Sure enough, the next day in the paper there's a story about the Hip gig and a huge riot in the parking lot with guys beating the shit out of each other." "It was just like a Western movie," said Baker. "People were getting chairs busted over their heads, and trays went flying."

"As it got bigger and bigger, that element was always there," Cripps continued. "A lot of testosterone. But you can't choose your crowd. Those people loved the band, loved the songs and the energy was palpable." Nothing could surprise the Hip in Hamilton after what they saw at their very first gig there years earlier. "Someone got stabbed in the head and another got knocked out cold right in front of me," recalled Baker. "It was an eye-opening experience for five young lads on their first trip to Hamilton."

"I remember seeing them play at this place outside of Hamilton," recalled their friend Mark Mattson, "like a motor sports place, and there were fires burning everywhere. I wanted to go visit the tour bus, but I was afraid for my life; there were these big biker guys guarding it behind a fence."

It wasn't just Hamilton, though. At one gig in Ottawa in 1990, 30 people left on stretchers. In Alberta, someone broke their neck while stage diving. Police cruisers would be parked outside gigs in the Maritimes, waiting for the inevitable fights to break out.

Reaction was not the same in the U.S. The MCA marketing department didn't help: the first press release they ever issued for the Hip called them "a quartet from Nashville," even though the accompanying picture showed five men. (At least it was the right five men.) "Fortunately, that moronic idiocy did not continue," said Bruce Dickinson, "but first impressions are hard to counter. The press department was restructured shortly after."

Nevertheless, the Hip were doing well enough. They played to a packed, enthusiastic crowd at punk mecca CBGB's in New York City and stayed up all night with a writer from Guelph, Ontario, only to discover that their van and all their equipment had been stolen by the morning. "They had a fair amount of college radio support," said Gregg. "The gigs were not great, but acceptable. We were seeding the marketplace and trying to break them the way we did in Canada: by having people see them." The Hip immediately found a home in Texas, Tucson, Detroit, Boston, Vermont, Chicago and Seattle, markets that remained loyal to the band for decades. Everyone who came to a show on that U.S. tour got a cassette of the debut EP. "It had a different cover, a bit snazzier. They only cost 25 cents each to make," said Gregg, who estimated he spent $250,000 of his own money on the band between 1986 and 1989, on tour support, recording, videos and promotion.

Only four months after *Up to Here*'s release, the Hip were in no mood to milk it. They were already planning ahead. In December 1989, they rented a house in Kingston's student ghetto to start writing more material: "Crack My Spine Like a Whip," "It's Just as Well," "Fight" and "On the Verge." Only the latter two would make it to the next album.

These were road tested in the winter and spring, starting out in the U.S. One day in March, while the band was on the West Coast, Allan Gregg got a call from Jake Gold.

"You've got to get Gord Sinclair on the phone, because they're refusing to do an in-store [appearance]. I don't know what's going on. You gotta talk to him."

Gregg called Sinclair, who said, "We just don't want to do the in-store."

"Why don't you want to do the in-store?"

"It's cheesy."

"Gord, the people who own that store and run that store don't think it's

70

cheesy. The retail guy who works for us doesn't think it's cheesy. They're going to think you're all cunts for not doing this. So if you want to piss off retail and piss off your sales force because you're too precious to do this, that's what you're faced with."

"Well, let me get Gord [Downie] on the phone."

Downie took the phone and was frank. "Look, if that's the price of fame, we'd rather not be famous."

"Gord," said Gregg, "it's your career, not mine."

They reached a compromise: only three of the members would do the in-store. The other two slept in the hotel, after what had been a long drive directly from Vancouver. They were woken up, however, with the news that they'd just won the Most Promising Group at the Juno Awards.

If ticket sales, record sales and radio play weren't enough to validate the arrival of a major new act, the Juno was considered prestigious in the mainstream media and at major record labels. The band wasn't having it: maybe because other than their friends in Sons of Freedom, the other nominees in that category were Indio, Brighton Rock and Paradox (go ahead, look them up). "We were always the kind of guys who would get together with a box of beer on Grammy night or Juno night and throw slices of pizza at the TV because it was such a gruesome show," said Gord Sinclair. "'That guy stinks! That guy sucks! How could they do that?' It was weird to find ourselves in the [opposite] position. We were mortified thinking of someone in their dorm room throwing pizza at us on screen." The Junos offered to fly the Hip to Toronto for the broadcast. They declined. "We thought if we're going to be the most promising band, then we should be where the most promising band should be—out working," said Downie.

An April 1990 gig at the Misty Moon in Halifax was filmed for a Much-Music special, which was later widely bootlegged among hardcore fans. In it, one can see the tightly coiled machine play a relentless set, sounding like the best garage rock band on the planet. Langlois displays his remarkable ability to sing strong backup vocals with a cigarette in his mouth the entire time. Between Downie's nasal voice and the haircuts on Sinclair and Langlois, the Hip look and sound a bit like a slicker version of the Gruesomes from Montreal, contemporaries who were too self-deprecating and DIY to ever break the big time. One can see the manic possession that overcomes Downie, the way his eyes roll back in his head, the way he appears to be channelling an energy from an unknown source. It's that unpredictability that has always drawn audiences closer to the "wild and crazy" singers, from Janis Joplin and humour ⤷

Joe Cocker onwards. It's what prompted the press to make odd, frequent—and unhelpful—comparisons to Charles Manson. (Was that supposed to be a compliment?!) One can also witness Downie as the referential music geek, who sings the chorus of "I Don't Wanna Know" by '70s British folkie John Martyn in the middle of "New Orleans Is Sinking"; though the song was covered by Dr. John and Blackie and the Rodeo Kings by the end of the decade, it was a decidedly obscure choice in 1990—and still would be today.

In July 1990, the Hip were home in Kingston and ready to prep their next record. They rented Grant Hall on the Queen's campus to rehearse new material, including "Long Time Running" and "Cordelia," the latter of which excited Sinclair because he and Fay "got to depart from the usual straight-ahead rock rhythm and get into some heavy funk metal." Not a genre one would historically associate with the Tragically Hip, necessarily, but it was 1991: the Red Hot Chili Peppers, Faith No More and Jane's Addiction were in the air. That influence is heard more clearly on "Twist My Arm."

The plan was to record again with Don Smith. The budget this time: $200,000. As much as they enjoyed their Memphis experience at Ardent, they wanted to try something different. And there is no place in North America anything like New Orleans. Their friend Colin Cripps had told them about Daniel Lanois's new space there; Cripps's band, Crash Vegas, had been the first to record there a year earlier. The studio still didn't have a name; the credit in *Road Apples* just reads, "Recorded in New Orleans." It would be soon known as Kingsway, one of the most prestigious new American studios of the '90s.

Kingsway was an old gothic mansion in the French Quarter, with 14-foot ceilings and big windows. Lanois and associate Mark Howard were slowly restoring the building, which was crumbling when they bought it. "Supposedly it was haunted by witches," said Michelle McAdorey of Crash Vegas. "There was some drama when we were recording there, and there was one moment when we had to exorcise something from the space." The band set up in the main room on the ground floor, beside Don Smith's control board; the drums were in the billiard room. "There was a lot of bleed between instruments while recording," said Sinclair. "Our ability to overdub was minimal. It was about capturing an energy—and, of course, that city exudes energy." Because of nearby residences, the studio had a curfew of 11 p.m. The city itself, of course, never sleeps. So with a clear cut-off time every day, the band explored as much of New Orleans nightlife as they could, visiting voodoo museums and even two-stepping to Cajun music at the Maple Leaf Bar.

When the band first arrived at Louis Armstrong Airport, they were picked up by a large African-American cab driver in a decked-out LTD. When he found out they were in a band in town to make a record, he gave them some advice: "You gotta make the young girls cry." He also recommended a local restaurant, with the suggestion that one should "eat that chicken slow, don't worry about them little bones." Downie thought that was odd, because at the time he was reading Timothy Findley's *Last of the Crazy People*, where a family's cat is named Little Bones. During that first week in New Orleans, playing pool in Kingsway's billiard room, it was so humid that Downie had trouble making shots because his cue finger was so sticky. All those elements, along with references to Jack Kennedy and recently deceased eugenicist William Shockley, came together in the album's opening track, "Little Bones," the album's lead single and the first sign that Downie was truly tapping into a new vein of creativity. *Road Apples* was the first album where he wrote all the lyrics—and it made a huge difference.

Gord Sinclair, who had written lyrics to many of the band's earliest fan favourites, conceded the point easily. "What makes [Downie's] lyrics special as they are is that they're very open to interpretation," he said. "And I say that from the vantage point of someone sitting beside him in the van as we were travelling, experiencing the same things he was being impacted by. He had the discipline and the foresight and the creativity to document all those things. I remember driving past the Golden Rim Motor Hotel [in B.C.]. I remember the hundredth meridian. They contain a certain meaning to me as a shared experience. But his real artistry is his ability to take our collective experience, diarize it and put it in a lyrical form that resonates on a universal level. That's why we tasked him with writing all the words—because he's so great at it."

"He was always very conscious that he was a spokesperson for us, that we weren't his backup band," added Baker, "that he was speaking for a broader group of people. He was conscious to include attitudes, and we'd find little snippets of dialogue appearing in songs."

Downie's lyrical approach was becoming more abstract and yet more explicitly Canadian. He wasn't going to write the northern equivalent of John Mellencamp's "R.O.C.K. in the USA" any time soon. Nor was he going to write about Canada as a distant memory, as Neil Young did in "Helpless" or Joni Mitchell did in "River." Canadian history and current events collided in the corners of Downie's imagination alongside Shakespeare, New Orleans lore and personal history. Sometimes it was oblique, like the expression "drop a caribou on you"—a play on "drop a dime," which refers to the cost of a payphone call in order to snitch on someone in the 1960s, the caribou referring to the tail side of a Canadian 25-cent piece: the cost of a payphone call in 1991. Sometimes it was an attempt at addressing current political events, like name-checking Sault Ste. Marie's city council decision to ban bilingual signs. Sometimes it was simply fantasizing about Canadian mythology, like the disappearance of painter Tom Thomson in 1917.

Downie's indirectness as a lyricist is not unlike Thomson's eye as a painter, if one takes in Northrop Frye's assessment that "Tom Thomson's eye . . . is continually scanning the horizon for some break into still greater distance. The tree in the centre of Thomson's *West Wind* seems deliberately out of visual focus: the eye is led to something behind it. Yet it seems also to be saying: 'Look, I belong here. I'm not just an obstacle on the way to the horizon.' It is an emblem of Canada itself, so long apologetic for being so big an obstacle on the way to somewhere more interesting, yet slowly becoming a visible object in its own right."

There was one song that was deeply personal for both Gords: "Fiddler's Green." Downie's sister Charlyn had lost her five-year-old son, Charles Gillespie, to a congenital heart disease in 1989; Sinclair had lost his only brother, Colin, to the same condition earlier. "Gord put his thoughts on paper as a gift to himself, to everyone, but mainly to his sister who went through that experience," said Sinclair. "We always had a real hard time playing the song, because it evoked some—not painful memories, but just memories. It's very personal." Despite being a fan favourite, and a song covered by Welsh band Stereophonics in 1999, the Tragically Hip didn't play "Fiddler's Green" live for years "because the wound was too deep," said Sinclair. In 2006, "we talked about it and played it one night and it was great and fun to play, and suddenly it became okay and it was good. It hasn't lost any resonance, but it became okay to perform it again." The Hip played it at their last-ever performance, in Kingston in 2016, where Downie dedicated it to his sister in the audience; it was one of the very few times during that performance where he was visibly emotional.

Musically, *Road Apples* was the first time the band had truly written all the material together; the album's closing track, "Last of the Unplucked Gems," was created while improvising in the studio. "I remember a review in the *Globe*," recalled Downie, "that was generally derisive. I don't know who wrote it—I can think of maybe a half dozen guys there who didn't like us—but it said 'Last of the Unplucked Gems' was a good sign for things to come. I totally agreed with that. The whole record was okay, but that was a new direction. It ushered in a new era of being able to write—I don't know, diaphanously, or something."

Don Smith took the tapes home to California to mix, without the band present. There, he called his friend Benmont Tench of Tom Petty's Heartbreakers to play piano on "Twist My Arm." Tench's contribution lasts all of two seconds. He was paid $1,500.

The album was set for release in February 1991. The band, Johnny Fay in particular, wanted to call it Saskadelphia, a geographical portmanteau that spoke to the dislocation felt by a band who played 200 gigs across North America in 1990. Management and label both balked. "Terrible fucking name," said Gregg. Nor were they impressed by the alternate suggestion, Call Me Ishmael, a reference to the narrator of *Moby-Dick*. The cover image had already been chosen, a shot of a horse in front of an RV park. That inspired what turned out to be the perfect title: *Road Apples*. It's a euphemism for horseshit, and in the frozen north those droppings would be used as road hockey pucks. It was both innocuous and subversive.

Management knew they had a hit on their hands. Jake Gold gathered as much of MCA Canada's senior staff as he could in a recording studio, where he pressed play and cranked the volume. "We hadn't heard a note up to that point, and we were blown away," said Kevin Shea, the head of the label's national promotions department. "Jake was so proud." MCA America was not impressed enough to pay for a video for "Little Bones." Allan Gregg shelled out instead.

No matter: *Road Apples* went platinum in 10 days. "It was like watching people you knew win the Stanley Cup," said the band's old high school friend Hugh Dillon, who by then had formed the Headstones.

To celebrate, Kevin Shea at MCA wanted to do something different than the usual framed plaques given to industry supporters of the band. Shea was a huge hockey fan. He wanted to do something with actual road apples. "I found a place in Quebec that would acrylicize anything, including horse manure," he recalled. "Then we wrote on the base of the plaque: 'Thank you for helping us get this hit'—with 'this' and 'hit' closely together. Jake and Allan took that idea to the band, who loved it."

At this point, the band could easily have headlined Massey Hall, the 2,750-seat Toronto venue that opened in 1894 and is considered a rite of passage for Canadian acts. In North America, it is second only to New York City's Carnegie Hall in terms of prestige, history and similar capacity. Instead of Massey, in March 1991, Gold and Gregg booked them for three nights at the 1,800-capacity Concert Hall (a.k.a. the Masonic Temple)—a general admission floor with benches on the balcony, an intimate club more amenable to rock'n'roll mayhem. Tickets sold out instantly. MCA marketing director Steve Tennant took out a full-page ad in *Now* magazine that read, "Even the scalpers are going to this one. But you can still buy the record." Ticket prices across the country were capped at $20, which Concert Promotions International told the *Toronto Star* was low. "Unheard of to date in the Canadian market" for the kind of artist with that level of demand. In August 1991, the Hip played three nights at the Ontario Place Forum, capacity 7,000 each night. The Skydiggers were the opening act. There was an unexpected after-party: fans stumbling through the park afterwards were surprised to walk by a waterfall that suddenly turned off; the wall behind it opened and the Village People performed.

The myth of the live Hip experience grew exponentially with the release of a radio-only promotional CD single for "Cordelia," which featured two live tracks as B-sides. "Twist My Arm" and "New Orleans Is Sinking" were both recorded by Don Smith at the Roxy in L.A. for the Westwood One radio network in May 1991. In this almost-nine-minute version of "New Orleans," Downie spends half of it spinning a tall tale characteristic of his mid-song rants at the time. "I had a job before this," it begins. "Ultimately it was that job that drove me into this." He then proceeds to tell of a time when he was a "clean and scrub" man working at a large government-funded aquarium, specifically in the "killerwhaletank" (one word) alongside Shamu and Bartholomew. After he unknowingly becomes part of an interspecies love triangle, he loses his left arm to a jealous whale. Underneath this bizarre tale, the band responds dynamically to both the narrative and the delivery; by the end, Baker is working his wah pedal to imitate whale sounds.

That side of Downie would never make it onto a studio record. But Jake Gold knew that fans were eating it up every night, and he wanted to feed them more—but not too much. As the track got picked up by various radio stations, and fans called in and requested it repeatedly, Gold didn't want to make it commercially available. Just as the live show was an ephemeral experience, so too should be the sensation of hearing this monologue on the radio. He knew that real music nerds sat in their bedroom with their boom boxes, waiting to press record when a rare song came on the radio. That sense of anticipation, that sense of achievement, of ownership, is what fuels real fandom—the sensation of scarcity that's hard to imagine in the "everything now" age of "infinite content," as Arcade Fire would say.

The "Killerwhaletank" rant would haunt the band for years. People would request it. Tribute bands would ape it. Downie insisted that it was a one-night thing, something spontaneous that could never be repeated. Which isn't true: a review of a Kingston show in August 1991 suggests that he was still using the monologue three months after that Roxy show.

That Kingston show, their second to be held at the historic Fort Henry site, was the Hip's biggest hometown date yet, in front of 4,500 people, with Blue Rodeo opening. Steve Jordan lobbied Mayor Helen Cooper to present the band with the key to the city, which she did. It was filmed for the one-hour CBC documentary *Full-Fledged Vanity*. Though the show was supposed to be a triumph, Jordan recalled that Downie was nervous and apprehensive beforehand.

Dan Aykroyd was going to be the MC. Though raised in Ottawa, the star of *Ghostbusters* has a family connection to Kingston going back six generations, and he owned vacation property half an hour north of town. He was frequently spotted in downtown bars, particularly blues clubs. It was natural that the town's biggest star should be on hand to MC a crowning moment for the next generation.

Jordan ran into Downie backstage. "Hey, how's it going? Isn't this great?" asked the CKLC DJ, who had MC'ed almost every Hip gig in town for the last five years.

"I don't know. Something doesn't feel right. You're not going to be bringing us on," said Downie.

"Dude, no one here, not even my own girlfriend, wants to see me on that stage."

"Yeah. All the same, I feel like it's a bad omen." With that, Downie walked away.

Shortly after, Johnny Fay walked up to Jordan. "What did you just say to Gord? We need to fix this."

Jordan found Aykroyd. "Dan, there's a bit of a problem. Gord's feeling a bit weird because I normally do this intro thing. Honestly? I don't care. You're Dan Aykroyd."

"Ah, good point, Steve, whaddya suggest?"

"Maybe if I came out and brought you on?"

"You know what? I've put on a few pounds. If I walk out there unannounced, people might not recognize me. Good call."

"That's how we solved that problem," Jordan recalled years later. "That whole familiarity thing, building a family around you—that was important to Gord."

The Fort Henry show capped an intense three-year period that turned the band's lives upside down, and not just professionally. All this flurry of activity occurred at a time when some members were settling down—if that's what you want to call it. Gord Sinclair and his wife, Chris, a psychology student he met when she worked at the Lakeview Manor as a waitress, had their first child, Colin, in 1989, the same year *Up to Here* came out. Rob Baker married Leslie Galbraith, who has a master's degree in art conservation, in September 1989, on a Friday; he left for tour on a Monday. Paul Langlois married his girlfriend, Joanne, in June 1991. Gord Downie married Laura Usher in February 1992 in Toronto. The reception was at the Horseshoe Tavern; Hugh Dillon's Headstones were the band.

None of those life events meant the band slowed down. A little more than a year after that Fort Henry show, the Tragically Hip released a record that would make them bigger than they ever imagined.

CHAPTER FIVE

ARE YOU BILLY RAY?
WHO WANTS TO KNOW?
THE BALLAD OF DAVE "BILLY RAY" KOSTER

*"Nothing can compare to how I feel when I'm by your side /
And nothing can compare to the world I see in your eyes"*

BLUE RODEO, "KNOW WHERE YOU GO"

HE WAS THE SLIM, handsome figure in an Australian hat, checking the microphones right before the lights went down. He was always standing at the side of the stage tuning guitars. He was the guy passing out set lists to the front row at the end of the show. They call him Billy Ray. His name is Dave Koster.

Dave "Billy Ray" Koster worked every single Tragically Hip show for the last 25 years of the band's career. "It's never been about a job. It's been a life," he told Joseph Boyden for a *Maclean's* article, one of the rare times he—or any roadie, anywhere, for that matter—was quoted in the media. Koster was Gord Downie's best friend, at his side not only for Hip business but solo projects and everything else. When the singer was diagnosed with brain cancer in 2015, it was a tightly kept secret: as one friend recalled, Koster was the only person not named Downie who knew about Gord's condition those first few weeks.

Koster was 18 years old in 1992. He was working for a Kingston audio company. One day, his boss sent him to set up a PA system at the Toucan, the tiny Irish pub on Princess Street adjacent to a haunted limestone alleyway. Koster was surprised when a crew arrived with the Tragically Hip's gear. He was a huge fan and knew exactly how to set up Johnny Fay's kit, impressing the Hip drummer. After the show, Koster's boss suggested he write the band a letter; they would probably need additional crew members soon. So he did. "Gord Downie always jokes that it was written in crayon, but it wasn't, it was typed out," Koster told George Stroumboulopoulos.

Koster was in his room at his parents' house a month later, listening to *Road Apples* at full volume. The phone rang. "Hi, it's Johnny Fay from the Hip." He leapt up to turn down the music. "We got your letter. Do you do guitars?" Koster had to admit he didn't, so Fay said thanks but no thanks. A week later, he happened to be driving by the Fay residence and saw Johnny and tour manager Dave Powell moving a couch out of a van. Koster offered his help and then introduced himself. He volunteered to go to an Ottawa show and work for free just as a trial. A few days later, Fay called him back: "Listen, we don't have a lot of money right now, but you're welcome to come out."

Koster started as Fay's drum tech. A month later, the band's guitar tech was moving on; Koster took that position as well. Before a show in Phoenix, Arizona, soundman Mark Vreeken showed Koster how to change guitar strings. On an Australian tour in 1993, Koster was doing monitors as well as serving as drum and guitar tech. "When I started with the band, they already had a Dave: Dave Powell was their tour manager. He'd been with them the longest of anyone at that time. So for the first month or so, they just called me 'the kid.' 'Tell the kid to get my amp.' I was fine with that, because I'm 10 years younger than those guys. But 'Achy Breaky Heart' [by Billy Ray Cyrus] was on top of the charts, and I had a mullet [like Cyrus]. One night on the bus, one of the guys said, 'Oh, come on, Billy Ray.' It stuck."

Back in Canada, Colin Cripps of Crash Vegas was looking for a new guitar tech—not an easy position, as Cripps is an aficionado for high-end guitars and used almost as many pedals as U2's the Edge. "[Cripps] thought he was getting Canada's premier guitar tech—the Tragically Hip's guy," said Koster. "He quickly realized, 'You don't know what you're doing, do you?' Rather than telling me to get lost, he taught me how to tear apart $10,000 Stratocasters from the 1950s and put them back together while he watched my every move. I've never met anyone who knows more about guitars than him." Cripps says Koster's greatest talent is the willingness to learn: "It's easy to show something to people who are interested, and he was very good. He had all of the ambition. It wasn't like I had to twist his arm."

As the crew evolved, Koster could have been promoted to production manager, or something less physically demanding. But he didn't want to leave the stage. He didn't want to miss one note of a sound check or a show—and he never did. He never got sick of it. "Now, when I listen to music, they're still my favourite band," he told Stroumboulopoulos in 2017. "That's the amazing thing. I've never lost the fire I had when I was 18 thinking, 'Man, these guys rock.' I used to take great pride in telling local crews in the States when we were setting up, when they'd ask, 'What are these guys like? Are they any good?' I would say, 'Just you wait, just you watch. Tonight you'll see something fantastic.'

"Even the nights Gord would consider a bad night were some of the best nights, because he would just destroy the stage; he'd go through seven mic stands. He had days where he'd break them and look right at me and I'd hand him another one and he'd just break it again. None of it is shtick. He gets up there and whatever is going to happen is going to happen.

"I've learned so much from those five guys. They're my brothers through good and bad. Like any family, you've got moments with different siblings, but I just love those five guys and I know they love me. They've proven that a lot of times. I'm not married, I don't have children. I don't regret it. I feel really proud and blessed. That night [in 2016 when] the whole country stopped to watch, the next day I didn't wake up feeling sad. I woke up feeling that something I was a part of was one of the biggest things this nation has ever seen. You can't help but feel good about that. And I was a very small part of it: if I was hit by a bus that Saturday morning, somebody else would have worked that show."

The bond between Downie and Koster cannot be understated. A lot of other groups have an auxiliary musician they consider "the fifth member" of the band: sometimes that's a producer, sometimes that's a keyboardist, sometimes it's a manager. With the Hip, the sixth member was Billy Ray.

"A lot of time, especially on this last tour, [Downie] would give me a kiss and say, 'I love you,'" Koster told Stroumboulopoulos. "There were nights as I scurried back down to guitar world that I just welled up. How lucky am I? Sometimes [Downie] was about to go perform in front of 25,000 people, and he'd say, 'You okay?' or 'You all right?' Again, he's thinking about me—not asking me if *his* night is going to be good. He's saying, 'Are *you* okay? Are *you* ready for this?' I've always said my hardest day at work, the worst day of my working life, still ends in a Tragically Hip concert."

CHAPTER SIX

SOMETHING FAMILIAR
1992—93: *FULLY COMPLETELY*

*"In the lineup where their souls can be sold /
They've never heard of this Canadian band"*

RHEOSTATICS, "ROCK DEATH AMERICA"

THE MOST CANADIAN sound on the most Canadian album by the Tragically Hip was not the Canadians' idea. And it came back to bite them in the ass.

It's the loon call at the beginning of "Wheat Kings," a campfire acoustic song about a wrongful conviction, with mention of the CBC and prime ministers of the past. The British producer, Chris Tsangarides, thought it was so Canadian he "wanted something to hammer the point home," said Gord Sinclair. "What's more haunting and universally Canadian than the sound of a loon calling out into the night?"

The band's manager, Jake Gold, was soon flying to the U.K. from Toronto to observe the sessions, so he was tasked with finding a loon call. He picked up a new age CD in the airport gift shop featuring sounds of the Canadian wilderness.

In 1992, hip-hop acts were only beginning to get into trouble for sample clearances; such a pitfall would never occur to a rock band, especially for a sound not created by a human. So Tsangarides sampled the loon and put it at the beginning of the track.

"And we got sued by a fucking duck!" he chortled.

Loon calls might be "universally Canadian," but the man who recorded that one, Dan Gibson, recognized the source right away. An award-winning documentary filmmaker, Gibson was behind the *Solitudes* series of CDs, which have sold 20 million copies worldwide. One of those copies got the Tragically Hip in trouble. "I don't think we were very wise on the clearances," chuckled Tsangarides. In a weird coincidence, it was his former client, Irish singer Gilbert O'Sullivan, whose 1991 lawsuit against rapper Biz Markie revolutionized the laws around sample clearances in the first place.

Still, the producer laughed, it was "unbelievable. It's like, 'You *what*? You recognize your *fucking duck*?'" Gibson's work had been used in pop songs before; Gordon Lightfoot had used his loon calls in two songs on 1983's *Salute* album. Gibson sued the Hip for copyright infringement. Thoroughly embarrassed, the Hip settled the case immediately, making a large donation to Ducks Unlimited, Gibson's favourite charity. They even sent Gord Downie to apologize in person.

That "duck" was the only rough patch to befall the album that contained "Wheat Kings." It sold 210,000 copies in its first five weeks and went on to sell more than million in Canada, a feat few of their compatriots have ever achieved. It came to define a generation of Canadian rock music. It was called *Fully Completely*.

———

The Tragically Hip were looking for a place to happen. "This record felt like the new beginning of songwriting for us, an arrival of sorts at a new place," said Gord Downie.

There had been many arrivals, many new places in the three years since the release of *Up to Here*. Every corner of North America, in increasingly larger venues. Inroads into Germany, the Netherlands, the U.K. Even the songwriting for their third full-length was itinerant. The lyrics to "Fifty Mission Cap" were inspired by trips to the Toronto Reference Library and the Smithsonian National Air and Space Museum in Washington, D.C. "Courage" was written at a Queen Street studio run by Ben Richardson of Toronto blues band the Phantoms. "Locked in the Trunk of a Car" emerged from onstage jams during "New Orleans Is Sinking" and "Highway Girl." "Lionized" and "We'll Go Too" were written while rehearsing at the house of a Kingston record store owner, Jon Sugarman of

House of Sounds. "Hundredth Meridian" debuted at Maple Leaf Gardens when the Hip opened for Rush. "Wheat Kings" was first developed in New Orleans as sessions for *Road Apples* wound down. Lyrics were pulled from Canadian Hugh MacLennan, Czech Milan Kundera and Russian Fyodor Dostoyevsky, as well as American noir, hockey cards and headlines from the Prairie provinces. The album was recorded in a suburb of London, England; the vocals captured in an isolation booth draped with Indian saris from nearby shops.

The Tragically Hip were once a band of small-town Canucks drawing from the American South. They were now cosmopolitan travellers about to make the most Canadian album of their career.

———

The Tragically Hip had enjoyed a meteoric ascent largely by not sounding like other radio acts. Their first two records were made by a man who'd worked with Tom Petty and Keith Richards, whose decidedly old-school methods appealed to the record collectors in the Hip.

As in any industry, the question then became not how to maintain a big success but how to make it even bigger. Time to fiddle with the formula. Think big picture. Time to modernize.

Bruce Dickinson, their A&R rep at MCA, wanted the band to work with Chris Tsangarides, who was hot off helping L.A. band Concrete Blonde land their first top 20 single ("Joey") and sell 500,000 copies of their third album, *Bloodletting*. Like the Hip, that band also straddled the alternative scene and commercial rock.

Chris Tsangarides started his career when he was 17, in 1975. He was tea boy during sessions for UFO's *Force It* album and worked with Canadian producer Bob Ezrin on Peter Gabriel's first solo album. "Bob Ezrin was the first guy who I thought was doing something amazing," he said. "Until that point, all I'd seen were jackasses from the record companies coming in, who knew nothing. They just ordered people about. Not Bob. He knew about arrangements and all sorts of important things. I had a classical music background on brass instruments, which has really helped my career. You had to learn about orchestrations and harmonies. In the '80s, bands would be petrified of producers, especially if they had a name, because they thought they would change their song. I'm glad those days are long gone."

When Tsangarides graduated from engineer to producer, he helmed many '80s records by Thin Lizzy and solo records by their guitarist, Gary Moore. Then came a series of metal records that came to define his career: Tygers of Pan Tang, Girlschool, Y&T and Canadian metalheads Anvil, including their 1982 breakthrough *Metal on Metal*. (Tsangarides can be seen helming a comeback album for Anvil in an acclaimed 2008 documentary.) He also worked with Black Sabbath, Judas Priest and King Diamond, and he made the first solo album by Iron Maiden singer Bruce Dickinson (not to be confused with the A&R rep). Before Concrete Blonde and the Hip, his main non-metal work was with Lords of the New Church, goth icons Sisters of Mercy and Killing Joke, remixing one track on 1987's *Brighter Than a Thousand Suns*.

Don Smith, the Hip's previous producer, had set the band up in a room and recorded them live. Tsangarides had a considerably different approach. "I'm going to record each of you individually," he told them, "and then you're going to let me create the live vibe." "We thought that was crazy," admitted Jake Gold, but said Dickinson insisted. "I loved what Don [Smith] had done," said Dickinson, "but I [wanted] a slightly bigger sound, ever so slightly more polished, without selling out the band. I wanted to grab people by the lapels and make them listen to the damn band."

One of Dickinson's motivations was to help break the band in Europe. An American producer like Don Smith was thought to prove to the American media and record company that the band was serious about America. Working with a British producer, ideally, would prove the same for Europe. Working with a Canadian producer wouldn't have proven anything to anybody. It's worth noting that over the course of the Hip's entire career, neither the name nor the nationality of a producer ever opened a door for them they didn't push down themselves.

The track listing had been more or less finalized before a surprise hometown show at one of Kingston's tiniest venues, the Toucan, on April 16, 1992. They played 15 new songs, including "Wheat Kings." The man who partially inspired the song, David Milgaard, had been released from prison that same day. On April 18, they played at Toronto's Horseshoe Tavern. It, too, was a surprise gig, hijacking the final night of a three-night stand by the Bourbon Tabernacle Choir. Tsangarides flew in to see what he was getting into. He knew next to nothing about the band other than a few tracks from the first two records. "Standing on the side of that stage," he said, "by the end of the gig it was like, 'What did I just witness here?' It was an epiphany. They were so intense. I was sold."

In the lead-up to the London sessions in July, there was a European tour of festival dates in Germany and the Netherlands, which concluded with a show at the Astoria in London. MCA Canada rep Kevin Shea, who'd seen the band dozens of times by that point, remembered it as "a show of all shows. The place was jammed. All expats, I'm sure: everyone was wearing something Canadian, whether it was an Expos sweater or whatever. Gord was at his best, hanging from a pipe above the stage. The band was unbelievable. A friend I was meeting there made us leave early, and I'm still upset about that 25 years later."

Then it was a quick jaunt home to play two shows on Canada Day, for a brewery-sponsored event called the Great Canadian Party, playing in Barrie, Ontario, and then flying immediately to Vancouver, where the show was broadcast live on MuchMusic. "Welcome to Molsonia!" Downie greeted the crowd. At the end of "Blow at High Dough," he replaced the Elvis reference in the lyric to be about Mordecai Richler, before breaking into Mary Margaret O'Hara's "To Cry About" as the lead-in to "Lionized."

Then it was directly off to London, the birthplace of so many of their teenage rock'n'roll dreams: the Rolling Stones, the Yardbirds, the Pretty Things. Except that Battery Studios, home to many landmark recordings, was located far northwest from the core, in Willesden Green. Their hotel was near the northeast corner of Hyde Park, a 25-minute cab ride from the studio and nowhere near the nightlife. "The area was bleak, grey and industrial," said Sinclair. "It was the complete opposite of New Orleans, where you had to discipline yourself to get back to the [studio] to do some work." On top of that, it was a cold and wet July. Most of the band's spare time was spent watching the Barcelona Olympics on TV or a slew of VHS tapes MCA had given them.

For most of the band, the first four weeks were excruciatingly dull. That's because only Fay and Sinclair were being tracked, as per Tsangarides's method of building tracks from the rhythm section up. The band played all together initially, but only as a guide for the bass and drums. All the guitars were recorded later, in four days near the end. "We wanted to see how other people made records," said Downie. They found out.

———

Following the release of *Fully Completely*, the Tragically Hip made several comments to suggest that, while full of praise for Tsangarides himself, they weren't entirely happy with the sound of the record. They got Don Smith to remix some of the tracks for the 2005 collection *Yer Favourites*. "In retrospect, we realized how incredibly naive we were at the time," said Gord Sinclair. "It's definitely a Chris Tsangarides record with the Tragically Hip, because he has his way of doing things." Rob Baker felt the title track "got compromised by the 'build it up from the bottom' process that served so many of the other songs so well. Live, we change gears seamlessly and in unison. Recording separately, the gear changes always felt clumsy and forced." He expressed similar concerns about "Locked in the Trunk of a Car" and "The Wherewithal."

Yet seldom do most listeners hear a modern recording where a band is playing in the same room together—the first two Hip albums being an exception. Up until the late 1960s, all recorded music was one band playing together, with the singer as close to the microphone as possible. Once multi-track recording became possible, a band with only one guitarist could layer several guitar parts and a singer could perform their own backing vocals. As technology advanced, every drum on the kit could have its own microphone and corresponding track. You only want the hi-hat louder? Just turn that track up—the rest of the drums will stay at approximately the same level.

Beginning in the late '70s, every single sound was isolated. Bands now usually play together with amps in different rooms, listening to each other through headphones. The singer is always in a separate booth. Usually, everything but the bass and drums is expendable and will be overdubbed later—as on *Fully Completely*.

The extreme example of this "build from the bottom" approach is Def Leppard, whose '80s blockbuster albums *Pyromania* and *Hysteria* were produced by Robert "Mutt" Lange. His peer Hugh Padgham said, "The guitar chords would be recorded *one string at a time*. And this was all on analog recording, way before ProTools was around and you could have infinite tracks. It was mad. There would literally be hundreds and hundreds of reels of tape. The job of the poor tape jockey, or the engineer, was a nightmare."

Why would Lange—or anyone—ever track every single note in a guitar chord? "Well, because he could," explained Tsangarides, who was a friend of Lange's at the time. "This is the weird thing: before Def Leppard, he'd done *Highway to Hell* and *Back in Black* with AC/DC. You don't get any more basic than that. That band played, and they were brilliant. Trouble was, Def Leppard wasn't." Songs were constructed around a basic drum machine, a glorified metronome. Drummer Rick Allen sat out—and this was even before he had an arm amputated after a 1984 car accident. "Then off they go, doing songs with one note per chord, all this nonsense," said Tsangarides. "It's spot on, doesn't waver. In fact, it's the most machine-like [rock band] you've ever heard. Then it's time to put the drums on. Of course, the poor sod can't play like a machine, so he's wavering, it's ridiculous. So the Fairlight sampler comes in, and there's the sound: simulated drums, not a real drum set. But that was the sound of the '80s, and Def Leppard sold 20 bazillion copies—so who's right and who's wrong, know what I mean?"

Fully Completely is a far cry from *Hysteria*, obviously. But it was drastically different from the electric energy of the Don Smith records. Johnny Fay in particular doesn't sound like a drummer here; he sounds like a time-keeper. Any swing he has in him has been bled out, not unlike Aerosmith's post-comeback records of that same era. That really doesn't serve the shuffle of "Courage" or "We'll Go Too." The album version of "At the Hundredth Meridian" is clunky and lifeless compared to any live version; it's no wonder it never hit anywhere but Canada, four singles deep into the promotional cycle. The title track suffers even more next to live renditions, where it was often the highlight of an entire set.

But if the Tragically Hip were going to prove they weren't a bar band, they had to stop playing like one. That meant harnessing the energy and slowing down the groove. "We spent a lot of time dialling the tempo back," said Johnny Fay.

"On the road, everything goes way faster," said Tsangarides. "You have to pull it down to the point of it almost feeling too slow: then you know it's right. I could feel where the right groove was. It's just a feeling." The man who produced the thrash band Exodus said that this is true even of metal groups. "It has to groove. If something is too fast, you can blow it; if it's too slow, you can blow it. Your head has to start nodding, your body has to start moving."

For better and worse, *Fully Completely* doesn't sound like a bar band; it's made for radio. Which was exactly the intention. A&R rep Bruce Dickinson flew to London while Tsangarides was mixing; the band had gone home. Tsangarides got ready to do the A/B test on different sets of speakers: the high-end speakers where one could hear minute detail, and smaller speakers where one could hear it the way most listeners would at home. Dickinson sat down and Tsangarides played him a track.

"Oh, wow! That's fantastic!" raved Dickinson. "Can we hear it on the small speakers?"

"That *was* the small speakers."

"No, no it wasn't."

"Yeah, it was. Here are the big speakers."

BOOM.

"I turned them on and blew his head off," Tsangarides recalled.

Dickinson sat still and let the music wash over him. He didn't say a word. When the song was over, he slapped the armrest of his chair and said, "Right, let's get lunch. End of meeting."

"I figured I was doing something right," said Tsangarides.

The producer coaxed a new kind of vocal performance out of Downie, who dropped his trademark tremolo for a more clear delivery. He was a huge fan of Johnette Napolitano's vocals on *Bloodletting*. "Her voice had a really honest, unaffected quality: strong, tough, real," he said. "With Chris, I thought I could find my own voice." Downie recorded all his vocals in a booth draped with Indian saris and supplied with wine and cigarettes—"a Moroccan tent affair," said Tsangarides. "On one song you can hear him light up a cigarette; it might be 'Hundredth Meridian.' You hear him spark up and take a drag."

Studio trickery was minimal, but included backward piano swells on "Courage," inspired by the slurping hi-hats on Jimi Hendrix's "Are You Experienced," which Tsangarides heard on the radio on the drive home from the studio one night. An entire afternoon was spent achieving a three-second sound to punctuate a lyric in "Pigeon Camera." "It's a tubular bell struck and then immersed in water," explained the producer; it creates a Doppler effect in which the tone rises and falls simultaneously. To record it, "You throw a microphone, double bagged in a condom, inside the water tank. You have to be pretty quick before you blow the whole place up." Tsangarides had only used this effect once before, on Japan's 1978 album *Obscure Alternatives*.

———

The sound of *Fully Completely* was one reason for its success. The other, equally if not more important, was the lyrical voice: not since the Guess

Who had a commercial rock band so clearly identified themselves as Canadian artists. A song dedicated to Hugh MacLennan, with a verse lifted from one of his novels. A song about Jacques Cartier encountering First Nations. A song about a Toronto hockey player who disappeared in northern Ontario. A song about a miscarriage of justice on the Canadian prairies. A song perceived to reference either the FLQ murder of a Quebec cabinet minister in 1970 or a serial killer in Ontario was, in fact, not written with either in mind, but by this point Canadians were ready to believe that every Tragically Hip song was meant to be a mirror. Writer Charles Foran thought *Fully Completely* "was engaged in a kind of musical royal commission on the Canadian psyche."

By dedicating the opening track, "Courage," to MacLennan, the album immediately announced its intentions. MacLennan, along with Sinclair Ross, W.O. Mitchell and Robertson Davies, was among the first generation of popular Canadian novelists who consciously set his work at home, mythologizing the streets of Halifax and Montreal. "I read *Barometer Rising* first," said Downie. "Once you read something by him, you want to read it all. *Two Solitudes* really struck me. My little brother was at Concordia at the time, so I was spending a lot of time there [in Montreal] and that book spoke to me." *Two Solitudes* is MacLennan's best known novel, about English and French relations in Quebec between the two world wars; *Fully Completely* was released at a time of heightened constitutional tension between all three of Canada's founding cultures.

However, the novel quoted in "Courage" is 1958's *The Watch That Ends the Night*, about a love triangle between a doctor—who leaves Montreal to fight fascism in the Spanish Civil War—his ailing wife and a McGill professor of English. Downie adapted a passage directly from MacLennan's text: "There is no simple explanation for anything important any of us do, and that the human tragedy, or the human irony, consists in the necessity of living with the consequences of actions performed under the pressure of compulsions so obscure we do not and cannot understand them." "If someone says it's preachy," said Downie, "well, I didn't write it."

The song is not about one thing, or one sentiment, though it was often quoted during the Hip's final tour. The song was originally titled "Courage My Love," after a vintage clothing store in Toronto's Kensington Market. The first verse is set at a gig, the second at a motel that reeks of urine. What the courageous act in question may be is not clear—and doesn't even take place at first, and apparently it doesn't even matter. When it does come later on, it's at the worst possible time. Why this song is viewed as an uplifting anthem in the face of adversity is mystifying. Charles Foran, in a piece for *Saturday Night* magazine, thought the lyric "castigated the national tendency to denigrate the local: 'And piss on all of your background / and piss on all your surroundings.'" "I'm not pissing on my surroundings," Downie told him, "I'm merely walking on pissed ground." No one, it seemed, had a simple explanation as to what this song was about. That includes Atom Egoyan, who included it in his Oscar-nominated 1997 film *The Sweet Hereafter*, which featured both a tonally incongruous use of the original Hip recording—the loud, uptempo rock song is jarring in the quiet, uneasy film—and a lullaby version sung by Sarah Polley.

The most explicitly Canadian song on *Fully Completely*, "Wheat Kings," is hardly a song to which one would wave the Maple Leaf (which, of course, happened anyway). It's about the release of a man wrongfully convicted of murder. Downie didn't initially write the song to be about David Milgaard, who was 17 when he went to prison in 1969 for the rape and murder of a Saskatoon nurse. Milgaard's mother, Joyce, fought for appeals for 23 years before the federal government finally referred the case directly to the Supreme Court, based on new evidence about a sex offender who confessed to other crimes in the city during that era. "It was Joyce's dogged and unrelenting belief in her son's innocence that got me the most," said Downie. "In my mind, I was always singing this song from Joyce Milgaard's perspective, trying to imagine her dance through that old and stubborn system, swallowing all the hopeless moments, her smiling face projecting only her utter and unshakeable determination."

If there's something truly Canadian about this story, Downie said, it's the passivity of the populace in the face of injustice—hardly something to celebrate: "The last verse sees a smug, 'wait and see' nation coming down from [sitting on] the fence—but only with David's freedom in sight. It is just so much noise around the quiet strength of a mother who never allowed her son to lose hope: 'Let's just see what tomorrow brings.'"

Downie had been reading a lot of crime fiction, both high-brow and low-brow: Fydor Dostoyevsky's *Crime and Punishment* and the 1950s thriller *The Killer Inside Me* by Jim Thompson, the American author sometimes called "the dime-store Dostoyevsky." Both novels depict brutal crimes, both in the first person. Stanley Kubrick, who collaborated with Thompson on the film *The Killing*, said *The Killer Inside Me* is "probably the most chilling and believable first-person story of a criminally warped mind I have ever encountered." After reading these books, Downie wrote a song called "Dumping the Body," soon to be renamed "Locked in the Trunk of a Car." Some lines were also pulled from the "double suicide" monologue heard on a popular recording of "Highway Girl."

Downie's narrator was deliberately modelled on *Crime and Punishment*'s Raskolnikov. He "appears first as an ageless shark moving through the centuries; then as Everyman at the gas station, getting the tank topped off," Downie explained. "It was never 'about' one historical incident. It was more trying to evoke the claustrophobic atmosphere around guilt and shame, the crushing effects of conscience, the machine-revving tension, the feverish state. I wrote and sang this in the first-person, the monster's-eye view, as it were. It is probably for this reason that this one has always made me vaguely uneasy. It is just so . . . graphic. I don't always feel like I can be near it, let alone own it."

Shortly after the song was released, Downie started distancing himself from it. Small wonder: southwestern Ontario was still reeling from the kidnapping, confinement and murder of two teenage girls, the second of whom was found six months before "Locked in the Trunk of a Car" was released in October 1992. In February 1993, Paul Bernardo, already suspected of being a serial rapist, was arrested for the schoolgirls' murders, after his wife, Karla Homolka, sought immunity in exchange for her testimony. The horrifying depths of the couple's perversity wouldn't be revealed until the trial in 1995, but in 1992–93, it was still a bit too chilling to hear a rock song on the radio about someone hiding a body in the woods.

In hindsight, Downie said he should not have put it on the album. "I wouldn't want it misinterpreted. I meant the song not as a kind of anthem for the serial killer, but as a metaphor for lost love and that sort of feeling of a loveless person, and the yearning for something else." He later elaborated, in an explanation that further muddied the waters, suggesting the central metaphor was intensely personal for him: "If you're in a love relationship and it's the best thing that ever happened to you—and you know it's the best thing that ever happened to you—and you manage to fuck it up, you're going to feel a certain amount of regret. I fucked up and felt really horrible and felt like I was being suffocated. I wasn't necessarily liberated from this relationship; I was drugged."

Because the Hip's popularity was reaching a fever pitch, strange accusations started coming out of the woodwork. The RCMP contacted Jake Gold about a case where a woman had been abducted from a flower shop in Toronto; she and her husband were both later found in the trunk of a car. The suspect told the police that he had met Downie backstage at Molson Park in Barrie, made a confession, and that Downie had written the song about him. "There were so many incidents of stupid stuff like that," said Gold. "I had a guy confront me once because he thought the band had stolen all the lyrics for *Road Apples* from him. It was in front of my office on Queen Street. I said, 'Well, when did you write those?' He said, '1994.' I said, 'It says right on the cassette you're holding that the record came out in 1991, so how is that possible?' *Then he attacked me!*"

Creepiness aside, "Locked" had another strike against it: the phrase "fucked up" in the lyrics, which made it a no-go for American radio when the band refused to edit it out. A station in London, Ontario, decided to edit it out themselves to clear it for prime-time play. Likewise, "Hundredth Meridian" had a "fucking." "Fucks" weren't common on Canadian radio; radio stations would only play such tracks (like the Who's "Who Are You") after either three p.m. or seven p.m.—definitely not on the key morning drive shows.

CKLC DJ Steve Jordan ran into Johnny Fay at the Toucan the night before the album's release and asked him on the air to do an interview. Fay agreed: "I'll go home, pour some scotch, call you and we'll go through it track-by-track at midnight." "Q107 [in Toronto] or someone was supposed to have an exclusive premiere, and MCA freaked out on my head," Jordan recalled. "I just said, 'Dude, talk to your drummer.' And also, who cares? It was midnight, in Kingston, so 2,000 listeners got a treat—pre-internet."

In its first five weeks of release, *Fully Completely* sold 210,000 copies; both *Up to Here* and *Road Apples* had sold about 325,000 copies by that point in time. Within a year, it would sell 500,000 copies.

———

The tour in the fall of 1992 kicked off with three nights at Toronto's Massey Hall—capacity 2,750—instead of headlining Maple Leaf Gardens, which they could have easily done. The larger venues were in the smaller cities: Halifax, Winnipeg. Major centres were purposely undersold, to maintain hype. Also, there were much bigger plans afoot: a travelling festival across Canada, headlined by the Hip with cherry-picked opening acts. It would be called Another Roadside Attraction.

The previous summer, in 1991, Perry Farrell of Jane's Addiction had launched something similar called Lollapalooza, with the intention of showcasing underground acts who were increasingly popular yet shunned by mainstream outlets. Headlined by Farrell's own band, that bill also featured Ice-T, Siouxsie and the Banshees, Living Colour, Butthole Surfers, and kickstarted the career of Nine Inch Nails. It would be a mainstay of the summer concert season for the next six years, eventually returning in 2005 as an annual weekend event in Chicago. Other festival tours sprouted in its wake, including H.O.R.D.E. (jam bands) in 1992, Ozzfest (metal) and Smokin' Grooves (hip-hop) in 1996 and Lilith Fair (female artists) in 1997. The idea is long since dead: destination festivals like Coachella, Bonnaroo and Osheaga have become the norm, much like the European model that inspired Perry Farrell and Jake Gold in the first place.

No Canadian band had ever attempted something like this. The closest comparison would be Festival Express in 1970, on which the Grateful Dead, the Band, Janis Joplin, Buddy Guy and Ian & Sylvia's Great Speckled Bird travelled together by train, making only three stops: Toronto, Winnipeg and Calgary.

Another Roadside Attraction was nine shows between Montreal and Vancouver, including a stop in Thunder Bay. "I don't think anyone thought it was possible," said Colin Cripps of Crash Vegas, one of five acts who played at every stop. "There were certainly [other] Canadian artists who were popular enough. Bryan Adams had one of the biggest records in the world at the time. But it wasn't just about the audience size; it was about the philosophy. [The Hip] didn't just do it because they had the ability to create those huge audiences; they wanted to embrace the community of musicians and invite a bunch of people, of whom they were big fans, and create this caravan. Nothing had happened to that degree before."

"Lollapalooza had played Toronto and Montreal, maybe Vancouver," said Gold. "We thought Canada deserved to have this kind of festival. I wanted to use different venues. We wanted a field, to build a city, to build cities wherever we go. We wanted it to be unique." That wasn't always possible, but the B.C. show was held on Seabird Island, a two-hour drive from Vancouver, east of Chilliwack. "It's like pulling off 10 weddings in a two-week period," Downie joked to MuchMusic.

The Hip stacked the bill with friends like the Pursuit of Happiness, Headstones, Andrew Cash, 13 Engines—all of whom appeared on various dates. "Certain luxuries are afforded to us now, most of them go unrecognized," said Downie. "But this one perk we really enjoy: playing with bands we love and getting to know them as people during the brief moments we have together. At the end of this huge mystery ride, it will be the relationships we've forged with these people that will sustain us into our golden years and not make us look back in anger."

They invited Daniel Lanois, whose two solo records were popular favourites on the tour bus. Irish band Hothouse Flowers were added to the bill to make the lineup less obviously all-Canadian; World Party and Pere Ubu also made appearances. But in case there were any lingering doubts about the viability of the bill, one more act was hired as a co-headliner: Midnight Oil.

The Australian band were renowned as one of the best live rock bands of the era. Their 1987 breakout *Diesel and Dust* sold 300,000 copies in Canada; 1990's *Blue Sky Mining* went platinum. They would headline the same venues in Canada as the Hip. They claimed to have a credo of never opening for anyone—which was not true, as they opened a North American tour for UB40 in 1985.

Why would Midnight Oil accept such a gig, instead of going out on their own? "It was an opportunity to broaden out and play with a band with whom we felt some kind of weird cross-hemisphere affinity," said singer Peter Garrett in 2016.

Allan Gregg was more frank: "We paid them a shitload of money, because now we're bigger than fucking Midnight Oil. That was the entire strategy." Jake Gold said it wasn't about Midnight Oil specifically, but that "it was about Canada seeing us as the biggest band in the land, bigger than anybody. We wanted to put a stake in it. It was actions speaking. People could say it, but we wanted to prove it." Gold clarified, however, that this was the mentality of management, not the Hip. "The band was never about that stuff," he said.

Gord Sinclair was characteristically modest. "The first couple of shows, going on after Midnight Oil was the hardest thing we'd ever had to do because they were by far one of the best live acts on the planet," he said. "They were so intense and so good musically. Nice people, but you knew they were out to steal the audience every night, and they played like it. That made us a way better band. We had to be."

The Tragically Hip were now dealing with the visible effects of their popularity as they faced tens of thousands of people every night. Garrett modelled some crowd-control tips. Pointing at two aggressive audience members in Markham, he bellowed, "You want to play fascist muscleman?"

before stopping the show, waiting for security to eject the offenders and then offering to reimburse the cost of their tickets.

"Most other artists don't really give a shit," said Garrett. "They care about their music, but they're not really thinking about the implications of playing in a certain place or the safety of their fans or the effect they're having more broadly. The Hip are very thoughtful people. Managing mass popularity is never easy. You don't entirely manage it; it manages you. There are some things you can do. Both [our] bands were on the side of ensuring that all women at a Tragically Hip performance should be accorded the same rights and respect as anyone else. Of course, at nine o'clock at night in a crowd of 15,000 people who've had a few beers, it's easier said than done."

Only a band with the power of Midnight Oil could have kept a rabid Tragically Hip audience from shouting them down with chants of "Hip! Hip! Hip!" Nevertheless, it started the second the Oils played their last note. Garrett said he didn't mind, "as long as they didn't do it during our show, you know? It was an amazing time, because the Hip had clearly broken really big. When a band reaches a point where communication with an audience is like a charge of electricity and it fires up a generation—that's no small achievement in any country. Watching that elevation happen was terrific, and they deserved all the success they had at that point in time."

CHAPTER SEVEN

STOLEN FROM
A HOCKEY CARD
PUCK ROCK

"When I lift weights, the Hip's always playing. I really like three songs: 'New Orleans Is Sinking,' 'Blow at High Dough' and some other one. But what I really like about them is that they're just regular guys, and I'm not saying that because it looks good in a newspaper. They're good old Kingston boys, respectful and, like me, big ambassadors for the hometown."

DON CHERRY, *KINGSTON WHIG-STANDARD*, 2016

KEVIN SHEA WAS head of national promotions at MCA Records Canada from 1991 to 1994. "As part of my job, I had dinner with the band on many, many occasions," he recalls of his times seeing the Tragically Hip at shows across North America and Europe. "We never once talked about music— ever. It was always hockey."

In the Hip song "Fireworks," the young narrator is baffled when he meets a girl who says she doesn't care for hockey. The notion is unfathomable to the boy. For large swaths of Canadian society, hockey is like the weather: it's always present, it's the subject of much cursing and you can talk about it with almost any stranger. Of course, as the girl in "Fireworks" illustrates with such beautiful profanity, a love of hockey is a fallible construct on which to frame a monolithic Canadian identity—much like the Tragically Hip's music itself. But there's no denying that a central part of the band's appeal is their association with Canada's sport.

Before 1992, Canadians could only assume the Tragically Hip played hockey—based on their haircuts alone. They were from Kingston, home of Don Cherry and Stanley Cup winners Doug Gilmour (Calgary Flames) and Kirk Muller (Montreal Canadiens)—both of whom started their NHL careers in 1984, the same year the Hip played their first gig. Most people didn't know that guitarist Rob Baker once played on a lacrosse team with Gilmour. They didn't know Gord Sinclair played league hockey until he was 13. They certainly didn't know that Gord Downie was a goalie whose teenage team won a provincial championship, let alone know that his godfather was Harry Sinden, former Boston Bruins coach, GM and president. They didn't know that the band would go on to sponsor a women's hockey team in their hometown or that Johnny Fay would one day marry a sportscaster whose father once owned the Oshawa Generals; the couple was introduced by Gilmour.

In 1992, all anyone knew for sure was that the Tragically Hip had written the best song about hockey to ever be played on commercial radio.

Actually, that bar is pretty low. The lowest, in fact. It was the *only* non-novelty song about hockey to ever be played on commercial radio. The song was "Fifty Mission Cap." It was stolen from a hockey card.

childhood
again???
All over the
place—hard to
keep track.

Gord Downie's connection to hockey royalty began before he was born, when his mother's schoolmate Eleanor married Harry Sinden. An Olympic silver medallist for men's hockey, the defenceman coached farm teams and minor-league hockey, including the Kingston Frontenacs at one point. Though Sinden had moved on to Minneapolis and then Oklahoma City, he spent summers in Kingston and dabbled in real estate; he sold the Downies their house in Amherstview.

By 1968, Sinden was the coach of the Boston Bruins. That same year, in May, Gord's younger brother Patrick was born, and their mother, Lorna, wanted to get them both baptized. Edgar Downie, whose Irish Protestant parents arrived in Canada by boat from Belfast, was not particularly religious, so that task had somehow slipped the Downies' mind when Gord was born four years earlier. A chaplain living across the street performed the service, and Harry and Eleanor Sinden were asked to be godparents. In a country where hockey is religion, that is no small role. Sinden coached the Canadian team in the Summit Series against the U.S.S.R. in 1972, a pivotal moment in Canadian sports history, documented in numerous books, films and commemorations. Gord Downie was eight years old in 1972, and he couldn't have been prouder of his godfather.

"Back in the day, we supported every move Harry made," Downie told Bob McKenzie, in the TSN sportscaster's 2014 book *Hockey Confidential*. "It wasn't just bias; we honestly believed in what he was doing. He had this blue-collar budget, trying to compete with white-collar teams. He made competitive teams in his own image, that shared his work ethic, and he managed to walk that tightrope with ownership. We really admire Harry in every way. He was a mentor. He taught us more than he will ever know."

The Downie brothers were Bruins fans for life. Patrick went to work for the team in Boston. He and Gord talked almost every day on the phone about their beloved B's: hence the song on Downie's 2017 solo album *Introduce Yerself*, "You, Me and the B's." Sportscaster Dave Hodge observed many Hip fans trying awkwardly to make conversation at backstage meet-and-greets. "If you could talk Bruins with Gord, you had a chance of having a longer conversation," said Hodge. "He always wanted to talk about the Bruins with somebody who could. It was always Boston, Boston, Boston."

Naturally, Downie and his brothers wanted to play. "You could turn anything into hockey, and would—in your rec room or in your garage or on a puddle that's larger than normal," he said. He started out a defenceman like his godfather. He soon moved to goal and became philosophical about it. He read about Jacques Plante, the Montreal Canadiens goalie who pioneered the use of the mask in the NHL. Plante called goaltending "the noblest position in all of sports," Downie told McKenzie. "I felt it was the position where you could have the biggest effect on the game. I liked everything about it. You can't play goalie harder or faster. Coaches never know what to say to the goalie. 'Go stretch, we'll get to you later.' I liked that independence. It's still the case, really; it's just a very different game than what everyone else is playing."

"My first year playing goal, I was on a really stacked team," Downie told Ron MacLean of *Hockey Night in Canada*, during a 2002 Olympic broadcast. "We went 16–0 and I had 14 shutouts. I was really into stats and would bore my family. In the championship game, it was the first time I was truly tested, and it was a goal that tied the game for this team we were supposed to walk over. We ended up winning 3–2, but it was tense."

Downie played for his local bantam team, Ernestown, which won a provincial championship with him in net. In one game, he faced off against David Shaw of Exeter, Ontario, who would go on to play for the Rangers, the Oilers and, yes, the Bruins. All the Downies came out to support young Gord in those playoff games, including one game against East Gwillimbury where he embarrassed himself by throwing a tantrum on the ice, after he very nearly let his team blow a 5–0 lead by letting in a series of goals in quick succession.

His parents were busy people with four other children. Most of the time, Gord had to get himself to and from practice. "My dad wasn't a hockey dad—he was the furthest thing from it," Downie told McKenzie. But every so often Edgar would sneak into a game. "He wouldn't be with the other parents, grouped under the heaters. He'd be alone, down in my end, and I would look up at him. He would just [raise his fist]. I'd make a flurry of saves, I'd look up and he would be gone. He had places to be. I was always very hard on myself; he would listen. I never really was told [by him] what I could have done better, but he always listened. When he showed up, when he raised that fist in the air, to me, it meant, 'I'm here, I'm with you, maybe no one else in the building is, but I am.'"

In 2006, Downie channelled that experience into the song "The Lonely End of the Rink." The first time Gord played it for his brother Mike, they drove down to Toronto's Cherry Beach and listened in the car. Mike cried first. Then Gord. "I just admire my dad so much and how he approached things," he told McKenzie. "By design or neglect, he was the perfect hockey dad."

The year after the championship, Downie played minor midget. But he was now in high school, the family had moved into town and he had other interests—like rock'n'roll. "Living in Kingston, instead of Amherstview, there was so much more to do," he said about his 16-year-old self. "Hockey just fell like a coat off my shoulders. I never looked back."

Once the Hip became successful, and life on the road less stressful, they tried to play hockey with members of their crew and opening acts before or after every gig. Sometimes that meant ball hockey in the empty arena while the stage was being constructed. Sometimes they'd seek out post-show invitations from locals to play on ice, even if it was just somebody's backyard rink. Skates and sticks and rollerblades were kept on the bus. So were books of official NHL stats. Downie ran the band's hockey pool, even writing weekly reports. Once, when opening for Jimmy Page and Robert Plant at the Philadelphia Spectrum in 1995, the band almost missed their slot because they were too involved in their game out in the parking lot. They made it onstage with fewer than eight minutes to spare.

At home in Toronto, Downie depended on Dave Bidini to help get him on the ice. Bidini's band, the Rheostatics, opened the 1996 Hip tour, and the two men bonded over hockey, literature and, of course, music. "He didn't have any hockey friends in Toronto, really, so for two or three years there we'd play several times a week in the west end," Bidini recalls. "At Wallace Emerson rink, we'd jump the fence and about a dozen of us would play. We'd just skate all night long. I'd bring him out to games at Dufferin Grove, and people would arrive by the time we were already out on the ice. They'd have no idea who was playing goal at the other end of the rink. In the dressing room, you'd hear, 'Holy shit, I think that's Gord Downie.' Gord treated it so seriously. He wasn't chuckling at the conceit that there was a rock star there. He just wanted to stop the puck."

When Downie moved to Toronto's east end, he would often suit up in his goalie pads and mask at home and then walk over to Withrow Park to play shinny with oblivious neighbours. By the time he was on the other side of 40, however, his passion for playing once again subsided—as his post-game Advil intake increased.

In 1991, with two multi-platinum records under their belt, the Tragically Hip were rehearsing in the living room of their drummer's parents. The Fays were away on vacation, so the boys pushed the furniture aside and set up their instruments. Gord Sinclair had a killer new riff. The band kicked in. Downie remembered he had a hockey card that he'd been carrying around in his pocket, because he found the story compelling. He pulled it out and recited it almost verbatim. The words stuck.

> *Although he was not noted for his offensive skills, Bill Barilko scored one of the most celebrated goals in NHL history during the 1951 Stanley Cup Finals between Toronto and Montreal. This series was the only championship final that required overtime in every contest. In Game Five, the extra session was nearly three minutes old when Barilko spotted a loose puck near the Montreal crease. He dove in from the blue line and fired a shot over Montreal goaltender Gerry McNeil's outstretched arm to give the Leafs the Cup. Unfortunately, it was the last goal of Barilko's career. He disappeared that summer on a fishing trip, and the Leafs didn't win another Cup until 1962, the year his body was found.*

The card was from a series made by the Hockey Hall of Fame, written by James Duplacey, commemorating photos of famous goals. "I believe it's the finest hockey photograph ever taken," Duplacey told Barilko biographer Kevin Shea, who, after his stint at MCA, worked for the Hockey Hall of Fame. The economy of his writing made Downie's job easier. "When you're writing cards," said Duplacey, "the space they give you is very restricted. I had 300 characters, so I had to try to find a way to get that one little piece of information in, as well as the fact the Leafs won the Stanley Cup and yet still give enough background about the genesis of the photo."

"I didn't know a lot about Barilko or his story, really," said Downie. "It was like going into a bygone era of hockey." He brought a new generation with him.

Bill Barilko grew up in Timmins, Ontario, with two siblings and a mother who was widowed when they were young. He first significant on-ice experience was at age 11, when he saved a 14-year-old who was riding a bicycle on a frozen Gillies Lake and fell through. Barilko's professional career began in California, for the Hollywood Wolves of the Pacific Coast Hockey League, a third-tier farm team for the Toronto Maple Leafs. He got the call up to the big league in 1947, on the team that won the Stanley Cup four out of the next five years. In 1950, they missed the finals after losing a semifinal game against Detroit, only because a shot from the Red Wings' end of the rink bounced off Barilko and into the Leafs' net.

"Hollywood" Bill Barilko, who referred to himself as "the Kid," was devilishly handsome, a popular player, confident, with a big smile. He was also a bruiser, leading in penalty minutes and unafraid to take on Maurice "Rocket" Richard when the Leafs faced the Canadiens. "Boop boop!" he would warn his opponents before crashing into them. "I hate that Barilko so much," Montreal coach Dick Irvin once said. "I sure wish we had him with the Canadiens."

The 1951 Stanley Cup was fought between the Canadiens and the Leafs. Toronto won three of the first four games, each of which went into overtime. If they won the fifth game, they'd take the Cup. Again, the game was a nail-biter in which the Leafs scored a tying goal with 32 seconds left in regular play. Two minutes into overtime, Barilko flipped the puck from the left faceoff circle to score the winning goal. Toronto erupted in celebration. The game was broadcast to the nation, called, as always, by Foster Hewitt. Barilko was 25 years old.

Four months later, "Hollywood Bill" was home in Timmins and decided to go on a fishing trip with a local dentist, Henry Hudson, who had a float plane. On the morning of Friday, August 26, he told his mother where he was going. She begged him not to go; her husband had died on a Friday when Bill was young, and she was superstitious. They argued. He left and never came back.

The story made national headlines for weeks. The search party was the largest and costliest in Canadian history, covering 100,000 square miles, involving 17 planes from the Royal Canadian Air Force, 135 airmen and 1,345 hours of searching. It was called off after a month. Leafs owner Conn Smythe offered a $10,000 reward for anyone who could find Barilko, "dead or alive." So mysterious was the death that cockamamie theories proliferated. One claimed that Hudson, being a dentist who did fillings, was a mule for gold smuggled out of the region. Another tapped into Cold War paranoia, suggesting that Barilko, the son of Ukrainian immigrants, had defected to the Soviet Union.

The NHL's 1951–52 season began on October 11. The Toronto Maple Leafs—Stanley Cup defenders, missing a star defenceman—did not do well and did not get better. In the next 10 years, they made it to playoff season only three times: losing twice to Detroit in semifinals (1954–55, 1960–61) and once to Montreal for the 1959–60 Cup. In 1961–62, however, they bounced back, and on April 22, they won their first Stanley Cup since Barilko's disappearance. Six-and-a-half weeks later, on June 6, the plane was found; the cause of the crash was determined to be pilot inexperience and bad weather. The Leafs won the next two Stanley Cups as well and one more in 1967—the last one the Leafs would ever win (at press time).

If Downie didn't know the story, Paul Langlois did. His father grew up in Smooth Rock Falls, a tiny town north of Timmins between Cochrane and Kapuskasing, and he told his son stories of all the search planes flying overhead looking for Barilko. Downie, however, felt he had more homework to do. He did what any good student in the 416 does: he went to the basement of the Toronto Reference Library and started poring over *Toronto Star* archives on microfilm. As he got to the point where Barilko's body was about to be found, he became so engrossed that he hadn't noticed the library's lights flashing, indicating closing time. A librarian then tapped him on the shoulder. "I jumped out of my skin," he recalled, "scaring us both."

As it turned out, Downie didn't use any of his research beyond what he'd found on the hockey card. For the chorus, he turned to something he saw while touring the National Air and Space Museum in Washington, D.C., on the same trip that inspired "Pigeon Camera." There, he learned of the Fifty Mission Cap, which was granted to Second World War pilots who flew 50 successful missions. The hat lacked a stiffening ring, in order for headphones to be worn over it. "It altered the cap to look crushed and battered, giving it a distinctive profile," said Roger G. Miller, historian at the Center for Air Force History, quoted in Kevin Shea's book *Barilko*. "It was technically out of uniform, but you could wear one if you'd paid your dues and proven yourself worthy by returning from a number of successful missions. The Fifty Mission Cap separated the fledgling from the battle-hardened survivor who had earned the right to wear it."

"I was taken with the idea of a veteran pilot whose ultimate goal is to stay alive, to fly 50 missions, that in itself is its own glory," Downie told Bob McKenzie. "Contrast that with Barilko's flashing moment—that 'is it better to burn out than to fade away' sort of thing." Downie decided to combine the two ideas in one song. "Back in those days, I was into collage or cut-and-paste writing," he said. "I wasn't comfortable with doing just a straight narrative of what happened to a hockey player."

"If it had been a blatant hockey song, I don't think it would have had the same appeal," says Kevin Shea. "There's enough mystery there that we want to hear more and try and figure it all out. That's what pulled us in."

Many fans tried in vain to connect the two stories; academics wrote theses on the subject, some of which are now housed in the Hockey Hall of Fame. Gord Sinclair offers his own theory: "I imagine winning the Cup is a lot like living to tell about it in a bomber crew or a rock band; you give your all for the collective and rise and fall on the heroics of each member. The sum is always greater than its parts."

With a lot to parse in a simple song, many missed the humour. What makes it comical is that the narrator—who has clearly not flown 50 missions but has merely "worked in" his cap to make it look like he has—is no hockey historian: he cops to the fact that the only reason he knows the Barilko tale at all is that he saw it on a hockey card. He's not an expert at anything: not flying, not hockey. He's an impostor, a poser, a con. He can't even come up with a second verse; he just repeats the first. Downie went to a library, but his narrator couldn't bother. When Downie performed this song, he often had an exaggerated, crazed look on his face as if he were saying, "Can you fucking believe this?"

By complete coincidence—some might say fate—the Leafs were doing their own reckoning with the Barilko legacy even before the Hip recorded the song in July 1992. The team had made plans to retire his jersey number on April 1, 1992, but an NHL players' strike shut down the league for 10 days. The ceremony was rescheduled for October 17, only 11 days after *Fully Completely* came out, which would have been the first time anyone heard the finished song. Toronto radio station Q107 jumped on the track immediately, and it went into regular rotation at Maple Leaf Gardens in between plays.

"When that song came out, you could probably count on two hands the people who knew who Bill Barilko was," says Kevin Shea. But at the Hockey Hall of Fame in the years after "Fifty Mission Cap" came out, the most requested photo was of Barilko winning the Cup. "I was a big Leafs fan: I knew the Barilko story and was a big hockey historian. It's a great story, but it was from 1951, for God's sake."

Sportscaster Mark Hebscher was more than familiar with the Barilko story. "If you were a real hockey nut like me, you knew the story inside and out," he says. "It's a legendary story. Right there, the Hip would have connected with a huge number of people, maybe way older than the demographic they were shooting for with a reference like that."

More important is that the fall of 1992 was the Leafs' first season with Pat Burns as coach, and Doug Gilmour—newly arrived from the Calgary Flames, where he helped them win the 1989 Cup—was a star. "At the same time the Leafs were winning 10 games in a row, the Blue Jays were also winning the World Series," says Hebscher. "Sports was at its highest level [in Toronto]. Then this song comes out. What song are they playing at Maple Leaf Gardens every single night? 'Fifty Mission Cap.' Now it's a Leaf anthem. The Hip guys get invited to the Gardens, they all get jerseys. They have unwittingly—because they certainly didn't write the song to coincide with the Leafs' success—started to ride a wave of nationalism, because Maple Leafs fans are everywhere."

Wait, doesn't the rest of Canada love to hate Toronto? Who outside the 416 was cheering for the Leafs? "They were on everyone's mind in Canada," insists Hebscher, the man who hosted Leafs games on Global TV. "With all due respect to the Montreal Canadiens, everyone was going nuts for the Leafs. Everywhere we went, it was a madhouse. So when you release a song that has a special connection to a team that is suddenly surging and heading for the Stanley Cup, that's a cocktail for success right there. The irony is that the Canadiens ended up winning the Stanley Cup in '93. And it was a big surprise. But had the Leafs beat Wayne Gretzky and the Kings [in the semis] and gone on to the finals, that song would have been even bigger. As it is, it solidified the legend and it forever linked the Hip with hockey."

The only other commercial rock song that might have been considered a hockey song at that point in time was Tom Cochrane's 1988 hit "Big League." Like "Fifty Mission Cap," it's about a young player cut down in his prime—only in this case that happens well before he makes it to the NHL. But if "Fifty Mission Cap" is mysterious, "Big League" is just depressing, undermining its appeal in a classically self-defeating Canadian way. The fist-pumping chorus, which sounds great in a hockey arena, doesn't really jibe with the second-last verse, in which the kid who's just landed a U.S. scholarship is killed by a truck driving in the wrong lane, leaving his father with PTSD every time he hears ice crack. It's a great song—but it's not going to bring you to your feet to cheer for the home team.

"Tom Cochrane's song is not about hockey," says Hebscher. "It's about a young man. There's no mention of any team. You don't know his name. You don't identify with the kid. You identify with the narrator whose boy was going to be a hockey player. That, to me, is not a hockey song. What the Hip wrote *was* a hockey song: a true story come to life, from a hockey card. 'Big League' could have been about a basketball player. But there's no basketball story where the guy goes down in a plane after making the winning shot for the NBA championship."

"'Fifty Mission Cap' is also tied to tragedy [as 'Big League' is], sure, but it's also tied to a Stanley Cup championship," says Shea. "I look at it as a celebration; I think the Leafs do, too. It just happens to be tied to the tragedy of a promising young hockey player."

Allan Stanley, Barilko's childhood friend, was playing for the New York Rangers in 1951. He was interviewed by Mark Hebscher after the song came out.

"The Maple Leafs should have won 10 Stanley Cups during that time period," said Stanley, who played for the team from 1958 to 1968.

"Oh, really? Why is that?" asked Hebscher.

"Because I was supposed to be in that plane, not Bill. If Bill had kept playing, and not me, the Leafs would've continued to win."

"I was shocked," says Hebscher. "I'd never heard this before. He then tells me the story of how he and the pilot, Henry Hudson, were really good friends. Hudson said he was going fishing for the weekend and did Allan want to join him? Allan wanted to, but he had a doctor's appointment, or something. But Allan said, 'You know, Bill has never been and I'm sure he'd love to go. He was asking me what the fishing is like there.' So Hudson calls Barilko and they go. On the Monday morning, they don't return, and Allan is feeling horribly guilty. He goes up in another plane and does reconnaissance. He knew the route. But he couldn't find the plane. He told me, 'I knew Henry Hudson was a reckless flier. Twice I was with him, on this pontoon plane, and we had to land it on the ground. I don't know why I told Barilko to fly with this guy.' It agonized him for years. When he heard the song, he broke down and cried."

Barilko's sister, Anne Klisanich, had been told that someone had written a song about her brother. She was incredulous. "I thought they were joking," she told Shea. "They said it was called 'Fifty Mission Cap.' I said, 'What's that got to do with Billy?' When I did hear it, I was a bit shocked at first to think that someone would write a song about somebody who died so tragically, but the more I listened to it, there was a lot of thought put into it. It was heartwarming to know that people were interested in Bill's life story."

She had no interaction with the band, however, until 1999, when the then-68-year-old found out the Hip were playing a show close to her home in Mississauga, at the Hershey Centre, home to the OHL's Mississauga Steelheads. She went to the box office as the crowd was filing in and asked a clerk if she could see the band.

"Where's your ticket?"

"Oh, I don't want to see the show, I just want to talk to the band."

The clerk rolled her eyes at the elderly lady. "Uh, no."

"Well, can you send them a message?" Klisanich insisted. "These boys wrote a song about my brother; it's called; 'Fifty Mission Cap' and my brother's name is Bill Barilko."

"Yeah, sure. You know, anybody could tell me that," responded the clerk. Klasinich produced her birth certificate, with her maiden name. A runner was then sent backstage to convey the message to the band.

Klasinich was immediately summoned to the dressing room, where the members of the Hip greeted her with big hugs, told her what a great honour it was to meet her, had a pleasant chat and posed for a photo. They invited her to stay for the show. She stayed for one song, but she couldn't handle the volume and left. She also had a very Canadian excuse: she was leaving for Florida in a few days and had to pack. But she did get to thank those nice boys for writing a song about her brother.

After "Fifty Mission Cap" and "The Lonely End of the Rink," there is only one Hip song that explicitly references hockey—and it's not about hockey. In fact, it's about everything else except hockey. "Fireworks" opens with a line about the '72 Summit Series, but it's really about the narrator meeting a girl who is indifferent to the sport and follows their relationship through to mid-life. It's about a boy moving beyond the myopia of his own interests. It was based on a true story. "There actually was a girl who said she 'didn't give a fuck about hockey,'" Downie told Bob McKenzie. "I had never heard a girl swear and I'd never heard someone say that before. It was like there was a whole other world out there, which is hard to fathom sometimes."

In "700 Ft. Ceiling," there's a reference to someone flooding a backyard ice rink. There is a dream about forgetting your skates in "It's a Good Life." But those are not hockey songs. Neither is 2004's "Heaven Is a Better Place Today," despite the fact it's dedicated to a hockey player who died in a car crash—and, unlike Tom Cochrane's protagonist in "Big League," this boy did make it to the NHL, playing for the Atlanta Thrashers.

Dan Snyder was a player from Elmira, Ontario. He spent three years bouncing between the Thrashers and their AHL affiliate, the Chicago Wolves. On the night of September 29, 2003, he was in a car driven by his best friend and Atlanta teammate, Dany Heatley of Calgary, the 2002 Calder Trophy winner who had led Canadian teams to gold medals in the World Cup of Hockey. That night, Heatley was going 130 km/h on a narrow two-lane road in Atlanta when he spun out of control and smashed into a fence. He had alcohol in his system but was below the legal limit in Georgia. Heatley suffered injuries to his lung, jaw, kidney and knee, as well as a concussion. Snyder had a skull fracture and died six days later.

Heatley was beyond heartbroken. He pleaded guilty to second-degree vehicular homicide. Snyder's family, knowing how close the two men were, made an appeal to the prosecutor for Heatley to avoid jail time. He got three years probation and returned to the NHL in 2005, playing for the Ottawa Senators.

"It seemed to me that Dany Heatley needed a friend after that," said Downie. "They were in that car together, they were buddies. He can pay whatever debt to society that society feels it needs him to pay, and that makes [society] feel better, but that doesn't help him. That's not the real punishment here." Downie was also struck by the forgiveness of the Snyder family. "It was like, 'We're going to handle this between us all,' all that pain," said Downie. "What they did outwardly and inwardly, I was so impressed."

I like the stories behind the songs, wrote about cool stuff.

The Tragically Hip met more than a few NHL players in their time. Dave Levinson, who worked for their management in the mid-2000s, remembered visiting the Vancouver Canucks' locker room with the band. "Watching each of them shake each other's hands, it was like little kids meeting their heroes—and it's mutual," he says. "A rock star meeting a hockey player, and each wanted to be the other. Seeing the deference and the respect they had for each other was cool."

One band who took the rock and hockey connection to the hilt was NoMeansNo, the Victoria art-punk band who were one of the most ferocious and inspiring live acts of the '90s. As NoMeansNo, they were deadly serious. But in 1984, they started a side project—or, as Western Canadians call it, a "fuck band"—called the Hanson Brothers, named after the three bruisers in the cult classic 1977 film *Slap Shot*. They played Ramones songs with new lyrics and titles like "Rink Rat" and "(He Looked a Lot Like) Tiger Williams." They only toured Canada during playoff season, never taking the stage until after that night's game was finished. As art-punks, NoMeansNo were decidedly DIY. As the Hanson Brothers, they were signed to a major label for their debut full-length, *Gross Misconduct*. The album was released in 1992, the same year as "Fifty Mission Cap." In 1996, the Hansons covered "The Hockey Song" by Stompin' Tom Connors on a split seven-inch single with DOA.

CBC Radio host Grant Lawrence, who hosted an annual "puck rock" special on his show *Radio Sonic*, was a huge Hanson Brothers fan. A goalie in his youth, Lawrence had left hockey behind to become the lead singer in a rock band—not unlike Gord Downie. In Lawrence's book *The Lonely End of the Rink*, he recounted a conversation he had with John "Johnny Hanson" Wright. "He told me that there really wasn't much difference between a great hockey team and a great band," wrote Lawrence, who spent 15 years fronting Vancouver garage-rock band the Smugglers. "For both to perform well, the members have to be completely in sync with each other. If one member of the band is playing out of time, it doesn't work; same thing as a hockey team skating up ice and a player going offside—the play is dead."

By the mid-'90s, all kinds of "puck rock" started coming out of corners across the continent, including "Gretzky Rocks" by the Pursuit of Happiness and "Hit Somebody!" by Warren Zevon. Suddenly, Stompin' Tom Connors was being played at hockey rinks, more than 20 years after he first recorded "The Hockey Song."

In 1999, national music monthly *Exclaim!* started hosting a musicians' league hockey tournament every Easter weekend in Toronto, which attracted teams from across the country; each team was also expected to perform a 15-minute set at a hootenanny, to ensure no one was stacking their team with non-musicians. Four years later, the Junos got in on the game, hosting an annual tournament between musicians and veteran NHL players. The musicians' team is usually captained by Jim Cuddy, and it has featured Sam Roberts, Kathleen Edwards, Classified and members of Barenaked Ladies, Sloan and 54.40. In Canada, no one will ever have a problem trying to find musicians who play hockey.

The Hip never participated in any high-profile musicians-versus-NHL games. They opted for more informal encounters, like the time former Montreal Canadien and fellow Kingstonian Kirk Muller invited Downie and Langlois to a summer game at Cataraqui Arena. Downie drove in from Toronto the night before and slept in his car so he wouldn't be late. During the game, former Maple Leaf Wendel Clark proved to be a tough opponent. "Gord's in net and Clarky's letting all these wrist-rockets go up around his mask," Muller told the *Whig-Standard*. "We told Wendel to back off, because if this guy takes one in the throat, there goes the band—and we love the Hip. I skated by Gord and said, 'You owe me one. That'll teach you for being a Bruins fan.'"

Dave Bidini established his writing career discussing both hockey and music. One of his many books is about both: *The Best Game You Can Name*, about the 2004 *Exclaim!* Cup. The Rheostatics have several songs that reference hockey, beginning with 1987's ode to a Maple Leaf, "The Ballad of Wendel Clark." Being a friend of Downie's, he says, "I can't tell you how many times in my life I've got a call from an editor that goes specifically like this: 'We would really love you to do something about hockey for us.' 'Okay, yeah, sure, great.' Then the conversation ends with, 'Do you think you could maybe ask Gord to do something, too?'"

One of those conversations was a request that both of them write letters to be read to Canada's world junior team in their locker room before a gold-medal game in 1996. Bidini and Downie each sent a missive and then watched the game on TV together in Toronto. "Every second song during the breaks was the Tragically Hip," recalls Bidini. "I said, 'Gosh, Gord, there's a lot of Tragically Hip being played here.' He said, 'It should *all* be Tragically Hip!'"

In all of the Tragically Hip's hockey moments, one stands towering above all. On February 10, 1995, the Tragically Hip headlined Maple Leaf Gardens for the first time. That alone was a huge thrill. "As a kid growing up, your whole orientation—hockey-wise, rock-band-wise, culture-wise— was toward this legendary mecca," said Gord Sinclair. "The first time you get a chance to walk into the venerable barn, sold out, performing in front of your crowd, it really doesn't get much better than that. Everyone since the 1930s has gone to that venue to see a significant event, and then all of a sudden there you are and *you* are the event in the same building."

John Sakamoto of the *Toronto Sun* reviewed the show. "At every Tragically Hip concert I've ever been to, there's always been that one instant in which a bunch of seemingly unrelated things rush together into a mind-boggling confluence, and you get to experience 'the Moment,'" he wrote. "Last night, 'the Moment' came six songs in during 'Fifty Mission Cap.' When Gord Downie got to the line, 'The last goal he ever scored won the Leafs the Cup,' 14,500 delirious fans looked up [guided by a house spotlight], pointed at the 1951 Stanley Cup banner hanging from the ceiling of the very building in which Barilko scored the goal in question and let out a cheer that was probably as loud as the one that greeted Barilko's feat."

What the rock critic couldn't possibly know was that Edgar Downie fell to his knees at that moment, overcome with emotion. He had just watched his son make hockey history: a different kind of championship, with thousands of witnesses, in a hallowed hall of the sport. He was no longer in the lonely end of the rink.

CHAPTER EIGHT

YOU WANT IT DARKER

1994–95: *DAY FOR NIGHT*

INTERVIEWER:
"Did you want to destroy your audience as soon as you got it?"

NEIL YOUNG:
"Turnover. Like in clubs where they turn over the audience. Did you ever notice that if the same audience stays, the second set usually isn't as good as the first set? But if they turn the audience over, the second set could be better than the first set? Because with me that's the way it is."

JIMMY MCDONOUGH, *SHAKEY: NEIL YOUNG'S BIOGRAPHY*, 2002

ROCK'N'ROLL SHOULD MAKE you scared. It's kinda what it does. Scared with the thrill of intoxication, of sexuality, of danger, of staring into either the darkest abyss or the most blinding light.

If you're the money man, however, your greatest fear is that the record just won't sell.

When Allan Gregg first heard *Day for Night*, he called Jake Gold. He told him, "Look, 'Nautical Disaster' is a radio hit. The rest is almost unlistenable. They're not finished. They have to go back into the studio." Gold brought this news to the band. It did not go over well. A meeting was called. "This is the finished record," the band insisted. Then, being Canadian, they offered Gregg a gentle out: "We think it might be better to have you as a friend than as a manager."

Gregg was ready for this news. He'd had a hell of a year, during which the Hip's continued ascent was the only good thing going for him. In the fall of 1992, he led the failed referendum campaign in favour of the Charlottetown Accord. One year later, he was campaign manager for prime minister Kim Campbell, in which the governing Progressive

Conservatives were driven to a fifth-place finish in the general election, threatening to wipe the country's founding political party off the map. On top of that, he was surrounded by cancer: both his father and his best friend died of it, and his wife was diagnosed with it, too. He wasn't totally happy with recent band decisions, either: they had gone to Australia and filmed a video for "At the Hundredth Meridian" that Gregg thought was a "fucking abomination."

He was exhausted. So when the Tragically Hip dropped off a mysterious, murky album on his desk with no obvious singles, he was less than receptive. "Look," he told them at the band meeting, "at the end of the day, your fucking name is on this record—not mine. If you can live with this shit, that's up to you. But I won't have any part of it." Though he remained a financial partner with Jake Gold in the Management Trust, Gregg receded from any advisory role in the Tragically Hip's career.

Day for Night sold 300,000 copies in the first four days of its release on September 6, 1994. It went on to sell 300,000 more. (*Fully Completely*, by comparison, took three months to sell its first 200,000 copies.) It spawned six radio singles and four videos. In February 1995, it allowed the band to launch the biggest-ever tour of Canada by a homegrown band, playing arenas in every major market, sometimes with multiple dates, as well as in secondary markets often missed by the biggest acts; it was a feat they would repeat two years later.

It was by no means a sure bet; Allan Gregg had every reason to be antsy. The Tragically Hip had gone dark. It's right there in the title, borrowed from a Francois Truffault film. They left the radio-ready ways of *Fully Completely* behind. They could have gone bright pop. They could have cashed in and gone grunge, playing catch-up with Pearl Jam. They could have wrapped themselves in the flag. They didn't. Because of *Fully Completely*'s blockbuster status, the Hip found themselves in a position to indulge. It was time to roll the dice.

———

An artist's first album after a massive success is always tricky. Do you try to climb the same mountain? Do you try to climb a similar mountain? Or do you try deep-sea diving instead? Fleetwood Mac's *Tusk*. Prince's *Around the World in a Day*. Bruce Springsteen's *Tunnel of Love*. Nirvana's *In Utero*. Radiohead's *Kid A*. All those records rejected a formula that had reaped considerable commercial reward just a few years before, a formula that made all those artists household names. All those records were welcomed by a collective WTF, only to later be embraced as classics, some sooner than later.

The Hip didn't necessarily know what they wanted, but they knew what they didn't: a repeat of the *Fully Completely* experience. Downie had described the London studio where it was made as a "fairly sterile environment" and that they "were lucky enough to pull a record out of it that we liked and had some sense of atmosphere. We vowed never to do that again." Gord Sinclair said that although the band had the Canadian music industry on their side, that industry "wanted us to make Fully Completely Part Two."

The Tragically Hip knew who they wanted to help them shake up their sound. The choice was obvious: Daniel Lanois, with whom they'd toured on the 1993 Another Roadside Attraction tour. His first two solo albums, *Acadie* and *For the Beauty of Wynona*, were Hip favourites. He'd made three of the biggest international records of the last 10 years: Peter Gabriel's *So* and U2's *The Joshua Tree* and *Achtung Baby*. Not to mention Robbie Robertson's solo album, the Neville Brothers' *Yellow Moon*, Bob Dylan's *Oh Mercy* and a slew of great Canadian new wave records in the early '80s (Martha and the Muffins, Parachute Club, Luba), as well as his work with Brian Eno on ambient music. The biggest new rock band in Canada working with the country's most internationally acclaimed producer: it seemed like a perfect fit.

Except that Lanois turned them down. Twice, as his name had been floated for *Fully Completely* as well. But the Hip were also friendly with Lanois's right-hand man, engineer Mark Howard, who was responsible for helping Lanois translate his ideas to tape and also assisted in setting up his studios in wonderfully weird parts of North America. It was Howard who, as Lanois's front-of-house engineer during the first Another Roadside Attraction, recorded the "Land" single in Calgary, featuring Midnight Oil, Crash Vegas, Lanois and the Hip. Watching him work was a revelation after *Fully Completely*. "When they saw how I made that song with them on the road," said Howard, "it opened their eyes to thinking, 'Wow, we could make a whole record like this.'"

The Hip decided to go back to New Orleans and hire Howard as co-producer. After years under Lanois's wing, this was his first production credit for a major client. Lanois wasn't around; he and Howard had just finished setting up shop in a Mexican mountain cave. "The walls were all natural rock and there was a grass roof over it and it looked over the Sea of Cortez," said Howard. After making that new studio functional, Howard flew back to New Orleans and started work on what would be *Day for Night*.

———

Mark Howard was born in Hamilton and started his career doing live sound, touring with local blues legend King Biscuit Boy. A bad motorcycle accident took him off the road, so he started working at Grant Avenue Studio, founded by Daniel and Bob Lanois and Bob Doidge. There, Howard worked on records by Sherry Kean (*Maverick Heart*) and the Shuffle Demons (*Bop Rap*) before Lanois took notice during an increasingly rare visit back to Hamilton, when he recorded the *Acadie* track "Ice" at Grant Ave. Lanois whisked Howard away to New Orleans, where the producer had been hired to make a record with the city's first family of funk, the Neville Brothers. At their first meeting in the Big Easy, Lanois told Howard he was leaving the next day to work with Brian Eno, and he wanted the 21-year-old engineer to find a location to make the Nevilles' album in a month's time. "I knew nothing about anything," said Howard. "I had to find a way to import most of the gear from England and Canada and get the rest from New York and ship it all to New Orleans." He found a five-storey apartment building for sale on St. Charles Avenue, in the city's Garden District, and convinced the landlord to rent it out for $1,500 a month for half a year.

While making *Yellow Moon*, Lanois lived in the penthouse; Howard, engineer Malcolm Burn, and saxophonist Charles Neville all had their own floors and the studio was on the second floor. Brian Eno flew in to help Lanois mix a Jon Hassell album. Bob Dylan dropped by to listen to two of his songs the Nevilles had covered. Enthused, he solicited Lanois for his next record. Plans to record it at Georgia O'Keeffe's estate in New Mexico were scuttled when Dylan told Lanois he wouldn't be able to sing at the altitude there; Howard then found another Garden District Victorian mansion on a short-term basis and reconstructed the studio again. *Oh Mercy* was made there, and Blue Rodeo's *Diamond Mine* was mixed there, by Malcolm Burn.

Burn and Howard were friends with another Hamiltonian, guitarist Colin Cripps, who brought his band Crash Vegas down to New Orleans to record their first album, *Red Earth*. That album inaugurated yet another New Orleans studio—the third and the last one of the Lanois era there—reluctantly scouted by Howard. "It was a ratty old Victorian mansion in the French Quarter," said Howard. "I went to see it and told Lanois, 'The place is a dump. It's too much work. It's full of rats.'" Lanois went on to sink a million dollars into the 13,000-square-feet, three-storey house at the corner of Esplanade and Chartres.

That's where the Tragically Hip recorded *Road Apples* with producer Don Smith in September 1990. Howard was there to help set up the studio before Smith arrived, but he didn't work on the album itself. In 1994, Howard had the band set up in the mansion's central ballroom, at the foot of a grandiose central staircase, with terrazzo floors and chandeliers. That was the only room that could accommodate the 14-foot-long API console that came from the recently closed Record Plant in New York City. (Howard drove it down himself, contracting a case of the measles on the way, and almost died.) The band set up behind Howard, so they heard the same playback he did. Like Lanois, Howard prefers to work without walls or glass separating producer and artist.

Sessions for *Day for Night* were preceded by having Howard visit the band between Christmas 1993 and New Year's, at their Kingston rehearsal space in the Woolen Mill, which was also the home of tour manager Dave Powell. Howard arrived unprepared for the weather; he spent the session huddled in a corner, wearing a Russian hat and other winter wear he cobbled together from a Kingston army surplus store. He wasn't just listening and making notes; he had a small recording rig with him, and he recorded the rehearsals to some ADATs. Two of those takes ended up on the album, with minimal overdubs later in New Orleans: "Titanic Terrarium" and "Nautical Disaster," the latter being one of the album's key singles—the one Allan Gregg thought was the only decently recorded song on the record. It had already been workshopped well before the winter sessions; the band had recorded a version that autumn in Amsterdam, at a nightclub/hostel/recording studio called Sleep In, where the band had stayed during a break in their European tour.

Inspired by recording as a live band again, the Hip were determined to make the rest of the album that way. Not only that, but they wanted to record in New Orleans as if they were on tour. "They had all the songs, and they were going to perform the record in a set, like playing it live at a show," said Howard. "They'd play one song, and then instead of doing a bunch of versions of the same song, they'd go to the next song to keep it fresh. That was a great concept, but I wasn't getting the kinds of takes I was hoping to get. There would be some kind of genius on each one, but also a flaw. Maybe a song had an amazing ending but not an amazing intro. After two weeks of this, I started editing. I'd take the best bits of each one and cut them together to come up with stronger songs."

Normally a producer takes a guitar pass from one take and places it over a rhythm track from another. Howard, however, "would use full-band blocks," cutting "miles and miles of tape" with a razor blade and then cutting that to another take of the same song. "That way I wasn't messing with performances. I was choosing the best."

As any producer would, Howard also helped shape the songs. "I'd be arranging the songs on the fly," he says. "We cut the song the way they thought it would be, and then I'd say, 'We need a more interesting intro here; let's make this section shorter.' I tried to build the songs so that they had form."

"So Hard Done By" had already been attempted with Chris Tsangarides in London; that version eventually surfaced on the *Fully Completely* box set, released in 2014. There, it's a typical Hip rocker of the *Road Apples* era: fine, but not remarkable. On *Day for Night*, it's a slinky, sparse and slow groove, driven by a grungy blues riff and a conga-enhanced beat. It sounds exactly like you'd imagine the Hip should in New Orleans, and it's easily the sexiest Hip song—which befits a song in which a stripper, albeit a reluctant one, is a central character.

"Fire in the Hole" boasts a tense, explosive performance that may well be Johnny Fay's finest recorded hour. Rob Baker sounds practically unhinged, his feedback-riddled lead guitar darting and dancing around the groove, a riff he called "pointy teeth." Meanwhile, Langlois keeps the steady rhythm while another guitar makes a long, low, lurching and groaning sound under all the fury. On top of it all, Downie delivers the most punk-rock performance of his Hip career, howling and screaming at the end of almost every line, some of which are borrowed directly from Hazel Dickens's harrowing bluegrass song by the same name, about coal miners' unions. He sounds terrifying. "I was really pushing them to take it more into Iggy Pop world, really over the top," says Howard. "I was jumping up and down, yelling, 'Further! Further! Let's go further!' Nothing else [on the record] had that kind of power behind it."

Uptempo rock songs are rare on *Day for Night*; they populate less than half the 14-song record. Here's the thing about Mark Howard: he doesn't make rock records. Look at his discography, with and without Lanois: Emmylou Harris's *Wrecking Ball*. Bob Dylan's *Time Out of Mind*. Tom Waits's *Real Gone*. Marianne Faithfull's *Vagabond Ways*. Lucinda Williams's *World Without Tears*. Vic Chesnutt's *Silver Lake*. Neil Young's *Le Noise*. The only real rock records he's made in the past 30 years, other than *Day for Night*, are Iggy Pop's *American Caesar* and Sam Roberts's *Chemical City*. "I grew up with Brian Eno and atmospheres and textures," says Howard. "Each record is different; *Real Gone*, there's nothing else that sounds like that. Making rock records can be a bit meat-and-potatoes; it's bombastic and there's a formula to it. Other than Led Zeppelin and those older artists, I'm not a fan of those kind of records, because there's nothing there that makes me jealous. That's how I judge something: if I'm jealous of it."

If opening tracks are meant to convey the tenor of an album—think "Blow at High Dough," "Little Bones" and "Courage"—then *Day for Night* lays its cards on the table right away with "Grace, Too." A mid-tempo boom-bap beat, a melodic bass riff and guitars that writer Sean Michaels described as "ivied." It seems like it might be building up to something, but never does—which is the point, in tune with the unresolved narrative in the lyrics about the plotting of a crime. When the pre-chorus kicks in, it doesn't hit you like a bomb the way "Blow at High Dough" does; it dissipates the energy through dynamics, rather than the textbook tricks of stop-starts or acceler-ated rhythms or a dramatic chord change. You don't pump your fist; you stretch your arms to the sky. It sounds like an ascension, even as the chord sequence descends. Over the band's modal riffing, Downie's melody alter-nates between only two notes, separated by an interval of a fourth. Then there's the coda: Baker's guitar never takes the lead exactly, but it starts off like a mist and gets increasingly denser with richer textures until he's conjuring snow squalls. By the time the song ends, he's making whale music. A decade after U2's the Edge redefined rock guitar solos heard on the radio, Baker took it a step further. Considering it's one of the Hip's most popular and enduring songs, "Grace, Too" is remarkable for what it isn't, rather than what it is.

Downie's lyrics are among his most elliptical as well—which is saying something. The narrator is a con man, trying to impress a woman with his wealth, his will, his determination. There's some kind of nefarious plan afoot. The lyrics are devoid of specifics. Over the roaring conclusion, the narrator sounds like an uncertain minion about to carry out a dastardly deed, questioning the who, where and when of the crime. He's howling like a victim locked in the trunk of a car, not a criminal pondering a fateful decision.

When asked directly about the song, Downie said, "All of our songs are about war. You can use them for any situation you desire, and I love 'Grace, Too' because of that. It's just UN peacekeeping language—'rules of engagement'—but definitely, the enlarged bits have their roots in the tiniest relationships."

Violence looms large on *Day for Night*. "Yawning or Snarling" was written about a gig in El Paso—a Texan border town along the shores of the Rio Grande—where armed cops went into an over-capacity club crowd at a Hip show to stop a mosh pit. The Canadians were worried. "Imagine these guys wrestling around in the pile with their guns on, and all I could think about was some kid grabbing one and firing off a few shots," said Gord Sinclair. "I mean, these cops seemed really anxious to start something, and they were all pretty young guys. Being from Canada, seeing that armed panic is a dangerous, dangerous combination."

"Nautical Disaster" is the most lyrically affecting piece on the record, perhaps in part because it's the most straightforward narrative: a man has a dream about being on a sinking ship off the coast of France where 4,000 people drown. He escapes in a lifeboat, kicking other survivors off his pant leg. The screaming fills his head, and, yet, in the opening line he says he "relishes" the whole experience; by the end of the song, he tells a woman named Susan—to whom he's been relating this dream—that their conversations seem only a faint memory to him now, likening their talks to the sound of fingernails scratching against the lifeboat. If that all seems like unlikely hit-single material, the song sets an endlessly circular chord progression to linear lyrics containing neither a chorus nor a single rhyme.

The lyrics were written while on tour in Europe, partly inspired by the sinking of the *Bismarck*, a German battleship in the Second World War that was downed by the British off the coast of France. For years, Downie claimed the lyrics were fairly spontaneous and that the entire song came together during the Amsterdam sessions. The lyrics were based on a single postcard he'd written—likely to Peter Howell at the *Toronto Star*, as the newspaper used it as a background image, underneath a headline, for a story on the front page of the arts section in 1993. In 2000, he recanted, however, having gone through an old notebook and finding "endless drafts of it. Endless, but they don't really change. Maybe I was experimenting with new pens." The song is haunting on several levels; Downie claimed that if he ever got remotely distracted while performing it and dropped a line, he could never find his way back in: "The song might as well end."

The Second World War is a recurring theme on the album. In "Scared," there's a reference to Russian soldiers evacuating an art museum so the Nazis can't pillage it. "Fire in the Hole" makes an oblique reference to Leni Riefenstahl's 1935 Nazi propaganda film *Triumph of the Will*. On tour in Germany in August 1993, this was all clearly on Downie's mind. At a show broadcast on German TV, he can be heard introducing "Twist My Arm" by saying, "This is for Leni Riefenstahl." About "Looking for a Place to Happen," he says, "This is a song about the *Bismarck*," and ad libs a dark joke, "I'm going to wash that race right out of my hair," inserting a genocidal twist into a lyric from the musical *South Pacific*.

Downie wrote most of his lyrics in isolation, in Toronto, while the band rehearsed in Kingston. Missing his bandmates and envious of the fact they were stretching their musical muscles every day, Downie would go on long walks in the big city and meditate on his themes. When he would arrive in his hometown for weekend rehearsals, he was prepared and ready to rock. "Love was the reward for hard work," he said, "and that's what I needed. For 48 hours, I would just be totally immersed in it. I'd missed these guys all week. So the electric energy was strong."

Some of Downie's best lyrics on *Day for Night* are on underrated songs: "An Inch an Hour" (which refers to the movement of a glacier, as per John Ruskin) and "Titanic Terrarium," featuring a treated guitar that sounds like a detuned banjo, underneath a lyric about respecting the power of nature. Both songs are dense with delightful lines and evocative imagery. If, on previous records, Downie had been a poetic lyricist, he was now a lyrical poet. His band and the producer were ready to meet him at least halfway or, as on "Titanic Terrarium," all the way. "Gord is such a good writer and comes from angles no one else can think of," said Mark Howard. "I took his songwriting and built around that atmospherically to go with the mood of his writing."

Howard would do what he and Lanois called "treatments," in which whatever sounds the band produced through various combinations of pedals and amps were treated with other effects on the sound board "to trip them out a bit more," said Howard. The lead guitar sound on "Greasy Jungle" is one example of this, as is the flange-like treatment on the drum loop in "Thugs" (made with an Eventide H3000 digital effects unit, popular with house music producers). The guitar solo on "So Hard Done By" was played through an amp the size of a cigar box, with a tiny speaker in it. Howard placed a microphone in front of it and boosted it in the mix: "You hear these Marshall stacks underneath and then this little sound on top like a barking dog."

"That was all part of the language of wanting to create a landscape in the music, to create more cinema in the story," said Colin Cripps, who'd known Howard, Lanois and Burn since the early '80s. "You'd take a drum sound or guitar sound or vocal sound and treat it. There was no automation [in mixing consoles] back then. I remember Malcolm and Mark would spend hours creating treatments so that they could create this possibility that might create a greater reaction, negative or positive. That philosophy definitely came from Dan's way of working—you can hear it in all of U2's records. It's the kind of record every band wants to make, a record that has a more dimensional feeling to it when you close your eyes."

"A lot of the guys in the band initially weren't very open to anything like that," said Downie. "When we get together as a group, the friction of people rubbing against each other, at best tends to push your ideals, and at worst it tends to bring out the bourgeois tendencies of your nature." That's why they hired Howard. "It was me pushing them along all the way, sound-wise," the producer claimed.

Once recording wrapped up, Howard went to the former Le Studio in Morin Heights, Quebec, to mix it. Once the site for recordings by the Police and Rush, it had recently been taken over by Pierre Marchand, best known as Sarah McLachlan's producer. (He, too, had been a Lanois protégé, of sorts; he played keyboards on Luba's *Secrets and Sins*, produced by Lanois.) The band insisted on being present. They didn't like being marginalized during the mixing process on the first three albums, and now they were assigning themselves the title of co-producer. This time they were hands on, literally, as they would all be crouched over the mixing board with Howard, working the faders for their own instruments (this was when automatic faders were increasingly common, but Howard preferred the old-school approach).

The band started to second-guess the experimentation that they'd hired Howard to deliver. "I mean, if you could have heard that record three months before we finished it, it was really out there," said Downie. Sinclair called it "goofy" and worried it would be hard to reproduce live. Howard was sent back to his own studio in San Francisco to clean it up; the Hip joined him there on a day off tour. Hot young New Orleans drummer Brian Blade—who would later become one of the most acclaimed drummers in modern jazz for his work with Herbie Hancock and others—had recorded some dual drumming with Fay, none of which made it onto the final record. Early mixes of "Grace, Too" and "Scared" leaned more on soundscapes. There was enough extra material and alternate takes that "they probably could have put a whole other record out," said Howard. "It's not rock." (Between 1997 and 1999, Olympic figure-skating medallist Kurt Browning performed a routine to a droning *Day for Night* outtake called "Antares.")

"Grace, Too" evolved from one of the more outré tracks into an anchor of the album and its most enduring song. "I didn't think it was going to be a single, in the beginning," said Howard. "As the process went on, it became obvious that it might actually be the *only* single. The mixes that came out of [Morin Heights] were too weird for them. I had to go in there and strip some effects off and make it more appropriate. In those days, record companies—man, if they didn't hear a single, then they didn't get it. They'd be like, 'What is this? A stoner record? We can't sell this.'"

It would not be the least bit unfair to call *Day for Night* a stoner record. "Well, they do smoke a lot of weed," said Howard. "I think they smoked a quarter pound of weed for the recording, and then when we mixed, it was half a pound of hash. I didn't smoke cigarettes in those days, and they mixed their hash with tobacco. After mixing the record, I started smoking cigarettes for the next 10 years. It's their fault!"

As on any morning after a bender, the band had doubts, even while peers immediately recognized the album's charms. Sinclair played it with trepidation for Colin Cripps and asked his opinion. Cripps said, "Well, what you went for, you've achieved. Everything is new to an audience who hasn't heard something—unless you keep making the same fucking record. Your audience will either love it or grow to love it—or not at all."

The doubt infected Howard as well. "At the time, I thought, 'Oh shit, I've made a record everyone's going to hate.' You know, their fans are hardcore: they'll throw beer bottles at you if they don't like it. It wasn't until years later that I went to a show and saw Gord [Downie]. He pulled me aside and said, 'You know that record we made together, it's one of my favourite records. I love listening to it.' I thought, okay, wow! It wasn't until then that I knew they actually liked it. The whole record has soul, and I think that's why people like it. It's heartfelt and you can really hear the emotion in Gord's vocals."

The shadow of Daniel Lanois lingered over the record's intentions, but it's hard to find much evidence of his sonic sorcery in the final product. Even if it had been Lanois and not Mark Howard behind the boards, the Hip were still essentially a bar band: arty atmospherics were never their strongest point. That side of them would not emerge again for another 22 years, when Kevin Drew and Dave Hamelin produced *Man Machine Poem*.

The record got mixed reviews, but support came from some unlikely quarters, including Greg Burliuk at the *Kingston Whig-Standard*, whose writing always had the air of someone being forced to say something good about the hometown boys. He wrote that *Day for Night* is, frankly, "dead brilliant, and that's coming from someone who has not been the biggest Hip fan in town." The *Globe and Mail*, on the other hand, took a pass: "There's little of the detail that made [Downie's] earlier songs interesting—but rather than offering anything so inviting as a hook, the rest of the band seems intent on providing trippy atmospherics and generic rock roar."

———

Day for Night sold almost half a million copies in the first few months after its release, even before the Canadian tour began in February 1995. The Tragically Hip became the first Canadian group to debut an album at No. 1 in *The Record*, a national trade magazine. Stores stayed open late the night before the release date, so uberfans could buy a copy at one minute after midnight. The HMV flagship store on Toronto's Yonge Street sold 600 copies in the first hour.

"That surprised us," said Langlois. "I don't think any of us was convinced that it was as accessible as our last records. We felt we'd made it—more this record than any other—for ourselves. We were really happy with it, but our expectations weren't that high." That modesty played into the tour as well. "We questioned the judgment of Jake and Allan in booking us in arenas," said Gord Sinclair. In fact, it was the biggest cross-Canada tour by any Canadian band at that time in history—partially because unlike Rush or Triumph or other internationally popular acts, it made better business sense for the Hip to spend so much time in their homeland. All the shows sold out instantly, faster than even R.E.M., who were on the road around the same time. Jake Gold, when he signed the Tragically Hip in 1986, told them, "You'll headline your first arena in 10 years." He was almost spot on: it was nine-and-a-half years later. "We were all left picking our jaws up off the floor because we'd never really had a sense that that was the scale," said Sinclair.

Frankly, that's hard to believe for a band who'd already headlined a touring festival, drawing at least 10,000 people a night, with Midnight Oil as the opener. Gold and Gregg's strategy from the beginning had been to undersell the band and create demand by booking them in smaller venues. If Sinclair is to be believed, the illusion clearly kept the band's own collective ego in check. So did the fact that after playing a sold-out arena show in Moncton, the band was turned away from a nearby nightclub "because the bouncer didn't like the way they looked," according to the *Toronto Star*.

The most shocking level of mainstream acceptance for *Day for Night* was when Howard was nominated for Producer of the Year at the Juno Awards in the spring of 1995; fellow nominees included David Foster for Céline Dion, Arnold Lanni for Our Lady Peace, Pierre Marchand for Sarah McLachlan and winner Robbie Robertson for his album *Music for the Native Americans*. It's hard to imagine what the sludgy sonics of *Day for Night* have in common with any of those records—it's like Elliot Smith performing at the Academy Awards. Howard didn't attend and didn't expect to win; the band, of course, had always kept themselves an arm's length away from the ceremony. "I know the Hip, and they didn't want anything to do with the Junos," Howard said. "They thought it was a bunch of crooked shit."

Even more surprising was when the Hip took Mark Howard's advice and employed Bob Lanois, Daniel's brother, to make two of the album's videos, for "Grace, Too" and "Greasy Jungle." Both videos used a technique called "video feedback," where "he'd put the film on the TV screen and then use his camera to feed it back into itself," said Howard. "After smoking some pot, it looked really cool." MuchMusic was known for programming a lot of oddball and groundbreaking videos, but "Grace, Too" in particular—which looks the way the earliest Eric's Trip records sound—is shockingly raw for something that was in any kind of rotation, never mind a focus track from the country's biggest band of the day.

The 19-date Canadian tour kicked off in February 1995, with the Odds and Change of Heart as openers. The band played hockey rinks from Halifax to Victoria, with stops in Moncton, North Bay, Sudbury, Sault Ste. Marie, Lethbridge, Kamloops and Red Deer—markets that other Canadian superstars never headlined at the height of their fame. Change of Heart's Ian Blurton had a theory about why *Day for Night* marked a shift toward mid-tempo, moodier material: "I was once told that Pink Floyd would go around and time all the auditoriums before they went on tour, and then adjust the BPMs of the set to fit, so that the echoes all line up. I believe that, because playing arenas can be a nightmare. The farther the back wall gets, the slower the tune has to be."

It marked the first time a new generation could see the Tragically Hip play indoors; prior to that, if you were underage, Another Roadside Attraction would have been a teenager's only chance to see the band. "We froze the young kids out," said Jake Gold. "We only played licensed places. The live thing was what made you go, 'Oh, *fuck*.' We chose to make it a rite of passage, consciously. There was no internet, no pics at the concert, no Snapchatting, anything like that. It was all word of mouth."

What should have been one huge word-of-mouth moment for the Tragically Hip was anything but. On March 25, 1995, their old friend and supporter Dan Aykroyd was a featured guest on *Saturday Night Live* (John Goodman was the host), and he pulled some strings to get the Tragically Hip as that week's musical guest. They played "Grace, Too" and "Nautical Disaster," both of which are odd introductions to the biggest audience of your career. In the clip, Downie is in one of his slightly unsettling states of semi-possession: twitching, trembling, entirely lost in the song, with a mischievous look in his eye.

He admitted he was distracted. He blamed his nephew, whose 11th birthday was that night. Downie promised the boy that he'd give him a special secret message on the air, by holding up his two index fingers to make the number 11. "In retrospect: not a very good idea," he recalled later, "because that's all I obsessed about: '*You cannot forget to do that!* You can't make a promise to an 11-year-old and break it.' So Danny's doing his intro, and the first line of 'Grace, Too' is, 'He said, "I'm fabulously rich."' I said, 'He said I'm Tragically Hip,' just repeating what Danny said, because I'm trying to do this 11 thing and I'm distracted. My inner elevator went from the penthouse to the basement instantly, because suddenly I don't know the next line. Because [normally] you get the first line and then it just flows. And then, boom, I pulled back on the joystick and we were off into the American consciousness for three-and-a-half minutes. But my sister-in-law claimed she had vicarious diarrhea, and there was a clenching of hands and nerves, nation-wide, I think, that night."

Over the outro of their second song, "Nautical Disaster," Downie slid in a quote of the Skydiggers' 1992 song "A Penny More," which shares the same chords.

How did the Tragically Hip celebrate their big moment on American television? Said Downie, "We went to a club called the Abyss in St. Louis the very next day and played to 42 people."

Two days after the *SNL* appearance, Robert Plant—on a reunion tour with Led Zeppelin's Jimmy Page—played the SkyDome in Toronto. The next day, Jake Gold got a call from the promoter, Donald K. Donald of CPI, asking if the Hip wanted to open some dates on the next leg of Page and Plant's tour in June, and another leg in October. Gold, who had sung Led Zeppelin songs in his own high school band, was over the moon. So were Baker and Sinclair, who learned Zeppelin songs together when they first started playing. "Robert Plant is a muso," said Gold. "That's why he loved *Day for Night*—not because it was a hit record. It's a musicians' record."

Plant loved having the Hip on tour. He'd play with Rob Baker's newborn son. After his own set, he'd go back to the Hip's dressing room, ask for a smoke and ask what he should do as an encore. Early in the '95 tour, during a Hip sound check, Downie noticed what sounded like Johnny Fay momentarily dropping the beat. When it resumed, it had a decidedly different feel. Downie turned around to discover the singer of Led Zeppelin sitting at the drum kit. "It was just buddies on the road, guys hanging out," said Gold. "It wasn't a mentor vibe. He was so normal that I never thought of him as Robert Plant. We met Jimmy once in 30 shows. Robert, we saw every day."

Sportscaster and friend Mark Hebscher travelled with the band on the California leg of the tour. Before one show, he was ferrying the band and Gold to the gig when they hit a traffic jam outside the venue. "Jake said, 'Just keep going, tell them it's the guys in the band,'" Hebscher recalled. "Paul had long hair and could have been mistaken for Jimmy Page. Jake said, 'Hey, just stick your hair out the window.' And we just drove by everybody. The guys were nervous: 'What if we get caught?' They were so down-to-earth, thinking maybe they shouldn't have done that, hoping nothing bad happens. They could easily have just said, 'Fuck you, we're the Tragically Hip.' But a leopard can't change its spots. These were five guys from Kingston."

Headlining a national tour of hockey arenas, playing on *Saturday Night Live*, hanging out with Robert Plant—what other rock fantasy could possibly come true for a bunch of small-town boys who grew up in the 1970s?

At their February 10 Maple Leaf Gardens show—their first time headlining one of Canada's temples of hockey—Jake Gold was standing by the soundboard with Arthur Fogel, of the promoter CPI, when the Hip launched into "Fifty Mission Cap," an electrifying moment for everyone in the room, one that tied together the history of Canadian rock'n'roll and the country's most beloved sport. Gold turned to Fogel and said, "Man, this is why I do this." Fogel turned to him and said, "Do you think the guys would want to play with the Stones this summer?"

Opening for the Rolling Stones, or any act at that level, is a résumé-padder at best. It's supposed to be a prestigious gig. It's not. You go onstage in full daylight, nobody cares that you're there—and even if they do, you're background music at best to everyone else, making for an alienating experience for everyone involved. No one buys your record the next day. If you're the Tragically Hip playing in front of 70,000 crossed-arm Germans wearing black leather jackets, the chances of you making any kind of impression are infinitesimal. "Basically, you have to live to tell about it," said Sinclair. "Literally, that was the objective."

There were four shows: Cologne, Hanover, and two shows at the Rock Werchter festival just outside Brussels. In Cologne, torrential rain—drops "the size of toonies," said Baker—started falling the moment the Hip hit the uncovered stage at 7:30 p.m. If they were shitting their pants, they didn't let it show: whether it was 70 people or 70,000, rain or shine, headlining or opening for heroes, a show was a show was a show. The Stones, curious about how their new tour mates would handle the situation, stood sidestage, and their jaws dropped—even Mick Jagger, who apparently never watched opening bands. "Afterwards," recalled Gold, "each one of [the Stones] came up to the band and said, 'Way to go! You guys are the real deal, real rock'n'roll guys.'" It all seemed to be a divine test: the clouds literally parted and the sun came out just as the Stones went onstage at nine.

After that, the legends extended a nightly invitation back to the "Voodoo Lounge"—not the general backstage party area but the more private area reserved for closest friends. The band who got their start playing a set comprised largely of Stones covers were now shooting pool with Keith Richards. "That was kind of my dream," said Baker, "but when you do that, it's kind of like meeting royalty. What are you gonna say? 'I-I-I'm your biggest fan, I got all your albums and, uh, can you tell me how you played the riff from . . .' You feel like an idiot, so instead you just nod your head politely and shake his hand and try not to break his fingers."

That was all a warm-up for the second incarnation of Another Roadside Attraction, a seven-date festival tour that kicked off on July 13 at Vancouver's Thunderbird Stadium. The lineup was rounded out by Kingston's Inbreds, Eric's Trip, Rheostatics, American power-pop song-writer Matthew Sweet ("Girlfriend," "Sick of Myself"), Spirit of the West, Blues Traveler and Ziggy Marley's Melody Makers. The latter may have seemed like an odd choice, particularly putting the non-rock band in the penultimate slot right before the Hip, a slot in which Daniel Lanois had been literally showered in abuse the year before at a Canada Day show. Then again, considering the stoner vibe of *Day for Night* and the jam-band scene the Hip were starting to be associated with—which would also explain Blues Traveler's presence—it wasn't that much of a stretch.

"We were struggling with who to schedule right before the Hip," admitted Gold, "and Ziggy was the last act that we booked." Gold had met him that spring during an annual Jamaican vacation. "I thought, everyone loves Bob Marley, and that's what Ziggy played—and he's the only one allowed! *This* is who we put on before the Hip, because no one can *not* like this! It's celebration music: tons of dancers onstage, a big show. So, Blues Traveler to Spirit of the West to Ziggy to the Hip, it was perfect." Blues Traveler had to miss the first date, however, because singer and harmonica player John Popper insisted on bringing his firearms on tour, which inevitably led to border problems—and the nickname "Gun Traveler" for the duration of the tour.

As with the first Roadside Attraction, it was designed as much as a travelling summer camp for the bands as it was an experience for the audience. "They had a whole approach to a communal backstage," recalled Spirit of the West's Geoff Kelly, "where all the dressing room trailers faced into the middle where there was a horseshoe pit and Ping-Pong tables to encourage everyone to hang out and be together. The first couple of gigs people were a bit aloof, but as it went on everyone was hanging out with everybody. They were the ultimate hosts. I have memories of the Inbreds and Eric's Trip being the first bands of the day, and the Hip were there every single day watching them from the side of the stage. You'd think that after a few shows you'd say, 'Don't have to see these guys again, just saw them yesterday.' Nope. They were always there." Sometimes they were among the only ones—even before the crowds showed up. Mike O'Neill of the Inbreds said, "Sometimes when we played, there would be two people throwing a Frisbee in the field and somebody still pounding stakes into the barrier, and that was kind of it."

If Another Roadside Attraction was yet another triumph in the best year of the Hip's career, they didn't rest on their laurels. Less than a week after they played in Newfoundland at the end of July 1995, they were back on the road in August, playing Rosie O'Grady's Good Time Emporium in Pensacola, Florida.

CHAPTER NINE

LET'S DEBUNK AN
AMERICAN MYTH
CONTINENTAL DRIFTS

*"In a huge country like the United States, a man with a
reputation such as I had here would have been prosperous."*

HUGH MACLENNAN, *THE WATCH THAT ENDS THE NIGHT*, 1958

ON MAY 24, 2016, the day Gord Downie's diagnosis was announced, I
was asked to be on camera for a short TV news segment. The fourth or
fifth question asked was: "Why do you think the Tragically Hip never
made it in the U.S.?"

I stammered out some kind of answer that refuted the question while
wondering if that sentiment was destined to be the band's epitaph. What
kind of country wraps their heroes' greatest accomplishment in an insecurity blanket?

At the Tragically Hip's final show on August 20, 2016, I sat in Kingston's
K-Rock Centre next to a guy who went to the same high school as the band
members. He saw gigs by their predecessors, the Rodents and the Slinks.
The Tragically Hip had been a huge part of his life and his hometown
pride. We talked of the various gigs he'd seen through the years and how
he'd visited their studio because he was a good friend of Dave "Billy Ray"
Koster's brother. During our brief conversation before the show started, he
told me, entirely unprompted, "It's mind-blowing that they haven't made

it in the U.S." He then paused, sipped his beer and continued, "They're way better than Nickelback."

Minutes before the last gig of the Tragically Hip's career, this myth of American failure was still on the mind of one of their biggest fans.

Mind you, his concern is true: Nickelback *is* bigger than the Tragically Hip—certainly in the United States, where Billboard declared them the biggest-selling group of the 2000s, of any genre (they edged out over Destiny's Child). As of 2017, Nickelback has sold 50 million records worldwide; the Tragically Hip, eight million. However, virtually all of those eight million Hip records have been sold in Canada alone; Nickelback's domestic sales total a mere three-and-a-half million. By some metric, that makes the Hip twice as popular as Nickelback in Canada. Nickelback, of course, are huge Hip fans themselves; on their 2017 tour, they covered "Blow at High Dough" in homage. Justin Bieber is also a fan and has covered "Wheat Kings" live. Before he became a teen sensation, he only had enough time and money to attend two big-ticket shows: the Tragically Hip and the Montreal pop-punk band Simple Plan. When Bieber relayed that anecdote in a 2010 *Rolling Stone* cover story, it was one of the only times the magazine had ever mentioned the Hip in print.

But this is not about numbers, it's about perception. This classic Canadian myth persisted until the very end: because the Tragically Hip never filled arenas south of the border as they did here, they were somehow unsuccessful. The fact that they were never a household name in America on the level of Alanis Morissette or Shania Twain was somehow a national Canadian shame. Yet for most of their career, they played 1,000-seat venues in every major U.S. market, despite little support from the press.

Many Canadian fans took the discrepancy to heart, further endearing the band to a home crowd who could claim the Hip as our own secret—a parochial outlook that runs deep in Canadian culture. One could trace it all the way back to at least Anne of Green Gables, the iconic character who eschews a scholarship on the mainland to stay close to her family on Prince Edward Island.

According to Allan Gregg, the problem started right off the bat with MTV. Both "Blow at High Dough" and "New Orleans Is Sinking" did fairly well on U.S. radio, as well as any new band from a foreign market could expect to do. The snag came with the video for "Blow at High Dough." On the back of an LP dust sleeve, Rob Baker had written down a series of images he wanted the director to use. "The video came back and it was exactly what we had asked them to do," said Baker. It featured the band playing in front of a blue screen projecting stock B&W footage of synchronized swimming, ant colonies, Japanese kaiju films, surfers, speeding trains and blasting rockets. The result was what one would expect from a band that started out playing garage rock inspired by the Monkees: it's intentionally kitschy. For Allan Gregg, that was a problem. "We got a very good director, with good credentials, and the band briefed him on what they wanted. It was a fucking mess. 'We want to see bugs crawling around'—and he took this literally, like he was the help. This was expensive, like, $75,000 for this first video." That equalled almost half the recording budget for *Up to Here*.

After the song went top-10 AOR radio in America, Gregg and Gold set up a meeting with MTV, who told them flat out that they didn't see the Tragically Hip as an MTV band, based on that clip. "They informed us that the Hip 'were not a video band' and that even if Steven Spielberg directed the next video, it was unlikely they would play it," said Gregg. To be fair, the band does look like it crawled out from under a rock. MCA was disheartened by the MTV decision: top-10 AOR was just so-so, in their eyes—but then again, no other MCA rock bands were cracking the top 10 of anything in 1989. MCA refused to fund another video for the next single, not wanting to spend good money after bad. So the Management Trust ponied up $6,000, hired a friend from Calgary and made a video for "New Orleans Is Sinking." "Again," says Gregg, "MTV wanted nothing to do with it; they thought it was shite. But MuchMusic played it and the record then exploded." "New Orleans" managed to replicate the limited success of the first single; it, too, went top-10 AOR. It did particularly well in Dallas, where the record held the No. 1 spot for 13 weeks, breaking a record held by home-state band ZZ Top. That started a long-standing fan base for the Hip in Texas, a market that was also the launching ground for the American breakthroughs of Rush and Triumph 10 to 15 years earlier. College radio was also supportive.

But the rest of the American campaign never recovered from the MTV snub, even as prospects in Canada got better by the week. In Canada, says Allan Gregg, "we start selling by the shovelful. The Americans are perplexed by this whole thing. They don't understand why they can't make any headway. In the meantime, the band is playing bigger and bigger venues, packed houses. They did really well at radio stations in all those places. We sold maybe 20,000, 30,000 copies of *Up to Here* in America [in the first year]." *Up to Here* went on to sell more than a million copies in Canada.

The band downplayed the discrepancy from day one. In 1990, Rob Baker said, "The States isn't the brass ring it used to be. And who cares? We're having a great time here. What we do here [in Canada] allows us to go to Australia and tour Europe. We're seeing the world." There's no question, however, that America was still a priority for the band and everyone around them—even if MCA America told Gregg that *Road Apples* had no "career-breaking hit singles." By the time *Fully Completely* came out in 1992, said Gord Sinclair, "We were still holding out hope for the equivalent American success. We did the math: 'Gee, we sold 300,000 copies of this record in Canada. There are 10 times as many people in the States, so 10 times 300,000 is . . .'"

It never happened.

I thought TH was bigger than it really is.

Album after album, one record deal after another, the Tragically Hip met a wall of resistance when it came to American media—and, by extension, mainstream success. No national radio hits. No *Tonight Show* or Letterman. No features in *Rolling Stone* or *Spin* or anything other than the occasional local newspaper. They only ever had one supporting slot on a big tour (Page and Plant, in 1995). The band who shipped multi-platinum at home in Canada never sold 100,000 copies of any album in the U.S., with *Fully Completely* coming the closest (in the first five years after its 1992 release, it sold 94,000). But by the mid-2000s, the Hip were playing the same venues that hosted Broken Social Scene, a buzz band Canadians believed to have "made it" in America.

Cam Carpenter, the band's Canadian A&R rep at MCA in 1995, recalls, "One of my proudest moments as a record-company guy was hearing Dan Aykroyd say on *Saturday Night Live*, 'And now, my friends from Kingston, Ontario, the Tragically Hip.' I still get goosebumps thinking about that. We'd hoped to break them two albums before that, at least, but to me that was making it: playing on *Saturday Night Live*, the same stage where I'd watched David Bowie and Elvis Costello."

Except that no one at the band's American label at the time, Atlantic, saw it the same way. One Atlantic promo rep complained, "There was no sales spike on Monday morning—and you always get a sales spike on Monday morning. No one cares about Canada down here." Brendan Canning remembers opening some American dates for the Hip just after *SNL*, with his band hHead. Gigs varied from a bowling alley in Omaha to the prestigious First Avenue in Minneapolis (capacity: 1,500).

By 2011, the Hip were still a joke to the American press. In a *Rolling Stone* cover story about Saskatoon rock band the Sheepdogs—who won a reader contest, the prize being a cover story—writer Austin Scaggs goes for a night on the town with the young band. He sets the scene in one bar by writing, "Blaring through the speakers is the awful yet extremely popular Canadian band the Tragically Hip, and occasionally the DJ will allow some inebriate to sing karaoke." That's what the Tragically Hip were to the U.S. press: an annoying musical backdrop that only surfaced in small-town Canada, a band whose only possible audience in America was expat Canadians.

Which is far from true. "When people would say to Gord, 'You never made it in America,' he'd say: 'You're completely disparaging our American fans,'" says Dave Bidini of the Rheostatics. "We toured with them in the States [in 1996]. I thought we'd be playing chicken-wing joints, you know? But we show up in Somerville, Massachusetts, and we're playing for 600 people in a soft-seater. They were playing great rooms all over the place." By the 2000 tour, those places included the Wiltern in Los Angeles (capacity: 1,850), Emo's in Austin (1,700), the Rialto in Tucson (1,200), and the Roxy Theatre in Atlanta (3,000). Two nights at each the Fillmore in San Francisco (1,150) and the Moore Theatre in Seattle (1,800). Three nights at the Metro Theatre in Chicago (1,100), a city where, at the House of Blues (1,800) in 2006, they played a televised New Year's Eve gig (with, um, Matisyahu). In New York City, where if you make it there you can make it anywhere, they played Central Park's Summerstage (5,000) and the Beacon Theatre (3,000). "Of course, they never made it to the national icon status they had in Canada," says keyboardist Chris Brown, who played on that tour, "but they totally succeeded in America."

Sportscaster Dave Hodge saw the Hip at the Austin City Limits festival in Texas in 2006. "I was curious to see how big the crowd would be and try to assess who made up the crowd. There were 75,000 people a day at that thing. It was bigger than I thought it would be, and everybody was singing along to every word. Were they all Canadians? Without going around and asking for birth certificates, you don't know."

Ian Blurton of Change of Heart opened for the Tragically Hip extensively between 1992 and 1997, which marked the band's commercial height in Canada, a time when the Hip's fellow citizens were developing severe insecurity complexes about their heroes' status down south. "Whenever we played with them in the U.S., there were always between 500 and 1,000 people there," says Blurton. "I know 300 bands who would kill for that statistic—and that includes American bands. That whole argument [about not making it in the States] is just ridiculous. What level are you putting the band on? How many bands sell out *everywhere around the world*? Maybe 50. Lots of bands are huge just in their own country—and that's a good thing."

Take the analogy to Britain in the mid- to late '90s. How many Canadians know who the Manic Street Preachers are? Their career is littered with gold and multi-platinum records in their native U.K. How about Stereophonics? They've sold eight million albums in Britain—the same number the Hip have in Canada. Manic Street Preachers headlined Glastonbury in 1999; Stereophonics in 2002. In North America, both those bands had a cult following at best. They played mostly to the same Anglophiles who flocked to Suede shows earlier in the decade, or to shows by Kasabian (six million records in the U.K.) in the 2000s, or to Cliff Richard gigs 40 years before all that. (Side note: Stereophonics are actually huge Hip fans and covered "Fiddler's Green" on a B-side.)

Downie said there was a while, in the early to mid-'90s, when the Hip's international audience was heavily populated by "expats, the homesick and student travellers abroad. I'd make jokes about performing for the troops in these far-off places, like the USO [United Service Organization]. They'd make themselves known in ridiculous ways. Sometimes I'd only notice after the show when I'd be standing around talking, and there would be one American saying, 'You guys were pretty good.' Then a guy from Canada would say [in a Don Cherry accent], '*Yeeeah! Fuckin' right!* They're good Canadian boys, they're *more* than pretty good!' Really defensive. I understood it: homesickness mixed with alcohol is a pretty potent brew. It might have been a guy who took a job down in St. Louis and thinks, 'All my friends think I'm a hoser because all I talk about is Canada and they're getting tired of it, so now I'm going to show them something from Canada.'"

The smug revenge of the meek Canadian could take more obnoxious turns, too. Diana Bristow, a Canadian living in Chicago, recalls one Hip gig there in 2002 with Sam Roberts, where the Canadian flags were everywhere in the audience, along with renditions of "O Canada." Bristow and another Canadian expat were not that demonstrative, but they did try to assert a spot near the front of the stage, behind a very tall man. The women asked him to move, to which he and his friends responded gruffly, "Are you *Canadian*? Only *Canadians* can move up front. *No Americans*." That led to heated grilling between the two camps over Canadian geography: the bully unconvincingly claimed to be from Newfoundland and had never heard of the Toronto suburb of Richmond Hill. "It was my first experience with aggressive Canadianness," she recalls, "which is pretty funny to encounter at the House of Blues in Chicago."

———

In the '90s, eight new Canadian acts made huge impressions in the U.S. Tellingly, only two were bands: Barenaked Ladies and Crash Test Dummies. The rest were solo women: k.d. lang, Alanis Morissette, Céline Dion, Shania Twain, Sarah McLachlan and Diana Krall. How did they do it?

Céline Dion found a Canadian mentor in the L.A. music scene when David Foster helped shape her English-language debut album, 1990's *Unison*, which sold a million records in the U.S. and opened doors for her to work with fellow hitmakers. In 1992, she and Peabo Bryson duetted on the title track of Disney's *Beauty and the Beast*, which was a top-10 hit; they performed it together at the Oscars, where it won Best Original Song.

k.d. lang had a head start, being signed to Sire Records in 1985 as a controversial country artist. She was a favourite of Johnny Carson's and first broke through with a Roy Orbison duet. It wasn't until she put out a smooth pop record, 1992's *Ingénue*—and made headlines as the first major North American artist to come out as a lesbian—that she sold two million records in the U.S.

Winnipeg folk-pop act Crash Test Dummies sold four million copies of their 1993 album *God Shuffled His Feet* based solely on the strength of extensive MTV play for "Mmm Mmm Mmm Mmm." No other singles cracked the American Top 10. It was their one and only hit album in the U.S.

Shania Twain was married to her producer and co-songwriter, Robert "Mutt" Lange, who had already been responsible for blockbuster records by AC/DC, Def Leppard and Bryan Adams. It was hard for him to make an album that *wasn't* a hit, and Twain's 1995 *The Woman in Me* reshaped the face of country music, selling 12 million copies in the U.S., 20 million in total worldwide.

In 1994, the 19-year-old Alanis Morissette had been dropped by her record company, but her music publisher hooked her up with Glen Ballard, who had co-written "Man in the Mirror" for Michael Jackson and several hits for Wilson Phillips. *Jagged Little Pill* came out in 1995 on Madonna's label and featured members of the Red Hot Chili Peppers, Jane's Addiction and Tom Petty's Heartbreakers. It sold 33 million copies worldwide.

In 1996, Diana Krall achieved the increasingly impossible for a jazz-based artist, from Canada or anywhere else, when her tribute album to Nat King Cole went gold in the U.S.; her next three albums went platinum. She, too, had some help from David Foster, but also from industry giant Tommy LiPuma, a producer and record executive who had guided blockbuster records by Barbra Streisand, Natalie Cole and others.

All six of those artists worked incredibly hard, but the *scale* of their success was—as is usually the case—largely due to flukes and connections. With the exception of Morissette, none would be considered rock artists. Very few lessons learned from studying their careers could apply to the Tragically Hip. But the stories of Barenaked Ladies and Sarah McLachlan, on the other hand, provide some context.

Both acts were managed by Terry McBride, a co-founder of Nettwerk Records (Skinny Puppy, Grapes of Wrath). With McLachlan, he was expecting big things in the U.S. from her third album, 1993's *Fumbling Towards Ecstasy*, after selling 225,000 copies there of her first album, *Touch*, and 558,000 copies of 1991's *Solace*—numbers that are more than impressive. But when "Possession," the first single from *Fumbling Towards Ecstasy*, didn't catch on at U.S. radio—it stalled at No. 73 on Billboard's Hot 100 chart—her American label, Arista, stopped pushing the album. McBride found that unacceptable and launched his own campaign to lobby radio and retail. "We discovered we could do a lot of things major labels do," McBride told *Wired* magazine. "Sarah had made this incredible album, and we felt that if we were just persistent, it would find an audience." McLachlan spent the next few years touring every corner of the States. In January 1997, "Possession" re-entered the charts and peaked at No. 19 on something called the "adult top 40 chart." By now, *Fumbling Towards Ecstasy* had sold 1.6 million copies in the U.S. That summer, she and McBride launched the landmark Lilith Fair and released the album *Surfacing*, which debuted at No. 2 on Billboard. It sold 16 million copies worldwide, eight million in the U.S. alone.

In Canada, Barenaked Ladies sold one million copies of their debut album, 1992's *Gordon*. Much of that was fuelled by their appeal to teens and college students, many of whom abandoned the band on their next two albums. But if they had suffered from initial oversaturation in Canada, their American fan base was growing slowly but steadily. "We took that initial amount of funds [from *Gordon*] and put it into the U.S.," says bassist Jim Creeggan. "We were always down in the States. We were all still young guys, probably living at our parents' houses, playing the same [American] towns four times a year, then going back and keeping it going. That's how we grew a fan base." When they finished making their third record, in 1995, they turned to McBride for help. He told the band that if they gave him 18 months of their lives, he could make it work. He knew they were a great live band, so he sent the band out to play every radio-sponsored festival, in-store appearance and backyard barbecue for contest winners. He also commissioned a live album: *Rock Spectacle*, released in 1996, sold more than half a million copies in the U.S. "The word-of-mouth following really built up," drummer Tyler Stewart told *Rolling Stone* in 1998, "and then the radio stations started to clue into that. They'd come and see a show and go, 'Wow, there's a lot of people here.' Then they'd start getting requests for the songs and they'd play them, and the next thing you know, we're a national sensation." That all laid the groundwork for 1998's *Stunt*, which sold more than four million copies and spawned a No. 1 hit, "One Week."

Sloan's Jay Ferguson heard someone accusing his band of not making it big in the States because they were "'lazy and didn't work hard enough.' And he was right. If we'd toured like the Barenaked Ladies, maybe we'd be a lot bigger than we were—or we might not be a band anymore."

Jake Gold recalls, "Gord always used to say to me, 'I want success on my own terms.'"

Comparing Barenaked Ladies' success to the Hip's, bassist Jim Creeggan says, "It comes down to this: when you see [the Hip] live, you get it. That's when you understand what it's about. It's a feeling. When you listen to the records, you don't see Gord illustrating the songs with movement. You don't get the sense of trance from the guys riffing and Johnny Fay just hammering it out. More people would have got it if they played down there as much as we did. Gord is an artist who can transcend any borders." The irony in comparing the two bands, however, is that Barenaked Ladies all but disappeared in Canada while they focused on the States. "I think we've lost Canada a bit," Creeggan admits. "People certainly know about us, but sometimes people don't think we've even existed for 10 years. You have to choose your battles."

The cultural nationalists will tell you that there's something inherently Canadian about the Tragically Hip that Americans en masse could never get—or at least the kind of Americans who were chasing commercial entities. That was the feeling in the MCA Canada office, says former MCA national promo rep Kevin Shea. "We'd be sitting up here thinking, 'How can they not get it?'" he says of his American counterparts. "You'd hear things like, 'Yeah, they're kinda a poor man's version of R.E.M.' Excuse me, *what*?! I was mesmerized by Gord Downie; I thought he was the best front man I'd ever seen. But guys down there would say, 'I don't see it. He's strange, man. Strange.' And they'd leave after four or five songs, claiming they had something else to see. It was so frustrating to me. Did [MCA America] give it a good effort? My guess is they gave it a couple of weeks and when it didn't hit, they moved on to the next thing."

In case one thinks the Tragically Hip is a unique case, take a look at other big Canadian acts of the day who failed to blow up in the States. 54.40. Pursuit of Happiness. Grapes of Wrath. Odds. Our Lady Peace. The Tea Party. I Mother Earth. Then there's the one group whose career has most resembled the Tragically Hip's for the past 30 years: Blue Rodeo. Like the Hip, Blue Rodeo had pockets of support in various markets in the U.S. Like the Hip on *SNL*, Blue Rodeo had two brief brushes with mainstream exposure: playing on *The Tonight Show* in 1991 and backing up Meryl Streep in the 1990 film *Postcards from the Edge*. Unlike the Hip, Blue Rodeo all but gave up on the U.S. later in their career—it wasn't worth the money or time to go there, and it's not like their U.S. audiences were getting any bigger.

The Hip never gave up on the U.S., though. They didn't need to.

———

The story of the Hip and America can only be told by one man: Bruce Dickinson, the vice-president of A&R at MCA Records who signed them in 1988. In his career, there are precedents and omens for the could've-beens and should've-beens of the Tragically Hip's trajectory.

Bruce Dickinson started out in the marketing department of CBS/ Columbia Records in the early '80s. He referred to himself as the "Department of Lost Causes." He had jazz fusion guitarist James Blood Ulmer. He had German new wave eccentric Nina Hagen. He had Miles Davis attempting a comeback after a six-year, drug-fuelled hiatus. He had Bob Dylan trying to reinvent himself as an evangelizing Christian song-writer. One day in 1982, his boss threw an album across his desk by a new Australian band. "Here, listen to this," she said. "We may have to put this out, so tell me what you think." The band was called Men at Work. The album was *Business as Usual*.

This was much more commercial than anything else he'd been assigned so far. He went to his weekly meeting with the head of marketing.

Dickinson told him, "I think it's a hit album with at least three hit singles. I love the guy's voice and the songs are great. I'd love to work on it." The marketing head looked at him and said, "Dismissed." At the next meeting he was told, "Okay, smartass, you got the band, we're putting it out. But you get zero dollars for a budget." The album shipped a mere 7,700 copies; even low-priority records shipped 22,000 at the time.

Dickinson scraped together money from discretionary budgets to put out a 12-inch white-label single for radio in April 1982: no band info, no label info, just the phrase, "Who Can It Be Now?" stamped on the cover. It was a strategy not unlike the one that launched the career of Winnipeg's the Guess Who 17 years earlier, although Dickinson was not aware of the precedent. "My idea was that every music director will have to play it just to see what it is, because they'll be afraid of missing the new Springsteen song, or Journey, or Toto, or whatever." Some thought it was a Clarence Clemons solo record—because, you know, saxophone. A couple of small stations picked it up. Nothing else. The album appeared dead in America, even as "Who Can It Be Now?" went top 10 in Canada that summer.

One day, Dickinson got a call from Jack Chase at the label's Dallas branch, asking about the Men at Work record. "Wow, you're from Texas and you're calling about Men at Work?" said an incredulous Dickinson. "Maybe I'm not the Department of Lost Causes after all."

"It's not a lost cause," said Chase. "I gotta tell you something: there's a store called Sound Warehouse in San Angelo. They sell half a dozen copies of this album every time they play it. So what kind of budget do you have?"

"I have nothing. Zero. No dollars. But look, I know CBS Canada has made some nice Mylar logo posters. They were putting displays in the stores up there."

"Ship me the posters."

A week later, Chase phoned back. "We're doing the same thing at the Sound Warehouse in San Antonio: every time they play it, they sell a dozen copies. This is no fluke. I have this promotion fund; I can have my local promo guy work this record at some Texas radio stations, on the QT."

The single was added to radio playlists in both San Angelo and San Antonio. "Which is good," says Dickinson, "but it's not going to change anyone's life. The record is selling in both those cities based on radio and in-store play. This is three weeks in. In the fifth week, KZEW in Dallas adds the record. At the time, there were four major Top 40 stations in the country where, if you got one of those stations, the rest of the radio business stood at attention and wondered what was going on. Usually you'd have to go get 15 or 20 markets first before KZEW would even listen to your record. So they add it. By Halloween, the band was on *Saturday Night Live* and had sold 500,000 copies."

Men at Work had already recorded a follow-up album that the label now wanted to rush to market in January. Dickinson told them to hold off and put out "Down Under" as a second single. "I said to my boss, 'We'll be platinum by Christmas.' She said, 'I'm not going to question you anymore on this record.' By *Thanksgiving*, we were platinum. I said, 'We'll be double platinum by Christmas.' By then, we were over two million. During the week we were away for the holiday, we sold another half million." In total, *Business as Usual* sold six million copies in the U.S. that year.

Like Men at Work, the Hip also had Texan radio support. But it never translated into a tidal wave. Dickinson blames his own label—both its reputation and its actions. In the industry, the joke at that time was that MCA stood for "Music Cemetery of America." "MCA had a reputation for not sticking by rock bands," says Dickinson. "In other words, they put the record out and maybe they'd pay the [independent radio promoters] for a couple of weeks, and then they'd pull the plug. The labels like Geffen, Epic or A&M—who had success with rock bands—they stuck with their bands, even if it took 10 or 12 weeks. They kept the band out on the road. They did a good job with the publicity. Unfortunately, MCA never really did that with the Hip. Radio thought, 'Why should I, as a radio programmer, stick my neck out for a band—even if I like them and think they're great live—if the label will not stand by them? I'm not going to be one of the five radio stations playing them, or else I'll lose my job.'

"It's hard to get radio to play almost anything. Radio looks for reasons *not* to play a record. It didn't used to be like that. In the era of call-out research, you're looking for a negative. If you're looking for a negative about anything or anybody, you can find it. You can only add so many records in any given week, or four-week period, or whatever. If you have 10 artists in front of you and you can only add six, which ones are you not going to add? It's going to be the ones by the company who doesn't stick by their artists."

The head of MCA Records in 1990 was Richard Palmese, who had been executive VP of marketing and promotion before that. "If you had a pop-R&B crossover artist, he was your guy," says Dickinson. "There was no one better in the business at that. But rock'n'roll? Everybody has their strengths and blind spots. MCA wasn't entirely any one person's fault. There was a new regime—and some survivors of the old regime—who didn't necessarily understand and/or like rock'n'roll, so they had other priorities. They were great at promoting New Edition."

But Dickinson knew all that from the beginning. "We knew radio wouldn't be opening their arms immediately" to the Tragically Hip, he says. "I thought, in the U.S., it would take two or three albums [to break], even though I thought it would be possible for something to happen—because things do happen. So I was looking for a way around the reticence of radio." The solution was, much like Gold and Gregg had done in Canada, to put the band in front of audiences. Dickinson figured the Hip could break like Bruce Springsteen did: "His first two albums sold not because of radio, but they sold really well off his touring—and they didn't sell huge numbers until [third album] *Born to Run*."

Dickinson had used the same approach to break the Psychedelic Furs when he was at Columbia. "I went to the powers that be and said: 'Don't give me money for radio promotion. We'll do great at college radio. Give me $47,000—I didn't say $50,000, because I had it down to the dollar—for tour support.' It worked. We sold records. We did it again for the second record. For the third record [1982's *Forever Now*], they burst through: Todd Rundgren produced it, they had the single 'Love My Way,' it went gold. Then those first two albums also went gold. That's what I envisioned with the Tragically Hip: just give us the tour support."

Major labels always get a bad rap from indie music snobs. The assumption is that bands on major labels have it made, that money is capable of buying success, that the proletariat would have better taste in music if corporations weren't constantly shovelling shit down our mouths. Indie snobbery is musical Marxism, for better and worse. Before the days of instant internet buzz, however, hard work and marketing ingenuity was the primary driver of commercial success. Indie or major, the team around the artist has always had to be inventive to make anything work. A major label deal has never been a guarantee of anything.

"You always had to think of ways *around* the record company, ways *around* the retailers, ways *around* the radio, especially," says Dickinson, who spent his entire career in the major label system. "A lot of record companies' biggest successes didn't start out because [an artist had] record company support as a whole. They've been successful because of two to six people in that record company. With Men at Work, it was me [and three others] who made that one happen. Loverboy: that was almost as bad as Men at Work. The label had refused to put out Loverboy until [manager] Bruce Allen came into the office with his contract and pointed out to the powers at be at Columbia that he had a guaranteed Stateside release if the band sold 'X' number of copies in Canada. And they had. That's how Loverboy's first record came out in America. I remember sitting with the [Columbia] product manager [responsible] for Loverboy, and he said, 'Radio's just not buying it. It's just some Canadian band.' I said, 'All right, just tell them it's the Canadian Foreigner.' He looks at me and goes, 'I can hang my hat on that.' And he made it happen. Sometimes you just need a simple catch-phrase. You need to put it in context for these radio people sometimes."

Jim Cuddy of Blue Rodeo says his band faced the same problem: "What we found in the States is that if you can't explain what you do in one sentence, people are not going to listen. [Blue Rodeo] never had a problem in [Canada] having two singers—never, not once. But that was everything in the States: who's the singer? Gord is an extremely recognizable character up here. We [Canadians] look at the Hip and we know who each of those guys is. They're like the ultimate Canadian boy band. The Hip represent why we are a different culture. We wouldn't expect them to be big in France."

Before Bruce Dickinson left Columbia for Chrysalis, he convinced the American label to pick up another one of its Australian acts: Midnight Oil. "At that point, I'd only seen videos of the band, but watching these videos was a holy-shit moment," he recalls. "These guys were unbelievable. The camera would be shaking because the whole venue was shaking. The band was note-perfect. Rob Hirst: I don't think I've ever seen a better drummer. He's like Keith Moon but with time. Obviously, Peter Garrett is the Gord Downie equivalent: he's the guy all eyes are on, the guy whose voice can sell a song. People can say he's not a great singer or he doesn't have great range: bullshit. Can he sell a song? All these guys, whether it's Downie or Garrett or Mick Jagger, they can sell a song.

"The first thing I said to Midnight Oil's management was: 'Bring them over and do two 60-date tours in the first year, and they'll break.' They did part of that and we had some success. Finally, what broke them was when they literally came here and established a home base in America as opposed to Australia, which is another planet away. It was the only way to do it."

Midnight Oil moved to Connecticut, putting them on the Eastern Seaboard and easily accessible to New York City, Boston, Philadelphia, Washington, D.C., and other major centres. "They played America like an

American band," says Jake Gold. "AC/DC did that in England, same thing. They were an Australian band who set up shop in London. They knew if they were going to break, they needed to be there."

"If the Hip could have done something along those lines," says Dickinson, "it would have been another way around radio. Allan and Jake and I always thought that if the band had been willing to move to Boston or maybe Atlanta for a year, either one would have worked. Boston would be a natural. Boston radio was still in its own little world. It would take a few more chances. A third of the city is college kids. At the same time, I understand that the band didn't want to leave their families. That's how it was explained to me."

It was also a point of pride and principle, according to Rob Baker. "We saw a lot of bands would move to L.A. and New York, and it bothered us that Canadians had to move to the States to make it," he said in 2017. "We thought, you don't have to do that—and if you *do* have to do that, then we don't want to make it that way. We'll make it in a different way, or we won't make it. We won't play that game."

Midnight Oil's success, coming from another corner of the Common-wealth, buries one Hip myth: that Americans were put off by geographically specific lyrics. Midnight Oil's breakthrough album, *Diesel and Dust*, which sold a million copies in the U.S., had a hit single, "Beds Are Burning," that referenced remote communities Kintore East and Yuendumu (it's also about Indigenous land claims, making it an even unlikelier hit single). There's a song called "Warakurna." The previous album had a track called "Kosciusko" and a song about an Australian boxing legend. Says Dickinson, "I'd say their songs are more Australia-centric than the Hip's are purely Canadian." American fans have also never had a problem with distinctly British acts.

Canadian fans want to believe the Hip are "too Canadian" to make it in the States only to validate our own self-worth. America has a problem with myopia, certainly, but to think American music fans can't handle the word "CBC" in a lyric is insulting to everyone involved. "I think we like to say that to inflate our own sense of taste," says the Rheostatics' Dave Bidini. "The Hip are often written about as if they only ever made it here. For a lot of people, that gives the band extra value in a country that doesn't have a lot of that, a country where a lot of people are always scrambling to make it elsewhere."

Part of the Hip's struggle in the States was that they chose to headline. Rarely, if ever, did the Hip get—or seek—any kind of opening gig, never mind an opening tour that would have put them in front of thousands of new faces. A short jaunt with smooth Texas blues guitarist Eric Johnson in 1991 was the closest they came to riding anyone's coattails until Robert Plant came calling in 1995, by which point an American breakthrough was beginning to look extremely unlikely. The Tragically Hip opened for Page and Plant for the prestige and for the thrill of observing childhood heroes up close. Same with the handful of times they opened for the Rolling Stones (four European dates in 1995, once in Moncton in 2005) or the one time they opened for the Who (in 2007).

What if the Hip were able to open for a known American entity while they were touring *Up to Here* or *Road Apples*? That wasn't what any of their handlers—Gold, Gregg, Dickinson or their American booking agent Wayne Forte—had in mind. The plan was to make the Hip "the hottest ticket in town at the club level," says Dickinson. "Book them in clubs that we know they can sell out. Get it to the point where people hear about the Tragically Hip coming to town, but they can't get a ticket because it's already sold out. That makes them hotter."

But if no potential new fans can ever get a ticket, can that not also backfire? "I can't think of any instance where that happened," Dickinson responds. "I was involved with the Clash early on [at CBS/Columbia]. Local promoters didn't believe the Clash could sell tickets. In Boston, we had them in the Harvard Square Theatre, and the tickets sold out in two hours. It was an 800-seater. Word of mouth happened: 'The Clash played last night, but you couldn't get in!' Then people thought this band must be incredibly hot. As long as the band actually *is* incredibly hot onstage, then this [strategy] works. The Hip had that quality; we knew it would work with them. The Clash, the second time they came to Boston, we put them in the Orpheum, a 2,800-seater, knowing the same thing was going to happen. They sold it out again in two hours. The promoter said, 'Oh man, I should have learned from the last time. I really fucked up.' We were like, 'Maybe you should have, but: goal achieved.' Of course, the next time they played an even bigger venue and that sold out as well. If a ticket becomes unattainable, people want what's unattainable. And they want to know *why* it's so unattainable: what is it about this band? You want to pique people's interest. If the band has the goods, that will work. If the band doesn't have the goods, you're screwed."

The Tragically Hip took that strategy of scarcity a bit too far when it came time to launch their third record, *Fully Completely*. The album came out in Canada on October 6, 1992, but it wasn't released in the U.S. until January 1993, when "Courage" was the single being worked in both countries. The Hip didn't play the U.S. on that tour until April 1993: six full months after the record came out in Canada. The lead Canadian single, the explosive riff-driven "Locked in the Trunk of a Car," was never released in the States, because the band didn't want to bleep out the word "fuck." "The idea was to really push 'Fifty Mission Cap' as the third track," says Dickinson in his defence. That would coincide with the spring tour—and the NHL playoffs. "I pictured programmers giving away tickets to playoff games, that kind of thing. I thought that would really bring the thing home." It didn't work. It was too late.

The Tragically Hip and MCA Records parted ways shortly afterwards. It was not the label's idea: the American numbers were "respectable," says Dickinson. "It was a little more than enough to keep MCA wanting to put out the next record." But patience was clearly wearing thin. "Prior to the release of *Fully Completely*," says Dickinson, "they flew in people from various markets in North America to Vancouver to have a grand listening party and promotion thing. They spent a lot of money on that. I remember having dinner with Richard Palmese and one of the sales guys, who said this album should really break them in America. Richard looked at me and said, 'Well, for your sake, it better.' I should have known right then and there that it wasn't going to happen—and that he was going to get rid of me."

Dickinson's only other success story during his tenure at MCA was the hard rock band Steelheart: their debut went double platinum in the U.S., the follow-up went platinum, and then they were dumped after the grunge revolution of 1992. His other signings? A band called Law and Order and another called, uh, Spread Eagle. The Tragically Hip was the biggest jewel in his crown—only if Canadian sales were considered a factor. The last thing Dickinson did for MCA was shepherd Meat Loaf's *Bat Out of Hell II: Back into Hell* to completion, a four-year process. When it was done, his bosses hated it. Dickinson was fired in June 1993, three months before the album was released—and went on to sell 14 million copies. He then went to Sony to work on reissue projects for its Legacy series, and never again signed a new band to a contract.

———

As soon as Gold and Gregg heard that Bruce Dickinson was out, they asked that the Tragically Hip be released from their MCA contract—which was not a problem. They did, however, stay with MCA Canada (soon to be rebranded as Universal Canada), who'd been more than supportive, and MCA International. They went looking for a new American partner. It took awhile. *Day for Night* was released in Canada before anything had been lined up in the U.S. The band did 20 American dates in the fall of 1994, selling the album at merch tables like any indie band would. "Practically speaking, it's maybe silly," said Downie at the time. "But at the same time, for general morale and sense of accomplishment, we never felt more bolstered and more energized. We knew that anyone who was at the show knew the band or had heard about us. There was no company buyout, no arms being twisted. In some cases, if we had 300 people at a show, we might sell 75 discs. In the past, even with record company support, we couldn't have sold 75 discs in a day. No way. It was getting back to the basics, but reacting to a situation. The by-product was at once rewarding and humbling."

A deal with Atlantic materialized later; the album came out in the U.S. in February 1995. That arrangement lasted a mere two years. "We went above and beyond [promotionally] with the group, but we were not able to surmount the boundaries that exist for them in this market," a senior VP of Atlantic Records told *Billboard* in 1998. "We got more radio airplay than [MCA], but it didn't lead to anything." The Hip's 1997 live album was released in the U.S. via a digital retailer.

Seymour Stein of Sire Records, the man who signed the Ramones, Talking Heads, Madonna and the Replacements, snapped them up. He had been a big Hip fan since he first saw them in Vancouver before the 1991 Junos. "I never expected to sign them," he told *Billboard*. "It has always struck me that, as with the Barenaked Ladies, there's no reason why their music shouldn't cross over [in the U.S.]." The band retained the rights to their entire catalogue, making them an independent act licensing the records to Universal Canada and Sire worldwide. Sire's general manager, Randy Miller, chimed in: "This is like signing R.E.M. when Warner Bros. did [in 1988]. The Hip could still be on the verge of their biggest commercial audience breakthrough [internationally]." The relationship looked promising: *Phantom Power* gave the Hip their best opening week in the U.S., according to a *Billboard* article—but that still only amounted to 13,000 copies. (The album would sell 45,000 in total on Sire.)

Six months later, Sire cut 20 per cent of its staff. In 1999, parent company

Warner merged Sire with London Records, a short-lived experiment that ended two years later, leaving many bands in its wake—including the Hip. When Gord Downie put out *Coke Machine Glow* in early 2001, he signed to Zoë Records in the U.S., a division of venerable folk label Rounder, devoted to adult-oriented niche artists, including an unusual number of Canadians: Cowboy Junkies, Sarah Harmer, Kathleen Edwards, Great Big Sea, Jann Arden, even Rush. Following suit, the Tragically Hip also signed with Zoë for 2002's *In Violet Light*; they remained there until the end.

Sam Roberts opened for the Hip extensively in both the U.S. and Canada, starting in 2002. "Whether or not they're a household name [in America] should not be the objective of any band," he says. "Bands who make music like the Hip aren't aiming for that. We realize there's a limitation to our range of potential influence and how many people we can reasonably expect to be into what we're doing. To go to Washington, D.C., and play a jam-packed 9:30 Club, I mean, what else do you want? With the Hip, [the Sam Roberts Band] played in some of the most beautiful theatres and rooms that, still to this day, I've ever set foot in. And we played to a packed, passionate crowd every night. I'm thinking, 'If this isn't the pinnacle of success, I don't know what is.' Because they're doing it on their own terms and making the records they want to make and can still compel their fans to be there, physically and emotionally."

Long after a breakthrough seemed possible, the Canadian press would not let the idea go—and in some ways, neither would the band. Ben Rayner of the *Toronto Star* was sent to the South by Southwest festival in Austin in 2007 to interview Downie, the angle being that the Canadian superstars were hustling at SXSW in the same way a bunch of 25-year-olds from Montreal were. A defensive Downie was suspicious of the writer's motives—unduly so, as Rayner is a big fan—teasing him about scribbling the same old story about the Hip's American fate. "We're essentially an indie act down here," Downie told him. "We're goin' it alone, so it makes total sense for us to be here. Within the Universal deal, we've always felt like an independent act. We've never been told what to do. We've used their resources to our own design. At this point, we've had not one shred of national-profile-enhancing anything [in the U.S.]. We've played on *SNL* and got not even a *Rolling Stone* review. Nothing. Which I'm not lamenting, really, but it gives you an idea of how we've been doing it, which is 50 people at a time—literally. We played in Dallas last night to a thousand people, but I can distinctly remember playing Dallas to 45."

In 2009, the *Globe and Mail* felt it necessary to reprint a *Wall Street Journal* article on the topic, with the headline: "The Hip's biggest mystery: where are the U.S. fans?" In it, Downie said, "If we were told we couldn't go to America anymore, we would be heartbroken. We're not trying to replicate our success. We go to America to work. We're not tourists. Music is meant to flow anywhere you want. Music isn't stopped at customs."

Minutes before the final show in Kingston on August 20, 2016, Prime Minister Justin Trudeau was interviewed by the CBC's Ron MacLean. He was asked what it was Canada was celebrating that night. The political leader of Canada, the son of a man who took great pains to differentiate the Canadian identity from the elephant to the south, gave a surprisingly typical response at once rooted in our national insecurity and summing up the collective evolution of many fans' thoughts, including that of the proud Kingstonian sitting beside me at the show.

"When I was in high school and university and they were playing on campus and we were celebrating them as our local band, a lot of Canadians would think it would be great if they made it in the States so everyone could see how great they are," said the 45-year-old prime minister. "In the back of our minds, we were always saying, 'Oh, at one point they will break through internationally.' It was always sort of too bad they didn't. Tonight, I'm thinking, 'You know what? I'm so glad they're all ours.'"

CHAPTER TEN
SUPER-CAPACITY
1996–97: *TROUBLE AT THE HENHOUSE*

"Buy a few acres do your own excavation / Lay down the forms,
build up the foundation / I'll gladly lend a hand if you need me
brother / 'Cause we are only wealthy through each other"

SPIRIT OF THE WEST, "WATER IN THE WELL"

IN 2017, "AHEAD by a Century" was licensed for use as the title credit theme for a new TV adaptation of *Anne of Green Gables*. Peak Canadiana, even more so than when, in 1998, Rick Mercer licensed "Blow at High Dough" as the opening theme for a TV show called *Made in Canada*.

In the infancy of its composition, however, "Ahead by a Century" was not the type of song you'd want to place in a family-friendly TV show featuring an iconic Canadian character. It was not the type of song that would have had much of the country singing along as the last song of the final Tragically Hip show in 2016. In its first iteration, "Ahead by a Century" was not a song that would be played on the radio, let alone in the hallways of elementary schools. It was, shall we say, rather blue.

"Originally," Downie told the *Georgia Straight*, the lyric was, "'First thing we'd climb a tree, and maybe then we'd talk / I will touch your cunt, you will touch my cock / then we'll be married, then we won't have to hide.' Those were [temporary] lyrics, but they stuck there. They said to me 'innocence,' and that's what I wanted. I thought, 'It's two little kids, and they don't know what a cunt is and they don't know what a cock is—they just heard them called that.'"

Rob Baker really liked it. The line survived many early incarnations of the song. It was Downie's friend, Tragically Hip guitar tech Dave "Billy Ray" Koster, who delicately pointed out that people would latch on to only those lines and not hear the rest of the song—it certainly wouldn't be played on radio. "People's ears are gonna race to those words and start having a little debate about what those words mean," said Downie. "I was going to have to defend one's right to use words that possibly offend other people, and I didn't really care to have a Lenny Bruce situation on my hands."

Downie then worked on excising the line, and "the whole verse crumbled like a house of cards. It took me about a week to rewrite that song, but the weird thing is I loved every minute of it. It was frustrating, but I loved it because it was a challenge that I had created for myself and that I met. And ultimately the song achieved kinda what I wanted it to."

The song's key line remained intact, the one that inspired T-shirts and tattoos and became a theme of the final tour. It was there from the beginning, and can first be detected in a January 1995 interview Gord Downie gave to Jennie Punter for *Impact Magazine*: "These tours aren't like dress rehearsals for life; they are life as it's happening."

As the song evolved from a folk-country riff by Paul Langlois, that first verse shifted to a more innocent tone, the acoustic guitars took over and the drum kit didn't kick in until halfway through the second verse. "Nobody thought it would make the record, but the lyrics were good," said Baker. The lyrics could be interpreted many ways: a boy marvelling at the maturity of girls, a father expressing parental concern for his children. The end result was the Tragically Hip's first No. 1 radio hit, a song with exponentially more reach than any other Hip song. And that was long before Anne of Green Gables showed up.

———

By the end of 1995, the Hip had marked the most successful year in their career to that point, in large part by sticking to their vision and resisting industry norms. So they decided to take even more control.

This meant building their own studio in Bath, just outside Kingston. This had been a dream ever since they first set foot in Daniel Lanois's

Kingsway Studio in New Orleans: to find a large, old house with an ambiance and vibe conducive to creativity, one that could double as a clubhouse and facility for friends' projects as well.

Right on Lake Ontario, off County Road 33 west of Kingston, near the Millhaven Penitentiary they immortalized in song, the band found an old carriage house built in the 1840s, once used as a stagecoach stop on the way to Toronto. It had been a B&B and then a farmhouse; the building had only ever had two owners before the Hip took it over and named it the Bathouse. The decor is homey: blankets and books act as acoustic baffling. Original album artwork hangs on the walls. The musicians congregate in a room on the main floor, playing live through headphones, with a vocal booth off to the side and the amps isolated in adjacent rooms. On the second floor, above the control room, is a billiards room with thousands of vinyl records and dozens of videos.

The job of assembling the actual studio fell to their live-sound engineer, Mark Vreeken, who in 1989 first started working for the Hip on monitors before graduating to front-of-house sound engineer. He'd been present in New Orleans and London for the making of the previous three records, studying the work of Don Smith, Chris Tsangarides and Mark Howard in detail, taking notes on their choice of gear. Steven Drake of the Odds helped them with some sound design.

Recording for *Trouble at the Henhouse* began while Vreeken was still assembling gear, in November 1995. Producing their own record had been a goal for years, but they didn't feel ready until after *Day for Night*, an album on which Vreeken and the band shared production credit with Mark Howard. This time out, the band figured Vreeken was all they needed. "Without a doubt, he's the sixth member of the band," enthused Gord Sinclair in a 1997 interview with *Canadian Musician*. "I think he knows the songs better than I do." Loyal roadie Dave "Billy Ray" Koster was also an invaluable help. "He's the jack of all trades," said Vreeken. "He can tech all the instruments and tune the drums and fix guitars and guitar amps. He helped me out a lot. I couldn't have done my job without him there."

With no clock to follow, the band felt free to explore previously unfinished ideas, to take songs that weren't working and recycle parts for something new. "Once you realize a song may not ever get on a record, you have to decide what to do about it," said Baker. "What we tend to do is start exploding it. You stick a bomb in it and you look for the most interesting pieces. You twist them around, try to reassemble it, change the rhythm of it or change the chords a bit here and there. Fooling around with the song may inspire someone to play a different lick and re-energize the tune."

"We wanted to make a record with no regrets, with no untried or unexplored ideas at the end of the session," said Sinclair. "That is the beauty of being in the producer's chair. We worked when we wanted to and knew how to stop when it wasn't going anywhere. Sometimes not playing is just as important to the creative process. There were times when we could play all day and night, while there were other days we would do nothing at all. We were all very conscious of the burnout factor." This was also the first time most of the band had young families: Sinclair's eldest was now six, but Langlois, Downie and Baker all had newborns or toddlers.

"Gift Shop" and "Springtime in Vienna" had already been performed extensively on tour. "700 Ft. Ceiling" came out of a song called "Win Win Win Situation." "Flamenco" had been a Gord Sinclair riff dating back years; the song was finally finished in a San Francisco session with Mark Howard, along with another new one, "Put It Off." "Ahead by a Century" was a riff by Paul Langlois, rebuilt from the ground up when Baker and Fay tried a take with a Linn drum machine and an open-tuned acoustic guitar. "Everyone lifted it up to another level," said Baker. "That's a full-band composition."

When it came time to mix, however, it was clear that outside ears were required. Steven Drake of the Odds, with whom they'd toured Canada in early 1995, got the gig. He arrived in the dead of winter and tried to make sense of what the band had come up with on their own. They wanted "someone to give us validation," said Sinclair, to know "we're not just losing our minds out here in the country, that we're actually making something that other people might enjoy." In choosing Drake, who was just starting to get production work outside the Odds, they were also helping out a friend— and at the right price. "It would have been easier for us—and I'm sure the American record company would have loved us [if we did this]—to have hired Bob Rock to do it at a million dollars a track," said Sinclair at the time.

"I made about $800 a song, or about $8,000 for the whole record," said Drake. "Meanwhile, they spent $80,000 on the guy on the last record. Jake [Gold] would say, 'Well, you can't ask for much money, because you're [inexperienced].' I did want to do it." Around the same time, Drake was also hired by 54.40 to mix *Trusted by Millions*.

Drake was very conscious that he was mixing a record for the biggest rock band in Canada. "It was fun to be working on 'Ahead by a Century,' because as it was coming down, I thought, 'This is a fucking hit.' I was by myself in the control room. Johnny called me up to see how it was going. I said, 'I don't know—bass and drums sound so good that this might just end up a reggae tune!' It was just one of those things, those clear moments, where you know it's going straight on the radio."

The album opens with "Gift Shop," a song inspired by a trip to the Grand Canyon, and an eerie Hammond organ played by Peter Tuepah of Kingston's Southbound Blues Band. When people talk about the notion of a "Canadian sound," Drake argued that Rob Baker's guitar on this track is it. Drake ran the signal out to a speaker in the barn adjacent to the Bathouse, then recorded the sound there—where it was -40 degrees, the point where Celsius and Fahrenheit meet. "That's what really cold air sounds like," said Drake.

Rob Baker considered *Henhouse* the most difficult record to make in their entire discography. "Part of that was not having a non-partisan soundboard," he said, "which is the number one thing a producer can do, is just be that voice of reason, to say, 'Guys, it's not working,' or 'This part is not helping the song.' That's part of it, helping with the arrangements and that fatherly advice."

It was Steven Drake—though he was hired as the mixer, not the producer—who played the role of mediator between the band members. "On the song 'Sherpa,' between the first and second verse, there was this big acoustic guitar thing reminiscent of 'Bluebird' by Buffalo Springfield," said Drake. As he listened to the track, something didn't sound right. He figured out that Baker had hit a bum note that was picked up on all the overhead mics, and it also threw Fay off the beat for a split second. It was impossible to patch over with overdubs. Several workarounds failed.

"Finally, I said, 'Why don't we just cut the two-inch [master] tape? I'll do a little half-inch edit [with a razor blade] and it will sound great. Gord Sinclair said, 'You can do that?'" The band had seen Mark Howard do this on *Day for Night*, but Howard was Daniel Lanois's right-hand man, whereas Steven Drake was just a guy from the Odds. "I actually did quite a bit of [splicing] on the 54.40 record I'd just finished," Drake explained. "The tech there showed me how to do it, and I was quite good at it. Of course, it's also a fantastic way to fuck up a master tape, like knocking the nose off a sculpture. So I wash my hands, clean them with alcohol, get the razor blade—and the whole house goes silent. Dead quiet, as if you're operating on your sister's baby. I do the cut and it works great, no problem. There's a collective sigh of relief.

"Then as I continue mixing the tune, each guy individually comes up to me, all five of them, and says, 'Hey, I didn't want to say anything in front of the other guys, but that's great that you cut that part out, because I didn't really like it.' *They all didn't like it!* But they were all so polite that they didn't want to offend anyone in the band. They had a certain respect for each other's ideas that they didn't want to chop anything."

One happy accident came at the San Francisco session with Mark Howard, when he suggested Rob Baker pick up a Jerry Jones model sitar for the closing track, "Put It Off." "I was looking for a sound that was so abstract and against the grain," said Howard. "I like a room to have a bunch of different instruments just sitting around. You know right away if something doesn't work. Working with Tom Waits is the same way. [Waits] would say, 'We need something on this song.' He'd walk around the room: 'Nope, piano won't work.' Then he'd come back with a huge pea pod from a 200-year-old tree and start shaking it, and he'd say, 'Yeah, that's it.'"

"Put It Off" has Downie claiming that he played the album *Love Tara*, by Eric's Trip, on the day his first child was born. The cultural nationalists who loved *Fully Completely* and *Day for Night* were distraught to discover that was the only Canadian reference on a new Hip album, unless you consider the flooded backyard rink in "700 Ft. Ceiling" to be exclusively Canadian. The shift was entirely conscious on Downie's part. A 1996 profile in *Saturday Night* magazine, by Charles Foran, noted that "the singer is actually no longer an outspoken cultural nationalist." Talking about the early '90s, Downie told Foran, "I was getting a sense of the country, a feeling for it. And I was watching as nationalism began to metamorphose into something creepy. Too much ill will was being generated by nationalistic feelings, both in English Canada and in Quebec. I had to bail out."

The lyric that raised the most eyebrows was in "Don't Wake Daddy," a reference to Kurt Cobain reincarnated as a sled dog. It had been only two years since Cobain's suicide, a raw wound for many rock fans. "The Kurt Cobain line was meant to place a well-known character in a very bleak landscape," said Downie. "It alludes to the line from [Nirvana's] 'Pennyroyal Tea' where he talks about a 'Leonard Cohen afterworld' where he can sigh eternally. When, in fact, you can't predict what your afterworld will be, or if there is one."

Downie and Cobain crossed paths once, on July 7, 1989, when Nirvana opened for the Tragically Hip in Madison, Wisconsin, at the O'Cayz Corral. Ticket price: four dollars. Nirvana was in town to scope out producer Butch Vig, with whom they were considering recording an album that would be called *Nevermind*. Interaction between the bands was minimal. "I was playing pinball in the back after sound check," said Downie, "and Cobain was lying on a table curled up in a ball. I was trying to make conversation: 'Pretty tired, huh?' They attracted a crowd of about 150, which dwindled down to about 40 when we went on. That was yet another of life's cruel lessons: never go on after a band from Seattle!" Downie reportedly told a friend later about this brush with a soon-to-be-legendary band: "They were late, they were drunk, they were assholes and then they left."

Near the end of Cobain's life, he turned to the blues, delivering a harrowing version of Leadbelly's "In the Pines" for Nirvana's MTV Unplugged special. The Tragically Hip, raised on the blues, could empathize. "The blues are still required," Downie told MuchMusic, quoting his own lyric in "Springtime in Vienna." "They're always required. The blues are not so much about heartache as they are about physical, molecular existence. Sing it like you feel it."

If *Trouble at the Henhouse* could at all be called a blues album, it's in its simplicity, its reliance on vibe, minimal chord changes, achieving an almost trance-like state on several tracks. It might have been exhaustion after an intense year and new family lives. Or it might have been the weed. There are very few uptempo rockers, and they're among the weakest tracks on the record—indeed, they're among the worst Hip songs ever recorded ("Butts Wigglin'," "Coconut Cream"). Even though it came out at the height of their popularity, you'd be hard pressed to find a Hip fan who considers *Trouble at the Henhouse* among their top three favourites, "Ahead by a Century" notwithstanding.

———

Trouble at the Henhouse was released in May 1996. Three surprise shows were announced, two at Toronto's Horseshoe Tavern and one at Le Spectrum in Montreal. To thwart scalpers, Jake Gold had a new plan.

He'd been to a conference where someone was selling Polaroid cameras with which you could imprint information on the image. When the shows were announced, people in line at the venue that morning got their picture taken with the date of the show on it. "I knew those were things that fans would savour forever, that it was their face on a Hip ticket," says Gold. "The scalpers out front knew who I was, and though I'd never support them, I'd smile and say, 'Hey guys!' That first night outside the Horseshoe, I went to check out the line, [and] they said, 'Picture tickets, huh, Jake? You fucked us this time.'"

Inside the Horseshoe, fans were treated to an unusual sight: Gord Downie playing acoustic guitar for most of the set, only putting it down for "Grace, Too." Along with the absence of Canadiana in the new material, this drastic change in the stage dynamic seemed like a deliberate ploy to dampen the looganism of some fans, who were giving the Hip's audience a bad reputation.

Canadians would have to wait until November for a full tour. The Hip spent the summer in the States and Europe, with one exception that put them in front of their biggest headlining gig to date: 55,000 people at something called Edenfest, held just east of Toronto, halfway to Peterborough.

In 1996, Canada didn't do big weekend festivals, akin to Glastonbury or Reading in the U.K. This was long before Osheaga or Pemberton or WayHome. There had always been single-day festivals, but nothing on the scale that an upstart Buffalo promoter attempted with Edenfest. Opening night headliner was the Cure. Saturday night was the Tragically Hip. Sunday was an elusive "mystery guest." The rest of the lineup reads like a list of '90s relics emblematic of alt-rock playlists of the day and since forgotten: Porno for Pyros, Live, Goo Goo Dolls, Seven Mary Three, Everclear, Bush, Mighty Mighty Bosstones, etc.

Organizers expected 100,000 people. Less than half that bought tickets. Having heard the sales numbers, food vendors understocked their trucks. Another 20,000 apparently entered the grounds through the adjacent forest. By the middle of the final day while an antsy crowd was trying to guess the mystery headliner, the food ran out. Ani DiFranco was scheduled to be the second-last act of the day. When announcers told the crowd that she was in fact the final act, that there was no surprise, that there might be some kind of "jam" afterwards, the riot began. Edenfest literally became one big garbage fire. The festival's office was later raided by the FBI after the organizer allegedly tried to extort $2 million from a bank, a charge that could land him in prison for 20 years. He disappeared.

The Hip's next Canadian gig was considerably more auspicious: a Vancouver show kicking off a 24-date tour even bigger than the one in 1994, once again playing multiple dates at arenas in major markets. No other

Canadian act had ever done this before, not Bryan Adams, not Rush, nobody. "Nothing against Rush, because they were doing it everywhere around the world," says Jake Gold, "and maybe they didn't want to put that much time aside to do [Canada]. We did three nights in Vancouver, two in Calgary, two in Edmonton. No one had ever done that before. And we still left money on the table. We did three nights in Toronto. Toronto is way bigger than Vancouver; we probably could have done a week in Toronto."

A 24-track mobile recording studio captured every one of the shows, including some in the U.S. They'd always recorded every gig, ever since the beginning, studying the previous night's gig on the tour bus the day after. This time, they were taking it much more seriously.

Though tape traders had followed the band early on, the band themselves were in no hurry to release a live album. "There were always new songs that demanded more immediate attention, so we never seriously considered the idea," said Sinclair. "The thought of doing a 'best of' live compilation culled from years' worth of tapes never appealed to us. The task of going through all that material is more than a little daunting. Besides, live records done that way often fall short of recreating the live experience. After all, a live show is just that: an experience, with every set having an ebb and flow all its own. That's hard to create if you're stitching together excerpts from over the years."

Downie was opposed to the idea, at first. He wanted to return to the studio immediately and start developing some of the material they'd been workshopping on the road. "After talking it out, I came to see that would have been too hasty," he said later. "I'm glad I was turned around."

Of all the tapes from the fall of 1996, one night in particular stood out: Cobo Arena in Detroit, which comprised the *Live Between Us* album released in May 1997. "It was as great as I remembered it," said Sinclair. "We had hit the ground running that night. From the instant the intro drum loop to 'Grace, Too' went up, there was a tingle of electricity. There was something there on tape beyond just the notes. We'd somehow managed to record the electricity of the moment. It gave me goosebumps, and as I listened on, the show got better and better."

Some fans were disappointed that there was nothing resembling the "Killerwhaletank" rant on the album. At one point, it sounds like Downie is pretending to wrestle a bear. There's a line that would eventually end up in "Every Irrelevance" on his 2001 solo record. Downie mostly sings quotes of other songs in the middle of his own: John Lennon's "Imagine,"

Jonathan Richman's "Modern World," "Into Temptation" by Crowded House, "China Girl" by David Bowie, "Don't Worry Baby" by the Beach Boys, "Temple" by Jane Siberry, "Bad Time to Be Poor" by the tour's opening act, the Rheostatics. There's also a snippet of the circa-1990 unreleased Hip song "Montreal." Enough for the trainspotters to chew on, but no defining moments.

"It's not like we're claiming this to be the best live Hip performance ever," said Sinclair. "Maybe it is, maybe it isn't. It has always been our fear that by releasing something live, we'd be sanctioning it as a definitive performance. We had managed to capture a moment in time, which is all that a live recording can be." Unlike most live albums, including some of the most iconic ones in rock history (*The Last Waltz*), there were no studio overdubs added later.

The tapes were sent to Don Smith to mix with Vreeken. The album was released almost exactly a year after *Henhouse*. The title, *Live Between Us*, was lifted from graffiti that stood in an alleyway in downtown Kingston that runs across from the Toucan—where the Hip used to play upstairs in a room called the Terrapin—and the restaurant Chez Piggy, opened and run by former Lovin' Spoonful guitarist Zal Yanofsky. The graffiti, which read "The Tragically Hip live between us," was written by the Hip's former saxophonist, Davis Manning—something the band themselves didn't realize until years later. Manning told the *Whig-Standard*'s Victoria Gibson that, being about 15 years older than the rest of the members of the Hip, he always felt more like a fan than a band member. "The mural's sentiment was directed to his fellow fans," wrote Gibson. "The Hip existed because of them, and between them. What mattered most was what brought the fans together, what kept them together. The boys of the Hip had gifted them with a common thread, of joys and pride and passion for what they brought to the stage each time."

Live Between Us was released just in time to announce the third—and what would be the last—iteration of Another Roadside Attraction, featuring Ashley MacIsaac, Los Lobos, Wilco, Change of Heart, Ron Sexsmith, New Zealand's the Mutton Birds and Kingston band Van Allen Belt. In addition to six Canadian stops, the tour also crossed into the U.S., at Darien Lake, outside Buffalo, and in Highgate, Vermont, between Burlington and Montreal.

This time out, the main support act would be Sheryl Crow, who was at her commercial peak; her 1996 self-titled album boasted the smash singles

"Everyday Is a Winding Road," "If It Makes You Happy" and "A Change Would Do You Good." As expected, her set was incredibly polished, with a seasoned band behind her, and she managed to win over a lot of people who thought of her as more of a pop star than a rocker. That said, being the only female solo artist and bandleader to have ever opened for the Tragically Hip at that point, even Sheryl Crow faced chants of "Hip! Hip! Hip!" during her set. "I think that threw her off," said Ron Sexsmith, who duetted with her during both his set and hers, on Badfinger's "No Matter What" and Elvis Presley's "Love Me."

Critical favourites Wilco had developed a reputation as one of the best live rock acts in America; their 1996 album *Being There* deservedly topped many year-end lists. They weren't much for mingling, however. Bandleader Jeff Tweedy kept to his trailer the whole time, emerging only to appear onstage for his set. So did Ashley MacIsaac, still riding high from his 1996 double-platinum *Hi™, How Are You Today?*, which set his Celtic fiddling to grunge and electronic beats. He was by far the wild card on the bill: as the only openly gay performer on the bill and having recently detailed some of his more unusual sexual preferences to the press, he revelled in baiting more conservative elements of the crowd. "He'd antagonize the Hip's audience so much," said Ian Blurton of Change of Heart. "It was amazing. He'd wear a dildo on his kilt, things like that." "I think he was pretty high most of the time," said Sexsmith; the Nova Scotian had a known crack habit at one point. "He was in his dressing room most of the day doing God knows what, and then he'd come out and do his show, which was always very entertaining. People went nuts for him."

Los Lobos were long past their commercial peak—they had scored a No. 1 hit with the title track from the movie *La Bamba* in 1987—but they were hitting their creative stride with producer Mitchell Froom, most recently on 1996's *Colossal Head*. They were the favourite of most of the other performers on the bill. Many of the members sat in on other acts' sets, and David Hidalgo sang a duet with Sheryl Crow on Marvin Gaye's "What's Going On." Los Lobos also did an area-specific cover at every stop, including the Guess Who's "Running Back to Saskatoon" in the titular city. Other acts joined in the community spirit. Sexsmith sang with the Mutton Birds. MacIsaac played on "Wheat Kings." Johnny Fay sat in with Van Allen Belt.

Change of Heart was the most punk rock band on the bill, and they found an odd kinship with the most mainstream act. "Sheryl Crow was amazing; I became a big fan," raved Blurton. "She blew me away, because she was doing things like recording drums in the 18-wheeler parked out back or renting penthouse suites with pianos so that she could record at night. She had [Kingsway studio engineer] Trina Shoemaker out on tour with her. The drummer from her band used to set up his drums side-stage during our set and play along. He was really into it." What Crow made of Blurton is less clear. "We played in Camrose, Alberta," he recalled, "and I was wearing all white clothes for some reason. I cut open my hand and my face, and I was covered in blood. I thought, if I'm going to bleed I might as well go all the way. So I wiped my eye and it looked like face paint. I turned around and Sheryl Crow was looking at me like, 'Oh my god, what is this?!'"

Being on Another Roadside Attraction was an unusual place to be for an American band, watching the Hip cast a spell over tens of thousands of Canadians every night. Ron Sexsmith would watch the Hip's set from the side of the stage, on bleachers dubbed the "Posers' Gallery," with members of Los Lobos and Sheryl Crow's band. "I think it was confusing to them," said Sexsmith. "Obviously, what they all are doing has this Americana thing about it, and Sheryl Crow is very song-oriented, like Tom Petty. They were scratching their heads a bit at how rabid the audience was. The Hip don't have typical songs, like the chorus to 'Everyday Is a Winding Road' or something. It definitely felt like a uniquely Canadian experience."

CHAPTER ELEVEN

ESCAPE IS AT HAND FOR THE TRAVELLING MAN

HELPING HANDS AND OPENING BANDS

"Oh, young lions / This is your kingdom / Roll out of the cradle / Climb out the window . . . / Loosen your collar / Shake off the wires / Run like a river / Glow like a beacon fire"

CONSTANTINES, "YOUNG LIONS"

JOHN K. SAMSON had heard all the stories. The ones about Daniel Lanois being pelted with bottles by thousands of Tragically Hip fans during an opening slot. The ones about fans shouting down opening acts with calls of "Hip! Hip! Hip!" (In industry parlance, this was known as "getting Hipped.") So the Winnipeg songwriter was nervous when his band, the Weakerthans, was invited to play some shows with the Hip in 2006, including a drunken New Year's Eve show at Copps Coliseum in Hamilton.

"I know the tenacity of their fans," he says. "Once I was up there onstage and there would be these murmurs and choruses of 'Hip, Hip, Hip' during quiet songs, I thought it would really bother me. But these people weren't insulting the opening act, they were just incredibly excited to the point where they couldn't contain themselves before what's about to happen. Then when you see the Hip come onstage, and you see the greatest front man I've ever seen engage with an audience, you realize why: it's a thrilling, emotional, beautiful thing. After that, I thought I don't begrudge the crowd at all. That was revelatory for me."

Samson is a magnanimous man capable of deep empathy, which is evident in his songwriting. Not every performer can see the beauty in being booed. Except maybe Jim Cuddy of Blue Rodeo, who got Hipped when they opened a 1991 show at Fort Henry in Kingston. "We were popular enough not to get Hipped, but we did," laughs Cuddy. "Maybe it's like being insulted by Don Rickles—maybe you *want* to get Hipped."

Once the Tragically Hip became successful enough to select their opening acts, the choices were often unconventional and occasionally challenging. The Hip ruled Canadian commercial rock radio; most of their opening acts would never get anywhere near those playlists. As a result, audiences were not always receptive, to say the least.

But to dwell on that would be wrong. It's certainly not a problem unique to the Tragically Hip, their former manager said. "Listen, I remember going to see Peter Gabriel in 1978 at Maple Leaf Gardens," says Jake Gold. "He did two nights in the concert bowl on his second solo album, and they had [glam pop star] Nick Gilder open for him. We were booing Nick Gilder: 'Get off the stage!' What is this, 'Hot Child in the City' opening for Peter Gabriel? We didn't want to hear that." Gilder was pegged in the head with a Frisbee, said, "Fuck this shit" and walked offstage. Gabriel was not sympathetic, making a derisive comment during his own set.

Not every one of the Tragically Hip's opening acts was told, "You're going to die, faggot!" Not every woman onstage was greeted by men making lewd gestures suggesting oral sex. Both those things happened, sadly, and such incidents are by no means unusual or isolated to the Hip's audience. The Tragically Hip appealed to millions of people: some of them happened to be vile assholes sitting within yelling distance of the stage.

But every single act who ever shared a stage with the Tragically Hip will tell you about the generosity of their hosts, of being treated like equals, of there being no backstage hierarchy. They will tell you about the valued mentorship they received, no matter how many years they'd already spent in the trenches of the music industry until that point. They will tell you about Gord Downie coming up to them after getting Hipped and saying, "It's got nothing to do with you, and it's got nothing to do with me or us."

"When we first played a show with the Hip," remembers Torquil Campbell of the band Stars, "it was a big festival in Calgary and there was a big fence up around the Hip's trailer, because they were the headliners. Someone said to me, 'I guarantee you that within 10 minutes of the band arriving, that fence will be down.' Sure enough, the band pulls up and they get out of their van; you see them looking at this fence around their trailers. Ten minutes later, not only was the fence coming down, but they were the ones pulling up the pegs."

The Tragically Hip helped instill confidence in entire generations of Canadian musicians. At the 2017 Juno Awards, Leslie Feist ran into Paul Langlois and Rob Baker, who were there collecting a Juno for an album co-produced by her friend Kevin Drew. She greeted them warmly and then gestured around the arena, which was called the Corel Centre when she had first played there as a member of By Divine Right, opening for the Hip. She told the Hip's guitarists, "You guys handed me this venue when I was 22 years old."

She admits, of course, that no one was paying attention at that 1999 gig. "I was playing to the backs of everyone, because they don't care, they're waiting for the Hip," she says. "That's a different kind of being forged by a strange flame—how to carry it off to people's backs, to a grand number of people not paying attention." It's the kind of trial by fire that can turn an amateur into a real artist.

———

The Tragically Hip did not have any friends. In the beginning, anyway. They didn't climb the ladder getting opening gigs for other acts; they were too busy playing three sets a night, six nights a week, every week, all around Ontario—the kinds of gigs where there are no opening acts. "We really had our head down," said Downie. "It bred a galvanized spirit: it was us, the five riders of the apocalypse, and no real time for fraternization. It was very insular. We would hole up in one hotel room, all of us, and smoke hash and do the show. Only over time did we manage to meet other musicians and start hanging out more, being more social and then getting turned on, obviously."

They liked playing with the Pursuit of Happiness, partially because guitarist Kris Abbott was an old friend from her time playing in Kingston cover bands. They liked playing with the Skydiggers, with whom they shared some stylistic similarities, and guitarist Josh Finlayson was one of Downie's closest friends when he first moved to Toronto. Those bands were like family. But most of the Hip's opening acts in the first three years after *Up to Here* were chosen by agents, management or the record label, with some input from the band.

One of the better matches of that time was Vancouver's Sons of

Freedom, a heavy guitar band who made the most of churning out relentless, chugging grooves over mostly one chord. They opened all dates on the *Fully Completely* tour in the fall of 1992. Signed to Slash Records in L.A. in 1988, Sons of Freedom had more in common with labelmates Faith No More than Canadian roots rock. "It was hard to find someone to tour with, musically, because there was nobody like us," says Sons of Freedom's Don Harrison, without a hint of arrogance—because he's right. They predated the grunge revolution and got lost in the fray once it started.

The Hip were big fans, Gord Sinclair in particular, who once mused about covering the band's "Dead Dog on the Highway" or "Circle Circle." The direct influence on the Hip is obvious in the stylistic leap between *Road Apples* and *Fully Completely*. "Sons of Freedom were one of the better bands I'd seen live at that time, and maybe will ever see," said Downie years later. "Power, heft, unbelievable. They were one of many bands that made me think, 'There's something we're going to have to follow.'"

"Not that the Hip had anything to worry about," says Harrison. "After our set, just before they went on, there would just be this incredible roar from the audience. We had our own fans there, which was great, but then it went from our applause to their applause—and there was a huge difference. It was one of the best tours I ever did, because of how well we got along with them and how well we were treated. It was three weeks all through Canada. I didn't want to come home—and I didn't normally even like touring."

As a point of contrast, the Sons of Freedom's next outing was the worst imaginable. Maybe the name should have been a hint: the Big, Bad and Groovy tour, featuring fellow Vancouverites Pure, a strung-out Art Bergmann—who'd been dropped by his label, had lost his band and had to take Greyhound buses to each gig—and headlined by Montreal funk-metal band Bootsauce. "It was a total fiasco," says Harrison. "I wanted off that tour within a week. I hated it. Everyone was getting treated really badly, especially from Bootsauce's management. They were complete assholes, truly nothing but trouble. Not sharing the P.A. and stuff like that. They were intimidated by a lot of people, I think because they didn't have a lot of confidence. Their tour manager was making things difficult for everyone the whole time, just completely unnecessary."

It made Harrison immediately nostalgic for the Hip and their crew: "They were perfect gentlemen. Because if you're the headline act, what do you have to worry about, really? You are *it*. People are paying money to see you, so be good to everyone else."

The Hip's generosity stepped up in 1993 when they staged the first of three Another Roadside Attraction tours. It was a thrill to play with idols Midnight Oil and Daniel Lanois for a month across Canada, but they also bonded deeply with Crash Vegas, featuring their friend Colin Cripps and vocalist Michelle McAdorey—one of the few women who ever fronted a Hip opener. "It was a very beer-driven, dude scene, which was interesting to be a part of," says McAdorey, who doesn't recall any negativity from audiences, despite their size and fervour in 1993. Backstage, she says, was an oasis of calm and nurturing. "After the show, we'd all be on the Hip bus, and one of their rituals was the peanut butter and jam sandwich. I was like, 'I don't know'—but then they'd make me one, I'd bite in and think, 'Oh, *yeah*! This is *exactly* what I need right now!' I felt like people were taken care of. It felt healthy, in terms of a rock'n'roll scene. No one was ever out of control. There was no hierarchy. I always felt like they had your back: they're looking out for you, and you're in this family."

That wasn't just a metaphor. "Gord [Downie] would say, 'Come to my house. Meet my family,'" says McAdorey. "I met his parents, lovely people, very open and exceptionally warm. I always felt listened to. Especially on the road, as a woman, there's a lot of male energy with the crew and everybody. With Gord, there was this softness: 'Hey, let's go for a walk and talk about poetry.' It was really nice to have moments like that. I cherished those. The shows were enjoyable, but the road is hard. At that time, too, you're wondering what the hell you're doing, and being able to discuss that with someone you feel is very smart and caring—it means a hell of a lot."

"Talking to Gord—he's not elusive, but he's a listener," says Joel Plaskett, who toured with the Hip in 2004. "I'm a talker, and he'd just be silently engaging me. Then he'd say a few things that would be everything I should have said in a condensed form. That's probably what makes him such a great wordsmith. He gives you just a few bits that you can chew on for a long time."

A call from the Tragically Hip could be a life raft being thrown to struggling bands. One of those was Change of Heart, a staple of the post-punk scene on Toronto's Queen Street since 1982; in 1993, they found themselves opening for the Tragically Hip. It couldn't have come at a better time. "We had done an absolutely horrible West Coast tour where our van broke down and we went about five grand in debt, and everything was crap," says bandleader Ian Blurton. "Then out of the blue we just got this call saying, 'Do you wanna come to the U.S. with us?' We had literally just lost our label, our manager, we didn't have anything, and they were like, 'Get in your stupid van and come with us.'"

Downie was drawn to Change of Heart's 1992 album *Smile*, which he thought was "really violent, original work. It really intimidated me, just from the stereo. Then I heard [Blurton] on this radio show, and someone asked him, 'What are you into lately?' He said, 'I like the Tragically Hip, I like the way they do things.' I thought, 'Fuck, no one's ever said that, especially a guy like him.'" By "a guy like him," one has to assume Downie meant a Queen Street denizen who silkscreened his own merch and whose punk band included a cellist, a percussionist, and a synth player who played more squelches than notes. "We're like the Becker's of pop music," Downie continued, "with one on every corner, and here is Ian Blurton and he sees that we're trying to do things independently within the confines of a major label. It was around the time of the first Roadside. We had this much-vaunted creative control. After that, I thought, 'Okay, now I can meet him because I don't think he hates me.'"

Change of Heart would also be invited to open the 1995 Canadian arena tour, along with the Odds. But their craziest Hip adventures were in the U.S. on that first jaunt in 1993, when Blurton was also breaking in a brand new rhythm section. "We did a lot of weird stuff on that tour, so it was nice for the Hip to accept us for who we were," he says. "We went to Waco, to see [cult leader David Koresh's] compound. We went to [grave robber] Ed Gein's grave and stuff. The Hip were like, 'What the fuck are you guys doing?'"

America had been a challenge for Change of Heart. "Every show we ever played there before that tour was always the worst: everything that could go wrong did. That tour, it was like, 'Oh my God, this can actually be fun.'" Or insane—like one memorable show in Dallas. "It was absolute fucking mayhem," says Blurton. "There was a guy in a wheelchair in the pit spinning around with the slam dancers. There was a pregnant woman lying on the stage holding her stomach. There were tornados of fights through the whole set, and people kept chanting, 'Hip! Hip! Hip!' I was in a particularly cranky mood, so I walked up to the microphone and said, 'Fuck you, the Hip fucking suck!' Gord Downie was sitting right there and started laughing. It was a really great show."

"That was a proud moment," Downie recalled. "I was like, yeah! That's what I would have done. Watching them [leading up to that moment], I thought, 'Why are these guys trying to be so nice and letting these people walk on them? Don't get on your knees for any man, or any Hip fan!' There would be some in our band that would have probably taken that personally, but—they don't watch the opening bands," he laughed.

If Blurton thought the Dallas show was one of the best, the worst was also with the Hip, this time in Seattle. "Everyone said it was going to be the best show on the tour, that we would just kill in Seattle," says Blurton, perhaps because Change of Heart was an infinitely superior band to 95 per cent of that city's exports at the height of grunge. "We did kill—the night before in Spokane. But in Seattle, it was not happening, and we started to get the Hip chant. I went into full-blown fuck-you mode. On the last song, I whipped my guitar up in the air. I aimed too high, and I thought it was going over our amps and into the Hip's backline, and I thought, 'Oh. My. God.' At the last moment, [the arc] died and it just ended up taking my guitar head off.

"I thought, 'Oh fuck, what else could go wrong?' There was a curtain around the stage that was super thick, and I got lost in it—I couldn't find the break. The whole audience was watching. Finally I managed to open it, and Gord is standing right there. I think he said something along the lines of, 'If you can't take the heat . . .'

"Then I thought, okay, I gotta leave this place and take a walk. All the 18-wheelers were lined up behind the venue. I couldn't get out, so I crawled under one to get around—but then it started moving, so I had to crawl along with this fucking 18-wheeler and then roll out." Fortunately, Downie was not standing there waiting for him with another witticism. "That would be the worst: like a puff of smoke and he'd be standing there in a wizard robe," laughs Blurton.

———

Every concertgoer has memories of opening acts who went on to bigger things, like seeing the White Stripes open for Sleater-Kinney, or Arcade Fire opening for the Unicorns. But openers are largely sacrificial lambs, there to pad the bill or because of industry horse-trading, providing a soundtrack to latecomers finding their seats.

Rob Baker said one of the most satisfying gigs of his life was opening for the Stones at a stadium in Germany, listening to a chorus of boos gradually evolve into cheers by the end of the set. The Hip opened for Rush at Maple Leaf Gardens in 1991; they were added to the bill at the last minute to boost flagging ticket sales. They debuted four new songs. "We got called back out for an encore, and the band wouldn't do it," says Jake Gold. "The Rush guys were like, 'Get out there!' Robbie said to me, 'Vegas rules: you don't do an encore if you're the opening act.'"

But the Hip did take the odd festival gig—really odd, in the case of Rockfest 2000 in Chicago, which found them opening for Metallica, Stone Temple Pilots and Kid Rock. "Metallica's fans were there from nine in the morning," remembers Chris Brown, who played keyboards with the Hip that year. "It was this corporate event where someone decided to put their logo on mouse pads. Well, guess what was flying at the stage all day, right? Then the Hip get up there and there's shit flying at the stage, and I'm so not into it. Then something hits my Leslie speaker: it's an Evian bottle full of gravel."

It was still early in the day; the Hip soldiered on and ended up getting positive notices from the Chicago press. The Boston folk-pop band Guster had gone on just before them. Lead singer Ryan Miller had been wary even before the mouse pads started flying. "It was the least thought-out presentation of a day of music," he says. "From the second I stepped on the site, it felt wrong. They were playing commercials between the bands. I was kind of freaking out. I told my manager that I needed to find Gord Downie and ask him what to do. We were getting paid a lot of money and I didn't want to let down my fans. I found him in catering and told him how I felt. He just looked at me and said, 'Speak your heart.' So I said something onstage, we got in trouble and they refused to pay us."

Barenaked Ladies were there too and went on right before Stone Temple Pilots. "As we were playing one of our first songs," remembers bassist Jim Creeggan, "a big, two-litre water bottle, full, came right at me and bounced off the strings of my double bass." It got worse from there, when the crowd starting chanting and calling them "faggots." Downie turned to Chris Brown and said, "These guys are going to get killed."

BNL's stage attire that year was matching pastel blue-and-green outfits. "We looked like crayons," says Creeggan. Ever the pro, singer Ed Robertson asked the crowd who among them hated the band the most and called the heckler onstage. "We got him to play the right hand of Ed's guitar and we did a little Van Halen 'Eruption,'" says Creeggan. "We made amends. But that was one of the hardest crowds to win over, for sure—having the whole audience giving you the finger."

Having a stadium full of people giving an artist the finger is not that rare. It happened to Joe Jackson on his Latin-tinged *Night and Day* tour in 1982, when he opened for the Who at Exhibition Stadium in Toronto. He took a picture from the stage and included it in his 1986 live album art.

Onstage in 2013, Gord Downie gave the finger to one of the most powerful men in the music industry, Eagles manager Irving Azoff. The Hip and Blue Rodeo were both opening for the Eagles in Grand Falls-Windsor, Newfoundland. "It was a big festival, 30,000 people, extremely hot day," recalls Blue Rodeo's Jim Cuddy. "Mostly Canadian bands, starting with Matt Minglewood at two p.m., and they were all amazing." So far, so good.

Blue Rodeo were supposed to go on right before the Hip, but the Eagles shoehorned into the lineup their friend James Dolan, a billionaire who owned the New York Rangers, the New York Knicks and Madison Square Garden itself, among other assets. Because he also had a vanity project called JD & the Straight Shot, that made Dolan the richest musician in the world, relegating Paul McCartney to second place. This, despite the fact that JD & the Straight Shot sold literally tens of copies of any given album they made.

"It was a blues band, and he was terrible," says Cuddy. "But he had to go on then because it was his plane that the Eagles were flying on. His set was long and people were throwing stuff at him, and I think he felt that was Newfoundland cheering. Then the Hip came on and they were on fire."

At the side of the stage watching nervously was Azoff, former CEO of Ticketmaster and a Live Nation executive. The 1990 book *Hit Men* called him "easily one of the most loathed men in the music business," adding that "his friends call him the 'poison dwarf.'" Azoff no doubt found the band's name amusing, if not familiar. In 1978, at a baseball match between the Eagles and their nemeses at *Rolling Stone* magazine, Azoff showed up in a jersey teasing the magazine's publisher: "Is Jann Wenner tragically hip?"

Azoff wanted the Hip off the Eagles' stage early, because James Dolan's blues band went over time. "So Azoff is standing there with the Eagles, and he's looking at Gord telling him to shorten the set, making gestures," says Cuddy. "It's making me furious, because I know the Eagles only want to shorten their own set so they can get on a plane and fly out, which they can't do after midnight or something. So Gord's doing his thing and continues on. Then the Eagles come on and do a miserable set, just sucking the joy out of the whole island.

"Afterwards I was sitting with Gord backstage and asked, 'Didn't that bug you?' He said, 'Pfft, I never thought in my wildest dreams that I'd be playing and have Irving Azoff telling me to shorten my set.' Gord is iconoclastic. He thought it was funny, and it fit right into his performance: he'd swirl around from facing the audience and have at it with this angry old five-foot-two man who's soaking the last few dollars out of the Eagles machine."

At least the Hip made some semblance of sense on a bill with the Eagles, and no doubt had the Newfoundland audience on their side. Sometimes an artist is booked somewhat randomly and incongruously on a bill, like in 1979 when the Ramones opened for Ted Nugent, AC/DC and Aerosmith at the CNE in Toronto and were mercilessly pelted with debris; six songs in, Johnny Ramone responded by flipping off 46,000 people from the stage and storming off. Sometimes artists deliberately choose an act that will challenge their audience: Jimi Hendrix opening for the Monkees in 1967; Prince opening for the Rolling Stones while wearing bikini briefs and a trench coat in 1981; Public Enemy opening for British goth band Sisters of Mercy in 1991; Sonic Youth opening for Neil Young in 1992.

Nothing that extreme happened at a Tragically Hip show, although, sometimes, like when Eric's Trip or the Inbreds or Jane Siberry or Ron Sexsmith opened, audiences might have wondered if the headliner was just fucking with them.

If the headliner had been Warren Zevon, he most certainly was, which Steven Drake can attest to. Drake's band, the Odds, had toured as Zevon's backing band in 1993. "The Odds would open the show, because he didn't want to pay another band," he recalls. "So we'd play to light applause, and then there would be a half-hour break. Zevon used that time rather unkindly. Just before that tour, Neil Young had put out that two-record live set, *Arc/Weld*. *Weld* was a regular show, and *Arc* was all the feedback between songs strung together." *Arc* is 34 minutes long, starts off abrasive and gets increasingly so; by the 32-minute mark, Young's bassist Billy Talbot starts moaning, "No more pain! No more pain!" "So he played *Arc* in between our sets," says Drake, "until the audience was literally screaming, 'Fuckin' turn off this shit! Fuck you!' You could hear them getting more and more pissed off: 'Make it stop!'"

It gets better/worse. "This was followed up by a Dutch-language instruction disc, which ran for about five minutes while we went onstage," Drake continues. "It would be a woman's voice saying, '*Weet je hoe je de wasruimte kunt vinden?* Do you know how to find the washroom?' Just random things in English that would then be translated into Dutch. Then when the band kicked into 'Play It All Night Long,' with the line, 'Grandpa pissed his pants again'—that would be the first line every night—the audience reaction would just be, 'Thank you! Oh my God!'"

Think of that next time you think you're being tortured by an opening act.

———

The Tragically Hip curated two of the greatest all-Canadian bills of the '90s. One went considerably smoother than the other.

The later one was a two-night stand at the Air Canada Centre on New Year's Eve 1999 and New Year's Day 2000, featuring many old friends and musical family.

December 31, 1999: Sharkskin (members of the Odds), Rheostatics (1996 tourmates), Starling (featuring Danny Michel), Hayden (1999 tourmate), Chris Brown and Kate Fenner (soon-to-be tourmates), Skydiggers (dear friends) and the Mahones (featuring Finn McConnell, who played with Downie and Baker in the Filters).

January 1, 2000: Sarah Harmer (old friend since the age of 16), Headstones (featuring high school friend Hugh Dillon), the Cash Brothers (featuring Andrew Cash), Julie Doiron and the Wooden Stars, the Watchmen (1993 tourmates), Treble Charger (whose Bill Priddle went to Queen's with the Hip) and Blurtonia (Ian Blurton's first post–Change of Heart project).

The Hip closed out 1999 with "Ahead by a Century" (of course) and a bit of "Last of the Unplucked Gems" to lead into the countdown; after the stroke of midnight, they ushered in the new millennium with "Save the Planet." Despite the fact that other high-profile New Year's shows that year were cancelled or had lower than expected ticket sales, both Hip shows were sold out and went off without a hitch.

Most important, no one got booed off the stage, which helped erase memories of 1994.

That was the year the Hip were approached to headline a Canada Day show at Molson Park in Barrie, Ontario. It was sold out. The Hip played a great show, debuting material from the forthcoming *Day for Night*. The lineup was incredible and eclectic: Spirit of the West, Jane Siberry, the Rheostatics, the Odds, Eric's Trip, Change of Heart, Treble Charger and the Mahones. Sadly, the show is remembered most as the one where Daniel Lanois was pelted with bottles and booed in the penultimate set of the day. The man who had released two gorgeous solo records—and had produced masterpieces by U2, Peter Gabriel and the Neville Brothers—had come home just to get Hipped.

"I was in tears," says Rheostatics drummer Dave Clark, "listening to Daniel Lanois and [his rhythm section] Daryl Johnson and Brian Blade play this beautiful music, with such majesty, amidst the most ignorant behaviour from a crowd I'd ever seen in my life. They were such a calibre above every other musician there that day, in many ways. I was completely inspired by it. Then I watched the Hip go on and saw Gord deal with that negative situation in a way that was very diplomatic." The first words Downie spoke upon taking the stage, introducing the yet-to-be-released "Grace, Too," were, "This is for the asshole who throws shit at musicians."

He'd taken the assault on Lanois personally. Downie had played a large part in curating the day's lineup and was excited to share it with his fans. "However, that day it struck me that I didn't really know why those [hecklers] were there, July 1 being a celebration of beer, money and Canada—in that order," he said later. From the stage that day, he told the crowd that 1867 was "the beginning of corporate and political opportunism in Canada."

Manager Jake Gold claims the Lanois incident didn't sour the larger accomplishment of the day. "Backstage, no one was walking around going, 'This is shitty,'" he says. "All the bands were in great moods."

Gold had been offered the gig by promoter Elliott Lefko, an old friend from summer camp who had promoted the Hip's first-ever American show, in Buffalo in 1989 (tickets were $4). He was now working at MCA Concerts. "We were between tours and they offered us a lot of money—and it was Canada Day," says Gold. "We were back and forth on what kind of acts to use, and Gord had his list of his favourite acts. We couldn't get anybody to agree: the band, the promoters. I said to Elliott, 'Let's just go on sale as 'Tragically Hip and friends,' and then we'll figure out support later. He said, 'You're insane! We need all kinds of support!' I said not to worry, it'll be fine. We went on sale on a Saturday and sold 21,000 tickets by noon. The park holds 35,000. So he called me back and said, 'Okay, whatever. Just figure it out.' He didn't argue with me anymore." Gord Downie got his wish list.

Jake Gold knew how outdoor shows worked. He knew that music fans would be interested in everything, and the kind of people who were only there for the Hip would spend most of the day in the beer gardens. "We were building a playlist, and the music had to fit the vibe of the day," he says. Jane Siberry's manager, Bob Blumer, tried to push for a slot closer to the headliner. Gold pushed back: "No, Bob, you need to trust me on this. You need Jane to go on at two in the afternoon when people are lying in the sun."

She did. But Siberry's set was the first sign that things might not go well. She'd recently released her masterpiece, 1993's *When I Was a Boy*, which Downie adored. By 1994, she was pushing her music in a jazzier direction; imagine Joni Mitchell playing *The Hissing of Summer Lawns* on Bruce Springsteen's 1975 *Born to Run* tour.

Jim Creeggan of Barenaked Ladies was Siberry's bassist that day. "I was playing beside her and a water bottle was thrown right between me and Jane," he says. "I looked over and said, 'Are you all right?' She came over, took my hand, raised our arms over our heads and said [to the crowd], '*Yeeeah!* I may look small, but if anyone throws anything else up onstage, I'm going to come out there and *tear your head off!* You can *puke* on yourself, go ahead—but I'm watching you!'

"And you know what? No more bottles. Then she went on to play some more free-form jazz shit. It was awesome."

Spirit of the West were third last. They, too, were greeted by a few bottles, but being the high-energy band they were, led by riveting frontman John Mann, they had no trouble keeping the audience's attention.

Then came Daniel Lanois.

When Lanois played Another Roadside Attraction the year before, they asked him why he hadn't toured behind his 1989 debut *Acadie*, why he didn't push his solo work more. "He said something to the effect of, 'Because then too many people I didn't want to be my fans would be my fans,'" says Gold. "Which is arrogant to say, but I understood what he was saying."

At the 1994 Canada Day show, Lanois insisted on going on right before the Hip. Gold tried in vain to talk him out of it.

"We have to go on in the dark," said Lanois, whose atmospheric material rarely rose above mid-tempo.

"It's not dark until 9:20," countered Gold. "That's when *we* go on. The kind of music you're doing, believe me, you do not want to go on right before the Hip."

The U2 producer persisted. "Daniel, you don't understand," said Gold, trying a different tack. "If you go on at eight o'clock, that's when we're shutting the beer tents down, because we want three hours for people to sober up before they get in their cars and drive home. But that means all those people who've been drinking beer all day will then be running to the front of the stage and looking for the Hip. It's a huge mistake. The people drinking beer in the tent—you don't want those people anyway. *You yourself* told me that *last year!* So why the *fuck* would you want to go on right before the Hip?"

The soft-spoken Lanois stood his ground.

"Fine," sighed Gold in resignation, throwing his hands in the air. "Your funeral."

"Everybody adored Dan, as a producer and sonic maverick," says his friend Colin Cripps of Crash Vegas. By "everyone," of course, Cripps means musicians and critics. "Now he was trying to carve out his own thing, and it was great, but it wasn't necessarily what every audience was going to appreciate. You get a 30,000-strong Hip crowd on a Saturday and it's 85 degrees out and they've been drinking for four hours and he comes out and does 'Jolie Louise'? No offence to Dan—it's brave and that's who he is and I applaud that—but, you know, c'mon."

Lanois opened with a long, trippy, snail's-pace instrumental. No matter how many classic rock fans in Molson Park might have claimed to be Pink Floyd fans, this did not go over well. When his second song succumbed to the same tempo, the boors from the beer gardens started the Hip chant. Then the bottles started flying. Lanois seemed unperturbed. His bassist, Daryl Johnson, one of only two non-white musicians onstage all day—Lanois drummer Brian Blade being the other—was not having it. "The Tragically Hip will be on soon enough!" Johnson scolded. "Now quit throwing the bottles, it's not cool. If you throw any more, we won't play."

"Well," says Gold, "if that isn't an invitation . . ." Frisbees, rolls of toilet paper and other debris rained down on the stage. The set eventually concluded with Lanois drawing out his song "The Maker" as long as possible.

"Sure, there were also a lot of dickheads in the crowd," says Cripps. "You can introduce an audience to something you think is great, and if they don't like it? Well, they're not required to like it. But at least you've given them the opportunity to experience something they may actually love. It's a great ambassadorship that the Hip have always tried to bring to their crowds, recognizing that it may not always work."

"There were some choices of opening acts we regret," said Gord Sinclair. "It was music that we were definitely into, but that maybe was in the wrong spot. It was tough watching Jane Siberry do her set. It was a cool, great set of music, but was it the best forum for it? Probably not. But it was always about exposing our fans to good music and spreading the word a little wider. Hopefully we gave people opportunities that we never really had. Nobody took us across the country; we always had to do it on our own. Loverboy never phoned us up! They never did nothing for us."

———

Not every band jumped at the chance to open for the Tragically Hip. Sloan turned them down in 1993. "We saw a bit of a divide," says Sloan's Jay Ferguson. "We thought of ourselves as upstarts from Nova Scotia who had our own label and all these cool acts. We wanted to distance ourselves from the Hip and Blue Rodeo and the Grapes of Wrath or whoever. Nirvana had created this cultural divide, and we aligned ourselves with the new. We didn't want to insult them or anything. It was more about just wanting to carve our own path and do all-ages shows."

Downie didn't take it personally. "I get it," he said. "We were asked to open a tour for Rush, and we said no. I know why it's not cool."

"Some acts have a policy of never opening for other bands, because you don't really build an audience that way," says Mike O'Neill of the Inbreds. "People get so excited about being asked to open for a band—and it is exciting, playing in places like those in front of that many people. But you never sell a ton. Think about yourself going to a concert: you might see the opening band, probably not."

"In the end, we did do some weird opening slots," says Ferguson, who adds that the shows Sloan did open for the Hip on a brief European tour in 2000 went well. "We opened for Alanis once, in 1999. I remember being onstage, thinking, 'This is stupid.' It was well paying, and we were on the second or third single from a record; we thought the gig would help stir up some interest in that. But I think the instances of an opening band really moving up the ladder are few and far between. I don't think it works 90 per cent of the time."

By Divine Right opened the Hip's 1999 tour. "We opened for them at Hamilton Place and sold so much merch," says bandleader José Contreras. "Then we played Hamilton six weeks later, across the street, at the Casbah, and there were, like, five people there. If even half the people who bought a record at the Hip show had showed up, we'd have filled the place. It just goes to show that it doesn't matter how many magazine covers you're on."

Touring with the Hip in Canada and in the U.S. were two totally different experiences, as By Divine Right discovered. On that 1998 Canadian tour, bassist Brendan Canning "drank too much, ate too much dessert, smoked too much weed. I came home and passed kidney stones four days later—which is painful. Then we did the American run with them after, which was a terrible idea. We went from being in a tour bus to being in a van, and six of us were sharing a hotel room, two of us were kind of dating at the time and we're judging our guitar tech for snoring. It was just messy, not a good time. Also, you're going from playing hockey arenas to WOW Hall in Eugene, Oregon, with 200 people there. Some shows were more fun than others, but why were we even on that tour? We didn't even have a record out in America."

That said, "I had a lot of respect for how the Hip treated people," Canning continues. "You'd go out for dinner with them, and they'd always pick up the tab—because they knew you were only making $350 a week, at best, back in the day." The Inbreds opened for the Hip on both sides of the border. "You'd wake up at the hotel and find that everything was paid for," says Mike O'Neill. "Dinners, too, and champagne and stuff. It was almost embarrassing; you didn't feel like you deserved it."

The thoughtfulness didn't end with a tour, either. Years later, when O'Neill was living in Halifax, he'd get phone messages from Downie before a show. "Gord gets in touch and he's like, 'We're playing in Halifax, so you have three on the [guest] list plus one. But you don't have to come. I just tell my friends because I think they get a kick out of it.' Then you're there, and he drops an Inbreds quote into a huge Hip song or talks about the Inbreds in front of the whole place. I mean, you still have to go to work the next day, but it's nice that they never forget."

The one act who benefitted the most from the Hip's benevolence is Sam Roberts, whose breakthrough single "Brother Down" had not yet been added to radio when Jake Gold invited him to open the Hip's *In Violet Light* tour. Downie didn't know Roberts; this was the first time in years he'd conceded to Gold the choice of opening band. But he, like the rest of the band, the crew and the fan base, was smitten right from the very first show, in Victoria in the summer of 2002.

"We weren't stepping onto the stage with any kind of reputation, so we just went nuts," says Roberts. "That was our strategy: don't give the audience a second to breathe. We went apeshit onstage every day, and whether they were liking the music or not, or just watching the spectacle, I don't know. But before [the audience] knew it, our 40 minutes would be up." Word of mouth among Hip fans spread: "It felt like we would show up at the next gig and people were ready to give us a chance," says Roberts. "Everything else happened from there: from the radio station who was playing our single half-heartedly who was now saying, 'Hey, that was all right,' to journalists writing positively about us right across the board. It all happened because of that tour."

Including one-off gigs like New Year's gigs or the Bobcaygeon show in 2011, the Sam Roberts Band opened for the Hip more than any other artist, on both sides of the border. Diehard Hip loyalists are now more than likely also diehard Sam Roberts fans. "For whatever reason, we were welcomed into the fold," he says. "I'd like to think that had that tour not worked out that we would've figured out a way to forge a career in music, but I'm not 100 per cent sure I can say that."

———

Part of the reason Gord Downie moved to Toronto was so that he could see live music any night of the week. He could often be spotted scouring the indie racks of record stores.

A friend of the Inbreds tipped them off that Downie had bought their first album, *Hilario*, at her record shop. On February 6, 1995, their friends in Change of Heart were opening for the Hip at the Kingston Memorial Centre; Blurton and company invited O'Neill and drummer Dave Ullrich onstage to sing an Inbreds song, "Prince." The band learned that it was Downie's 31st birthday that day. So Ullrich found a brown lunch bag and stuffed it with an Inbreds shirt and a copy of their new album, *Kombinator*. He gave it to Downie and shook his hand. The Hip played Maple Leaf Gardens a few days later; the morning after, the *Toronto Star* ran a picture of Downie wearing the Inbreds shirt. "That's Dave's promotion at its best," quips O'Neill. "That's what I've been missing in my solo career: brown paper bags." Later that year, the Inbreds were invited to join Another Roadside Attraction, and they also opened up gigs in the U.S.

Sometimes Downie cold-called the people who made his favourite records, which is what happened with By Divine Right's 1997 album *All Hail Discordia*. Downie and José Contreras became friends, going out to shows and biking around the back streets of Toronto together until sunrise. Contreras was finishing his next record, 1999's *Bless This Mess*, when By Divine Right was asked to open the *Phantom Power* tour. He rushed to finish it in time. "As with most of my records of that era," he says, "it was greeted with huge disappointment by everyone on board. But Gord thought it was cool, and all of a sudden we were cool. It was so transparent, oh my God."

Bassist Brendan Canning, who had opened for the Hip as a member of hHead in 1994, had recently quit By Divine Right to become a DJ. One night, he ran into Downie at the Bloor Cinema. "Bad time to leave the band, buddy," Downie told him. Canning rejoined. In the meantime, Contreras had enlisted a young Calgarian guitarist who was new to Toronto; her name was Leslie Feist. Contreras taught her all his guitar solos, "because I thought it would be cool for all the girls at the show to see another girl playing lead guitar in a rock band in a hockey arena." On tour, Feist watched Rob Baker closely. "I remember she said to Robbie, 'Hey, you're pretty good at guitar!'" says Canning. "It was such a funny, innocent compliment. He was like, 'Yeah, well, uh, thanks. I've been playing for a while, I guess.'"

Playing with the Hip made some acts want to step up their game. Rich Terfry, a.k.a. Buck 65, opened for the Hip at Toronto's Air Canada Centre in 2006. "I was a bit more nervous than I would be on any other night," he admits. "I've played to lots of large crowds, so it had more to do with the Hip and wanting to understand that crowd. My manager told me, 'If you don't want the night to end with you being completely forgotten, what are you going to do?' I studied video of Gord but also Freddie Mercury and Jacques Brel and other all-time great performers. You've got to be big, to play to the back row. I had to up my game. I felt it went well—not that I won them over or stole the show, but I didn't get destroyed. Maybe Hip fans were so into the band enough to know that I wasn't just some randomly chosen person, that I was handpicked."

"What you learn from that experience is that there is no mailing it in," says Sam Roberts. "To have a lesson like that taught to you at an impressionable stage in your career is a key ingredient to keep going past whatever the average lifespan is for a band with a couple of hits on the radio—which is what, four or five years? Not long.

"Watching them play every night, it was always growing," Roberts continues. "At the first show, we thought, 'Well, it can't get any better than that.' Then there was the next one. By the time we went from Victoria to Edmonton, the third night in Edmonton would be 10 shows into the tour, and how much could they possibly have left in the tank? Yet there was always that feeling of this growing energy rather than a diminishing one. Maybe if you come into the tour at certain points and see them in Toronto one night and Halifax two weeks later, you might feel like one night is better, or there's been a shift. But when you see it every day, you just marvel. You wonder how the hell they can dredge that much energy out of themselves."

For indie rockers who were a bit rough around the edges, playing with the Hip was a serious wake-up call. "I remember watching them and thinking, 'Wow, our band sucks,'" says Canning, of his time with By Divine Right. "I thought, 'This is just not achievable for us.'"

Others felt the same way. Right before By Divine Right played the first show of the Hip's 1998 tour—a surprise show in Kingston at the Iron Horse Saloon—Contreras was taken aside by the tour's promoter, Patrick Sambrook (who became the Hip's manager in 2005). "I hope you guys are ready to get booed," Sambrook told Contreras. "Change of Heart just got booed." "He was so happy about it, I wanted to punch him in the face," says Contreras. "Then, of course, we were the first band that *wasn't* booed. It might have been the arc of their audience: it was now more female, more artsy, ready for us. We never got Hipped. It started a little bit in Ottawa, but Leslie said, 'Really, guys?' And it stopped immediately."

Sometimes it wasn't enough to be Hipped. Sometimes a Hip fan would actually take the trouble of tracking down an artist's post-office box and send them a letter in the mail. Chris Brown and Kate Fenner kept one such correspondence on their fridge in Brooklyn for the longest time.

It read simply, "Why the fuck are you opening for the Tragically Hip? You are nothing like the Tragically Hip. The Tragically Hip are the band I love the most."

———

Gord Downie's support for young bands wasn't just offering them opening slots; sometimes, it wasn't even that. After he heard *David Comes to Life* by Toronto punk band Fucked Up, he sought out singer Damian Abraham to rave about it. Abraham was shocked. As a doctrinaire young punk, he had hated the Tragically Hip, as a knee-jerk reaction in alliance with the hardcore underground. As a grown-up, he worked in a video store Downie frequented and was disarmed by the rock star's gentlemanly demeanour. The first time they met properly, backstage at a show by their mutual friend Dallas Green of City and Colour, Downie helped Abraham's toddler retrieve a dropped pacifier and washed it for him. Two years later, Downie asked Green for Abraham's email address, and they began a correspondence. Abraham eventually worked up the nerve to ask Downie to sing on a new Fucked Up song, "The Art of Patrons." He happily obliged. Both Fucked Up and Downie had records out in June 2014 on the Arts and Crafts label, which booked them both for the Field Trip festival in Toronto. During Downie's live set, he covered Fucked Up's "Generation." Abraham couldn't believe it.

Downie and Abraham never shared the bonding experience of touring together. "The reality is, I hardly know Gord," Abraham wrote for a 2016 piece in *Vice*. "We have talked here and there and collaborated once in the studio. But the effect has been profound. In our few conversations, he has offered wisdom that changed the entire way I look at my situation singing in a band. I can't ever thank him enough for that."

Several Hip openers admit they weren't fans before they got the call, or they were lapsed fans, or they had a love/hate relationship. Bry Webb of the Constantines was one of the latter. "I went to a school just outside of London, Ontario, and it was kind of a farm school. People came from all the neighbouring towns. I remember thinking of the Hip as a jock band, a band that the guys who were kicking my ass for skateboarding were listening to. Then I heard *Fully Completely* and really thought the songs were beautiful. I might even have heard it in art class, which says something about how those songs resonated with people of different leanings in a small-town high school. I listened to it more and realized there was some incredible writing and singing and interesting musical ideas.

"I fell out again as I got into hardcore punk rock, and I wanted to disassociate with all that stuff. Then in my early twenties, maybe it was *Phantom Power*, realizing that it was amazing, this reassertion of their art as a singular rock'n'roll band in the greater context. That record blew me away. A lot of it had to do with the lyrics. Then I just got busy making my own music."

The Constantines opened for the Hip in 2007, three dates in Canada and several weeks in the States. "The Canadian dates were incredible," says Webb, who had never seen the Hip live before. "There were some really strange moments. Maybe one of the most inspiring performances I've ever seen was at this casino in Atlantic City, at a banquet hall that was half full. It was not a good Tragically Hip show. All the others were good shows, with devoted fans, but this one fell apart in an amazing way. It was a bad vibe in that space. So they played a shorter set, and it ended with Gord lying on the stage, yelling, *'You people air-condition EVERYTHING!'*

"It was this incredibly beautiful moment, the most honest thing that could happen. There wasn't going to be any bullshit about it. He was just laying it out there—literally. That's what I want from people at that level. It was not something that was so rehearsed and ready to deliver in the same way every night. That was the experience of that particular night."

———

"A band at their scale was still listening to promising weirdo bands to expose their audience to," says Mike O'Neill. "There wasn't any government grant for them to have a policy like that. It's like you hear Gord say on [the opening track of 1997 live album *Live Between Us*], 'Thanks to the Rheostatics—we are all richer for having seen them tonight.' That was the attitude. What a giving, generous gesture, for both the band they're featuring and their audience."

The Rheostatics' Martin Tielli was on the catwalk in the rafters of Cobo Arena in Detroit on the night that album was recorded. When he heard Downie shout out his band from the stage over the opening of "Grace, Too," "I was shaking in my boots, mortified," says Tielli. "And that night he sang bits of every song from [the Rheos' 1997 album] *The Blue Hysteria*. I was grateful as hell."

Opening for the Hip was a rock'n'roll high school. "It was a lesson for a band who not only wants to do this with their lives but to do it well and to do it the right way," says Sam Roberts. "This was how you treat your opening band; how you treat the staff in the venues; how you relate to your crew and make them feel like they're part of the family, that they're not just worker bees. It's one thing keeping your band together, it's another keeping your crew together. That's how you survive. That's how you put on shows with any kind of consistency. That's how you have the confidence to get up onstage, knowing that when—not if, but when—the shit hits the fan, that you're in good hands. That's something we saw in them and stayed with us ever since."

"It can't be underestimated what good guys they've been to all of us for so long," says Dave Bidini. "That's what chokes a lot of people up. For a lot of bands, especially the smaller bands, it'll never get any better than it was playing with them."

CHAPTER TWELVE
THE BERLIN PERIOD
1998–2000: *PHANTOM POWER, MUSIC @ WORK*

> *"It ain't about the dollar or trying to go fast / unless you take pride*
> *in what you're doing, it won't last / Craftsmanship is a quality that*
> *some lack / You got to give people a reason for them to come back"*

BUCK 65, "CRAFTSMANSHIP"

STEVE BERLIN COULD hear thousands of people chanting his name. It was distracting. Sheryl Crow was onstage at Another Roadside Attraction in Camrose, Alberta. Berlin was backstage with Jake Gold, who was asking Berlin if he wanted to produce the next Hip record, and then—*Oh, right, she'd asked me to sit in on one of her songs and that's where I was headed when Jake stopped me.* He quickly exited the conversation and joined Crow onstage. Later that night, he watched the Hip's set considerably more closely than he had in Vancouver. The next stop, in Winnipeg, he found the band playing underneath a spectacular display of heat lightning. "And the band was on fire, too," says Berlin. "I'd say from then on I was in way deep."

———

Best known as the saxophone player in Los Lobos, Berlin had produced debut albums for San Francisco funk-metal band Faith No More (1987, featuring "We Care a Lot"), Toronto folk duo Lava Hay (1990, "Waiting for an Answer") and the multi-platinum arrival of Winnipeg's Crash Test

Dummies (1991's *The Ghosts That Haunt Me*, featuring "Superman's Song"). Los Lobos was also hitting a creative peak: 1992's *Kiko* was a kaleidoscopic masterpiece that appealed to musos everywhere, no doubt including the Tragically Hip. The Hip were longtime fans: they'd covered the early Los Lobos song "Don't Worry Baby" in the first year of the band, when they had Davis Manning on saxophone playing Berlin's part.

The Hip had self-produced 1996's *Trouble at the Henhouse* and found that their democratic creative process was better served with a mediator in the middle, a job that had fallen to mixer Steven Drake. That album's "Ahead by a Century" broadened the band's appeal even further beyond the hundreds of thousands of fans who bought *Fully Completely*. Steve Berlin wasn't hired to give the Tragically Hip another "Ahead by a Century"—although with the song "Bobcaygeon," he did exactly that. On the rest of the album that was to be called *Phantom Power*, he did much more.

"At that point in the Hip's career, they could have phoned it in for the rest of their lives and people would [have been] happy," said John K. Samson, who in 1998 had just left hardcore punk band Propagandhi and started the Weakerthans. "Then they came out with this bustling, really vivid and forthright record that sounds like a band's first or second record. Those are usually the ones that are the most exciting and durable; you build a body of songs that are really tested—all those reasons why the first couple of records by a band really define a band. *Phantom Power* feels like one of those records, even though it's 10 years after the debut."

Steve Berlin was the first producer the Hip hired who was known primarily as a musician; everyone sitting in that chair before him had built his career on one side of the studio glass (or, in the case of Howard, no glass). Hence, the two albums in the Hip's "Berlin period," including 2000's *Music @ Work*, find the notoriously tight-knit band broadening their palette, bringing in more guest musicians: keyboards, pedal steel, backing vocalists, cello, tabla. "We had so many cool ideas to mess with, so many colours to pick from," said Berlin.

Most of Berlin's production jobs before this were for debut albums; this time, he was working with a band who had five records behind them. "In many ways, they were a lot like my band: guys who had known each other since they were teenagers and played together for a very long time. They had developed this pattern: 'This is where we set up the guitars; this is what the guitar sound is.' They all had their corners. Paul and Bob are both great guitar players, but they sound a lot alike. They're both playing Mesa

Boogie amps and they're both playing Les Paul guitars. It was a wall. The parts were effective, but not imaginative. I said, 'We could do a lot more texturally if these guitar sounds were different, rather than one just being a trebly version of the other.' I made them rethink a lot of stuff. A lot of their prior songs were a riff and then the chorus would be a louder version of that same riff. I wanted more."

The first sparks of *Phantom Power* were in March 1997, when the band started recording demos at the Bathouse. Some were complete, road-tested songs ("Vapour Trails," "Escape Is at Hand," "Save the Planet"), while others were snippets that would later be shaped into songs, like "Poets." The tapes they sent to Berlin knocked him out. "They rocked so hard on everything. I knew right away we had the makings of a great record."

The album's lyrical triumph is "Fireworks." It's a story song that opens by reminiscing about a hockey moment that "everyone" recalls: the nail-biter Canadian triumph over the Russians in the Soviet Series of 1972. The rest of the song details the ennui of a marriage dissolving into what Downie describes as a Cold War standoff, each side hoping for a victory just like that goal back in '72. Yet removed from expectations—of nation, of tribes, possibly of gender roles—it's amazing what can be accomplished, sings Downie, even if the most spectacular sights, like, say, fireworks, are only "temporary towers," leaving a dazzling display that outshines the heavens, a triumph of temporal pleasures in the grander picture. The song itself is one of the Hip's greatest rock songs in a pop format, driven by a classic riff with a boogaloo push, with hints of the Romantics' new wave hit "What I Like About You" and the Who's "I Can't Explain." At one point, there were four trombones playing the guitar riff. "It got to the mixing stage before we realized it was a really silly idea," said Berlin.

But *Phantom Power*'s primary rock tune is the opener, "Poets," the one time in the Hip's recorded career when their worship of the Rolling Stones comes directly to the fore. The guitar break right before the chorus is ripped from Keith Richards's playbook. The maraca-enhanced drumbeat is signature Charlie Watts. There's a swagger here that dates back to the Hip's earliest days doing '60s R&B covers; this is exactly the kind of song they would have covered at the Lakeview Manor.

Except, of course, Downie is at his most obtuse and Beck-ish on "Poets," subverting what should be a straightforward song with allusions to porn, imaginary Himalayas, bare-breasted women, archetypal fathers, frozen-food sections and more. Even the most devout Downie fan has trouble piecing this one together. The song originated from live jams in the middle of "Hundredth Meridian," which would sometimes stretch out for 10 minutes—longer than both finished songs put together. But it was still a random collection of ideas until Berlin helped them paste it together and turn it into a song with a chorus and a bridge. Once they did, they nailed "Poets" in the second take.

"The way the band used to write their original tunes really changed somewhere after *Phantom Power*," said the Odds' Steven Drake, who had mixed the Hip albums before and after it. "All those records prior to that were really written in jam sessions where the band hung out with a big pile of pot in the middle of the table and everybody rolling these big joints. They'd mess around until finally Gord [Sinclair] would play a bass line that somehow stuck. Johnny Fay would come up with his drum part almost immediately. The basic groove is instant for him, and once he's found that, that's what you get. Paul would start to play his rhythm, and Robbie would start soloing. Meanwhile, you'd see Gord over in the corner pawing through his notebook with a pencil, grabbing the mic and saying something like, '*I've got vermicelli underwear!*' Or whatever." Starting with *Phantom Power*, songs were assembled from component parts contributed by different band members.

One song stood out from the rest, one that Gord Downie brought to the band intact: "Bobcaygeon." Driven by a lilting bass line from Gord Sinclair and featuring an aching pedal steel part from Bob Egan, the country-tinged song finds Downie spinning a relatively direct narrative: big-city cop finds refuge from riots and mayhem at his lover's house in cottage country. End of story.

Downie had recently been smitten by the songs of Ron Sexsmith, whose 1995 major-label debut had vaulted the St. Catharines native from obscurity in Toronto to international acclaim, racking up accolades from many high-profile songwriters, such as Elvis Costello and Steve Earle. He and Downie had first met in New York City in 1996, when the songwriter was opening for Moxy Fruvous at the Wetlands. After the set, Sexsmith walked through the crowd and ran into Downie, who told him he'd come just to see his set and how much he liked the 1995 record. "I was really flattered," said Sexsmith. "We hung out that night. The next day, he called my room and asked me if I wanted to come to his show. He came and picked me up in a car. We ended up at Madison Square Garden, where they were opening for Page and Plant. I had no idea—I just thought they were playing a club somewhere. I was a little shy around him, a bit starstruck." Back in Toronto, Downie invited Sexsmith over to his house for coffee and to talk shop. "At the time I met him," said Sexsmith, "he was really getting into playing the guitar. He was really interested in songwriting in general. He'd ask me, 'How'd you write that "Lebanon, Tennessee" song?' I had a song called 'So Young' I remember him saying he really liked."

In its melody, feel and straightforward narrative, "Bobcaygeon" is far closer to Sexsmith's work—or to that of Gordon Lightfoot, of whom both Downie and Sexsmith are enormous fans—than anything in the Tragically Hip's catalogue up to that point. And yet there are obvious Downie-isms, like rhyming the words "dull" and "hypothetical" to describe a cloudy sky.

Then there's the use of the descriptor "Aryan twang" in the lyric to describe the timbre of a fictitious singer's voice. Aryan is a loaded term, used frequently by Nazis to mean "white Nordic Christians" as distinct from and genetically superior specifically to the "Semitic" people, among others. The Sanskrit term actually dates back to ancient Persia (hence: Iran), but in the 1840s was used by German linguist Max Müller to reference Indo-European languages. In the 1850s, French aristocrat Arthur de Gobineau adopted it in his "Essay on the Inequality of the Human Races," which used the term "master race" to refer to what he called racially pure "Aryans." The concept of white supremacy was certainly nothing new, but de Gobineau's writing provided faux-scientific justification for waves of rancid, racist philosophy ever since. His ideas quickly took root in British, American and Russian thinking—and, obviously, in Germany. There's no two ways about it: any use of the word "Aryan" since the 1920s in inextricably linked to Nazi Germany.

Is Downie's use of the term a dog-whistle to white supremacists? Isn't this the same lyricist who referenced Leni Riefenstahl on "Fire in the Hole"? What's going on around here? The song's video—directed by Downie—depicts neo-Nazis disrupting a gig and an ensuing riot. The video concludes with the band picking up the pieces the next morning and carrying on in the wreckage; Rob Baker's guitar bears the same slogan sported by Woody Guthrie: "This machine kills fascists."

Still, leaving the word "Aryan" dangling in a pop song is dangerous. One tourmate remembered Downie asking mischievously, "Isn't it so dark when I sing, 'Their voices rang with an Aryan twang,' and you see all these people singing?'" The musician responded, "I don't really think that's because of the lyric, I think it's the just emotional pinnacle of the song."

Indeed, it comes in the bridge, riding a pedal-steel swell and a reference to Toronto that never failed to elicit a rapturous live reaction in Downie's adopted hometown. The checkerboard floor in the lyric is understood to be the Horseshoe Tavern in Toronto, where the Hip played dozens of times. "I'm saying that this [Aryan business] happens in Toronto, too," the singer explained. "It's not just a thing for rednecks in the bush."

That same bridge references "the men they couldn't hang"—which, unlike so many fictional bands in Downie's oeuvre, is a very real band from Britain whose brand of Celtic (Aryan?) rock made them contemporaries of the Pogues. (One of them played in a punk band with a pre-Pogues Shane MacGowan.) The real Men They Couldn't Hang also had a song called "The Ghosts of Cable Street," celebrating a 1936 incident when hundreds of thousands of Jewish and Irish protesters clashed with police while halting a fascist parade in London.

Because of the word "Aryan," the riot reference in "Bobcaygeon" is widely assumed to be about an incident in Toronto's Christie Pits in 1933, where a Nazi gang known as the Swastika Club interrupted a baseball game between a largely Jewish team and one sponsored by a Catholic church. The Jewish youth were the targets of assault, and Catholic Italians and Ukrainians—outsiders in WASP Toronto—joined in their defence. The scene escalated as more and more people joined the fight, which police were unable to control until about 12 hours later. It's the most well-known race riot in the city's relatively uneventful history. But one doesn't have to reach back to the 1930s to find police riots: there were several in the 1990s, when the austerity policies of Progressive Conservative premier Mike Harris prompted protests by the Ontario Coalition Against Poverty. Riot police on horseback clashed with activists on the steps of Queen's Park, where, in 1995, 17-year-old Sarah Polley—future Oscar nominee and co-producer of *Secret Path*, who sings "Courage" on the soundtrack of *The Sweet Hereafter*—was clubbed in the stomach and elbowed in the jaw, knocking out two of her teeth. Neo-Nazis were active in Toronto in the 1990s, and there was a high-profile case of an undercover CSIS agent ascending the ranks of the most prominent Nazi group. Canadians like to think their racist and/or most brutal incidents are far in the past, but Downie's song is easily set in the 1990s—not the 1930s.

Bobcaygeon, population 2,500, is a peaceful Kawartha cottage town located 90 minutes northeast of Toronto, between Lindsay and Peterborough. Now largely a retirement community, it's located on the

Trent-Severn Waterway and is known as the houseboat capital of Ontario. In 2016, when *Maclean's* writer Adrian Lee travelled there to examine the town's relationship to one of the Tragically Hip's greatest hits, he found Toronto Hip fans who had relocated there to start new businesses, local shop clerks who appreciated the song's role in tourism, and a karaoke host who said he only gets about three requests a year for the track. In 2011, the Hip played a much-hyped show in the tiny town, in front of 25,000 people, which was the subject of a concert film directed by Andy Keen. "There isn't really a romantic, beautiful reason they wrote that song, as far as I can tell," said Keen. Downie once admitted to a radio interviewer, "You could use any small town, really. Bobcaygeon rhymes with constellation . . . sort of."

When Jake Gold went to Universal to talk about the follow-up single to "Poets," the conversation went a little something like this:

"Geez, Jake, we're having a real hard time picking the next single. So-and-so thinks it should be this, and that guy thinks it should be that."

Gold said, "Well, what's *your* favourite song?"

"Bobcaygeon."

"Okay, what's everybody's favourite song?"

"Bobcaygeon."

"Well, what the fuck's the problem?"

"Well, 'Bobcaygeon' isn't really a single, now, is it, Jake? How are they going to say 'Bobcaygeon' on the radio when it's the single?"

"Listen, EVERYBODY'S FAVOURITE SONG IS THE SINGLE. *THAT'S HOW THIS WORKS*. This is no mystery. We're going to go with fucking 'Bobcaygeon.'"

When asked about this, Gold responded simply, "These kinds of conversations happened all the time."

"Bobcaygeon" is about a (relatively) long-distance relationship, which is a recurring theme through much of *Phantom Power*. "Thompson Girl," about a remote community in northern Manitoba, is similar. "Vapour Trails," "Chagrin Falls" and "Escape Is at Hand for the Travelling Man" are all travel songs. "Fireworks," "Emperor Penguin" and "Something On" are all love songs of sorts that had largely eluded Downie's oeuvre until this point. These were all written as the band's families were growing, a time when touring meant being away from more than just one loved one. The other common themes are considerably more random: Antarctica, something called a "superfarmer" and edible audio equipment.

Steve Berlin said there was nothing random about Downie's lyrical process at the time. "We would have silly—I wouldn't say arguments, but he would want me to push back on whether he should say 'a' or 'the.' What was more powerful to say? It seems silly, but it mattered to him," said the producer, whose own band co-wrote and performed a song with Paul Simon on *Graceland*. "I don't know if I necessarily felt like it had to be one or the other, but he really wanted that engagement: 'If you think it should be "the," then tell me why it should be "the."' 'Uh, okay, well . . .'"

The quality control on *Phantom Power* is unusually high for a band about to be exiting their prime. It's every bit as glossy as *Fully Completely*, but with actual rock'n'roll energy and signs of evolving musical tastes: the country of "Bobcaygeon" and "The Rules" and the motorik beat and droning, swirling guitars of "Escape Is at Hand," which owes a debt to the German instrumental band Neu!, particularly their 1971 track "Hallogallo." There are plenty of nods to their own past, not just the Stones in "Poets." "Save the Planet" could have been culled from *Up to Here*. "Membership" recalls mid-'80s R.E.M., as do tracks on the Hip's baby blue EP. Until "Thompson Girl," not since "Boots or Hearts" had the band delivered an acoustic song with such a stomping, insistent rhythm; the song was later covered by their friend Sarah Harmer, and one can see why—melodically it sounds like it comes right from her own songbook.

Steve Berlin doesn't recall there being any kind of mission statement to push forward or to harken back—but the band did require a bit of pushing. "Like any band, including mine, there's a comfort zone that's hard to escape," he said. "You think it's your vocabulary, but it's a cocoon that's safe. Producers are supposed to tell you to try things a different way. There was a bit of pushback from the guys, but it didn't last long. 'Fireworks' was one where in the studio everyone was set up in their corners [in the Bathouse], and then we moved everyone into the kitchen. Johnny was playing this little cocktail [drum] kit. Just literally taking them out of their comfort space was revelatory and helped them grasp the idea of changing the paradigm of everything."

If the Hip trusted Berlin in the studio, they weren't as keen on his choice of mixing engineer, Jim Rondinelli, who had produced Sloan's *Twice Removed* and the Odds' *Bedbugs* and whose mixing credits included Matthew Sweet's *Girlfriend* and Wilco's *Being There*. Only three songs from Rondinelli's mixes made it to the final album: "Bobcaygeon," "Something On" and "Chagrin Falls." Berlin described the rest of Rondinelli's work as "a bit too outside for [the Hip's] sensibility." Mark Vreeken mixed "Thompson Girl," "Fireworks" and "The Rules." They brought back Don Smith, who helmed *Up to Here* and *Road Apples*, to mix the rest without Berlin present. "I thought Don had done some great work, but not with the Hip," said Berlin. "I thought he'd taken some of the cool stuff out. We had this summit meeting where we bartered: I'd get two Jim mixes if Don gets a mix, with a couple of rough mixes Mark Vreeken did. It was a little messy. But even when we were arguing, they were Canadians: kind and gentle."

That reputation extended to the Tragically Hip's performance at Woodstock '99 in Rome, NY, in front of 100,000 people (another 300,000 would show up over the course of the day). "Michael Lang, the original guy from Woodstock, said that the Tragically Hip was the only band on the bill that weekend that represented the ethos of the original Woodstock," said Jake Gold.

Not that it would matter. The Hip were the first mainstage performers on the Saturday, on a bill where the three main headliners were Metallica, Rage Against the Machine and Limp Bizkit. "It was a very aggro environment—the whole vibe there was," said Gold. "I remember being in the audience going out to see what was going on, and Limp Bizkit was telling people to 'fuck shit up' in their song. People started tearing down the PA, where the front-of-house sound was set up. They were taking the plywood and passing it around the audience. The promoters felt the need to shut off the sound, because it was getting insane. Limp Bizkit's manager was tearing up the backstage area and wasn't even thinking about potential safety concerns for the audience."

The next night, after the Red Hot Chili Peppers' set, the festival finished with massive bonfires and vandalism. What was supposed to be yet another celebration of the apex of the hippie movement—a time idealized and commercialized ad nauseum by baby boomers since the day it happened in 1969— had ended with multiple reports of rape in full view of the crowd, along with even more reports of sexual assault, as well as rampant destruction and hooliganism. If there was ever one moment that displayed the death of the hippie dream, and the consequences of corporations controlling rock'n'roll culture, and the coming nihilism of the 21st century, this was it.

Coincidentally or not, Gord Downie was getting tired. Emboldened by "Bobcaygeon," he started writing different kinds of songs. Songs that didn't need the masculine muscle of a rock band behind him. Songs that worked at a whisper. Songs that would never get him booked to play in front of

100,000 people. Songs that—*heresy*—might be better served outside the Tragically Hip. Songs that would find a home sooner than later, on a 2001 album called *Coke Machine Glow*. One song was called "Every Irrelevance," which he played with the Rheostatics in 1997 on the CBC show *Radio Sonic*. One of them was called "The Never-Ending Present," which he debuted live with just Johnny Fay behind him when they picked up an honorary degree from Kingston's St. Lawrence College in 1999.

———

The Hip's next album was also looking for a home. Unsure where to make it, they came up with the idea of riding the rails: Dan Aykroyd had a converted Pullman train car he was going to lend the band for two weeks, where they would write and rehearse, leaving from Chicago with stops in New Orleans and Los Angeles to record the results. A week before the adventure was to begin in September 1999, Aykroyd told them the train was not operational and wouldn't be any time soon. With studio time already booked at Kingsway in New Orleans, they flew down to share the song ideas they'd been developing separately. Sitting in a semi-circle in the hallway of the converted mansion where they'd made *Road Apples* and *Day for Night*, it took the Hip merely two days to come up with 20 songs in various stages of completion. Steve Berlin had been hired to produce again, but his Los Lobos schedule didn't free him up until December. For three months off and on, the Hip woodshedded back in the Bathouse, sending Berlin tracks and taking his suggestions. When he arrived for three weeks in December, all the writing and pre-production was finished. They recorded one song a day, debuting many of them at two shows at the Air Canada Centre on December 31 and January 1.

The shows went off with only one hitch, right after the stroke of midnight. "We had a big balloon drop that didn't work," said Downie. "It was supposed to come out of the mouth of a dragon. The stage was littered with balloons. Someone had left the back door open to the rink, and it was like an Arctic gale was blowing on the stage. For me, as a singer, it's not good; you want warm, humid. You can't trust what you're going to sing. I kept asking them between songs to close this fucking door. My reaction to that was: I fell on a balloon and it went pop. There were 8,000 balloons on the stage. I decided that I was going to kill every balloon on the stage with my body, and I didn't stop. It was a fit of rage. There was nothing artistic about it. It was so ridiculous, and I think it got to the point where the crew were all in tears—and not from laughing. Like, 'Wow, I'm witnessing the worst blowout I've ever seen.'" Downie started jumping on every balloon on stage, screaming, "THIS IS ROCK'N'ROLL GENOCIDE!"

Then it was back to the Bathouse, where they invited more guests into the studio than ever before. That means more than two: *Phantom Power* featured Bob Egan's pedal steel and Steve Berlin's keyboards and flute; *Music @ Work* brought in keyboardist Chris Brown, cellist Sarah Pinette, someone referred to only as "Mr. Hussein" on tabla and Julie Doiron on backing vocals. Berlin once again provided additional keyboards, percussion and saxophone. The tabla was a long time coming: Fay had studied it in high school, and in the late '90s he was a fan of Asian Dub Foundation, a London band melding electronic beats and Indian instrumentation. However, it was the first and last time a tabla appeared on a Hip record.

Julie Doiron is one of only two credited backup singers on any Hip record—Sarah Harmer is the other, on 2012's *Now for Plan A*—and she's an odd choice. Doiron grew up in Moncton and in 1990 co-formed Eric's Trip when she was 18. The Cure and Neil Young were formative influences, and CBC's *Brave New Waves* radio program "opened up everything," she said. Doiron first met Downie when Eric's Trip was invited to play the 1994 Canada Day show in Barrie. In January 2000, Downie called and asked if she would sing on the new Hip record. "I was honoured and in shock that they would ask me to do that," she said. "My brother, who is a really big Hip fan, was kind of super confused." Downie booked her a train ticket to Kingston; he and Langlois picked her up at the station and drove her to the Bathouse, where the entire band was in the mixing room, watching her learn four songs on the spot. "I was like, 'Uh, are you guys going to be there the whole time?'" she recalled. Doiron had just spent a couple of years working with Ottawa band the Wooden Stars, known for unconventional harmonies. "Gord doesn't necessarily pick conventional melodies, either," she said. "I don't know if I was actively making unconventional harmonies or whether it was the Wooden Stars' influence, but I know I wasn't doing major thirds or fifths. But after a couple of passes, the band was super encouraging. I was there for two days."

Doiron and Downie work well together, but she is all but lost on the dense rock song "The Completists," where she sings a very Langlois harmony. The dreamy "As I Wind Down the Pines" is much more revelatory, and on the elegiac "Toronto #4," her presence is devastating and a clear precursor to her work on *Coke Machine Glow* and other Downie records.

Other than "Pines," another outlier on *Music @ Work* is "Tiger the Lion," which opens with Chris Brown literally crawling inside a prepared piano, as well as a ghostly cello loop and a huge Black Sabbath riff that never lets up. The song is punishing and divisive—in a good way. "Some people think it's the cat's ass and others just don't know how to respond to it," said Sinclair during the 2000 tour. Downie's lyrics quote avant-garde musical icon and philosopher John Cage extensively, with lines about making room in daily existence for what Cage called "purposeless play." In Cage—and Downie's?—view, art is less important than living a real life; art should not be about striving toward a masterpiece, art should be about being alive to possibilities in your own life. This was a time when "going to work every day was a break from raising small families," said Berlin. "They seemed to really enjoy time in the studio, as opposed to dealing with stuff."

As recording wrapped up, Berlin was feeling disillusioned. Not having been there at the start of the process, he was not as involved as he'd been on *Phantom Power*. "A couple of times, I thought I should walk away because they just weren't listening to me and I didn't think they liked me anymore," said the producer. "I remember feeling very defeated. I packed my bags and I didn't even tell them; I thought I would split. But I woke up the next day and decided to stick it out. I thought, if they want me gone, they'll just fire me—and that's okay, I'd been fired before."

After bartering over mixes on *Phantom Power*, the Hip decided to go back to Steven Drake to mix all of *Music @ Work*, with Berlin sitting over his shoulder. It was the first Hip record to be made with Pro Tools, "but we were still bouncing it over to the 24-track to mix it," said Drake. "It was stressful. It wasn't quite completely finished when I showed up—because that's what Pro Tools does to you, it allows you to keep going. Some stuff had to be edited. I was given a lot of creative leeway."

That leeway drove Berlin bananas. "Steven is a wonderful human being and very talented musician, but as a mixer? He just about killed me," Berlin said. "It was at the Bathouse in the dead of winter. It was a lot like *The Shining*. I didn't have a car, there was six feet of snow—did they even have a TV? I don't remember. Also, I'm not a pot smoker at all, and Steven had a joint attached to his mouth all day, every day. Unbelievable amount of weed.

"He mixes in this bizarre way where things sound not just bad but horrendously bad, for hours and hours," Berlin continued. "He wasn't even listening to the whole track, just the bass and the floor tom, or the bass and the room mic. It didn't sound like the song. He would stay awake for two days and then sleep for a day-and-a-half. He had his telescope and his astronomy kit with him, so he'd take a break to look at the stars and then come back in. Suddenly, the mix would come into focus and it would sound like a supertanker coming out of the mist. That was one of the toughest, hardest experiences of my producing career."

Downie took the train back to Toronto with the producer; both the American producer and the Canadian superstar realized that they'd somehow boarded in Kingston without their wallets, with only two dollars in change between them. "I think we had to literally panhandle to share a single beer to toast our moment," said Berlin. "That will always stand out to me. It was very special. I'm as proud of those two records as anything I've ever done. Those were certainly highlights of my career."

The album's first single was the title track, simultaneously one of the Hip's most monstrous rock songs and one of their greatest pop songs, right down to the fact that a guitar solo is supplanted by Downie singing "la-de-das." Broken Social Scene's Brendan Canning remembered the song being a reference point for his band during the recording of 2002's game-changing *You Forgot It in People*. "[Producer] Dave Newfeld would put on 'My Music at Work' and say, 'Listen to this!' He loved the way the drums sounded. He wanted our tunes to pop out of the radio the way that one song in particular did."

If "Ahead by a Century" and "Bobcaygeon" had broadened the Hip's appeal to a pop audience, *Music @ Work*'s "Lake Fever" and "Stay," both featuring a prominent drum machine—not unlike the one heard on Sarah Harmer's "Basement Apartment" or other adult pop hits of the day—were the most radical departure for the rock band. *Music @ Work* was met with a universally lukewarm reception, perhaps inevitable for the band's most musically diverse set yet: an album that included the punishing crunch of "Tiger the Lion," the soft pop of "Stay" and the abstract acoustic delicacy of "As I Wind Down the Pines." But also, like *Henhouse*, on most of the straight-up rock tracks the band just sounds tired, going through motions. Even Jake Gold admitted, "There was a lull at that point. A dip in the overall vibe." The public picked up on this. *Music @ Work* sold fewer than 200,000 copies. Tickets for their Massey Hall shows did not sell out instantly.

When the record was finished, Gord Downie reached out to Chris Brown and Kate Fenner with a curious proposal: to see if the former members of the Bourbon Tabernacle Choir wanted to join the band for the 2000 tour—not just as an opener, but onstage with the Hip for the entire set. This would mark the first time since Davis Manning's departure in 1986 that any musician would be allowed into the inner sanctum of the Tragically Hip; Fenner would become the first woman to join them onstage since Georgette Fry duetted with Downie on Otis Redding songs.

"I was pretty terrified," said Fenner, "and it turned out to be with pretty good reason. I love *Music @ Work*, and I initially thought I was just doing Julie [Doiron]'s parts, which were manageable, and maybe a couple of other things." She and Brown showed up in Bath for a two-day rehearsal; Fenner expected that Brown might be expected to learn the whole catalogue and that she'd be brought in just for a certain part of the set. "Gord said, 'Oh, no, I want you onstage the whole time, so just find something to do wherever you can.' I was like, 'What?'" Fenner went back to her home in Brooklyn and sat at her kitchen table with one earphone on, one off, "trying to sing all these songs that I knew as a fan, and trying to figure out what on earth to add."

Brown and Fenner had been making music together since they met at Lawrence Park Collegiate in Toronto in 1985, which was also the site of the first gig by the Bourbon Tabernacle Choir (which included, among many others, future Broken Social Scene guitarist Andrew Whiteman). For the next 12 years, the Bourbons were a big live draw in Toronto and across the country, with all eight or nine members—and Brown's Hammond organ and fridge-size Leslie speaker—piling into one van. Their take on '60s R&B and soul and their popularity on campuses made them kindred spirits of the Tragically Hip, although the two had not crossed paths until the Hip hijacked a Bourbon gig at the Horseshoe in Toronto in April 1992, in order to showcase for producer Chris Tsangarides right before recording *Fully Completely*.

That 1992 show was Fenner's induction to the Hip experience. "I was completely blown away. I had no idea," she said. "The roadhouse-blues thing wasn't for me, but standing side-stage, experiencing Gord's performance, the mystery of his lyrics terrified me—in a good way. I felt a deep connection to the urgency of Gord's performance—obviously many people do, but it was a big event for me. It wasn't just 'Oh, that's a killer rock band.' It was earth-shaking. There are lots of different levels on which you can appreciate something—on craft, power, expertise—but that one was really visceral. After that, I'd buy every album; I knew every song."

In the early '90s, Fenner lived in Toronto with Brown and other Bourbons on Dundas Street East near Sherbourne Street. It was a frequent site for parties after Bourbon gigs—or for any reason at all. The practice space in the basement hosted many jams with musicians from the Bourbons' extended social circle, including Downie. Fenner later had another connection to Downie: her sister was the Downie family nanny. The Bourbons relocated to New York City in 1995, with the intention of using it as a home base for more American touring. Shortly afterwards, the band broke up. Brown and Fenner stayed on, releasing their debut, *Other People's Heavens*, as a duo in 1998.

That same year, Brown got a call from Barenaked Ladies. It was a call that came with mixed emotions: the Ladies' keyboardist, Kevin Hearn, had been hospitalized with leukemia and was about to undergo a bone marrow transplant. The band's new album, *Stunt*, was just about to come out. The day Hearn received the transplant, their song "One Week" hit No. 1 on the Billboard charts. Hearn would not be able to tour for the next year. Brown, who'd known Hearn since they were both students at St. Michael's Choir School for Boys, was offered the temporary gig. At the time, Brown was gigging with Fenner three times a week in the NYC area and working at a Korean restaurant to pay bills. Within a month, he was playing huge shows and festivals with the Barenaked Ladies across the U.S. During any rare downtime, he and Fenner recorded the album *Geronimo*, one of the great unheralded albums of that era in Canadian music.

When they got the call to join the Hip, Brown and Fenner had just come off a gruelling tour where they'd barely broken even. "I thought, 'What are we doing?'" said Fenner. "Chris is the eternal optimist: if there are only five people at a gig and they all love it, then he thinks we've done our job. Which is a nice way to think, but—well, the call from the Hip came just as I was re-examining my career direction."

Having known members of both Barenaked Ladies and the Tragically Hip for so long made the gigs appealing for Brown: "They were both real, authentic bands that had grown up together and had achieved fame doing what they naturally do. They were not a project that had set out to acquire some portion of market share." In a lesson key for any support player, Brown also learned not to over-identify with his employers. "You just have to allow it to be what it is," he said. "If they need your left leg, just give your left leg and put your arms to use somewhere else."

Except that neither Brown nor Fenner were sure which limb to put where. "There was not a lot of feedback or instruction," said Fenner. "There is so much stealth musicality in that band. Things that I would gravitate toward, thinking, 'Oh, this would be a good part,' I didn't realize that Paul Langlois was already doing something embedded somewhere in there. He just doesn't pop out; he's part of the fabric. I always wondered if I was stepping on someone's toes, but no one ever said, 'There, you should go up a third'—nothing. That was hard. I'm also not sure how together they were on the desire to have two extra people on the road. Some people were really warm, and some weren't."

Fenner was given a spotlight on "Flamenco" and "Yawning or Snarling," on both of which she and Downie would trade verses. When that happened, the audience would consistently roar with approval—in part because she sounded fantastic, in part because for the first time in the set the crowd could actually hear what the lady onstage was singing. "Most of the time, I wasn't sure anyone even knew I was there," admitted Fenner. "Maybe it would have been the smart thing for me to say, 'There is no purpose to having me onstage for "Hundredth Meridian" or "Blow at High Dough" or all those big boy-rockers.' I played a lot of tambourine." *Toronto Star* reviewer Vit Wagner noted, "There were times when backup vocalist Kate Fenner must have felt like the most superfluous person in the house."

"I'm sure the fans were like, what is this?" said Julie Doiron, who saw the tour at the Bell Centre in Montreal. "I remember thinking, 'Thank God they didn't ask me to do this gig.' There's no way I'd have the stage presence to pull that off. I get pretty scared being in front of a bunch of people. When I'm in a room and everyone's singing the lyrics, I cry—there's something about that energy. I'd probably be crying onstage the whole time."

Brown's keyboards also largely bled into the background, except when he was given a solo turn for the intro of "Gift Shop" that seemed to be a direct nod to Garth Hudson's flights of fancy before the Band's "Chest Fever." "Maybe you bring in a Hammond and piano and a woman's voice— if you're not used to using that palette, what do you do with it?" said Brown. "It was cool to feel that their fans responded to the door being opened and air being let in the room. But then that door would shut. I don't know if that was the same pullback on *Music @ Work*, where they were probably heading off in new directions but then didn't. If they'd gone that way and just been mind-blowing, it would have been a different record."

So why were they there? "I'd offer the Billy Preston equation," theorized Steven Drake, referencing the keyboardist who played extensively with both the Beatles and Stones in the '60s and '70s. "Which is: sometimes you invite someone on the road just to change the personal dynamic in the group. That's why George Harrison kept dragging Billy Preston into Beatles sessions toward the end, because then everybody would be civil to each other. I don't think the Hip were having trouble being civil, but it was the idea of changing the mood and having different people onstage just purely for emotional reasons, to make it new again." Downie told a live MuchMusic audience, shortly after the Massey Hall shows, that with Brown and Fenner on board, "it feels like a whole new band."

Whether the Hip wanted to be a whole new band was another question. Communication inside the group was not good, exacerbated by the fact that Downie had been recording a solo album the month before the 2000 tour began, to the chagrin of the rest of the band. Brown and Fenner could tell something was up: they came of age in a band of high school friends and recognized passive-aggression when they saw it. So Brown called a band meeting before a show at Philadelphia's Theatre of the Living Arts, a month into the tour. "Downie said to me, 'This is the first band meeting we've had in five years,'" said Brown. "I said, 'Oh, really? *I wouldn't have noticed.*'" The band erroneously thought Brown and Fenner were part of Downie's new solo project, which they perceived as a threat. "I think they thought we were some kind of Jake-Gord conspiracy," said Brown. "When we dispelled that, it was like, oh, okay. When you're in a group like that and you depend on each other for your mode of expression, it becomes very precarious. Things become very threatening. I think we both understood that, which is why we wanted to clear the air."

Camps were definitely drawn, however, and Downie did become close with Brown and Fenner. "I think Gord was less lonely then and really liked having us around," said Brown. "I had a [portable] turntable in our hotel room, and we had it backstage and would listen to it pre-show. We'd buy vinyl on the road. And we'd listen to tracks we were all working on. Gord would sit in the hotel room with us and play mixes from *Coke Machine Glow*. I found a first-edition *Call of the Wild* and gave it to him because I knew he loved Jack London. We would hang out with everyone else, too, listening to music late at night on the road. There was a lot to it that was healthy. But the difficulty [Kate and I] prompted [in the Hip] was probably cathartic. Whether some people wanted us there more or less, we got good vibes from everybody. When they asked us to do the second leg of the tour in Canada, we were like, 'Really?' Totally surprised."

The *Music @ Work* tour concluded on December 23, 2000. Chris Brown and Kate Fenner were not asked to tour with the band again. Gord Downie was getting ready to shake up the Tragically Hip in a whole new way.

CHAPTER THIRTEEN

IS IT BETTER FOR US IF YOU DON'T UNDERSTAND?
BAND OF RINGOS

"Within the Kingston community, opinion was divided. There were some who thought we were just a university frat-boy band, too smart for our own good, and then others who thought we were working-class bums."

GORD DOWNIE, 2000

Michael,

I like you and I like the guys in the Hip but I don't really think I can add anything to their story. I actually think they are mostly terrible and remain shocked that people love them so much. Of course, I have met them and they are all super nice and I believe they have attempted to challenge their shittier fans with gentleness and poetry, but it is still not my bag. Maybe when someone has the "courage" to write a book on the Emperor's New Clothes aspect of that band, I'll contribute and get assassinated. Good luck!

[name withheld]

That email is from a peer of the Tragically Hip. It doesn't matter who it is. The sentiment is not uncommon.

More than 11 million Canadians watched the final Tragically Hip concert via a CBC broadcast. Many were fans. Some others tuned in for the Terry Fox moment; some others tuned in merely out of curiosity, because it was a hyped live event like an Olympic hockey game or even the Academy Awards. It was the Thing We Were All Supposed to Watch. Many of these "others" left scratching their heads.

What is it we're supposed to like about this band, exactly? Listen to that singer, barking away madly about God knows what. That long-haired guitarist keeps playing the same solo, and it ain't "Freebird," that's for sure. The other guitarist just stands there. The drummer just keeps the beat—nothing interesting there. What do bassists even do again? Is this long section where nothing happens what you call a "jam"? This is the Great Canadian Band we've heard so much about? No wonder they didn't make it anywhere else.

The Tragically Hip have sold far too many records to be considered a cult band, or niche. But for a band held up as a cultural pillar of a time and place in Canadian culture, they're an odd choice. Bryan Adams, Loverboy, Céline Dion, Blue Rodeo, Sarah McLachlan, Shania Twain, Alanis Morissette, Our Lady Peace, Diana Krall, Nickelback: all of these acts are easy to understand and contextualize even if their music isn't your thing. The Tragically Hip feel like something you should understand if you're a rock'n'roll fan. If you don't get it, does that make them a terrible band? God forbid, does it make you less Canadian?

Iconic though they may now be in Canadian culture, the Tragically Hip were never sacred cows. The music critic at their hometown newspaper could never figure out what the fuss was about. Neither could segments of the national press. Witness this 1995 review of Another Roadside Attraction in the *Globe and Mail*: "At full speed, the Hip are impressive to behold. Unfortunately, the Hip don't operate at full speed all the time. And when they do slow things down—the band heading off on meandering, neo-psychedelic jams; Downie tracing the same three-note melody over and over—only the presence of self-indulgent wankers such as Blues Traveler save them from being the most tedious band on the bill, if not Earth."

What confused this reviewer and others was how a '90s rock band who didn't adhere to trends in metal or grunge or even '70s rock revivalists, a band who didn't have a marketable image, who didn't write pop songs, could command such a large and devout following.

"I was a non-believer until I saw them live," says *Now for Plan A* producer Gavin Brown. "That was my own ignorance. I've humbled myself at the feet of music a long time ago, when I was a 16-year-old fucking asshole and thought I knew everything." To his teenage self, Brown would now say, "Go ahead: write a hit song, asshole, go ahead and try. It's the hardest thing, to connect to hundreds of thousands, if not millions, of people. Anyone dissing the Hip can suck my balls through my drawers, to quote Jay-Z. Anybody looking at success from down below and saying that it's crap, that's their own problem. The Hip are magic. When they get their shit going two-thirds of the way through the show and they take it to another level, there's nobody better."

Expectations of rock music had changed by the '90s. The music's rebel spirit had long been bled out of it. Dangerous tightwire acts were no longer acceptable. Rock bands, at least ones who reach a certain level of success, were expected to deliver a consistent show. Margins of error were minimized. That's partially why a wild card like Nirvana was so refreshing. It's also what led to the rise of the jam-band circuit—two seemingly opposed fan bases in which the Hip created an overlap. One of those fans is Toronto music historian Stuart Henderson. "When I go see a band live and there's absolutely no chance they'll do something that surprises me, it is not a great show for me," he says. "Even if they play everything perfect. Perfect doesn't do much for me. The Hip were rarely perfect because they had this character in the middle of everything who was all about chaos. That's incredibly exciting."

Exciting for some. Erratic for others.

———

The Tragically Hip are a band of Ringos.

That's not a slight, although it sounds like one. Generations of know-it-alls raised on the mostly white playlists of classic rock stations have dumped on the Beatles' drummer for not being the Who's Keith Moon or Led Zeppelin's John Bonham. Ringo Starr is not flashy. He doesn't draw your attention to his drum patterns. He has no desire to be the star of the show. For those acts of modesty, Starr is spat on and deemed unworthy of being in the Beatles. When in fact he's one of four equally important reasons why they were so influential.

Put Moon or Bonham in the Beatles, and you'd have a terrible band. You'd have a showboat who tries to distract from often-intricate pop songs and disrupt the chemistry that made the Beatles what they were. Chemistry is something you can't quantify. It's certainly not dependent on virtuosity. For every Who or Zeppelin or Rush or Police, there are groups like the Band, U2 or R.E.M.: all have chemistry, all would falter if a member were to be replaced (which happened to R.E.M.), but those latter bands don't have an explicitly obvious skill set that makes a lay audience think of them as individual musicians first. (Even if their talent is more than evident to other musicians.)

The same could be said of the Hip's single biggest musical influence: the Rolling Stones. Mick Jagger is obviously a great front man, but a singer? Nope. Keith Richards? Like any great blues player, he's all feel—and you only know it when you feel it. Charlie Watts? Keeps the groove, never demands more; his most brilliant flourishes are the most subtle ones. Bill Wyman is of a piece with Watts and Richards. Brian Jones, Mick Taylor, Ron Wood: all fine guitarists, but there are few memorable guitar solos in a band that has primarily functioned as a rhythm section.

Which is exactly how many peers and associates describe the Tragically Hip: a rhythm section with a front man. A different kind of rhythm section, one anchored by Johnny Fay and Paul Langlois, with Gord Sinclair playing both a rhythmic and melodic role ("Grace, Too"), intertwining with Rob Baker's lead work, which, with the exception of the occasional song like "New Orleans Is Sinking" or "Greasy Jungle," is rarely at the forefront. Nobody would ever describe the Hip as an R&B band, but—as anyone who saw them in Kingston in 1986 can attest—that is their genetic makeup, musically. Much like the Rolling Stones. And, much like the Rolling Stones, there's a massive audience who don't stray from the greatest hits; there's an exponentially smaller cohort who follow every twist and turn, who tolerate the downturns, who appreciate the deep cuts.

In many ways, the Hip's career is analogous to another of their '90s peers: Pearl Jam. Both bands enjoyed a quick ascent due largely to the charisma of their singers. Both peaked commercially right out of the gate, between the years 1991 to 1995. Both attracted the bootleg community, the tape traders who collect live recordings and study nuances from night to night. Both straddled so-called corporate rock and the vibrant underground of the day. Even their sales numbers in Canada are comparable; as Pearl Jam's multi-platinum days waned in the U.S., they routinely sold twice as many records in Canada, proportionally, than in their native country (consistently gold in the U.S. but platinum in Canada). Both have deserved reputations as upstanding, philanthropic, intelligent gentlemen. But both could also be accused of spinning their wheels—either from album to album, or from note to note during onstage jams. Unlike the expansive reach of Wilco or My Morning Jacket, the explorations of both the Hip and Pearl Jam owe little to jazz, to psychedelia, to experimental music, to anything that explodes possibility; more often than not, it just sounds like a rock band playing for a really, really long time.

Of course, when talking about so-called jam bands with a massive cult following, one band prevails above the rest: the Grateful Dead.

Full disclosure: I've always hated the Dead. Still do. I can admire the economics of the massive counterculture they created and the Talmudesque studies of the tape traders. I even understand and can appreciate Dead descendants like Phish, but my feelings about the Dead have been confirmed in numerous blind taste tests.

Never in my life would I have guessed the Dead and the Hip would share a significant fan base. But when I travelled to Kingston for the final Hip show, the first people I met that day, in a downtown parking garage, were Deadheads: Fran and Bob Stanhope from Raymond, Maine. As a Canadian, I was naturally intrigued by the mythical unicorn known as the American Hip fan, so I asked Fran how she discovered the Hip. It was in 1998, at a tailgate party while skiing in Vermont, where some Canadians turned them on. "It took three years after Jerry [Garcia] died before we found the Hip," said Bob. "We tried a couple of Phish shows," said Fran, "but the camaraderie with the Hip shows is a lot like the Grateful Dead."

"It's not [about] the music, per se," says Dave Levinson, a Vancouver Deadhead who worked with the Hip's management in 2003–05 and helped them market their archive of live recordings online. "It's the collective vibe and collective energy on any given night, which influences [everything about] the show: the collective high, the collective buzz and how everyone recognizes each other. There's a parking lot culture: everyone gets together and trades and talks about the shows. With the Hip and the Dead and Phish, they're searching for something every night, and they need the crowd to get there. The crowd needs the band, and everyone needs each other—everyone plays a part. It's different than the standard concert, where everything has cues and the set lists are the same.

"Musically, it's not the Dead," he admits, "but the extraneous variables are there. There's nothing like the whole being greater than the sum of its parts. Whether that be music, weather, climate, venue, vibe—everything. Dead fans respond to every little nuance: they'd break it down to the solos, even the notes, and react on such a specific level. I found the Hip fans were like that. They always picked up on little comments Gord would make. Everything had meaning."

One must grant the Grateful Dead this: they never sound rote. If they sound lost, at least they're searching.

The Tragically Hip are a conservative band. They don't particularly push the envelope created by their own design. They lack the anything-goes spirit and left turns—and the frequent silliness, for better or worse—of their peers the Rheostatics or Barenaked Ladies. What improvisatory impulses they have are always indulged in a select few standards, primarily "Hundredth Meridian" and "New Orleans Is Sinking." Many Hip songs, "Ahead by a Century" among them, developed out of onstage jams during these tracks. On one hand, it's a revealing peek at the band's creative process. On the other, it sometimes meant Downie was singing in seemingly a different key, or that Baker, Langlois and Sinclair were pulling in different directions, new chord choices clashing within the structure of whatever song they're jamming.

The Hip had a loose affiliation with the jam-band circuit, starting in 1995 when they brought Blues Traveler on Another Roadside Attraction and shared some bills with them in the States—including the H.O.R.D.E. (Horizons of Rock Developing Everywhere) festival, a travelling roadshow founded by Blues Traveler in 1992 and, like ARA, modelled after Lollapalooza. H.O.R.D.E. gave birth to the modern jam-band scene, nurturing groups like Phish and the Dave Matthews Band. In 1998, the Hip played five nights in a row at the Wetlands in New York City—"which is Deadhead central right there," says Ian Blurton, who did sound for opening act Hayden at those shows. In 2007, they played the 10,000 Lakes Festival in Minnesota, on a bill with Phish's Trey Anastasio, the Grateful Dead's Bob Weir, the Derek Trucks Band, Zappa Plays Zappa and Gov't Mule. If that's not an embrace from the jam-band circuit, nothing is.

All jam bands have one thing in common: musical virtuosity, in at least one member, that allows those never-ending solos to go somewhere. (Ideally.) In the Tragically Hip, it was Gord Downie's erudite extrapolations and lyrical expeditions that mutated the most from night to night. There has never been a bass solo or a drum solo at a Tragically Hip show. The two times they toured with a guest keyboardist, there was a tiny window of freedom in "Gift Shop," but that's it. In later years, Rob Baker would play an extended acoustic intro to "Ahead by a Century." For most of his career with the Hip, he rarely staked out a solo section that differed from anything found on a record.

Maybe we shouldn't expect much more from a band of Ringos.

Rob Baker always told friends that his ultimate musical goal was "to have a signature sound, like when people hear Santana or Keith Richards." Former manager Jake Gold says, "Robbie plays lead, but it's not traditional jerk-off lead guitar. That's not Robbie's MO, never was. It was always taste and riffs and sounds, as opposed to Guitar Hero lead stuff." One of Baker's favourite guitarists is Smokey Hormel, sideman to Beck, Tom Waits and Johnny Cash, a master of the understatement, always in service of a larger vision.

"I've never been so much into the guitar theatrics," says Baker, "although I appreciate Joe Satriani, or for that matter Jeff Beck, who I really love and always have. But I'm much more into the guys that are maybe not in the spotlight. They're standing back and they're playing a supportive role, making the song better. My approach, whether it's playing single note stuff or lead stuff, is to play as little as you can. Leave as much space and as much open room as you can. The editing is more important than the flash, showing what you can do. It's more important to know when to do it." Just like Ringo.

"The best guitar players aren't necessarily the best players," says Colin Cripps of Crash Vegas and Blue Rodeo—one of Canada's best guitar players by any measure. "They're the ones who have the signature, where you hear three notes and you know who it is. You can't manufacture that. They don't have to be the greatest guitar players, technically. Some signature players are great technicians. Then there are lots of amazing technicians, but they sound like a hundred other guitar players—even to other guitar players. Robbie is a signature guitar player. I always knew it was him [on a track], even before I'd hear a note of Gord's vocals. That's the best place any musician could get to. That's where you make your name: 'That's Jimmy Page.' 'That's the Edge.' Also, when you get put in a nucleus that celebrates each distinctive personality, you get to [bring out] more of that signature."

After the first three Hip records, Baker became enamoured with different tunings, particularly open tunings. Gord Sinclair once jokingly complained, "He's got a whole pile of guitars over at home, each one seemingly tuned to a different key. When I'm over, I can never pick up a guitar and play it, because I don't know how he's got it tuned." This creates interesting textures in tandem with Langlois and generates a sound unlike a lot of other rock bands.

Paul Langlois may well be the most underrated member of the Hip, mainly because few people understand what exactly a rhythm guitar player does: to punctuate the beat, to be lockstep with the drummer, to colour the song underneath the lead. Says producer Steve Berlin, "Paul is truly one of the most amazing rhythm guitar players I've ever worked with. He's got such an incredibly deep knowledge of how rhythm guitar parts work." By Divine Right's José Contreras agrees, adding, "Paul is like a mist on a mountain. He lets his notes ring and they float around." His subtlety stems from his personality, says Chris Brown: "Paul is the only guy who can smoke on the bus and no one notices it." Perhaps he's the most Canadian member of the Tragically Hip.

Steven Drake, who mixed *Trouble at the Henhouse* and *Music @ Work*, explains what exactly Baker and Langlois do together: "The band does this pentatonic modal thing, where they get these textures going between the two guitars and the bass, where they're doing two or three different pentatonic scales that combine to create quite dense chord structures. It's a little thing they do that nobody else does, and you hear it occasionally. 'Gift Shop' has quite a few moments like that. Gord [Downie] floats on top of that, doing a lot of tetrachordal melodies, little four-note phrases, against these moving textures of modal pentatonics. It's an interesting sound."

"At first I couldn't figure it out, then I realized they're masters of the understatement," says Ian Blurton of Change of Heart, perhaps the greatest guitar player to emerge from Toronto's Queen West scene of the '80s. "Sometimes with guitar players like [Baker and Langlois], it takes you awhile to realize what they're doing. What I've heard of them playing separately, you can tell that they're a partnership. They're like [the band] Television without the extended solos. Sinclair has an almost Cure or New Order–ish thing going on. I always thought he was the anchor and everyone else plays around him—especially live when they go on extended jams."

Gord Sinclair needs no explanation: he is clearly the musical engine of the band. If anyone is going to be accused of being Ringo, of course, it's the drummer. Johnny Fay has taken hits from critics over the years, maybe because a drummer always gets blamed when extended jams lag in energy. Maybe it's because on so many Hip songs, Fay does little more than the bare minimum.

"Johnny Fay is miraculously underrated," says producer and drummer Gavin Brown. "I told him, 'I can set my watch to you, dude; you're as tight as shit.' He plays exactly what's needed, and when you don't expect it, he adds a little flourish you wouldn't think about."

In the band's earliest days, Steve Jordan says, "Sometimes I'd watch Johnny the entire show. As riveting as Gord is as a front person, I found Johnny just as riveting. His style was not like your typical Kingston cover band drummer." Evidence of this can clearly be found on early bootlegs from 1986–87, where Fay drives the backbeat like any great R&B drummer, although one can also hear some laughably clunky drum fills on a very early live version of "Smalltown Bringdown." (Totally forgivable: the guy was still in high school, after all.) But listen to the upside-down beat that opens "Little Bones." Or the explosive energy of "Fire in the Hole," "Fireworks" or "Family Band." Or the way he holds the pulse on the delicate "Throwing Off Glass" while Sinclair's bass floats around like Jaco Pastorius on Joni Mitchell's *Hejira*. "Johnny is a monster drummer, not a nuance guy," says Kate Fenner. "Part of that is probably Gord Sinclair's idiosyncratic bass playing. If you had a more impressionistic drummer as well as an impressionistic bass player, you'd have—Phish!"

"Drumming is about energy and metabolism," says Hawksley Workman, who started his career behind the kit as a session player. "Implicit in the playing of the iconic rock drummers of the world is the sound of a willingness to self-destruct. I think of the beat that opens 'Poets' or the hot snare intro into 'Cordelia'—Johnny Fay's energy always feels breathless to me. He plays ahead of the beat, he hits hard, it's super physical. He plays big, beautiful Paiste cymbals. He's a tough player with a street-fighting energy, which you can hear on all those records. I don't know if he's a natural drummer, which many of the big Canadian rock drummers are not."

Wait, what's a natural drummer? "Steve Gadd [Paul Simon, Chick Corea] is a natural drummer," Workman explains. "Dave Clark is a natural drummer. Neil Peart and Johnny Fay are not natural drummers. Neil has an intellectually driven style of drumming. Some people have it in their bones, and some people have to work a little harder to get there. Johnny Fay could probably save 30 per cent of his energy every night by making a few adjustments to his style, like tuning one's golf stroke, but the exciting thing is that he's hitting hard, to within an inch of his life. Rock'n'roll is the sound of destruction and metabolism cranking at its peak. I feel Johnny is still there."

Together, the Hip have a chemistry that be neither adequately explained nor quantified. "There's this telepathic thing that happens when you're a musician playing in a really tight unit," says Kris Abbott of the Pursuit of Happiness. "It's like you can feel the distance of everyone onstage without even seeing them. You can almost crash into each other but never touch.

Or you can feel the space that will come after the snare shot, before it even happens, because there is this heightened sense of spatial awareness that happens when you're in that bubble. It's very different than when you're just in a good band supporting a good singer. We're not talking about being a good band; we're talking about that string of energy that actually connects people. That is super rare. It's not something to ever take for granted. It's absolutely a spiritual thing. It's a high."

Dave Clark shared a drum teacher with Fay, Gavin Brown and other Toronto luminaries in the late jazz great Jim Blackley. "With the Hip, they're playing rock'n'roll," says Clark. "Rock'n'roll doesn't come out of a book. Johnny's going to lay down a heavy backbeat and it will sit in the mid-tempo and they're going to do their thing. Listen to Howlin' Wolf or Lightnin' Hopkins: they don't move too far away from what they do, but what they do has nuance and character. That's why people love it: it feels good. And the Hip have this low-end, mid-range punch in their music that hits people physically, viscerally. And look at Gord!" Clark lets out a belly laugh and concludes, "Let's face it: he's not bad."

———

What if Gord Downie didn't front the Tragically Hip? That's not a hypothetical question, of course, because he put out three records with the Country of Miracles and one with the Sadies. All have great merit. None connected to audiences in the way the Tragically Hip did. Downie's magic spell would likely not work with any random collection of all-star musicians. Just look at Neil Young.

Neil Young has a long and varied discography with an ever-evolving cast of characters, many of them ace players from L.A. and Nashville. But he keeps coming back to Crazy Horse, a scrappy garage-rock band whose almost willful amateurism made Young's peers like David Crosby and Stephen Stills recoil in disgust. Many didn't understand why he was wasting his time with these bumpkins, why he didn't either a) hire a band who wasn't prone to bum notes, or b) stick to the California country-rock that would have made him as rich as the Eagles' eccentric Canadian cousin. Crazy Horse clearly have chemistry with Neil Young, in ways Young has been unable to find elsewhere. So even if they're notorious for doing just one thing and doing it, at the very least, adequately—certainly infused with their unique spirit—that's a comfort zone in which Young has produced most of his greatest work. But even the biggest Neil Young fans have a tolerance limit with Crazy Horse—and Neil Young, for that matter.

"I love Neil Young and I worship his music and I love Crazy Horse on record," says Dave Clark. "My friend Paul goes to see Neil with Crazy Horse, buys the floor seats directly at the front and has a mental orgasm as Neil Young plays the same three notes for 25 minutes on his solo. Whereas I sit up in the stands and wait for them to get back to singing, because they're amazing singers. I love Neil Young's guitar playing, but I only need one solo. I don't need the excessive jamming. I appreciate it, but the gold is in the singing. They still sound like teenagers: the harmonies are shocking and beautiful."

Hawksley Workman recalls, "I saw Neil's *Le Noise* show at Massey [Hall in 2010], and within that same year I also saw Crazy Horse. I found both shows just preposterous, just horrible. But I've also never talked so much about a concert as I have either one of those Neil Young shows. Which has me feeling: is this art within the art? Is he disappointing us because he wants us to see that someone we idolize can disappoint? Watching Neil, I thought, 'There is a room full of disappointed people here. The disappointment is palpable. What is the problem?' But then is his thing to push us in that way? To tell people like me, 'I'm not going to bend to you.'"

Many casual Hip fans feel the same way about the band's jams and Downie's "rants." Most of those fans also probably didn't buy a new Hip record after 2000. "You should be loyal to artists you believe in," Workman continues, "even if you don't think their latest shit is great. I've had that with my sense of ownership as a fan of Bruce Cockburn; he's put out some records where I think, 'What the fuck is this?' But then I think, my faith in this guy has to speak more than my first response to what he's doing. And I give Neil that as well."

Being a hero of the baby boomers, Neil Young is given the benefit of the doubt that few younger artists command. Our attention span is too short. We are constantly exposed to all kinds of new music, from every corner of the world and every point in history. Who knows if the much-maligned Hip records of the 2000s would have received critical reappraisal were it not for the band's premature end, or even if 2016's *Man Machine Poem* had not suggested a new creative renaissance and garnered their best reviews in at least 15 years.

One thing is certain: the public is no longer enraptured with rock'n'roll heroes. The Tragically Hip may very well have been one of the last

Canadian rock bands to headline arenas. In the 2000s, few other than Nickelback, Billy Talent and Arcade Fire followed in their wake. Drake became the new Canadian cultural icon. Rock music, as it's been defined for the past 60 years, is going the way of jazz: for increasingly older and niche audiences. And so when one-third of Canada rallied around the final Hip show in 2016, two-thirds of Canada may have wondered from what they were being excluded.

———

Headlines across the country in the summer of 2016 had variations on one that ran in the *Globe and Mail*: "One nation under Gord." Social media was filled with quaint pictures of natural settings with the hashtag #GordDowniesCanada. The Tragically Hip had been ordained, by the Canadian media and even the current prime minister, as the sound of Canada, as essential to the national character as a loon call or maple syrup or a canoe. Of course, loons, syrup and canoes are all emblematic of the rural or small-town Canadian experience, not that of the increasingly urban face of Canada.

If you grew up in small-town Ontario in the '90s, there's no question the Hip were a monolithic cultural force. In the cities: not so much. Ryan McLaren is a Toronto concert promoter who grew up in a tiny town in the Niagara area. "When I was in high school, there wasn't a lot of access to the world beyond the borders of that town, where there were 2,000 people and no paved roads. I remember a friend bought me *Up to Here*, and then I thought, 'There are Canadian bands? I thought all bands were American.' When *Day for Night* came out, they played in [nearby] Hamilton, and the next day everyone was wearing a Hip shirt. But when I moved to Toronto, people were so down on the Hip. Nobody thought they were great. Here I was thinking this was the most important band that meant so much to all kinds of people—which they did, in a small town."

For many urban Canadians not of European descent, the Hip were merely a curiosity, an almost exotic look at what Canada was thought to be, an image that didn't square with the multicultural suburbs of the 21st century. The rapper K-OS said that listening to the Hip helped him understand "white Canada." This was further explored on a panel convened by Ontario public broadcaster TVO after the final show. There, Toronto writer Navneet Alang explained that in the '90s, although he was "definitely one of those brown kids that listened to rock, the Hip always seemed like they belonged somehow to rural Canada or a white Canada to which I didn't feel particularly connected. The Hip, in my mind, belonged to Muskoka or Sudbury or B.C., but somehow not diverse Toronto. That may not be fair or even very logical, but it was definitely how I felt as a teen."

His fellow panelist Anupa Mistry, one of the country's most insightful music writers, took this idea a bit further. "This rigid definition of Canadianness has not changed over the course of my life," she said, "and while I am grateful for the benefits of my citizenship, this culturally mandated take on patriotism mostly just feels like low-key xenophobia." Citing the fact that one-third of Canadians watched the CBC broadcast, she continued, "That stat gets my back up. You know what's bigger than *one*-third? *Two*-thirds! I promise I'm not trying to be contrarian here, because I actually do believe the Hip and Gord are worthy of acclaim, but what bothers me is social exclusion: the idea that the myth perpetuated by the musical preferences of this one-third makes people like me, who just had other things to do, somehow lesser." What was Mistry doing the night of August 20, 2016? "I was at a friend's house on a quiet [Toronto] street, dancing to soca and Afrobeats with my friends who grew up across the GTA [Greater Toronto Area] in very Canadian communities, like mine."

"What's with this fascism of feeling?" chimed in media critic Jesse Brown on his *Canadaland* podcast. Even though he claimed to be a Hip fan, the parade of patriotism in 2016 left a bad taste in his mouth. Speaking of the fawning media coverage, he said, "What happened during that concert was an assertion of dominance on a romantic or sentimental level. '*My* feelings about Canada define Canada. *My* songs define Canada. *My* connection to this band defines Canada.' Nobody gets to say their shit 'defines Canada'. . . . We collectively said that we as a bunch of white-guy Canadians are *more* Canadian," he argued, than the two-thirds of the country who tuned out.

Rollie Pemberton, a.k.a rapper Cadence Weapon, says the notion of the Hip's final show as being a moment for "white Canada" resonated for him to some degree, but "it's hard for me to be cynical about it," he says. "I can see that especially for relatively new Canadians, they don't get it at all—it doesn't speak to them. I have this nostalgia for it. I feel it's something you should experience, whether you know the music or not. I had a respect and appreciation for the bravery of the performance. But there is this assumption from the hive mind that we all have to watch things like the Super Bowl; there's a sense of not wanting to be left out of the cultural conversation. The Hip's music doesn't exclude people. The band doesn't exclude people. You can't help who your fans are."

That sense of social exclusion is by no means limited to ethnicity or any other demographic factor. Ask anyone who doesn't give a fuck about hockey how they feel when an Olympic hockey moment is said to be something that united "all" Canadians, or even just when making small talk with (mostly white) strangers. Ask Albertans how they felt about the "national mourning" during Pierre Trudeau's funeral. Ask Newfoundlanders or Quebecers about almost anything. Assuming that a cultural moment—especially a musical one—is going to rally 33 million people around the flag in unity is a specious supposition at the best of times. That doesn't make that supposition xenophobic or deliberately exclusionary, just short-sighted.

It's simply not possible for the music of one rock band to unite a country, and Downie himself—who railed against the concept of nationalism for years—would have been the first to agree. The human drama of his final years, the new take on the Terry Fox narrative, was what compelled so many Canadians—that doesn't mean those people had to be Tragically Hip fans. Many may have been paying attention to the Hip's music for the first time or were reminded that it left them cold long ago. Undoubtedly, however, many rediscovered what they loved in the first place, and, maybe, some even finally figured out what the fuss is about.

CHAPTER FOURTEEN

IS THE ACTOR HAPPY?

2001: *COKE MACHINE GLOW*

*"You must experiment. You do things in which you eliminate
something which is perhaps essential, but to learn how essential it
is you leave it out. The space then becomes very significant."*

HENRY MOORE, 1986

IN 1999, GORD Downie was restless. He was tired of playing arenas. He'd
been inspired by the opening acts he'd curated for Hip tours and Another
Roadside Attractions. He was writing songs he knew wouldn't fit with
the Hip. He had itches that couldn't be scratched. It was time for artistic
infidelity.

In any other band with 12 years of recording behind them, this wouldn't
be a surprise. It's more unusual when this *doesn't* happen. But inside the
Tragically Hip, it was blasphemy among brothers. Several sources said that
Downie's decision came at a time of poor communication and passive-
aggression, and it caused a degree of discomfort for much of the next
decade. "When Gord started doing solo albums," Rob Baker admitted in
2017, "none of us liked it, because he had a voice with us."

I put the question to Jake Gold: what led to Downie's decision to make
a solo record, and how was it received inside the band? The normally forthcoming Gold paused slightly, gave a steely glare and responded, "I'm not
going to talk about that."

Coke Machine Glow came out in March 2001 and caused as much confusion as it did excitement. The Tragically Hip could still be heard constantly on every classic rock station in Canada; those stations did not play *Coke Machine Glow*, with its dirgey country songs and poetry set to soundscapes, an album where there are only two uptempo songs: one sounds like the Velvet Underground's "White Light / White Heat," the other is a polka with a tuba and banjo. The indie scene was inherently suspicious of a rock star slumming in its world. The new band was scrappy, loose and exploratory, not a tight rock'n'roll machine.

Mainstream press were likewise baffled. "Maybe Downie wanted the creaky-boards feel of a coffee-house poetry reading," wrote the *Kingston Whig-Standard* reviewer (and later Michael Bublé biographer), who cited the "clompy percussion with timid acoustic guitar and Downie's hesitant vocals in an under-produced sound that has the deliberate unfinished feel of a demo tape." The *Globe and Mail* wanted to know "how someone so demanding of his words can be so complacent about the music."

Gord Downie would never make another record like it again. Yet it became one of the most beloved albums in his discography. A popular music blog took its name from the album title. Musicians who played on it say that strangers still ask them about it all the time. *Coke Machine Glow* is to Downie what *Nebraska* is to Bruce Springsteen or *Tonight's the Night* to Neil Young: an album full of songs shunned by radio and rarely performed live, yet adored not only by certain fans but by people uninterested in almost everything else by the artist in question. *Coke Machine Glow* became a secret whispered from one sympathetic ear to another. Like its title, it was a beacon of light in unfamiliar surroundings from a widely recognized brand name.

———

The album was born on a train. Travelling from Kingston to Toronto, Downie asked Steven Drake for ideas about how to make a solo record. Drake told him to just get a good group of people and record it all live. A solo project would inevitably be a home for songs that fell outside of the Tragically Hip's oeuvre. But Drake said Downie was "more interested in a certain combination of people and what that would bring about."

The first person he had in mind was Josh Finlayson of the Skydiggers. "He was really the first friend I made in Toronto," Downie said. "We've been like brothers ever since." It was Finlayson who convinced him the project could work. Drake was hired as producer, engineer and bassist. Recording at the Bathouse was out; Downie wanted something totally fresh. Not a single piece of equipment, not even a guitar, would be borrowed from the Hip's clubhouse.

Downie booked the Gas Station studio, at 53 Fraser Avenue in Toronto's Liberty Village, run by Dale Morningstar and Don Kerr. Kerr was in the Rheostatics and had toured with the Hip on Another Roadside Attraction in 1995 and on an arena tour in 1997. On the last night of that tour, there was an after-party at the studio, which is where Downie first fell in love with the space. Morningstar and Kerr had once been bandmates in the Dinner Is Ruined, an often chaotic, noisy avant-garde band that started out on the outer reaches of grunge, with nods to Sonic Youth, and got progressively stranger with each record. The Gas Station was their playground, stocked with junkyard instruments and odd artifacts. When Kerr left the Dinner Is Ruined, Morningstar and keyboardist John "Dr. Pee" Press continued as a duo until original Rheos drummer Dave Clark signed on. Kerr remained a partner in the Gas Station, a studio that birthed many beloved records of the late '90s, including Thrush Hermit's *Clayton Park*, Neko Case's *Furnace Room Lullaby* and Godspeed You Black Emperor's *Slow Riot for a New Zero Kanada* EP.

In the 1990s, Liberty Village was full of disused factories and loft spaces. It was a corner of Toronto that time forgot, colonized only by film crews and artists looking for maximum space at minimal rent. Today, it's a bustling village of towering condos, prime office space, upscale bars and high-end grocery stores. At the Gas Station in 2000, you still had to load your gear onto an old freight elevator and down a dusty hallway before entering the magical playroom, with its 12-foot-high ceilings and huge windows that offered a panoramic view of the city. "It was a Fibonacci room," says Drake, "meaning the height of the ceiling to the width of the wall was 1:1.618, the Golden Ratio. Those proportions are comforting for people." The acoustics are inherently impeccable in such a room.

Morningstar was assisting Drake with the studio set-up in late March 2000 when he got a call saying the studio was being evicted. The next week, Morningstar staged an anti-gentrification protest outside his landlord's office, which rallied other artists and got some local media coverage. That night, he had a Dinner Is Ruined gig at College Street venue Ted's Wrecking Yard. Having always been the kind of band to walk a tightwire act, with no script or plan, the Dinner Is Ruined was known for having an erratic live show. "DIR is like someone plugs the thing in and you never know if it will hop, buzz, fizzle or explode," said Dave Clark. When they were on fire, however, as they were that night at Ted's, they were mind-blowing. Gord Downie was in the audience that night, witnessing Morningstar, Clark and Press channel their eviction blues into a strange performance piece about the birth of the universe. Downie was grinning in the middle of the room; one could almost see a light bulb going off over his head.

That week was the first of two scheduled sessions for *Coke Machine Glow*, with Kerr on drums and Kevin Hearn on piano. It started out, recalled Hearn, as a series of "very mellow, stoned afternoons." Until it wasn't. "The people directly below the studio were having some sort of eviction party," said Hearn. "They were trashing the place—hurling couches, smashing appliances, throwing bottles at the wall. Gord was trying to do a vocal take, but the noise was too much. He took off his headphones, walked downstairs and calmly walked into their party. I tagged along. Everything stopped when Gord walked in; it was like an old Western movie. Wearing a plaid shirt, jeans and cowboy hat, he politely asked if they could please give us an hour, so he could finish his last vocal take. Everyone in the room, a little shocked, said yes, of course, sorry, et cetera. We went back upstairs and finished his vocal, accompanied by beautiful, reverent silence."

That first session resulted in only two songs, "Chancellor" and "SF Song," along with a rocking, Lou Reed–style take on "Vancouver Divorce" before both Hearn and Kerr had to leave for tour commitments with Barenaked Ladies and Ron Sexsmith, respectively. They were scheduled to return for a second session in June, but the Gas Station was being evicted on May 15. Morningstar called Downie with the bad news; Downie begged to reschedule for any time available before the eviction.

Dave Clark heard about this and knew that Kerr couldn't finish the record. He asked Morningstar to tell Downie he was available if needed. Morningstar was reluctant; he didn't feel he knew Downie well enough to put in a word for a friend. But he did. "*The* Dave Clark?" asked an enthused Downie. "I didn't think he'd be into it—but yes!"

Dave Clark joined the Rheostatics when he was a teenager in 1980. His last three records with the band—1990's *Melville*, 1992's *Whale Music*, 1994's *Introducing Happiness*—garnered a massive word-of-mouth cult audience, comprised mainly of fellow musicians, including Neil Peart of Rush. Clark was one of four very different and charismatic characters in the Rheos, whose live shows would veer from the triumphant to harrowing to downright silly. He would often play around the beat rather than delivering a standard rock pulse.

He joined the Dinner Is Ruined on the day he quit the Rheostatics in 1995. He then focused on his improv band, the Woodchoppers Association, while also doing "different joe jobs: a lot of office cleaning and deliveries, some consulting for music festivals," he said. "I was still delivering *Now* magazine at that point."

Many people didn't understand why Dave Clark would leave the Rheos for the Dinner Is Ruined, or why Gord Downie would possibly hire that band to comprise the majority of his. "With DIR," said Dave Clark, "it gave me the ultimate faith in any sound, any thought: just make it, if you believe in it. Playing with that band, I learned how to give in. I used to delineate between improvisation and playing songs. I was wrong. You can do what you want." That freedom was what Downie went looking for.

When sessions resumed, Morningstar started out plucking the strings of the piano with a guitar pick on "Blackflies" and ended up playing on most of the tracks. "He was like fungus," said Steven Drake, when talking about Morningstar. "He just grew into it."

Musicians sat in a circle. Finlayson and Drake knew the songs; Morningstar and Clark were learning as they went. Overdubs, including vocals, were minimal. Drake conducted the band while playing bass; at the end of a take, he'd run back to the control room to work the board. No one wore headphones except Downie, who used a small set of what Clark described as "airplane Walkman headphones, just to get a bit more attenuation on his vocals. We played at a whisper. The record sounds much bigger than what it is."

"We didn't have any amplification," said Drake. "We were playing at an acoustic level, so we could hear Gord singing in the room. I just had a kick drum mic and a single overhead on the drums. Gord was singing in a BeyerDynamic Ribbon mic from the '50s, the same kind of mic Stan Getz used on his horn for 'Girl From Ipanema.' He was playing his Martin nylon string [acoustic guitar], and he was quite awkward on his guitar."

"I'd never experienced that before," said Clark, "but the sound was phenomenal. The tones are so clear and we're playing together, so it's very dynamic."

"There was a magic on that record," said Morningstar. "There was a map, but I don't think anyone knew the direction. That's not a bad thing; we were just moving forward. Some things just happened. The original title [track] was 'Insomniacs of the World, Goodnight.' That song came about when I was in the other room, jamming away on the pump organ by myself. Gord was walking through and said, 'Hey, is that something? Can I use that?' So he got Steven to come in, mic it up. Gord had his lyrics and they just did it, right then and there. Then they layered on Dave doing some swells and Julie [Doiron] on backing vocals. Gord was so open to stuff like that, the spontaneity of those moments."

Some of those moments were glorious mistakes—mostly from Dale Morningstar. "If Dale plays what sounds like a wrong note at first, he'll lean into that thing until it's the right note," said Clark. "He'll bruise that note until you stop feeling the pain and it starts tasting sweet. He's magical that way." By Divine Right's José Contreras, who played organ on two songs, was there when Morningstar played an atonal, screeching note right before the third verse of "Vancouver Divorce." "I remember Steven Drake: [makes pained face, covers ears] '*Fuckin' HELL,*'" said Contreras. "I was sitting there going, 'That's fucking beautiful.'"

"Dale was the studio rat character," said Drake. "He's a funny guy. I don't know if he was shitting me or not, but I remember I turned to him and said, 'Oh, that's a D.' He said, 'Huh? I don't know what that is.' Then he played a D. If I played it, he could play it, but he didn't know the names."

"What's beautiful about the record is the vulnerability, and surrendering to these people that [Gord] trusted," said Morningstar. "Nobody there sounds like a session player, or like they're phoning it in or following orders. And there are songs like 'Trick Rider': I can't imagine the Hip doing something that delicate. That set of lyrics also strikes me as the strongest."

"Trick Rider" is one of the most beautiful songs about parenting ever written, and the most straightforward, emotionally vulnerable set of lyrics Downie had penned since "Fiddler's Green." It's not particularly original subject matter: the narrator marvels at the innocence of his children, long before the hypocrisies and failures of the future can corrupt their idealism. He cannot bear to watch them perform dangerous, carefree acts, even as he admires their fearlessness. In Downie's hands, of course, the song avoids cliché, and the harmonies with Julie Doiron of Eric's Trip make it even more haunting.

"I absolutely adore 'Trick Rider,' which I think is one of the greatest songs he ever wrote," said Clark. "Julie is amazing on that song. The lyric is heartbreaking. I liked that it addressed being an adult with children. A lot of people hide who they are, and Gord did not. He's a dad. There's nothing more rock'n'roll than being a dad—oh, wait, yes there is: *being a mom!*" Clark's daughter is the same age as Doiron's and Downie's eldest children; all were about five years old at the time of *Coke Machine Glow*. The song would routinely move Clark to tears while playing it live, even 10 years later. Doiron called it "one of the most beautiful songs ever written." She's not wrong.

Doiron was not given much notice before the session; when she got the call, she was leaving for a Swedish tour in two days, so she went to Toronto a day early before her flight. "Trick Rider" just happened to be the song scheduled for that day. "No one said, 'We've been waiting for you to do this one,'" Doiron recalled. She played piano, which she rarely does, only because there were three other guitarists there.

Doiron and Contreras were two of several players outside the core band brought into the main session. Jaro Czerwinec, who played accordion on the Cowboy Junkies' *Trinity Session*, provided a direct link to one of *Coke Machine Glow*'s inspirations. Andy Maize of the Skydiggers played trumpet. Filmmaker Atom Egoyan played classical guitar. Los Lobos drummer Louie Perez co-wrote one song. The Sadies' Travis Good played fiddle and mandolin.

For a record that was supposed to be entirely Hip-free, one guest was more than conspicuous in his presence. Paul Langlois, Downie's oldest friend in the band, contributes his unmistakable harmonies on "Lofty Pines" and "Yer Possessed." It was a last-minute decision. Because the entire album was being recorded to only eight tracks, Travis Good's fiddle got wiped from those two songs to make room for Langlois.

Contreras credited Downie's faith and Drake's expertise with the album's success. "It was incredible, musically," he said. "'Vancouver Divorce' was three takes: every take, different set of lyrics. No lyric book in front of him. Maybe he'd have some papers to look at. But he'd sing a lyric and you'd think, 'That verse is incredible.' Then he'd not do that verse in the next take. And you can't be like, 'Oh, don't forget that verse.' Because these other verses are just as great."

That said, Contreras felt a clash between what he perceived as the straight half of the band—Drake and Finlayson, both coming from musically conservative rock bands—and the weirdoes from the Dinner Is Ruined. "Steve very much believed in the songs and thought it could be a hit record," said Contreras. "Because that's what he does. You can take that really any way you want. There was a lot of tension in the air because Dale and Dave did not click with Steven Drake. I'd had a video hit and I was 29 and Steven pulled me over to get me onto his team: 'C'mon, José, you like hit records, buddy; we want to make a hit record here, don't you think?' Then Dale and Dave did the same thing, pulling me into another room and grouching about 'fucking corporate rock' and how shit it is, and the attitude. There was real tension in the studio, but Gord was either oblivious or rose right above it. Not a word about it, zero."

Contreras was only in the studio two days. The others dispute his version of events. "The sun would be shining in the windows," said Clark. "Everyone was very happy, joyous, very relaxed. Gord and Steve had a vibe together that made sense. There were times when I wasn't sure if Steven was making the right decisions, but I listen to the record now, and it really makes me happy."

"I don't think there was any uneasiness," said Morningstar. "I think we were all trying to harvest those songs. I was trying to play as sparse as I could and not overstep. I was the colour man. That's how I saw myself. It was the first chance I'd had to play with a singer, an outside singer, and really try to play off his voice, or complement it. That's what everyone was trying to do: not step on the music."

"I mean, Steven Drake did an amazing job," said Contreras. "If you listen with the idea that one person in the room was producing and engineering and also in close touch with Gord about what the idea was, *and* he's playing bass while looking around the room, too—and then you listen to the bass playing—you realize he's a fucking master."

———

For his first solo performance outside the Tragically Hip, Gord Downie could not have chosen an environment more unlike the rock clubs where he cut his teeth. That said, it did involve beer.

Held on February 3, 2001, at the newly opened Steam Whistle Brewery in the shadow of the CN Tower, the Do What?! Festival was curated by Dave Clark and Terence Dick of the Woodchoppers Association. Downie was a featured performer, alongside performance artist Sook-Yin Lee, Toronto avant-garde veteran "sound poet" Paul Dutton, dance performances by Andrea Nann and Lisa Prebianca and art installations including one by Reid Diamond of Shadowy Men on a Shadowy Planet, who'd died of cancer months before. Tickets were $10, available only at College Street record store Soundscapes. They sold out immediately. Judging by the dress code of the crowd at this freaky event, a significant majority were mainstream Hip fans unsure what they were in for.

"It was the kind of gig I'd normally do with the Woodchoppers," said Clark, "dancers, singers, visual artists, musicians all together. Gord worked out these dance pieces with Andrea Nann, who is one of the greatest living exponents of modern dance Canada has ever produced. He improvised with the Woodchoppers. We had a huge band, and everyone was dressed up in everything from hockey gear to princess and fairy outfits. Gord kicked it through the post, man. It was really good. I remember some people being beside themselves, freaking out at how much fun it was, and others were just shocked." Nothing about the evening was predictable or rote. Downie looked delighted, completely at ease in this environment.

In July 2001, Downie debuted his "Goddamned Band" with Finlayson, Morningstar and Clark, as well as John "Dr. Pee" Press from the Dinner Is Ruined on keyboards and Julie Doiron, who would alternate between guitar and bass with Finlayson. Their first gig was playing a webcast for the Umbrella Music site. "We'd rehearsed a bit, but I didn't feel like I really knew the songs yet," said Doiron. "I went up to Gord and said, 'I'm sorry I'm so nervous! I'm freaking out. What am I doing here? Why me?' He said, 'Julie, you're here because I need you here.' He could have easily had any studio musician who would know all the parts. But he didn't want that. I don't think he's ever looked for that. He wants people he wants to be around, creative people, not necessarily technically good. That's what makes working with him so cool, because he trusts whatever it is you're going to do. I've never been given any guidance. He's like, 'You know what to do.'"

That was followed by a few select dates at summer folk festivals, starting the weekend of July 27 at the Calgary Folk Festival and the Hillside Festival in Guelph, Ontario. Those shows threw a lot of Hip fans for a loop, even if they had bought *Coke Machine Glow* a few months earlier. "Sure, some hardcore Hip fans just hated it," said Morningstar. "But I'm sure some thought, 'This is different, this is great.' People didn't shout out for Hip tunes. We thought that might happen, but it didn't at all. Gord was just proud—proud of the band and what we were doing. He would say stuff like, 'I love this band. I believe in this band. This is my band. I'm really good at putting bands together.' He didn't give a fuck what anyone thought. He wanted to make it good from his own perspective and from ours."

The Goddammed Band, later renamed the Country of Miracles, was a relief valve for Downie. If the Hip had become entrenched in an all-too-familiar working method, with audiences cheering the loudest for songs written 10 years prior, this new band had something to prove every night. And they were fearless players.

"Things would get *outside*," said Clark. "That band was able to go in on a dime. Lots of vocals, some really bluegrassy stuff. I ended up playing tuba; we all played different things. When we went to New York City, we'd play in the middle of the audience. We'd stretch things out; Gord would extemporize. Every time we'd go on tour, there would be a lot of taking the piss out of each other and loads of jokes. After gigs, we'd put on some music and dance and sing on the bus. We'd hang out and talk about music. Everybody in that band is a hyper nerd."

It wasn't just Downie learning from his band; the exchange was mutual on all fronts. Clark praised Doiron for influencing his own playing. "She's a monster of a musician," he said. "She's one of the hardest-working musicians I've ever met and manages to raise a gigantic family of kids. She had this vibe, this groove, this pocket she could get into, which helped me out as a player a lot. I tend to get adrenalized and can push things too hard. She made me aware of some things that could work better, and I thought, 'I should listen to this person. She knows what she's talking about.'"

It was also a band of singers. Having just toured with Kate Fenner as a temporary member of the Hip, Downie relished the even bigger harmonies his new band could provide. So did Clark. "I love singing with people, probably more than I love drumming," he said. "Sometimes I'd be onstage and it would be like, 'Holy fuck, man, I'm singing backups with Gord Downie!' I'd look around, and there were all my friends I'd known for years and we're onstage together and the whole thing's bouncing and we're having a good time. Then my brain would shut off and I'd start listening and be part of the band again."

Cover songs appeared in many of the sets, the first time since he had a record contract that Downie regularly sang other people's songs live. The Goddammned Band did some Randy Newman, some Bob Dylan, some Taj Mahal, some CCR. And one particularly memorable version of Neil Young's "Tonight's the Night."

"We ended up headlining the Edmonton Folk Festival, at night," Clark recalled. "The amphitheatre there is on what looks like a ski hill, and people light candles so it's like looking at stars at night. The band before us was

Baaba Maal's big band, from Africa, an 18-piece band with dancers. I remember standing at the side of the stage with Dale and saying, 'Jesus. Who thought *this* was a good idea, to put us on after these guys?' But we got up and had, to my mind, the best set of the tour. We started with 'Tonight's the Night.' Gord walked out there and just grabbed it—every night."

When there was time, the Dinner Is Ruined booked shows for off nights in the same town. Again, Edmonton was a highlight. At a gig at the Liquid Lounge, Finlayson joined them on bass, and Gord commandeered the mic while the five of them improvised an entire set of music. In an odd twist, said Morningstar, "One big DIR fan after was like, 'Ah, man.' He was bummed out that Gord Downie was on our stage. I'm like, 'Oh, c'mon.'"

Something similar happened in Yellowknife. "They put us up in a house for five days," recalled Morningstar. "One night, a Monday or Tuesday, we went down to the local watering hole, where they had an open mic. We went and said, 'Can we hit the stage?' Josh was home sleeping. We took over that room. It was Gord freestyling. It was the DIR with Julie on bass. The crowd had no idea Gord Downie was going to play. They were all standing on tables. No songs, we were just jamming. It was the peak of his freestyling, just going for it."

Whether or not Downie knew what he had been looking for when he stepped outside the framework of the Hip, he had most certainly found it. This was a new family of freaks, of dancers, of kindred spirits. Even if they never took precedence over the Tragically Hip, even if they only did two other records and tours over the next 16 years, these were people with whom Downie felt at home. The feeling was more than mutual.

"The time we spent together was special and intense and instructive," said Clark. "More than anything, we developed a lifelong friendship. I don't have to see Julie for years and when I see her, it's beautiful. I go out walking with Josh, and I start laughing before we even open our mouths. All those people who played on the first record: Andy, Don, José, Kevin—they're all friends. My whole point for playing music personally is to commune with people. I don't go to church; I'm not a religious person. Where I go to church is when I get onstage with people. I want to be with people. I want to sing. I want that endorphin rush. I want to be a part of something. With Gord and that crew, there was a real community and a real family and I'm deeply grateful for it."

CHAPTER FIFTEEN

A HEART-WARMING MOMENT FOR LITERATURE

WORDS AND GUITARS

*"Like a jazz musician with the word as her instrument, reading and performing
these poems is an extension of the creative process for the work . . . These
poems breathe, they are alive. Sit quietly with them, read them aloud or
shout them in public places. And remember: always a poem, once a book."*

LILLIAN ALLEN, *WOMEN DO THIS EVERY DAY*, 1993

COKE MACHINE GLOW, the album, confounded many people when
it came out in 2001. That the singer in the Tragically Hip had put out a
solo record was newsworthy enough. That he simultaneously released a
book of poetry, with the same title and cover design, was something else
entirely. For the first two weeks both were on sale, they were available
only as a bundle—and they sold 10,000 copies in 36 hours. When they were
put on sale separately, the book sold another 10,000 copies, a total that
exceeded sales for Michael Ondaatje's then most recent collection, 1998's
Handwriting. Poets were feeling particularly sensitive to this news: it had
been only three years since pop star Jewel released her first and only book
of poetry, which was also a bestseller, despite scathing reviews.

What was this big rock star doing slumming with literary company
equally revered and reviled, in the least commercial literary medium possible? What does a songwriter know about poetry? Isn't it a completely
different medium? Didn't Jim Morrison ruin this for everyone?

But Gord Downie was hardly a pariah among poets. *Coke Machine Glow*
came out the same year as the inaugural Griffin Poetry Prize, one of the

richest literary awards in the world, presented every year to one Canadian and one international poet. Downie performed at the first gala. But his book was not nominated—that would have been quite a coup, for a writer's first book to take a place beside Anne Carson and Don McKay on a shortlist. To that crowd, Downie's work may have been a curiosity at best. A rock star with a poetry book? Yeah, right—why don't we just give Bob Dylan the Nobel Prize for Literature. Oh, wait . . .

———

Two young Canadian poets, one in Ottawa and one in Toronto, were talking on the phone in 1998.

"Did you hear the new Tragically Hip single?"

"No, why?"

"It goes, 'Don't tell me what the poets are doing.'"

"Uh oh."

Both those poets, Ken Babstock and David O'Meara, were Hip fans and got to know Gord Downie in the coming years—they were even referenced in his lyrics. The first track on *Phantom Power* features the tongue-in-cheek chorus, the one that so concerned the two young poets in question. "Poets" is one of the most straight-ahead, Stonesy rock songs in the Hip's catalogue, with nothing remotely abstract in the music that might deter people suspicious of poetry. The chorus quickly became a cliché referenced countless times in headlines and stories about Downie and/or other lyricists and poets.

Poetry has a bad rap in our culture. Novelist David Mitchell says, "Too many people think it's an elitist pastime, like polo; or twee verse; or brain-bruising verbal Sudoku. Poetry isn't these things—or if it is, you're reading the wrong stuff. Like music, you need to explore a little to find poets whose work speaks to you, and then you have a lifelong friend who'll tell you truths you didn't know you knew."

Rock'n'roll culture in particular doesn't want to know what poets are doing. The exceptions are rare: Bob Dylan, Lou Reed, Patti Smith. Though Leonard Cohen and Joni Mitchell wrote poetry and ran in rock circles, no one would argue they made rock music, no matter how many rock musicians they influenced. Anyone after Patti Smith was either a) nowhere near the mainstream, like Vic Chesnutt or Neko Case, or b) a cut-up surrealist, like Michael Stipe or Beck or Stephen Malkmus, more in love with the sound of language than its content. Pop music fans who wanted poetry were far more likely to find it in hip-hop than rock music.

Except in Canada, where Gord Downie's lyrics leapt out of radio playlists not just because of wordplay, or because of references both known and mysterious, but because his use of language was so evocative, so rich with meaning and allusion—coded messages that often deserved to be deeply examined. Sure, some were more successful than others. Some were plainspoken and should never be read on the page: "Fifty Mission Cap," "Courage." Some were impenetrable nonsense, such as, ironically enough, "Poets." But with each passing album, his language became as compelling on the page as in the music—more so, in some cases.

"The greatest compliment you can give a poet is to say she's a rock star," says Damian Rogers. "The greatest compliment that you can give a musician is to say he's a poet. Gord Downie is both."

If anyone, Rogers should know. The Detroit-born writer has been deeply involved in the Canadian poetry scene since she moved from Chicago to Toronto in 2002. She's been a poetry editor at the *Walrus* magazine and at House of Anansi press, the creative director of the youth program Poetry in Voice and co-curates the Basement Revue with Jason Collett, a performance series that mixes music and the written word. She's also sung on a Smog record, co-written with Jim Cuddy and is married to drummer Mike Belitsky of the Sadies. "I think of Gord as part of a continuum of great Canadian songwriters who are actually poets," she says. "When I was growing up, it was Leonard Cohen, Gordon Lightfoot, Joni Mitchell. That's who influenced me as a poet."

Not surprisingly, Downie has cited all those as key influences, as well as David Byrne, Van Morrison and, yes, Jim Morrison; Downie sang a few Doors tunes in his early days. Lou Reed's 1973 album *Berlin* was also big. "We gathered around that record like you would around a campfire," said Downie at a Reed tribute in 2013, where he performed "How Do You Think It Feels." "We inhabited that record."

His literary education came a bit later, in university. His friend Mark Mattson recalls first meeting Downie at the Prince George Hotel in Kingston, with Queen's classmate and future Governor General's Award–winning poet Steven Heighton, while blues band the Lincolns played in the back room, and students in the front bar discussed Margaret Atwood and Northrop Frye. "When I first started reading poetry, it was Irving Layton, Leonard Cohen and Al Purdy, and then it kind of moved into Sam Shepard and Raymond Carver," said Downie in 2001. "In every case I was finding things that I could relate to: the plainspoken language of the last two, and Purdy is very welcoming, obviously. Then I moved into almost anything I could get my hands on, guys like John Ashbery, very impenetrable. Then I got into this real great, Canadian, mostly first-time poet jag with Ken Babstock, Paul Vermeersch, Chris Chambers and Rob McLennan. That was the stuff that was really humbling to read."

It's Al Purdy to whom Downie most often gets compared, less so for an approach to verse than for the fact that both men defy the stereotype of a poet being an aloof academic, either twee or in tweed. Both were commanding orators who felt perfectly at home performing in pubs.

Margaret Atwood's foreword to a Purdy collection published in 2000 could just as well apply to Downie. Writing about his breakthrough work, 1965's *The Cariboo Horses*, Atwood wrote of Purdy, "I found that the drunk in the bar was also a major storyteller and mythmaker, though still wearing his offhand and indeed rather shabby disguise. This is poetry for the spoken voice par excellence—not an obviously rhetorical voice, but an anecdotal voice, the voice of the Canadian vernacular. Yet not only that, either, for no sooner has Purdy set up his own limits than he either transcends them or subverts them . . . In a Purdy poem, high diction can meet the scrawl on the washroom wall, and as in a collision between matter and antimatter, both explode."

Perhaps Purdy's most famous poem is "At the Quinte Hotel," set in Belleville, just west of Kingston. In it, the narrator, a self-professed "sensitive man," attempts to joke with the bartender, comparing his beer to half fart and half horse piss and all "wonderful yellow flowers." He gets pulled into a bar fight, which ends with him sitting on the thug and saying, "Violence will get you nowhere this time, chum. Now you take me: I am a sensitive man and would you believe I write poems?" He wins over the crowd with a recitation, moving them to tears in what he says is a "heart-warming moment for Literature."

It's easy to see why "Quinte Hotel" appealed to Downie: it's funny, it's unpretentious, there is the threat of violence and it's set in exactly the kind of century-old Canadian Shield hotel bar where the Tragically Hip spent much of their youth. In 2002, Downie acted in a five-minute short film based on the poem, with Purdy's own recitation on the soundtrack, and Downie performed it himself in the 2015 documentary *Al Purdy Was Here*.

When the Tragically Hip performed on MuchMusic's *Intimate and*

Interactive in June 2000, when Downie would have been working on *Coke Machine Glow*, they performed the song "Tiger the Lion," which quotes the writing of composer and philosopher John Cage extensively. Downie dedicated the song to Al Purdy and recited most of "Quinte Hotel" over Rob Baker's guitar solo.

The comparison of Downie to Purdy doesn't scratch below the surface, argues Andrew Whiteman of Broken Social Scene. "Gord's lyrics aren't like Purdy because Gord is going somewhere more intellectual; his language is elevated in ways Purdy's wouldn't be. Gord's lyrics are not everyman. Jim Cuddy and guys like that, they're everyman writers. They would never write something with the kind of urgency heard in 'Freak Turbulence' from *Music @ Work*. Purdy is a traditional poet in that he is recollecting; with Gord, you're there—it's happening now, like with [New York School poet] Frank O'Hara."

Trying to situate Downie among other lyricists or poets is a mug's game, says poet Damian Rogers. "I think of whose voice sounds authentically their own, who sounds the least like they're trying to be someone else. As a poet and a huge music fan, that's always more telling to me than comparing two different aesthetics. Gord has an incredibly consistent body of work. So does [American songwriter] Will Oldham, but they're radically different, and I wouldn't try to think of comparing them in any way that would be evaluative. The Tragically Hip as a band represents something in Canada, a kind of unapologetic inhabitation of this place, elevating that to the highest level in a way that is difficult to compare. Someone like Stephen Malkmus [of Pavement], as a lyricist, can't compete in terms of a large-scale resonance that the Hip has been able to achieve." Downie was a big Malkmus fan. "He seemed to eschew lyrics and make them seem like they're less than meaningless, but they're so obviously not to me," said Downie. "They're so beautiful and strange."

Malkmus, though he works with the American poet David Berman, admits that while he's deeply influenced by poetry, his lyrics are not to be read as such. "I don't really know where the songs are coming from often," says Malkmus. "Many of the best things I made up were just off the top of my head. With lyrics for me, it's usually musically based. It's not really poetry- or writer-based. It's rock-based. It doesn't mean that I'm aping rock lyrics, but I'm writing from a music standpoint. I'm thinking more of music heroes, if they're in my mind. Not William Blake or John Ashbery— sometimes maybe I thought of him a little bit. Or Wallace Stevens. I don't even really fully understand either of them." Downie, on the other hand, based the 2002 Hip song "The Dire Wolf" on Wallace Stevens's "Sea Surface Full of Clouds."

"No one else writes like Gord," says the Weakerthans' John K. Samson, one of the only rock songwriters in Downie's wake who could be considered a poet. "He can work in the abstract and still somehow be really specific. He lets parts of his consciousness in [in ways] that most songwriters aren't able to do, myself included. I don't feel like I have that access to the surreal and the somehow beautifully meaningful non sequitur that fits perfectly. I can never figure out how he does that. Still, somehow the songs feel rooted in a place. [Fiction writer] George Saunders said something about how the role of the writer is to build a more detailed world. That applies to Gord's body of work. There's something really political about that: a more detailed world is a more complicated and complex world, and therefore a more empathetic one. Gord's lyrics are exceptionally empathetic. The fact that they cross all those cultural cliques and boundaries really amplifies that."

Downie was a big Samson fan. In 2000, he read the lyric booklet for the Weakerthans' *Left and Leaving* before listening to the CD. "It was interesting even the way it was laid out," he said. "It had a sensibility with which it spoke, that of a poet. It seemed like prose, and I read it accordingly. Then, hearing the music and where the rhymes fell and where the obvious line breaks were, it altered it a bit. That was part of the permission process for me. I think I'm a better writer now."

Shadrach Kabango, a.k.a. the rapper Shad, finds Downie to be a writer of "precision. I feel like the impression I'm left with is what he intended. John K. Samson would be another example of that. In hip-hop, there are a lot of people like that, from Black Thought to Kendrick Lamar, and across genres, [country singer] Jason Isbell would be another. With all those, you can tell that this person really nailed it. They conveyed emotionally what they set out to do."

"There are so many levels going on in his lyrics," says David O'Meara, whose 1999 poem "The War Against Television" was quoted in Downie's "Leave," from 2002's *In Violet Light*. "If you look at a lot of lyrics in popular music, it's facile and just there to fit the music. Downie had a way bigger game in his songs. Images and bits of narrative lead you toward independent thought. 'We live to survive our paradoxes'—you can think about that line for days. Whenever I hear it, I think about what it means to bounce it off my own life, maybe where I was 20 years ago and what I'm planning on doing next. He wants people to think beyond the everyday, to think about the gift we've got from being here. He wants us to think about it, not just feed it to us."

That is the very essence of literature, Northrop Frye argued in his 1963 Massey Lecture. "There is no direct address in literature," he wrote. "It isn't what you say but how you say it that is important. The literary writer isn't giving information, either about a subject or a state of mind: he's trying to let something take on its own form, whether it's a poem or novel or whatever." Let's imagine Frye might have included song lyrics in that mix as well—maybe even some lyrics from *Man Machine Poem* that quote Frye directly.

Downie described his lyrics as "user-friendly. Here they are: you deal with them. Sometimes that's not good enough for certain people. Maybe if you don't understand what they're about, that's okay. Even if you get a sense of the mood or the landscape or a character or even if it takes you off somewhere so you're not listening to lyrics by the end of the song, then it's succeeded. It functions as sound."

That's true of most song lyrics, where a clever line or catchy rhyme rolls off the tongue in unexpected ways—that's what makes one lyricist stand above another, like Dan Bejar of Destroyer. The best songwriters can tell a story or encapsulate a theme with just a few lines, but for most listeners, lyrics are fleeting, ephemeral, blink-and-you-miss-them while a song plays on the radio, or in the background, or over a PA system in a crowded venue. In those situations, one key line might be all a song needs—the rest functions, as Downie said, as sound.

Or more. Superfan Hugh Larkin from Livonia, Michigan, says, "Gord's lyrics and the Hip's music really did educate me, or bring me to a higher level. I'm not much of a reader or writer. Before the Hip, I never listened to lyrics much. I was the kind of guy who just knew the first few lines and the chorus. When I started going on [fan site] Hipbase, I started thinking that there was a lot more to this band. I started to relate more to the Canadian fans, because I could see why they were so passionate. After I'd been a fan for two or three years, I listened to the music over and over again, I literally know maybe 85 per cent of the lyrics by heart."

Downie gave fans like Larkin a lot to chew on—and in many cases, sent people to the library (in pre-Google days). For someone growing up in a small rural town, as songwriter Hawksley Workman did, artists like the Hip or Bruce Cockburn or David Bowie were gateways to a bigger world. "I was always interested in these larger, bigger figures who had their fingers reaching into the human experience—especially for a teenager, it felt so grand and authentic. That always came from the Hip for me. It wasn't somebody's rehearsed party repartee. I'm a high school dropout, and these guys [like Downie and Cockburn] read all the books I probably should have and gleaned them all with substance. Gord has this scholarly command with lines like 'football, Kennedy-style'—you're always feeling you're dealing with someone with a severely developed, muscular understanding of things. There was never any sense that this guy was a pretender in any way."

"He's always paddling forward as a writer," says Samson. "There is no recycling, like other writers do—like I certainly do. I always go into listening to a new record by Gord solo or with the Hip and think, 'Well, I know what this is going to be, lyrically.' Then as every song starts, I think, 'Oh, I have no idea where that comes from.' He has this entirely original voice, both literal and metaphorical."

That's not a universal opinion, of course. A 2012 concert review in the *Vancouver Sun* read, "Comparing this guy as a poet to Leonard Cohen is akin to comparing Steven Seagal and Daniel Day-Lewis as actors. But he gets the job done and often is entertaining."

One of the Hip's producers admitted he found Downie's lyrical left turns unnecessary. "Gord and I had a lot of discussion at the beginning about lyrics—and then we didn't," he said. "Everyone in the band would diplomatically comment on each other's musical stuff, but you can't talk to Gord about the lyrics. When the band said, 'Hey Gord, that one's really good,' he would change it. Why? I find simplicity to be the highest form of art, in a lot of ways. Art needs to be; you walk into a room, there's a painting, and you feel it or you don't. I don't know what Picasso did between 1938 and 1939, and I don't give a shit: do you feel something or not? The Hip are lucky in that some people are going to pay attention to their records no matter what, but there's an arrogance to that, too."

"Overall you get this sense of an intriguing artist you want to understand, because of how obviously intentional he is," says Shad. "I'm thinking of the line [from 'Flamenco'], 'Maybe a prostitute could teach you how to take a compliment.' He just leaves that there. There could be two more lines after that in that verse, but he leaves you wondering what is going on with that character that he would say that. It's charming and funny."

"Right from the outset, I felt like Gord built so much room into his songs," says Samson. "He made me think of songwriting as full of boundless possibilities, that a song could really contain multitudes."

"His songs are intimate," says Andrew Whiteman, who adapted the works of American poet Alice Notley into music for his band AroarA. "In some tunes, it's the voice of a lover, like in 'Bobcaygeon.' But in 'Locked in the Trunk of a Car,' it's like, 'Hey buddy, the shit is going down.' He often starts in the middle of a caper or a caper is just about to happen or just did happen, and he's pulling you in close to let you know what the fuck just went on. The urgency of his phrasing is so key."

"He talks about some existential things," says O'Meara, "everything from 'Locked in the Trunk of a Car' to 'Nautical Disaster,' things about crucial life decisions and crises. Yet behind it, there is a great tune going on. One of the strengths of the band is that they often create more of an atmosphere than a song, a sound that creates space for Downie. Like 'It's a Good Life,' the music is just a cloud that builds at certain points, but Downie gets what he wants to say in there."

One person who doesn't pay much attention to Downie's lyrics is Rob Baker. "I don't generally read the lyrics anyway," he said in 2002. "I just listen to it and go for a more intuitive understanding of the song. Gord comes up with fascinating lyrics, but I don't think you need to know he was inspired by [Raymond Carver] in order to enjoy the song."

But what is Gord Downie without Rob Baker and the rest of the band behind him? Someone once asked Bob Dylan if he was a songwriter or a poet; Dylan famously answered, "I'm a song-and-dance man." Before 2001, Downie would have said the same, without hesitation. With *Coke Machine Glow*, the book, Downie was decidedly casting his lot as a poet.

———

Oh look, there's Bob Dylan again. You can't have this discussion without him, Nobel Prize or otherwise. He forever changed the parameters of the popular song, in the way Jackson Pollock changed painting, in the way Miles Davis changed music more than once. Dylan's influence ranges from the Beatles to Kendrick Lamar and everything in between, even to artists who don't count themselves as Dylan fans. Leonard Cohen would never have written a song if Bob Dylan didn't make him think it was possible to do so. Joni Mitchell, Gordon Lightfoot, Neil Young: none would be possible without Dylan. But you already know that.

Because Dylan was so revolutionary, because he drew direct inspiration from beat poetry and because baby boomers like to think they rewrote every rulebook in existence, it came to be argued that Dylan was not just a songwriter, but a poet. That his songs demanded much closer inspection than Woody Guthrie or Chuck Berry or Smokey Robinson. That his works be included in curricula.

In 2016, Dylan was awarded the Nobel Prize in Literature. It's safe to say that no one saw that coming. He was the first American to win it since Toni Morrison in 1993. Though it had been given to poets and playwrights before, it had never been given to a songwriter. If the prize was going to go to an American poet, why did it not got to long-shunned but highly influential John Ashbery? (Ashbery died in 2017, which made the Nobel decision even more infuriating for Dylan's detractors; Nobels are not awarded posthumously.) Bestowing the Nobel upon Dylan seemed to answer the age-old question about whether or not song lyrics are poetry. Or did it?

"Lyrics are not poetry," says Andrew Whiteman, who has worked with publisher Book Thug to pair poets with musicians. "I don't care if you're Bob Dylan: you're not a poet. Dylan is a master lyricist, master songwriter. Lou Reed is also a student of poetry—but he's not a poet, he's a songwriter."

"Is Bob Dylan a writer?" asks Dave Bidini. "Yes. Are his lyrics and songs among the greatest in the 20th-century musical canon? Yes. Should his work be recognized as literature? No . . . the lyric dances with voice and instrument while prose is left to stand naked against a tree. The lyric hides its weaknesses through melody, while prose has to be strong enough to withstand the vacuum of its own existence. Bad lyrics can be good lyrics"—one could cite dozens of cringe-worthy examples, the Beatles being the most obvious, though Bidini cites AC/DC—"but bad prose is usually just that."

"I'm a Dylan fan," tweeted Scottish novelist Irvine Welsh the day of the Nobel announcement, "but this is an ill-conceived nostalgia award wrenched from the rancid prostates of senile, gibbering hippies." Salman Rushdie, who once wrote lyrics for a U2 song, was on Team Dylan. "From Orpheus to Faiz, song and poetry have been closely linked," he tweeted. "Dylan is the brilliant inheritor of the bardic tradition. Great choice." Many American poets expressed their support for the decision, including former U.S. poet laureates Billy Collins, Rita Dove and Juan Felipe Herrera.

One of the knocks against Dylan's Nobel was that his words are effective only when performed, when sung—ideally by Dylan himself—where vocal inflections and phrasing can be as evocative and important as the words themselves. Because that's what music is: it's not the notes, it's how you play them.

"Gord's lyrics work on paper as poetry, 100 per cent," says Shad. "And as someone who performs lyrics myself—this is my total bias—but I think there's an added degree of difficulty writing lyrics. There's stuff I've written where I think, 'I've totally got this right on the page.' Then it takes me forever to get it right in the studio. I don't really understand someone who writes poetry turning up their nose at lyricism like it's not poetry. A lot of the time it is—with a higher degree of difficulty. It's really hard to deliver certain lyrics right. Gord does on record, certainly, but onstage he's a beast."

"There is a common sense that poetry exists in a world of pure language, but a poem is, in fact, both the music and the words," wrote poet and book critic Craig Morgan Teicher in the *New Republic*. "Poetry's sonic aspects—such as syllable sounds, rhyme, rhythm, assonance, dissonance and meter—are meant to accompany the content, to set the mood, to refer to and elicit a sensory experience related to the emotions and images of the poem. Dylan's lyrics alone don't compare to a poem, but a complete song—words, music, arrangement, instrumentation, all of it taken together—does. No, Dylan isn't a writer of literary books. But perhaps no living artist has shaped the American soul, or plumbed its depths, as profoundly as Bob Dylan. And what's literature for if not that?" Transplant that same argument to Canada, and we'd be talking about Gord Downie.

Should we be delineating lyrics from poetry? "As soon as you draw a line in the sand somewhere," says poet and critic Paul Vermeersch, "someone will come along and blur it and do something innovative. Songwriting and poetry are certainly related on some level. You don't have to go far down the street to get from poetry like Amiri Baraka to a recording artist like Gil Scott-Heron. They're pretty close together on that continuum. But Amiri Baraka might have more in common with James Baldwin, and Gil Scott-Heron might have more in common with Chuck D."

In 1982, Jamaican-Canadian dub poet Lillian Allen sold 8,000 copies of her debut collection, *Rhythm an' Hardtimes*, and did so independently—those are bestseller numbers in the world of Canadian poetry. She later set some of those verses to music, on the Juno-winning reggae album *Revolutionary Tea Party*, on which the musical cadence of her voice is a key part of her poetry.

Leonard Cohen is the biggest bridge in this debate, as someone whose literary credentials were in place well before he wrote his first song: he published two novels and several books of poetry—one of which won the Governor General's Award shortly after he released his debut album. His 1993 collection, *Stranger Music*, compiled both poems and song lyrics as one body of work, which could be seen as either a deliberate artistic choice, or simply a crassly commercial one.

Then there is the spoken word movement of the late '90s, which blurred lines between poetry and performance. It rose and faded relatively quickly, but is still practised by the likes of Penticton's Shane Koyczan. "The thing about spoken word is that it's meant to be heard in the moment," says David O'Meara. "It has to be more transparent. Its strength isn't subtlety. Whereas with a poem on a page, you want to sit there and read it two or three times and pick up new things each time, because you have the luxury of sitting with it. If you don't get a spoken word piece right away, it has failed. And when you read that stuff on the page, it can feel flat. It's about different genres in the same art form, like cubist paintings versus realism. They bring different strengths to the presentation."

Rollie Pemberton, the Polaris Prize–shortlisted rapper who performs as Cadence Weapon, was appointed poet laureate of his hometown of Edmonton in 2009. If rock lyricists have trouble being taken seriously, rappers have an even bigger hill to climb in the world of poetry. "I caught a lot of flak," he says. "At that time, I was arguably one of the best-known artists coming out of Edmonton, so who better to represent the word coming out of Edmonton than the rapper, right? The previous poet laureate thought it was a joke. He didn't come to my appointment. But the other previous poet laureate, Alice Major, did come, and she was very supportive. Some people get it, some people don't. Even at the time, 2009, I felt this was such a dated, tired way of seeing rap. I didn't think anyone in the world still felt like that.

"The *Globe and Mail* had this thing where they put my lyrics beside Shakespeare, but the lyrics would be from one of my party tracks. I'm like, 'This is totally not fair! Why don't you get one of Shakespeare's scribblings on a napkin?!' But the backlash I got really pushed me to be a better lyricist." Pemberton published his first book of poetry, *Magnetic Days*, in 2013.

———

Coke Machine Glow shared a title and a cover design with the book of the same name, which made it appear to be mere merchandising. It did include some lyrics from the album, but also some lyrics that would appear in later songs, and a lot of material from his sketchbooks that he sculpted into poems, with the help of editor Susan Roxborough. Downie wanted to be challenged; he encouraged her to question every line. He admitted that he had to consciously stop hearing musical phrases while looking over his notes. "That can be done by just pulling out a well-placed rhyme," he said. "Once you do that, the whole thing comes tumbling down and you can reconstruct it."

Downie had always carried a notebook with him, since he was a kid. "I really do like collecting words, lines, sentences, billboards—it's happening all the time," he said. "If you're listening to conversations, people are doing it all the time: the language they select for the choices they make. It's fascinating and it's all kind of beautiful. That's how you can make the ordinary ecstatic—and the other way around, I suppose." His bandmates would often say they recognized their own conversations and road observations in Hip lyrics.

Some of the poems in the book *Coke Machine Glow*, like his lyrics, were written on the road. But he also craved a more disciplined writing practice, working from 10 p.m. to two a.m. every night after his kids went to bed and the house was quiet. "I went to bed grumbling some nights, reluctant other nights," he said. "I would go over in my mind what constituted a good night or a bad night. I wouldn't know a seminal moment if it pissed on me, but it became interesting because I'd never really thought about how to feed your head properly."

His wife and children are present in *Coke Machine Glow* in ways they are often not in Hip songs. One poem, "L. vs. Al," finds Downie reading Purdy's *Cariboo Horses* while cradling his infant son. Downie often quoted Tess Gallagher, the poet and widow to one of his favourite writers, Raymond Carver; in the introduction to a posthumous Carver collection, she said that poetry was a chance to be ample and grateful to those people dearest to your heart. "I use that as words to live by," said Downie.

Hugh MacLennan would agree. The author argued that a writer "must feel that he is writing for friends if what he writes is to be good. If he pretends to write only for himself, he lies, or lets his pride deceive him. He must convince himself that a personal relationship exists between himself and individual members of his audience. He must think of those individuals as valuable personally, each a person whose soul is inviolate . . . The greater [literary art] is, the more intimate it is. The more universally it comes to be loved, the more local has been its origin." That would be advice Downie would take directly to heart on one of his final albums, 2017's deeply personal *Introduce Yerself.*

Did *Coke Machine Glow* work as a book of poetry rather than a footnote to Downie's recorded legacy? It received mostly positive reviews, with more than a few "don't quit your day job" comments. "Unless I miss my guess," wrote Vit Wagner in the *Toronto Star*, "the poetry readers of this country—that little but loyal cadre dedicated to the careful dissection of distilled dispatches from Christopher Dewdney, Lorna Crozier, Roo Borson et al—haven't been praying quietly for the day when they, too, can marvel at the mind behind the Tragically Hip's lyrical genius, without having to endure the three-guitar assault that usually accompanies it . . . As poets go, Downie is a darn good songwriter."

Some poets were more forgiving than the pop critics. "[Downie's] gentle irony and clever conceptual turns are thoroughly contemporary and undeniably original," wrote poet Kevin Connolly in *Eye Weekly*, adding that the book "possess[es] a distinct, personal vision and reintroduces whimsy and humour to an art form often hobbled by its own self-importance—laudable achievements for any first book."

"I found it very interesting, but I read it the same way I would Nick Cave's lyrics," says David O'Meara. "It's hard for them to exist without the music. It reads like a sketchbook. It's more successful than a lot of songwriters' books, though."

A particularly damning review came from *Quill & Quire*, a widely read trade magazine for the book industry. It was written by Paul Vermeersch, who argued that the book would not have been published were it not for Downie's celebrity. "On the whole, the poems in *Coke Machine Glow* are lyrically, structurally and stylistically weak, rife with clichés . . . and occasionally garnished with exhausted rhymes," he wrote. "I even have to wonder how many of these poems are actually stillborn song lyrics recycled, however unsuccessfully, as poetry."

Years later, Vermeersch's opinion hasn't changed. "I don't want to be a Grinch," he says. "I do think Downie is in the highest class of songwriters and lyricists. His gifts are no small thing, and he's certainly influential and deserving of the highest praise. But if you ask me specifically about this work as a book, I think it's not successful. The phenomenon of these rock stars who turn poet—and it's usually just for one book—comes down to a matter of access, like travelling to Nepal or skydiving or something. It's just something they've always wanted to do, and now they have the ability to do it and someone's willing to pay for it. I don't want to make a declaration about whether or not Billy Corgan's *Blinking with Fists* is legitimate poetry. Sure it is: it's just not very good."

Don't people like Downie provide a gateway for new readers to discover poetry? "I don't know that the audience he reached with that book overlaps much with people who are reading Karen Solie or other literary poets in Canada," says Vermeersch. "I don't think he brought more attention to Canadian poets, and I don't think he distracted attention away from them, either. I don't think it was the same audience. The primary audience for that book was Tragically Hip fans, who would have picked it up as extended liner notes for the album."

"I hardly know anyone who reads poetry," said Downie. "So, in a moment of vanity, I think it'll be cool if *Coke Machine Glow* means more people will go into the poetry section of the bookstore . . . How much humility is there in actually making something that has no demand? No one needs this. No one requires it. I just want people to go buy more poetry. Poetry characterizes a nation, and if Canadian poetry doesn't rule, then Canada doesn't."

Who was the bestselling Canadian poet of the next generation? In 2017, 25-year-old Torontonian Rupi Kaur, who got her start posting poems to Instagram, sold 2.5 million copies worldwide of her debut collection, *Milk and Honey*. It was the bestselling book in the U.S. that year—not just the bestselling book of poetry, but beating out fiction and non-fiction titles alike. Critics howled.

CHAPTER SIXTEEN

AS MAKESHIFT AS WE ARE

2002–05: *IN VIOLET LIGHT,*
BATTLE OF THE NUDES, IN BETWEEN EVOLUTION

*"Remember when we had them all on the run / and the night we
saw the midnight sun / Remember saying things like 'we'll sleep
when we're dead' / And thinking this feeling would never end"*

JAPANDROIDS, "YOUNGER US"

"IT'S A GOOD Life if You Don't Weaken." It's the title of the first single
from 2002's *In Violet Light*. It's the title of a 1996 graphic novel by Guelph,
Ontario, cartoonist Seth. It's an oft-quoted aphorism from the 1958 novel
Saturday Night and Sunday Morning by British writer Alan Sillitoe. It's a
truism that seems obvious.

Yet it's also an impossible standard: of course, you're going to weaken.
Unless you lead a perfectly happy life until the moment you die peacefully
in your sleep, you will weaken. You will not be at your best. You will experience loss, confusion, pain, illness. You can try to keep your head above
water all you want, but the fact is you're still swimming, and there are times
when you will tire. That Edenic island will forever remain on the horizon.

In 2002, the Tragically Hip were fallible. Everyone knew it. They were
coming off a 12-year run that even the luckiest artists in rock'n'roll history
would have had trouble maintaining. Trends change; audiences, radio and
press all grow weary. Just as in the early '90s, new waves of rock bands were
sweeping away the old. No matter who you are, no matter the genre, it's
incredibly hard to get anyone excited about your eighth and ninth records.

Gord Downie had put out a solo record and a book of poetry and was writing a second set of songs for his new group of friends to record. The Hip's former co-manager was embroiled in a bankruptcy that ruptured the entire Canadian music industry. Between 2003 and 2006, the Hip would be represented by three different management companies, having severed ties with Jake Gold after 17 years. It was a time of tumult. The Hip dealt with it the only way they knew how: never slow down, plow ahead.

Don't weaken. Easier said than done.

———

By the end of the '90s, Allan Gregg had sold Decima Research and co-founded a new firm, the Strategic Counsel. He also hosted an interview program on Ontario public broadcaster TVO and became president of Viacom Canada. But he remained a partner in Jake Gold's Management Trust, bringing the multi-platinum band Big Wreck into the fold, working with blues guitarist David Gogo and trying to launch the career of Kingston artist Chris Koster, brother of longtime Hip roadie Dave "Billy Ray" Koster. In 1999, Gregg took on a considerably larger challenge that would prove fatal to his career in the music business: creating a new major label in Canada. He saw a large hole he thought he could fill. Instead, he fell into it headfirst.

Canada's independent scene had suffered a huge blow in 1997 with the bankruptcy of Cargo Records. Started in 1987 by three record-store employees, the Montreal-based distributor tapped into demand for punk, new wave and other underground genres in the lead-up to the grunge and independent boom of the early '90s. It was primarily a distributor for American labels like SST, Dischord and Sub Pop, but also Canadians like Mint, Murderecords and Sonic Unyon. It doubled as a record label with direct Canadian signings. In 1995, it struck platinum when two artists on Epitaph Records, Rancid and the Offspring, landed mainstream radio hits and started selling hundreds of thousands of CDs. Two businessmen with little knowledge of the music industry had taken over the label the year before, and a combination of hubris and ignorance led to the complete unravelling of the Canadian company in 1997, leaving nearly 500 unsecured creditors—almost all of them tiny labels with no capital to fall back on. Classic Canadian albums by the likes of Shadowy Men, Change of Heart and NoMeansNo were out of print.

It was a lesson that Allan Gregg should have studied closely. Though new players stepped onto the scene—like Outside, Fusion III and Sonic Unyon's transformation into a distributor—Gregg thought he could single-handedly consolidate various factions of Canada's independent scene and navigate a rapidly changing market with old-school methods. The company would be called Song Corp.

In 1998, 90 per cent of the Canadian market was controlled by five major record labels. Gregg thought the rest was his for the taking—and likely even more. Consolidation among the majors resulted in those companies either shedding smaller labels, or those small labels feeling they were getting lost inside an ever-widening corporate umbrella. That was the story of Al Mair's Attic Records, founded in 1974 and responsible for success stories ranging from Hagood Hardy to Triumph to Maestro Fresh Wes. It was distributed by Polygram before that company merged with Universal in May 1998. Attic would be a key component of what Gregg hoped would be Song Corp.'s new empire. "I saw that there was no strong indigenous Canadian music industry," Gregg told *Toronto Life* writer David Hayes, which would have been news to many on the indie scene. Hayes paraphrased Gregg's intentions: "Song would combine the virtues of size with an independent's flexibility and street credibility. It would be kinder and fairer to its artists, grooming them for long-term careers."

Gregg began Song Corp. in July 1999 by acquiring and merging three separate entities: Attic Music; The Music Publisher (TMP), founded in 1986 by '60s independent label pioneer Frank Davies; and Oasis distribution, a new company started by a former head of Polygram's distribution wing. Merging a label, a publisher and a distributor under one wing was central to Song's plan. Gregg then raised $12.5 million with the help of an investment banker. Together, they convinced venture capitalists that the music industry was more bankable and stable than other entertainment industries, especially for record labels. After all, as Gregg told investors, "We loan artists money to build their house, and when they've paid off the house, we own it."

Originally housed in four separate locations, in June 2000, the various wings of Song Corp. moved into a 14,000-square-foot building in Toronto's Liberty Village and began renovating the property to the tune of $1 million. The opulence was embodied in a grandiose spiral staircase made from imported Italian marble. The four principal partners put themselves on salary at $250,000 each. There was a staff of 80 people in five offices across Canada, a payroll considerably bigger than comparable independent companies. This was a corporation whose biggest domestic acts at the time were Maestro Fresh Wes (biggest hit: 1989) and the reunited Grapes of Wrath (biggest hit: 1991). The label's only radio hit at the time was "Who Let the Dogs Out" by the Baha Men, who, despite being a cultural meme, was not the type of artist that sold actual units.

Song's nod to the new indie rock underground came by acquiring Teenage USA, the label that released the first EP by sexual provocateur Peaches and a lot of shoegaze and math rock—none of which was likely to cross over to mainstream appeal, nor even move the kind of numbers that would influence a balance sheet. Gregg himself began to quickly question the acquisition of Teenage USA, which was supposed to be a pillar of Song's so-called street credibility. "We'd go out and see their bands and everyone would say, 'Holy Jeezus, this is terrible!'" said Gregg. "Anything the Song A&R guys liked, [the Teenage USA guys] hated. It was clear that the prospect of all of them working together was slim."

Because Song's promotional and distribution staff was largely staffed by major label refugees, they didn't know what to do with the more obscure labels that Song snapped up for the sake of quantity over quality: 99 labels in all, "some with 100 artists, some with just one," said one former employee. There were three promo reps working those titles for all of Canada; a major label might have a national staff of 20. "It was a studied decision to have all those offices, all those marketing and promotion people in major markets, working radio," said Gregg. "But when you have Head Fuck Records—which we did, by the way—what radio promotion does it need? It's not going in Music World at [Toronto's] Yorkdale Mall. It's going to be in the grungy heavy-metal store on Kingston Road. But we never serviced those [smaller stores]. I talked about 'the Song Difference,' the independent mentality, but no matter how much I stamped my hoof in my hankie, I had a hard time getting people's heads around it."

Song's first year of business was rocky to begin with. But the sound of Song's death rattle came from nine horrifying zombies from the cornfields of Iowa.

Slipknot, a nu-metal band, was on Roadrunner Records, a U.S. label that launched the careers of Metallica and Slayer. Attic's Al Mair had signed a distribution deal with Roadrunner in the late 1980s, which was grandfathered into Song. In 2000, Slipknot's debut album went platinum in Canada, making them the one act whose sales numbers bolstered Song's bottom line to any degree at all, bringing in $2.5 million that year.

But Roadrunner's contract with Mair was due to expire on December 31, 2000. The label's owner flew to Toronto and visited Song's office. He was shocked at the opulence in light of what little sales the label seemed to have. Meanwhile, Universal offered the label a $2-million deal too good to refuse, rumoured to be a deliberate provocation to kneecap Gregg. Roadrunner took it, leaving Song in the lurch.

In January 2001, Allan Gregg assembled Song's staff in the boardroom and told them, "The experiment is over. I've failed terribly." He was emotional, bordering on teary. Recently acquired office supplies were returned to Grand & Toy. Thirty of the company's 80 employees were laid off that day. Those who took a lump sum severance were paid; those who opted for a staggered paycheque were stiffed. The distribution wing limped forward for another five months. Some employees had bought shares to the tune of five- or six-figure amounts. That money vanished with the bankruptcy, which was declared in May 2001. Song owed $8.2 million to creditors after only 20 months in business.

At the time of its demise, Song Corp. controlled publishing rights for more than 4,700 Canadian songs, including the catalogues of Tom Cochrane, Honeymoon Suite, Teenage Head, Crowbar, Junkhouse, Jane Siberry, Eddie Schwartz, Ron Hynes—and the Tragically Hip. Anyone who wanted to license that music for film or television had no one to contact. None of the songwriters represented by Song received royalty cheques between September 2000 and November 2002. Hynes told the *Globe and Mail* that he made between $12,000 and $20,000 every year from his publishing royalties. His song "Sonny's Dream" had been covered by more than 30 artists, including Emmylou Harris. Going two years without that income had forced the then 51-year-old performer back into a "brutal" tour schedule. In 2000, Molly Johnson sold 10,000 copies of her jazz album released by Song—no small feat for a jazz artist. When the company went bankrupt, she was owed $50,000, a small fortune for any independent artist. On tour in 2001, she begged audiences not to buy her record at stores, because all the money would only go to Song's bankruptcy trustee.

As with Cargo's bankruptcy, Song's demise also left dozens of album masters in limbo, including Molly Johnson's. Artists like Maestro, Teenage Head, Lee Aaron and the Nylons found their master recordings purchased by yet another company, Montreal-based Unidisc—that was not about to sell them back to the artists. Artists tried in vain to smuggle product out of the warehouse, which was padlocked. "Boxes of CDs were chainsawed, under order to destroy the product," said one former employee. "It was a debacle, and people were desperately hurt: creatively, financially and spiritually."

A year later, Gregg saw himself as the visionary whose failure to tend to the details did him in. "I had no interest in running the day-to-day operations of a music business—none, zero," he said in a *Toronto Life* profile titled "Song Corpse." "I was persuaded that the guys we'd hired were perfect. They would run the company. I would think big thoughts, run a publicly traded company, which I would be good at because I'm a good talker." This was the man whose career in the music business started in 1969 at age 17 in Edmonton, when he brought Led Zeppelin to town—but also lost $35,000 that same year by booking another band who fraudulently claimed to be the Yardbirds.

The president of the Canadian Recording Industry Association said bluntly, "This was a grand scheme that probably wasn't based on reality." Gregg was suitably humbled. "I'd been successful in so many other things that I didn't anticipate failure in this," he said. "Having been involved in the periphery of the music business for a number of years, I knew the basic economics, the basic structures. I thought that was enough." He told *Billboard*, "This is the single worst business experience in my adult life."

The Tragically Hip's debut EP was also affected, as was their catalogue from the first four albums. Rob Baker told the *Globe and Mail* they had no idea their songwriting had been consolidated into Song and only learned as much when they read a news story about the bankruptcy. Yet if the band members themselves were shareholders in Song Corp., they would have seen the prospectus when the company first went public—which repeatedly cites the Hip's catalogue as Song's crown jewel. Nonetheless, the Hip filed a legal action, which ended up costing them $100,000, claiming that Gregg had violated their management contract.

When they had signed to the Management Trust in 1986, the first EP came out on Gregg's Rock Records (temporarily licensed to RCA); 50 per cent of their publishing, the administrative half, was signed over to Roll Publishing. The lawsuit "was partly their misunderstanding of business," said Gregg, "but also because I had unduly tied up an asset—which was entirely within my fiduciary right—that if anyone had a claim to, it was the band, not the trustee or another publishing company they knew nothing about. Typical of their lack of willingness to confront things in a real and forthright and mature way, they never even raised it with me. So it was never a conversation, let alone a fight."

It was an unprecedented legal case: no publisher had ever gone bankrupt in Canada before, and the Hip were hoping the rights would revert to the artist. Instead, the judge ruled in favour of the creditors. The band did not have the money to buy back its own songs from the bankruptcy trustee. Even if they did, they'd still need to work with an actual publisher to capitalize on the catalogue by licensing the songs to film, television, compilations and other uses—even though that was something the Tragically Hip had studiously avoided in the past, on principle. "That's why you get a publishing deal in the first place, so that you have people in the field working your music," said Rob Baker in 2002. Publishers also chase down money owed to songwriters in both domestic and international markets—a task most artist managers don't have the infrastructure to do. (Though the Management Trust did.)

In November 2002, Song's publishing assets, valued at $2.2 million, were purchased by the Canadian division of Peermusic. Peermusic was founded in 1928 by Ralph Peer, an A&R man who launched the careers of Louis Armstrong and the Carter Family, and who helped popularize Latin music in the U.S. It's an international company with offices in 28 countries. Before 2002, its active Canadian catalogue was infinitesimal: a mere 200 songs, compared to the more than 4,700 it acquired after the Song bankruptcy. With Gold's guidance, the Tragically Hip signed a lucrative deal with Peer after the court case, making the whole debacle a bit of a shell game; the only thing they lost was money spent on lawyers and any personal money individuals may have invested in Song Corp. shares.

Gregg had not been directly involved with the band since 1994, when they turned down his advice to re-record *Day for Night*. He was still a financial partner with Jake Gold in the Management Trust. "Alan was the vision guy and Jake was the get-the-job-done guy," a diplomatic Baker told the *Globe and Mail* in 2002. "They worked very well like that. In the end, we proved very frustrating to [Gregg]. He had major nations of the world asking his advice, and here he was offering his advice to us, and we seemed intent on charting our own course and not taking his advice."

"They got to the point where they didn't want a Svengali," said Gregg, "and they had got a bit of shit on the side, too: 'Allan Gregg's sugar babies'—there was that undercurrent in the press, and one guy called them exactly that. They are very proud and have tremendous integrity, so the notion that they were someone else's puppet was not flattering or consistent with their self-image."

Gold had only an arm's-length arrangement with Song Corp. and had resigned from the board of directors in April 2001, a month before the company folded. "I had nothing to do with the running of the company," he said. But the stain of the Song debacle coincided with the timing of Gold's contract renewal with the Hip.

Two months after the band signed their own deal with Peermusic, the Tragically Hip fired Jake Gold. Allan Gregg opened his door one night in January 2003 to find Gold on his doorstep, devastated.

———

Jake Gold is a character, all right: hero, villain, hustler, angel, bully, business mastermind. "Forget about the Hip," one musician told me. "Write about Jake. That's who your story should be about."

Ian Blurton recalled the first time he encountered Jake Gold, in 1988. "I was out postering for Change of Heart at Brunswick and Bloor, and he came right along and postered right over ours. I was just like, 'What the fuck?' In my mind, he was accompanied by a tall blonde in a fur coat—but maybe that's just how I remember it," he laughed. "Jake and I are like oil and water, but we respect each other. The most amazing thing I ever saw him do was at the [1997] Another Roadside Attraction show in Barrie. It was an early call, like six a.m. or something, so we were hanging out all day. Pepsi was trying to get as much advertising on that space as possible. I watched him make them take down all these triangle [plastic bunting] flags that went all around the perimeter. They said, 'No, we're not doing that.' He's like, 'Yes, yes, you are. Right now. Down.'"

"The band didn't want any sponsorship, whenever possible," said Gold. "So if those were the rules, I was the enforcer. I insisted that if [the promoters] wanted us to do Roadside at Molson Park that it couldn't say Molson Park. I didn't want any signage. I got the actual sign for the highway, the exit sign that said, 'Molson Park this way,' to say, 'Another Roadside Attraction this way.'"

"All day he was bossing people around," said Blurton. "It was amazing. If you're a band at that level, you need someone to do that, otherwise you're getting ripped off left, right and centre."

"To us, Jake was always a really nice guy," said another musician who toured on Another Roadside Attraction. "He's a classic music manager: if you're on his good side, he's golden. But it's like Artie Fufkin in *Spinal Tap*: you don't want to be on the other side of Jake."

"I did three deals with the guy," said Steven Drake. "He'll take you out for steak dinner afterwards and pour you some $60 bottle of wine and roll a hash joint and joke about shit, but during the negotiations he's impossibly competitive and volatile. But he's the guy who said, 'I don't care if people think I'm an asshole; I'm the guy who's gonna get what I want for my band.' He would have jumped in front of a train for those guys."

The band themselves were not immune to Gold's volatility. "I wore short sleeves onstage once at a show around 1989," said Rob Baker. "When I walked offstage, Jake said, 'Don't ever do that again!' I said, 'What?' '*You have arms like ham!*' I don't wear short sleeves to this day because he said that. It's not the worst thing he ever said, but I love him dearly."

The Hip would have achieved some level of success even without Allan Gregg and Jake Gold on board. But there's no question that Gold's acumen, loyalty and dogged daily persistence aided the Hip's ascent by no small measure. Most important, the Tragically Hip's much-admired independent streak would not have been possible without someone of Gold's fortitude manning the barricades.

In 1993, Another Roadside Attraction was Gold's idea. In 1994, he ensured the Tragically Hip were one of the first artists with their own website. In 1997, they became one of the first artists to sell their music directly online, when *Live Between Us* didn't get American distribution. *Newsweek* magazine lumped them in with David Bowie as digital innovators, interviewing Gold for the story. In 2002, when digital privacy had started to decimate the music industry, Gold included "Hip Club" cards inside every CD of *In Violet Light* that allowed paying fans to access bonus tracks online; Hip Club members also had access to presale tickets. At a time when the band's massive popularity was starting to wane, Gold wanted to ensure that the core audience was still energized.

On a considerably more trivial note, every music editor and ad designer who worked in Canada in the '90s has a story about Gold berating them on the phone, insisting that the word "the" must appear before the Tragically Hip's name in any copy or advertising and that it must be capitalized—*Canadian Press Style Guide* be damned. (That was the directive from Rob Baker, the art student.) No detail escaped his view.

When asked why he was fired, Gold said with a shrug, "It had prob-ably run its course: 18 years." He suspected that, in 2002–03, the band had trouble coming to terms with the fact they were entering a second phase of their career.

"I knew the arenas were getting tired," he said. "I said: 'Let's do some big festival-type shows in the summer, but make the tour exclusive.' We'd been playing for low ticket prices, and we needed to raise prices. But going into arenas and raising the ticket prices wasn't going to work. I said, 'Let's go smaller, do multiple nights [in one market], bring in big production and make these things events again. Sell 'em out, make it crazy.' I knew they were meandering a bit at that point, and we needed to mix it up."

Hip Club members bought 80 per cent of the tickets to the 2002 tour before they were available to the public. "The fans were loving it," he con-tinued. "They were members, so we had their name, their address, we had this massive database. I knew we needed to build that, because that's where things were going. I said to the band, 'This is the Freedom 55 plan: we're taking a step back so we can take 10 steps forward.' They thought I was taking them smaller, but they didn't understand; they probably do now. I noticed the reviews on the previous tour [in 2000] weren't as good. We weren't getting buzz. Now we were getting buzz, and off a record that didn't do that great. It didn't have any big hits or anything. But now we had buzz and reviews—back when reviews counted—that said things like, 'The Hip have once again proved they're the greatest band in the country.' Which is what I wanted: to have people not forget that." The 2002 tour was also the first time in 10 years that Gord Downie let Gold pick the opening act. It was Sam Roberts, who ended up opening up for the Hip more than any other act and was warmly embraced by their audience for years to come.

But the 2002 tour was not the Hip's only issue with Gold. His brash Toronto personality had clashed with the small-town band for years. Some of that was because Gold had to assiduously guard the lines in the sand that the band had drawn; he was the bad guy on behalf of the notoriously polite band. Other times, the band discovered decisions Gold had made on their behalf that they weren't comfortable with. Steven Drake of the Odds said that on their 1995 tour together, "[The Hip's] crew guys were getting paid less than ours. They eventually straightened that out, once the band got wind of that—they realized it was fucked." (Jake Gold denied this.)

"A lot of relationships got soured by Jake not realizing that he'd won and continuing to be nasty when he'd already won," said Drake, who had produced Gord Downie's first solo record, *Coke Machine Glow*, a cherished experience that soon went sour. He claimed Gold wanted to renegotiate a handshake deal between the producer and Downie. "It's one of my favourite records I've ever done," said Drake. "It's too bad, because all the negotiations with Jake totally fucked everything up. Gord and I lost our friendship over that, and it was terrible. I got Jaked." They did finally come to an agreement Drake found to be fair, "but it's the principle."

However, Drake credited Gold's personality for ultimately strengthening the bond between the band members. "Jake was such a force of nature himself that he actually made the band more cohesive," he said, "because the band had to have some kind of clear mandate in order to work with Jake. He's a divide-and-conquer guy, too, and the band could not allow that—so it made them a tighter unit. That's one thing that kept the Hip together."

Though Downie and Gold may have seemed drastically different—the sensitive artist and the loudmouth manager—they worked well together. A friend once asked the singer why the mild-mannered band had Gold as a manager. Downie responded, "If you're going to court, you want the most brutal lawyer you can possibly get. He's the guy who will get the job done. It's not going to be someone with our personality; it will be with someone like Jake." Downie and Gold also shared a key trait in common. "They have a personal drive that most of us don't have," said Steven Drake. "They wake up in the morning and they're the man with a plan. Gord was always like, 'What's next? What's today?' He could be relentless in his pursuit of getting to where he wanted to be."

"Jake came out on tour a bunch," said Dave Clark of Downie's Country of Miracles. "He was hilarious and a super nerd. All that bluster is a cover-up for a guy who's vulnerable like most people, and he loved being on the bus. He loved rock'n'roll. We had fun. The other stuff? I don't care. That's their business."

Gold continued to represent Downie's solo career for the release cycle of *Battle of the Nudes*, which came out in June 2003. By that time, Gold had stepped out from behind the scenes and had a new career that made him a household name: he became a judge on *Canadian Idol*. The show ran for six seasons; the season-one finale is among the highest-rated TV broadcasts in Canadian history.

The Tragically Hip worked with many talented producers over the course of 13 albums. Some were recommended to them, some were peers, some made the band's favourite contemporary records. Only one was a childhood hero: Hugh Padgham.

"I had to go to summer school because of Hugh," said Johnny Fay. "When [the Police's 1983 album] *Synchronicity* came out, I ditched my exams so that I could be the first person in Kingston to own it."

Any serious rock or new wave fan who grew up in the late '70s or early '80s knew Hugh Padgham's name. His production credit can be found on many landmark recordings: the Police's last two albums and all of Sting's solo albums, records by Genesis and Phil Collins, David Bowie's *Tonight* and the Human League's *Hysteria*. He engineered and/or mixed Kate Bush's *The Dreaming*, *H2o* by Hall & Oates and the early albums by XTC and Split Enz.

Most notably, he engineered Peter Gabriel's third solo album, on which Padgham gets credit (or blame) for creating the "gated drum" sound that came to define the '80s sonic palette. It can be heard on the Gabriel track "Intruder," featuring Phil Collins on drums, and then Collins's own "In the Air Tonight" single recorded six months later, produced by Padgham—which, of course, features perhaps the most famous drum fill of the 1980s. It's created by combining the sound of microphones close to individual drums with an ambient room mic to capture the natural reverberation, but clipping the release of the reverb at half a second, creating a much punchier sound. It became ubiquitous, but it is not Padgham's signature; though beloved by Collins, it's not inherent to any of the producer's other clients.

When the Tragically Hip came calling, Padgham's work schedule had slowed down significantly, due in part to a new family life. His last major commercial success was Melissa Etheridge's 1993 breakthrough *Yes I Am*; by the turn of the decade, his only major releases were by the American band 311 and the British band Mansun.

Padgham knew the Hip through reputation. "I used to read *Billboard* and see the charts from around the world," he said, "so you knew if your record was number two behind the Tragically Hip." When he got the call, he was intrigued. Other than 311, he said, "I'd done a lot of records with women around that time, so I quite fancied having some male testosterone. Then I listened to some of the previous records, like *Music @ Work*, and I loved the band. There was something completely different about them, in terms of Gord's lyrics. He's an amazing poet in a rock band. I've always been attracted to good and thoughtful writers." He paused, and added, "Sting was a pretty good lyricist as well."

Writing the record took place in Kingston in June 2001, shortly after the release of the *Coke Machine Glow* album and accompanying book. Downie had just come off his first experience working with a poetry editor going over his work line by line, and he thought he could arrive at rehearsal with fully formed, carefully edited works that looked great on the page. "I got up to the mic and guess what? It was really clunky," he said. "So I had to start cutting things out on the spot, a word here and a word there, to make it seem like it was all just occurring to me. What I learned from that session was that you have to prepare and refine, but you also need time in front of a microphone, just singing it."

The last three Hip albums had been made in Kingston at the Bathouse. Being relaxed and close to families had its advantages, but *Music @ Work* in particular suffered from overcooking and last-minute twiddling. If it's easy to keep rolling tape, that's what you're going to do. Johnny Fay said in 2002 that *Phantom Power* "took eight months to make. I never knew when we were finished or when we had started. I'm happy with that album, [but] I can't listen to it. I think you could accuse us on the last couple of records of screwing around with stuff too much."

This time, the Hip wanted to go back to the method of their first four records: a work-intense vacation to an exotic place full of musical history. They chose the Bahamas.

Compass Point was a studio opened by Island Records founder Chris Blackwell in 1977. Bob Marley was one of the first artists to record there. Grace Jones made her classic early '80s albums there, as did Talking Heads. AC/DC's *Back in Black* was made in the same tropical paradise, as were records by the Rolling Stones, Iron Maiden and Judas Priest. In 2002, it was run by engineer Terry Manning, whose career dates back to early '70s albums by the Staple Singers and Led Zeppelin and who ran Ardent Studios in Memphis when the Hip made *Up to Here*.

With Padgham and Manning behind the boards, the Hip wanted to limit themselves to a 24-track tape machine to avoid the fussiness of *Music @ Work*. At a time when the industry was turning toward the infinite possibilities of digital recording, the Hip wanted to keep it old school.

It was also the last time they would have an old-school budget, totalling approximately $300,000. That paid for five weeks of recording in late 2001 and five more weeks of overdubbing and mixing in early 2002. If there was any remaining uneasiness surrounding Downie's solo work, or the collapse of Allan Gregg's attempt at a music empire, or post-9/11 anxiety—which made its way into some of the lyrics—the time in the Bahamas built a renewed bond, determined to "get friendship right," as Downie says in "It's a Good Life."

Though the surroundings were idyllic, the studio itself contained no windows. "When Chris Blackwell built it," explained Padgham, "he did that on purpose so that the bands couldn't be distracted by the beautiful blue sea and all that. When we were actually in the studio, it was dark and studio-like."

Along with boating, casino visits and other Caribbean activities, Compass Point also provided a museum experience of sorts, with guitars that once belonged to Bob Marley, Eric Clapton, Jimmy Page, Duane Eddy—even Robert Johnson, whose guitar Baker was allowed to hold, but not play. "I'm not a vintage snob," he said. "I'm a utilitarian when it comes to guitars; they're just tools. But there was something special about those guitars."

Guitar parts were the one area in which Padgham pushed his own arrangement ideas: he wanted less of them. "Hugh doesn't like to hear guitar solos per se," said Baker. "Unless you are Clapton, he doesn't want to hear you winding out for several choruses. Basically, all the parts had to serve the song, so it was a matter of stripping back."

After the 10-hour shifts of the initial sessions before Christmas, the pace was quite different for the overdubs and mixing. "I would get up at my leisure," Baker recalled, "have breakfast by the pool, take a walk and then slip in to see [what the others were doing]. We all popped in and out every hour or two. You hire the best people that you can and let them do their thing."

Hugh Padgham doesn't recall taking any direction from the band whatsoever. "I'm not sure how much of a producer I was, in a way, other than being the keeper of the sessions," he said. "They wrote the songs they presented to me. I don't know if they wanted me to turn them into something else. I don't remember sitting down and having any discussion about that. I'm not sure I'd have the ability to do that anyway. They probably chose the wrong bloke if that's what they wanted; [if so] they should have chosen Trevor Horn [Art of Noise, Yes's *90125*]."

When *In Violet Light* was released, many expected more from a producer of Padgham's pedigree. The *Toronto Star*'s Vit Wagner offered the most passively Canadian response possible, writing, "*In Violet Light* is a solid effort that made me wish I actually liked the band's music more, rather than admiring it from afar with detached, respectful indifference." One of *In Violet Light*'s bonus tracks is called "Ultra Mundane." Had it been included, the title would have provided more fodder for the album's critics. Bill Reynolds in the *Globe and Mail* wrote that the album "suffers badly from the hands of their hired producer . . . they got jobbed. He might as well have wrapped mummifying gauze around them."

The latter is a tad unfair: Padgham is known more for pop and new wave records than he is for recording rock bands. "I'm more of a chameleon as a producer," he said. "When I started working with the Police, they did want a sound that was different than a three-piece playing live off the floor. That was my remit. I wasn't given that with the Hip. It was just, 'Let's turn up in the Bahamas and make a record.'"

But it's true that the rockers on *In Violet Light* fall flat; small wonder that the lead single was the moody, unconventional and pretty midtempo track "It's a Good Life," on which Padgham's penchant for sonic textures shines through, or that the album's second-strongest song is the gorgeous "Throwing Off Glass," which is an inverse companion to *Coke Machine Glow*'s "Trick Rider." This time, it's the daughter conveying concerns about the world's dangers, while the parent offers reassurances about the exquisiteness of existence. The 6/8 swing of "A Beautiful Thing" is about a three a.m. phone call from a friend; the narrator jokes that the interruption had better be about a life-or-death matter—and it is.

Overall, *In Violet Light* sounds like a successful, middle-aged rock band, comprised of old friends, recording in the Caribbean. No blood, no sweat, no tears. "It was all quite nice, really," said Padgham. "Sometimes making records when the atmosphere is too nice isn't very good. I made *Synchronicity* with the Police on a Caribbean island, when they all hated each other and were arguing all the time. 'Another shitty day in paradise,' we always used to say. But the tension of the arguments held in a lovely place really came out in [*Synchronicity*] and made it something special."

With *In Violet Light*, said Padgham, with 15 years hindsight, "If anything, you could say that any weakness was probably due to the band's familiarity. They all got on really well. Perhaps it was like being in a long marriage at that point. Perhaps there wasn't an amazing spark. But I listened to the album again a couple of times recently, and I'm really proud of it. And I remember it being a lot of fun."

———

For the next two years, Gord Downie was in a hurry. His next record was made in 10 days, not 10 weeks. *Battle of the Nudes* was the first studio album to capture the live energy of the Country of Miracles: Julie Doiron, Josh Finlayson, Dale Morningstar, Dave Clark and John Press. Made at Morningstar's new Gas Station studio on Toronto Island and at the Bathouse, *Battle of the Nudes* was Downie's first punk rock album. It's raw, rough and noisy, with a horn section adding to the occasional cacophony, and the quieter moments coloured by kalimba, bells and tongue drum. There's even a song called "We're Hardcore"—albeit, it's about parenting. It has little of the delicacy of *Coke Machine Glow* and none of the polish of the Hip—not that it needs either. "It was more in the box, more powerful, more precision," said Dave Clark. "All of us had way more muscle."

"Gord Downie seems intent on tearing apart everything we think we might know about him," wrote Ben Rayner in the *Toronto Star*. "This is a good thing. If *Battle of the Nudes* came from some 22-year-old indie-rock kid's basement, it would probably be hailed as genius. As it stands, this literate hodgepodge of ramshackle fuzz-rockers, creaking ballads and hallucinatory poetic interludes will likely be greeted with distrust from both the Hip fans put off by Downie's wayward solo debut, *Coke Machine Glow*, and its ideal audience—i.e., the people who'd normally buy records by such Downie bandmates as ex–Eric's Trip bassist Julie Doiron and the Dinner Is Ruined's Dale Morningstar."

Downie took his band on the road for a much more extensive tour than the one for *Coke Machine Glow*, including many dates in the U.S. While there, he was increasingly distressed by the politics of the George W. Bush era, which crept into the lyrics he was writing for the next Hip album, which, like *Battle of the Nudes*, was made quickly with no fuss, no muss.

In Between Evolution was made in Seattle, in part at Heart's Bad Animals studio, with producer Adam Kasper, who'd made recent records by Pearl Jam, Foo Fighters and a band credited by many for reinventing hard rock, Queens of the Stone Age. If that was your idea of rock music in the early 2000s, then *In Between Evolution* was considered the Hip's most powerful album since *Fully Completely*. Kasper's own reference points to the Hip sound like they came out of a campus paper review of *Up to Here*: in the album's official press release, he claimed that "if the Rolling Stones and R.E.M. were to have sex, the result would be a five-headed baby called the Tragically Hip." Hmmm, never heard that before. Kasper told the band that he enjoyed their live show but not any of their previous records. He wanted to make a record with them that sounded the same way their concerts did. In an industry experiencing freefall, the Hip also knew they could no longer afford to dick around in the studio. Sinclair said, "We wanted to create this environment: we're on someone else's nickel, the meter's running and this is costing us."

Naturally, the album was touted as a "back-to-basics" move for a band who were further and further away from their first three records, records that got more spins on classic rock radio than their latest material. Downie said there was no conscious move on the band's part to go retro. "I spent a year on one of the songs, 'You're Everywhere'—a year solid—and at no point in any part of the process did I think about anything we'd done before or anything we needed to do with relation to fans . . . It's too delicate; it's too profound and special to process a work of art, to sully it with thoughts of what it might do for you, what impact it might have, what nostalgia it might carry."

The lyrics have a tone of wartime anxiety, resilience in midlife challenges and a belief that brotherhood and family make you stronger. Sinclair said that "One Night in Copenhagen" was inspired by a show at the end of the *In Violet Light* tour. "Professionally it was a difficult time for us," he said, "and yet, amidst it all, the group was playing better than we ever had. The stage, and the five of us, became a real refuge. Everything is falling apart around you and yet there's this life raft and the life raft happens to be the five guys in this band onstage."

More interesting than the actual music on *In Between Evolution* was the cover art by 23-year-old Cameron Tomsett, a Kingston student who spotted Rob Baker dining at local café the Sleepless Goat and invited him to his small art show behind a bookstore. Baker was smitten and brought Tomsett's art to the band, who decided to name the album after one of the paintings. His animation was used in the video for the first single, "Vaccination Scar."

It was the first—and only—album the Hip made under their new management, Macklam Feldman, a West Coast powerhouse. Sam Feldman had been a business partner of industry giant Bruce Allen since 1972; Feldman's booking agency was Canada's biggest, while the management company with Steve Macklam represented international artists like Elvis Costello, Norah Jones, the Chieftains and Canadian icons Diana Krall and Joni Mitchell. Costello no longer being considered a rock artist, that made the Tragically Hip singular on the roster.

If anything indicates a band is at a crossroads, it's a greatest hits collection. That contractual obligation came in 2005, with a fan-sourced 2-CD set called *Yer Favourites*. It was also rolled into the *Hipeponymous* box set, which came with the band's first proper concert film, *That Night in Toronto*, and a DVD compiling their videos and featuring a documentary and short visual vignettes. It was well received, selling platinum and picking up a Juno for best packaging. But it was clear that the band wasn't excited about being boxed. "It's something that someone felt like we needed to do," said Downie. "It's not a career retrospective. When we do one, I guess you'll know it."

By the time he spoke those words, the Hip had already been inducted into the Canadian Music Hall of Fame at the Juno Awards, held that year in Winnipeg. Neil Young was in the audience. Sarah Harmer gave the induction speech. The tribute reel included then–prime minister Paul Martin, figure skater Kurt Browning, David Suzuki, Wayne Gretzky, Atom Egoyan, Barenaked Ladies and Rush. The Hip then performed—the first time in their career they'd ever agreed to do so on the Juno telecast. Maybe because it was the first time they needed the Junos, rather than the other way around.

They played "Fully Completely," during which Downie said, "I'm going back in time to the worst time in the band's career! 'Bring me back in shackles . . .'" They then played "Grace, Too," slipping in a lyric from the Weakerthans' 2000 song "Aside": "And I'm leaning on this broken fence between past and present tense / and I'm losing all those stupid games I swore I'd never play and it feels okay." Interesting choice.

As the year wound down, the Hip decided to switch management again, leaving Macklam Feldman. There was talk of rejoining Jake Gold at Management Trust, but the band couldn't reach a consensus. Instead, they turned to old friend Bernie Breen, one of Paul Langlois's best friends. Breen had started out his career co-owning the Copper Penny II in Kingston township, with his brother Dave. It was a roadhouse restaurant and occasional live venue. In their earliest days, the Hip once played to five people there at a Saturday afternoon matinee after a sold-out show at the Lakeview Manor the night before. In the late '80s and early '90s, he promoted large events in Kingston, including the Hip's Fort Henry shows. Breen had worked for the band directly before: he was production manager for the 1992 tour and tour co-ordinator for the first Another Roadside Attraction. Gold made him a partner at a Management Trust subsidiary from 1996 until 2001 where he worked with the Headstones, Big Wreck and Crash Vegas. During the Song debacle, Breen then struck out on his own, taking longtime Management Trust employee Sarah Osgoode with him.

When the Hip came to Breen in 2005, he was sharing office space with Patrick Sambrook's Eggplant Entertainment. Sambrook had discovered Sarah Harmer in her Weeping Tile days and had been Jake Gold's roommate from 1994 to 1998; his other big client in 2005 was Kathleen Edwards, and he was also co-managing Sam Roberts. Sambrook and Breen would now be co-managers of the Tragically Hip, both of them having learned valuable lessons by working intimately with Gold. When Gregg heard that Breen and Sambrook were the Hip's new managers, he told Gold, "You taught them everything they know, Jake, but you didn't tell them everything *you* know."

Returning to work with Breen seemed a much more natural fit, historically and geographically, than the Feldman connection. The brief time with Feldman "was almost necessary, like a rebound relationship," said one source close to the band, who said the split was amicable. They retained Feldman as a booking agent.

The first half of the decade had been incredibly productive. "I'm on my fifth record in five years," Downie boasted to the *Toronto Star*. Two of those, of course, were solo records. He put his solo career entirely on hold for the next five years. The direction of the democratic group was now firmly in the hands of its singer. That included the controversial choice of its next producer.

CHAPTER SEVENTEEN

THE DANCE AND ITS DISAPPEARANCE

PERFORMANCE

"Every activity I engage in has to contain the possibility of internal growth; otherwise it ends up as either 'making a living' or 'passing the time'—two ways of going through life that feel to me like a living death. I want to know with every passing moment that I am alive, that I am conscious, that with every breath I take there will be some possibility of growth, of surprise and of complete spontaneity."

ALAN ARKIN, *AN IMPROVISED LIFE*, 2011

SHANNON COONEY WAS a small-town girl who studied ballet and tap. She went to York University in the early '90s to study dance. She performed with Toronto's Dancemakers from 1994 to 2006 before moving to Berlin. In 1991, she was into Nirvana and listened to the outer reaches of the musical underground on CBC's *Brave New Waves*. On a trip to Vancouver, her friends took her to see the Tragically Hip at the Commodore Ballroom. She was blown away.

"Body, text, poetry, improvisation, time-space travel, expression, all seemingly coded and yet not at all—it was all readable and totally present," she recalls with reverie. "You surrendered and felt like you're a part of it. Your presence as an audience member fed the moment. Watching Gord [Downie] in the Commodore—and I shouldn't say watching, because it was a sound, poetry, multi-level thing—it was an inflection of the movement. I was halfway through my training at York, and then I saw this man who was doing what we're learning, but without any inhibition and no training, and he's a phenomenal dancer. Then everyone in the room had licence of freedom to move through gesture and expression, to hug each other.

"Someone like Jim Morrison might go on some poetic trip, but it would be dangerous because he's not in control and it could get ugly. But with Gord—no way. He goes on a fully embodied, conscious trip. Language is felt. Thought is not a radio frequency in your head. Thought is in the body, and as you try to articulate something, it comes through the body."

In 1999, Downie told journalist Laurie Brown, "If you're singing well and you're expressing your heart and letting your voice soar, that becomes a great drug. Then your body wants to help, in terms of getting it across. I think my body is basically giving subtext. For anybody out here who is big on meaning, then they can look at my body." He paused to laugh at himself. "'I give you my body!' And with my voice I'll give you the confines of my heart, which is illegible. It's more of a feeling, a mule kick to the chest."

Rich Terfry, a.k.a. the rapper Buck 65, was asked by Downie to open some Hip shows on the 2006 *World Container* tour. Terfry, who grew up listening almost exclusively to hip-hop, came to the Hip late in the game, drawn primarily to Downie's use of language. He was flattered by the invitation and nervous; he'd opened for large acts before, like Moby, but felt he should go to some of the secret warm-up shows before the tour to see what he was getting himself into.

"I thought I could learn from this," he recalls. "I want to be the best performer I can be, and here's this guy: he's the best. I watched him very closely to try and pick up on little things. I'd done the same thing with Springsteen, going to a couple of concerts and watching videos. It was easier with [Springsteen]: I could see what he was doing with his posture, with his legs, with his eyes. But with Gord, I thought, 'I'm not walking away with anything here. There's nothing I can personally pick up on, because I don't know what he's doing and I don't think it can be imitated.'

"As soon as he walks out on stage—and having had the chance to hang out with him, I'd say it starts even before that—I had the sense he was on another plane. Watching him from a few feet away, it's like hearing the Windsor hum, you feel like you're caught up in the Force. Up close, there's something almost terrifying about it. Whatever it is that takes over for him is so strong. To see someone wielding so much power in an unpredictable way, there's something scary about that. He's a tall guy, kind of an imposing figure, and we're in awe, which makes a person seem even bigger. He's also armed: he's using the mic stand. I had the sense like, 'Am I a total fraud? Because I'm not what this guy is at all. This guy's from another planet.'

"I've toured with a lot of people where you watch the first night and you're blown away by all the great moments, or a joke that's told with perfect timing, and you think they're a genius. Then on night two it's the exact same thing, and it's a bummer. It's all a script, and you wonder how long it was worked on. With Gord, it's a completely different ride every night, with different dance moves and new conversations, new profound things being said. I've seen Iggy Pop and Tom Waits and James Brown and Bruce Springsteen—I've seen them all live. But I've never seen anything quite like that, ever. It's hard to imagine that I ever will."

———

Gord Downie was obviously not a tightly choreographed pop star like Michael Jackson or Madonna. He was not a theatrical master like David Bowie or Annie Lennox. He was not a strutting peacock like Mick Jagger or Freddie Mercury. He was not a messianic figure like Bono or Jim Morrison. He's not the maelstrom of punk mayhem of Iggy Pop. He was not a grunge-era macho man like Eddie Vedder or Chris Cornell. And he couldn't hold a candle to the likes of Prince or James Brown or anyone in the R&B tradition.

That's not the point. Anyone looking for that kind of archetypal front man will be disappointed. Downie's appeal as a performer is, like the band's music, enigmatic. It's something that seems unlikely to work, but it does. Maybe that's a Canadian thing. Maybe it's just the mark of intangible singularity, in the way that there only ever be one Ian Curtis, or one Frankie Venom, or one John Mann. It's also something in the air, created by the band and Downie together, something best felt in a room, not on archival video clips. "I felt the same way watching Patti Smith live," says the Constantines' Bry Webb of watching Downie. "I can't describe what it's like even watching Patti Smith just stand on a stage, but her presence is so inspiring and electrifying."

"I surrender," Downie said in 2009. "I throw myself on the altar of song and I see my own personal musical life in fast flashes of faces and names and colours and sounds. I get lost in the euphoria of standing up there like Howlin' Wolf or Otis Redding or David Bowie with a mic in my hand and an audience that's ready . . . For a show to be great, something's got to happen. I go for it; I sing, I dance, I listen to this great band, I do what the music urges. My brain tries to get a step ahead: jump there, turn, kick, spin, drop to your knees. Dab brow with white hanky. Throw hanky into crowd. It's just all really so fun and improvisational and cool and when things break or fall down or go wrong, it can be even better."

Except that it's not entirely improvisational. It's a craft, a practice. Says his friend Mark Mattson, "As much as everyone thinks that Gord just did these things—or was drinking, or was high, which I hear all the time—they don't have any clue how hard he worked to get up there and do that whole show."

"The people who do this well—they're in control," says Michelle McAdorey of Crash Vegas, herself one of the most engaging and enigmatic performers of Downie's generation. "It might look really dangerous, but they take you there and then bring you back and then you're weeping and you're laughing and you have licence to scream. It's an amazing thing to come together and do."

Like every singer in every rock'n'roll band ever at the beginning of their career, there was a time when a young Gord Downie didn't know what to do with his hands when he wasn't singing. Once you step back from the mic stand, what should you do? Should you cling to that mic stand like life support? Should you just stand there and shake your sweaty mane all over the front row? Should you dance around and risk jostling your bandmates on the tiny stages you're playing?

Downie did all of that, but soon he started pontificating, spouting nonsense, eventually forming stories and narratives or workshopping new lyrics while the band chugged away underneath him. Many thought these were improvised every night; that's not necessarily true, especially in the case of two of the most widely bootlegged Hip performances ever: the "killerwhaletank" version of "New Orleans Is Sinking" and the "double suicide" rant in "Highway Girl." The latter was based on a screenplay Downie wrote for a film class at Queen's. "Killerwhaletank" evolved over time. Sometimes Downie would pull from something he found in his notebook before the show; sometimes it was the news of the day; sometimes, as can be heard on *Live Between Us*, he just started singing favourite songs by others in the middle of Hip songs.

"Gord's thing was a privilege to witness," says Kate Fenner, the only backup singer to ever tour with the Hip. "Only the two of us wore in-ear monitors on stage; everyone else just rocked out. That meant I could hear all his narratives. The first time I commented on them, he said, 'Oh! You're the first person who's ever heard them.' Because it's true—normally you

Golfing in the rain: the Tragically Hip's first-ever photo shoot, for the *Queen's Journal* in 1985. L-R. Gord Sinclair, Davis Manning, Johnny Fay, Gord Downie, Rob Baker. PHOTO BY PAUL FAULKNER

———

Hanging out at 585 Brock Street, where Sinclair, Downie and Langlois lived in 1985–86. Langlois, who was not yet in the band, is donning a fake moustache and pretending to be Davis Manning. PHOTO BY PAUL FAULKNER

Gord Downie onstage at the Horseshoe Tavern in Toronto, Nov. 12, 1988. PHOTO BY BISERKA LIVAJA

Backstage at the Horseshoe Tavern, Nov. 12, 1988, the night
Bruce Dickinson (centre) signed the Hip to MCA Records.

PHOTO BY BISERKA LIVAJA

———

The Tragically Hip, February 1990.

PHOTO BY MARKO SHARK

Recording a radio session in Toronto, November 1989.
PHOTO BY MARKO SHARK

Downie and Dale Morningstar recording *Coke Machine Glow* at the Gas Station in May 2001. PHOTO BY BARB YAMAZAKI

———

Steven Drake recording *Coke Machine Glow* at the Gas Station in May 2001. PHOTO BY BARB YAMAZAKI

Paul Langlois and Gord Downie at the
Molson Amphitheatre in Toronto, July 1, 2004.

Rob Baker at the Molson Amphitheatre,
July 1, 2004. PHOTO BY DAVID LEYES

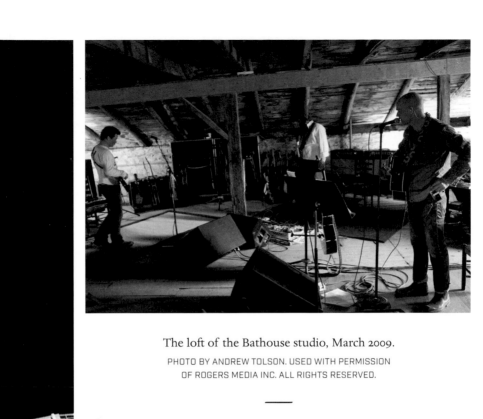

The loft of the Bathouse studio, March 2009.

———

Julie Doiron, Downie and Josh Finlayson with the
Country of Miracles, at Ottawa Bluesfest, 2010.

Charles Spearin, Downie and Kevin Drew performing *Secret Path* at Roy Thomson Hall in Toronto, Oct. 21, 2016. PHOTO BY JEFF HARRIS

———

The *Secret Path* band (L-R): Drew, Spearin, Dave Hamelin, Downie, Josh Finlayson, Kevin Hearn.

PHOTO BY MATT BARNES

Gord Sinclair at the Molson
Amphitheatre in Toronto, July 1, 2004.

Gord Downie and the Sadies perform at the Harvest Picnic
outside Hamilton in 2012. The Sadies are (L-R): Travis Good,
Sean Dean (obscured), Mike Belitsky, Dallas Good.

PHOTO BY NANCE FLEMING

———

Sam Roberts and Tasha the Amazon present Paul Langlois
and Rob Baker with the 2017 Juno for Group of the Year,
just before Langlois is cut off mid-speech.

THE CANADIAN PRESS, PHOTO BY SEAN KILPATRICK

"Every syllable was important," says producer Steve Berlin. "Gord had—oh God, it looked like a phonebook, a binder that was literally bursting with ideas."

——

Playing the school gym in Fort Albany for the Great Moon Gathering, a 2012 gig later immortalized in "Goodnight Attawapiskat."

Downie performing with Northern Revolution, including guitarist Braiden
Metatawabin and Roseanne Knapaysweet, in Fort Albany, Ontario.

———

The Tragically Hip at FirstOntario Centre in Hamilton, Aug.
16, 2016. Downie is wearing his silver "Patrick" suit, named
after his younger brother. PHOTO BY JEFF HARRIS

Justin Trudeau, Daisy Wenjack and Pearl Wenjack join Downie at
WE Day in Ottawa on July 2, 2017. This was Downie's last public appearance.
THE CANADIAN PRESS, PHOTO BY JUSTIN TANG

———

Sinclair, Fay, Baker and Langlois on the red carpet at the TIFF premiere
of *Long Time Running*. THE CANADIAN PRESS, PHOTO BY FRANK GUNN

just catch these mysterious bits, and they're still effective because the way his mind works is very captivating.

"Hearing the orchestrations of his narratives was fascinating," she says. "He had these stories, these extrapolations on songs that are like plays: he'd have two characters talking together, and then they'll go off and do something else. Sometimes the speaker of the song would change. Sometimes [an improvisation in a song] would have the same idea [night to night], but they would never be the same. It was thrilling."

From what could be discerned in the audience, it wasn't always successful. It could be baffling and ripe for parody. His ongoing boxing battles with "the microphone stand who thinks it's a man!" certainly got tiresome during the last 15 years of the band's career. And, of course, the "rants" could be interminable and distracting. "I'd be going on and on and [the band would be] looking at their wristwatches," said Downie. "But never once, God love them, did they ever say to me: 'Do you mind wrapping it up?' Well, maybe they have a few times. They have their ways of letting me know the soup's getting cold.

"But once that taps out and you realize you're doing it as a kind of matter of course, then you move into other forms of expression. You don't want to be the last left to turn out the lights on a shopworn idea. So I moved on."

Choreographer Shannon Cooney says, "The art I'm attracted to is not about reproduction. It's about presence: what is presence, how to expand presence, how not 'to show' but to be embodied. I think Gord was constantly orienting to this. It's not just a state; it's how to manifest being here now, not thinking about where you're going or show what you're doing, but still have it be a performance."

Cooney met Downie through their mutual friend Dale Morningstar; in 2002, the three of them worked on a choreographed piece at the National Arts Centre in Ottawa, based on the love letters of legendary Montreal Canadiens goalie Jacques Plante. By that point, Downie was taking dance very seriously.

Around the same time he was writing *Coke Machine Glow*, Downie started studying pantomime with his friend Andrea Nann, a professional dancer who was performing with the Danny Grossman Dance Company. They improvised works together onstage with Dave Clark's Woodchoppers Orchestra. They performed together in a 2001 dance piece called *Reveries*—which was savaged in the *Globe and Mail*, but no matter: Downie wanted to bring that practice into the Tragically Hip. He no longer wanted to go through the motions; he wanted to create new ones. His work with Nann was transformative and cannot be underestimated.

"He's in a band that is somewhat musically restrictive," says keyboardist Chris Brown. "His whole pantomime thing was the place that could open up and be new and unchallenging to the others onstage. Whether they liked it or not didn't matter: point being, that's where it could happen. Gord was finding all this theatre and this way of accessing what he needs to and becoming this enigma, and satisfying this artistic premise, this chimeric kind of trickster."

Not that Downie became James Brown or anything. "I don't think he had any illusions about being an extraordinary dancer," says Patrick Finn, associate professor at the University of Calgary's school of creative and performing arts. "Most musician movement is a direct emotive expression of the moment"—a grand hand gesture, a high kick, a twirl, jazz hands, head-banging. "What he's doing is adding articulated stuff that is another craft piece, much like a solo is constructed. His movement pieces are abstractions of the lyrical journey. He's doing what you see in modern dance, this iterative practice, taking a movement to extremes, taking a hand gesture three or four times, exploring the movement component."

Offstage, Downie's eccentricities could be socially awkward. He was a listener, not a talker. And the way he conversed was rarely in linear language; beneath the darting eyes, one could always sense the gears turning, searching for a different expression or a tangential association, always a step ahead in the conversation. It's the kind of intelligence that all funny people have—irony and humour were a big part of his stage persona—but it also meant that he often had trouble finishing sentences, because he was always on to the next thought. This is evident in most long-form radio or television interviews he did. If he hadn't been the front man in a rock band, Downie would be one odd duck. "A lot of guys who were creative or artistic in some way, rock music was a way you could be creative and not get the shit kicked out of you," says Finn. "Painting and poetry would get the shit kicked out of you. Performance is the way Downie expresses himself. There are some people who express themselves entirely in the lyric or in the way that they sing. He is a performance artist. He really connects with people through his performance."

Many people on the fence about Tragically Hip recordings were sold once they saw the live show. Rapper Rollie Pemberton, a.k.a. Cadence Weapon, is one. He first saw the Hip when they shared a festival bill in Calgary in 2008. "I knew 'Ahead by a Century' and had an idea of what they were, like good-ol'-boy Canadians, but literate," he says. "But that performance was very physical, which I didn't anticipate. I was gripped." Fellow rapper Shad felt the same way—and it wasn't even at a Hip show, but a Downie cameo with City and Colour at Montreal's Osheaga Festival in 2011, on the song "Sleeping Sickness." "He hopped up there, and he was just a monster—his voice exploded," says Shad. "Within seconds, I thought, 'Man, this is one of the best performers I've ever seen.' *Within seconds!* His voice and presence exploded out of him."

"There was a beauty in his performance that I really loved," says Michelle McAdorey, "which is this licence to express, to let go, to find expression through this happening of music and exchange of energy that, to me, is my religious experience. I find it really powerful. It's given a lot of meaning to life for me, or a means to make sense of things. The last time I saw Nick Cave [on his first tour after his teenage child died], that was one of the heaviest shows I've ever seen or felt or heard. I was bawling my eyes out and I was jumping out of my chair in that temple that is Massey Hall. The bullshit meter is very subjective: do you believe this person? Like Nick Cave—you can laugh or whatever, but I'm right there, I *believe* him. It's not a self-aggrandizement or an ego journey. I try to understand what that is; it's like this big act of generosity, and you're exchanging it. This person can reach *you*, no matter how many of 'you' are there. There's something really honest in it, even though there's performance in it."

Broken Social Scene's Andrew Whiteman had been a Hip fan for more than 20 years when, in 2015, he took Ariel Engle—his spouse and partner in the band AroarA—to her first Hip experience, at the Bell Centre in Montreal. "She knew nothing going in. It was fabulous," says Whiteman. "She went in there stone cold, and she was like, 'Holy shit, he's a catharsis machine. He's creating the conditions for us all to have a catharsis through him.' That's a mantic function of very old, shamanic poetry tradition, pre-poetry-on-the-page."

In order for Downie to do that, however, the musicians behind him must create the necessary conditions. Describing the same 2015 show, Whiteman says, "At their best, this is a trance band; they start this churning and turn it into a tornado. Bobby Baker's style is perfectly suited for that, because his 'solos'—I wouldn't even call them that—his phrasing barely goes beyond the 16th notes, he just stays on the eighth notes. He won't go all out; he won't be epic. His solos elevate, they rise, but he doesn't grandstand. It's slow, languid, it ebbs and falls. Think about the Stooges: the sax player goes for these skronky solo things that one could say don't go anywhere. But it's not about going anywhere, because you're *here*: this is the moment you're in right here, the present. There's something mystical and ineffable about it. It's really important that Bobby is that kind of player; it's an essential puzzle piece for Gord."

"In order for that band to work, there has to be ballast and foundation," says Dave Bidini of the Rheostatics. "Those long jams where Gord can become untethered and fly out into all of these melodic zones and do these interesting things—the band has to establish that seven-minute jam and continue to keep the flame high, keep things interesting. The interplay between the two guitars is sublime. On tour with them once, I thought, 'I'm just going to listen to the guitars tonight.' What was illuminating was the jams where—because we're always focusing on Gord we often miss this—those guys are doing a lot of interesting things. You almost have to look underneath the carpet occasionally to think, 'Oh, wow, this is really interesting. How'd *that* get in there?' Johnny Fay is commanding, confident, serving the song, really fun. It's a unit. It's like a chevron of geese with Gord at the front. If he were alone, he'd probably fly away and have no home to return to."

Patrick Finn thinks Paul Langlois is a crucial anchor to this framework. "With everybody other than Paul and Gord [Downie], you get this male machismo thing. Gord is trying to be a poet, and Paul is the softening influence. This was a hard-edged band that was writing hard-edged stuff, very male aggressive, and it's Paul who is the soft guy. He is the George Harrison. Without him, I don't think Gord gets to be the more poetic artsy guy. That's partly reflected in their stage construction"—childhood friends Baker and Sinclair together on one side, high school friends Langlois and Downie on the other. "I don't think the Hip would be the same without Paul being there. They might still be playing AC/DC-style music."

There is no more softening influence than the acoustic guitar, which Downie started playing onstage in 1996; he'd only learned to play it 10 years before that, when Langlois gave him one. It was a move no one expected— or necessarily wanted. That includes people in the band and crew. "You could never hear Gord's acoustic guitar in the mix," says Brendan Canning, who opened the 1999 *Phantom Power* tour as part of By Divine Right. "I think it was more of a comfort blanket than anything."

"I just felt like playing guitar," Downie said with a shrug, "as well as wanting to become a better singer, and there was no better way to do this than to play with a band. It was a real trial by fire. The first bunch of gigs were very embarrassing because it was hard to sing and play. But a small decision begat a whole new landscape where I'm plugged into the band in a way I never was before. All of a sudden I'm able to converse with them."

It took years before he looked anything less than uncomfortable with a guitar in his hand, however. "I always thought it was an odd dynamic," says Steven Drake, who toured with the Hip in 1995—the last tour before Downie picked up a guitar. Because Downie didn't start playing seriously until later in life, Drake argues, "Gord missed out on one of the most important parts of being a young guitar player, which is developing your stance. Me, I used to practise with a light behind me, looking at my silhouette. Developing a stance is really what it's all about when it comes to selling it onstage. Take a look at Robbie: he's got his stance totally down. Same with Paul. And Sinclair is king of stance!"

"I feel like I'm playing the washboard more than the guitar," Downie said in 1996. "My friend called me 'the scrubber' the other day. I really liked that."

The acoustic guitar toned down Downie's manic energy on stage, especially on songs like "New Orleans Is Sinking." Normally an end-of-set climactic number during which the crowd would wig out alongside the unhinged front man, now Downie was anchored by his acoustic guitar, which served no discernible musical purpose on a rhythm-based rocker. It changed the tenor of the set, starting with the testosterone level on- and offstage—a welcome change after years of women getting pushed out from the front of the crowd or opening acts being pelted with bottles.

———

"We're witnessing the return of the girl at the Tragically Hip show," Downie said in 1995. "The woman is reborn and alive again in the front row. That's good, because I was getting a little tired of the sea of testosterone and regretting the fact that the girls were getting muscled out."

"The Canadian fans were a bit boorish in the '90s, a lot of heavy drinking," says Hugh Larkin, a firefighter from Livonia, Michigan. He saw more than 100 Hip shows over 20 years, travelling far and wide to see them, always arriving two hours early to situate himself directly in front of the band. "Those early albums are very high-energy rock, and when you add alcohol and testosterone, it was very hard for my wife and I to be at the front at these shows. While I'm pretty big and strong, and it was okay for me to be there, I was always afraid for my wife. I was like a wrestler trying to protect her and stop the fights."

The Rheostatics opened the 1996 tour where Downie introduced the acoustic guitar. Dave Bidini felt like the crowd had almost completely changed from the first time the two bands gigged together on Canada Day, 1994. "That was the low ebb," he says. "Almost imperceptibly, in that 18-month span, the Hip audience went from being largely assholes who would have gone to see shitty metal or hard rock acts to being people who looked and dressed like them but were really interested in respecting music and having a great time and putting all that shit behind them."

That's a rather harsh assessment of the early fans, to say the least. But even if it was true, what changed? Surely it's not just the acoustic guitar. "Our musical tastes as a listening nation were changing at the same time the Hip were changing," says Bidini. "If the Hip did engage that, open up ears a little bit, everybody was pulling it open. We needed different flavours. We were maturing as a nation, and the Hip were a huge part of that."

As Downie's performance evolved, it became less of a masculine archetype. Downie never played with gender roles in ways explored by almost every genre of popular music in the '80s, but his portrayal of masculinity was one that increasingly embraced flamboyance and vulnerability. A more defined approach to dance and movement was a big part of that. One first sees it in the video for 1998's "Poets" (perhaps the first half-decent video the band ever made), and even more so in the choreography in 2000's "My Music at Work," directed by Kid in the Hall Bruce McCulloch. By the late 2000s, Downie was practically prancing around the stage, doing pirouettes with a white hanky in his hand. Here was a performer beautifully comfortable and unafraid of what any dude might think. Try to imagine how that would have gone over at a biker party in 1990.

"I feel like he challenged the context, but in a way that never seemed malicious," says Bry Webb of the Constantines. "The Hip came up playing in bars and playing for drinking bros; there's certainly that element to being in the audience at a Hip show. But the way Gord moves and presents physical expression of the experience of each song, it pushes at what I perceive as the challenge of that context. He's pushing at the guys who kicked my ass as a kid. Not in a macho way at all—in the opposite of that, in a way that says, 'This is possible in this space; it's transcendent and better when it's like this.' I can't imagine it wasn't intentional in some way—knowing how much intention he puts into everything. But whether or not it was intended as such, it was an affront to that machismo."

"Gord has this effortless manliness," says Hawksley Workman, a dandy who regularly performed with feather boas. "He was this Boston Bruins guy, rock'n'roll chronicler, that invited a swath of people who wouldn't necessarily be attracted to overly poetic rock music. But the tenderness was always right there. I felt such a determined feminine energy from Gord. And in the accepted list of pop and rock archetypes, you can be a weird girl more than you can be a weird guy. There is no male analogue to Tori Amos. There is no analogue to Björk. But Canadians do quirk better than Americans, because we're not obvious people."

———

When the final Tragically Hip tour was announced, people marvelled at the fact Downie considered himself physically and mentally able to do it after having had two brain surgeries. But there's also the emotional component: How do you conduct your own living wake in front of thousands of people every night? How do you maintain composure during such a prolonged farewell performance? People expected that the shows would be sombre. They were not. The Tragically Hip were total pros here, armed with skill and determination.

"Grace, Too" ended the final encore of August 14, 2016, the final of three Toronto shows. The song has always concluded with Downie screaming the words, "Him? Here? Now?" The lyric is mysterious. Perhaps the narrator is being asked to kill another man. Who knows? Point being, something terrible is about to happen to that guy. On this tour, that lyric meant, for the audience, the very real possibility that Gord Downie could have a brain seizure on stage and die in front of their eyes. "Him? Here? Now?" Everyone at every show walked into the venue knowing that—maybe not even realizing it until they heard Downie sing that line.

That night in Toronto, someone uploaded a clip of that moment. It was viewed more than million times in the next year. In it, Downie screams the line with increasing intensity, as he had done for years. (Many people watching this tour had not seen the Hip in years, so this may have been new information.) Then his face appears to crack with emotion, and the audience finally sees the catharsis they've been seeking: a look of real pain and distress that lasts at least 30 seconds, as he continues to scream. He follows that with a brief flailing, seemingly helpless and frustrated dance. Through the entire show, he's been a model of strength under clearly compromised circumstances. This is the moment where he loses it.

Or does he? Those screams are in time with the music. A split second after the band lands on the final extended, climactic note, Downie says, with his usual authoritative tone, "Thank you very much. Thank you, Toronto." He then turns toward the drum set to retrieve his mic stand. He picks it up. As the band prepares their final punctuation, Downie lands the mic stand right on the beat. Is that a man who just had a breakdown on stage?

No. That's a professional.

"That's performance," says University of Calgary drama professor Patrick Finn. "If I'm working with an actor, I say, 'We're going into the scene where *this* happens.' By knowing that and bringing thoughtful craft to the moment, you can say in rehearsal, 'This is the moment where I'm going to potentially let myself be totally open, and then I'm going to come back out of it and I've got a way out.' Otherwise, what would happen? How do you break down like that and then come back? You don't. This is a problem with method actors: yeah, they have an emotional moment, but then they can't put themselves back together."

Wait a minute, isn't that nothing but cold calculation? "What could be more emotional than letting that feeling be there, knowing that everyone is trying to capture it and knowing that the audience is wanting this, in a sense?" Finn counters. "He wants to share it; he is ever the performer. There may well even be an ego-driven component of wanting this 'greatest possible moment.'

"Some people think that moment was constructed and some think it was real: I think they're both right. On one night maybe you're only getting a glimpse; on another night it could be very real; on yet another night it's really real. What is certain is that you know it's coming; you know it's here; and you know the way out.

"That is craft. That's a good thing, not a bad thing."

CHAPTER EIGHTEEN

ROCK IT FROM THE CRYPT
2006–09: *WORLD CONTAINER, WE ARE THE SAME*

*"Bob Rock is Bob Rock, right? It's not like you're wondering,
'What would happen if . . . ?' He has a very strong
hand, and he's going to Bob Rock it."*

CHRIS BROWN, 2017

BRUCE ALLEN IS an undisputed giant in the Canadian music industry. He orchestrated the international success of artists such as Bachman-Turner Overdrive, Loverboy, Bryan Adams and Michael Bublé, as well as Prism, Trooper, Payola$ and Tom Cochrane. He was involved in the later careers of Anne Murray and Jann Arden. He was not a fan of the Tragically Hip.

"I get pissed off that too many artists are given the label 'great' when they haven't earned it," he once ranted to *Vancouver Magazine*. "I do not believe the Tragically Hip are great. I believe they're a Canadian act that wouldn't even be in existence today if it wasn't for Canadian content." CanCon radio regulations were a bugaboo for Allen: he was convinced that talent, marketing and his own bluster could bully just about anything onto the charts. Mostly, he was right. He wanted to go big or go home. And despite the Hip's undisputed reign over Canadian rock'n'roll since 1989, they didn't cut the mustard in the eyes of the West Coast kingmaker. The band themselves joked about Allen's anti-endorsement over the years, both on- and offstage. Allen had long been an arch-villain to Vancouver's indie and punk scenes, people with whom the Hip felt a closer kinship than the likes of Loverboy.

Which is why it's weird that Bruce Allen was indirectly responsible for helping make two albums that may well have saved the Tragically Hip—or damn near destroyed them, in the eyes of some fans.

Allen's roster included Bob Rock, the Payola$ guitarist turned producer who helped make Metallica into superstars in 1991 and helmed multi-million-selling albums by Mötley Crüe (*Dr. Feelgood*: 10 million albums sold), Bon Jovi (*Keep the Faith*: four million) and Canadian platinum records by the Moffatts and Our Lady Peace. He also played a memorable supporting role in the 2004 Metallica documentary *Some Kind of Monster*, in which, as the band's temporary bassist, he sat in on group therapy sessions while recording *St. Anger*. In the summer of 2005, Rock and Metallica severed a 15-year relationship that had served both parties immensely well. Allen then suggested to Rock that he should produce the Tragically Hip.

Behind the bluster, Allen had a begrudging respect for the Hip. He apparently said to Rock, "Hey, listen, the business has changed. These guys are a great band. There's a reason why they're still around. They just need to make a better record, and I think you can do it."

The band had nothing to lose. The last two or three Hip albums appealed to hardcore fans only. They'd just delivered to their record label a greatest-hits set, a box set and a concert film—a hat trick that suggested the end of an era. Gord Downie had put out two solo records in the last four years. They were about to change management for the second time in three years. But something else had to change or they'd be spinning their wheels forever more.

The Tragically Hip made two Rock records: 2006's *World Container* and 2009's *We Are the Same*. To paraphrase a Superchunk album title: here's where the strings came in. And the airport-lounge ballads. And the operatic backing vocals. And the toy pianos, pipe organs and accordions. And the trumpet solos. And the song with a pseudo-ska beat. And the waltzing metal song that switches between 6/8 and 9/8 time. And the nine-minute-long suite. And the single that somehow simultaneously sounds like the Smiths, Talking Heads and . . . Rage Against the Machine? What the Rock was going on here?

Bob Rock said he'd always wanted to make "the great Canadian record." He came close a couple of times in the 1980s with the Payola$, where the songs he wrote with singer Paul Hyde—notably "Eyes of a Stranger" and "Where Is This Love?"—won the band numerous Junos and made them a bridge between Vancouver's new wave underground and mainstream success.

Rock (yes, that's his real name) was born in Winnipeg and raised in the Victoria suburb of Langford, where his love of British music led him to classmate Paul Hyde, a U.K. expat from Yorkshire. After high school, they both spent time in London but failed to get their music off the ground. Rock moved to Vancouver; Hyde had a brief stopover in Toronto before returning to the West Coast. They formed the Payola$ in 1978. That same year, Rock started working as an engineer at Little Mountain Sound under the tutelage of Bruce Fairbairn, for whom Rock assisted on records by Prism and Loverboy. On his own time, he helped the first wave of Vancouver punk bands sound miles ahead of their peers in Toronto, Montreal or even L.A., on records by the Pointed Sticks ("The Real Thing"), the Subhumans ("Slave to My Dick") and Art Bergmann's Young Canadians ("Hawaii"). His star rose considerably when he worked for Fairbairn on Bon Jovi's *Slippery When Wet* in 1986 (12 million copies) and Aerosmith's smash comeback *Permanent Vacation* in 1987 (five million copies). He then produced the debut by Colin James, and within three years he was with Metallica.

Bob Rock figured he could finally make his "great Canadian record" with the Tragically Hip. It started in Maui.

In the summer of 2005, Gord Downie went to Rock's home in the small town of Paia, where their lunch conversation continued late into the night in Downie's hotel room, with a side trip for some wave-watching in between. Downie played him some demos. Rock was shocked, particularly by the song "Fly." "It got to me right away," he said. "I had never heard a song like that from the Hip: it was so direct and pop-like."

Except it wasn't a Hip song. It was a Gord Downie song that he was considering for his next solo record. When the singer played it and others for Rob Baker, however, the guitarist wanted to do them with the Hip. The band had been talking—as they often did—about reuniting with Don Smith, the producer with whom they made *Up to Here* and *Road Apples*. Downie rolled a Rock up that hill.

Excited but ever cautious, the band convened that September for what were deemed trial sessions with Rock, held at Bryan Adams's Warehouse Studio in Vancouver. Rock said the trepidation cut two ways: "Was I the metalhead, as rumoured? Were they stubborn and fixed in their musical ways?" The first day was spent rehearsing and throwing ideas around. Rock was surprised to find out the Hip were such big fans of the Clash and David Bowie—both huge influences on Rock; Bowie guitarist Mick Ronson produced the Payola$' 1983 album *Hammer on a Drum*. The Hip even copped to having a soft spot for Mötley Crüe's *Dr. Feelgood*. The next day they recorded four tracks: "Family Band," "Last Night I Dreamed You Didn't Love Me," "The Kids Don't Get It" and "Fly." So far, so good. Everyone was excited.

They reconvened in February 2006, at Toronto's Phase One. Again, the band was focused and ready for Rock, recording "Yer Not the Ocean," "The Drop Off," "Luv (sic)" and "The Lonely End of the Rink." For such a makeover record, *World Container* was proving remarkably painless to make. "Bob works the room in the rehearsals," said Downie, "saying to each guy [different things] to make the song more interesting to each member. Whatever he asked for, the band could deliver. Very agile. Which maybe even I had forgotten."

"Family Band" was easily their poppiest rock song since "My Music at Work" and perhaps the single most underrated Hip song. Rock successfully lobbied the band to channel the Who on "Yer Not the Ocean." "Luv (sic)," a version of which had been recorded for an earlier record, is just as strong, thanks to a new hook and bridge written during the Rock session. "The Lonely End of the Rink" draws from two-tone ska in the verses; it's a refreshing change on the familiar rhythmic limitations the Hip usually placed on themselves.

Then it came time to "Bob Rock it." In March, sessions resumed in Vancouver at Armoury Studios. Rock brought in keyboardist Jamie Edwards, formerly of Our Lady Peace, whom Rock had met while recording that band's 2001 album *Gravity*. The three tracks with Edwards are the ones that has purist fans wringing their hands: "World Container," a monstrous piano power ballad that, for better and worse, veers into Queen territory; "Pretend," perhaps the single most schmaltzy song in the Hip's discography, in which one can picture Downie in a velour suit, holding the mic while leaning against a piano; and "In View," the song with a plinky piano and mini-Moog playing the hook that would give the Hip their third and last No. 1 radio hit. "That song keeps giving you more and more," said one of the Hip's peers. "'In View' has four choruses. I've listened to that song with musicians while in a van on tour, and I'd say, 'No, wait! There's two more choruses that are going to hit.' It doesn't stop, it's so good."

Did it sound like the Hip? No, but it certainly did sound like a band having fun. Downie admitted the band's approach had become static. "You begin this dogged pursuit of your own sound as a group, and you cling to it and it quickly becomes a control issue: to have control of your own sound," he said. "You want to protect everything. In the process, you tuck all those influences, all the fun stuff of your youth, under the hem." By reconnecting with those teenage crushes, "lo and behold, it's fun to recognize your place in the grand scheme of things, in this river of rock."

Those influences came to the fore on tour. There was a new cover every single night: sometimes tied in to the city they were in (not unlike Arcade Fire's approach on 2013's *Reflektor* tour), sometimes just an excuse to revisit their old record collections. They did Elvis Presley's "Suspicious Minds" in Las Vegas. ZZ Top's "Tush" in Dallas. The Replacements' "Bastards of Young" in Minneapolis. Teenage Head's "Picture My Face" in Hamilton. In Sudbury, it was, yes, "Sudbury Saturday Night" by Stompin' Tom Connors. Iggy Pop, Neil Young, the Rolling Stones, Eddie Cochrane, Cheap Trick, the Beatles, Gordon Lightfoot, Johnny Cash, the Who, the Clash all made at least one set list—even Bob Marley ("Is It Love," which, though slightly awkward, is much better than their take on the Clash's "Magnificent Seven").

Downie was more vocally ambitious, hitting much higher notes than ever before, particularly on "In View." It had been 10 years since he quit smoking in order to preserve his voice. "I love Tom Petty," he said, "but those cigs get you singing the same song after a while, because you can't really explore other places. More range means more possibility."

His lyrical voice was also different. The Hip's discography was notably devoid of love songs, or at least anything that might be obviously recognizable as a love song. On *World Container*, Downie talks about being lovesick, about words he carries in his heart, about dreams of a spouse's abandonment and muses on Northrop Frye's claim that "love is the only virtue there is." "I was probably avoiding it all those years for some highfalutin reason," he said, "being heady about it. I probably didn't trust myself not to lapse into some sappy sentimentality. Sentimentality is really dangerous in my line of work. Since I've started, I realized that taking a crack at it is the important thing."

When *World Container* was released in October 2006, Rock and Downie talked each other up like new BFFs. Downie told CFOX in Vancouver that it was the best record the Hip had ever made. Rock was slightly less effusive and had some qualifiers. "I think it's one of their strongest," said the producer. "I like the band, but I didn't really understand them much [before this]. I really forced them to write good songs and do the work. I really challenged them, because I thought that's what was needed." Downie didn't disagree. "We wanted to be good for Bob," he said. "He was a focusing influence on the group. He was interested in what our influences were and showing that to people." In 2007, when Rock was entered into the Juno Hall of Fame, it was Downie who gave the induction speech. A year later, Rock joined the band onstage in Ottawa for a cover of David Bowie's "Queen Bitch." Clearly, this love affair was just beginning.

But the really weird thing about that Bruce Allen quip? The one slagging the Hip as a substandard CanCon joke? He made it in 2007, the year after *World Container* came out.

———

In 2006, Downie was excited about this new chapter for the Hip. He put his solo career on hold. The energy he would normally devote to his solo career was instead channelled into a new cause championed by his old Queen's friend Mark Mattson, who way back then was a roommate of two Harmer sisters, Barbara and Mary. Mattson was now an environmental lawyer, who had been horrified when, in 2000, seven people died in Walkerton, Ontario, after drinking the town's tap water. With Kristyn Tully, Mattson launched Lake Ontario Waterkeeper in 2001, dedicated to mounting legal challenges against polluters in and around Lake Ontario. Sarah Harmer played Waterkeeper's first-ever fundraiser that same year. The organization's stated goal is to lobby for a "swimmable, drinkable, fishable" future.

The message resonated with Downie, who once said, "I'm more likely to call myself a citizen of Lake Ontario than anywhere else." He grew up across the street from Lake Ontario, near Breakwater Park in Kingston— adjacent to a swimming pier that, in 2017, would be renamed the Gordon Edgar Downie Pier. "As kids, we spent every waking moment up and down the rocky shore," he recounted. "We used to tie a skipping rope to a pitchfork and try to spear big carp. We never got one. My kids love that story, very *Lord of the Flies*." In the mid-2000s, he said, "I'd lost contact with the lake and the water and assumed it belonged to someone else. In fact, it belongs to us. It's in the commons, the public trust. The water is a definite influence on my life. The Lake Ontario of my mind. It's in everything I think about and everything I do. When I go to express myself, that's where

I go." The Bathouse studio was on the water. So was Dale Morningstar's Gas Station studio, on Toronto Island, where Downie recorded with the Country of Miracles. When his family bought a fishing lodge in 2006 in Prince Edward County—near the Glenora ferry, with a view of Main Duck Island, and the nuclear reactors of Oswego in New York state visible on the horizon—he and his kids would swim off the sandbanks almost every day.

In 2006, the Lafarge cement company announced they were going to be building a kiln to burn tires, plastics and household garbage near Bath. No public hearings were being scheduled. The Ontario ministry of the environment approved the project. Waterkeeper, two other environmental groups and the Tragically Hip appealed the licences, spent $150,000 on expert assistance and won. Lafarge filed an appeal; the company lost. Downie knew he was lucky; other communities would not necessarily be so.

"Gord is the hardest-working guy you've ever met in your life," said Mattson. "He surprised me on environmental issues: read everything, worked hard, wrote. He's a huge researcher. Gord always said he didn't know what he was talking about—but of course he did. We did half-hour radio shows where he'd talk about these issues and he was brilliant. Gord's influence wasn't so much that he was famous, but that he worked with me and Krystyn and we went through the courts and won based on law, science and argument. [His] fame was there—people were nervous about [using] it, but people were surprised he didn't use it more. He showed up at every hearing, by himself, took notes. He never did press releases. I always said: don't argue the case on the front steps of the courtroom unless you're losing in the courtroom. A lot of environmentalism is on the front steps, using the court as a backdrop. But I like to win the cases."

Canadians' attitude toward its fresh water supply is "cavalier at best, criminal at worst," said Downie, "how we take it for granted." Waterkeeper's message was, and is, simple: "They're not asking people to use different light bulbs or drive different cars," said Downie, "they're just reminding people there are perfectly good laws in the books that say if you pollute, you have to clean it up."

Water as both a metaphor and something quantifiable also appealed to him. "You can hold up a glass full of lake water and it's hard to deny what's in that glass," he said. "Whereas emissions are a lot easier to fudge. Anything that comes out of a stack or runs off the land ends up in the water and in the plant life and then the fish. So it's a natural line in the sand, a natural place to start . . . We're all lulled into thinking in some paternalistic way that some benevolent uncle is protecting the environment. In fact, none of that takes place without a push."

In 2006, Mattson assembled a travelling road show to raise Waterkeeper's profile. Downie was the singer. Andrea Nann was the dancer. Tanis Rideout, an old friend of Sarah Harmer's, would be the poet. Mattson would be the advocate. He thought his job would be easy: just get up and talk. Downie had to teach the lawyer a few lessons. "I didn't realize until I toured with him that we had to practise," said Mattson. "I never practised. I should. I have since. Practise my speeches, the choreography, prepare, take voice lessons. Find your voice. Deep breaths. 'What are you going to do when the lights go down?' He would get [to the venue] early, 11 o'clock, and the thing wouldn't start until seven. I mean, what the hell?! He'd want to meet everyone who was involved."

The Tragically Hip had embraced easy, apolitical causes in the past: Camp Trillium, for children with cancer (in 1994, the Hip raised one-quarter of Camp Trillium's annual budget); the United Way; Kingston hospitals; Olympic athletes; War Child, assisting youth in international conflict zones. All important and valuable, none of them controversial. The most political event they appeared at would have been the Live 8 concerts, advocating for increased foreign aid in the budgets of G8 countries.

The exception, of course, was the 1993 Clayoquot Sound protest against clearcutting the rainforest on Vancouver Island's west coast. The Hip were on the Another Roadside Attraction tour with Midnight Oil, whose front man Peter Garrett took an acute interest in the cause. Midnight Oil performed at the barricades in the "Peace Camp," on a stage made from charred clear-cut logs. Downie joined them to take in the scene. David Suzuki was dancing in the front row. Later on the tour, in Calgary, the Oils and members of the Hip, Crash Vegas and Daniel Lanois recorded a charity single, "Land," with proceeds going to the activists' legal defence fund. The protests were the largest act of civil disobedience in Canadian history—and ultimately proved to be effective. By the end of the year, the Nuu-chah-nulth and the provincial government signed an interim agreement halting the cuts; in 2000, Clayoquot Sound and the surrounding area was designated a UNESCO biosphere reserve.

"Peter Garrett showed [the Hip] a lot about what could be done," said Mattson, "about how their fame could bring all these people together and how they could have an impact. Maybe that was unfortunate—given that it was [the Hip's] first big cause, that [success] wouldn't always be the case. I say this to artists all the time, and Gord knew this: when we start out doing something, we're only going to have 20 people there at the beginning—unless you bring the whole band, but that's a massive undertaking involving agents, other people and money. But to actually get out there and really understand and learn these issues and start from scratch, the audience is very small, even if you're famous. You can bring the band in when an issue is already famous, that's one thing. But to make an issue famous? Especially like water quality, which wasn't on everybody's radar? If we took on climate change or pipelines, that's when people will show up. But I was more focused on issues that affected small communities like Port Hope, Whitby, Kingston."

———

Bob Rock, having rescued Metallica from the brink of a breakup, may or may not have applied his mediating skills to help the Hip do the same. But that's what they needed to happen. "When we first worked with him, we had this thing: just trust in Bob. And we still do," said Johnny Fay in 2009. "He's a triple threat: engineer, producer and a great musician. You have everything there." All parties felt there was unfinished business after *World Container*. "It seemed like we were just getting to know each other as the album was ending," said Rock. "It was done three or four songs at a time. We knew that we had to try at least to raise the bar a bit. We knew we had to come up with something different, not just what we did before." Funny, then, that the album was called *We Are the Same*.

The title is unspeakably banal. What does it mean? *Hey, old fans, don't forget about us! We're now going to recycle every motif we've beaten into a cliché over the course of our career, with the help of the same producer we used last time.* It wasn't promising—or true, thankfully. Of course, it was a concept Downie was toying with, in a line from "Now the Struggle Has a Name" as well as the song "The Exact Feeling." It's the assumption that relationships remain static, rather than evolve—or fade. The assumption that finally getting to kiss your high school sweetheart as an adult is going to be an act of time travel rather than a rude awakening. The assumption that doing that drug again will deliver you the same experience you had the first time. "'The exact feeling' is an impossibility," he explained. "There is no such thing. And yet we continue chasing the impossibility. This record is full of [that]. The title in itself is an impossibility. It's something to shoot for but at the same time entirely a delusion."

Replicating their experience with Bob Rock started with a shift back to home turf: three sessions at the Bathouse, the first time in eight years the band had chosen to stay close to home. "I've always been a fan of going away to make a record," said Baker. "It makes you work more intensely, more quickly. But we revamped our studio, and it got to a point where we were saying, if we're not going to use it, why do we have it?"

We Are the Same has rock songs on it, but it is a far cry from a rock'n'roll record. It's a mid-life crisis record, from top to bottom. It's the existential dilemma heard in "Honey Please." It's the anxiety attacks and false comforts in "Morning Moon." The regret and departures in "The Last Recluse." The fanciful infatuation with a youthful ideal in "Coffee Girl." The haunted history of "Now the Struggle Has a Name." The diagnosis and denial in "The Depression Suite." The rural retreat and search for renewal in "Queen of the Furrows" and "Country Day." The marital crisis in "Speed River," "Frozen in My Tracks" and "Love Is a First"—in the latter, the word "first" is routinely interchanged with the word "curse."

It's also the most musically decorative the Hip have ever been, much more so than on *World Container*. On Hammond organ is veteran keyboardist John Webster, from Tom Cochrane's Red Rider and Idle Eyes ("Tokyo Rose") and a session player heard on records ranging from Suicidal Tendencies to Jann Arden, as well as many Bob Rock production jobs. Kevin Hearn of the Barenaked Ladies plays accordion and piano. Bob Buckley, who wrote the 1981 power ballad and No. 1 single "Letting Go" with his band Straight Lines, did the string arrangements. On tour in 2009, singer/songwriter Jim Bryson, also known as Kathleen Edwards's key sideman, was hired to flesh out the sound onstage.

If Downie explored his upper range on *World Container*, he went in the opposite direction on *We Are the Same*. Some vocals were recorded with portable gear in Rock's hotel room; in interviews, Downie talked about using his "hotel voice." Referring to his vocal approach, he said he used to have "a certain expectation that [if] you're going on record forever, you need to give'r. [But] there is intensity in restraint. That's what Bob has taught me. There are certain emotions, sentiments, expressions that are better whispered."

We Are the Same opens with "Morning Moon," the most country-esque song in the Hip catalogue, with uncharacteristically lush backing vocals, pedal steel, cello and perhaps the only time Gord Sinclair ever locked into a standard root-fifth pattern. "Honey Please," like "In View," is driven by

Kevin Hearn's piano hook and bears an uncanny resemblance to Barenaked Ladies—small wonder, then, that Steven Page later covered it in 2016. "The Last Recluse" opens and closes with what sounds like a pipe organ; there appears to be an operatic man chorus swelling in the latter third of the song, though no backing vocalists other than Sinclair and Langlois are credited. "Queen of the Furrows" opens with acoustic guitar, mandolin and hand drums before a crash of metallic(a) guitars come bursting into the chorus, followed by some arpeggiated wah-pedal noodling on the solo. Then there's the triumph of "Love Is a First," with a bass line similar to Talking Heads' "Psycho Killer," a guitar riff that chimes like the Smiths' Johnny Marr, a hard-rock chorus that wouldn't have been out of place on *Fully Completely* and an erratic, all-over-the-neck guitar wig-out that finds Baker emulating either a squiggly Bernie Worrell synth solo or Tom Morello of Rage Against the Machine. It's easily the most WTF single the Hip ever released to radio, but it's also a great pop song and became a Top 20 radio hit. There's nothing musically surprising about "The Depression Suite," other than how seamlessly three separate songs are linked together, an idea credited to Langlois and executed by Rock.

"The Depression Suite" was mocked for its ambition—which tells you something about the conservatism of rock fans—but it's "Frozen in My Tracks" that's the only clunker here: an awkward waltz with a heavy metal chorus and whoa-oh gang vocals, a direct nod to Mötley Crüe's "Dr. Feelgood." Far more successful is the equally uncharacteristic "Hush," an iTunes-only bonus track that finds Baker playing jazzy chords, the rest of the band dancing delicately behind him and Downie diving deep into his lower range.

Fan vitriol was reserved for "Coffee Girl": with its hip-hop drum machine beat, its Herb Alpert–esque trumpet solo and the image of a middle-aged man fawning over a young barista, it's anathema to everything the Hip built their career on. But as a pop song, it's entirely successful. There's nothing inherently creepy about the lyrics, no malice in the narrator's intent; it's simply a tale of tiny observations. Perhaps the lyrics' only crime is its avoidance of the Downie-esque oblique: in being easy to grasp, it's easy to dismiss.

Sadly muddled is "Now the Struggle Has a Name," a song with nods to the Canadian government's then recent apology for Indigenous residential schools and their abuses. The lyric uses the terms "truth" and "reconciliation," but it could just as well be about a domestic argument. It frequently refers to a character named "Honey Watson," a reference to Downie mis-hearing the name of CBC foreign correspondent Connie Watson, who had a story about Haiti follow a news report Downie was watching about the Truth and Reconciliation Commission. It's a MacGuffin that derails the entire lyrics. Turns out the struggle did not have a name after all.

In a hilarious takedown on the now-inactive blog *Coke Machine Glow*, one writer with a major hate-on for Bob Rock claimed, "Gord Downie and the boys fucked this one up royally. Really, nothing else in their back catalog comes close." Blame is placed only partly on "the bed of melo-dramatic strings that Rock drapes over the mess like he's a production designer on cable access television." Those are among the kindest things said in the 1,000-word review.

The Hip's second Bob Rock album proved to be one of the most divi-sive records of the Hip's career. Love it or hate it, they were, most defi-nitely, not the same.

CHAPTER NINETEEN

ARE WE THE SAME?
SURVIVING AS A CANADIAN CLASSIC ROCK BAND

"Retirement is not something I would ever do. My greatest hero is Howlin' Wolf. The stories of him are legendary, at 55, climbing the velvet curtain with the microphone clutched under his arm and singing from 35 feet above the stage. What would I retire to? It's what I do. It's what I love. It's what I'll always do."

GORD DOWNIE, 2009

HOMER AND BART Simpson are at the state fair. A band of grizzled rockers takes the stage.

"Who are these old men?" asks Bart.

"It's BTO!" says Homer. "They're Canada's answer to ELP. Their big hit was 'TCB.' That's how we talked in the '70s. We didn't have a moment to spare."

"Hellllllllloooooo Springfield!" says Randy Bachman. "We're going to play all your old favourites. But first, we'd like to dip into our new CD."

"'Taking Care of Business!'" hollers Homer.

"Don't worry, sir, we'll get to that," assures bassist Fred Turner.

"No talking! No new crap! 'Taking Care of Business,' now!"

They play it for fewer than 10 seconds, before Homer interjects again: "Get to the 'workin' overtime' part!"

"I don't believe this." Yet the band obliges. Homer dances. Happy as a pig in manure.

Cut to the next song, "You Ain't Seen Nothin' Yet." As soon as it's over, Homer yells out, "You Ain't Seen Nothin' Yet!"

"We just did that."

"Whatever."

"Be sure to stick around for the battle of the elementary school bands," says Fred Turner before he exits the stage.

That episode aired on Gord Downie's 36th birthday: February 6, 2000. This skit would not yet ring true for the Tragically Hip. Maybe it never did. They never played greatest-hits sets at county fairs, and they certainly never opened for a talent show. But a not insignificant part of their audience would have been happy if they'd only ever stuck to their first three albums—that's the entire reason Hip cover bands still exist. It's also part of the reason they toured behind a reissue of *Fully Completely* in 2015, playing the album in its entirety. To quote the Kinks, give the people what they want.

The *Fully Completely* tour prompted a skit on CBC comedy show *This Hour Has 22 Minutes*. In it, Shaun Majumder and Susan Kent are watching a band portraying the Hip, with Mark Critch as Gord Downie, playing "At the Hundredth Meridian."

"I love this song!" exclaims Majumder. "It's my favourite album, this is so awesome!" says Kent.

Then Critch/Downie stops singing and starts preaching: "I'm a super fan! Like only Bobby Orr can! I get money back on my *taxes*! I said to Merv, my tax guy, do you take new clients? He said, *yeeeah!*" The couple's look of delight quickly turns sour.

"Oh god," moans Kent, "he's doing a Gord Downie spoken-word rant thing."

"Wanna get a beer?"

"Yeah, we won't miss anything."

Cut back to Critch/Downie: ". . . full of hypocrisies and lies—*I've seen the Diefenbunker!*"

"Yes," intones a voice-over, "the Hip will play the entire *Fully Completely* album—if Gord Downie can ever get through a damn song." Cut to the couple at the bar, who now hear "New Orleans Is Sinking" in the distance and run back to the stage.

"*Swim! Swim!*" screams Critch/Downie, before going off again. "I was never a strooooooong swimmer. I remember a gym class, everybody got different colour ribbons like in Participaction . . ."

Every band is haunted by their history. The past is always present. No one cheers for new songs; they take a bathroom break.

That's true even for artists whose crowds are supposedly open-minded. In 2017, a story circulated online about Radiohead fans at the Glastonbury Festival applauding for an extended guitar-tuning break, thinking it was a new song. It's funny because it's—oh, wait, actually, it wasn't true at all. The story was a joke. The real Radiohead gig in question featured the normally innovative band revisiting their 1997 album *OK Computer*; they even played their breakthrough hit "Creep," long considered an albatross and left off set lists. That same year, U2 postponed the release of a new album, their 14th, so they could play *The Joshua Tree* in its entirety, for its 30th anniversary, on a sold-out stadium tour.

The Tragically Hip evolved throughout their career: some fans fell off after the first three or four records. Some prefer the latter-day pop hits. Some loved it when the band went the furthest out of their comfort zone, like on the Bob Rock records. But many would have likely been just as happy had they stuck to a script. "We never wanted to make *Up to Here*, parts 5, 6 and 7," said Sinclair, adding that because of their commercial cushion in Canada, no one from their American label ever pressured them to do so. "If something excites us in the studio, then we'll put it on the record. I'm sure [the 2000 track] 'As I Wind Down the Pines' makes some people cry every time they hear it, and I know for a fact other people hate it. But it's great to be in a position where you can indulge yourself musically."

"If they made 10 *Fully Completely*s, people would be fucking happy," says Gavin Brown, who produced 2012's *Now for Plan A*. "I don't think AC/DC has worries about their 10th or 12th album, because they're going to do what AC/DC does and be very happy about it. It's when people start putting themselves ahead of their fans and feel the need to grow into another thing, like 'this is my blue period.' Your fans don't want a blue period! They liked green on your first seven records. New Coke is not here anymore, you know? If you can make that one little blip and make it your own, then you win! You don't need to try and go somewhere else because you're insecure or whatever your issues are."

"We have about 12 to 14 songs that we have to play every night," says Neal Osborne of 54.40, whose first album came out in 1984 and whose last real radio hit was in 1998. "We don't mind, because those are the songs people get excited about." 54.40 have continued to release new records every three years since their major-label contract expired, but they add only "three to five new songs in the set. Maybe one of those songs is successful enough that you keep that one amid the next new batch of songs. When I saw Elton John live, he squeaked in two new songs. Which was good, but if he'd played any more, I don't think anyone would have been happy. Your biggest competition is your old catalogue—which is okay."

Even Neil Young, who's usually more than happy to piss off his audience, knows that. Sure, he might occasionally decide to debut an unrecorded rock opera about eco-justice for the entirety of one tour (*Greendale*, 2003), but most of the time his live show sticks to tried and true classics, regardless of how many new records he's released in the last 12 months.

Playing to the crowd is easy enough. If you want anyone to be interested in your new material, a radio hit is your best bet—and that's near impossible for any band long in the tooth. New records by Blue Rodeo, 54.40, Rush and other CanRock stalwarts don't get played on radio; neither did much of the Hip's later material, with rare exceptions ("In View," "Love Is a First"). Bands who put out their first records 30 years ago are, by definition, classic rock. "Playlists have become pretty locked," says Osborne. "We're fortunate to be there with our old catalogue. When we released *Lost in the City* [in 2011], we hired radio promoters and told them, 'If they don't play the new songs, just tell them to play anything by us.' A lot of [the promo cycle] is radio station visits. They love it when you drop by and say hi, and then you can play your new song live in the studio. Then you're reaching right through them to their listeners."

Why not just ride your own coattails and cruise on your catalogue? Gordon Lightfoot seems to be fine with that, among hundreds of other acts. Why put out new records at all? "Because we always have," says Osborne. "It's always been the fuel, our reason for being. Without that, it just doesn't feel as good."

Then there are acts who put a twist on the catalogue, like in 2017, when Barenaked Ladies recorded a new album of old material with the Persuasions, a veteran a cappella group from Brooklyn. In 2016, 54.40 put out a record of acoustic reworkings of their hits. The Vancouver band followed that with some "unplugged" shows—which were only a problem if they weren't advertised as such. "The worst gig was a casino in Calgary," says Osborne. "Some fans were expecting a rock show and got our acoustic show. It got a little hostile. It was almost like a political rally where there were supporters of the band who knew what was going on and then casual fans of the hits wanted to hear them the way they knew them. There was a lot of drinking, and both sides started arguing with each other—and with me. After the show, we went to the casino lounge to hang out, and a few guys came up to us: 'You guys sucked! That was awful!' Other fans got involved, security got involved—it was like 1981, being accused of selling out."

Many veteran artists release some of their greatest work late in their career after years of duds. Sometimes it gets its proper due: Bob Dylan's *Time Out of Mind*. Sometimes it's little more than a blip on a few radar screens: Paul Simon's *Stranger to Stranger*. It's not like either of those artists should have given up long ago. But if a fan happens to be taken with a new record by a veteran, it's best to catch that tour—because those songs will never resurface again. Or will they?

———

It was Belle and Sebastian who changed the live-music industry—ironic, for a band who put out three records before they ever played two consecutive dates.

The Scottish band started in 1996 as a studio project for Stuart Murdoch, a shy shut-in who was recovering from chronic fatigue syndrome. Live shows were few and far between in the band's first four years, even though their wispy folk-pop albums garnered them a devoted fan base on both sides of the Atlantic. They did not tour.

In 1999, they held a festival called the Bowlie Weekender, held at the Camber Sands resort in southeast England, between Brighton and Dover, in a beach town where fans and artists mingled easily. They invited many of their favourite artists from near and far. In 2000, it was rebranded All Tomorrow's Parties, and eventually expanded to several annual events around the world, each curated by an artist or band.

In 2005, All Tomorrow's Parties started the ironically titled Don't Look Back series in London, in which an artist was invited to perform a beloved back-catalogue album in its entirety. It started out with Belle and Sebastian's *If You're Feeling Sinister*, which was not even 10 years old at that point. But because it was an album that was never performed live when it came out, the Don't Look Back show was seismic for the band's fans. It even spawned a live record.

The only known precedent was a year earlier when Brian Wilson toured behind the long-lost album *Smile*, recorded in 1967 but not released until 2004. Again, this was music that had mostly never been played live, hence the novelty.

The trend quickly expanded beyond never-performed material. The underground embraced it first, largely at All Tomorrow's Parties. Suicide, Slayer and Sunn O))) all did it. Obscure but beloved bands no one ever thought would ever perform live again, like Slint or the Raincoats or Young Marble Giants, did it. In 2008, absurdist cult heroes Sparks performed all 21 of their albums over 21 consecutive nights in London—because they're Sparks. By the time Bruce Springsteen started doing it in 2015, the idea had become thoroughly mainstream and cross-genre. Public Enemy, Nas and Kanye West all did it; k.d. lang did it in 2017. So did Change of Heart.

In 2011, Gord Downie pooh-poohed the concept when asked about it directly. "I don't know that a band should get overly involved in the business of defining its own epochs," he said. "As long as you're giving the audience what you want, and emotionally and artistically and soulfully at that, you'll be good and true—maybe even entertaining."

Three years later, however, it was the Tragically Hip's turn, with *Fully Completely*. In November 2014, they reissued the album in a "super deluxe" package with a remastered version of the original and a live disc recorded at the Horseshoe in September 1992. The third disc was the long out-of-print doc *Heksenketel* on DVD. Also included was a book that featured an oral history of the album—which conspicuously did not include producer Chris Tsangarides—and plenty of archival photos, posters, artwork and clippings, even a reproduction of the original hockey card Downie quotes on "Fifty Mission Cap."

Touring behind it was a no-brainer. Although the Hip were no longer a band that inspired fever pitch among fans—and hadn't been since probably 2000—they weren't in their "gold watch and goodbye" phase, exactly. But starting that decade with a couple of tepid records followed by a pair of Bob Rock records that divided their audience and a 2012 record that appealed mostly to diehards all added up to an appetite for a victory lap. It's not like they never performed these songs: at least half of *Fully Completely* routinely made set lists right until the end. But audiences had a deep attachment to the entire record, an album that would stay on repeat at parties and never leave the car's tape deck. *Fully Completely* wasn't just a bestselling album in 1992–93, it was a cultural moment.

The Hip were not the first Canadian band to jump on this trend. In

2012, Sloan had put out a deluxe box set of their 1994 album, *Twice Removed*, and toured behind it, playing the album in its entirety. Sloan's Jay Ferguson had first mulled over the idea in 2009, the album's 15th anniversary. A year later, Sloan was a not-so-surprise guest at Sappyfest, an indie rock festival in Sackville, New Brunswick, co-founded by Julie Doiron. The surprise was that they came out and played *Twice Removed*. The crowd went nuts. Tears of joy. The more skeptical members of the band were won over. Ferguson went to work on his archives.

"I'm a big fan of reissues and digging deeper into albums I love," he says. "I thought there might be a thousand people out there who would buy this and enjoy it. I wanted to create a well-curated, expensive box set that fans would really dig. It's not done haphazardly." The *Twice Removed* box was so well received that Sloan did it again in 2016—both a box set and tour—for their 1996 album *One Chord to Another*. That proved to be even more successful than exhuming *Twice Removed*.

"Some think you should never look back and always look forward," says Ferguson. "I don't think in those terms. I always want to make new music. But why would we turn our back on something just because it's 20 years old, if we still enjoy playing it? It brought out a lot of people who had not been to a Sloan show in a long time. They liked us in college but then got a job, got married, had kids and hadn't been to a rock show in 10 years. But if we're playing one of their favourite records, then they *have* to go see that show. Talking to them after the show, they tell you they're so excited about seeing you again next time. Leapfrogging a new album and a reissue could really stretch out our career."

Broken Social Scene's Brendan Canning was the opening act on the *Fully Completely* tour, playing a DJ set before the show. "I think it was a good time for the Hip to do that," he said. "Maybe they'd have done a *Road Apples* tour next. There would be some grumbling in the band, but it's also not a bad way to make a living." Even Gord Downie had come around to the idea and suggested it to Canning. "Gord was telling me that [Broken Social Scene] should go out and tour [2002's] *You Forgot It in People*. But I mean, we don't even have a catalogue yet. We're only on our fourth real band record, after 15 years." No matter: Liz Phair had put out only five records by 2008, which is when she resurrected her 1993 debut *Exile in Guyville* on tour to celebrate its 15th anniversary.

The trend is not without criticism. Performing an album in order eliminates the element of surprise that was once key to a live experience.

Though in every area of modern life, consumers don't want surprise: they want safe. "What the audience wants is to hear the album like they remember it," wrote *Exclaim!* editor James Keast in a 2013 opinion piece. "Yet the more successful the band are, the closer this gets to total irrelevance. The more it sounds like the album, the more reason fans have to just stay home and listen to it. What I'd like to hear is the artist you are today interpreting your material, approaching it as a contemporary artist revisiting earlier material"—he cites Björk as an example—"not some bizarre time machine that pretends the last bunch of years never happened, artistically, culturally or musically."

Some artists cave in to demand with the caveat that they're putting a nail in the coffin. Ferguson recalls that "Sonic Youth, when they did *Daydream Nation* [in 2007], they said, 'That's it, that's the last time, we're now going to put this behind us.' They like to put something out, tour it and say goodbye. But I'm a fan of our band. I like to make use of the things we own and—not to sound crass—monetize them and make them available to a public who wants them and encourage people to come to shows.

"It's hard to get people interested in your 12th album. We're lucky enough that we own all our catalogue. Why let it just sit there?"

———

One of the most remarkable things about the Tragically Hip is that the same five people heard on their first recording in 1987 also played the final show 29 years later: no substitutions, no deaths, no ins-and-outs, and the band never went on hiatus nor spun into commercial oblivion. At the level of multi-million-selling success the Hip had, there are only three other rock bands in history who crossed the 30-year mark in the exact same scenario: ZZ Top, U2 and Radiohead. Even bands who make it to 20 active years with original members are rare. All others either don't have the same level of success, or they changed, dropped or added members at some point—including Rush, whose first album was made before Neil Peart joined. The Hip's friends in Los Lobos were together for 11 years before they added Steve Berlin to the band in 1984.

Rob Baker and Gord Sinclair met when they were toddlers. Gord Downie and Paul Langlois were friends since grade 11. None of them knew Johnny Fay when he auditioned for the band, but the 18-year-old came from the exact same background, high school and mindset; he fit in instantly. Hanging around your old high school friends on such an intimate basis when you're on the other side of 50 can be more of a curse than a blessing for some people. Not these guys.

Sam Roberts has known his bassist, James Hall, since they were both three years old; they started a band together with keyboardist Eric Fares at 16. They're both still in his band. "We had this very long vetting process," Roberts says. "If you can survive the rigours of house league soccer and swim team and high school dances together, then you figure out if they're someone you want to spend time with. Nobody gives you any tutelage on longevity. That's when you have to plant the seeds."

Barenaked Ladies lost their first keyboardist early on, almost lost their second keyboardist to leukemia and famously had an acrimonious split with one-half of the singing/songwriting duo at the core of the band. "When a band can stay together, even if it's not all the original members, it comes down to this: does everyone believe in the music they're playing?" says bassist Jim Creeggan.

For R.E.M.'s Peter Buck, the answer to that question was obvious. After 31 years together—having lost their drummer halfway through—Buck admitted, "We made a couple of albums [in the 2000s] where I thought, 'I don't even know if this is a record. It's just some sounds we put together.'" In 2011, they had a band meeting where singer Michael Stipe announced, "I think you guys will understand: I need to be away from this for a long time." Peter Buck said, "How about forever?" Bassist Mike Mills added, "Sounds right to me." The end.

"You have to be able to acknowledge where you're at," says Creeggan. "When you can give and when you can't. It's a family. How do you make a family work? How do you make any kind of team work? Everyone can relate to that. With the Hip, it's a testament to how they respected each other and supported each other. It's tough when you have a guy like Gord who is a really strong personality. He's the main lyrical and ideological thrust of the band."

Gord Downie recorded and toured with two bands other than the Hip; he rarely played Hip material in either configuration (you could count the instances on one hand). Even if the Hip had split up for whatever reason, it's unlikely you would ever see him performing "Little Bones" with anyone else. Certain bands have a chemistry that can't be replicated, which is obvious to anyone who's seen Sting play Police songs without Stewart Copeland and Andy Summers, or—well, take your pick. Jay

Ferguson picks Guided by Voices, whose original lineup dissolved in 1996, though bandleader Robert Pollard forged forward with rotating members until 2004. When that first lineup reunited in 2010, "I thought: *that's* the sound," says Ferguson. "The drummer's kinda shitty, the guitar sound is not amazing, but they have the gel that creates something that is impossible to recreate. When Robert Pollard hires other guys to play the same songs, it just sounds like Pollard with a cover band. I like the idea of original members; it's authentic."

54.40 guitarist Phil Comparelli left his band in 2005, after 22 years. That was a tough blow, Neil Osborne concedes, but the decision to continue "was an easy decision to make because it was a question of the band's survival. When [bassist] Brad Merritt and I started this band in high school, our manifesto was one word: survive. Make sure we always have another gig, or do what it takes to make a record, or whatever it was. That's inherent. It never went away because we got along so well and went through so much from age 17 onward."

Band members "have to have your back when things are tough," says Sam Roberts. "You have to be able to hash it out when there's a conflict, and you have to speak your mind without fear of the band disintegrating. Most important, how you mesh on a creative front will fuel the happiness of the band, or lack thereof."

The biggest challenge for any band past the 20-year mark, of course, is meeting their own expectations, rather than just phoning it in and collecting a paycheque. "Meeting expectations isn't as fun," said Downie. "That can happen with the Hip a lot. You come out [like that carnival game where you] swing the big mallet, and the thing goes up and rings the bell and you're supposed to do that. But you can still challenge people, and there's a lot to challenge them with." Sometimes that challenge works, sometimes it doesn't. "You're allowed to make shit records," says Crash Vegas's Michelle McAdorey. "Look at all my favourite artists: Neil Young, Nick Cave, whoever. I might not like the latest record, but why would I expect everything they do to be the thing I always loved?"

When music is truly your life's calling, the transcendence it delivers never goes away, even if the urgency diminishes. "We were on a mission," says Neil Osborne. "We thought we could change the world. There was a sense of panic and urgency. I felt like I would die, if that's what it meant to get to that place. It sounds weird and silly, but that's the way we felt. Today, as seasoned older people who have lived a life, it's really about the subtlety.

When we're up onstage and we're all in the pocket together, it's almost as if everything around us slows right down. We'll all be ready to hit that first chord of 'I Go Blind,' and we are so there. Just hitting that note, knowing all the vibrations that go with that, it's like riding an amazing wave on a surfboard, when you can slow it all down. Even though it's only for 10 seconds, that's the infinity I want. That's the difference between being twenty-something and fiftysomething."

If you're fiftysomething and only playing to the same people who came to see you 30 years ago, your options are naturally going to diminish. There are still plum gigs to be had: April Wine still pack 'em in at suburban soft-seat theatres where 70-year-olds, who bought tickets as part of a subscription series, nod their head quietly in approval—perhaps even letting out a whoop.

What set the Tragically Hip apart is that "their audience was always getting younger," says Sam Roberts, who played with them between 2002 and 2014. "It wasn't just aging gracefully with the band. It was young people to whom the music had been passed down by their parents or discovered the same way I found out about the Kinks or something. The front row of people was always young—or maybe I was just getting older and so they looked young. But to witness that rejuvenation of the fan base means that there was life left in the band. They were still vital, still pertinent."

CHAPTER TWENTY

OH YEAH, *THIS* BAND
2010–15: *THE GRAND BOUNCE, NOW FOR PLAN A*

"Someone asked me how I know what's a Hip song [and what's saved for a solo project]. I don't think about it—I just use it up. As dire as it sounds, I don't even know if I'm going to be here tomorrow, so I don't get too precious or cute about it."

GORD DOWNIE, 2010

THE TRAGICALLY HIP released only one album between 2010 and 2015, called *Now for Plan A*. It came out in 2012. Before and after came a lot of Plan Bs.

New solo projects started. Some were brought back to life. The new Hip album was their weakest seller, failing to go platinum. They followed it up by reissuing their biggest seller in a deluxe box set format and touring behind it. Several band members lost parents and in-laws. One became a parent for the first time. One lost all hearing in his right ear. One was being treated for hip pain, of all things. One spouse battled and survived breast cancer. No one said turning 50 is easy. Neither is being in the same band for 25 years.

———

It was the day after Halloween, 2008. Dale Morningstar was walking on the beach near his studio on Toronto Island when his phone rang. It was Gord Downie. "It's time," he said.

The Country of Miracles had been on hold for five years. Not that anyone noticed. "No one ever said we were having a hiatus," said Julie Doiron. "We did that [2003] tour and then a Hip record came out. I wasn't sitting around wondering about the next gig. When Gord called me to say we were making another record, I was like, 'Oh yeah, *that* band!'"

Doiron had kept busy with her own solo records, including 2007's *Woke Myself Up*, which was shortlisted for the Polaris Music Prize. She played supporting roles on tour in the French band Herman Dune and New Brunswick's Shotgun and Jaybird; there were also some Eric's Trip reunion shows. Josh Finlayson had soldiered on with the Skydiggers. The Dinner Is Ruined had slowed down, but Dale Morningstar remained busy producing other people's records at his Gas Station studio. He and Dave Clark travelled to Africa, collaborating and recording with musicians in Mali.

Downie wasn't sure he was going to make another solo record, until he met Chris Walla, the guitarist in Death Cab for Cutie. Formed in 1997 in Bellingham, Washington, Death Cab revolved around the earnest lyrics of Ben Gibbard, endearing the band to doe-eyed teens of a new generation. Walla produced all their records. In 2002, he produced the debut EP by Victoria, British Columbia's Hot Hot Heat, which led to work for the Decemberists, Tegan and Sara (2007's *The Con*, 2009's *Sainthood*) and others. He also helped his Death Cab bandmate Gibbard on his million-selling side project the Postal Service. In 2008, Walla released his debut solo album, *Field Manual*, as well as Death Cab's *Narrow Stairs*. He met Downie that July at the Pemberton Festival in B.C. They hit it off immediately. "In an hour's conversation, I was able to determine that he was a guy without a hint of snobbery and an encyclopaedic knowledge of music past, present and future," said Downie. One morning back in Toronto, Downie was listening to *Narrow Stairs* in his car. When he got home, he called Walla and told him they were going to work together. "Sure," responded Walla.

"What I find interesting about Death Cab records—and I didn't even realize this until he was mixing my record—is that the way he mixes turns every song into an event, or a series of events," said Downie. "It doesn't go linearly. Every eight or 16 bars, you're turning a corner, with the addition of an instrument or some other element. He's just changing the atmosphere of the song, so they unfold very elegantly."

Everyone except Doiron, who was now living in Sackville, New Brunswick, convened at Josh Finlayson's house to start learning Downie's new material. Walla drove from his home in Portland, Oregon, to Toronto in July 2009 to join them. Studio time was booked at the Bathouse in August, which is when Doiron took a train to Kingston to meet her old bandmates.

Doiron wasn't sure where to fit in: everyone else already knew the songs, and there were four guitar players there already, including Walla. Downie wanted her to play guitar, too. "I thought I would just sing on everything," she recalled. "I didn't know what else I could bring to it." With Walla's encouragement, she played on everything. "I ended up coming up with a lot of guitar parts I really loved. It pushed me out of my comfort zone. They had faith in me. I wasn't good at collaborating. Even after all those years of being in the Country of Miracles, I was really insecure and intimidated by all these guys who are really sweet and really cool and good at what they do."

The sessions were joyous. Everything was tracked live in the front room of the Bathouse, which resembles a ramshackle library more than a recording environment. "Happy days collapsed into sunken evenings," said Downie. "We recorded and swam, had some laughs and raised our glasses." Dave Clark credited Walla for enabling such an easy session. "He knew the minutiae of what people were doing, musically, in a great way," he said. "He's a beautiful player. He was deeply respectful and kind and happy." Downie was in an emotional and reflective state of mind. "I am grateful," he wrote when the album was finished. "Grateful for the words, for expression. Grateful to the band and to Chris and to my family. Grateful for the chance to try for an emotional event that unfolds gradually, elegantly, beautifully."

That it does. *The Grand Bounce* is Downie's most fully realized solo record, probably the most underrated work in his entire catalogue. It has the beauty of *Coke Machine Glow*. It has the energy of *Battle of the Nudes*. It has the melodicism and songcraft of the Bob Rock records. It brings out the strength of every player on it. Downie and Doiron's harmonies sound like that of siblings.

Much of *The Grand Bounce* reflects Downie's recent move from Toronto to Prince Edward County in 2006, including "Moon Over Glenora." The album opens with the soaring, Springsteenian folk-rock anthem "The East Wind": a melody worthy of Lightfoot, the chorus lyrics borrowed from a farming neighbour. "Broadcast" is another Downie ode to Lake Ontario. "As a Mover" is driven by a droning organ, throbbing bass and railroad rhythm; the lyric addresses the uncertainty of a man uprooting his family. "Gone," if it is to be read autobiographically, suggests the move did not go well.

"The Hard Canadian," written in a hotel room in Detroit overlooking the Ambassador Bridge, takes its title from a phrase uttered by *Trailer Park Boys* director Mike Clattenburg, a friend of Downie's. "Yellow Days" is one of Downie's finest melodies and lyrics, while the arrangement immediately situates the listener in a hot, muggy August night; Dave Clark's malleted ride cymbal sounds like what Joni Mitchell would call "the hissing of summer lawns." "Pinned," the intimate closer, takes an original piano passage played by Downie's teenage daughter and loops it. Over top, he placed a recording of himself whispering a melody on a train, en route home from a funeral. The daughter was not happy about the surreptitious recording; he gave her songwriting credit as consolation.

"The Night Is for Getting" had been tried by the Tragically Hip before, but John Press's cascading piano line and Doiron's harmonies, along with the punk rock energy, serve the song much better. After purposely redirecting all his energies toward the Hip for the last four years, Downie was now telling the press he no longer worried about segregating his material. "That would give me a headache," he said.

The title was a curious choice, however, as it's 19th-century American military slang for desertion. "Desertion is everywhere, all the time," said the then-46-year-old singer during a campus radio interview. He seemed to cherish running with the theme. "We desert ourselves, our values, our convictions, our morals, our better judgments, our memories, our promises, our nature, our god. Wedding vows: in sickness and in health, until death do us part—'I'm not deserting you, honey, I'm just dying!' Fight or flight. It seemed bottomless to me; that's why I chose it as a title."

The most surprising thing about *The Grand Bounce* was the cover image, painted by Downie himself. Rob Baker was always the visual artist in the Hip—he painted the cover of *In Violet Light* and played a key role in art directing all Hip album covers. But the entire band shared an interest; in 1997, a Kingston gallery even asked all the members to loan favourite pieces from their collections for an exhibition. Downie offered works by the abstract expressionist landscape artist Manfred Mohr and local Kingston artist Daniel Hughes.

The Grand Bounce cover was the first time fans had any inkling that Downie himself was also painting. That became more evident on the tour, where Downie had an overhead projector onstage, set up next to his microphone. Either before or during songs, he would manipulate watercolours and food dyes on top of transparencies, creating gorgeous fluid accompaniment to the music. There was some recent local precedent to this: Toronto artist Stephanie Comilang used a projector to create layered shadow plays on tour with Owen Pallett in 2006; Shary Boyle did live drawings on a projector for both Feist and Christine Fellows. The work of those women was different from each other and from Downie's work with paints. He was drawn to the ephemeral nature of the process, at a dawn of a new cultural moment—three years after the iPhone launch—when audiences were determined to document their experience rather than enjoy it. "You can film it on your phone," he said, "but you're really only getting 10 per cent, so you're better off putting your phone away and taking it in. You can try and explain it later, after gauging what you took in, what you got from it and what you want to get more of."

The visual element happened only during the theatre tour in the fall of 2010. The preceding summer dates were largely at outdoor festivals, including a sweltering early afternoon set at Coachella in California. Downie was not necessarily playing in front of a sympathetic crowd at festivals—a challenge he relished. At the Edmonton Folk Festival, he saw one woman in the audience plugging both her ears "in full view of everyone, needing me and everyone to see that she entirely disapproved," he said. "But I was really happy about that; my punk rock self was really happy about the prospect of garnering disparate levels of reaction from 'I hate what you do' to 'I love what you do.' That's the dream you dream as a musician, to elicit strong feelings. No one wants a five out of 10."

The Inbreds' Mike O'Neill saw the Country of Miracles at the Rebecca Cohn Auditorium in Halifax on that tour. There, too, Downie spotted an audience member plugging their ears. This time, it agitated him. He asked a stagehand for some tissue, then left the stage, walked up to the person and said, "Do you want this in your ears?" Later, backstage, Downie expressed some regret. "I was a bit of an asshole there, but it was so distracting I just wanted it to end," he told O'Neill.

The arc of the set contained a dynamic range of moods, but Dave Clark conceded that it was a loud band. "It was the loudest tour I'd ever been on," he said. "It wasn't as out-of-the-box musically as it was visually. Gord worked really hard connecting those two. And on my end, there's always the challenge of balancing excessively physical playing with more dynamic, orchestral approaches to the music. The band was super tight."

The tour ended in November 2010; the next summer, the Country of Miracles did a one-off gig at Daniel Lanois's Harvest Picnic outside

Hamilton, on a bill where Emmylou Harris and Lanois's band performed her 1995 album *Wrecking Ball*. Clark couldn't make the gig; Johnny Fay subbed in for him. Downie was delighted. "It meant a lot to Gord that Johnny did that gig," said one friend.

The Country of Miracles was created from a recording project consciously meant to be as Hip-free as possible. Yet Downie still called Paul Langlois to sing on 2001's *Coke Machine Glow*. And at the last gig the Country of Miracles would ever play, he had Johnny Fay behind the kit. Gord Downie would always be a member of the Tragically Hip, first and foremost. Because he loved them.

———

By 2010, Downie was no longer the only Tragically Hip member with a solo project. In 2005, Rob Baker had started working with Craig Northey of the Odds, with that band's rhythm section and Doug and the Slugs keyboardist Simon Kendall—that lineup had called themselves Sharkskin since 1999. With Baker in the band, the new project was called Strippers Union; the guitarist who got his start playing after dancers at the Lakeview Manor believed burlesque dancers and rock musicians had a lot in common. Baker had a lot of musical ideas stored away, ones that never made it into the Hip; Craig Northey added lyrics and helped him shape the songs into more than sketches. A self-titled debut album appeared in 2005, and a follow-up, *The Deuce*, in 2011. Baker and Northey claimed to be heavily influenced by R&B—which explains the presence of horns—yet the band is a far cry from the Stax/Volt records said to have been an inspiration, or even from the young Tragically Hip's take on songs by Marvin Gaye and Otis Redding. For hardcore Hip fans, however, it was a treat to hear Baker's rich baritone take a few lead vocal turns, considering that he'd never once stepped to a mic during a Hip show.

Hip fans were familiar with Paul Langlois's voice, and even his specific writing style: he'd written "She Didn't Know" and "When the Weight Comes Down" on *Up to Here*, before the Hip fully democratized their songwriting method. He didn't expect to ever make a solo record. He kick-started his extracurricular activity in 2005, by producing a record at the Bathouse for his old high school friend, credited to the Hugh Dillon Redemption Choir. Dillon was having trouble finding a label to put it out; Langlois decided to step up and start his own, Ching Music. Ching focused on Kingston-area artists: Jim Tidman, Greg Ball, My Friend Andy, and the Campfire Liars Club, the latter a collaborative project for all Ching artists.

In 2010, knowing that Downie had slotted some time to tour behind *The Grand Bounce*, Langlois decided to follow Baker's lead and start sorting through years of musical ideas he'd shelved. He went to the Bathouse and started to play drums along with the tracks. It worked better than he expected. He then decided to write lyrics and play the rest of the instruments himself. The result, *Fix This Head*, was released in December 2010. Langlois wasn't the only one pleasantly surprised: the guitarist—who'd once contemplated trying to make a career in Nashville before he joined the Hip—could easily stand on his own. His voice largely stuck to a Lou Reed–ish singing-speaking style, which served his storytelling. He returned in 2013 with the more accomplished, less tentative follow-up, *Not Guilty*. On both records, the invisible guitarist in the Tragically Hip displayed exactly what it was he brought to the band, and they served as a calling card for Langlois as a producer as much as a solo performer.

Gord Sinclair joined Baker in backing up local Kingston artist Miss Emily Fennell, but was largely happy to stay behind the boards. He made four albums with Peterborough band the Spades, led by James McKenty. He produced the fourth album by Nova Scotian hard rockers the Trews, 2011's *Hope and Ruin*; he co-wrote 10 of the 12 songs, including one co-write with Dave Rave of Teenage Head and one with Newfoundland songwriting legend Ron Hynes. Sinclair played bass on one track on *The Falcon Lake Incident* by Jim Bryson and the Weakerthans—it's the one track the Weakerthans didn't play on. Johnny Fay spent some time in B.C., playing drums with Kelowna band the Sleddogs and joining an all-star group in Vancouver called Stellar Band of Neighbours, featuring the Odds' Steven Drake, Kevin Kane of the Grapes of Wrath, Simon Kendall, Wyckham Porteous and Del Cowsill. He later joined a country band led by Grant Tingey of Gravenhurst, Ontario.

Two years after *We Are the Same* and a flurry of solo activity, the Hip hired Gavin Brown to produce the next record. He was sent some demos everyone had been working on. "The demos were so interesting—because there was nothing there," said Brown. Confused, he called manager Bernie Breen and asked, "Are you pulling one over on me here, buddy?"

Gavin Brown first met the Tragically Hip in November 1996. He was playing drums in the last incarnation of Crash Vegas, opening a Hip show at the Buffalo Auditorium. It was also the first time he'd ever seen the Hip play live. He was bowled over by the power of "Grace, Too" and others.

When Brown was a young punk rocker, playing in arty hardcore band Phleg Camp—Sean Dean, later of the Sadies, was the bassist—the Hip were not the kind of band he would be into. By the time Phleg Camp released their final album, 1992's Steve Albini–engineered *Ya'red Fair Scratch*, the Tragically Hip ruled the country while Brown and his friends were listening to *Goat* by the Jesus Lizard. "I never bought a Hip record," he said, "because every place we'd load in, a Hip record was playing. In the '90s, they were ubiquitous."

Brown's hardcore days didn't last long; he soon became a gigging drummer with the Skydiggers, Crash Vegas and Big Sugar. In 1998, Brown joined Danko Jones, a garage-rock power trio named after its tongue-wagging, sexually charged singer, who was gleefully out of place in the polite world of Canadian rock. (He later became a minor star in Scandinavia.) During Brown's brief eight months in the group, he co-wrote and produced the single "Bounce," which proved to be the national radio breakthrough for a band barely known beyond Toronto's Queen Street West at the time. It preceded the commercial return of garage rock by two years. Brown had struck gold with his first-ever foray into producing.

"Within a few months, Danko Jones went from a band that played one riff for the whole song to having actual songs," Brown said in *Too Much Trouble*, a Danko Jones biography. "I thought the next idea was to have amazing songs." The band, however, did not want to write songs that could be sung: they wanted to snarl and sneer. At one practice, Jones chided Brown about a new song, saying, "This is shit; it sounds like Tears for Fears." "Tears for Fears are amazing," responded Brown. Years later, when reminded of the incident, Brown dug in: "Tears for Fears are a great band and will go down in history as a far more important band than Danko Jones."

At that point in time, Brown had a young family of three to feed. He made more money in one session gig than he did in one month as the drummer in Danko Jones. When they fired him, it was no skin off his back.

He went to Bernie Breen for advice. Breen was working for Jake Gold at the Management Trust and had managed Crash Vegas. They met in Breen's office. In the background, Toronto "modern rock" station the Edge was playing.

"Look, I like this producing thing. I'd like to do more," Brown said to Breen.

"Well, what have you done?"

"Bounce" came on the radio at that very moment.

"I did that!'

That was on a Wednesday. Breen gave him $200 to work with a new teen artist signed to Management Trust, Alexandra Slate. Brown and Slate co-wrote three songs that weekend. On the Monday, the president of EMI Publishing offered him a publishing deal. "What's publishing?" asked Brown. "I thought: 'Great! I'm going to buy Pro Tools and all this equipment.' [The publisher] said, 'No. I'm going to buy you a guitar—*so you can write songs.*'"

Brown and Slate wrote 24 more songs together and recorded in L.A. with Green Day producer Rob Cavallo. More tracks were recorded at the Bathouse, with Colin Cripps producing and members of the Hip playing on it. When released, Slate's album barely made a blip, but Brown's new career was about to take off. In 2003, Brown produced two of the biggest rock records of the year: the self-titled debut albums by Three Days Grace and Billy Talent. *Billy Talent* sold 300,000 copies in Canada, as did its Brown-produced follow-up in 2005. *Three Days Grace* sold more than a million copies in the U.S. alone.

Any traces of his teenage punk rock snobbery were long gone. He played drums for Great Big Sea and Jim Cuddy while producing the Cancer Bats and the Tea Party. Closer to the Hip camp, he made two records with their old friend Sarah Harmer: 2004's *All of Our Names* and 2010's *Oh Little Fire*.

In February 2011, he went to the Bathouse to meet the Tragically Hip. Gord Sinclair had already recorded demos of five songs. Everyone was now presenting "thought sketches," said Brown. "We then sat in the room and grew these seeds to flower. It was a beautiful time, in the winter; great dinners, great talks." Brown is a firm believer in pre-production: arranging and workshopping songs well before anyone presses the record button. That happened for two months early that year, on and off, "three days a week, just to reacquaint everybody," he said.

By June, the Hip hadn't played a show in a more than a year, and they had a big one coming up in Bobcaygeon, Ontario. The cottage-country town of 2,500 people was expecting a crowd of 25,000 for the Hip's show there, largely because, of course, Downie had immortalized the place in a hit song. Fifteen years after Brown had last seen the band play live, he was in the Bathouse watching the Hip rehearse when they broke into "Grace, Too"—and he broke into goosebumps. "Oh yeah," he thought. "*This* band."

———

Work on the record ground to a halt in August 2011. Downie's wife, Laura Leigh Usher, was diagnosed with breast cancer. The music stopped.

Downie stayed home, caretaking, cooking, learning how to be the spouse of someone stricken with disease. "My jobs were very menial and basic," he said. "But in the moral support side, I fell short—a lot. Which maybe only a husband can. A man should be satisfied with the little joys that sacrifice can bring. But a man should also consider those things long after the fact. In the middle of it, it's useless. My wife's health and happiness is its own reward, obviously. That's all I really care about. So many of her friends are going through this. [She's] a woman who's done all the right things, eaten the right things, exercised right and is trying to make sense of it. She would listen to almost everybody but me."

He was not writing during her chemo and recovery. It didn't feel right, or useful, or remotely rewarding for anyone. When she recovered, his writing changed. "Everything [I wrote] had to achieve a standard of reality," he said. "Illusion wasn't really cutting it. To the extent that I've contributed to the illusion machine all these years, and to the extent that I tried to extricate myself from the illusion machine now, was very basic. I wanted to write very clearly, openly. Having said that, I still write the way I write." Of the lyrics on *Now for Plan A*, he said, "Maybe [the meaning] is not entirely obvious, but it would be obvious to the people to whom it would be obvious."

When pen finally returned to paper, Downie wrote songs like "Man Machine Poem," "Take Forever" and "Done and Done," none of which could be accused of being obvious. "Every song doesn't have meaning," Downie said. "Maybe these don't either, but they mean something to me." "About This Map" and "The Lookahead" could well be about disease, or they could be of a piece with the mid-life marital songs that coloured *We Are the Same* and *The Grand Bounce*. Two songs that journalists and fans presumed to be about Usher had in fact been played live before her August 2011 diagnosis, as seen in the *Bobcaygeon* film shot two months earlier: "At Transformation" and "We Want to Be It" (the refrain of "drip drip drip" supposedly referring to chemo treatment). "Please don't make it a cancer album," Usher told him.

When the album came out, very few critics picked up on any of this, other than the staff of CBC Radio's *Q*, where Downie was asked if the songs were about mortality; his response was cagey. After filming an interview with Wendy Mesley for CBC's *The National*, however, Downie called her back and asked for a do-over. And another. And another. He kept coming back, eventually doing four takes of the interview. He wanted to choose his words with utmost care. It was the most personal interview he'd ever given up to that point in time.

Mesley was an ideal interlocutor: she had been diagnosed with breast cancer in January 2005, when she was 47. In 2006, she returned to work as host of *Marketplace* after two lumpectomies, chemo and radiation therapy, and she produced a documentary called "Chasing the Cancer Answer," about potential links between environmental toxins and the prevalence of cancer.

Downie spoke to Mesley about the song "The Lookahead," a song "where I was trying to help, mutely, in the way a man around breast cancer tries hard to help. It's a struggle. You make so many mistakes. Mortality is not even relevant. There are decisions to be made here. As cold and as calculated as those decisions seem, it's at least an oasis of comfort, because at least you're moving toward something."

Usher survived. At the same time, however, Paul Langlois was worried he might never sing with the Tragically Hip again.

On December 8, 2011, Langlois woke up and thought his ears were plugged. He walked his daughter to the bus stop for school and noticed he had trouble hearing her. The situation didn't improve the rest of the day. That night, he went to Toronto to see Ryan Adams at Massey Hall and stayed over in a hotel. Testing the phone in his room, he realized he had no hearing at all in his right ear. He googled "sudden hearing loss." It was a thing: rare but not entirely unusual. He feared he'd be unable to sing harmonies live. Because there were no gigs on the horizon, he toyed with headphones and in-ear monitors in the Bathouse, figuring out how to adjust. His usual stage set-up, on the right side of the stage, meant that the band was always to his left—so that was some consolation. At the next Hip show, on the remote shores of James Bay, no one was the wiser.

———

Joseph Boyden had been a friend of Gord Downie's since 2005, the year the writer published his first novel, *Three Day Road*. Set in Moose Factory, Ontario, and the First World War battlefields of France and Belgium, the book's combination of European military history and a rarely documented area of Canada appealed to Downie's sensibilities. The singer tracked down the writer's email address and dropped him a line with a one-word subject header: "Woah." He invited Boyden over to his house for a visit. Two months later, they went fishing together in James Bay. They both became high-profile supporters of Lake Ontario Waterkeeper. In 2009, Downie hired Boyden to write a press release for *We Are the Same*. Boyden interviewed Downie for *Maclean's*.

In February 2012, Boyden had been invited to be the keynote speaker at the Great Moon Gathering by the former Fort Albany chief Edmund Metatawabin. Held on the shores of the Albany River near James Bay, the educational event gathered youth from all the surrounding reserves. That area included Kashechewan—which for years had been the focus of dire headlines for its boil-water advisories and suicide crises—and Attawapiskat, which, in October 2011, had declared a housing crisis, a crisis that helped kick-start the Idle No More movement a year later, demanding that Indigenous issues be part of the mainstream political conversation. The Great Moon Gathering sought to provide local youth with some rare positivity. In his initial phone call to Boyden, Metatawabin made a request familiar to all of Downie's close friends: "And, uh, do you think you could ask Gord to come?"

Gord wanted to come. So did the rest of the Tragically Hip. And their crew. And their management. And Gavin Brown. And CBC Radio host Shelagh Rogers. And filmmakers Nicholas de Pencier and Jennifer Baichwal. And photographer Andrew Tolson from *Maclean's*. And Waterkeeper's Mark Mattson. They all piled into a small prop plane and flew over the exact spot where Bill Barilko's body had been found, en route to Fort Albany. Volunteers from all around the Albany River ensured that the necessary sound equipment arrived, and that the visitors would be fed fresh food in a town where a head of lettuce cost eight dollars. They all did it, wrote Boyden in *Maclean's*, because "we decided that we needed to initiate a guerrilla act of love for a people who are so thoroughly underrepresented but now, somehow, overexposed for only their shortcomings. A guerrilla act of love to show the rest of the country what strength and artistry, grace and humour the Cree possess."

The Tragically Hip played in Fort Albany's high school gym. The green room was the school library, where they were served moose stew. There were five local opening acts comprised of teenagers. Downie joined one, Northern Revolution, on their version of Bob Dylan's "Knockin' on Heaven's Door," a song he'd once sang with the Slinks and the Filters as a young man. "We do the Guns N' Roses version," the band asserted. Right before the show, he learned that their singer, Roseanne Knapaysweet, was going to sit the song out. "You mean you guys bumped your singer for me?!" Downie yelled at her bandmates, only half-mockingly. "Don't do that! This is your singer! You never bump your singer for anyone!" They all insisted, including Roseanne. After she sang the first song on her own and left the stage, Downie stepped to the mic and called her back for "Heaven's Door." She sang harmony through the whole thing. The guitarist, Braiden Metatawabin, played what Downie called a "gym-melting solo." Afterwards, Roseanne wrote that the experience taught her she "shouldn't let the word 'fear' bring me down. I need to face it." Her sister was crying with pride. "Everything that people said about me [that night] made me feel more confident about myself," Roseanne continued. "I don't even think about the negative stuff anymore."

The whole band returned from the trip feeling inspired and changed. The ice fishing, the snowmobiling, the sweat lodge, the sense of community they experienced "was a great bonding thing for us," said Brown. "It was short, but seemed longer and deeper. You can go on tour with a band, but this was special. I learned a lot, saw a part of Canada I'd never seen, and it gave me a lot of context."

Downie wrote a new song, "Goodnight Attawapiskat." When it was released, some people—even some people who actually listened to it—assumed it was a protest song. It wasn't. Unless, of course, portraying the people of Attawapiskat as full of promise and hope is inherently political. Which it is. "I'm trying to paint a picture that isn't the one we all accept and forget about," he said.

"The song is about a band showing up in Attawapiskat to play," said Downie. "'Good evening folks, we're the Silver Poets. No one ever got laid telling people what to do. We're just a band here in our thousand-mile suits. We're here to play.' I try to make it like a Chamber of Commerce piece: 'Oh, Attawapiskat, the city by the bay! Diamond, dazzling, you are on your way!' But they are not 'on the way.' It's a fly-in community."

Back in their own community, the Tragically Hip were the subject of heated debate in city council chambers. Kingston city councillor Brian Reitzel wanted to honour the band with a landmark in town. Various options were on the table, including naming a park, or erecting a sculpture, or meekly promising to merely "incorporate information about the band in the city's Heritage Interpretation Program." Reitzel wanted to change the name of the street running in front of the new K-Rock Centre from Barrack Street to Tragically Hip Way. Kingston being a conservative town with a proud military history, some felt this would be the first step on a slippery slope to dismantling Fort Henry. The final compromise was that only a one-block section of Barrack Street, immediately in front of the arena, would be renamed.

The band were simultaneously tickled and nonplussed. Gord Downie couldn't help but dwell on the decision-making process. "Kingston city council voted for it seven to six. Do I have to say anything else?" he laughed. "'We'd like to honour you with a debate of your work for six months, and then [conclude with] a close, nail-biting council vote.'" In a twist that would make Jake Gold smile, the original signs delivered to the city read "Tragically Hip Way," not "The Tragically Hip Way"—and therefore had to be returned. New signs were ordered to comply with the band's perpetual insistence on the definite article. "The additional letters made the new signs longer than any other street sign in Kingston," noted the *Whig-Standard*, "so long that city workers had to fashion new brackets to give them additional support."

Shortly after the sign went up, former Toronto Maple Leaf Doug Gilmour, now general manager of the Kingston Frontenacs, walked out of the K-Rock Centre onto the newly renamed street. A car pulled up and someone yelled, "Hey, Gilmour! Get the fuck off my street!" Confused, the former NHLer turned to address the laughing heckler. It was Paul Langlois.

Back at the Bathouse, the Hip continued to workshop the new songs. They didn't press "record" until June 2012, 16 months after they had hired Gavin Brown. Which the producer thinks was as important as anything they did once they entered the studio: "We mostly just spent time hanging out. Playing golf. Having a few pints. That was the mandate. If I could create camaraderie in the building, that would translate into the music."

Brown said people forget that for all the musical and technical knowledge required to be a producer, being a psychologist "is the number one job I do at all times, with every project. Recording? There are wonderful, talented engineers for that. People in the industry have no idea what I do. I produce results. The hardest people to convince are young bands. If I'm not touching the computer, they think I'm not doing something. I tell them, 'You know what's funny? All of a sudden, the songs are great, it sounds fucking amazing, it's on time, we're on budget and it's going to be a hit. *You* tell *me* what I did.'"

That was never a problem with the Hip, of course, all of whom by this point had several outside production credits: "At no point did the Hip ever make a comment on a microphone or an EQ," said Brown. "They come from the world of working with Hugh Padgham and Chris Tsangarides and Don Smith, where they have great respect for everybody in each chair. That's lost on young bands who own a Pro Tools rig and think they're producers. I say, 'No, you can make some *sound*.' I can make a film; does that make me Scorsese? When I was 18, Steve Albini produced my record [with Phleg Camp]. I'd say, 'Dude, I want to do this thing where—' He'd stop me and say softly, 'We can turn it *up*—or we can turn it *down*.' Because he's always said he's an engineer, not a producer."

Brown had his own goals distinct from some of the band's. "Some of them wanted to try the weirdest things they possibly could, and some of them said, 'No, we're the Hip, we should at least stay within the range of what we are.' Which is quite a broad range. There was a mild discussion about the word 'radio,' which is an important thing in my life because I like to have hit songs."

The initial plan was to work at the Bathouse and track everybody individually, much like Chris Tsangarides did on *Fully Completely*, which is Brown's preferred way of working. After standing side-stage at the Bobcaygeon show, however, Brown knew that wouldn't work: he realized what was wrong with the recordings they'd started to make at the Bathouse, "which is that they weren't playing together"—a lesson the Hip seemed to keep relearning throughout their entire career. "The Bathouse wasn't equipped to do what I wanted to do," said Brown.

Brown booked 10 days at Noble Street Studios in Toronto's Parkdale neighbourhood, where he often worked. Itchy after a long break and entirely comfortable with the new material, the band banged out a song a day. "Those two weeks were magic, fantastic," said Brown. "I felt completely alive. Gord was wailing away. Johnny was playing amazing. We'd get there, have a little lunch, watch some stupid shit on YouTube, run through the song about five or six times, and 50 to 60 per cent of the record has vocals from live takes—partly to keep the lyrics from evolving. I knew from the very beginning that Gord was the kind of painter from whom you'd have to take the canvas away; he wouldn't let the paintbrush leave the canvas."

Brown's engineer, Lenny DeRose, did some mixes that played up the more "rock" elements. Some of the band was very happy. Downie, Brown and others wanted something different, so the tracks were sent to mixing engineer Michael Brauer, whose hundreds of clients include Coldplay, My Morning Jacket and Leonard Cohen. "I was into the ambient, textural side of things: that's what I love to do," said Brown, an odd admission for a man who'd made a million-selling record for a neo-grunge band. "Guitar-bass-drums is a little old—like saxophone! Robbie is amazing at textural stuff, and we had some keyboard stuff, and I made some noises. Some of that depth is really great: 'Man Machine Poem' is fucking unbelievable. That's a very mature thing they couldn't do on their earlier records."

The *Now for Plan A* song "Man Machine Poem"—not to be confused with the songs "Man" or "Machine" on their 2016 album *Man Machine Poem*—was neither an ode to Kraftwerk's 1978 album nor a nod to futurist Ray Kurzweil. It's the most cryptic lyric on the record; Downie said it was about himself, struggling to be the supportive husband, the "man machine," and his wife being the "poem." Musically, however, it was bold: huge ringing chords over a sparse beat, with Downie holding long whole notes at the top of his range, like he's hollering across a canyon. It's enormous and hypnotic.

A surprise guest on the title track and "The Lookahead" was Sarah Harmer—surprising only because it took that long for their old friend to appear on a Hip record, though they'd backed her up on her song "Silver Road," recorded for the 2002 film *Men with Brooms*. Her cameo was not at all premeditated: she showed up for a barbecue at the Bathouse one day and ended up behind a microphone, becoming only the second female voice to ever appear on a Hip record, after Julie Doiron in 2000. It was more than a happy accident: "Now for Plan A" is one of the loveliest songs in the Hip's entire catalogue. She also starred in the video for "We Want to Be It."

That song's title came from *An Improvised Life*, a 2011 memoir by the actor Alan Arkin. In the book's preface, he recounts the story of making a film with Madeline Kahn and marvelling at her myriad skills: actress, pianist, comedian and in possession of an operatic voice. "I asked her which of her talents she considered to be her primary focus," he wrote. She had trouble finding an answer, so he asked her what her first impulse was as a child and he started listing off her talents. Dancer? Singer? Actress? She denied them all. Finally, she said, "I used to listen to a lot of music. And that's what I wanted to be." Arkin asked her to clarify. "I wanted to *be* the music," she replied. Arkin was taken aback. "With that one statement, I realized that what she'd said about herself was the impulse behind all of my own interests, all of my needs, all of my studying, compulsions and passions . . . So much had been invested in craft, in externalization, in looking for something solid out there that would fill the void, create a sense of flight, of getting out of the oppression of self. We didn't want to *do* it; we want to *be* it . . . This is dedicated to everyone who wants to be the music."

As the Hip prepared to release *Now for Plan A* in the fall of 2012, they were also set to release the concert film from the Bobcaygeon show. It was directed by Andy Keen, who had impressed Downie with *Escarpment Blues*, a 2006 documentary about Sarah Harmer's battle to protect part of the Niagara Escarpment from a planned gravel mine. *Bobcaygeon* would most definitely not be a documentary about the Hip themselves: they'd purposely avoided that with 1993's *Heksenketel* and 2005's *That Night in Toronto*. They didn't want to do it in 2012, either. The film was supposed to be about the fans, and it is—but it's not what fans wanted. It's a decent documentary, but, like *Heksenketel*, it's more about the logistics of putting on a show than it is about the art of making music. One fan dubbed it "Dudcaygeon," and other reviews were not much better. For a Tragically Hip film, there's not much Tragically Hip in it—although when Keen showed it to the band, one of them said, "Wow, we're in it for more than we thought."

Now for Plan A was released in October 2012. To launch it, the Hip booked a week of shows at the Supermarket, a restaurant in Toronto's Kensington Market with a live space in the back that can fit about 150 people. In addition to five-song evening shows for a select few, every afternoon, for five days, they would play three songs on the restaurant's patio for the general public; they'd then mingle with fans and sign copies of their new vinyl record. The multi-million-selling icons were now running a pop-up store in a bustling neighbourhood. Fans were ecstatic and passersby were intrigued, but the underlying symbolism was obvious: the band had to hustle to get their new music heard.

The record got good reviews; the live show, not so much. Though Downie had upped his singing game in the studio, some fans were discouraged to hear him screaming through many live shows of this period. The *Vancouver Sun* accused the band of plodding through the new material and "verging on caricature," concluding, "the Hip could lose many who don't want to swim in lukewarm waters of barely 50 per cent good performances. Blue Rodeo and 54.40 are still out there giving it their all."

———

Gord Downie wanted more. He had an incredibly successful, beloved rock band with radio hits. He had a ramshackle group of creative friends in another rock band that could play folk festivals. But there was another rock band he wanted to join: the Sadies.

The Sadies revolve around Dallas and Travis Good; their father Bruce was a member of successful '70s country band the Good Brothers, with whom young Travis played as a teenager on the county fair circuit. Travis grew up taking lessons from Gordon Lightfoot's guitarist, Red Shea. Dallas went a more punk rock route, eventually playing with post–Shadowy Men band Phono Comb and Rick White's Elevator. The Sadies started in 1997, with Phleg Camp's Sean Dean on bass and Sloan's Andrew Scott on drums; Scott was replaced by Mike Belitsky, of Halifax's Jale. The Sadies got their big break as Neko Case's touring band, which led to many gigs backing up roots and punk legends like the Mekons' Jon Langford, X's John Doe— even Neil Young for one session. They have an encyclopaedic knowledge of all guitar music; they're just as likely to cover early Pink Floyd as they are Teenage Head or the Louvin Brothers. Blue Rodeo's Greg Keelor was an early champion, frequently guesting with them and telling anyone who would listen they were the greatest rock'n'roll band on earth. Gord Downie didn't need convincing.

In 2005, CBC producer Bill Stunt had a show called *Fuse*, hosted by Amanda Putz. The concept was familiar to anyone on the folk festival circuit: put two performers on a stage and have them play on each other's material, perhaps even write something new together. There were some odd pairings, like country singer Fred Eaglesmith with the electro-goth of Austra's Katie Stelmanis. More often than not, the guests were singer-songwriters or folkie bands. But nothing was as raucous as the day in 2007, when Gord Downie and the Sadies walked into the CBC Ottawa studio and blared through a nine-song set that opened with a very early Guided by Voices song (1992's "Over the Neptune"); included covers of obscure songs by Neil Young, Johnny Cash and Roky Erikson, two Sadies songs, one Hip song ("Fire in the Hole") and one Downie song ("Figment"); and concluded with an explosive blast through the Stooges' "Search and Destroy." The gig went like gangbusters. Everyone wanted more.

There was no rush, however. Downie was deep into the Bob Rock period of the Hip and then dove into *The Grand Bounce*. The Sadies were never short of work or collaborative offers; they released six albums in the next six years, either on their own or backing up other artists. Between 2008 and 2014, the two parties would occasionally get together and record: the Sadies providing the music, Downie the lyrics. Released in 2014 on the Arts and Crafts label, the self-titled album was credited to Gord Downie, the Sadies and the Conquering Sun. It was mixed by Bob Rock.

Some songs skewed close to the Sadies' signature sound, like the stunning "Budget Shoes" or the country ballad "Devil Enough," while others were the most punk rock thing either artist had ever done: "Crater" or the sizzling "It Didn't Start to Break My Heart Until This Afternoon." Outside of 1994's "Fire in the Hole," Downie had never before sounded this raw, like he was ready to shred his throat. Fittingly, one of the covers they worked out to pad their live sets was "Generation," by Fucked Up. That Toronto band's vocalist, Damian Abraham, built a career on amelodic screeches on top of his band's high-concept hardcore punk; "Generation" was no different, and it was riveting to watch the 50-year-old Downie scream through a punk song that consists solely of this refrain: "Generation / holding my breath / no hesitation / freedom or death." Downie and the Sadies performed it at the Field Trip festival that summer, on a bill curated by the Arts and Crafts label that also featured Fucked Up; Downie joined them on stage to recreate his cameo on their song "The Art of Patrons."

The Tragically Hip played only one gig in 2014, a free show on October 8 in Toronto's Yonge-Dundas Square sponsored by the NHL to kick off that year's season. Earlier, in May, Johnny Fay and sportscaster Kathryn Humphreys, who were married in 2007, became parents to twin boys.

————

The next move was to reissue *Fully Completely*, and to hit the road in February 2015, playing a set that included the album's entire track listing in its running order. Fitting the concept, this time there was no opening band to expose the audience to new ideas; instead, they hired Broken Social Scene's

Brendan Canning to DJ before the set, playing good-time rock'n'roll: CCR, Los Lobos, Link Wray, Weezer, Muddy Waters, Chilliwack.

All major Canadian cities were covered on the first leg in February, playing at the large hockey rinks. Broken Social Scene's Andrew Whiteman went to the Montreal gig at the Bell Centre. "That show was flat-out riveting," he said. "I hadn't seen them since 2000. The fact they were doing *Fully Completely* did not take away one iota from the tornado that was happening onstage." What few people noticed was that Downie was in physical pain. Yes, the Tragically Hip singer had hip pain. He enlisted a Toronto Maple Leafs trainer to help with therapy.

From April to October, the Hip played anywhere and everywhere: Kirkland Lake, Kamloops, Prince George, Medicine Hat and casinos in Windsor, Moncton and Orillia. They played a gig at a farm in Creemore, Ontario, and a birthday party in a Hamilton backyard. The year's run ended on the West Coast of the U.S. and with three dates in Texas. One former associate saw one of those final 2015 shows. "I'd never heard them so goddam tight in my life—like, holy shit," the colleague raved. "They were right in the pocket. I went back to say hello, and you could see that it was a great vibe, everyone was in a great place, they were all hanging out together. It was a beautiful sight. That's why it was so great onstage— because it was so great offstage.

"Gord became a different person," the colleague continued. "There's a difference between the Tragically Hip and what I'll call Gord Downie and the Kingston 4—and I think they had become the latter at some point. I've heard tell there was a point where he took everyone aside and said, 'I'm sorry, I've been a real dick for a while.' Then they had it out, which every great family or friendship or marriage eventually does. After that, they were in such a great place. Then 30 days later, he collapsed. That's what makes this all even more sad."

CHAPTER TWENTY-ONE

THE INEVITABILITY
OF DEATH

2015–16: *MAN MACHINE POEM*

"It takes the greatest rhetoric of the greatest poets to bring us a vision of the tragic heroic, and such rhetoric doesn't make us miserable but exhilarated, not crushed but enlarged in spirit."

NORTHROP FRYE, 1986

THE COUNTRY'S MOST beloved rock band, who once sang "Summer's Killing Us," didn't want to ruin Canadians' first long weekend of the summer. So they waited until the day after.

The morning of Tuesday, May 24, 2016, the Tragically Hip issued a statement on their website.

Hello friends.

We have some very tough news to share with you today, and we wish it wasn't so.

A few months ago, in December, Gord Downie was diagnosed with terminal brain cancer.

Since then, obviously, he's endured a lot of difficult times, and he has been fighting hard. In privacy along with his family, and through all of this, we've been standing by him.

So after 30-some years together as The Tragically Hip, thousands of shows, and hundreds of tours . . .

We've decided to do another one.

This feels like the right thing to do now, for Gord, and for all of us.

What we in the Hip receive, each time we play together, is a connection; with each other; with music and its magic; and during the shows, a special connection with all of you, our incredible fans.

So, we're going to dig deep, and try to make this our best tour yet.

Later that morning, managers Patrick Sambrook and Bernie Breen held a press conference at Sunnybrook hospital, alongside Downie's neuro-oncologist, Dr. James Perry. Perry explained that Downie suffered a seizure in Kingston in December 2015 and that an MRI revealed glioblastoma multiforme, a cancerous tumour that originates in the brain. It was on his left temporal lobe, affecting short-term memory and speech. Most of it was removed in an emergency procedure. Downie had radiation treatments and chemotherapy between February and April 2016. The swelling in his brain had subsided.

But what about the tour? "All of my patients have trepidations about returning to their jobs and their daily lives, wondering what the future holds," said Perry. "You can imagine what a unique position I was in, to give advice to one of the most iconic individuals in the country, about a task such as a tour across [Canada] . . . We all know he doesn't sit down in a rocking chair and play a banjo." But Perry insisted that Downie was up for the job.

A journalist asked Breen what this loss means for Canada. "Can't speak for Canada," he laughed awkwardly, "but there's no loss here. We're going out to play a tour. Gord is dealing with his issues of health, and we're confident, comfortable and happy to get at it. What loss?"

The working men were going back to work. It would be the last time.

———

This wasn't to be a farewell tour. The band took great pains to clarify that it was not a "final tour," and that the media should not refer to it as such. No, this was the *"Man Machine Poem* tour," named after—naturally—a new album to promote, this one having been made with producers Kevin Drew and Dave Hamelin.

Kevin Drew first saw the Tragically Hip when he was 13 years old, at the Ontario Place Forum in 1990. A few months later, he started at the Etobicoke School of the Arts, a *Fame*-like high school where his classmates included Emily Haines of Metric, Amy Millan of Stars and others who would make a splash in Toronto's music scene of the 2000s. Though the Hip had blown him away, Drew was mostly into Sonic Youth, Dinosaur Jr. and My Bloody Valentine, with an odd affection for Italian film composer Ennio Morricone. After high school, he went to college to learn about the music business, and in 1998, he started an instrumental studio project called KC Accidental with Charles Spearin of Do Make Say Think.

With Brendan Canning, Drew then formed Broken Social Scene, whose ascent was the most unlikely success story in Toronto music history: a shoegazey, ambient band with too many people onstage, a set list of brand new songs every night and singers who may or may not show up. Within a year, they were playing more conventional sets that included fist-pumping anthems, with some New Order and bossa nova on the side. Nothing about Broken Social Scene made much sense, but their anything-goes approach to genre and flouting of all industry rules captured imaginations in Canada and abroad. Both their 2001 debut, *Feel Good Lost*, and the triumphant 2002 classic *You Forgot It in People* featured, among many others, the Hip's old Queen's classmate Bill Priddle of Treble Charger.

Kevin Drew's forays into production were limited outside his own band and solo records. That changed when he befriended elder Montreal-born songwriter Andy Kim, who is best known for writing "Sugar Sugar" in 1969 and other AM radio staples. By the 2010s, Kim had put out a couple of attempted comeback records and was still an engaging performer who hosted a popular annual Christmas party in Toronto, starring an eclectic, inter-generational lineup. Drew had always enjoyed the company of older peers: he was the baby in Broken Social Scene, while bandmates like Brendan Canning, Andrew Whiteman and Jason Collett were industry veterans who'd already done time in more than one band. With Kim, Drew formed a special bond that produced 2015's *It's Decided*, four years in the making, a striking reinvention on which Kim sounded like Bono singing Daniel Lanois ballads.

It's Decided was co-produced by Dave Hamelin of the Stills, a band signed to Drew's Arts and Crafts label. The members of the Stills had been together since they were 12 years old, going through a metal phase, a punk phase, a ska phase and eventually emerging in the 2000s as a brooding rock band on the spectrum between Echo and the Bunnymen and Interpol. By the time *It's Decided* was finally released in March 2015, Drew and Hamelin had already made an album called *Secret Path* with Gord Downie.

Now Downie wanted them to make a Tragically Hip record. "It was Gord's idea, obviously," said Drew's bandmate Brendan Canning. "And Robbie's a really open guy. Kev always likes to be in the thick of whatever's going on. He's there in a crisis: 'Hey, you guys need some help? I'm here for you right now.' He's always been that guy."

"They are two guys who kinda grew up listening to our band," said Baker in July 2015. "Now they're working with us and pushing us around in the studio like we've never been there [before]. They have their own ideas of what the band is and what the band should do. I don't know that I could describe it. It's atmospheric and big and dark and heavy and trance-y."

"I think [Downie] trusted us because of our process during *Secret Path*," said Drew. "I had no business being there unless they wanted us there." Drew asked Baker what he wanted to achieve with a new record. "I just really want four new songs to add to our set," the guitarist told him. Drew responded, "They play all your hits on the radio, so we're free to do whatever we want."

There was no material ready to record. Even though they were touring *Fully Completely*, the band that once cranked out an album every two years like clockwork was now rusty. "When you're a 25-year-old kid, being on the road is great, and when you're not onstage you have a guitar in your hotel room, writing songs," said Baker. "When you're 54 years old and you're not onstage, you're getting physiotherapy and trying to get some real sleep. When you get back together to play, you're not as sharp as you were a year ago when you were firing on all cylinders and there's this unspoken communication and it's like you're all on the same wavelength. You have to nurture that again and build it up. A band is really a band when they're playing. When you put down your instruments and walk away and everyone is in their own homes, you're not a band, you're just five guys who work together."

The first writing session for the album, before Drew and Hamelin arrived at the Bathouse, had produced "Tired as Fuck," a jazzy riff of Baker's, and "In Sarnia," which was the first completed song of the recording session, featuring one of Downie's most harried vocal performances. Twenty years after the Bathouse opened, Baker now suggested ditching the main room and moving into the hayloft over the garage. "There's lots of room for everyone to spread out and play as a band," said Baker. "That's preferable to me than everyone having their amps in isolation and having headphones on, [which makes it] really hard to lose yourself in the music. You can't get your head in the clouds." No better way to get your head in the clouds than to play in the loft. The drum sounds are unlike those on any other Hip album: just as raw as the Don Smith records, but deeper and richer. Fay's playing is also interesting, the space in the music allowing room to appreciate his nuances.

Most of the album was written in the loft—and quickly. "I would just sit and listen and say a few things here and there," said Drew, "but when [a band has] that much history together, [they] have an incredible synchronicity and melodic patterns. It was interesting to watch them come together. [One day] they finished a song and I said, 'Okay, let's see if you guys want to jam out another one.' I went downstairs, cracked open a Guinness, poured it, came back up to the control room and there was a song playing. I said, 'What's this?' Paul said, 'Just something I'm working on.' They were just so fast." That song was "What Blue," played almost exactly as it can be heard on the final album. The acoustic, psychedelic "Ocean Next," in a lilting 8/8 rhythm alternating with a 6/8 chorus, had a similar birth. On that song, Downie's lyrics quote Neil Young's producer David Briggs on his preference for spontaneity while recording: "You think, you stink." Young's influence also surfaces when Downie purposely mispronounces "interest" as "innarest" in the song "In a World Possessed by the Human Mind"—"innarest" is a vocal tic of Young's left intact by biographer Jimmy McDonough throughout the book *Shakey*.

"Dave and Kevin were very funny to work with," said Baker. "They were often on opposite sides of the fence. Kevin would say, 'This song "Here in the Dark," I think we should slow it down and go more spacey with it. Maybe have a total breakdown with a rap section in the middle.' And Dave Hamelin would say, 'No, this song needs more four-on-the-floor, we have to pick the tempo up and cut it as a live track.' The two of them would go back and forth and [the band would] sit in the middle and watch it like Ping-Pong. It was highly entertaining. It's fun to be the vets in the studio. We've been around this track a few times, and then to bring in a couple of know-it-all kids is kind of fun."

Drew and Hamelin weren't the only ones on opposite sides of a fence. As with almost every Hip record of the previous 20 years, a certain contingent of the band wanted to rock, and Downie wanted to do something else. Juggling a passive-aggressive group of alpha males who've been a band for 30 years doesn't help, but perhaps having those arguments embodied in two producers, rather than one, helped smooth band relations.

The title of the album was recycled from a song on *Now for Plan A*, but Downie had also titled two new songs "Man" and "Machine." The latter was a fully formed song, driven by a Gord Sinclair bass line, but as the band jammed in the studio they developed a coda that took on a life of its own, which became "Man." That song, which begins the record, opens with the discombobulating sound of Downie's voice manipulated on a tape machine: it's easily the most jarring opening to any Hip record and a signal that *Man Machine Poem* was going to be decidedly different.

The rest of the band wanted to open with "Machine," which became one of the only new tracks they played every single night of the 2016 tour. "It seemed like a natural lead-off track to me," said Baker. "Gord Downie heard it another way. In the end, we decided it was something we hadn't done before. We've done 'obvious' before."

Even the band couldn't believe how good the record was—as in, they had trouble believing they actually played certain parts on it. During the mixing process, Drew and Hamelin had to assure them that although the producers provided some keyboards and some percussion, that all drums, guitars and backing vocals were absolutely performed by the band—even if at times it sounds like nothing else they'd ever done before.

The album was a concise 10 songs, including "Man" and "Machine." A lot was left on the floor. "There's a whole shadow record," said Baker. "We've done that on a few records, where there's a light album and a shadow album. There are probably eight or 10 tracks of really interesting tunes. Some of them felt like they were too personal or awkward somehow to put on the record."

"I'm grateful we didn't make a rock record or an acoustic fireside album," said Drew. "We made something that has blood."

———

Man Machine Poem was going to come out in early 2016 with the title *Dougie Stardust*, a play on David Bowie's *Ziggy Stardust*. Downie commissioned Izzy Camilleri, a celebrated Toronto fashion designer—whose work appeared on Bowie himself in the 1997 video for "Little Wonder"—to make a series of shiny metallic suits he planned to wear onstage when it came time to tour the record. David Bowie died on January 10, 2016, and suddenly the album title didn't seem appropriate. A few other things got in the way, too. But those suits came in handy.

If 2015 was spent celebrating the reissue of their biggest album while simultaneously creating one of their best, it wasn't a joyful year. Tragedy struck Gord Sinclair's family first, in April, when his mother, Leona, died of intestinal cancer. And Gord Downie's personal life was in disarray. For starters, his beloved 84-year-old father, Edgar, was ailing. Recording at the Bathouse allowed Downie to spend precious time with the man he admired more than anyone.

In 1991, all members of the Hip were asked some boilerplate questions by the *Whig-Standard*: astrological sign, favourite food, favourite musician, etc. When asked to name an idol, Rob Baker and Gord Downie both cited their fathers. "He's the coolest," said the 27-year-old Downie of Edgar. He often spoke of his dad throughout his career, citing the old man's magnanimity and graciousness with everyone he met. In 2016, Canada was struck by the sight of the five men in the Tragically Hip kissing each other on the lips onstage—that was something Downie and his brothers got from their father, who was not shy with affection.

Edgar Downie died on October 27. The obit read, in part, "All men die—some never live. Edgar avoided such a fate: he lived, he loved, he laughed, he hugged, he kissed and he had a special way that put everyone he met immediately at ease . . . He saw the good in people and they in turn saw it clearly in him . . . Everyone should be so lucky as to have a father like Edgar. He taught us firsthand about the big stuff in life: honesty, loyalty, dedication and above all kindness."

Downie had another reason to spend more time than usual in Kingston: he was separating from his wife of 23 years, Laura Usher. Downie had written many songs hinting at mid-life marital strife in the past 10 years; on *Man Machine Poem*, the song "Here, in the Dark" nods to Joni Mitchell's "A Case of You," sharing her images about a star in the darkness as a metaphor for an oblivious male lover preoccupied with the life of the mind.

In early November 2015, the couple's Toronto house sold for almost a quarter-million dollars *under* the asking price—unheard of in Toronto's white-hot real estate market at the time. The identity of the former homeowners somehow made it into the *Huffington Post*, the one and only time in the Tragically Hip's history that their personal lives were the subject of celebrity gossip. Coincidentally, Downie's brother Patrick—who had been living in Boston, where he once worked for the Boston Bruins—had also split from his wife. The two brothers were about to become closer than ever before.

In December, Gord Downie collapsed while walking down a Kingston street with his family. He'd had a seizure. He was taken to Kingston General and attended to by Douglas "DJ" Cook, a fan and friend of the band who had become a certified neurosurgeon just three years earlier. In the operating room, Cook was able to map out Downie's language area while the singer was awake. Downie's tumour was in a relatively accessible area of the brain, which meant that most of it could be removed in the first surgery. Downie was told that his best-case scenario was four or five years, with no further neurological decline.

Some brain cancers start elsewhere and eventually spread to the most important organ in the human body. Those ones are more easily treatable—though in 1988, that's what killed one of Downie's literary heroes, Raymond Carver, at age 50, when his lung cancer reoccurred as a brain tumour.

Glioblastoma, however, starts in star-shaped cells in the nervous system and spreads quickly. Visualizing it involves a Cronenbergian eye: it's been described as a "hand with fingers, all interlocking into the brain, reaching in like the brain was jelly." Glioblastoma affects four to six people per 100,000 in Canada. In 99 per cent of cases, the cause is unknown. The median survival rate is 15 months. There are extremely rare exceptions in which people live much longer, but overall only five per cent survive more than two years after diagnosis.

Symptoms can include memory loss, balance difficulties, intense head-aches, vision problems or seizures. Rare is the diagnosis made in the early stage; usually by the time symptoms show, the tumour is in full bloom. By that point, steroids are used to reduce swelling in the area around the tumour before surgery—it's impossible to remove it all, because of the manner in which it's attached. You don't want to mess with the brain, which makes chemotherapy a delicate balance as well. And "multiforme" means that different cells will respond differently to various therapies. There is no easy way out. The cancer will keep coming back with a ven-geance, often in different areas of the brain and with a different genetic profile. It's the deadliest game of oncological Whac-A-Mole imaginable.

In February 2016, Downie had a second seizure, followed by another craniotomy. He then started six weeks of radiation and chemotherapy. Dr. Perry described Downie's form of glioblastoma as "more amenable" to chemotherapy treatment than most. Patrick Downie became his guardian, taking him to all his appointments, attending to his medical reg-imen and playing music to comfort him. After the first week, Paul Langlois went to see his old friend, whose memory was incredibly foggy. Downie could barely stay awake. He was unable to form sentences. But he wanted Langlois to stay. The guitarist accompanied him to all remaining radiation treatments.

"We were supposed to tour, right?" Downie asked Langlois. "We've got this record coming out, right?"

"Yeah, supposed to come out in June, as far as I know."

"Well, we're going to tour, right?"

"Honestly, I just don't know."

After radiation and rest, Downie wanted to put the band back together. They were more than nervous—Rob Baker in particular. But they knew how important it was for Downie to do this, how crushed he would be if he didn't at least try, how badly he needed to have a goal—however impossible it may seem.

Astute fans started to catch wind that something was amiss. A Tragically Hip album called Dougie Stardust appeared on retail sites for pre-order in March, before being withdrawn after a couple of days. (Some vinyl copies with that title—same artwork, same tracklisting—were pressed and circulated, then recalled and destroyed. Rob Baker has one of the only surviving copies.) Downie was uncharacteristically absent from the annual Lake Ontario Waterkeeper gala in Toronto on April 21. Rumours were starting to float around Kingston. When the entire band was given honorary degrees from Queen's on May 19, Downie was again a no-show. Five days later, the entire country knew why.

On May 24, Downie's condition was made public and the band announced their intention to tour: 15 dates over the course of a month, starting in Victoria and concluding in Kingston. No show in Montreal or anywhere east; no U.S. shows.

That morning, José Contreras and By Divine Right were scheduled to record "Ahead by a Century" for The Strombo Show; George Stroumboulopoulos and his team, oblivious to the diagnosis, had been slowly commissioning Hip covers for a radio special celebrating the 30th anniversary of the Hip's debut EP in 1987. Contreras now wondered whether or not he should still show up at Strombo's house, if he could even get through the song. "I got there," said Contreras, "and George said, 'How you doing?' 'Fucked up.' 'We're all fucked up now.' Those first few days—not even being a big fan, but loving them all as people, really believing in them—I realized how important they are, how life-changing they were to me on many levels. It hit me really hard. It was really fucking heavy." He was not alone.

"I would get very jumbled emails when he was in treatment, or texts at odd hours of the night," said one former musical colleague. "When he first said they were going on tour, I said, 'Are you okay? Are you sure?' Then I understood his reasoning, not the least of which was doing it for the guys, which was really lovely, and I thought, 'Of course. You're a rock'n'roll band. You're family.' And [doing it for] his own family as well, to put something in the coffers for his kids."

———

Man Machine Poem was released on June 17. Fans breathed a sigh of relief. Critical and popular opinion had been sharply divided on everything the band had done since *Phantom Power*, but the consensus was that this was easily their best record since then. The headlines may have helped open ears, but the record had legs; it won Junos and was longlisted for the Polaris Music Prize—a first for the Hip—a full year after its release.

Former producer Steve Berlin, of Los Lobos, raved that *Man Machine Poem* was "some of the most powerful stuff they've ever written. That's hard to do, let me tell you, as a guy who's been in the same band for 40 years or so. To hit one out of the park in your third decade? Not an easy trick."

"It was something completely different," said Sam Roberts. "It was the most emotionally raw record [from them] I'd heard in a very long time. Sometimes you have to wander away from things to write a seamless record like this. You have to be allowed to take these adventures, these sidesteps, incorporating new things, new musical elements, a new way of delivering songs. Eventually, if you stick with it long enough, you'll come to a place where it all feels very natural."

Kate Fenner had a physical reaction the first time she heard the track "Great Soul." "It was a thousand degrees in New York City and I was walking through Washington Square Park listening on earphones, and I felt like [the song] just went right through me. When it was over, I went to rewind and listen again, but for once, I said, 'Do not try to get that back. You got that. That's past.' I literally felt like a hot wind went through me."

Ticket demand for a final tour would have been high to begin with; the fact that the new record was one of their best upped the ante.

Long-dormant fans started coming out of the woodwork. So did scalpers, naturally. The day the tickets went on sale, they disappeared in record time, and then within minutes started appearing on secondary-market sites for hundreds of dollars over face value. That was not at all unusual in the era of ticket bots and digital scalping, as any fan of arena-level artists can testify. But a frustrated ticket buyer can imagine that there will always be another Beyoncé or Coldplay show, or that Fleetwood Mac will reunite in some form again. The Tragically Hip were never coming back.

The uproar became a political issue debated in provincial legislatures. CBC's *Marketplace* reported that two-thirds of tickets for the tour were purchased by "ticket brokers," a term that simply describes scalpers who operate online, with or without the help of ticket-bot software. Because the brokers score most of the best seats, this means most fans have little choice but to use them. This practice is by no means unique to the Hip tour. It is simply unfettered supply-and-demand capitalism at work. Demand is highest the day tickets go on sale: when fans discover they can't get legit tickets, they get emotional and may decide to immediately shell out exorbitant amounts for good seats.

But in the months leading up to the event, many fans in Western Canada found tickets being offered for face value or only slightly more. The Vancouver *Province* reported that for the shows there, "the resale factor was so bad [that week] that thousands of tickets on StubHub were being sold at discount prices." That was far from true for the final Ontario dates, by which point the rave reviews from the West had come pouring in. Unsurprisingly, some tickets for the last four shows were selling for thousands of dollars.

The Tragically Hip's management held "ticket lotteries" and "ticket drops" on the day of each show; several patient fans got lucky by scoring face-value tickets at the last minute. Management also held a fair number of tickets for their own use—again, completely common practice for every artist and every tour. But this was a beloved band with decades in the industry, which meant a lot of professional and personal acquaintances would want to witness the swan song. That includes fellow musicians and the most diehard fans; the band and management had always nurtured relationships with those who travelled far and wide to see them. There were no freebies for anyone: anyone who obtained a ticket through management paid full price. If you were a fair-weather fan who suddenly decided you had to see the Tragically Hip, you were likely out of luck.

The band themselves knew the stakes were high. They tried to shut out as much of the exterior noise as possible as they began rehearsing. At the first rehearsal, Downie didn't know the names of any songs. He didn't know any lyrics. He used a teleprompter. The first song at the first rehearsal was "Escape Is at Hand for the Travelling Man." As rehearsals continued, progress was slow. "We would finish a song like 'My Music at Work,' where he says, 'music at work' 50 times at the end," said Billy Ray Koster, "and then he'd look at me and say, 'Billy, what's that one called?' And then he'd write it down." During breaks in the music, Downie would do stretches or hop on a stationary bike and exercise. He was not going to give up. "Don't tell Gord he can't do something," said his brother Patrick.

A month after the tour announcement, on June 29, Rob Baker was one of several prominent Canadians invited to Ottawa to watch Barack Obama address the House of Commons. CBC Radio host Rich Terfry was another. They chatted on the chartered bus on the way to Parliament. Terfry had just watched *I'll Be Me*, the documentary about Glen Campbell touring with Alzheimer's; he told Baker that he couldn't finish watching the film, it was too heartbreaking. Baker had seen the whole thing, and it was certainly on his mind. Hip rehearsals were still rough, and the first gig was now three weeks away. Downie's memory was still shaky. The crew was still working on a teleprompter solution for the live show; he eventually ended up using six. The encouraging sign was that the melodies were still there—or at least they would be after a few run-throughs of any given song. Baker was still nervous about the whole endeavour. Now Terfry was, too.

"I care about Gord so much, and the band, and I started to think about the Glen Campbell thing," recalled the CBC host, whose peers were preparing to broadcast the final show in Kingston. "I understood all the great reasons to document this and broadcast it, but I was terrified: what if it doesn't go well? You don't want to broadcast something that is painful." He went to his manager at CBC. "If we get the sense from anyone involved that it's hard and maybe not going well," he told him, "you'll want to think seriously about if this is something you want to do."

The first show was July 22 in Victoria. Trepidation was still prevalent on all sides, despite the sign-off from Dr. Perry. "I never thought it was going to happen," said Gord Sinclair. "Even by the time we went out to Victoria, I didn't think it was going to happen. If [Downie] had come to me in the middle of the show and said, 'I don't think I can do it,' I would've put my guitar down and walked off stage in a second."

"It was the rare thing that was out of our control," said manager Bernie Breen. "The safety net was pretty thin. Up until the start in Victoria and the end in Kingston, it could have ended at any point in time."

Stephen Dame, curator of the fan website the Hip Museum, knew a critical care doctor who had urged him to "fly out west and see those early shows, because he's not going to make it to Ontario." The doctor's husband took her word for it and flew to Edmonton.

The venue in Victoria was one of the smallest on the tour, holding 7,400 people. The band rented it out for rehearsal for two nights before the first show. Dr. Perry was there, as he was for all but one show in the tour. There was also a personal EMS team on hand for Downie. "There are a whole bunch of people involved, medically," Perry told the CBC during the tour. "He's had the same team—trainers, chiropractors, masseuses—for a long time. His problems [on tour] aren't so much the brain tumour as the fact that we're not getting any younger."

The first show opened with "Boots or Hearts," with the line about the title objects disintegrating, falling apart.

Except it didn't fall apart. The online review in the Victoria *Times Colonist* that night opened with the line, "Breathe easy, Canada. Ol' Gord has still got it." The only time Downie addressed the crowd was before "The Lonely End of the Rink." "Here's one for my good ol' dad," he said. "He's gone. Shit happens." Later in the set, the Hip played "The Luxury" from *Road Apples* for the first time in 16 years, a song about being so preoccupied with one's current condition that you can't appreciate your immediate surroundings. They also played "Little Bones," with the line about not mistaking fatigue for near-death, a line delivered with determination and defiance.

Manager Patrick Sambrook went to the soundboard to watch the show. He found Dr. Perry standing there by himself—bawling. "He'd had all this weight on him," Sambrook said, "because, ultimately, we'd all turned to him and said, 'Can we do this?' And he'd said yes. He'd been carrying that until that moment, and here he was, and he lost it. And then I lost it."

"It's unbelievable what [Downie has] been able to do," said Perry, halfway through the tour. "He's performing better than he has in years. No doubt drawing on all the emotion and the crowd, no doubt knowing that this may be his last time in front of such a major audience . . . When I wondered if he would have the stamina, I never imagined him leaping around in a pink leather suit with a feathered cap. It says so much about the guy."

Onstage, the normally lithe and animated Downie was noticeably restrained, employing discipline worthy of tai chi to the most subtle of gestures. Recurring among his typically amusing dance moves was one that evoked a centenarian doing a vaudevillian soft-shoe. The teleprompters were clearly visible beside every monitor. The improvisatory poet with such a bountiful command of language was now following a tight script—by crippling necessity. That didn't stop him or the band from putting on unforgettable shows.

"I saw a lot of different expressions between the band members," said Jim Creeggan of Barenaked Ladies, who saw one of the three Toronto shows. "Johnny came out and was like, 'Yeah!' at the end. Paul came out and just cheered with the audience in a very sombre way. It's confusing: here you are doing something while something unknown and traumatic is happening, such as cancer. You're presenting to your fans and you haven't quite figured out what the shows are yourself. Gord was playing with all the emotions: there is not one resolute emotion or perspective. It's painful, conflicted, happy, sad."

"It was pretty intense every night to watch an arena full of people cry," said Billy Ray Koster. "The mission of the band was to go out there and do what they've always done. To not have people feel sad." The tour was not the rock'n'roll equivalent of a casket criss-crossing the country by train, with parades of spectators hailing a fallen leader. "I was really worried that it would be like a funeral every night," said Baker. "It wasn't. The second I walked onstage in Victoria, I knew I didn't have anything to fear. It's a celebration, not a funeral. It would be very easy to be overwhelmed by the emotion: we would look out into the audience and see people overwhelmed, every night. But you have to compartmentalize and just go up and do your job. We're very good at compartmentalizing."

"Gord was doing a public transformation, which is always a very potent thing," said Chris Brown. "You're exposing vulnerability inside the public ritualized space like that, and suddenly people are themselves feeling vulnerable. All their associations that are so deeply pinned on this entity, which is apparently dissolving in front of them—you have to reckon with that."

Almost every Canadian has been cursed with cancer in some way: if not personally, then through family or friends. Hearing stories of Downie's triumph was cathartic for many—especially those who suffered from glioblastoma themselves.

Joanne Schiewe was nearing the end of the 18 months her doctors told her she was likely to live after her glioblastoma diagnosis; a huge Hip fan, she was crushed when she couldn't get tickets to the Winnipeg show. Fellow Hip fans banded together and offered her tickets; one offer came from a man from Halifax who was going to fly in for the show. "It just goes to show that Canadians and Tragically Hip fans are a pretty special breed," she told the CBC. She attended the Winnipeg show with her husband and died a week after watching the Kingston show on TV. She was 36.

Yaron Butterfield of Vancouver was diagnosed at age 29 in February 2004; he's an incredibly rare long-term survivor. Since then, he's had two tumours removed, got married, had a child, ran a marathon in Iceland, played hockey and continued to work. He's a bioinformatics coordinator at the BC Cancer Agency. He went to see the Tragically Hip play their last show in Vancouver. He sat in section 108. He felt like Downie looked him directly in the eye and winked.

Darren Sawchuck of Winnipeg was a lawyer who retired after his diagnosis and decided to open a vinyl record shop; he was also the singer in a Hip cover band. He had front-row tickets to the Winnipeg show. He told the CBC, "I'm not counting Gord down and out, and I'm not counting myself down and out. I hope that there are lots of these last tours to come." Sawchuk died in March 2017. He was 51.

Jason DeRoche of Moncton, 39, was diagnosed with glioblastoma shortly after Downie. The only consolation in this news was that he had the same disease as his longtime hero. His wife, Amanda, posted his story on Facebook, hoping she could somehow get him tickets to the Kingston show—the only tour date that would work with DeRoche's radiation treatments. Johnny Fay's brother Paul heard this story and reached out to the DeRoches to offer them his tickets. Prior to the show, DeRoche had lost feeling in one side of his body; it was difficult to stand up for two hours at a time. At the show, DeRoche was on his feet for six hours straight, no problem.

There was also tragedy behind the scenes. The Hip's longtime front-of-house sound engineer Jon Erickson—he'd been with them for 10 years—had worked on production meetings leading up to the tour. But mere days before the Victoria show, Erickson himself was diagnosed with cancer and started treatment almost immediately. He was able to make it out to the last Toronto show, as a guest. Mark Vreeken, who mixed the band from 1989 to 2006, came back to the fold to take Erickson's place, but he had previous commitments for the last five dates. Those were mixed by Lee Moro, an old friend of Erickson's. Moro told his hometown newspaper, the *Windsor Star*, that the singing crowd at the Toronto shows drowned out the P.A.

"We can't forget to celebrate," said Sarah Harmer that month. She took her 84-year-old mother to one of the Toronto shows, and she attended the Kingston show with her sisters who, 30 years prior, had dragged their then-16-year-old baby sibling to Tragically Hip shows around Ontario. "This is us honouring the life force," said Harmer. "Celebrating is a duty."

That celebration was embodied in Downie's choice of wardrobe, which signalled strength and power to distract from notions of fragility. Izzy Camilleri had designed leather suits for the singer on the 2015 tour. This time, Downie wanted her to make something with more spectacle, something metallic. Originally, he wanted just silver and gold. He eventually asked for five more colours. Each was named after a person: the purple one was "Prince," the white one "Bowie"—two recently departed demi-gods whose shadows lingered over 2016. (Downie's offstage uniform in the last year of his life featured a Prince pin on his denim jacket and a ball cap from First Avenue, the Minneapolis club in *Purple Rain*.) Gold was "Paul," for Langlois, and green was "Jenn," for longtime management assistant Jenn Pressey. The hot pink one was named "Izzy," after Camilleri. Silver was "Patrick," for his younger brother, and turquoise was "Edgar," for his father. Every one of them illuminated Downie brilliantly, literally lighting up the solemnity of the occasion, giving him an eerily angelic glow.

Downie was also inspired by Bob Dylan's attire on the *Desire* album cover, so Camilleri enlisted milliner Karyn Gingras to create similar hats with pheasant feathers and porcupine quills that would become a signature of the tour. Gingras stitched some of her favourite Hip lyrics into the interior of each hat. Likewise, ankle boots designed by Jeff Churchill had the lyrics to "Ahead by a Century" engraved on the soles.

The set each night was broken up into thematic suites: four songs at a time from any given album; encores would be two or three songs from an album. Songs five through eight were always from *Man Machine Poem*; the only other album to be featured every night was *Phantom Power*. *Fully Completely*, *Day for Night* and *Trouble at the Henhouse* were all featured at 13 of the 15 shows. Audiences at seven shows would get both *Up to Here* and *Road Apples*; everyone else got one or the other. Every night would have a wild card from the back half of the discography: four songs from one album released between 2000 and 2012. They only played *We Are the Same* once, in Edmonton; *In Violet Light* twice. The other albums of that period got three shows each. The opening night in Victoria, it was *World Container*, produced by Victoria native Bob Rock. The closing night in Kingston, attended by all the families, it was *Music @ Work*, which features a song about Downie's maternal grandmother.

The first eight songs were played on a no-frills stage set-up in which the band played in a tight circle, no further apart than they would have been at the Lakeview Manor in 1986. It's unusual for a band playing in an arena to do that, and the visual metaphor was obvious to everyone: this is a tight unit of brothers who stayed together for 30 years. That's sweet, but drama professor Patrick Finn theorized there's also some spiritual medicine and performance practice involved. "They were building the support of energy there, to get Gord to where he needed to be," he said, "to get that feeling that's required to connect with an audience, which can be so draining. I think they were helping him concentrate that energy and be comfortable and protecting him, because he's drawing more directly on their energy." There was then a quick set change to a more traditional arrangement: the band farther spread out, Downie with more room to roam, a suspended cage of neon icicles framing the stage. Downie would re-emerge in a metallic suit of a different colour, and in yet again a different one for the first encore.

Downie spoke very little at any of the dates. Sometimes he acknowledged someone in the audience, like Winnipeg music writer John Kendle. Sometimes he joked about how few people the Hip played to on their first visit to that night's city 30 years earlier. Sometimes he stopped to thank the women for coming to the shows, even in the years when the men were acting like meatheads.

On the first night in Toronto, during the extended outro to "Grace, Too," Downie turned to look at one of the cameras onstage and told the audience, "The film hasn't been working this whole time. Everything is delayed." He then crouched down at the front of the stage and stared directly into the camera in front of him, his image projected on the screens. What was a strangely intimate and uncomfortable moment—the giant face of this icon who is staring down death now staring directly at an arena audience—transformed into something magical when Downie began mouthing something in incredibly slow motion, over the course of two full minutes.

If you were at the front, you might have missed it. Only if you were in the back and paying close attention could you tell that he was saying three words: "I. Love. You."

At the end of every night's first encore, Downie would stand and address the crowd in silence. Making eye contact. Pointing, waving, smiling. It could have come across as an ego trip: the rock star standing there, doing nothing, gorging on the adoration. Downie, for all his self-deprecating claims, must have known that the audience needed this, this personal moment, this chance to say goodbye. Because he needed it, too. This was an exchange of gratitude. Downie's music and words had meant the world to these people for almost 30 years. In turn, the support these people had invested in Downie's art had given him the creative life he'd always wanted, with his best friends at his side, four men with whom he took great pleasure and comfort kissing on the lips in front of thousands of people every night of the tour.

After a few minutes of this suspended moment in time, this deafening silence, this recognition that art in our time is far less important than our daily lives, this impression of the never-ending present, the strangest solo ever performed in the history of arena rock, one performed without a note of music, finally came to a close. Downie waved goodbye—only to come back for another encore and kick cancer in the ass a bit more. Because we don't want to end on a maudlin note, now, do we?

Rob Baker didn't. "At the last night in Kingston, it was just another day at work," he said. "We'd done it a thousand times. I don't think that show the CBC aired was our best show, or even necessarily a great show. But it's what we do every night. It's emotional for other people—and it was for us, too, but you have to keep that at bay. You just have to know that at the end of the show you're cleaning out your wardrobe trunk, cleaning out your desk and going home."

CHAPTER TWENTY-TWO

EXIT, STAGE 5
CANCER AND OTHER CURSES

"I believe that the purpose of death is the release of love"

LAURIE ANDERSON, 2013

FEW TALKED ABOUT the morbid humour Gord Downie displayed by wearing a *Jaws* T-shirt onstage during his final tour with the Tragically Hip. Underneath the metallic leather suits was the image from that 1977 movie poster: a swimming innocent on the verge of a deadly surprise attack from a monster lurking below. As with everything Downie did, the symbolism was there, if you cared to find it. But could a terminal cancer patient possibly wear something funnier onstage?

There were other theories about the *Jaws* shirt, mostly revolving around Downie's specific reference to the film in the 2002 song "The Dark Canuck." In both his lyrics and his improvisations onstage, death in the water was a frequent theme. Not as often cited in fan theories was Hugh MacLennan's *The Watch That Ends the Night*, the book quoted directly in the lyrics to "Courage," which has this eerily illuminating passage: "Little did I know—though I believed I knew all about it—how little I actually knew of the enormous and terrible implications of absolute finality. The shark in the ocean may be invisible, but he is there. So also is fear in the ocean of the subconscious. A man standing on a rock may believe himself strong enough to stand there forever. But if an earthquake comes, where is he? *What* is he?"

When that earthquake comes—or the shark, or the lightning strike, or whatever natural metaphor one uses for terminal disease—the measure of an artist is put to a test. If they are able—and that's a big if—what they choose to accomplish with limited time can be transformational.

Neurosurgeon Paul Kalanithi wrote *When Breath Becomes Air*, a best-selling, posthumously published 2016 memoir about living with Stage 4 lung cancer. In it, he wrote, "I woke up in pain, facing another day—no project beyond breakfast seemed tenable. *I can't go on*, I thought, and immediately, its antiphon responded, completing Samuel Beckett's seven words, words I had learned long ago as an undergraduate: *I'll go on*. I got out of bed and took a step forward, repeating the phrase over and over: '*I can't go on. I'll go on.*' I would have to learn to live in a different way, seeing death as an imposing itinerant visitor but knowing that even if I'm dying, until I actually die, I am still living."

———

"I want to go out with a bang, not a whimper. I don't think that after all these years of proud road-warriorship that we should go out with a whimper. We need to knock it out of the park."

That's not Gord Downie or a member of the Tragically Hip. That's their friend Vince Ditrich, drummer in Spirit of the West, speaking in 2015. The two former tourmates shared many commonalities: they both started in 1984, they both had riveting front men, and in 2016, both bands played their final shows, tainted with tragedy.

Singer John Mann had already beat colorectal cancer—and wrote a musical about it with playwright Morris Panych—when he was diagnosed with early onset Alzheimer's in 2014, at the age of 52. The next year, the band decided to do one last tour across the country, including their first and only time headlining Massey Hall in Toronto. Like the Tragically Hip, the tour was contained to a month (12 shows versus the Hip's 15). Spirit of the West played their final three shows at Vancouver's Commodore Ballroom, their "home ice," in April 2016. They wanted to go out on top: "We didn't want it to become embarrassing," says Mann's co–front man, Geoffrey Kelly.

Mann's guitar duties were passed off to one of the newer members of the band, Matthew Harder. Accordion player Tobin Frank operated a foot pedal that controlled lyrics displayed on a tablet in front of Mann's microphone. Mann's wife, Jill Daum, acted as a nurse on the road, ensuring he had the proper rest, nutrition and exercise, because he needed every brain cell in order to perform each night. In every town, old friends and well-wishers wanted to come and pay their respects, which the band had to put a lid on. "We'd keep the visiting to a minimum and have a little after-party, but mostly quiet," says Kelly. "Right before each gig, we'd listen to music in the dressing room, which would get him in the mood. Music for him broke through everything. He'd be very quiet all day, and then he'd come alive at sound check. He didn't differentiate between sound check and the gig; he'd be dancing around, everything. It was a lot to get him ready to perform for 90 minutes. As a big family, we were able to get through it. If he had a bad night, he'd get mad at himself, but he wouldn't let it linger. He'd let it go pretty quickly. We were all hyperaware of his condition that we all knew when it would be time to call it off."

Sportscaster Dave Hodge saw Mann perform a solo show at an Ontario winery, using an iPad for lyrics. "He needed it, and stumbled over some words and the technology," Hodge recalls. "Later on, someone at the winery told me that an audience member wanted their money back because they'd paid for a professional performance. I just shook my head. How could you? I hope that was the only person in the crowd who didn't know what they were watching and why it was the way it was. But I guess somebody stumbled in and paid $75 that they hoped would be more polished."

At the final show at the Commodore, the band enlisted some old friends to sing lead vocals: Paul Hyde of the Payola$, Skydiggers' Andy Maize, Steven Page, Colin James and Jim Cuddy. "It was a once-in-a-lifetime celebration," says Cuddy. "They put me in the encore, which was very nerve-wracking. I sang one of their songs, 'Not Just a Train.' I had wanted to say a little something, so when I went out, I stepped to the mic and looked down and everybody there was crying, just weeping. I couldn't tell that from the side of the stage because there was so much cheering. Of course, I teared up right away. I said a few words and did my thing and there were a few encores, but when they finally came off the stage it was an incredibly sad thing. Because that's it."

Kelly says he held it together until the final note of the last song on that last night. "It wasn't even our song," he says. "We'd been covering a song by Hunters and Collectors from Australia, 'Throw Your Arms Around Me.'

It's gorgeous, it seemed appropriate and John sings it beautifully. When we got to when John was holding that last note, I just started crying.

"I had been pretty good until then. I felt like I had to guide the ship through all of this. John couldn't use the mic very much to do the intros, so I became the de facto front guy addressing the crowd. For me, the overall feeling was sad and heartbreaking but also uplifting. We all felt incredible about how the gigs went, and John did so well, especially on the final night: he sang beautifully and seemed to be more present than he had been in weeks."

Mann's final bow was not without precedent. In 2011, '60s and '70s pop and country icon Glen Campbell, then 75 years old, went public with his Alzheimer's diagnosis and toured extensively for more than a year. Offstage, as detailed in the harrowing documentary *I'll Be Me*, the Rhinestone Cowboy's train of thought could be derailed within seconds, and he didn't recognize himself in old home movies. Onstage was a different story.

"I saw his show at the CNE in 2011, and it was great," remembers Sloan's Jay Ferguson. "There were teleprompters all over the stage: wherever he walked, they were there. You could see him looking for them everywhere he went, but still reacting with the audience. A fan in the front row gave him a cowboy hat, and he put it on and started singing the song. After, his daughter Ashley, who's in his band, came over to him and said, 'Hey, Glen, where'd you get that hat?' He said, 'I . . . don't . . . know.' I don't know if he was joking or didn't remember. But his guitar playing was so intact and phenomenal. He would also go outside the parts he'd normally play, super musical and stuff you wouldn't expect. It was mind-blowing to see this guy who is losing his faculty and still have his talent intact."

Jessica Grahn is a neuroscientist at the University of Western Ontario. She told the CBC, "It's not an unknown phenomenon for those who have trouble speaking or with their memory to still be able to sing. Music tends to activate emotional centres and we know that emotional centres really solidify memories. Some of our strongest memories are the ones that are associated with strong emotions. And another thought is that the music helps support the memory for the lyrics because it's another thing that's always coupled, so it's another cue . . . whereas with speech there's no supporting information."

"I know there are people who don't understand why we've gone out on tour and why we've exposed this illness so publicly," said Glen Campbell's wife, Kim Woolen, in the documentary. "Why we've allowed a loved one to go onstage and take the risk of making a fool out of himself. But it's something he wanted to do and it's healthy for him and it's worth the risk. He's still living his life to the fullest. It hasn't got to the point where he's embarrassing himself. The fans are so supportive. They want him out there. They don't care if he messes up. They love him, and he loves them."

Campbell continued to perform until November 2012, at which point he did embarrass himself. At what would be his final show, in Napa, California, he repeatedly dropped lines, rambled incoherently and even flubbed a guitar solo—the one skill he'd maintained throughout his entire ordeal. "This is terrible," he told the audience after the solo. That's when his family decided to call it off. The documentary came out in 2014. Campbell died in 2017.

Watching a performer battle with disease onstage can be as inspiring as it is uncomfortable, especially if, like Downie, the artist's work is rich with allusions to death and mortality. Then there's emotional pain—and there is no greater emotional pain imaginable than the death of a child. Can you even begin to present that pain onstage? Should you?

Nick Cave lost one of his 15-year-old twin boys in July 2015; he fell off a seaside cliff near the family's home in Brighton, England. Cave had already started writing and recording his next album, *Skeleton Tree*; the ghost of his boy haunted the rest of the session. Ghosts have always haunted Cave's work, of course: his deep catalogue is full of devils, murderers and unsavoury characters. Cave can be campy as often as he is truly terrifying; that he blurs those lines willingly can be confusing for many. Now he was re-emerging from an intensely private pain with a new album. "It's almost as if by thrusting himself into the spotlight during his darkest hour, Cave was issuing a form of karmic payback, penance for the pain and reckoning he's inflicted on so many characters in his songs," wrote Stuart Berman in *Pitchfork*. "Grieving doesn't happen on a standard timeline—you don't just hole yourself up for three months of weeping and then emerge fully recovered. Grief is a wraith of love that haunts your soul, emerging when you least expect it from the most mundane triggers and surroundings."

After his son's death, Cave invited filmmaker Andrew Dominik to film the rest of the recording sessions for a documentary—shot in 3D, no less— called *One More Time with Feeling*. "After a time, [my wife] and I decided to be happy," he says in the film. "This happiness seemed to be an act of revenge, an act of defiance. To care about each other, and everyone else, and to be careful. To be careful with each other and the ones around us."

"The big problem with a film like this is: should you even make it?" says Dominik. "There's a certain amount of discomfort, to look at ourselves in the worst possible way as being these people that are exploiting a tragedy to sell records. That's not really the real intention behind it at all, but that does exist in it. Is there something disgusting about the fact [that] this film, on one level, [is] a promotional tool to sell a record? We were always trying to work out where was this film a legitimate portrait that has some kind of integrity, and where was it grief porn?"

Audiences may have had trepidations about Cave's tour that followed. But Crash Vegas singer Michelle McAdorey says the Toronto show on May 31, 2017, was one of the most cathartic experiences in her life, musical or otherwise. "I was going through heavy stuff at the time, but I went to that Nick Cave show because I needed to be there," she says. "I was bawling my eyes out and jumping out of my chair in the temple that is Massey Hall. I was the crazy woman there. But then I looked around and saw several other 'crazy women.' I wasn't the only one. Everybody just let go and reached out. We can't figure out all this stuff rationally."

"Nobody has ever described [the final human struggle] truly in words— nobody can," wrote Hugh MacLennan in *The Watch That Ends the Night*. "But others have described it, and I can tell you who they are. Go to the musicians. In the work of a few musicians you can hear every aspect of this conflict between light and dark within the soul. You can hear all the contradictory fears, hopes, desires and passions of Everyman fissioning and fusing into new harmonies out of the dead ones. You can hear—you can almost see—the inward process of destruction, creation, destruction again and re-creation into the last possible harmony, the only one there can be, which is a will to live, love, grow and be grateful, the determination to endure all things, suffer all things, hope all things, believe all things necessary for what our ancestors called the glory of God. To struggle and work for that, at the end, is all there is left."

———

Cancer was once the disease that dare not speak its name. Hard to believe, in a culture filled with Run for the Cure and Marathons of Hope and pink ribbons galore. Yet, as *Breaking Bad* and the 2003 Sarah Polley melodrama *My Life Without Me* suggest, some people prefer to keep their diagnosis incredibly private, perhaps even from family members.

In Susan Sontag's landmark 1978 essay "Illness as Metaphor," she reported that in France and Italy, it was the rule for "doctors to communicate a cancer diagnosis to the patient's family but not to the patient; doctors consider that the truth will be intolerable to all but exceptionally mature and intelligent patients." She added that in the U.S., mail correspondence from cancer hospitals did not include a return address, lest the diagnosis be a secret from the victim's families. Though cancer became considerably less stigmatized over the next 30 years, concealing a cancer diagnosis was still prevalent in 2016.

In the case of Jack Layton, federal leader of Canada's New Democratic Party for eight years, he was open with the public about his battle with prostate cancer in early 2010 and continued to serve as leader. He was in remission by the time he led his party to a historic second-place finish in the May 2011 election. By July, he'd been diagnosed with a new cancer, requiring him to take leave. He was dead a month later. His family never did reveal what the second cancer was; they didn't want Layton's experience to unnecessarily frighten people with the same diagnosis. "People know it's a cancer, it's cancer cells," said Olivia Chow, Layton's wife, fellow NDP MP and herself a thyroid cancer survivor. "It's not as if we're not saying what he died of—he died of cancer. We don't need to go into what kind of cancer because those people that have that kind of cancer will not react well, and why inflict that on people?"

"My sister lasted 10 months from the time she was diagnosed with a brain tumour," says Don Harrison of Sons of Freedom, who opened for the Tragically Hip's fall 1992 tour. "My friend Graeme Nicol, who was our lighting guy and went on to work with Sarah McLachlan and Sheryl Crow, lasted a year [with the same diagnosis]. My sister didn't tell anyone it was terminal. Only her husband knew. She didn't want to worry any of us. Most people just want to live day to day, just keep on doing what they're doing—which is probably the best thing you can do, keep going until you can't anymore."

Toronto illustrator Teva Harrison—no relation to Don—was diagnosed with Stage 4 metastatic cancer in 2013, at the age of 37. She didn't tell anybody about her condition for the first year, a year in which she started making the drawings that would eventually turn into a graphic novel about her day-to-day struggle, called *In-Between Days*.

"When people suggested to me that the drawings might be helpful to other people," she says, "I thought, 'I might have only a tiny bit of time left. What am I afraid of? How is being public going to make it worse?' Whatever I was afraid of was just gone. I'd always been private with the dark stuff. Which is not unusual, and social media encourages us to share the good stuff and keep the rest to ourselves. Then I was in a position where it was so bad, so dark, and I was so sad, and I felt alone with my feelings. I thought if someone else is feeling alone with their feelings and they happen to pick up my book and it makes them say, 'Yeah, me too!' then maybe that's worth it. Not talking about something doesn't make it less scary. It makes it loom larger."

Invisibility is its own kind of death. She wrote in her book, "We're encouraged to slip away because people generally prefer it that way . . . What is lost when we allow sick people to disappear?" When posed her own question in conversation, she answers, "I think we lose the depth of the human experience. The extremes of emotion—extreme joy and extreme grief—are where our deepest commonalities exist, no matter where that joy or grief comes from. That's where we meet. By not talking about it, we are limiting the depth of our connections with other people, our own opportunities to feel and live. But I also think we lose the stories and knowledge and experience of a person. We don't have as much of a sit-around-and-tell-stories culture. Maybe that's part of why Gord Downie being so public is so meaningful to people, because he's a major national storyteller, one of Canada's biggest. That warm invitation that storytelling gives, that foundation of community, is part of what we're losing, part of what we're trying to hold on to."

Publishing a book and going on a book tour was not the end of Harrison's final journey. She continued to work on new art projects, display her work in galleries across Canada and write books. In *In-Between Days*, she wrote of having "more hunger for life and experiences . . . I really have nothing to lose. So I am going to say yes even more. Live like a tornado, when I can. I'm going to suck the marrow out of life and see what I've been missing." The key there is "when I can"—Harrison is aware of the notion of being "able-ist," of projecting a model of strength that masks the utter helplessness that other cancer victims experience.

"Sometimes people say, 'I don't know how you do it. I could barely get here today.' Sometimes *I'm* that person who can barely do it," she says. "It depends what you're willing to do, and how important it is to you. Obviously there are times when you simply can't, when you have mobility issues, for example. My palliative care doctor gives me Ritalin to use if I have a speaking engagement and I'm so tired I can't do it. It's not ideal, but there are ways to fake it. This changes how you live. You're simultaneously living your life but engraving your own death. Which feels like it should negate itself in a way."

"If need be," says one of the protagonists in *The Watch That Ends the Night*, "she must be enabled to live her own death. She is one of the very, very few who can." He and the other central character are discussing the ethics of allowing a loved one to either die or undergo a second surgery that would result in her living a compromised existence. "Her life isn't completed yet. She wants to paint more pictures."

Will Munro was a Toronto artist who died of glioblastoma multiforme in 2010. In addition to his provocative art, he was a popular DJ and curator of Vazaleen, a monthly queer dance party celebrated for its eclectic cross-pollinations: of music, of communities, of scenes. He was diagnosed after a seizure in 2008, when doctors found a seven-centimetre tumour in his brain. They gave him three months to live. He immediately wanted to put on another art show. And another party. For two years, he kept working and working, through four brain surgeries and multiple chemotherapies.

"That whole chapter in Will's life, besides being excruciatingly heartbreaking, it's also the most humbling thing I've ever experienced," filmmaker Bruce LaBruce told Munro's biographer, Sarah Liss. "The courage that he displayed, and his fight, just his grace, having that last show. I can't imagine how I would respond to something like that, and I would never imagine that I could face it with such aplomb. It just shows what kind of spirit he had."

Liss says that the concept of "one more show" from someone on death's door "involves a very complicated mix of defiance and humility. In both Will [Munro]'s and Gord [Downie]'s case, they knew how physically compromised they'd become. There is a confrontation with vanity, with the ego. That amazing willingness to let yourself visibly falter and fail in front of the people who have admired you—maybe that's part of it, a necessary act of being seen. I can't imagine that Prince would have wanted that. Prince had so much invested in presentation." That said, Prince did spend his final year in public sporting a cane—which he needed for the pain in his hips, the pain for which he took the opiates that killed him.

Liss is wary, however of "sanctifying sickness," the notion that "these figures were empowered to make their greatest statements by virtue of this immersion into their own mortality. The 'noble cancer' narrative can turn someone into a saint. It can lead to hagiography, and the rough edges get smoothed off." Liss says she's grateful that Will Munro's many caregivers were willing to be candid with her about their frustrations. Dealing with the demands of a terminal person hell-bent on a final project is not easy. "He was being such an asshole—and, goddam, I can't blame him," one friend said. "There was a real reaction in [Toronto's queer and arts] community to immediately turn Will into an uncomplicated saviour figure," says Liss.

She sees some parallels with the canonization of Downie, who, like Munro, was "this incredibly galvanizing figure, well loved by many people who identified as his friends, even if he wasn't necessarily super connected with them. [Downie is] such a universally recognized figure, such an icon in a country that doesn't have a lot of icons. We know so much about him—and yet we don't know that much about him at all, as a person. I feel like there hasn't been a lot of complication of the hero narrative, and I don't know if we'll get that. There is a reason that the candour I got [from Munro's friends] came years after Will died, rather than in the moment."

———

David Bowie—who, like Downie, was decidedly deliberate in every aesthetic decision leading up to his death—started recording what would be his final album, *Blackstar*, in January 2015. Bowie had liver cancer, but he had yet to be diagnosed as terminal. Contrary to popular belief, Bowie did not believe he was making a final statement, though he was aware of the possibility. When sessions began, "He just came fresh from a chemo session, and he had no eyebrows, and he had no hair on his head," says producer Tony Visconti, "and there was no way he could keep it a secret from the band. But he told me privately, and I really got choked up when we sat face to face talking about it." Obvious or not, some of the musicians later claimed not to know he was ill.

"People are so desperate for *Blackstar* to be this parting gift that Bowie made for the world when he knew he was dying, but I think it's simplistic to think that," says Francis Whately, an old friend of Bowie's who directed a BBC film called *David Bowie: The Last Five Years*. "However, he must have known there was a chance he wasn't going to recover, so to do an album with a certain amount of ambiguity in it, is Bowie playing the cat-and-mouse game he always played." The term "blackstar" refers to a pre-malignant lesion in breast cancer. In astrophysics—not an unlikely topic of research for Bowie—it also refers to a collapsing star that never transforms into a black hole, trapped in an infinite transitional state.

Bowie's chemo appeared to be working. By the middle of 2015, he was in remission—though apprehensive. *"For now*, I'm in remission, and we'll see how it goes," he told Visconti. By November, Visconti told *Rolling Stone*, "He's in fine health. He's just made a very rigorous album."

That same month, however, Bowie discovered his cancer was, in fact, terminal. That's when he shot the "Lazarus" video. In it, Bowie is strapped to a hospital bed, his eyes covered in bandages, with tiny plastic eyes from a children's craft project placed eerily in their stead. A mysterious figure emerges from his closet and hides under his bed, reaching up to touch him. That's intercut with scenes of a twitching, jittery Bowie at a desk, writing furiously—a last will and testament, perhaps? The video concludes with Bowie retreating into the closet from whence came the intruder, closing the door while still facing the camera.

Director Johan Renck had already come up with the concept of Bowie being bedridden; the singer had pushed for a more traditional performance clip. "I immediately said, 'The song is called "Lazarus," you should be in the bed,'" says Renck. "To me it had to do with the Biblical aspect of it . . . it had nothing to do with him being ill. I found out later that, the week we were shooting, it was when he was told it was over, they were ending treatments and that his illness had won."

David Bowie died on January 10, 2016, three days after the release of both *Blackstar* and the video for "Lazarus."

Two months later, Malik Taylor died at age 45 of complications from Type 2 diabetes, which he'd been living with since 1990. Taylor was better known as Phife Dawg, one-third of beloved hip-hop group A Tribe Called Quest, one of the most influential acts of the '90s. They split up somewhat acrimoniously in 1998, which was tough on Phife; he and fellow MC Q-Tip had first met at church when they were both four years old. Q-Tip was the star of the group, featured on prominent collaborations with everyone from the Beastie Boys to Norah Jones, and was quick to launch a solo career. Phife was largely left behind. Tribe reunited in 2006 for a tour and selected live dates in the coming years. Phife always wanted to make another record. Q-Tip claimed he was on a "sabbatical."

On November 15, 2015, A Tribe Called Quest performed on *The Tonight Show* to mark the reissue of their debut album. Sparks flew. Hatchets were buried. This time, Q-Tip agreed that it was time to make a new album.

It would be their first in 18 years. Phife started flying from his home in California to Q-Tip's studio in New Jersey twice a month, spending just as much time rebuilding the relationship with Q-Tip as actually working on music. Guests like Kendrick Lamar, André 3000, Busta Rhymes and Jack White—even Elton John—dropped by. Literally no one phoned it in: all vocals were cut together, in person. "I hadn't seen Phife that happy since we were kids," Q-Tip told the *New York Times*. But the travel took its toll on Phife's physical well-being. "Doing this album killed him," said Tribe member Jarobi White. "And he was very happy to go out like that."

Phife Dawg died on March 22, 2016. Eight months later, A Tribe Called Quest released their final album, *Thank You for Your Service, We Got It from Here*. It debuted at No. 1 and was one of the best-reviewed albums of the year, miraculously managing to tap into the group's original aesthetic while simultaneously sounding entirely modern. The surviving members performed on *Saturday Night Live* and the Grammy Awards, unveiling a mural of Phife during his verses on "We the People," an anti-xenophobia anthem that took on extra resonance after the 2016 presidential election. The group toured without him in 2017, gesturing to an empty microphone as his vocals played on the backing track.

The day before the final Tribe album was released, the world found out that Leonard Cohen had died after a fall, likely caused by effects from recently diagnosed leukemia. The Venn diagram illustrating fans of both artists is small, but not entirely negligible. Cohen was 82 when he died, and the shadow he cast was enormous, just as large as that of Bowie or Prince, who died on April 21, 2016—a year that was an emotionally exhausting *annus horribilis* for fans of eclectic music.

Cohen had been riding a magnificent fourth act, a comeback that began in 2008 and spawned two albums of new material and no fewer than four live albums culled from sold-out arena tours—arenas!—around the world. His final album came out only two weeks before his death—the same day as Downie's *Secret Path*. Cohen's album was called *You Want It Darker*. By that point in the year, no one really *did* want it darker, but the album proved to be one of the best of Cohen's illustrious career. Tastefully co-produced by his son, Adam, and featuring the male choir from his childhood synagogue, as well as longtime collaborator Sharon Robinson, it featured songs about "killing the flame," "leaving the table" and being "out of the game," even intoning at one point, "I'm ready, my Lord."

Maclean's Brian D. Johnson asked Cohen if he thought this would be his last album. "Not specifically," responded the singer in his last Canadian interview, "but at this stage in the game, you know that all your activities are subject to abrupt cancellation . . . [I'm] a little too weak to get out there and boogie, and a little too healthy to die. Work is not always sweet, but it's always sustaining."

"There were only a few hours a day that we could work," Adam Cohen told Johnson. His father was largely confined to an orthopaedic chair, due to multiple compression fractures in his spine. "I was dealing with an ailing old man, but an ailing old man who was showing paranormal levels of devotion and focus, and that rubbed off on everybody. The encounters were urgent and sweet and meaningful. It was as if we were riding some kind of mysterious wind . . . There were fits of laughter woven throughout what was a very serious endeavour. There were episodes where I saw an incapacitated old man stand up and dance in front of the speakers. There were hilarious, esoteric arguments fuelled by medical marijuana. There were episodes of blissful joy that sometimes lasted hours, where we'd listen to one song on repeat like teenagers. There were smiles and an inner glow that I can actually hear on the record."

There were at least three songs finished after *You Want It Darker* was done. Cohen clearly wanted to keep going. "I'm not much of an optimist," said Patrick Leonard, Cohen's co-producer and co-songwriter, two months before the artist's death. "But Leonard won't be done until he's done, and I don't think he's done. His strength is profound. He's going to keep going, as long as he can put a pencil to paper and get to a microphone."

Talking about other famous deaths to set the tone for Downie's passing.

Johnny Cash recorded eight albums of material between 1994 and his death in 2003; four of them were released posthumously. They were all produced by Rick Rubin, who wanted Cash's voice to be as unadorned as possible. Much of the material featured skeletal arrangements, often just Cash and a single acoustic guitar. The gravity of the Man in Black's baritone had never sounded so stark and chilling, or as beautiful. His commanding authority was still very much present: to some, it sounded like the voice of God. The first two Rubin albums were a late-career game changer for Cash.

At the age of 65, in 1997, four years into his comeback, Cash was experiencing tremors and dizziness. He was diagnosed with Shy-Drager syndrome, affecting the nervous system. Touring was no longer an option. He put all his energy into recording as much material as possible with Rubin, on which he sounded increasingly frail and vulnerable with each new record. By the time of 2002's *The Man Comes Around*, the voice of God was in tatters, suffering from asthma and diabetes. Six months after its release, his beloved June Carter Cash died during heart surgery. In September 2003, Cash died from respiratory failure—and a broken heart. Three years later, *A Hundred Highways* debuted at No. 1. It featured covers of Gordon Lightfoot's "If You Could Read My Mind," Ian Tyson's "Four Strong Winds" and the traditional gospel song "God's Gonna Cut You Down." It also contained one of Cash's last compositions, "Like the 309," in which the artist muses about meeting "doctor Death" and prepares for a final train ride—in a casket.

The Rubin records enabled Cash to reach an entire generation of new listeners, but there was no shortage of criticism. There were accusations of stunt casting: of purposely choosing songs like Depeche Mode's "Personal Jesus" or Soundgarden's "Rusty Cage" as a marketing ploy to amp up the goth appeal of the Man in Black on his death bed. The video for "Hurt," a Nine Inch Nails cover, was maudlin. Rubin, who also owned the record company releasing the albums, was accused of propping up a dying man and milking him for every last breath. Considering the wealth of material—or the glut, depending on how you look at it—it did appear that Rubin was trying to, um, cash in.

Rubin says Cash ruled everything around him. "I know he wanted to be able to do more than he was physically able to do," says the producer. "He had suffered for a lot of years, and yet he could still get the job done whenever he wanted to. But now, for the first time, he was experiencing times when he wanted to be working, and the frustration of either physically not being able to do it, or mentally not being able to stay focused, or voice-wise, not being of strong voice. This was all new to him, and it was very difficult for him to deal with. Sometimes he felt embarrassed, and it really took the people around him to say, 'This is beautiful, and we love it.' And again, he trusted the people who were saying that, because we really did feel that way."

In 2002, Cash had an exit strategy, but didn't know when he was leaving. Warren Zevon did. That same year, Zevon's doctor told the acerbic singer-songwriter he had three months to live.

Zevon had lived a hard life. At the height of his success, he guzzled several bottles of whisky a night, along with other intoxicants. He got black-out drunk and was impossibly cruel to his friends and lovers, to say nothing of strangers. He scored a novelty hit in 1978 with "Werewolves of London," but his sharp wit and strength as a songwriter made him much more than a one-hit wonder. Zevon got sober in 1984, by which point his commercial prospects had dried up but, miraculously, he still had many loyal friends who held powerful positions in the music industry. In 2002, he was two albums into a modest comeback when he appeared at the Calgary and Edmonton folk festivals, gigs he was reluctant to take because he thought they were beneath him. While in Alberta, he was short of breath. He thought it was stress and anxiety and lashed out at festival staff. He hadn't seen a doctor in 20 years; he relied on his dentist to tell him if anything was wrong. When he got home to California, he finally went to a doctor and was told he had inoperable lung cancer.

Zevon suffered from OCD and had a superstitious fear of cancer his whole life. He once told his manager that any time he heard the word "cancer," he had to return or get rid of anything he'd bought that day: clothing, food, didn't matter what it was. He'd once ordered cases of his favourite kind of cigarette before a trip, but tasked his assistant with ensuring the word "cancer" didn't appear on the packaging. Any other warning was fine: lung disease, infertility, gum disease, whatever. Just no cancer.

Now that he had it, Zevon asked his friend Mitch Albom, author of *Tuesdays with Morrie*, "So, am I supposed to die with my boots on? Is that my fate? Is that how I'm supposed to approach this?" He told Albom that he was in the most creative period of his life: sober and on a songwriting roll. "I want to make as much music as I can possibly make before I go," he said. "I've got all these ideas, and it's coming better now than it has in 20 years."

He sought different spiritual leaders and entertained different ideas about how to spend his final days. He eventually told his ex-wife, "My job is music. It's all I can leave the kids and people I love, so I'm going to make a record." The man who once wrote a song called "I'll Sleep When I'm Dead" told his manager, "We have to go into showbiz mode. I'm giving you permission to use my illness in any way that you see fit to further my career right now." Pre-diagnosis, a best-of album had already been planned for release; the cover image was a skull smoking a pipe. The record company was horrified that it would suddenly appear highly inappropriate; Zevon insisted it stay. He joked to *Rolling Stone* that he didn't really care how long exactly he had left to live, except that his fate came in handy in line at the supermarket: "Excuse me, I have terminal cancer," he'd tell the cashier. "Can we speed this up a little?"

Zevon rejected chemotherapy and started working on his final album, *The Wind*, right away. "Do they still make EPs?" he joked to his longtime collaborator Jorge Calderon. Plenty of friends and admirers were enlisted to play on the record: Bruce Springsteen, Jackson Browne, the Eagles, Dwight Yoakam, Ry Cooder. (Yes, Ry Cooder helped play Zevon's self-penned eulogy.) There was even a cover of Dylan's "Knockin' on Heaven's Door." Many of the songs were personal love letters. "If I can let someone know what I felt about them," he said, "that's more important than passing off some bullshit insight I've had about living on the planet."

On October 30, 2002, David Letterman devoted an entire program to Zevon's final public performance; the two were old friends, and Zevon occasionally filled in for Letterman's bandleader, Paul Shaffer. It was an incredibly rare display of vulnerability and mortality in popular culture. "Playing your own wake is a rare opportunity for a show business personality," said Zevon. "It's one most performers would not take on. It's not the easiest thing to do . . . I don't think I've been in denial about death, but I've been in denial about doing 45 minutes of live network television."

Once *The Wind* was finished and the Letterman experience was over, Zevon started drinking heavily again, mixing $500 bottles of scotch with liquid morphine. He figured he didn't have anything to lose. He lived a full 13 months after his diagnosis, 10 months longer than his doctors had given him to live. In that time, he got to see *The Wind* go gold, see Bob Dylan perform his songs live, attend his daughter's engagement party and witness the birth of his grandsons. When Letterman asked Zevon what he had learned from this experience, the singer said simply, "Enjoy every sandwich."

———

Bowie, Cohen, Cash and Zevon made final records, but they didn't go on tour. That's a whole other cup of meat, as Levon Helm of the Band might say—Helm, of course, beat throat cancer in 1998 and came back in 2004 with a productive final act before the cancer returned and killed him in 2012. Carl Wilson of the Beach Boys was diagnosed with lung cancer in March 1997; he continued to tour with the band that summer while undergoing chemotherapy, playing guitar while sitting down. He died in February 1998. Def Leppard's Vivian Campbell has been battling Hodgkin's lymphoma since 2013, scheduling tours between treatments.

Then there's Bob Marley, who ignored a diagnosis of skin cancer in 1977, which started under a toenail; he initially thought it was a soccer injury. Doctors recommended amputation; Marley refused on account of his Rastafarian beliefs. He released four more albums and a live album between then and September 1980, when he collapsed while jogging in Central Park. The cancer had metastasized to the rest of his body, including his brain and lungs. His doctor said he had "more cancer in him than I've seen in a live human being" and told him he "might as well go back out on the road and die there." Bob Marley played his last show on September 23, 1980, in Pittsburgh. He sang Queen's "Another One Bites the Dust" repeatedly at sound check. He then cancelled the rest of his tour and went to Germany to seek holistic treatment. When that failed, he decided to fly to Jamaica and die there. He had a stopover in Miami. He didn't make it home. He died on May 11, 1981, at the age of 36.

Lemmy Kilmister of Motörhead died two days after being diagnosed with a brain tumour in 2015. Two weeks before, he was celebrating his 70th birthday at the Whisky A Go-Go in L.A., with fellow legends of metal and punk. He'd flown back from a European tour the day before; he was supposed to go back there in the new year for more shows. For the last three years of his life, diabetes and a heart arrhythmia had led to some shows being abruptly cut short. He'd stopped his inhuman intake of Jack Daniel's and switched to vodka and orange juice. In the last two weeks of that final tour, he skipped sound checks. In one of the last interviews he did, with podcaster Marc Maron, Lemmy's weakened voice was barely audible. But the show had to go on.

"To really think of what energy and the balls that took to still play shows for the fans," said Todd Singerman, his manager of 24 years, in a *Rolling Stone* obituary, "to do the last fucking show two weeks ago and then drop— that's like a *Rocky* story to me."

Two days after his birthday party on December 13, Lemmy went to an emergency room with chest pains, but was dismissed. His manager and friends were worried he might have had a stroke, as his speech was getting worse. On December 27, the results were in: it was brain cancer and he was given two to six months to live. A shift of homecare nurses was set up, and a video game console from his favourite bar, the Rainbow Room, was brought into his bedroom. He died there two days later, on December 29, 2015.

"Here's the shocker for me and everyone else," said his manager. "He's been to a thousand doctors and hospitals throughout the world, but nobody caught this. To be told you have terminal cancer with all the blood tests he's taken in his life and everything else? It's very hard to grasp that."

———

Other than Gord Downie, there is only one other performer who both recorded and toured, fully conscious of their disease, right up to her dying breaths. Sharon Jones died 11 months to the day before Downie. In 2017, Jones's *Soul of a Woman* and Downie's *Introduce Yourself* were released within three weeks of each other.

Every album Sharon Jones put out was better than the last. If you didn't know the story behind *Soul of a Woman*, you'd never guess that it was made as her body was falling apart; the record is full of the fire and energy her audience had come to expect.

A late bloomer, Jones found herself on a path toward success in 1996, at age 40, with a group of young musicians called the Dap-Kings, who were thrilled to discover a gospel-trained singer who was as invigorating a performer as she was a vocalist. In 2006, Amy Winehouse may have borrowed Jones's band to make *Back to Black*, but Jones's band stuck with her until her final days in hospital. She died of a stroke after two bouts with pancreatic cancer.

After the first bout, which postponed the release of 2013's *Give the People What They Want*, Jones was bedridden for 10 months. That killed her spirit; she was downright miserable. Once in remission, she went back on the road: bald, no wig, not hiding the ordeal she'd been through. When the cancer came back in 2015, she decided to stay on the road—even while doing chemotherapy. It's a final lap that exceeds even Gord Downie's: his final tour was only 15 dates. Sharon Jones played 30 shows in 2016, the final one in September, only two months before her death.

"There were a lot of voices—friends, family—telling her not to push herself, not to go on the road, to rest," says Dap-Kings bandleader Gabe Roth. "There was a side to it that we all understood, and that she made very clear, that being onstage and singing was when she felt best. That was her therapy: getting on stage and connecting with people, looking them in the eye, feeling the music in her body."

It wasn't an easy place to be. "She'd be in pain backstage and having a hard time walking or eating or talking," says Roth. "We'd be really concerned. Then we'd get onstage, and she'd somehow connect to the music and the audience and summon this energy, this power, out of what seemed like thin air. Vocally she was getting stronger and stronger. As someone who'd been standing behind her for 20 years, I was still amazed at the way she was singing. The sheer power of it defied the reality of her health situation."

In between legs of a tour, she'd go into the studio to make what became *Soul of a Woman*, where that vocal strength is audible in ways not heard on other artists' exit statements; Downie's 2017 album *Introduce Yerself* being the only other exception. "She only came in to the studio when she felt strong," says Roth. "There was no reason for us to get her on tape when she felt weak or sick. That's not how she saw herself or how we saw her." That extended to the lyrical content as well. "It wasn't like we were trying to construct a goodbye letter," says Roth. "It wasn't a swan song, a final opus. It felt the same way all of our records felt: it's about being alive, about that moment. And cancer was part of that moment."

The last show Sharon Jones ever played was with Hall and Oates at the MGM Grand hotel in Las Vegas. "It was a cavernous arena-type place, and we were the opener," says Roth. "It was half-empty. It wasn't a particularly romantic or inspiring last show. It was very sad. She got onstage and tried to do what she does, and it was the first time she physically didn't have the air in her body to do what she wanted to do. She came offstage and we had oxygen for her. I remember her crying. That was the first time it felt like she wasn't invincible. Through all that cancer and all that stuff, we'd get onstage with her, and no matter what the doctors said, it was hard to believe that she wasn't a superhero."

The Dap-Kings didn't book any shows after that. And Jones had to turn down the one gig she'd been waiting eight years to play—in some ways, waiting her whole life to play. "She'd been talking about getting to the White House ever since Obama got into office," says Roth. "She was so excited, leaning on management and the booking agent, 'When am I going to get to the White House? When are we singing for the Obamas?' Finally, the invitation came through and everyone was so happy for her, but [the White House] only wanted her—not the band, just her and a couple of people.

"Sharon said, 'I'm not going unless the whole band goes. All nine guys, background singers, everything.' She held out, against all our advice: 'Sharon, you've been wanting to do this forever! We don't care, just go and do it.'" The White House acceded to her request, but she contracted pneumonia just before the gig. "When you're dealing with that kind of intense cancer and that kind of brutal therapy, even a common cold is a very serious thing," says Roth. "So she told us to go without her. It was an incredible sign of how loyal she was, how much solidarity there was in the band. Every band talks about being a family, but there was really something there." The Dap-Kings played the White House show with long-time backing singers Saundra Williams and Starr Duncan Lowe, who had been singing behind Jones ever since they were all in a wedding band; they had also released their own record with the Dap-Kings backing them up. "They're very capable of putting on a show—we can put on a show without Sharon, but it's not Sharon Jones and the Dap-Kings, that's for sure," says Roth. "It was a great little show, but it was done with heavy hearts."

All the Dap-Kings were by Jones's bedside during her final days. "She suffered a few strokes," Roth recalls. "She couldn't speak, couldn't say hello or her name or follow simple commands." At one point, bandmate Binky Griptite started playing guitar, and Jones started moaning and eventually singing. Everyone joined in. "Day by day, even though her body was deteriorating, something in her brought back her voice and she was singing with us," says Roth. "She was forming words, and we were singing these gospel tunes: 'Go Tell It on the Mountain,' 'His Eye Is on the Sparrow.' She was singing beautifully, even harmonizing and improvising—all these things that you would think require some amount of brain function, she was all there at that point. She couldn't answer a single question, but for days all she wanted to do, all day and all night, was sing to her last dying breath. It was so essential to who she was." She died on November 18, 2016.

The album concludes with "Call on God," a gospel song left off a 2007 album. She had written it "in the late '70s or early '80s," says Roth, for the church choir she led. At the memorial service for her at that same church, former choir members flew in from all over the country. There, Jones's younger musical brothers in the Dap-Kings convinced her older gospel sisters in song to swing by Daptone Studios—where Jones herself once helped install the electrical wiring—and overdub backing vocals onto the old track. "They got to sing with Sharon one more time, with her in their headphones," says Roth. "It was a beautiful way to complete the album, with something very personal, with something that connected with something she'd done her whole life, that connected the Dap-Tones with the church people to honour her together."

After her death, the Dap-Kings were unsure what exactly to do next. They took some studio work, including a Smokey Robinson Christmas album. But unlike Prince's Revolution, who toured without their former leader in 2017, the Dap-Kings were not going to hit the road on their own or with a new singer. "It's not even a question of taste or the optics of it, because I don't care about that, really," says Roth. "On one level, here's a great band that spent 20 years cultivating a sound, who loves being together and playing together—we're musicians and that's what we want to do. That's not an easy thing to say goodbye to. But the other side of that is the special connection we had with Sharon, and we know that there's no sense in chasing that high. We were never higher than when we were behind Sharon onstage."

However this goes on for too long and feels like unnecessary info. ⌐ Filler.

Kevin Hearn was on stage with Gord Downie at the last performance of his life, on November 29, 2016, as part of the *Secret Path* band at the Rebecca Cohn Auditorium in Halifax. The day Hearn learned that Downie died, October 18, 2017, he had a gig at the same theatre with Barenaked Ladies.

Hearn and Downie discussed cancer often. In 2000, the keyboardist had played on two songs on *Coke Machine Glow*—a time during which Hearn was battling leukemia, a cancer of the blood cells that originates in bone marrow. It was a time in Hearn's life when he danced with death almost on a daily basis. Years later, he was musical director for Lou Reed's band, and he became very close to the rock legend in his final days as he battled liver cancer; one of Reed's last recordings is the guitar solo on the Hearn song "Floating," about having an out-of-body experience in a hospital bed. Reed died on October 27, 2013. "Floating" appears on Hearn's album *Days in Frames*, which Gord Downie loved and listened to every day when it came out in 2014—almost exactly a year before Downie had his brain seizure. Downie appeared at a Lou Reed tribute show in early 2014 organized by Hearn and featuring Reed's band; the Hip singer sang "How Do You Think It Feels?"

Hearn was diagnosed with leukemia in 1998. He was 29 years old. His doctor told him he might only have five months to live. He required a bone-marrow transplant from his brother; the day of the operation, his bandmates in Barenaked Ladies called him to sing "happy transplant to you" on the phone—and to tell him that their song "One Week" had just hit No. 1 on Billboard. Hearn didn't exactly hit the town to celebrate: his recovery period required a month in an isolation room at the Princess Margaret Hospital in Toronto. *⌐ I do not like the cancer talk I'm getting anxious.*

Hearn's ordeal took its toll on his bandmates, at a time when everyone's lives were changing quickly. "Kevin was just a shadow of himself, going through chemo," recalls Barenaked Ladies bassist Jim Creeggan. "I remember visiting him; he was just bones. I wish I'd visited him more. I wonder how much I was there for him, when I was scrambling as a human being myself, not even being that happy with success. I had never gone through that before. I couldn't quite process it because everything was moving so fast. I can relate to where the Hip were at on their last tour. If anything, I identified with the mixture of celebration and mourning all at the same time, not knowing from one moment to the next where I was standing."

Building a new immune system after a bone-marrow transplant is a five-year process—and a harrowing one. "I wanted my life back," says Hearn. "I wanted to feel like myself. I know Gord had similar feelings. I probably shouldn't have been out there, but I was fighting for my life, and your body needs your mind to move forward and not give up. Fear is human but also self-defeating. You need faith, not just hope." He took advice from his nurse, who told him, "Don't become a full-time patient. Get out there and do what you love to do, as much as you can."

Not without peril, however. When he rejoined Barenaked Ladies on tour in 2000, Hearn was on a series of medications to help him deal with graft-versus-host disease, a medical complication following the receipt of transplanted tissue. "I was on so many medications, it got out of control and threw my blood sugar out of whack," says Hearn.

One day in Salt Lake City, the band had a day off before their gig. Hearn was particularly low on energy and opted to sleep it off in the hotel. When singer Ed Robertson went to visit, Hearn had no idea where he was: he was delirious and thought he was on a boat. The band gathered and demanded that Hearn phone his doctor while they all listened in on the call. The Toronto doctor knew people at the Salt Lake City cancer clinic and set up an immediate appointment. "His blood was the consistency of oatmeal: he was 12 hours before organ failure," says Creeggan. "The fact that we let him sleep the day off in his hotel room—he could have died there. He wasn't able to even make the decision himself. He was going to die."

That Hearn's condition deteriorated that much is the downside of the "show must go on" mentality of the business. "You have this machine, the tour is moving, and to counter that, you try and maintain yourself—it can get away on you," says Creeggan. "You don't realize that your partner's life is being threatened. Everyone props up the artist just to get the show done."

A year later, Hearn recorded a series of songs he wrote while in the isolation room at Princess Margaret Hospital. The album, *H-Wing*, wasn't entirely about cancer, but songs like "Death Bed Love Letter," "The Good One" and "Bonefight" dealt directly with his battle with the disease. The album struck a deep chord with many. John Mann of Spirit of the West, who'd never met Hearn before, wrote him to say how much he enjoyed it. So did Lou Reed, who at that time only knew Hearn through a mutual business acquaintance. "Lou said I'd been somewhere most people don't go, and I'd come back to report on it," Hearn recalls. The keyboardist was incredibly moved: in high school, Hearn had a picture of Reed in his locker, and Reed's elegiac 1992 album *Magic and Loss* was a favourite. "That album has one of my favourite Lou lines," says Hearn. "'Life is good, but not fair at all.' It also has one of my favourite Lou songs, 'Cremation,' which Lou and I played on our tours together.

"I feel so blessed to have worked with both Lou and Gord," says Hearn. "Two beautiful souls, two beautiful poets. Sweet poet friends I'll always love and miss with all my heart, who explored mortality in a serious manner."

———

By the time Gord Downie was diagnosed with brain cancer, he had already recorded *Man Machine Poem*; the album was mixed and mastered. Nonetheless, upon its release, on June 17, 2016, a month after his disease was made public, fans parsed the lyrics and his vocal performances for clues—there were none, other than the fact mortality and a fierce sense of carpe diem had infused Downie's work from the beginning. *Secret Path* was finished even earlier. His diagnosis had not informed his decision to exhume an old story of a dead child, but his dedication to educate the public about the horrifying legacy of residential schools was most certainly fuelled by the desire to maximize his remaining time.

With the final Hip tour finished and *Secret Path* launched into the world, Downie quickly turned his attention to other musical projects. And at the urging of *Globe and Mail* writer Ian Brown, Downie started penning a memoir of his post-diagnosis life. One of the singer's favourite expressions came from the writer Raymond Carver, a phrase Downie used in the chorus of a 2002 Tragically Hip song: "Use it up," Carver told his wife, fellow writer Tess Gallagher. "Don't save anything for later."

CHAPTER TWENTY-THREE

THE STRANGER

2012–17: THE SECRET PATH TO RECONCILIATION

"It's the privilege of mass delusion"

FUCKED UP, "THE ART OF PATRONS"

Very glad this is being brought up!!!

where I'm from

IT WAS OCTOBER 2012 when Mike Downie, Gord's older brother, was driving in his car and listening to a CBC Radio documentary by Thunder Bay reporter Jody Porter. It was called "Dying for an education," about Chanie Wenjack, a 12-year-old Indigenous boy in northwestern Ontario who fled his residential school in 1966 and froze to death on train tracks he believed would lead him home. Mike Downie knew about Canada's residential schools only in the abstract. "I *think* I know what that is," he thought, "but I don't know what it is." The story shook him. He drove back to his own home, safe in Toronto with a son the same age as Wenjack. He started researching online and discovered the story originated in a 1967 *Maclean's* article by Ian Adams.

That night, Mike went to see his brother sing. The Hip were playing in Kensington Market, doing a five-day pop-up promotion in the storefront of a restaurant. He met author Joseph Boyden there, a friend of Gord's. "I just heard the most incredible radio doc today," he said, and relayed the tale. Boyden told him about the Truth and Reconciliation Commission (TRC) that began in 2008; in Winnipeg in 2010, the author had attended the first of seven national gatherings where survivors of residential schools could testify about the abuse and neglect they suffered. "What," said Mike, "you mean Truth and Reconciliation like what happened in post-apartheid South Africa?" He didn't know it was happening in Canada.

Mike Downie is a professional documentary maker who, at that point, had worked with David Suzuki, Dave Bidini, CBC's *Dragons' Den* and with Inuk filmmaker Zacharias Kunuk on something called the National Parks Project. While working together on Baffin Island, Kunuk had mentioned how kids there had been taken by the government to go to school and that the parents would follow them to town, ending an ancient nomadic lifestyle and no longer living off the land. Mike Downie was shocked to learn that this had happened during his lifetime.

The next day, the two brothers spoke on the phone. "Joseph was telling me about this Wenjack story," Gord told Mike. "What's the story?" They met for a previously scheduled lunch at Allen's on the Danforth, during which they'd planned to talk about starting a production company together to make fictional films. Mike had printed out the *Maclean's* article and showed it to Gord.

"We have to tell this story," said Gord.

It was a story that would define the final act of Gord Downie's life, a story that over the course of the next four years would be as central to his legacy as 30 years of music with the Tragically Hip.

———

Chanie "Charlie" Wenjack came from the town of Ogoki Post on the Marten Falls reservation. He was sent to the Presbyterian-run Cecilia Jeffrey Indian Residential School in Kenora, Ontario, in 1963, starting in grade 1, when he was nine years old and spoke only Ojibwe. There were 150 students there—75 boys, 75 girls—in a nearby school that was more of a dormitory; children slept there but studied at a local school. Escape was easy. On the warm October day Wenjack sprinted away, he was with two other boys, one of whom had run away three times already, one month into the school year. Ten children in total fled that day; all except Wenjack were eventually caught.

Wenjack and his two friends, Ralph and Jackie MacDonald, were headed 32 kilometres north to Redditt, where they planned to stay with the MacDonalds' uncle, Charles Kelly, and his wife, Clara. There they met another runaway, Eddie Cameron, who was also a nephew of Kelly. The

Kellys referred to Wenjack, the only non-family member taking refuge in Redditt, as "the stranger." When Kelly took his nephews on a canoe trip to a trapline, there was no room for Wenjack. The boy figured he would walk and meet them there. He asked Clara for some matches. She gave him seven and sealed them in a small glass jar. After rejoining the Kellys at the trapline, he ventured forth to Ogoki Post on his own.

As Ian Adams wrote, "Charlie had more than half of northern Ontario to cross. There are few areas in the country that are more forbidding. The bush undulates back from the railroad tracks like a bleak and desolate carpet. The wind whines through the jackpines and spruce, breaking off rotten branches, which fall with sudden crashes. The earth and rocks are a cold brown and black. The crushed-rock ballast, so hard to walk on, is a pale-yellow supporting ribbon for the dark steel tracks. Close to the tracks, tall firs feather against a grey sky. And when a snow squall comes tunnelling through a rock cut, it blots out everything in a blur of whiteness. The sudden drop in temperature can leave a man dressed in a warm parka shaking with cold."

Wenjack had only a cotton windbreaker as outerwear. For the next 36 hours, he walked through the wilderness in below-zero temperatures and freezing rain. He only made it 20 kilometres. He fainted and died of exposure.

The next morning, a train engineer spotted his body and alerted authorities, who retrieved the child's corpse. Later that week, the body was sent back to Ogoki Post; his three younger sisters joined him and never returned to residential school. Travelling with them to Ogoki Post was the school's principal, a Cree from Saskatchewan who had attended a residential school himself; he broke an arm there when he was six; it became gangrenous and had to be amputated. The Cree principal had a family member die the exact same way Wenjack did: a runaway later found dead of exposure next to railroad tracks.

Ian Adams was working on a story in Kenora about Indigenous issues. He spotted two paragraphs in the local newspaper that mentioned "an Indian kid who had been found dead beside the railroad tracks," he told the CBC in 2016. "It didn't even mention his name. How could a kid who had apparently run away from school just die, and nobody knew his name?" Adams started asking questions and went to the inquest. The Wenjack family were not told an inquest was being conducted. They found out about it when they read Adams's story called "The Lonely Death of

Charlie Wenjack" in the February 1967 issue of *Maclean's*. It got a lot of attention—some of it unwelcome, in the case of the CEO of Maclean-Hunter publishing, who wrote Adams a letter saying, "he didn't think that my kind of writing belonged in a magazine," said Adams. "So I started looking for other work. Shortly after that, I became a freelancer."

Chanie Wenjack's story was not at all unique in the history of residential schools, which began in 1876. In 1902, Duncan Sticks ran away from a school in Williams Lake, B.C., and died of exposure. "Hardly a day goes by that one or more [students] do not take leave on their own account," said one "Indian agent" in The Pas, Manitoba, in 1928. The TRC report claimed that, overall, "at least 33 students died, usually due to exposure, after running away from school." Parents who didn't return runaways to school could be prosecuted; in 1937, one Manitoba father was jailed 10 days for this so-called crime. Children were prosecuted for "stealing" the school uniforms they were wearing when they ran away. Repeat runaways could be sentenced to a reformatory school until the age of 21.

What were they running from? Shoddy, poorly kept buildings where tuberculosis was easily incubated; Indigenous children died from TB at a rate five times that of the non-Indigenous population. "Parental requests to have children's bodies returned home for burial were generally refused as being too costly," notes the TRC, citing evidence of mass graves at some schools. Children were forced to do agricultural work that benefitted only the school's staff, while gruel or thin soup was served to the students; some were part of "starvation experiments" conducted by scientists and bureaucrats to test new supplements or additives. "Errant" children were locked in closets or cells for days at a time and given only water; some were shackled to their beds and whipped until they bled. Fort Albany chief Edmund Metatawabin wrote of how he and his classmates were victims of sexual abuse at the hands of staff and other students, subjected to an electric chair as punishment, forced to eat their own vomit and denied bathroom visits at night—and then forced to wear feces-stained underwear on their heads in the morning. To non-Indigenous Canadians, it sounds like an even more sadistic version of Mordecai Richler's dark children's tale *Jacob Two-Two and the Hooded Fang*. Except there was nothing remotely funny at all about this, and no dream for the children to wake up from. And it's true.

At least 6,000 Indigenous children died in residential schools; TRC head Murray Sinclair estimated the number is much larger, perhaps

10,00

exponentially so, because records were either incredibly poorly kept or intentionally destroyed. There were at least 37 attempts by students to burn down their schools.

That's why Wenjack ran.

This all happened at schools children were forced to attend. The 1920 revisions to the 1894 Indian Act made it legal for the government to compel any Indigenous child to attend residential school—though, again, technically it was never compulsory for all Indigenous children. Many parents willingly brought their children to the schools, having been convinced—or strong-armed into thinking—that it was for the best.

And yet: the TRC heard stories of the "trains of tears," filled with children forcibly removed from their homes and placed on trains headed to residential schools. One train conductor in northern Manitoba told the commission about stopping the train and watching the Indian agents herd the children on board. "The parents were crying, the children were crying, and he knew how wrong this was," said Ry Moran at the National Centre for Truth and Reconciliation (NCTR). "He knew it wasn't right. But he was one man hired to drive the train, and he didn't do anything about it. He is now in his 70s, and teared up while talking about this." Sometimes there would be a two-day delay before departure, during which the trains would remain stationary, full of wailing children.

"Kids were abducted, literally stolen, snatched," Moran continued. "The Indian agent would drive into town and forcibly grab kids walking on the side of the road, throw them in the back of the car and drive them to the residential school. Parents wouldn't know where their kids were. It was forced. It was planned."

———

"Down south, none of us—I'm 52—heard a darn thing about what was happening up here. Not at all," Gord Downie told Chanie Wenjack's sister, Pearl Achneepineskum, when he went to visit her in Ogoki Post in September 2016.

"I knew nothing," said Mike Downie, on a podcast with host Karim Kanji. "It's not a great feeling. I'm a documentary filmmaker. I've been all over this country, and I know a good story when I hear one, but I knew nothing about this. It's important when talking to people to be honest: you may be coming late, but it's okay. A lot of us are just discovering this story."

The Downie brothers were hardly alone in their ignorance. It went straight to the top. In 2009, prime minister Stephen Harper told an American audience that "Canada has no history of colonialism." Former prime minister Joe Clark was an honorary witness at one of the Truth and Reconciliation gatherings. "When I came to take my place this morning," he said that day, "I knew the storyline, if you will. I knew what had happened. I had some idea of the consequences, but I had no real idea because I had not been able to witness it before . . . the multi-generational emotion that is involved in what has happened to so many of the victims of the residential schools . . . I heard, 'We are only as sick as our secrets.' That is an incentive to all who have kept these emotions and this history too secret, too long, to show the courage that so many of you have shown, and let those facts be known."

For decades, residential schools were a blip on the radar of most post-secondary history students. No one in the general public education stream would have learned about them as part of their curriculum. References in popular culture were next to non-existent, other than a few lines in Buffy Sainte-Marie's 1966 song "My Country 'Tis of Thy People You Are Dying" and Bruce Cockburn's 1987 track "Stolen Land."

In 1975, the NFB released a film called *Cold Journey*, about a residential school runaway who freezes to death beside railroad tracks. It appears to be loosely based on the Wenjack story; it's not, though the story's commonalities only confirm that the circumstances were far from unique. It does, however, open with a version of the song "Charlie Wenjack" by Willie Dunn, which had appeared on the first two albums by the iconic Mi'kmaq songwriter, filmmaker, and activist, in 1971 and 1972.

Cold Journey was directed by Martin Defalco, who made many documentary shorts for the NFB from the '60s through to the '80s; in 1973, he co-directed a film with Willie Dunn about the Hudson's Bay Company, called *The Other Side of the Ledger*. Defalco first became aware of residential schools while shooting a fishing film on a reserve in northern Saskatchewan in 1966; one day he witnessed all the children being taken away for school. He later met Noel Starblanket, an aspiring NFB filmmaker who would later become president of the National Indian Brotherhood, the precursor to the Assembly of First Nations (AFN). Starblanket pitched a film about residential schools; Defalco wrote a fictional script and insisted on hiring Indigenous actors in the principal roles—a first in North America. Dan George, nominated for an Oscar for *Little Big Man* a year earlier, appears in a cameo. Shot in Pelican Narrows, Saskatchewan, and The Pas, Manitoba, *Cold Journey* was rejected by the NFB for being too depressing and for its wooden acting. (Both are entirely fair criticisms, but the same could be said of any Canadian movie of the era, starting with *Goin' Down the Road*.) Upcoming filmmaker and activist Alanis Obomsawin convinced the NFB the film was important and worth releasing, at the very least to Indigenous communities. *Cold Journey* actually premiered at Cannes—where a *Variety* critic called it "a bleak undertaking." No commercial distributors were interested, so the NFB took Obomsawin's advice and screened it in theatres and Indigenous community centres on the Prairies.

In 1989, CBC aired a feature-length TV movie called *Where the Spirit Lives*, starring Michelle St. John as a residential school student and Ann-Marie MacDonald as the one benevolent teacher in the school. The film doesn't shy away from the issue of family separation, cultural genocide and abuse—though the teacher's embodiment of the white-saviour archetype and a happy ending where the student gallops off to freedom seem designed to make it more palatable to a prime-time audience.

That same year, Canada was rocked by a scandal at the Mount Cashel orphanage in Newfoundland, where sexual abuse survivors took the Catholic Church to court, exposing not just abuse but a massive cover-up with far-reaching implications. This was not directly related to residential schools, but taboos were now broken around calling out institutional abuse and subsequent cover-ups. Mount Cashel predated similar scandals in Ireland and the United States. (Americans were shocked in 2002 by a sexual-abuse scandal in the Boston Archdiocese, later documented in the Oscar-winning 2015 film *Spotlight*; by that point, this kind of story was very old news to Canadians.) After Mount Cashel, former residential school students felt emboldened to make their voices heard.

On October 30, 1990, Phil Fontaine, head of the Assembly of Manitoba Chiefs—later head of the AFN—dropped a bomb on prime-time television. While interviewed by Barbara Frum on CBC-TV's *The National*, he spoke candidly about the physical and sexual abuse he experienced at a residential school. He became the first prominent Aboriginal leader to address the issue, giving credence to some smaller, isolated court cases across the country, like the 1988 case in Lytton, B.C., where eight former students sued the Anglican Church and the federal government for sexual abuse; a settlement was reached before trial, and the case did not make major headlines. A similar case in Williams Lake, B.C., against the Catholic Church, was settled in 1990. Fontaine called for a full inquiry into the residential school system, "to undertake a healing process, to make our people whole. So that when we talk about the future, we talk about the future as a whole people, not as a people with many, many individuals who have missing parts and pieces and gaps in their being."

The apologies began. The United Church of Canada, which operated 10 per cent of all residential schools, had been the first back in 1986. The Anglican Church of Canada formally apologized in 1993. The Presbyterian Church, which ran the school Wenjack attended, did so in 1994. As of 2018, the Catholic Church has yet to do so—claiming that because only 16 of their 70 dioceses were involved, the Church on the whole was not responsible, even though it ran 67 per cent of all residential schools. For what it's worth, in 1993, the Canadian Conference of Catholic Bishops did issue a statement that acknowledged how "various types of abuse experienced at some residential schools have moved us to a profound examination of conscience as a Church." In 2009, Pope Benedict XVI expressed "sorrow" and "sympathy" to a Canadian delegation of Indigenous Canadians, including Phil Fontaine and Vancouver Canuck Gino Odjick.

The last residential school closed in 1996.

In the fall of 1990, the federal government launched the Royal Commission on Aboriginal Peoples. It delivered its final five-volume report in 1996, with a list of 440 recommendations. Residential schools was but one of dozens of issues addressed. Based on that report, in 1998, the federal minister of Indian Affairs, Jane Stewart, made a "statement of reconciliation" that acknowledged the government's role in residential schools and apologized to victims of abuse. At that point, the feds were being sued by 79,000 survivors in what was then the largest class-action lawsuit in Canadian history, launched in 1995 by Mi'kmaq Nora Bernard. A $1.9-billion settlement was reached in 2006, which opened the door to a formal apology from a prime minister. After initial stonewalling by the new Conservative government, Stephen Harper rose in the House of Commons on June 11, 2008, and, in the presence of Phil Fontaine and others, addressed victims.

Residential schools, Harper said in his speech, "were based on the assumption Aboriginal cultures and spiritual beliefs were inferior and unequal. Indeed, some sought, as it was infamously said, 'to kill the Indian in the child.' Today, we recognize that this policy of assimilation was wrong, has caused great harm and has no place in our country."

"The burden of this experience has been on your shoulders for far too long," he said to the victims. "The burden is properly ours as a government, and as a country. There is no place in Canada for the attitudes that inspired the Indian residential schools system to ever prevail again. You have been working on recovering from this experience for a long time and in a very real sense; we are now joining you on this journey. The Government of Canada sincerely apologizes and asks the forgiveness of the Aboriginal peoples of this country for failing them so profoundly."

Fontaine praised the apology, saying that among other effects, it "stripped white supremacy of its authority and legitimacy."

That same day, Harper announced the inception of the Truth and Reconciliation Commission. Seven years later, it filed its final report. "Ongoing public education and dialogue are essential to reconciliation," it stated. "Governments, churches, educational institutions and Canadians from all walks of life are responsible for taking action on reconciliation in concrete ways, working collaboratively with Aboriginal peoples. Reconciliation begins with each and every one of us."

That all sounds great. But if a government commission report lands on the prime minister's desk, does it make a sound? In 1996, it certainly didn't. In 2015, there were concerns the TRC report would meet the same fate. "To be a white Canadian is to be sunk in deep denial," says Sto:lo writer Lee Maracle.

A June 2016 Environics Institute poll, co-sponsored by the Truth and Reconciliation Commission, showed that 66 per cent of Canadians had heard of residential schools: not a great number, but not the worst. But of that 66 per cent, only 42 per cent knew of abuse or molestation—and that was the element that had the highest awareness. Only 31 per cent realized it involved separation of children from their parents. Only 29 per cent associated residential schools with "mistreatment of Aboriginal peoples." Only 18 per cent realized students were forbidden to speak their own language. The TRC report itself was familiar only to 42 per cent of non-Aboriginal Canadians. Perhaps that's not so surprising, considering the level of civic engagement and voter turnout in Canada. The number of voters who pay attention to government reports on any topic can be expected to be minuscule; outside of an election campaign, most people can't even name the opposition leaders.

The 2015 Syrian refugee issue needed the photo of Alan Kurdi—a five-year-old boy found dead on a Turkish beach, en route to Canada, to mobilize public opinion. The horrors of the Holocaust have been explained to children with *The Diary of Anne Frank*. The issue of residential schools and reconciliation needed a face. It belonged to Chanie "Charlie" Wenjack.

———

In 2013, the Downie brothers' plan was to find a writer who could turn the *Maclean's* article into a novella that could be adapted into a script. Mike assembled a research package and sent it to some writers he thought might be interested, including Joseph Boyden. They waited for a response. Nothing.

Then one day, Gord called. "I have some news."

"Oh, did you hear back from one of the writers?"

"No, but I've written a poem about Chanie."

Around the same time, Kevin Drew of Broken Social Scene called Gord. The two bands had shared a few festival gigs together, but were not close. In the summer of 2013, Drew was working on a solo album at the Bathouse, which is when he and Downie connected. Drew is a gregarious, passionate extrovert, so it was not at all odd that he would have the chutzpah to say to Downie that August, "I want to make a record with you." Gord was open to the idea.

"Do you have anything we could take into the studio sooner than later?" asked Drew.

"No, actually, nothing at all—oh, wait . . ."

Downie had once told Gordon Lightfoot that he'd always wanted to write a commissioned work with set parameters, like the elder Gord's "Canadian Railroad Trilogy." Now he realized he had exactly that. He and Drew started recording with Dave Hamelin of the Stills in November 2013. But Downie didn't tell his younger collaborators what his lyrics were about, let alone that they were making a concept record together. Themes of escape, of death, of estrangement—none of these would be unusual on a Gord Downie record. About halfway through the process, the singer started to spill the beans. The history of residential schools was new information to the thirtysomething musicians, just as it had been for the Downies, just as it would be to most people who would eventually hear the album.

Drew and Hamelin were proud and excited—and crestfallen when Downie told them it wasn't going to come out for another two-and-a-half years, to coincide with the 50th anniversary of Wenjack's death. That's when Downie figured it could have the most impact.

The first song on the album is "The Stranger." It was what the Kelly family called Wenjack when he showed up at their door. But it also recalls a poem by Douglas LePan, "A Country Without a Mythology," cited in Margaret Atwood's *Survival*. In the poem, someone called "the stranger" is travelling toward no discernible goal through a land without "monuments or landmarks," among "a savage people" who are silent and moody or, when they speak, incomprehensible. "The stranger" must live off the land on berries and fish, snatching what he can get and "forgetting every grace and ceremony." LePan was clearly writing from a settler's standpoint, but his poem can easily be inverted through Wenjack's eyes, redefining who the "savage" is in the narrative but still lost between two worlds.

Sometimes—perhaps at the tentative fall of twilight—
A belief will settle that waiting around the bend
Are sanctities of childhood, that melting birds
Will sing him into a limpid gracious Presence.

While the album was being recorded, Mike reached out to Wenjack's surviving relatives, starting with one of his sisters, Pearl Achneepineskum, who still lived in Ogoki Post, a fly-in community 600 kilometres northeast of Thunder Bay, on the Albany River, halfway to Fort Albany.

"Hi, I'm Mike Downie. I'm a filmmaker. My brother is Gord Downie—do you know Gord Downie?"

"No."

"He's in the Tragically Hip. Do you know the Tragically Hip?"

"No."

Mike started to explain the project. Pearl was hesitant. She let the line go quiet for extended periods of time. Almost 50 years ago, when her brother had died, she had prayed that his life not be forgotten, that one day his story would be told. It had been told once before, by Ian Adams in *Maclean's*. And now someone wanted to tell it again. Which was weird, because she had just been sitting in her cabin, thinking about how to get a hold of Oprah Winfrey. She thought Oprah might be interested in Chanie's story. Then this Mike guy called.

Eventually, the ice broke, and she gave the brothers her blessing.

With just rough mixes from the recording session, in December 2013 Gord reached out to illustrator Jeff Lemire, who balanced work on comics like *X-Men* with graphic novels like *Essex County*, a bestseller comprised of three linked stories about orphans, hockey players, nurses and the secrets they all hold. The Downies thought Lemire might work as a screenwriter—maybe for an animated film? Lemire told them he was very interested but was booked up with work for at least the next year and was in the middle of *Roughneck*, a book about an Indigenous hockey enforcer from Moosonee. All this appealed to the Downies; they'd clearly found a kindred spirit.

Just hours after that meeting, the artist sent Gord a picture that he'd drawn as soon as he got back to his studio. Lemire said it had felt like his hand was being guided across the page. It was a picture of Wenjack on a swing set. Gord forwarded it to Mike, with the subject header: "You'd better sit down for this." Mike opened it and got a chill. Lemire was on board—although he still wouldn't be able to start until September 2014. He finished it two months later.

When Lemire finished, the trio of Downie, Drew and Hamelin made a surprise appearance at Toronto's Opera House, during an event called No More Silence. Organized by Boyden, A Tribe Called Red, songwriter Jason Collett and poet Damian Rogers, it was to focus attention on the issue of missing and murdered Indigenous women. Also on the bill were Jennifer Castle, Lee Maracle, Naomi Klein, Leanne Betasamosake Simpson and Cris Derksen. The Downie trio were the only white men onstage, other than organizers Collett and Boyden. They played two songs: "Secret Path" and "Here, Here and Here." That was December 18, 2014.

The album was still not scheduled to come out for almost two years, in order to give Boyden time to work on a related novella, and for other associated projects to gestate. Gord's cancer diagnosis came in December 2015. Now the Downies wanted to do something even bigger with the project, knowing Gord's time was limited.

Mike had done some work for the business-pitch reality show *Dragons' Den*, produced by Stuart Coxe. Coxe expressed interest in the project. So did filmmaker Sarah Polley, who set up a meeting for them in the spring of 2016 with CBC-TV's general manager of programming, Sally Catto.

"So, what is it you guys want to do with this?" she asked.

"We want to animate this book and we want it to be on the CBC on the 50th anniversary of his death, on October 23."

"Okay, done."

"We were all sitting around the board room at the CBC, crying," recalled Mike. "This was the craziest pitch you've ever seen in your life."

Animator Justin Stephenson was brought on board in June. He had designed title sequences for David Cronenberg and made videos for the Rheostatics and others. Now the rush was on to complete everything—film, book, album packaging—and be ready to air and launch by October. At his home, Stephenson worked 18-hour days, seven days a week for three months straight to finish the animation. It was incredibly emotional for him, to the point where his wife asked him, "Do you just sit in the basement and cry?" The final cut of the film was completed a week before the CBC broadcast.

In September, after the Hip's final show, the three Downie brothers, including youngest brother Patrick, and a small film crew travelled to Ogoki Post to meet four of the five living Wenjack sisters. They arrived with the music, the book and "The Stranger," the first clip to be animated. Not all the sisters were as into the project as Pearl; their very private pain, which was theirs and only theirs for the last 50 years, was about to be very public. The Downie brothers certainly understood this. They were in a unique position to do so.

————

Secret Path was finally revealed to the public on September 9, three weeks after the final Hip show, with the clip for "The Stranger" and a long statement that outlined Downie's motivations for the project, including this passage:

> *Chanie haunts me. His story is Canada's story. This is about Canada. We are not the country we thought we were. History will be re-written . . . I have always wondered why, even as a kid, I never thought of Canada as a country . . . I never wrote of it as so. The next hundred years are going to be painful as we come to know Chanie Wenjack and thousands like him—as we find out about ourselves, about all of us—but only when we do can we truly call ourselves, "Canada."*

It was a throw-down to the incessant flag-waving that took place during the Hip's final tour that year—indeed, that took place during their entire career. Here was Captain Canada himself telling his country it was guilty of an original sin, that the smug "angel complex" was a lie, that—like something out of *Jane Eyre* or, more appropriately, *Wide Sargasso Sea*—there was an estranged relative we'd been trained to ignore, locked up in the attic.

On October 18, 2016, Gord Downie debuted *Secret Path* at the National Arts Centre in Ottawa. In the band were Kevin Drew, Dave Hamelin, Kevin

Hearn, Josh Finlayson and Charles Spearin. Before the performance, in a private ceremony backstage, Algonquin elder Claudette Commanda told those assembled, "Look around this room and see the beauty: see survival, strength, life. This is beautiful. Thank you, Gord Downie, for bringing us together." During the performance, birch-bark baskets were circulated through the crowd to collect soggy tissues; "the firekeeper will offer the tears to the fire as a connection to our ancestors," said Commanda.

During the show, the animated film was projected above the performers. Indigenous leaders, writers and the Wenjack family took up the first few rows. "Before the performance started," wrote Anishinaabe academic Hayden King, "the large group at the front were loud, joking and laughing. Meanwhile the crowd behind them was stoic and serious. When Downie sang and wailed, they did, too. They moved to the music in their seats. They cried, at times. And after the musicians left the stage and a short video began, showing the tall birch trees among boreal forest of Marten Falls, they raised their arms, whistled and celebrated home. They did what the concert was unable to: they showed that they are not merely victims. When the end of the world came, they persevered, and they endure today in the most inexplicably vivid ways."

The short film that was shown after the performance documented Downie's trip to Ogoki Post, in which Pearl Achneepineskum says, of Downie, "He is the right person to tell the story. Because the Creator chose him. We didn't. I didn't. And I'm glad it was Gord. He will be forever remembered."

Three days later, the same performance was given at Roy Thomson Hall in Toronto. It was held the same week as imagineNATIVE, an annual festival focusing on modern Indigenous filmmakers. That festival got a fraction of the press the *Secret Path* event did.

The evening opened with a short speech by Mike Downie in which he promised, with the evangelical zeal of a convert, that we would all "be a part of history and reconciliation tonight." Ian Adams was in attendance, as was the Wenjack clan, as well as members of the Tragically Hip, Barenaked Ladies, Cowboy Junkies and others of Downie's generation in music. As with in Ottawa, after the performance and the short doc, Mike Downie got up to introduce every person involved in the project: the musicians, Lemire, the filmmakers, Adams, and Downie's two brothers. Mike was the only one speaking.

It was all beginning to sound like a best man's speech at a white family's wedding, until Mike invited 25 members of the Wenjack family to the stage. Then the evening's spotlight shifted. Two of Wenjack's grand-nieces gave short speeches. Pearl talked about her memories of dancing with Chanie to an old country song he loved, "Ashes of Love." She sang a traditional song that was every bit as moving as Downie's performance. "Ashes of Love" then played over the speakers, while everyone onstage stood around somewhat awkwardly, clapping along, while Pearl started weeping and Gord embraced her. It was beautiful, uncomfortable, moving and downright odd to see all this happening on the stage of Roy Thomson Hall, in front of a sold-out audience, some of whom had paid $1,000 per ticket to sit in the VIP section and witness white guilt manifest itself. It was also necessary.

Secret Path aired on CBC-TV on the evening of October 23, the 50th anniversary of Wenjack's death. In Peterborough, a special screening was held at Wenjack Theatre, the largest lecture hall on the campus of Trent University; it was so named in 1973, four years after the institution became the first in Canada to offer a Native studies program. Until *Secret Path*, the plaque in front of that theatre was the only place Wenjack's story lived on. In 2017, Trent renamed its program the Chanie Wenjack School for Indigenous Studies.

The author of the original *Maclean's* story, Ian Adams, now 80, was interviewed in 2016 by CBC Thunder Bay's Jody Porter, the woman whose radio documentary struck Mike Downie. Adams said that he often felt as if he "wasted his life telling people stuff they didn't want to hear." Then he added, "Don't let the cynics tell you journalism is written to be forgotten."

"We can talk all we want," said Indigenous writer and activist Jesse Wente on a CBC-TV panel that aired immediately after the *Secret Path* premiere. "It's important for Canada to understand that there has to be action after the listening. As great a work as this is, this is not the end. This is just part of the conversation. Engaging with this isn't reconciliation. It's not even close."

———

Secret Path was not just a new album for Gord Downie or just a natural extension of his ever-widening political engagement. It became his life's mission—with what little of his life he had left. He wanted to channel the

371

nation's sympathy for a rich, white, privileged rock star and redirect it toward the greatest victims of the Canadian experiment. He considered it the most important work he'd ever done. He wanted it to be his legacy. On top of the larger societal impact, it gave meaning to his own life as it approached its tragic end. "He knows what it's like," said Pearl Achneepineskum, "seeing this little boy losing his life, which is the stage [Gord] is in. The two of them come together. They have to do this together."

Downie was being heaped with hagiographic praise and premature eulogies after his diagnosis was announced. Throwing himself into *Secret Path* was a way of dealing with that. "Personal fame counts for nothing if your life isn't, in itself, a life of virtue," wrote philosopher Rebecca Newberger Goldstein, about ancient Greece. "Being song-worthy is the whole point of being extraordinary. It's in *kleos*, in glory and fame, that the existential task of attaining a life that matters is fulfilled. Living so that others will remember you is your solace in the face of the erasure you know awaits . . . Perform exceptional deeds to earn the praise of others whose existence is as brief as your own. That's the best we can do in the quest for significance."

What does that make the rest of the Tragically Hip's discography? Chopped liver? The Tragically Hip were entertainment. *Secret Path* aspired to reset the way in which we think about Canadian history. "Does 'important' mean having a profound impact on people's lives? Then yes, *Secret Path* is his most important work," said Mitch Champagne, an educator in Peterborough, Ontario, who has used Hip music in grade 7 and 8 social studies courses. "But I'm not so cerebral that I don't realize how important [the Hip's] music is to people's lives as well. It gets people through stuff, it expresses feelings they didn't know they were having. But *Secret Path* deals with more people. It's Canada's history, but it's also Australia's history, it's America's history. This is beyond just music. And it's making a difference."

Downie had touched on political issues previously in his career. The wrongfully convicted in "Wheat Kings," one of the Hip's most powerful songs. Bilingualism in "Born in the Water," which is most definitely not one of the Hip's most powerful songs. Environmentalism in "Titanic Terrarium," which Downie considered one of his favourite set of lyrics. None of those get into specifics. And he discarded a song around 2004 that railed against the central African terror campaign of warlord Joseph Kony, a song inspired in part by the band's support of the charity War Child.

This time, however, he was going all in. And he knew he had an audience. Downie's illness unquestionably boosted the project's profile. After the splash and mixed reaction to *Coke Machine Glow* in 2001, his solo projects attracted a fraction of the attention that any Hip record would. If *Secret Path* had simply been the follow-up to *The Grand Bounce* and *Now for Plan A*, it might be a curiosity at best. Instead, it was a media sensation with an enormous ripple effect.

As *Secret Path* entered the world, so did something called the Gord Downie & Chanie Wenjack Fund. The name was seen by some as problematic: why is the white man's name here, a man who had no real role in the Wenjack story until he willed it to be? If Eddie Vedder expressed a sudden interest in 50-year-old civil rights cases in the U.S., would he start an Eddie Vedder & Emmett Till Fund—and how would that go over? The obvious answer is that Downie was well aware of his celebrity status and was putting it to use; he also had the full participation and blessing of the Wenjack family. His predominantly white audience would soon forget the name of a new charity unless Downie's name was front and centre, much like the equally new Gord Downie Fund for Brain Cancer Research.

But what was the Downie-Wenjack Fund for? "The money goes directly to real reconciliatory actions," Mike Downie explained. "Ideally, they bring Indigenous and non-Indigenous people together to improve the lives of Indigenous people." That could involve sponsoring educational programs in schools, cultural exchanges between northern and southern students or the creation of "legacy rooms" in public spaces to raise awareness of residential schools. Mostly, however, the money is spent in co-ordination with the National Centre for Truth and Reconciliation in Winnipeg; the NCTR's education lead, Charlene Bearhead, is also the co-chair of the Downie-Wenjack Fund. The fund has been very careful to put Indigenous voices front and centre and in leadership roles, lest it be seen as a white competitor to the NCTR.

Gord Downie had been aware of the pitfalls of celebrity activism early in his career. He watched Midnight Oil's Peter Garrett dive deep into environmental and Indigenous issues and display a deep commitment that Downie himself didn't feel ready for then—and maybe never did until 2016. "All I can do is say, 'Let your actions speak louder than your words,' and maybe direct people toward the experts," Downie said in 1995, discussing the Clayoquot Sound clear-cuts. "I could say, 'Listen, I don't know enough to be up here telling you what you should think. And maybe no one should tell you what to think. But maybe, if you're interested, read some of [David Suzuki's] books. Make some time for yourself to learn.'"

From the outset, Mike Downie's hope was that *Secret Path* would be used as an educational tool, as part of school curricula. Almost right away, some teachers started using *Secret Path* in their classrooms as a teaching tool in the 2016–17 school year. So did literacy programs in prisons, where the rate of Indigenous incarceration is 10 times that of the non-Indigenous population; justice reform advocates refer to the prison system as "the new residential schools." Mitch Champagne, who teaches at Trent University's school of education, started developing a curriculum with his practicum students, a way for primary and high school children to interact with Jeff Lemire's book. When they were finished, the white educator worked closely with Bearhead and the NCTR to get it into schools.

How effective can *Secret Path* be as an educational tool about the effects of colonialism—especially when the music and book, and even the curriculum, are by white men? It's a start, said Hayden King. "Canadians need to know what happened in residential schools, that this was systemic, that there were deliberate attempts to kill children by making them sick, exposing healthy children to tuberculosis, all the sexual violence, all the brainwashing—all that stuff needs to be told. But as long as we're telling that story in a singular fashion, in a one-dimensional way, then Indigenous people get trapped in this narrative of the victim, of the crying Indian, helpless, requiring people to save them. That is disempowering. I think there is a way—I do this in my classroom when I teach—to tell those truths but also motion toward the way Indigenous people have survived, the way Indigenous people resist, and the vision for education we currently have, which is an ongoing struggle. That's the key to having this discussion in a way that doesn't contribute to an emergent stereotype of the Indigenous as victim, the Indigenous as powerless."

Even aside from issues of representation, there's the narrative itself, which is far from straightforward. Downie's lyrics are characteristically opaque; he doesn't even mention the word "school" once. "Gord told me that he really just wanted his words to tell the story," said his friend Mark Mattson, "that it wouldn't be overt, direct, it would be very much like his music; people would find their way in and it would resonate in certain ways." To contrast, Willie Dunn's "Charlie Wenjack" song communicates the narrative clearly and concisely, in a traditional folk song style not unlike Woody Guthrie or Phil Ochs.

Lemire told the story largely through flashback and dreams and First Nations symbology. One has to know the broad strokes of the Wenjack story, and of residential schools, before approaching the work in order to fully grasp *Secret Path*. So why not teach Ian Adams's *Maclean's* article, rather than *Secret Path*? Why not play Willie Dunn's song in class? Or why not teach curricula based directly on the TRC report?

"The beauty and tragedy of Chanie's story is that it's a simple story of a boy trying to get home," said Mike Downie. "You don't need to know much else. You don't even have to have kids [to understand] the idea of trying to get back home to those who love you. Then when you realize what the circumstances were at the residential school, that you realize this was done to 150,000 kids over 100 years—all those details can come next. But this is a great on-ramp story that puts you on the highway where you're going to learn a lot more about this, and maybe be inspired to do something about it."

Hayden King said *Secret Path* can be effective "only if it's taught by people with the sensitivity to teach it, which is common with texts of this nature." That might be a big ask. "It's graphic. There are very painful images. I'm curious what an Indigenous author with a connection to residential schools would have done with Downie's material, and whether or not we'd have seen a different product—I think we would have. Both the book and the album are helpful tools to have this conversation, but there is a lot of navigating of misrepresentation that is required."

Mitch Champagne thinks that Lemire's graphics bring the story to life in ways that Downie's lyrics don't specifically. "I think Gord realized the album was more vague—maybe that's to let readers bring what they have in them, and then watch the video and get something out of that." But the music is most definitely central. "There's music on in my [grade 7 and 8] class all the time when we're working," said Champagne. "At least once a week, someone would say, 'Put on *Secret Path*.' I'd hear them humming it at other times. Our choir did a great version of 'Here, Here and Here.' The music is an entrance to this very difficult story."

"The film only alludes to the horror of it all," said Jeremy Hoyle, the singer in the cover band Strictly Hip. "My 14-year-old daughter watched it, and I had to explain to her afterwards what was really happening. I don't think there's a way to fully illustrate, artistically, what happened—I mean, there probably is, but Gord's not going to do that." Hoyle has appeared at *Secret Path* events organized by Mike Downie and has long performed

"Hip Talks" in Canadian schools, in which "I go to schools with my guitar and I tell stories about Hip songs, putting them in the context of Canadian identity and whatnot. It's hard to keep high school kids focused. But when I play 'The Stranger' from *Secret Path*, it changes everything. You tell that story and you play that song—it's like church. It's that powerful."

On December 6, 2016, the Assembly of First Nations honoured Downie during a blanket ceremony, a teaching tool that details the history of colonization and cultural genocide. Upon the recommendation of elders, AFN National Chief Perry Bellegarde bestowed upon Downie the Lakota name Wicapi Omani, which translates as "man who walks among the stars." It had been just over three months since the Tragically Hip's final show, when Downie suddenly transformed into an activist. "We're here to honour Gord for what he's done in such a short time period to elevate all of our issues," said Bellegarde. "When he made those statements at his concerts about getting things done, he raised a spotlight on our issues, and we wanted to take the time . . . to honour this man." Referencing "the next 150 years" weeks before Canada's sesquicentennial year, Downie said, "This is the first day of forever, the greatest day of my life."

Almost as much as *Secret Path*, it was those few short minutes at the Hip show that intrigued Indigenous leaders. "Here we have a highly recognized, respected [individual] admired by millions and millions of people across this country and internationally," said Federation of Sovereign Indigenous Nations Chief Bobby Cameron. "And for him to say what he did there, during the concert and during our ceremony the other day: pretty significant. Because it says we have to improve the lives of Indigenous peoples. Indigenous peoples deserve that quality of life. Indigenous people deserve to heal from the injustices of residential schools and the Sixties Scoop."

"I don't think being non-Native or being white is the strength here," said Isadore Day, the AFN Regional Chief of Ontario. "In his own time of reflection about his own mortality, he has drawn a line of truth about what's important."

———

Seven months later, it was announced that all members of the Tragically Hip would be appointed to the Order of Canada. Downie, however, would receive his insignia from then governor general David Johnston earlier than the rest of the band, at a ceremony on June 19, 2017—a day dedicated to people recognized for their leadership role on Indigenous issues, including urban community organizer Sylvia Maracle, NHL player Jordin Tootoo and *Angry Inuk* filmmaker Alethea Arnaquq-Baril. Downie was the only white honouree that day—for work that he'd only been doing publicly for the last 10 months.

"Given Gord's cancer diagnosis, it made sense that the honour be bestowed sooner rather than later," wrote Mi'kmaq comedian and radio host Candy Palmater, who'd been a Hip fan since she saw them at the Misty Moon in Halifax in 1990. "But when I read that he was receiving the Order of Canada not just for music but for his leadership as an Indigenous activist, I was stunned. Surely this was a misprint. After all, I know so many Indigenous people who have given their whole lives to furthering our cause without ever being recognized. Not only that, but so often their lifelong anti-racist work has taken a toll on their health and careers."

"At the Governor General's ceremony, I saw a white man honouring another white man," wrote activist Clayton Thomas-Müller. "One was the official spokesperson of the Queen of England. The other was being honoured for his work on Indigenous issues in a space meant for our residential school survivors and the very best of our Indigenous leaders . . . Indigenous people do not need white interpreters for the world to understand our stories, our traditional knowledge or its value . . . Settler allies can do effective work when teaching others how to increase understanding toward reconciliation and reparations with Indigenous peoples. But these allies must not take up space meant for our own front-line voices."

Since Downie's diagnosis, he was conspicuous for *not* taking up space: he did only two interviews during that time, and after the three *Secret Path* shows, you could count his public appearances on one hand (the AFN and GG ceremonies, two WE Day appearances). He spoke very little at any of them. At all of them, he was surrounded by Indigenous leaders and/ or Pearl Achneepineskum. The man himself was not courting media, but he knew its power. "The white man will only listen to the white man," said Algonquin elder and law professor Claudette Commanda. "If Gord Downie's gonna be the white man that is going to go out there and raise the social conscience of Canadians and government, so be it."

These conversations came at a fraught time in politics and literature, when issues of cultural appropriation were reaching a critical mass: Who gets to tell the stories of marginalized communities? Who gets to judge when stories are told with respect and when it is done with arrogance and white privilege? Is it the fault of the dominant culture in general or that of the individual white artist for whom more doors are opened? It's a debate that goes at least as far back as Rudyard Kipling, through to the birth of jazz, the "African" paintings of Henri Rousseau, Elvis Presley, the Rolling Stones, W.P. Kinsella, Paul Simon, Farley Mowat, Eminem—the examples are endless, the verdicts decidedly mixed.

All these questions came to be embodied in Downie's friend Joseph Boyden. The author's debut novel *Three Day Road* won, among other prizes, the McNally Robinson Aboriginal Book of the Year award in 2005. Boyden was an outspoken advocate of Indigenous issues, leading up to and through Idle No More and the TRC. He was an occasional writer for *Maclean's* and a popular guest on the literary and arts gala circuit. He was generous in his support for Indigenous writers, many of whose work featured blurbs from the bestselling author. He spent a fair amount of time in Moosonee, raising money for an Indigenous youth camp there and teaching courses at Northern College when he wasn't at his home in New Orleans. He shepherded his southern friends up there, including the Hip, to raise awareness of northern issues—*Secret Path* would likely not exist without him. He collaborated with musicians Tanya Tagaq and A Tribe Called Red. He rarely turned down a media request. "Whether it be the CBC or the *Globe and Mail* or a tiny radio station in the rural North with a listenership of 50," he wrote in *Maclean's*, "I was more than willing to stand up and be vocal."

But Boyden had been the subject of suspicion in Indigenous circles for years. His widely praised 2013 novel *The Orenda*, set in the early 1600s, received blowback from some Indigenous critics who took issue with the accuracy of the bloodthirsty historical narrative; others, like Wab Kinew, host of CBC Radio's *Canada Reads*, championed the book enthusiastically. Boyden sold 500,000 books in Canada, won many awards and, it can fairly be argued, "took up a lot of space." Normally that would sound like typical Canadian tall-poppy syndrome, directed at an incredibly gifted, articulate and handsome writer. But in a country that rarely listens to Indigenous people themselves, the fact that Boyden became an attention magnet was a major sore point for some Indigenous writers and activists—as was his seeming inability to provide clear answers to obvious questions of interest to Indigenous people, like from what tribe he claimed to be. Especially when he made careless and/or ignorant mistakes like identifying as Metis, which has a very specific legal meaning in Canada. Or when, in one 2011 interview, he referred to himself as a "two-spirit person," claiming it meant mixed ancestry—when, in fact, anyone with a cursory knowledge of Indigenous and/or queer culture; or anyone who's ever read Tomson Highway; *hell, anyone with access to Wikipedia* could tell you that it comes from an Anishinaabe term that refers to someone outside of binary gender norms: queer, trans or gender-fluid in some way. After all that, he claimed that something called "blood memory" came to him when he was writing and that he "had to trust that voice." This sounded a little bit like a young Jim Morrison seeing a traffic accident in New Mexico that killed a truck-load of Natives and later claiming in the poem "Dawn's Highway" that "the souls of the ghosts of the dead Indians . . . leaped into my soul." Which, you know, made that white rock star all the more mystical and/or exotic.

Who was this writer, many Indigenous people wondered, and why are white people listening to him tell and define our stories?

Boyden, like Downie, had taken up the Wenjack story. He wrote a novella, *Wenjack*, that came out the same month as *Secret Path*. He appeared on A Tribe Called Red's acclaimed album *We Are the Halluci Nation*—also released in September 2016—playing the character of an inmate talking to the ghost of Wenjack. He most likely would have become a prominent spokesperson for the Downie-Wenjack Fund.

But in December 2016, a few weeks after his friend was honoured in a blanket ceremony by the AFN, Boyden was the subject of a deeply researched takedown by the Aboriginal Peoples Television Network, which challenged his claims to Indigenous heritage. An even more in-depth story was published in the *Globe and Mail* in August 2017. The ballad of Joseph Boyden was fascinating for the fissures it created in the arts community and among Indigenous people—some of whom came to his defence, extremely wary of policing bloodlines or falling prey to the settler concept of "blood quantum." Issues of Indigenous identity and inclusion are incredibly complex and divisive, to say the least, and largely defined by government agencies and legal terms. (It's not something that will ever be explored adequately in a book about the Tragically Hip: go listen to Chelsea Vowel or Lee Maracle discuss this instead).

Indigeneity was central to Boyden's brand, from which he profited greatly. Boyden, who grew up in an Irish Catholic family in suburban Toronto, has always maintained that "a small part of me is Indigenous, but it is a huge part of who I am." Plenty of North Americans have a story about an "Indian" branch in their family tree, but after centuries of colonial appropriation of land, of artifacts, of bones, of symbols and of stories, modern-day Indigenous people want the right to welcome people into their circle as they choose—by marriage, by adoption or ceremonially—rather than witness someone independently proclaim Indigeneity. Some of the writer's best friends were Indigenous. But Boyden's work was presented to and understood by white Canada as an Indigenous voice. Even his friend Wab Kinew argued that, regardless of ancestry, Boyden should only ever have been read as a "talented outsider" because he never claimed to be Cree, Huron or Haudenosaunee, the nations he wrote about in *Three Day Road* and *The Orenda*.

As the argument played out, many decided they didn't want to hear from him anymore, or at least any time soon. *Seven Matches*, his next novel, highly anticipated and originally scheduled for a fall 2017 release, was postponed while he lay low. It was the most stunning reversal of literary fortune since James Frey's *A Million Little Pieces*. Meanwhile, *Secret Path* sold 100,000 copies in six months.

Why was Boyden raked over the coals, while Downie received acclaim and awards? What's the difference between these two men? Are they not both "allies" in the reconciliation process?

Downie stayed in his lane. He created the work, donated all the proceeds and then stepped back to let others, largely Indigenous people associated with the NCTR, talk about it—which he would likely have done regardless of his health. "There's a right way to do things, and I think we managed to do that," said Mike Downie. "The [Downie-Wenjack] fund is Indigenous-led. We have an Indigenous-majority steering committee. Our program director is Indigenous. You have to do what you can and educate yourself, but you're not going to be perfect and you'll be open to criticism. If I'd been smarter, I would have been more concerned about that: why would a couple of hosers from Kingston be telling this story? I don't have an answer for that. We wanted to tell this story to white Canada. We can reach white Canada. When I say white Canada, I mean non-Indigenous Canada. We wanted to reach Gord's fans."

"The conversation about Gord Downie was an opportunity to get into the conversation about 'taking up space' generally," said Hayden King. "I can't recall many attacks on Downie himself. But Boyden was actually dishonest and benefitted immensely from his dishonesty. That's a significant difference in how Downie had approached his project and how Boyden has approached his. My feeling is that Downie has only come from a genuine and honest place, and this is a learning experience for him—and you can see it. Whereas Boyden has approached his literature, his relationship with Indigenous communities, his discussions in the public sphere in ways that perpetuate some of the problematic stereotypes we're trying to move away from as Native people. It's artificial and arrogant."

"I've never claimed to be anything other than what I am," said Jeff Lemire, who was first shown around Moosonee by Boyden in 2013. "I've never claimed to be a spokesperson for Indigenous rights, or anything like that. I'm just a white guy. For any artist, you're trying to learn something. For me, this was a big part of our history that I didn't know enough about, and I still don't know enough about. By going up there and doing these books, I know more than I did, and maybe if I can share what I learned with people who otherwise wouldn't read about this stuff, then it's worth doing."

At the same time, Lemire also fully admitted his own mixed feelings about both *Secret Path* and *Roughneck*, and a new superhero he created for DC Comics named Equinox, a teen girl from James Bay. "I don't know if I should have done the books, to be honest," he said. "These are not my stories to tell. You fall in love with the story and you have to do it, for better or worse. They won't let you go. At the same time, look at the impact *Secret Path* has had: the fact that children will be learning about residential schools. Gord and I never learned about this in school. Which is why we wanted to do it in the first place. So I look at that and I think it's worth it. And the fact the Wenjack sisters embraced us and supported the project, it makes me feel okay about it."

Secret Path was a blockbuster in the world of Canadian publishing. Proceeds went to the National Centre for Truth and Reconciliation. The Downie-Wenjack Fund was off to an auspicious start. But *Secret Path* should never be the beginning and end of Canadians' engagement with Indigenous issues, argued Candy Palmater. "In no way do I mean to disrespect the memory of Gord Downie," she wrote in *Chatelaine*. "But Canadians need to wake up and realize that collectively feeling bad for little Chanie Wenjack dying on the tracks all those years ago will never change the future for one Indigenous child today. Activism is not warm and fuzzy. It is not about embracing a famous person who makes an album about a situation. It is about facing the hard truths that may make you feel uncomfortable. It's about getting out of the way of the Indigenous people who have been demanding change for decades now. It's about realizing you may be part of the problem and figuring out how to use that knowledge to move toward change."

In April 2017, *Secret Path* won the Juno for Adult Alternative Album of the Year, a category designed for music nobody knows what to do with otherwise. In his videotaped acceptance speech, Downie said, "Canada is celebrating 150 years this year. For me, Canada has to begin the next 150 years, the next seven generations, now. We're rebuilding the country. To truly call this Canada, we need everyone. We need to recognize how kept in the dark we've been, how much we've been deprived . . . My dream would be that this record, with Jeff Lemire's drawings, might help people, might give teachers something to help teach our young ones. This next generation will truly be the first among us to truly know about our country's worst aspects, the first of our true Canada . . . Thank you from me, Wicapi Omani, the man who walks among the stars."

Best chapter in the book, should have been longer (2 chap) but prob wasn't possible since Downie had terminal cancer.

L still could've.

Doesn't feel right going back to "regularly scheduled programming" after that.

CHAPTER TWENTY-FOUR

THAT NIGHT IN KINGSTON
AUGUST 20, 2016

"If I'm lucky . . . there will be time for me
to bid goodbye to each of my loved ones.
If I'm lucky, they'll step forward
and I'll be able to see them one last time
and take that memory with me.
Sure, they might lay eyes on me and want to run away
and howl. But instead, since they love me,
they'll lift my hand and say, 'Courage'
or 'It's going to be all right'
. . . If I'm unlucky . . . , well, I'll just
drop over, like that, without any chance
for farewell, or to press anyone's hand."

RAYMOND CARVER, "MY DEATH," 1984

IT'S THE MOST gorgeous August day one could hope for. Hot: not too hot. Humid: modified by slight breeze. Sunny: a few clouds. Everyone is excited. Even the security staff are smiling while frisking bags outside the pedestrian-only downtown core. Locals are riding the buses for free today. Tragically Hip music is blasting from every storefront. I park my car in a municipal parking lot close to the core. The event parking fee for this historic event: $3.15. Ah, Kingston.

The woman who fills the meter just before me is Fran Stanhope from Raymond, Maine, who has travelled here with her husband, Bob, and seven friends. The Stanhopes, who used to be Deadheads, have seen the Tragically Hip 42 times since 1998. This week, they got tickets to shows in

Hamilton and Ottawa and decided to tack on a visit to Kingston to watch the outdoor screen in the band's hometown. In the past, they've seen a few shows in Montreal, but don't normally see the Hip in Canada. "We've seen them in Portland, Maine, with 300 people, so why would we come to Canada?" asks Fran. This time, of course, "We knew chances were they weren't going to do a U.S. tour."

Tony Ingram of Cornwall, Ontario, is waiting behind me for the parking meter. He first saw the band a mere year into their existence, back in 1985. "They were playing at a stock-car track outside of Ottawa. There were eight bands playing that day. Nobody had ever heard of these guys. They went on at midnight. My wife and I thought, wow, what a great band. When they got on the radio years later, we remembered that they were the band we saw."

William Walton of Syracuse, NY, drove up with his daughter to watch the show in the square. He first heard the band only a few years ago, via a friend from Buffalo—where one can easily pick up Canadian radio signals. "I've never seen them in concert before, just on YouTube," he says. "We've had a lot of cancer in our family, so we also came to support Gord. And my brother-in-law is here from Kentucky."

Down in Market Square, a crowd of what will eventually reach 25,000 people is assembling. A couple with lawn chairs is perched between two storefronts, next to an optician's office where one can also buy farm-fresh eggs. Moe Peters has lived in Kingston all his 82 years; his wife, Dee, is a relative newbie, with only a mere 66 years in town. They arrived at 10 a.m. to scope out the city's big day. "Most people, even if they're our age, are very excited," says Dee. The Tragically Hip mean more to the elderly couple's children than to the elderly couple, but they live down the street from Gord Sinclair's parents and met him at a wedding once. Gord Downie's type of brain cancer, glioblastoma, is exactly what Dee's sister died of 12 years earlier. "Her doctor was on the big screen over there earlier, explaining that since then they do have more hope [for these patients]; they can extend life, to a point. It would mean a lot to her for us to be here." Have they ever seen an event like this in Kingston before? "We came down because we'll never see anything like this in our town again. We had the blues festival [in 1999] with what's-his-face, Aykroyd. That was kinda neat, but not crowds like this."

I spot my old friends Sam Baijal and Nancy Floyd dining on a patio. Baijal books the Hillside Festival in Guelph, Ontario. He's seen the Hip a dozen times, the first being a university show he booked in the late '80s for about 400 people. In 2006, the Hip wanted to play Hillside; Downie was impressed with the festival when he played one of his first big solo shows there in 2001. Baijal thought the Hip would overshadow the rest of the lineup, so instead he booked them for a single night a month before the festival, with Buck 65 and the Weakerthans. Like the Stanhopes, Baijal too is a former Deadhead. "The amount of emotion that's going on with this tour is phenomenal, and the only thing I can equate it to is Deadheads," he says. "The actual circumstance of what's taking place, there's nothing like it. I think all of us are feeling a place that we're occupying in this story."

A man who identifies only as "Steve from Toronto" is outside the venue looking for tickets. He saw the third Toronto gig and says, "It was everything I wanted in a concert. The band is going out on a high note." He is prepared to pay "$700 at the most" for a ticket. "Can't do more than that. I saw a guy selling for $1,500 each."

While I'm talking to Steve, I hear a small commotion gathering around me. I turn around to see Prime Minister Justin Trudeau about 10 feet away, having just walked out the back door of the K-Rock Centre, dressed in denim and glad-handing his way down the street. In the most Canadian thing I see all day, the crowd immediately forms two lines so he can pass easily. I follow the hubbub back downtown for a while, because, hey, I've never seen a prime minister up close before. Less than a year after his win, Trudeau is still enjoying a honeymoon with the electorate, and he really is a rock star: people are downright giddy with excitement to get close to him. It makes total sense that he's here: he's the same age I am and was in late high school and early university years when the Hip were in their prime.

Walking back to the venue, I encounter three guys with matching homemade Hip shirts. Keith Johnson of Austin, Texas, drove up with his two brothers—Jeff of Oklahoma City, Jerome from Temple, Texas. They got tickets through two Canadian friends, Joe and Melanie Dobroski of Niagara Falls, whom they met at a Tragically Hip show in Boston several years ago. Keith's fandom stemmed from a random discovery: he listens to a tech podcast from Canada that played a Hip song as an outro on one episode. Texan fans are not that rare, of course; the brothers Johnson saw the Tragically Hip at the 1,000-capacity club Emo's on a recent tour.

What's with all the Americans here? Maybe they do look different than Canadians, which is why I end up approaching so many of them. Lucas Murray is from Philadelphia and is here because "you have to pay homage to a guy who's given so much to a generation." Wait, what generation? How many of his Philly friends have heard the Hip? Murray was exposed in 2002, via a roommate from Halifax—"and from being in hockey locker rooms, where they were the soundtrack." Murray went to see the Hip every time they played Philly. "The friends I have up here [in Canada] are always jealous of the shows that I go to, because [the Hip] will play to 17,000 people in Toronto, but in Philadelphia, at the Theatre of the Living Arts, they'll play to 200 people. At the show was me, my two buddies, half the women from the Princeton hockey team and some guys from the AHL [Lehigh Valley] Phantoms and [Hershey] Bears. Afterwards, the band came out and just sat at the bar and drank with us and showed a genuine appreciation for who we were."

Steps away from the K-Rock Centre, at 1 The Tragically Hip Way, Murray is helping Jason Stanton of London, Ontario, to hold corners of an enormous Canadian flag, approximately 10 by 20 feet, which Stanton bought for $100 after he made plans to come to the final show. Stanton wanted to get as many of the 7,000 attendees as possible to sign well wishes for Downie and somehow direct it to the stage during the show, "to let Gordie know he's always in our hearts." Stanton was also circulating copies of the lyrics to "Courage," hoping he could get the crowd to sing the song to Downie during a break between encores. (He didn't get a chance. The roar of the crowd was too deafening.)

Inside the venue, I have to prompt the woman at the will-call to ask me for ID. I'm seated next to Keeley Renwick, a native of Kingston now living in Toronto. I ask him if he knew the band way back when. "Oh yeah, went to the same high school." Kingston Collegiate? "Yeah, they were a bit older than me, though. One of their fathers taught me." So when was the first time you saw the Tragically Hip? "At KCVI." Wait, you mean when they were still the Slinks or the Rodents, punk bands playing in the cafeteria? "Yep, they were exciting." What songs were they covering back then? "No idea, but they were great even then." How many times have you seen them? "Eight. But this trumps everything. This is Kingston bowing down to the Hip and saying thank you."

———

The mood in the arena is electric. People are in their seats and standing and cheering a good 20 minutes before the band goes on stage. There is a spontaneous yet inevitable round of "O Canada." There is a large banner that reads, "Thank you Prime Minister Downie."

The PA system plays Jimmy Cliff's "The Harder They Come, the Harder They Fall."

At 8:30 p.m. sharp, our hosts arrive. The first song is "Fifty Mission Cap," a song about a Canadian hero who mysteriously disappears without a trace on a late August day in Ontario. Gord Downie is making a heroic and very conscious decision not to disappear. In 2000, Downie told me the Barilko story is "almost the greatest example of being struck down in your prime. You do something great and unique, and then when you're not paying attention: boom."

The band is stationary, workmanlike, stoic. The change in Downie's voice is immediately apparent; it's gruff, slightly wavering, occasionally struggling with pitch. No one cares. Downie remains within one square metre. Paul Langlois and Rob Baker are dressed in white; they look like angels framing the two sides of the stage.

"Courage" has become an anthem this summer, if only for the titular word alone. Is it coming at the worst time? Or the best time? If it doesn't come at all, does it really not matter? Did this song ever actually make any sense? Downie unzips his metallic jacket right before the third verse, the one from a book about a man who chooses principle over his personal life by leaving his wife and daughter behind to fight a foreign war against fascism. Beneath Downie's jacket is the *Jaws* T-shirt, the signifier of the dark Canuck.

"Wheat Kings" is a song about a man condemned to a fate he didn't deserve, about the strength of a family who believed in him. It's a song partly set in a high school with pictures of prime ministers past. It's being performed with a sitting prime minister in attendance, at a venue two kilometres away from the high school where this band met, a high school founded in 1792, a high school attended by the first prime minister of Canada. Downie digs into his vocal performance here, giving the song a ferocity it does not normally require. Tonight, it does.

The one and only sign of the night when things seem somewhat amiss is in "Hundredth Meridian," when, during the bridge, Downie stumbles and, ironically, misses a key line—a line that happens to be about memory. Downie had once said, "The idea of 'remembering every single fucking thing I know' was interesting to me. Of course, to remember everything would be a curse. The way I understand it, when we forget what we read, culture begins. I wanted 'Hundredth Meridian' to seem a cursed person's lament." The curse is lifted by the next part of the song, the half-rapped verse about dying in vanity, where he demands that Ry Cooder sing his eulogy, in which there are hints of disease and a dramatic burial.

Next: four songs from the new *Man Machine Poem*. My seatmate decides to go get another beer, because no beer will be sold after 9:45 p.m. Meanwhile the band plays the single "In a World Possessed by the Human Mind," a song I missed at the Air Canada Centre show in Toronto because I spent 80 minutes in a will-call line—80 minutes that included the first 30 minutes of the show.

Onwards, more new songs: "What Blue" and "Tired as Fuck," the latter with a line about wanting to stop so much that he actually doesn't want to stop. Contradictory? Nah, Gordie, baby, we know exactly what you mean. But the man is a machine. Hence: "Machine," the first verse of which he sings an octave lower than the recording; never in my life did I expect Gord Downie to try to sing like Stephin Merritt. Any trace of pitchiness in his voice is now gone; the singer is in full command. Gord Sinclair's bass line wouldn't sound out of place on the Cure's *Disintegration*. This song deserved to be a long-running live staple in the Hip's set. It will only ever have been played live in the summer of 2016.

Over the intro to "Machine," Downie gives an incredibly uncharacteristic political endorsement. Noticing a sign in the audience, he reads, "'Thank you Prime Minister Downie.' Well, you know, Prime Minister Trudeau has got me. His work with First Nations. He's got everybody. He's going to take us where we need to go. And we gotta be a country; it's gotta take 100 years to figure out what the hell went on up there. But it isn't cool, and everybody knows that. It's really, really bad. But we're going to figure it out. You're going to figure it out." And then right into the song.

That is—well, pretty weird. The Tragically Hip have supported many causes in the past, but being the everyman band they are, they've never been known to flat-out endorse or condemn a political leader.

Then there's a break, 35 minutes into the set. The stage is reconfigured; the band's stations are now spread out. The audience watches four minutes of nighttime thunderstorms over a lake in the Canadian Shield, forced to contemplate nature's fury, its potential destruction, singling out isolated locations at random.

When the band returns, Downie is in a purple suit. We've lost Prince this year, but Downie is still here. Until this point, he's spent a lot of time on stage right, beside Paul, his oldest friend, facing the side of the arena where family and friends are seated.

Every set list on this tour has featured a wild card: songs from an album from the 2000s, an era when the band entered a slow commercial decline, a.k.a. the songs most fans probably aren't that excited about hearing.

Tonight it is 2000's *Music @ Work*, which starts with the rousing title track, about a night that is so long it actually hurts. On "Lake Fever" he sings about wanting to break everyone's heart. Before "Toronto #4," in which he praises someone for being a unifying force in his family's life, he addresses his mother in the audience: "Okay, Lorna. This is someone we know." It's a song written about his late grandmother. This chapter concludes with "Putting Down," about wanting desperately not to be afraid, about beginning to choke on one's own words.

Then we're back to the classics, this time from 1991's *Road Apples*. "Twist My Arm," with a line that disparages the concept of martyrdom yet claiming to enjoy it vicariously. Downie adopts a simian swagger, one of his oldest moves, and mimes throwing salt over his shoulder for good luck.

Another disappearance in "Three Pistols," this time a reference to Tom Thomson. "Your country seems to be very famous for its disappearances," Downie said in 1992, introducing this song at Massey Hall.

Downie stops to explain a part of his wardrobe: "In the glowing days of the band, with the help of a good friend, we invented a scarf made of two socks. A singer needs to keep his or her voice always warm. It only took me 28 years to figure that out. Thank you. Thank you people, for keeping me pushing, for keeping me pushing. You here, Char?"

He's looking for his eldest sister, the one for whom September 17 is Mother's Day: that's when, in 1989, she lost her five-year-old son to a congenital heart condition. Downie wrote "Fiddler's Green" for her. The song that was too painful to perform live until 2006. This is a night for facing pain. Fans dissected every moment of this tour, looking for signs of frailty; many thought they saw it in a clip of "Grace, Too" in Toronto that went viral. Others argued Downie was performing a character, and/or mirroring what he was seeing in the audience. That's all up for debate. But performing this song, on this night, in this town, is the first time visible emotion undeniably crosses Downie's face. He wipes away tears and a runny nose in between lines. His delivery never falters, however. If the cameras weren't offering close-ups, we'd have no window into this moment except in our imaginations.

But wipe away those tears, here comes "Little Bones." The crowd goes apeshit in ways I've only ever seen when Bruce Springsteen breaks into "Born to Run." Downie exits the stage while the band jams the outro and then goes into the largely instrumental "Last of the Unplucked Gems," a trippy slow burn. Downie returns to complete the song, ending it with a falsetto wolf call.

In a town that still vividly remembers the January 1998 ice storm, they cheer for "Something On," from *Phantom Power*, with its line about ice-covered trees. Then "Poets," one of the most beloved rockers in the catalogue. Rob Baker delivers perhaps his best solo of the night.

In "Bobcaygeon," the audience sings the bridge, after Downie drops it—only the second mistake he makes all night. The set closes with the (explosive!) "Fireworks," during which Downie changes a line to read: "Isn't it amazing what we can accomplish when we don't let First Nations get in our way?"

Sorry, geeks, no "Escape Is at Hand for the Travellin' Man."

The band takes bows, embrace and kiss each other and leave the stage. This is normally the part of this show where Downie stands and addresses the audience silently, looking people in the eye and waving goodbye. It usually lasts several minutes. Tonight it merely lasts one, before he picks up the mic.

"Thank you, we all appreciate it," he tells his neighbours. "We started here, as you know. We opened up to 13 people. Then our next show, we had 28. The next Kingston show after that, we had six." Pause. "This is my favourite gag to do on this trip." Laughs. "We played here a thousand times, played all the rooms. Really glad to be here in Kingston; we could play the university, and we could play for the bikers. Our idea was that everybody is invited, everybody is involved. We tried to write that way, we tried to think that way. We went through a period there where we had to work very hard to get the girls to come. Because the guys were just scrapping and being really weird. Somehow, we got the girls to come back. And thank you— whoever did that. Whoever was the cause of that one. On behalf of the boys and the men and women of our crew, thank you for a great tour and a great show." Starts to choke. "We enjoyed the hell out of it. Now we're going to go in the back and pretend we've left and you're going to cheer and then we'll come out and play."

First encore: "New Orleans Is Sinking," a song about not wanting to surrender to the forces of nature, about trying to stay afloat in disaster.

The band looks and sounds a bit tired, perhaps emotional. Someone in the crowd throws up an inflatable killer whale. "New Orleans" was always a point in the show where Downie would improvise, either with a surreal rant or by working out a new song. But there is no improv tonight—because there are no new songs. There will be no new songs. Just the hits, boys, just the hits.

On "Boots or Hearts," Downie sings about blocking off Main Street for a "faith parade." They most certainly did: I hope the 25,000 people watching the show around the corner in Market Square got a charge out of that, as with the line about telling a lover's answering machine that he's on his way home.

On the night when they actually are shooting a movie in his hometown, Gord Downie jumbles and adds to the opening to "Blow at High Dough": *They shot a movie once, some kind of Elvis thing / everybody was in it / just to hear me sing.* No mention of "in my hometown." Maybe that was a fuck-up. More likely, the contrarian singer omitted it on purpose. Rob Baker once said that his favourite part of any Hip show was during this song, when the whole band kicks in after the opening. Tonight, he has a look of immense satisfaction at that moment, enjoying it for the last time.

The band again takes bows and starts to leave the stage. Downie remains.

"Thank you to this fine building. To the fine community. To the men and women behind the show. Helping us put on the show. Thank you to the prime minister for coming to our show. It really means a lot to all of us. But mostly, thank you everybody, thank you very much."

It looks like Downie will now do his extended goodbye. Instead, he delivers a speech that shakes the nation.

"There are problems in this country. I met the m—, I was going to say the mayor, I meant the prime minister. He's going to be looking good for at least 12 more years. I don't know if they'll let him go beyond that. But he'll do it. We're in good hands, folks. Real good hands. He cares about the people up north, people we've been trained to ignore, trained our entire lives not to hear a word about what's going on up there. What's going on up there ain't good, maybe worse than it's ever been. So it's not all on him to improve. We're going to get it fixed. We got the guy to do it, to start, to help. Thanks for listening to that. Thanks for listening, period. Have a nice life."

The show could have ended there, and been perfect. But now it's time to get dark. From *Day for Night*, a haunting "Nautical Disaster," a devastating "Scared" and a triumphant and cathartic "Grace, Too." During the song's outro, he reclines on the mic stand, sensually, before jumping up to bark the "him, here, now" part. He starts play-acting but then, seemingly prompted by seeing someone in the audience, he soon succumbs to a quivering lip and unmistakable sobbing. He breaks to deliver three final screams in time with the music, before dropping the mic and surrendering entirely to the moment: rubbing his eyes, crossing his arms, weeping. The audience is biting their nails. Frankly, they're worried for his life, unsure what is emotional or physical anguish—or both. Then the pro impulse kicks back in again: sensing the song's impending conclusion, Downie snaps out of it, places the mic back on the stand and takes a bow.

Seconds later, he's laughing with Rob Baker, pointing out people in the crowd, kissing Gord Sinclair. The band is waving and taking bows, looking exhausted. Downie kisses and embraces Fay. Fay carries him down the back steps.

That's it, right?

Not a chance. A third encore opens with the rarely performed "Locked in the Trunk of a Car." The singer who was recently inside an MRI machine is now heard howling, *"Let me out!"* Penultimate pleasure "Gift Shop" is lovely but ghostly, a song about looking down on the world from above.

The last song is not one for the diehard fans, is not worthy of the wild speculation that preceded it. It is the Hip's biggest radio hit, "Ahead by a Century," an acoustic-based pop song about childhood innocence, a song that is to a later generation of Canadians what Neil Young's "Heart of Gold" was to baby boomers, a song that has had gymnasiums full of Canadian children united in song, a song with the lyric that has been quoted endlessly during this tour, in every review, on T-shirts, even inscribed on Gord Downie's boots: it's a line that Queen's prof Robert Morrison said is infused with "an insistence on living as fully and genuinely as possible: *'No dress rehearsal/This is our life.'"*

Over Baker's extended guitar solo on the outro, Downie is repeatedly striking poses, ending each with a ta-da moment that begs approval, before he stops, shrugs dismissively and then tries another one, even more grandiose. He looks like he's performing a figure-skating finale, a vogue dance, a ballerina's final pose. He's walking like a matador. He's workshopping his grand exit in front of our eyes. "You like this one? How about this one?" he seems to be saying.

Finally, he starts framing the audience like a director or cinematographer would, holding out two L-formations with his thumb and forefinger, documenting these final minutes. Then he mimes painting on a canvas, first facing the audience, then his brothers onstage. Capture this. Make it last. Put it in a frame. These days in frames.

The song ends. It feels like the end of a century. Bows are taken. Kisses exchanged. "You're wonderful. Thank you for that." Those are Gord Downie's last words onstage as a member of the Tragically Hip.

That night in Kingston, the humidity gave way to a massive windstorm. Rain fell through the night, in real time, as we all went back to our homes or hotel rooms to drink, to discuss, to reflect, to write.

Canadians are a stoic bunch, imbued with optimism. Both inside and outside the venue, there are tears, yes. But tonight, many are holding out hope that this is not the last time. People travelled from down the street and across the continent not necessarily because they even liked the Tragically Hip, but because they wanted to "be there for Gord." To bear witness. To be a part of the never-ending present.

———

Months later, I asked the band's peers where they were and what they were doing on August 20, 2016.

Kris Abbott, the Pursuit of Happiness

I was in the K-Rock Centre, in the family and friends section. Right underneath Trudeau! Everybody in this town knows this band, or has gone to school with them, or is a friend of one of the sisters. It was hard not to reminisce about their history and not think of both the comfortable and uncomfortable parts of my own past. I was trying to focus on celebration and the energy and the positive uncertainty of the future and what the residual effects of all this will be. The gift they gave was not forced down anyone's throat. They just put it out there and everyone got into it.

When [my wife] and I went downtown on the bus that day, it was packed. The city made buses free for the day. Everyone was happy and excited. They had security checkpoints going into Market Square, for everyone's benefit, and they were very easygoing people. There was no badness. Reports of any incidents were incredibly minimal. I think there were maybe two, and they were people who were escorted out by people, as opposed to the cops.

I was so blown away by the musicianship of the band. The performance was amazing, but I couldn't stop taking in the band. I used to play with them quite a bit, but I hadn't seen them in many years, and I was blown away at how great they were.

Sarah Harmer was sitting a few seats in front of us; she was on her feet the whole show. She had her running shoes on, because she had come to dance. That's the way everyone was thinking. Everyone was there just to soak it in and enjoy it. It was a gift.

Stephen Dame, curator, the Hip Museum

Kingston was hot and humid and had a different feeling than the other shows I went to; the AC was either off or inefficient. It was almost delirious—and I'm not trying to be overdramatic, it was a feeling of delirium, with so much joy and jumping. It did not feel like a goodbye. It really felt like a celebration, a collective moment. There was something special about it.

Allan Gregg, former manager

I watched it on television. My kids literally grew up on Gord's lap, at band meetings in my basement. I brought them to the Air Canada Centre show [in Toronto]. We didn't go backstage. The show was remarkable. I should've felt deadeningly sad, but I didn't—because Gord didn't. He looked like he was having the time of his life. I told my kids that they'll be singing "Bobcaygeon" 50 years from now. That will be Gord's legacy: the songs. Those songs will be here forever and part of the Canadian fabric when you're an old, old man.

Colin Cripps, Blue Rodeo, Crash Vegas

I was playing at the Molson Amphitheatre [in Toronto] with Blue Rodeo that night. We played "Bobcaygeon" as a tribute. Somehow [the tech crew] got a feed to show [the Hip] playing live on our screens, and they were also doing "Bobcaygeon." Total fucking fluke. We had no idea that was happening. Suddenly people started going crazy, and we looked up and there's Gord. It was an amazing Canadian moment. People were crying. You couldn't help but feel all the history you have together.

I watched about a third of [the Kingston show] later. I couldn't watch the whole thing, to be honest. I went to two of the shows, one in Toronto and one in Hamilton. I stood at Billy Ray's station at the side of the stage. It was an amazing show, both times. I was blown away. That was enough for me. The last show was too much. They're my buddies and I'm a big fan. If I was watching it in the moment, it would be different. But to go back and watch it? No. It was a communal experience of religious proportions. People were celebrating the Hip but also all of us being a part of that community and feeling that through music, which is such a powerful thing.

Michelle McAdorey, Crash Vegas

I was at the Blue Rodeo show. That was really intense, for so many reasons, for me, personally. Backstage at this Blue Rodeo gig, everyone was watching the Tragically Hip show. Then Blue Rodeo did their Tragically Hip tribute [by playing "Bobcaygeon"], and I had a friend there who was so riddled with cancer—and that was the last time I saw him. There were so many emotions. I'd watch a bit of the Hip show, then a bit of the Blue Rodeo show, then I'd be talking to my friend. It was such a gorgeous moment, that "Bobcaygeon" moment. But it was hard to watch.

Chris Tsangarides, producer, *Fully Completely*

I was here [in England], in my studio, watching it through tears. To watch him break down, you felt his pain. Everyone in that room felt the anguish and unfairness of it all. One of the worst things that can happen is knowing you only have so much time to live. That must be godawful. I don't know how he could carry on. The best way about it is to go when you don't know, because then you carry on in your merry old way. [In 2014, Tsangarides contracted Legionnaire's disease and was placed in a medically induced coma for 10 days. He died of pneumonia on January 7, 2018.] Then a few months later, I saw the blanket ceremony [where Downie was honoured by the Assembly of First Nations], and I broke down watching that. I have a real thing about Native Americans, an amazing people with an amazing ethos. It brings it home just what a bunch of shitheads we were to these people all these years ago, and still are today.

Steve Berlin, Los Lobos, producer, *Phantom Power, Music @ Work*

I was quite literally crying the whole summer. I managed to see the show in Calgary. For [the Kingston] show, Los Lobos had a gig in Kentucky or somewhere, and we were just about to go onstage when, out of a clear blue sky, this weird storm shows up and shuts down this whole festival we were playing. The show was cancelled, so I got to listen to the entire Hip show. I got to sit and listen and cry like everyone else. [As told to Steve Dawson]

Dave Clark, Country of Miracles

I'd been watching it on my TV [in Toronto], and it sounded amazing in the house with the windows open. I went outside to see what the city was doing. Everybody had their windows open. People all over my neighbourhood, no matter where I walked, it was like a living boom box. Then bars and cafés and courtyards on College Street were hanging bedsheets and projecting it outside. It was blasting out of wide-open doorways. It was amazing. And putting the prime minister on the hot seat in front of Canada—that was a really good thing. Whether you like the Hip or don't like the Hip, man, you can't deny that stuff. That night that they galvanized Canada. It was a really special national moment. I was glad to witness it. It made me cry.

Bruce Dickinson, former A&R executive, MCA Records

I've had my own medical issues in recent years. That afternoon of the show, part of having been ill, I was very dizzy. I fell off a bus and landed square on my chin. I went into an ER at Columbia Presbyterian, a few blocks from where I live [in New York City], with a mild concussion and my shirt was covered with blood. They looked at me and said, "You're going to need 14 stitches." I looked at the doctor and said, "Here's the deal. I have to be walking out of here at 7:30." "What if we want to keep you here for observation?" "No. I'm walking out of here at 7:30. Do what you have to do so that can happen." Because the show was going to start at eight o'clock! I came home, kind of woozy, and watched the show on my Mac. It was very bittersweet. I was extremely proud of the guys. They were phenomenal. To see Gord Downie be able to summon what he did to do that show—my throat is catching as I describe it to you. It's part of what makes him a great artist. He's got that inner drive and that inner spirit.

I saw that right away, way back at [the first time I saw them, at] Massey Hall [in 1988]. This is a guy who will not be denied. That's what you need. You need an artist who will grab you by the lapel and go, "I have something to say and you're gonna listen." And you could see the love and support from the other guys. When Gord might have been about to falter on some words, Paul could see it coming, and he was right up there next to Gord, doing a harmony so the lyrics came through. Baker and Sinclair were watching Gord throughout the show, ready to do whatever needed to be done to support him. When they did the encores, Johnny was literally carrying Downie down the steps at the back of the stage. All of that stuff added up to one of the most powerful things—if not *the* most powerful thing—I've ever seen on a stage.

Dale Morningstar, Country of Miracles

I was at [my spouse's] mother's house in Manitoulin Island. Her whole family was there: brother, stepdad, sister and her husband. We were all down in the basement. They knew I had an association with Gord, but they didn't know how close. We're watching it, and I'm saying, "The best part of it is when the band leaves the stage and Gord delivers a soliloquy. It'll drive you to tears." As soon as the band left the stage, there was a storm, and—boom—no signal. It was like, "Wait, what?" The timing was impeccable. The TV kicked back in for the last song of the last encore. I went out for a swim after, alone. It was still storming out. I was just yelling at the sky.

Julie Doiron, Country of Miracles

When I heard about the tour, I made the decision that I just had to be in Kingston. I was touring across Canada, and the way my tour was booked, I would have missed it. About a month before, I cancelled my shows on the way home and drove a straight shot from Vancouver to Kingston in five days. We got to Kingston the day before. I ended up sitting next to [engineer] Aaron Holmberg, who was working at the Bathouse when we were doing *The Grand Bounce.* I was singing all the words. I wanted everyone else to be doing that, too, but there were a few women in front of me texting or on Facebook. I wanted everyone to be 100 per cent into this. Some people who were there just wanted to say they were there. I ran into Kevin Drew outside, and some people were trying to go to an after-party—I didn't feel like doing that. I wanted to process what I'd just witnessed. I really, really loved it. If I hadn't got tickets, I would have been in the square. I just believed it would work out.

Steven Drake, producer, the Odds

I kinda watched it and didn't watch it. I'd just seen them a few weeks before in Vancouver. I had the broadcast on while I was doing other things in the house. I think I was building a telescope or something. I couldn't sit there and watch it; it was too intense. But I couldn't turn it off.

José Contreras, By Divine Right

I didn't watch it. Friends of mine from Edmonton, the Wet Secrets, asked me to play a show at the Drake Hotel in Toronto. No one checked the calendar; we only realized 10 days before that it was the same night of the Hip show. I called the Drake and said, "Can we broadcast the show, eight to 10 and then play our show after?" They said they had an event and couldn't do it. I was really torn up. Then I realized I got this gig for the same reason I played with the Hip: because a friend offered it to me. I'm a working artist; that's what I do. I don't have management, a label or a booking agent. I take what comes to me. It sucked, loading into the Drake, bumping into friends, who asked me, "What are you doing?" "Um, loading into the Drake." "Okay, weird. Bye!" But you know what? We had a great show. Lots of people there. I took a picture of the Wet Secrets during their set, when they hit that moment when they were great. I remember thinking: this is worth it. This is music. This is life. This is my life.

Dave Hodge, sportscaster

I consciously did not go to the Kingston show, even though I had the opportunity. I'd seen the first of the ACC shows, and I saw the Hamilton show. I thought Kingston would be too overwhelming. I didn't watch it on TV, either. I preferred to remember the way I'd seen them last. I've never seen a show that included so much other thought, apart from the music. You want to say to each of them—but you don't—"I wish I could hear you one more time." That would really be uncomfortable, because they know damn well that they're going to miss it, too. Other bands say, "This is it," and then they come back two years later. That's not happening here.

Mike O'Neill, the Inbreds

I chose not to watch it. A couple of people were saying, "Come to Kingston and see it," like Virginia Clark and Sarah Harmer. I didn't, and I don't regret it. I saw a bit of the Mansbridge interview, and I found that really hard to watch. It answered all the questions I wanted to know in an achingly honest way.

Dave Ullrich, the Inbreds

My family watched it on a backyard screen. We had all kinds of buffering problems—it was pretty bad. And it was the wrong crowd to watch it with. The kids were not into it.

Sam Roberts, the Sam Roberts Band

One of my relatives from South Africa was here. We had a big party at another cousin's house: brought the TV outside, speakers out. My cousin, who had never heard this music before, was saying, "What is this about? What am I listening to?" But after half an hour, 45 minutes, there was definitely the dawning of something [for them]—which to me suggests that [the Tragically Hip's music] is not just this impregnable fortress, where if you're not literally born to it that you're not going to understand it. Whether it was the music itself, or the delivery, or the performance or Gord's character coming through—I don't know what it was, but it left an impression.

The grief [for the rest of us] was very real. Very deeply felt. It was not superficial in any way, and it was collective. I went to see them in Ottawa and found myself not even thinking about Gord and his health, and I just watched the band play and go further and deeper than I'd seen them before. It's how he and they as a band make you feel. That joy: what better thing could you bring to people's lives? It's the mark of a great band, the level of sacrifice you're willing to take on to pour into what you do. The humour was there, too. Life is funny—even the bad parts. Most bands have a fountain-of-youth syndrome. What they did that year is chronicle the sadness and humour that goes with your life, of feeling less than you were, that feeling of being diminished in some ways but growing in ways you never thought you would and fading away in others. It's the rare band who takes that on.

Bry Webb, the Constantines

I watched it on TV. The most moving thing about it was Gord's vulnerability and his response to his own vulnerability, or his own fight—the guttural release coming from him in moments of that set and the look of peace and bliss and enlightenment on his face. Two minutes later, he would be bestial, just catharsis and release. It was everything I value about him and performance and art—it was all there. It was pretty punk, from five men kissing each other full on the lips before taking the stage, to watching him drop a few lines and be aware of it and just say "fuck it!" There was a lot of great punk rock energy to that show. The shout-out to JT was full of intent and was a really interesting decision. It wouldn't make sense, in terms of the energy of that moment, to say "fuck you" about this issue. It was Gord saying, "Here's some energy. I'm putting a spotlight on this at the moment, in a way that I can." Knowing the intention with which Gord does things, I felt that was what was happening at that moment.

Andrew Whiteman, Broken Social Scene

I watched it with Evan Cranley [of Stars] at his house in Montreal, watching it on a super system. We loved it. I was excited by a couple of the newer tunes, which they played really well. Gord called out Trudeau, which I loved, because I can't stand Trudeau. It was emotional, but in a selfish way for me: come to Montreal, you fuckers! I really wanted to see one more show.

Hugh Larkin, American mega-fan

I'm so thankful I live in Detroit, because we get CBC Windsor here. I was able to watch the final show live in my family room. My wife and I just sat there, side by side, holding hands, teary-eyed. It was very impressive to me that the prime minister was there. I'd never heard of the president or vice-president of the United States going to some rock concert. The fact that the Hip had such an attachment to Canadian culture and Canadian society that the prime minister felt it was important to be there was really impressive to me.

Hayden King, Anishinaabe educator

I was taken aback when Downie made that reference to the prime minister and demanded change. My initial satisfaction over that gave way toward the end, when he expressed optimism—but I'm willing to give him the benefit of the doubt. Considering his path through life—and death—I'll afford the man some optimism. We did just come out of 10 years of a Conservative government that was aggressively anti-Indigenous, and here's Trudeau during his campaign and the early days after the election—and even today—saying a lot of sweet things to Indigenous people. If you're listening to a prime minister say those things right after being elected, it's okay to check your cynicism. Now, two years later, we realize none of those things have come to pass, and if Downie said the same thing about Trudeau today, I'd be more critical. Part of me wished that Downie was more critical, but I'm also happy that he demanded action at that particular moment in time.

Rollie Pemberton, a.k.a. Cadence Weapon

Me and my girlfriend watched it on TV in Toronto. I have a friend in Montreal, who is from New Brunswick, and he loves Canadiana. He's the most Canadian guy I can think of. We were texting each other during the show. He was crying. My girlfriend was watching it just out of respect; she's not a fan whatsoever. She doesn't get down with any big public events; she doesn't care. We had three different perspectives on the show. For him, it was this defining moment. For her, she couldn't give less of a shit. For me, I felt a kinship and a need to be a part of it, as a fellow songwriter. I had some tug of Canadianness, but I didn't have a personal stake in how the show went. There was a wide cross-section of people who watched it for different reasons.

Navneet Alang, journalist

I watched the concert on TV, partly out of a strangely morbid empathy, but also because I'm a sucker for collective events. I don't like hockey, either, but you can bet I watched the 2010 [Olympic] gold medal men's hockey game in Vancouver. Moments like that form part of a kind of collective consciousness, I think, linking individuals to narratives of nation or identity. And what is a nation or country but a narrative—or a narrative constantly retold, over and over, each time in a slightly different way? I think we look to those instances to mould a relation to this thing—a country—that gives us a sense of place in the world, or a way to understand our connection to the broader social and political realities in which we are imbricated. That seems extra important as the era of monoculture appears to be on the wane. [As told to Chantal Braganza]

Patrick Finn, academic

The Hip have an ecumenical approach, in that the hosers love it at the exact same time the singer is saying, "I hate nationalism." That's a very Canadian thing, that weird mélange of all viewpoints being sustained. The person who voted for Stephen Harper and the person who voted for Jack Layton are both singing along. There's one person there because of a Hugh MacLennan reference, and another person is a biker who's there because he likes that kind of music. What's Canadian about the Hip is this vision that we all get along. There was a performance of Canada itself at that final show: the singing of the anthem, the circulating of the flag, the CBC broadcast, the presence of the prime minister. It's like the audience decided, "We're going to get all our Canadianisms out tonight. Let's just be the *good* Canada tonight." It's idealistic, but it's not a bad idea to talk about what we can do collectively rather than what it is that separates us.

Shadrach Kabango, a.k.a. Shad

I was playing a show in Vancouver that night. After sound check, I was catching up with a friend at a bar, and it was on TV—it was 5:30 p.m. out there. There are not a lot of moments like that, when everyone is watching. It was beautiful and inspiring. Part of why people like sports is that there's this human drama happening that is real, but veiled by the fact that it's just a game. Whereas this was really just the human drama, with music.

Kate Fenner, singer / songwriter

I couldn't do any of those shows. I didn't see any. Just couldn't. [My family and I] went to Greece and Malta. I was born in Malta, but I'd never been back. I was on a rock in the middle of the Mediterranean. [The next day] I got a coffee and opened the paper, and—mother-fucker!—the *Times of Malta* had a huge picture of the last show. It was unbelievable.

Brendan Canning, Broken Social Scene

I went to a Toronto show and thought it was sweet how tight they were onstage. And it was nice to hear new material as opposed to just all the old songs again. But the last show? I wasn't interested. I'd been on tour with them in 2015. I've been watching them play since 1989. I didn't need to see another Hip show. Everyone was talking about it, and I was like, "Yeah, yeah, I get it." I was in the Bathouse with Broken Social Scene that night. Kev [Drew] went to the show. I'm not one for fanfares of that regard. It's a heavy emotional thing—which is the understatement of the year—but I don't need to be there for it. Any chance I can be at the studio without a bunch of people around, I'm going to take it.

Mark Hebscher, sportscaster

I wanted to go, but I knew it would be too emotional for me. People said, "Are you nuts? This is the last chance you'll have to see them play." I saw them play many, many times, often up close. I was sure that this time I would just lose it, and I wouldn't enjoy it. When I watched it on TV, at home, by myself, I just cracked. I had the lights off. I turned it up loud. I danced. I was watching the crowd shots and thinking, "Man, it's great that you [are] there to see this, but you should have seen them at their best and not because you felt you had to see them now." Watching them play six nights in a row, on the road [over the years], was spectacular. You have to be a pro to go out there night after night and kill.

Shannon Cooney, choreographer

I watched it [where I live] in Berlin, where there is a six-hour difference, so it started at two a.m. I was worried I wouldn't be able to watch it, because CBC video content is usually blocked outside the country. But the CBC unlocked it, and I realized I couldn't miss this. All of Berlin was sleeping while I watched this show until five in the morning. I danced in my living room. But then I was kind of emotionally destroyed for the next few days. It was hard to explain to my German boyfriend just how much Canada loves Gord and that whole band. They could have broken up long ago; Gord could have been a solo artist, but he's a loyal member. What a show! It was political: he was talking about strong women, and he called out Justin Trudeau on our dirty, dark secrets that we didn't all know we had until the reconciliation process.

Music is present, but it's also a marker of time. We went from the late '80s until now with this presence, this poetry that you either completely love or you push up against because you don't like it, but it runs through these generations. It has personal resonance; it's not just about watching these people onstage. I don't think [his condition] inhibited his performance. That's the thing about being present, which I think he's constantly orienting to: [being present is] not just a state, it's how to manifest being here, now. I loved that it wasn't maudlin. It could have been, and maybe people wanted that.

Award-winning Canadian novelist (name withheld)

That was a weird concert for me. In a secret way, it was disappointing. This feels awful to say—I don't mean that Gord or the band let anyone down. But if I'm honest with myself, what I most wanted from the Hip's final show was a demonstration of Downie's fragility. Evidence, onstage, of the show's terrible significance—because it meant so much to me. Many fans, I think, will have felt this selfish desire: to glimpse the vulnerability of the band we loved, to see our own sorrow mirrored back by the musicians in the floodlights. If this was really a farewell, the Kingston performance was the closest thing to closure that fans were likely to get. And yet the band, and Downie, had a different set of objectives. For them, it was important to show that they were *not* fragile. That Gord was *not* weakened. That he and they were mighty, thunderous, strong as ever. That maybe he would live forever. And for me at least there was a dissonance: the concert rocked too hard and too well. The gig didn't give me what I wanted because what I wanted was almost cruel. I felt this bizarre sense of disappointment, a sense of disappointment that seems unkind to even entertain. Does that make any sense?

Jim Creeggan, Barenaked Ladies

I'd already seen one of the Toronto shows. Gord was in control and he always has been, but for me I went to learn about how I felt about it. It's almost like he was able to really lead everybody through it, the transition. The one moment at the very end where he just knew everybody cared about him, about their attachment to him, the memories they shared with him: when he stopped at the end and looked at each section of the audience and gave them a long look of gratitude, I will always be grateful for that. After all the clowning—which turned up the volume on everything, right down to the scream, the full-on scream of pain and anguish and all that stuff—then he just looked at the audience and said, "I acknowledge you and I acknowledge what you're giving me." At the Toronto show, there was also a moment when he was playing with the camera [that fed the overhead screens], staring right into it. His look was probing, almost: "Why are you here? Are you just a voyeur, or are you expressing something for yourself? Are you here to say goodbye to the Hip? Why are you here?" That's one thing about Gord: you cannot fuck with him! He always holds the line of truth. He's right beside it all the time.

I watched a bit of the final show on TV. I was on a family vacation, sleeping in a cottage on P.E.I. Down the way, some neighbours were blasting it. The ocean wind was blowing, and it was this ethereal Hip experience. It was good, because then I had time as I was falling asleep and listening to the sound blowing around to process how I felt about it. It was a good time to reflect.

Neal Osborne, 54.40

In the 1980s, we were in Saskatoon at some festival: it was Spirit of the West, us and Tragically Hip. I hadn't seen them much until then; I knew they were starting to grow a following. It was really rainy. Spirit went on and it was drizzly and rainy, and I felt bad for them. Then for some reason, for us the clouds broke and it was all nice and the sun was setting. Then a storm came in and just poured, and there was lightning, and Downie was out in front just givin' 'er, and I thought, "Okay, I get it. This guy is committed." That's when I became a fan. I always think back to that gig, because both those guys [Downie and Mann] have gone through some trials. I saw two shows on the last tour: the first one in Victoria and then one of the Vancouver shows. I was quite moved, obviously. [On the night of the Kingston show] we were playing in Saskatoon, actually. We did a shout-out to them and then we managed to catch the last couple of songs in the hotel lounge; we finished our show early enough to do that.

Vince Ditrich, Spirit of the West

The final concert took place not terribly long after Spirit was forced into retirement due to John Mann's early onset Alzheimer's. At the very same time, I underwent a kidney transplant and was in the midst of a long recovery period. That day my house was full of guests, lots of activity, people coming and going. There wasn't a lot of eagerness or enthusiasm about the Hip's final show, just a pall of sadness. To my friends and family, Spirit's end was difficult, and for such a similar thing to afflict our friends just seemed doubly sad. Personally, I felt the tectonic plates in Canadiana shifting, as if some hand was gently sliding us all aside to make room for new, fresh ideas and concepts. It was a changing of the guard, writ large.

I reluctantly turned on the TV and found the network audio mix to be tragically unhip. At that moment, I was less engaged in the music than the memories of touring with them in 1995: remembering Rob Baker's insanely rude hotel check-in name, which he used with mischievous glee, or Gord Downie shrinking with embarrassment as our bumbling bus driver tried to make a U-turn in the middle of a main street in Chicago during the height of rush hour. I thought of watching Johnny playing his ass off, but losing grip on one stick that went clattering off into the wings. I grinned and pointed a "gotcha" at him, as he put his head down in a snarl, like he'd missed a penalty shot. I thought of the show we did together in Wichita, Kansas, where one audience member was such an obnoxious drunken boob that we wrote a song about him.

But, of course, I couldn't stay tuned. I was too sad for all of us and simply had to change the subject, as I watched the tangible evidence that time was moving on, past all of us in that musical generation.

Jennie Punter, journalist

My husband doesn't really like that kind of music, so we had plans to go to the Markham Jazz Festival to see Lonnie Smith that night. We had to eat first, so we went to a pub. They had the show on, and it was just starting. I could imagine what it was like to be in Kingston, because the *Whig-Standard* building used to be right there, off the square. I didn't feel like I wished I could be there. But I was very emotional inside. I was with my husband and my daughter, so it was a very private thing for me.

It was a surreal experience: I was in a bar in a town I never go to, going to an event I've never been to, in a pub I'll never go to again, in this festival setting with ice-cream booths and people tying balloons and all the stuff you see on a street closed to traffic. Then there's this event that all of Canada is watching, and I'm not one of those people. It made me aware of how big an event it was. If I'd watched it at home alone in a room with the door closed, I wouldn't have thought about that factor.

Virginia Clark, Kingston promoter

I was sitting in the family section at the venue [in Kingston], and there was a lot of crying—pretty much non-stop for three hours. It was crying but also elation and joy, not just sadness. All the feelings! I'd never felt this way during any performance, ever, and how many shows have I seen in my life? Countless. I held on to that show for at least a week, with melancholy. I was depressed and exhausted. I don't know how to describe it.

Steve Jordan, founder and director, Polaris Music Prize, former CKLC DJ

I don't go back to Kingston often. My wife and I walked up and down Princess Street; every single place was blasting Hip songs. Went to Zap Records. [Owner] Gary [LaVallee] was playing some bootleg he had from '88, which gave my silent memories a soundtrack. The gravity of it was getting weird. Went to the Toucan for some pre-drinks. All the people I'd see at the shows all the time back then, that was their HQ. Right upstairs, in [a room once called] the Terrapin, was the first time I saw the Hip, capacity: 40. That's when the reality of it really kicked in.

I thought I'd have two tickets; when I went to pick them up at about 11 a.m to avoid any nonsense, there were four tickets there. What do I do with these extras? It felt like a test. I called Virginia Clark, to see if she knew someone in desperate need of tickets, or who might be terminally ill and couldn't get one. Then a lightbulb went off: the first guy I listened to at the radio station when I was growing up, who now teaches at St. Lawrence College, Jim Elyot. He was the guy who first indulged me on the request line when I was 12. He gave me my first free record: Bob Seger, *Stranger in Town.* I gave him the tickets; he and his wife, Julie, sat next to us. I think she once worked with Gord's sister Paula, so I'm also pretty certain I first heard of the band through them.

Second song in was "Courage," and I thought, "This is the last time they'll play this song—ever." I just crashed and started crying out of my pores. It was more than sorrow; it felt like I was feeling every single emotion at the same time. At my wife Michelle's behest I did my best to take it all in and live in the moment. Then I'd catch a snippet of a lyric that, in that moment, would take on a more urgent meaning and

407

I'd start crying out of my pores again. I'd always thought the band were great players and somewhat overlooked in that sense, but on that tour they were an unstoppable force. They were just so generous to each other and the audiences. It was beautiful to watch and to hear. They weren't just barely holding it together; they thrived. That was informing my emotion, and I'm just some guy who sort of knows them, who by circumstance was lucky enough to see the very early beginnings. I'm a mess, and I'm not even *in* the band. How are *they* even functioning? How did they do this for three weeks? I can't even imagine what kind of shit they're going through.

Jake Gold, CEO, the Management Trust

I saw six shows on the 2016 tour, including two in Vancouver and the show in Kingston. I hadn't seen them play live since I [last] worked with them [in 2003], so, 13 years. It was great to watch them as a fan. It was good. It was interesting. While I think for others there was melancholy, I saw it as a celebration. I completely saw where Gord was coming from. He was saying goodbye to everyone he loved. That, to me, was how I walked in the door. It was really emotional, don't get me wrong, but I didn't shed a tear until the day after the Kingston show. Kingston was so beautiful the day of the show. It was everything you want for a Hip show: hot and sweaty and sunny out all day. The next day, I woke up and it was pouring rain. I broke down and started to cry. But it didn't happen until that day.

———

He was on a fishing trip. In the remote north, in a land where the many not born there dare not go. Where some get lost. Where some go to get lost.

Days earlier, this quiet man had held much of the entire nation rapt, millions watching as he summoned all his strength to tackle his terminal condition, to fend off—however briefly—the inevitability of death. To testify one more time. It would turn out to be the last show of his band's 30-year, multi-million-selling, award-winning career, a fate many suspected at the time.

But things were much quieter now. Just a few close friends on a starry night in front of a campfire on James Bay.

There were a few others there, though, most of whom knew enough to respect the privacy of the cancer-stricken man who had travelled hundreds of kilometres to disappear. Nonetheless, someone piped up.

"Gord, I always wanted to ask you: how do you get the energy to make it so real every day? I think if I put myself out there like that, on the line, and make people emotionally connect with me, I feel like I couldn't ever do it again, because I'd get bored or I just couldn't summon the same amount of emotion. And it seems like you get up there every single time and give it!"

The man slumped a bit. Paused. Then he got up, silently, walked over to a pile of wood, picked up two logs and returned to put them on the fire. Not a word. He stoked the fire until sparks came out. The poet whose metaphors had inspired generations of rock'n'roll fans had nothing more to say—with words, anyway.

Do the work. Create the spark. Then sit back and see what happens, because it's not like you can control it. Sit down. Shut up until it's time to do it again. See where those sparks land. If you work hard enough and you're lucky enough, you'll leave an eternal flame.

CHAPTER TWENTY-FIVE

THE LUXURY
2016–17: EPILOGUE

> "It was almost a law, [Raymond] Carver's law, not to save up
> things for some longed-for-future, but to use up the best that
> was in him each day and to trust that more would come."

TESS GALLAGHER, 1989

GORD DOWNIE GAVE only one television interview in 2016, to Peter
Mansbridge on CBC's flagship news program, *The National*. It aired a
week before the release of *Secret Path*. It was the first time Canadians saw
Downie offstage and talking about his condition. The singer's syntax was
slow, measured, ensuring the right words came out. His face alternated
between extreme focus and an almost childlike delight; he even giggled at
a few points. It was both heartbreaking and joyful to see him so vulnerable,
so emotionally raw and yet positive and zen.

Downie admitted on camera he was terrified to do the interview,
"because I don't know what my brain's going to do." He'd written down
"Peter" on his arm, "just in case I call you 'Doug,'" he told Mansbridge.
He admitted he had trouble remembering the names of his four children.
While talking about *Secret Path*, he couldn't remember the term "residential school"—Mansbridge let him struggle for a few seconds before helping
him out. He talked about spending a lot of time with his father before he
died in 2015. He said he wasn't in pain. He said he was "resigned to the
direction this is heading." When asked what worried him now, Downie

said, "I want my kids to be good. I want them to be safe and have a great, long life. And [to] take what they need from me and leave what they don't— definitely leave what they don't . . . I don't want to die, because my son is 10, my youngest son. And that really scares me, obviously. But I sure want to do this right on the way out, so he's not worried."

When asked about the Hip's connection to Canada, Downie said, "I mentioned it a lot in lyrics. But I was never like, 'Aren't we the best?'" He said that Canada's Indigenous character was "what's missing as we celebrate doughnuts and hockey—over and over and over and over again." Mansbridge asked if Canadians' ignorance about Indigenous issues was indicative of racism. Downie denied it. "I don't think we are. Racist—no way. Just no exposure. It's a chance at a whole different world waiting for us, and I don't think we're racist at all . . . We've got to really help out our friends up north. I'm not putting it all on my death. But it's put me in a position where I can actually get some attention."

"What will make you at peace?"

"Just doing things."

Downie concluded the interview by telling the anchor, "I love you." Mansbridge responded in kind and extended a hand; Downie took it and reached in for a kiss on the lips.

———

Secret Path was now two-and-a-half years old, but it was new to the public. It consumed the next three months of Downie's life.

It would take some work to perform it live: the first show was October 18 at the National Arts Centre in Ottawa, with another at Roy Thomson Hall in Toronto on October 21. Co-producer and drummer Dave Hamelin asked keyboardist Kevin Hearn to help orchestrate the band, which would include Kevin Drew on keys, Charles Spearin on bass and Downie's old friend Josh Finlayson on guitar. Hearn was more than comfortable in the role. He was a two-time cancer survivor himself (most recently in 2014), and he served as Lou Reed's musical director for the last few years of Reed's life.

"With Lou, I'd rehearse the band for maybe three or four days before Lou would show up," said Hearn. "Lou would say, 'Kevin, thank you so much for what you've done. You've taken the weight of a cow off my shoulders. I don't have enough hours in my day to sit there and teach people the songs.' Also, with Lou's band, I'd intentionally screw up the lyrics or go back to the first verse; I'd say, 'This is what's going to happen, guys. He's gonna be different every night, and we as a band have to know how to navigate those situations.' It was similar with Gord.

"Dave Hamelin and I got together and worked on sounds and programming for a couple of days. I didn't want Gord to be sitting around while we worked on songs. But as soon as the band started rehearsing, Gord said, 'I don't care if you're just workshopping. I just want to be there. I'll just sit on the couch or whatever.' He was totally into it from the moment he got there, singing with total feeling. He didn't ever do it less than 100 per cent. His emotions were in it at every rehearsal. We could get through the whole album once a day, and then go over a few areas that needed to be worked on, but that was about it. It was too intense to do it over again."

Rehearsals were held in Hearn's apartment. The plan was to move to a proper studio eventually, but Downie was comfortable and wanted to stay. He even insisted the Mansbridge interview be held at Hearn's place, no matter how crowded it was with the band, managers, Downie brothers, musical equipment, the TV crew and Mansbridge himself. It was where the singer felt safe.

Full-production rehearsals for the *Secret Path* show, where the band learned to play in synch with the animated film for the first time, were held at the Algonquin Theatre in Huntsville, where Hearn has a family home. He wanted to get the band out of the distractions of Toronto before the first show. Hearn also thought that travelling through the Canadian Shield to Ottawa via Algonquin Park—rather than from Toronto via the 401— would be more inspiring, especially at the same time of year that Chanie Wenjack embarked on his now-fabled walk.

Joining them on the bus was *Globe and Mail* writer Ian Brown. He and Downie talked about his memory problems, about being the roadie for his 16-year-old son's first gig the weekend before, about his desire to build a cabin in Ogoki Post and live there, about his beloved late father. Mostly they talked about how *Secret Path* was the most important thing he'd ever done. "If this is the last thing I do," he told Brown, "then I'm happy."

The Ottawa show went off without a hitch. The Toronto show started late due to a box office snafu, but the performance was flawless; it was filmed by the CBC for broadcast one year later. The next night, the *Secret Path* band made a surprise appearance at Massey Hall for Hayden's Dream Serenade concert, alongside Barenaked Ladies, Broken Social Scene and others. A few weeks later, they made a brief appearance at the Ottawa WE Day event for youth on November 9. A final show took place in Halifax, at the Rebecca Cohn Auditorium, on November 29. It would be the last show of Downie's life.

"I loved seeing how good Gord felt after we performed," said Kevin Hearn. "How he always wanted to book more shows, which sadly weren't to be. Gord always had time for people. He offered genuine kindness, not showbiz kindness. It could be too much for him, and he avoided going out in public while we rehearsed. Once I started working with him on *Secret Path*, I started receiving gifts for him, requests for photo shoots, requests for charity appearances, endorsements, etc. I can only imagine what his life was like and how overwhelming it must have been.

"I loved those days," concluded Hearn. "Hearing Gord sing, working with him again, sharing a few laughs, having deep talks about cancer. Those were precious days."

———

There was more work to be done. In December 2016, at the Gas Station on Toronto Island, Dale Morningstar recorded the debut record for a band in which Downie's 16-year-old son played drums. Downie was going to come and watch a session, but he called Morningstar to cancel. Then he said, "I really want to make one final record with you. I don't know how we're going to do it, or with who or what, or with all the guys [in the Country of Miracles] or just you." It turned out to be the Dinner Is Ruined—Morningstar, Dave Clark and John Press, who are also three-fifths of Downie's Country of Miracles. The trio went to the Gas Station one day in March 2017 and rolled tape. Downie was going to lay down some vocals in June, but Toronto Island was flooded, so Morningstar took the files to Downie's garage. "He put headphones on, and there were 20 tunes or something, and he went at it, full throttle, for an hour-and-a-half or whatever it was, because he wanted to be in the same zone we were," said Morningstar that month. "We didn't have any ideas, we had just free-styled it—so he did, too. He didn't overanalyze the words or anything; it just came out in that one night, and he's been tinkering with it since. It sounds stark and great. I'm not sure what will be added, if anything. There's something about the starkness of it."

There were other projects in various stages of completion, including an album Downie wrote and recorded with Bob Rock, a concept record about a rail derailment. But there was one very personal project he was determined to finish. In February 2017, Downie completed a second session at the Bathouse for *Introduce Yerself*, an album he started with Kevin Drew in January 2016.

Drew had been told about Downie's diagnosis on Christmas Eve, 2015. Drew took the news hard; the two men had been through a lot together in the last three years. On Christmas Day, Drew left his family dinner early and sent Downie some piano demos. Downie responded at 11:30 p.m. that night, sending the files back with vocals recorded on top. This went on for several days. Finally, Downie asked, "What are we doing here, Kev? It sounds like we're making a record." Drew wrote back: "That's what it sounds like to me."

In early January 2016, they went into the Bathouse with Dave Hamelin, engineer Nyles Spencer and Billy Ray Koster. Four days later, they had 17 songs. Most of the lyrics were written during snowy walks along the shore of Lake Ontario before each day began. "We were documenting how he was feeling, very quickly," said Drew. "There was an urgency that pushed us to create as much as we could. We knew that we needed to focus on pressing record. You couldn't say, 'Hey, it's going to be okay.' But it felt like we were creating more time by being in the studio. If this was the way that we got to be with him, then that's what we were doing." Shortly after the sessions ended, Downie had another seizure, prompting another craniotomy followed by radiation and chemotherapy. Then came the Hip rehearsals and tour, followed immediately by *Secret Path*. When sessions finally resumed in February 2017, another 10 songs were recorded in four days.

The music was unlike anything Downie had ever done. There were more than a few trace elements of *Secret Path*: Drew's sombre piano, Hamelin's soundscapes. Though there were many dead-slow, heavy-hearted numbers, there was also a playfulness on the uptempo tracks, with New Order–ish bass lines and grooves that sounded like Broken Social Scene minus the 12 layers of guitars. The songs were all love letters: to his family, friends, bandmates, his dog, to bodies of water. The tone was not unlike *Songs for Drella*, the album Lou Reed and John Cale made about their mentor, Andy Warhol, after his death; a more recent, less elegiac parallel would be Stephen Merritt's *50 Song Memoir*—though that 2017 album was released a month after *Introduce Yerself* was finished.

The title track is about an old trick to cover for memory lapse: when you can't remember someone's name, get an adjacent friend to introduce themselves, prompting the mystery person to self-identify. The song is specifically about "Billy Ray" Koster. Downie had considered having "introduce yerself" tattooed on his arm, to show to Koster if the singer was blanking during a social occasion. The entire album is Downie convening the most important people in his life and introducing them to each other— but without ever saying their names.

Introduce Yerself is also a celebration of the specific bond between Downie and Drew those last four years of the singer's life. "It means everything—he means everything to me," said Drew. "His family, the Hip and everybody took me in and were really good to me. So much love. He had so much love in the end. People leave [this world] angry—I've seen it. He did not. That was something that was so spiritually educational."

When it was released in October 2017, *Introduce Yerself* got rave reviews everywhere: including *Rolling Stone*, *Pitchfork*, the *New York Times*, the *Washington Post*—the American press that had ignored the Tragically Hip for 30 years.

———

The broadcast of the final Kingston show won several Canadian Screen Awards in March, for sound, production design, photography, performance and for Best Entertainment Special. Paul Langlois gave the acceptance speech. "The tour we did last summer was tough for all of us to do, for obvious reasons, especially that last show in Kingston that was broadcast—that was particularly difficult to get up for," he said. "Fortunately, when we hit the stage, that all fell away. It was a unique night. There were a lot of feelings circulating out there: kindness, empathy, sadness, hope, celebration and love, a sense of community. Maybe, for some, even a shared sense of Canadianness. I want to assure everyone who watched that night that none of it was lost on us. We felt it all. We all felt it. We felt your support. We felt the connection."

That awards ceremony went considerably better than the Junos, held a week later in Ottawa.

Historically, the Tragically Hip had always distanced themselves from the Junos, treating the annual industry event with suspicion and downplaying its importance. This year was different. On April 1, at the pre-broadcast ceremony, they won Rock Album of the Year for *Man*

Machine Poem, and *Secret Path* won Adult Alternative Album of the Year and Recording Package of the Year. During the telecast, Gord Downie won Best Songwriter for three songs from *Secret Path*. Though there were initial plans for him to perform, he submitted a prerecorded acceptance speech instead.

The Hip won Group of the Year, and Rob Baker and Paul Langlois were there to accept from presenters Sam Roberts and Tasha the Amazon. They used the moment to thank the tight team that had surrounded them for so long. "Some of these people we've worked with, it's been 25 or more years," said Baker. "They're family, people we love very dearly. They're the people who have the unenviable task of getting us to look good, and sound good, and get us to the gig on time. I want to thank Billy Ray, [tour manager] Tristin Chipman and [security director] Ricky Wellington. Some sound people: Mark Vreeken, Lee Moro, Jon Erickson, Juice . . . there are lighting people, catering people, caterers, drivers—every one of them deserves a thank you. They make every band roll across this country. They're the group of the year, *every* year."

Paul Langlois then took the mic, saying it was an honour to be in the same sentence as the other nominees. "To all the bands in the country who haven't been nominated—that will make you stronger," he said, as the show's director started playing music to wrap up the speech. "Oh, you're actually going to play me out? Okay," laughed Langlois, before continuing. When he started thanking family members, the music changed to one of his own songs, "Ahead by a Century." "Oh, I love this," he chuckled. "Hey, go to commercial! This is my arena, not yours! I want to shout out to Gord Downie—" With that, Langlois's mic was cut, at the exact moment he was paying tribute to his dying friend. The head of the Junos, former Universal Records exec Allan Reid, apologized the next day.

Rob Baker didn't mind at all. "It made it special to me," he said later. "Much more fun. We laughed about it. It was fine. People got worked up about it, but—c'mon." The next day, the Hip's Twitter account simply posted: "#MyArenaNotYours."

———

It was announced in June 2017 that the Tragically Hip would be appointed to the Order of Canada. This was considered to be a great honour. In fact, it was an insult.

There are three levels of the Order of Canada, the highest civilian honour in the country. The highest is "companion," which the Governor General's official website describes as recognizing "national pre-eminence or international service or achievement." Only six non-classical musicians have ever received this: Oscar Peterson, Joni Mitchell, Leonard Cohen, Gordon Lightfoot, Anne Murray and Céline Dion.

The next level is "officer," recognizing "national service or achievement." Non-classical musicians achieving this rank include k.d. lang (1996), Roch Voisine (1997), Sarah McLachlan (1999), Bryan Adams (2003), Diana Krall (2005), Shania Twain (2005), Tom Cochrane (2008), Rush (2014) and Blue Rodeo (2015).

The final level of the Order of Canada—the introductory level, if you will—is the "member," which "recognizes outstanding contributions at the local or regional level or in a special field of activity." This is what the Tragically Hip received.

Look at the Tragically Hip's peer group on those lists: k.d. lang was appointed "officer" 20 years before the Hip were appointed a mere "member." If the Hip cared about these things—which they more than likely don't—it would have been an ego bruise in their friendly rivalry with Blue Rodeo to see that band appointed "officers" the year before the Hip were considered worthy of only being "members."

If it's any consolation, Neil Young is also stuck at the "member" level, as are Raffi and the McGarrigle sisters. One can be promoted up the order: Bryan Adams and Rush both entered as members and were promoted to officers more than a decade later. The same will unlikely happen to the Hip, seeing how their career was cut short the same year as their appointment.

Something similar played out years before at the Governor General's Performing Arts Awards. In 2008, the Hip didn't win a Lifetime Achievement Award—which Michel Pagliaro received that year—but a lower-tier level called the National Arts Centre Award, meant primarily to award "work of an extraordinary nature" particularly "in the past performance year." (One has to suppose that *World Container* made a big impression on the committee—maybe Bob Rock did make "the great Canadian record" he'd always wanted.) In the years following, Buffy Sainte-Marie, Bryan Adams, Rush, Daniel Lanois, Blue Rodeo and Sarah McLachlan all received Lifetime Achievement Awards. Not the Hip.

Downie received his Order of Canada on June 19; the rest of the band on December 17. Perhaps a more suitable tribute was the one assembled by their friend George Stroumboulopoulos, who aired a special four-hour episode of *The Strombo Show* on January 1, 2017, featuring interviews with the Hip's peers and often-revelatory covers by their contemporaries and a musically diverse selection of descendants—in one case, their literal descendants in the band Kasador, featuring Rob Baker's son and Johnny Fay's nephew.

More of a book for fans. → Review on Back

Gord Downie was a haunting presence around Toronto in the final year of his life. He quietly showed up to friends' gigs: the Skydiggers' Christmas show at the Horseshoe; Julie and the Wrong Guys, featuring Julie Doiron with members of metal group the Cancer Bats; prolific singer-songwriter Daniel Romano; he was easily visible side-stage at the Field Trip festival watching Broken Social Scene, A Tribe Called Red and Feist. He went to Massey Hall for shows by PJ Harvey, Nick Cave and Spoon. He was photographed at a Maple Leafs game in April, beside Bobby Orr. At a Raptors game in May, where he had courtside seats, Downie spotted Drake and walked over to greet him. The rap superstar, the only significant Canadian artist since Downie to sing so specifically about his surroundings, bowed down and wrapped him in a warm embrace. The clip of the two seemingly incongruous, intergenerational icons instantly went viral.

There were only two onstage appearances. In February, he appeared with Blue Rodeo and the Sadies at Massey Hall, singing "Lost Together." He didn't look well. The Sadies' Travis Good covered for him on the second verse, which Downie was presumably supposed to sing; during the keyboard solo, Downie improvised a largely inaudible melody and played air guitar. As lovely as it was to see him with his comrades in the Sadies, his peers in Blue Rodeo and his old friend Colin Cripps—on the very stage that landed him his first record deal—it was bittersweet to watch.

In his very last public appearance, Downie appeared at a WE Day event as part of Canada 150 in Ottawa on July 2, once again calling on Canadian youth to reckon with the legacy of residential schools. A children's choir sang "The Stranger," the opening track from *Secret Path*. As with the blanket ceremony, the emotion and pride on his face was palpable. This, it seemed, meant much more to him than the Hip's final show or the Order of Canada or the millions of records he sold.

And then: the dancer disappeared.

September saw the release of *Long Time Running*, a documentary of the 2016 tour by Jennifer Baichwal and Nicholas de Pencier. Baichwal is the acclaimed director of visually striking documentaries like *Manufactured Landscapes*, about photographer Edward Burtynsky. De Pencier had worked for Baichwal as a cinematographer; he'd also shot Brian D. Johnson's Al Purdy documentary. Together they'd provided the interstitial visuals for the *Man Machine Poem* tour (i.e., the lightning storms during the first set break). Five days before the tour started in Victoria, the filmmakers got a call asking them to come and film the whole experience. "Make the film I've never seen," Downie told them. The movie was Downie's idea. The band was reluctant. There was enough pressure on the tour already.

Baichwal and de Pencier filmed every show, racked up 15 hours of interviews with Downie and talked to many of the band's friends and associates. The Hip had only two conditions: the directors couldn't film inside the dressing room, and there would be no on-screen interviews with the band. In the end, they agreed to both. There is a brief backstage scene in the film where they're seen dissecting the Edmonton set while undressing. There's also a beautiful scene in which a shirtless and decidedly unglamorous Downie shines his shoes and suits up before a gig, concluding with him decked out in his silver suit and looking invincible. His youngest son gives him a warm embrace. It's wonderfully intimate scene and—as per his wish—is not something ever seen before in a rock doc.

The interviews were trickier. Other than Downie, the band did not want to talk about the most difficult and emotional period of their lives on camera. "That kind of crumbled in the end," said Baker. "In post-filming, they felt they needed the interviews and we relented on that. We don't want our story told by someone else. They can tell it, and they'll have their perspective on it, but if this is going to be a final document on the band, it would be advantageous for us to have our voices in it." The Hip's voices are key; they're the entire reason the film works. Almost none of those additional interviews with peers were used: only Dr. James Perry, Patrick Downie, Bernie Breen, Patrick Sambrook and tour manager Tristin Chipman appear more than once.

Contrary to its title, *Long Time Running* is only 97 minutes. But in that time, Baichwal and de Pencier capture the drama leading up to the first gig of the tour, provide a glimpse at the band's beginnings and explore a lot of emotional terrain in between. There are only four full songs in the film—it's not a concert movie. Fans had already watched the Kingston show, so that wasn't necessary. But they pack a lot of musical snippets into a minimal amount of time, and the tracks are carefully chosen for mood and—as diehard fans would notice—for the lyrical underpinnings.

It's not a complete picture of the band; it's not meant to be. It's a human story about the long, strange summer of 2016, a unique moment in Canadian cultural history and the five men at the centre of it all. It was produced by Banger Films, which makes metal documentaries and had made the acclaimed Rush doc and HBO's Emmy-winning *Hip-Hop Evolution* series. Producers Sam Dunn and Scot McFadyen know how to tell a rock'n'roll story; Baichwal and de Pencier know how to make artful films that find beauty in the ordinary. Together, with an undeniably compelling narrative at the core, they made one of the most satisfying rock films ever made—at the very least, it was finally the film the Tragically Hip had always deserved.

At the end of the film, Rob Baker relates the following story: "I received a letter from a musician in Philadelphia. He followed the band for years, and he watched the last concert by himself. He bawled his eyes out. He said, 'Rock'n'roll and bands are like hot air balloons that go up. If you're really lucky, you get up to the jetstream and you travel really far and you see a lot. But at the end, you're going to come crashing down. There's always a bad end for a band.' He said, 'I've never seen a band—especially after a 30-year journey—land the balloon safely. They landed the balloon, and it was glorious. And everyone was there to cheer when it landed.'"

The musician in question is Dave Bielanko of the band Marah, a Springsteenian Americana band who were signed to Steve Earle's label in the early 2000s and were renowned for their live shows. As a 14-year-old Philadelphian in 1988, Bielanko bought the Hip's debut EP just because he liked their name and the cover. Though he tried in vain to turn friends on to the band, their music was very much a secret between him and his brother Serge, with whom he formed Marah years later. "Our vantage point was just so strange, being lost in America and in our own upheaval of lives," he said. "We heard rumours that this band was playing to 30,000 people. That made no sense to me. Because in my book bag, the Hip's tapes were there right beside the Dead Milkmen and Jimmy Reed and dark-horse things I've always been drawn to. They're very much a dark-horse band who pulled themselves into the light of an entire country. I think my letter gave Rob a perspective that he was probably wondering if it even existed out there. I could tell by their response that it went around the whole camp: the families, the wives, the managers. It helped them make sense of how emotional that [last show] was, and how unusual."

The weekend it opened, *Long Time Running* was No. 2 at the Canadian box office, second only to the blockbuster adaptation of Stephen King's *It*. The film ran for several weeks in most markets, a rarity in Canadian film. When it was released on DVD on December 1, 2017, the deluxe package included Bielanko's letter in full, as well as a poster inspired by the letter, designed by Steven Wishart, a fan in Barrie, Ontario.

———

The rest of the Tragically Hip showed up for the September 13 gala premiere of *Long Time Running* at the Toronto International Film Festival; Downie did not. He had every intention of performing at the Polaris Music Prize gala on September 18, an event run by one of the band's earliest supporters, former CKLC DJ Steve Jordan. *Secret Path* was on the Polaris shortlist, alongside A Tribe Called Red, Feist, Leonard Cohen, Tanya Tagaq, Weaves and eventual winner Lido Pimienta. Two weeks before, Downie called it off. Rumours started circulating around Toronto that his health was deteriorating; texts sent from friends were not returned. Obituaries were prepared, if they hadn't been already.

"We had nicknames for each other," said Kevin Hearn, of his 20-year friendship with Downie. "He was Snowman, and I was Flapjack. Over the years, every text would start with, 'Hey, Snowman.' Near the end—this was a sad day—he texted me and said, 'I know you're Flapjack, but who am I again?' I started crying."

On Sunday, October 15, 2017, windstorms of 90 km/h hit Toronto, leaving 25,000 people without hydro. "I was going to go see Gord that day," said Kevin Drew, "but his brother Pat said it was an intense time with family right now. When I saw those trees going down all over my neighbourhood and my power was out for eight or nine hours, I thought, 'He's going.'"

On Monday, October 16, Mike Downie had been scheduled to represent the Downie-Wenjack Fund at a Calgary school event. He had a plane ticket, accommodations, the students had been working on Wenjack-related projects in anticipation of his visit—but he cancelled abruptly that day. Two days later, everyone knew why.

Gordon Edgar Downie died at 9:15 p.m. on Tuesday, October 17, "with his beloved children and family close by," said an official statement released the next morning. "Gord said he had lived many lives," it continued. "As a musician, he lived 'the life' for over 30 years, lucky to do most of it with his high school buddies. At home, he worked just as tirelessly at being a good father, son, brother, husband and friend. No one worked harder on every part of their life than Gord. No one."

Exactly a year earlier, to the day, Downie had been talking to writer Ian Brown about mortality and being with his late father just before he died in October 2015. There was a long pause in the conversation. Brown watched Downie formulate his thought. "That could be my sensation as I'm going out," Downie mused. "'Oh, there's Edgar.' That'd be fabulous."

———

The day Canada learned that Gord Downie was dead, the flag on the Peace Tower on Parliament Hill flew at half-mast. There was a moment of silence in the House of Commons. The carillon bells of Parliament played "Bobcaygeon." Prime Minister Justin Trudeau shed genuine tears during a brief media scrum, rarely seen in any politician of any stripe, on any occasion. "We lost one of the very best of us," he said. "We are less of a country without Gord Downie in it. We all knew [this day] was coming but we hoped it wasn't." He paused, swallowed and his voice broke with raw emotion. "I thought I was going to make it through this, but I'm not. It hurts."

Ron MacLean of *Hockey Night in Canada* gave an interview praising not just Downie but all the Hip. "They were a hockey team," he said. "They really propped up their Gretzky. They were not jealous; they were supportive. [Gord] dealt with the audience, and they were the engine. Great team, great band, they played in a way Harry Sinden would have loved." Talking about his last conversations with Downie, MacLean said the singer's final days were an extended mission of gratitude to all those who had given him the life he led. That's when MacLean—the national voice of hockey in a country where the sport is a religion—suddenly choked up on camera, much like Trudeau earlier that day.

To paraphrase that Rolling Stones song, Gord made the grown men cry.

That night in Kingston, there was an impromptu candlelight vigil in Market Square. A few young men with acoustic guitars led the crowd in song. People lined up to sign a large scroll. Someone parked their van on the side of the square, with a TV and sound system in the back of it, and played the *That Night in Toronto* DVD. The LED display on the front of all city buses flashed the message, "We'll miss you, Gord."

Greg Keelor posted an original tribute, "Gord's Tune," written and recorded after the final Tragically Hip show: "Many a mile from where we came / but each man endures / from the days of 'shall not be the same' / til the last song fades away / Thunder and lightning / no word could explain / with the echo of this choir / falling one voice at a time." Leslie Feist posted a solo cover of "The Stranger," just as she had posted a cover of "Flamenco" the day of the diagnosis. Our Lady Peace debuted a new song, "Ballad of a Poet," about Downie.

Twitter tributes poured in: from Gordon Lightfoot ("Canada has lost one of its bright stars"), from Drake ("Rest in peace, legend"), from Arcade Fire ("a great artist and inspiration"), from Bryan Adams ("thanks for the music"), from k.d. lang ("Swift rebirth, Gord Downie") and from far less expected corners, including Chuck D of Public Enemy and—Paula Abdul. Vancouver duo Japandroids performed "Nautical Disaster" during their set at Massey Hall a couple of days later; likewise, Tori Amos covered "Ahead by a Century" at the same venue at the end of the month.

A week after Downie's death, Rob Baker and Gord Sinclair played two shows at the Isabel Bader Centre in Kingston, backing up Miss Emily Fennell, a local artist they'd been accompanying in recent years. At these shows, she played "Wheat Kings," with a palpably emotional Sinclair taking a verse and dedicating it to Wicapi Omani.

Torquil Campbell of the band Stars called into CBC Radio's Q the morning Downie's death was announced. "When I think of Gord Downie," he said, struggling through tears, "I think of a guy who would sit on guitar cases at the side of the stage at festivals all day long before he went on as a headliner, and watch every band and cheer for them and clap for them and sing their songs and know their names and tell them they were beautiful and exemplify what it means to be an artist and a citizen and a friend and a community member. And that's not just Gord, that's *everybody in the Hip*. Everybody in music and art in Canada who has ever worked with the Hip or interacted with them, everybody knows this: those gentlemen exemplify kindness, professionalism, open-heartedness, fun, warmth, strength. They really were the gold standard of how to be a band. Gord was the gold standard in how to be an artist and how to be a person."

On October 24, one week after Downie died, more than 3,000 people gathered at Nathan Phillips Square in front of Toronto City Hall, in an event organized by Choir! Choir! Choir! Led by Daveed Goldman and Nobu Adilman, this vocal ensemble/social club had a viral video hit in 2016 after conducting hundreds of David Bowie fans in a rendition of "Space Oddity," recorded at the Art Gallery of Ontario after his death; they also filled Massey Hall after Prince died so that 2,700 people could sing "When Doves Cry" together. Downie's death hit Canadian music fans just as hard as those other two icons, and so C!C!C! circulated lyrics to 10 Hip songs—and "The Stranger"—and invited everyone to the somewhat impromptu wake.

There was no choir on stage, just Goldman on acoustic guitar and Adilman nominally conducting the crowd. There were some of the expected favourites: "Gift Shop," "Bobcaygeon," "Courage," "Wheat Kings," "Last of the Unplucked Gems." Some geniuses in the crowd started chanting "Hip! Hip! Hip!" at one point, as if attempting to drown out this twee act would usher in a surprise appearance by the surviving rockers. Former Rheostatic Don Kerr altered the lyrics to "Fiddler's Green," substituting October 17—the date of Downie's death—for the September 17 in the original lyric. Comedian Pat Thornton and a buddy inexplicably clowned their way through "Poets" over the original Hip track, "combining the worst aspects of karaoke and lip synching," they boasted. It was slightly inappropriate and entirely absurd, and one couldn't help but think that the big *Trailer Park Boys* fan in Downie would have approved.

Shifting gears, a solemn Mike Downie then gave a speech thanking everyone for their support and then spoke about the Downie-Wenjack Fund. In the past year, he'd become an incredibly effective speaker, with the cadence of the best politicians. Then the studio version of "The Stranger" played over the PA; rather than singing, people mostly listened quietly and intently. The choir leaders then led everyone in "Grace, Too"—not exactly an acoustic campfire number, but they made it work.

At the back of the crowd, by the illuminated Toronto sign by the fountain, manager Bernie Breen could be seen taking videos with his phone. He'd been beside the band almost every step of the way for 33 years. Back in 1986, Breen practically lived at the house on Brock Street in Kingston where Sinclair and Downie asked their roommate, Langlois, to become the new guitarist in the Tragically Hip. He promoted their first huge hometown show, at Fort Henry. He was production manager on the 1992 tour, was tour co-ordinator for the first Another Roadside Attraction. He worked for Jake Gold in the '90s. He became the Hip's manager in 2005. He had to face the media on the day Downie's diagnosis was made public. Now, he was just like any other fan there. He stood by himself: singing a little, shuffling his feet and eventually heading home before the closing number, "Ahead by a Century," even began. He left to the sound of the crowd singing Downie's line about hailing from downtown—beneath Toronto City Hall in the town Breen and Downie had both adopted as their home.

Breen could afford to leave early: this wasn't his gig. Not anymore. There was lots to do at the office—*Introduce Yerself* was being released in three days, as had long been scheduled—but there was nothing for him to do at this show, unlike at every Tragically Hip show in the past 12 years, and hundreds before that.

Back on the stage, after 3,000 people sang "Ahead by a Century" together, Goldman and Adilman bid the crowd adieu and said the show should end with a rocker, the way the Hip always did. And so the studio recording of "New Orleans Is Sinking" started blasting over the speakers.

The people sitting on the bleachers behind the stage came down to dance while the crew packed up. The thousands-strong crowd remained in the square and sang along. Some joker even yelled, "Killer whale! Killer whale!" They all sang along to the one Tragically Hip song none of us probably ever need to hear again in our lives, but on this night, we did. The audience danced in front of the stage, as audiences always do—except now the stage was filled with people who looked just like the crowd. The performers were gone. Some kind of Elvis thing had left the building.

There was no Gord Downie here, no Tragically Hip. There never would be again. Just the everyday people, singing their songs.

ENDNOTES

Note: some material in this book first appeared in articles the author wrote for Macleans.ca and print editions of *Maclean's* between August 1, 2016, and October 18, 2017. Reprinted by gracious permission of editor-in-chief Alison Uncles, with thanks to Sue Allan, Adrian Lee and Jason Kirby.

Abbreviations used:

G&M = *Globe and Mail*

KWS = *Kingston Whig-Standard*

LTR = *Long Time Running*. Directed by Jennifer Baichwal and Nicholas de Pencier, Banger Films, 2017

TRC = *Final Report of the Truth and Reconciliation Commission of Canada, Volume One: Summary*. James Lorimer & Company, 2015.

TWTETN = Hugh MacLennan, *The Watch That Ends the Night*, Macmillan, 1958

All author interviews conducted in 2016–17 unless otherwise indicated.

Gord Downie and Gord Sinclair were interviewed in October 2000 for the book *Have Not Been the Same*; both interviews were co-conducted by Jason Schneider. The author also interviewed Downie in December 2000 for *Eye Weekly* and in 2004 for a Sarah Harmer feature in *Exclaim!* magazine.

PREFACE

"The Hip have to": *Bobcaygeon*. Directed by Andy Keen, Universal Music and Regular Horse Productions, 2012.

"It is probably a good thing": Hugh MacLennan, "Victory." *The Other Side of Hugh MacLennan: Selected Essays Old and New*. MacMillan Company of Canada, 1978.

"Anyone can write": Jane Stevenson, "The Hip must go on." Toronto Sun, Oct. 21, 2017.

"We always knew there was": LTR.

"Because I love them": Mayan Freeborn, "Don't tell me what this poet's been doing." Calgary Journal, Sept. 15, 2010.

Also referenced:

Howell, Peter. "Red-hot Hip melting its way across Canada." Toronto Star, Feb. 9, 1995.

Howell, Peter. "Fest more than just Another Roadside Attraction." Toronto Star, July 20, 1995.

Q. CBC Radio, Nov. 16, 2012.

Zivitz, Jordan. "Meaningful music can pack a wallop, too." Montreal Gazette, Nov. 27, 2004.

CHAPTER ONE: IN A BIG COUNTRY

Author interviews with Steve Berlin, Dave Bidini, Ian Blurton, Chris Brown, Jim Cuddy, Bruce Dickinson, Gord Downie (2000), Steven Drake, Kate Fenner, Mark Hebscher, Dave Hodge, Dave Levinson, Mark Mattson, Mike O'Neill, Joel Plaskett, Damian Rogers.

"Singing the world into existence": Bruce Chatwin, *Songlines*. Penguin Canada, 1987.

"Aboriginals could not believe": Ibid.

"If he was lucky enough": Margaret Atwood, *Survival*. House of Anansi, 1972.

"We hit the Canadian music scene": Greg Burliuk, "Kingston's Tragically Hip grabs 'most promising' Juno." KWS, March 19, 1990.

"I don't see *Fully Completely*": Alan Cross, liner notes to *Fully Completely* super deluxe edition. Universal Records, 2014.

"On a personal level": Ibid.

"Sometimes": Ibid.

"If you drop a stone": Hugh MacLennan, "If you drop a stone." 1952 essay from *The Other Side of Hugh MacLennan: Selected Essays Old and New.* MacMillan Company of Canada, 1978.

"Like a Molson Canadian": Burliuk, "'They're a real Canadian hard-rock kind of band.'" KWS, Feb. 7, 1995.

"One young woman": Vit Wagner, "Tragically Hip greeted with full-swing singalong." Toronto Star, June 24, 2000.

"There are few things": Al Purdy, *Rooms for Rent in the Outer Planets: Selected Poems 1962–1996.* Harbour Publishing, 1996.

"A *Heritage Moment*": Adrian Lee, "Searching for the Tragically Hip's mythical Bobcaygeon," Maclean's, July 15, 2016.

"There's an adherence to motifs": Q. CBC Radio, June 4, 2009.

"He was probably thinking": Mitch Potter, "Kingston guys take a ticket to ride," Toronto Star, March 30, 1990.

"A lot of bands have": Nicholas Jennings, "From the Hip." Maclean's, Dec. 11, 2000.

"When you have five children": Burliuk, "They're chips off the old block!" KWS, April 8, 1991.

"Songs are only half-finished": *George Stroumboulopoulos Tonight.* CBC-TV, Oct. 16, 2012.

"As a 10-year-old kid": Laurie Brown, interview with Gordon Lightfoot and Gord Downie. Soundcloud.com/gord-downie, Feb. 4, 2010.

"As if scripted": Laurie Messerschmidt, "Tory pollsters picks Kingston rock group." KWS, Jan. 28, 1988.

"We summon a sense of rage": Potter, 1990.

"We'd never be like Poison": Burliuk, "They're all for one and one for all." KWS, Feb. 22, 1991.

"KCVI is one of those schools": Sarah Crosbie, "The Tragically Hip—at home, at last." KWS, Sept. 11, 2004.

"We feel like Carrie": Chris Dafoe, "Top Junos go to James, Dion." Toronto Star, March 4, 1991.

"I've often said we're like a five-way marriage": Crosbie, 2004.

"I've always thought that if there was": Gabrielle Bossy, *Hippie Historian* podcast. June 30, 2017.

"We're basically fairly dull and regular": "The Tragically Hip," *Egos & Icons*. MuchMusic, date unknown.

Also referenced:

Connors, Stompin' Tom. *Stompin' Tom and the Connors Tone*. Viking, 2000.

Einarson, John. *American Woman: The Story of the Guess Who*. Quarry Press, 1995.

Greenwood, Therese. "Tragically Hip's status in Toronto may come as surprise to hometown." KWS, Dec. 3, 1991.

Guralnick, Peter. *Last Train to Memphis: The Rise of Elvis Presley*. Back Bay Books, 1995.

Jennings, Nicholas. *Lightfoot*. Viking, 2017.

Kelly, Cathal. "Canada's Song Bird sings a happy tune." G&M, Aug. 5, 2017.

MusicCanada.com.

TheCanadianEncyclopedia.com.

Tragically Hip live at Thunderbird Stadium. Vancouver, July 1, 1992, MuchMusic special (YouTube bootleg).

Varga, Christine. "Hip finale to festival." KWS, Aug. 30, 1999

Wharton, Edith. *The Age of Innocence*. Vintage Classics, 1920.

CHAPTER TWO: I CAN ONLY GIVE YOU EVERYTHING

Author interviews with Kris Abbott, Jeffrey Barrett, Virginia Clark, Gord Downie (2000, 2004), Jake Gold, Allan Gregg, Sarah Harmer, Peter Hendra, John Kendle, Mark Mattson, Jennie Punter, Gord Sinclair (2000).

"Love This Town," lyrics by Joel Plaskett, reprinted with permission.

"When I first": *Q*. CBC Radio, June 4, 2009.

"Grew up in a house": Gabrielle Bossy, *Hippie Historian* podcast. June 30, 2017.

"You can tell if": Ibid.

"We're just beginning": Greg Burliuk, "They're chips off the old block!" KWS, April 8, 1991.

"Taylor just has this": Jim Kelly, "Guitar summit 2000." Canadian Musician, May 2000.

"Robbie was like God": Adam St. James, "Interview with guitarist Bobby Baker of the Tragically Hip." Musician's Friend, date unknown, circa 2004.

"We played high school dances": Bossy, June 30, 2017.

"I just wanted in": Gord Downie Facebook page, live chat with fans, June 22, 2010.

"As great as that one show": Joe Pater, "Learning to rock with Gord in the Slinks." Blogs.umass.edu/pater, Aug. 18, 2016.

"We thought: 'We're a really good band'": LTR.

"From the moment I saw him": Peter Hendra, "Moves like Iggy Pop . . . swagger of Mick Jagger." KWS, May 24, 2016.

"We played the worst gigs": Ibid.

"I went up to the room": Hendra, "A wild, winding beginning." KWS, Aug. 20, 2016.

"He had seen other people": Ian McAlpine and Michael Lea, "The Tragically Hip earned success, fans say." KWS, April 11, 1991.

"I had live Police tapes": Julian Mainprize, "Percussion 2002." Canadian Musician, Nov. 2002.

"I told her I was just": Ibid.

"There's one skit": Steve Newton, "25 years ago." Ear of Newt, Oct. 26, 2014.

"Gord Sinclair writes the basic songs": Ted Emerson and Paul Faulkner, "Long-haired monsters? Just good clean boys." Queen's Journal, Oct. 1, 1985.

"A guy came up to us in London": James Cowan, "The band doesn't get Downie's lyrics either." National Post, June 17, 2002.

"What else is a judge's boy": Therese Greenwood, "From jazz to hockey rock." KWS, Feb. 29, 1992.

"I didn't like lifting gear": Bossy, June 30, 2017.

"But *this is* Thursday!": Q, June 4, 2009.

"Three stylish female dancers": Don Munro, "Hip to Head in music and muck." Queen's Journal, October 22, 1985.

"I ended my high school": LTR.

"Who are we to say": Burliuk, April 8, 1991.

"He'd been there": Sarah Crosbie, "The Tragically Hip home at last." KWS, Sept. 11, 2004.

"I can't put my life": Ibid.

"We were the name band": Greg Barr, "Tragically Hip: unaffected by all the hoopla." Ottawa Citizen, April 12, 1990.

"He knew how to play": Mark Hebscher and Liz West, *No Fun Intended* podcast. July 3, 2017.

"When the band called": Burliuk, April 8, 1991.

"Jake is far more aggressive": "Allan Gregg and Jake Gold make music their business." *Venture*, CBC-TV, 1989.

"It was really, really rough": Laurie Messerschmidt, "Tory pollsters picks Kingston rock group." KWS, Jan. 28, 1988.

"That was a bit of a blow": Burliuk, "Local band takes its shot at success." KWS, Dec. 10, 1987.

"We played at the Whippletree": Q, June 4, 2009.

"It's sort of a secondary": Bossy, June 30, 2017.

"This record can't compete": Burliuk, Dec. 10, 1987.

"The Diamond Club's manager": John Kendle, liner notes to *Yer Favourites*.
    Universal Music, 2005.

"On day three": Bossy, June 30, 2017.

"Like any rock band": Kendle, 2005.

Also referenced:

Boyden, Joseph. "'Life's too short for bad coffee.'" Maclean's, April 13, 2009.

Chiang, Jack. "On the road with the Tragically Hip rockers." KWS, April 6, 1991.

Hendra, Peter. "Blushing Brides still get satisfaction from covering Stones." KWS,
    April 21, 2017.

Krewen, Nick. "The Hip in the Hammer." Hamilton Spectator, Dec. 5, 1996.

Love, Noah. "Meet Hugh Dillon: Mr. hard-core star." KWS, Jan. 15, 2005.

Punter, Jennie. "The Hip's early years: hot times in local bars." KWS, April 10, 1991

The Tragically Hip live at the Copper Penny II. Kingston township, Ontario, 1985
    bootleg recording (YouTube).

The Tragically Hip live at the Shady Lady Disco. Renfrew, Ontario, 1987 bootleg
    recording (Soundcloud).

CHAPTER THREE: EVERYBODY KNOWS THE WORDS

Author interviews with Joe Foley, Dan Hiltz, Jeremy Hoyle, Todd Sharman.

"I can't imagine": "The fans interview the Hip." Canoe.ca, Nov. 5, 1996.

"The whole purpose of Road Apples": Robert Hough, "Not quite the Tragically
    Hip." Toronto Life, Nov. 1995.

"I don't really have a problem": Canoe.ca, Nov. 5, 1996.

"When I hear the original songs": Philip Marchand, "Shania Twin, Skinny
    Leonard." Toronto Star, Jan. 14, 2006.

"It kills me when people compare": Hough, Nov. 1995.

Also referenced:

Keeping Up with the Hip. Directed by Catherine Legge, 2006.

"Record store owner, Tragically Hip cover musician passes away from cancer."
    CTV Winnipeg, March 18, 2017.

"Winnipeg Tragically Hip cover band singer battles terminal cancer." CBC News
    Manitoba, Aug. 3, 2016.

CHAPTER FOUR: ON THE VERGE

Author interviews with Colin Cripps, Bruce Dickinson, Gord Downie (2000), Jake Gold, Allan Gregg, Steve Jordan, Michelle McAdorey, Kevin Shea.

"By walking I found out": Irving Layton, *Selected Poems 1945–89: A Wild Peculiar Joy*. McClelland & Stewart, 1982.

"It was such a weird night": Mitch Potter, "Kingston guys take a ticket to ride." Toronto Star, March 30, 1990.

"A real band you could just": Greg Burliuk, "Tragically Hip signs MCA worldwide record deal." KWS, Dec. 23 1988.

"This weird ghost town": Bob Mehr, *Trouble Boys*. Da Capo Press, 2016.

"This song is about a podiatrist": Peter Howell, "Road warriors thrash Hip-o-drome." Toronto Star, July 4, 1991.

"It had this huge, spooky effect": Potter, March 30, 1990.

"These are the things": Mark Hebscher and Liz West, *No Fun Intended* podcast. July 3, 2017.

"It sounds like there's an amplifier": Greg Barr, "Tragically Hip." Ottawa Citizen, Sept. 29, 1990.

"He's not a wild creator": Ibid.

"I remember really concentrating": Jeff Leake, *The Verge*. SiriusXM, June 17, 2016.

"It was just like a Western": Nick Krewen, "The Hip in the Hammer." Hamilton Spectator, Dec. 5, 1996.

"Someone got stabbed in the head": Ibid.

"We were always the kind of guys": *The Tragically Hip: Full-Fledged Vanity*. Directed by Don Allan, Revolver Films, 1992.

"We thought if we're going to be": Burliuk, "Kingston's Tragically Hip grabs 'most promising' Juno." KWS, March 19, 1990.

"Got to depart from the usual": Burliuk, "They're all for one and one for all." KWS, Feb. 22, 1991.

"There was a lot of bleed": "The Tragically Hip's 'Road Apples' 25th anniversary special." *Sideshow*, KRock1057.ca, June 9, 2016.

"What makes his lyrics special": Ibid.

"He was always very conscious": Hebscher and West, July 3, 2017.

"Tom Thomson's eye": Northrop Frye, *Divisions on a Ground: Essays in Canadian Culture*. House of Anansi Press, 1982.

"Gord put his thoughts on paper": *Sideshow*, June 9, 2016.

"Because the wound": Ibid.

"We talked about it": Ibid.

"It was like watching people you knew": Ibid.

"Unheard of to date": Peter Howell, "The Hip hits Hot Stove then heads for Europe." Toronto Star, May 15, 1991.

Also referenced:

"A night with the Hip in New York." CBC.ca, Aug. 19, 2016.

Barr, Greg. "The Tragically Hip go wild." Ottawa Citizen, Dec. 30, 1999.

Burliuk, Greg. "Fans jam Fort Henry for Tragically Hip, Blue Rodeo benefit gig." KWS, Aug. 30, 1991.

Newton, Steve. "The Tragically Hip bring Road Apples to the Town Pump—and that's no horseshit." Georgia Straight, Feb. 21, 1991.

Schneider, Julia. "Alone, together, band members, spouses, must accept time apart." KWS, April 9, 1991.

"The jailbreak that time forgot." Kingston Life.ca, date unknown.

The Tragically Hip Live at the Misty Moon. MuchMusic special (YouTube bootleg).

CHAPTER FIVE: ARE YOU BILLY RAY? WHO WANTS TO KNOW?

Author interview with Colin Cripps.

All "Billy Ray" Koster quotes from *The Strombo Show*, Feb. 5, 2017.

"Know Where You Go," lyrics by Greg Keelor and Jim Cuddy, reprinted with permission.

CHAPTER SIX: SOMETHING FAMILIAR

Author interviews with Colin Cripps, Bruce Dickinson, Gord Downie (2000), Peter Garrett, Jake Gold, Allan Gregg, Kevin Shea, Gord Sinclair (2000), Chris Tsangarides.

"Rock Death America," lyrics by Dave Bidini and Dave Clark, reprinted with permission.

"Wanted something to hammer the point home": Alan Cross, liner notes to *Fully Completely* super deluxe edition. Universal Records, 2014.

"This record felt like the new beginning": Ibid.

"We thought that was crazy": Ibid.

"The area was bleak": Ibid.

"We wanted to see": Ibid.

"Got compromised": Ibid.

"We spent a lot of time": Ibid.

"Her voice had a really honest": Ibid.

"Was engaged in a kind of": Charles Foran, "Shooting from the Hip." *Saturday Night*, June 1996.

"I read *Barometer Rising* first": Q. CBC Radio, June 4, 2009.

"There is no simple explanation": TWTETN.

"If someone says it's preachy": "The Tragically Hip," *Egos & Icons*. MuchMusic, date unknown.

"Castigated the national tendency": Foran, June 1996.

"It was Joyce's dogged": Cross, 2014.

"The last verse": Ibid.

"It was never 'about' one": Ibid.

"Appears first as an ageless shark": Ibid.

"I wouldn't want it misrepresented": Peter Howell, "Tragically Hip's postcard from the edge." *Toronto Star*, July 22, 1993.

"If you're in a love relationship": *Egos & Icons*.

"It's like pulling off 10 weddings": Ibid.

"Certain luxuries are afforded": Ibid.

"You want to play fascist muscleman?": John O'Callaghan, "Touring the Canadian way." G&M, July 26, 1993.

Also referenced:

Greenwood, Therese. "Hip, hip, hooray! Band debuts new songs in surprise Kingston gig." KWS, April 18, 1992.

CHAPTER SEVEN: STOLEN FROM A HOCKEY CARD

Author interviews with Dave Bidini, Mark Hebscher, Dave Hodge, Kevin Shea.

"When I lift weights": Patrick Kennedy, "Hockey and the Hip." KWS, Aug. 20, 2016.

"Back in the day": Bob McKenzie, *Hockey Confidential*, quoted in "Fully, Completely." TSN.ca, May 24, 2016.

"You could turn anything": Kevin Shea, *Barilko: Without a Trace*. Fenn Publishing, 2010.

"The noblest position": McKenzie, May 24, 2016.

"My first year playing goal": Ron MacLean, Salt Lake City Olympics coverage. CBC-TV, Feb. 23, 2002.

"My dad wasn't a hockey dad": McKenzie, May 24, 2016.

"I just admire my dad so much": Ibid.

"Living in Kingston": Ibid.

"Although he was not noted": Shea, 2010.

"I believe it's the finest": Ibid.

"I hate that Barilko": Jordan Reis, "The Tragically Hip legend of Bashin' Bill
    Barilko." *Detroit Hockey Report*, Aug. 26, 2011.

"I jumped out of my skin": Alan Cross, liner notes to *Fully Completely* super
    deluxe edition. Universal Records, 2014.

"It altered the cap": Shea, 2010.

"I was taken with the idea": McKenzie, May 24, 2016.

"Back in those days": Ibid.

"I imagine winning the Cup": Cross, 2014.

"I thought they were joking": Shea, 2010.

"There actually was a girl": McKenzie, May 24, 2016.

"It seemed to me that Dany Heatley": Ibid.

"He told me that there really wasn't much difference": Grant Lawrence, *The
    Lonely End of the Rink*. Douglas & McIntyre, 2013.

"Gord's in net": Kennedy, Aug. 20, 2016.

"As a kid growing up": Shea, 2010.

"At every Tragically Hip concert": Cross, 2014.

Also referenced:

MacLennan, Hugh. "It's the U.S. or us." Maclean's, Nov. 5, 1960.

"Dany Heatley avoids jail time." CBC Sports, Feb. 4, 2005.

CHAPTER EIGHT: YOU WANT IT DARKER

Author interviews with Colin Cripps, Gord Downie (2000), Jake Gold, Allan Gregg,
Mark Hebscher, Mark Howard, Geoffrey Kelly, Mike O'Neill, Gord Sinclair (2000),
Dave Ullrich.

"Did you want to destroy": Jimmy McDonough, *Shakey: Neil Young's Biography*.
    Anchor Books, 2002.

"Fairly sterile environment": "The Tragically Hip," *Egos & Icons*. MuchMusic,
    date unknown.

"Imagine these guys": Greg Barr, "Northern exposure." Houston Press, Aug. 3,
    1995.

"Love was the reward": Jennie Punter, "The luxury of gradual evolution." Impact,
    Jan./Feb. 1995.

"Dead brilliant": Greg Burliuk, "Hip reach new heights with fifth album." KWS,
    Sept. 24, 1994.

"There's little of the detail": Chris Dafoe, "Cryptic lyrics demand work." G&M, Oct. 17, 1994.

"That surprised us": Elizabeth Renzetti, "The Hip favour the Odds." G&M, Feb. 4, 1995.

"Because the bouncer": Peter Howell, "Red-hot Hip melting its way across Canada." Toronto Star, Feb. 9, 1995.

"In retrospect": Q. CBC Radio, June 4, 2009.

"We went to a club": Ibid.

"The size of toonies": Gabrielle Bossy, *Hippie Historian* podcast. June 30, 2017.

"That was kind of my dream": Jim Kelly, "Guitar Summit 2000." Canadian Musician, May 2000.

Also referenced:

Howell, Peter. "Tragically Hip's postcard from the edge." Toronto Star, July 22, 1993.

Lanois, Daniel. *Soul Mining*. Farrar, Straus & Giroux, 2010.

LeBlanc, Larry. "MCA gets Hip with No. 1 hit." Billboard, Oct. 15, 1994.

Wilson, Scott. "Daniel Lanois: The Mercy Seat." Magnet, 2005.

CHAPTER NINE: LET'S DEBUNK AN AMERICAN MYTH

Author interviews with Dave Bidini, Ian Blurton, Diana Bristow, Chris Brown, Brendan Canning, Cam Carpenter, Jim Creeggan, Jim Cuddy, Bruce Dickinson, Gord Downie (2000), Allan Gregg, Jake Gold, Dave Hodge, Sam Roberts, Kevin Shea, Gord Sinclair (2000), Hawksley Workman.

"In a huge country": TWTETN.

"The video came back": Christopher Ward, *Is This Live? Inside the Wild Early Years of MuchMusic, The Nation's Music Station*. Random House Canada, 2016.

"The States isn't the brass ring": "The Tragically Hip," *Egos & Icons*. MuchMusic, date unknown.

"There was no sales spike": Michael Barclay, "Stuart Berman: Broken Social Scene." Radio Free Canuckistan, Oct. 28, 2009.

"Blaring through the speakers": Austin Scaggs, "Meet the Sheepdogs." Rolling Stone, Aug. 18, 2011.

"We discovered we could do": Jeff Howe, "No Suit Required." Wired, Sept. 1, 2006.

"The word-of-mouth following": Gary Graff, "Barenaked Ladies are kings of the world." Rolling Stone, Oct. 15, 1998.

"We saw a lot of bands": Gabrielle Bossy, *Hippie Historian* podcast. June 30, 2017.

"Practically speaking": Jennie Punter, "The Luxury of Gradual Evolution."
    Impact, Jan./Feb. 1995.
"We went above and beyond": Larry LeBlanc, "Tragically Hip's live Universal set
    welcomed in Canada." Billboard, June 7, 1997.
"I never expected to sign them": Larry LeBlanc, "Sire makes Tragically Hip deal."
    Billboard, May 9, 1998.
"This is like signing R.E.M.": Larry LeBlanc, "Tragically Hip shows 'power' in
    U.S." Billboard, Aug. 8, 1998.
"We're essentially an indie act": Ben Rayner, "Canada's rock titans crash the
    hipster party." Toronto Star, March 18, 2008.
"If we were told": Jim Fusilli, "The Hip's biggest mystery: where are the U.S.
    fans?" Wall Street Journal, June 1, 2009.
"When I was in high school": "Trudeau says the Tragically Hip is 'anchored in
    Canada.'" YouTube.com/CBCNews, Aug. 20, 2016.

Also referenced:
LeBlanc, Larry. "Radio leaps for Ladies." Billboard, June 20, 1998.
LeBlanc, Larry. "Sarah McLachlan comes to the fore on Arista set." Billboard,
    June 28, 1997.
Mason, Anthony. "Sarah McLachlan is back in the game." CBS News, July 27, 2014.
"Nickelback named band of the decade." Canadian Press, Dec. 15, 2009.
Scaggs, Austin. "Welcome to Justin Bieber's world." Rolling Stone, April 29, 2010.

CHAPTER TEN: SUPER-CAPACITY

Author interviews with Ian Blurton, Brendan Canning, Gord Downie (2000), Steven Drake, Jake Gold, Ron Sexsmith.

"Water in the Well," lyrics by John Mann and Geoffrey Kelly, reprinted with
    permission.
"The lyric was": Steve Newton, "Hip at Home." Georgia Straight, Nov. 8, 1996.
"People's ears are going to race": Ibid.
"The whole verse crumbled": Ibid.
"These tours aren't like dress rehearsals": Jennie Punter, "The luxury of gradual
    evolution." Impact, Jan./Feb. 1995.
"Nobody thought it would make": Gabrielle Bossy, *Hippie Historian* podcast. June
    30, 2017.
"Without a doubt": Paul Myers, "On the road with the Tragically Hip: from the
    'henhouse' to your house." Canadian Musician, Feb. 1997.

"He's the jack of all trades": *Trouble at the Henhouse* promotional material, TheHip.com.

"Once you realize": Ibid.

"We wanted to make a record": Ibid.

"Everyone lifted it up": Bossy, June 30, 2017.

"Someone to give us validation": Myers, Feb. 1997.

"It would have been easier for us": Ibid.

"Part of that was not having": Mark Hebscher and Liz West, *No Fun Intended* podcast. July 3, 2017.

"The singer is actually no longer": Charles Foran, "Shooting from the Hip." Saturday Night, June 1996.

"The Kurt Cobain line": "The Tragically Hip," *Egos & Icons*. MuchMusic, date unknown.

"The blues are still required": *Egos & Icons*.

"There were always new songs": *Live Between Us* promotional material, TheHip.com.

"After talking it out": Larry LeBlanc, "Tragically Hip's live Universal set welcomed in Canada." Billboard, June 7, 1997.

"It was as great": *Live Between Us*, TheHip.com.

"It's not like we're claiming": Ibid.

"The mural's sentiment": Victoria Gibson, "The Tragically Hip exist all around Kingston." KWS, Aug. 21, 2016.

Also referenced:

Gerichter, Daniel. "Remembering Eden Fest's 1996 meltdown." Aux, Jan. 15, 2015.

Lawrence, Grant. "The Tragically Hip's Rob Baker at the Bathouse Recording Studio." YouTube.com/CBCMusic, July 12, 2013.

CHAPTER ELEVEN: ESCAPE IS AT HAND FOR THE TRAVELLING MAN

Author interviews with Dave Bidini, Ian Blurton, Chris Brown, Brendan Canning, Dave Clark (2000), José Contreras, Jim Creeggan, Colin Cripps, Jim Cuddy, Gord Downie (2000), Leslie Feist, Jay Ferguson, Jake Gold, Don Harrison, Michelle McAdorey, Mike O'Neill, Joel Plaskett, Sam Roberts, John K. Samson, Rich Terfry, Martin Tielli (2000), Dave Ullrich, Bry Webb.

"Young Lions," lyrics by Bry Webb, reprinted with permission.

"When we first played": *Q*. CBC Radio, Oct. 18, 2017.

"We had done an absolutely horrible": Peter Hendra, "Many bands have

439

benefitted from the Hip's 'ultimate rock-and-roll mentorship program.'"
     KWS, Aug. 20, 2016.
"It was the least thought-out": Joshua Kloke, "What it's like to tour with the
     Tragically Hip." Toronto Star, July 22, 2016.
"Easily one of the most loathed": Frederic Dannen, *Hit Men*. Vintage, 1991.
"The reality is": Damian Abraham, "How I learned to love the Tragically Hip and
     still be punk." Vice, Aug. 9, 2016.

     Also referenced:
"The fans interview the Hip." Canoe.ca, Nov. 5, 1996.
Hagan, Joe. *Sticky Fingers: The Life and Times of Jann Wenner and Rolling Stone*.
     Knopf, 2017.

CHAPTER TWELVE: THE BERLIN PERIOD

Author interviews with Steve Berlin, Chris Brown, Brendan Canning, Julie Doiron,
Steven Drake, Kate Fenner, John K. Samson, Ron Sexsmith, Gord Sinclair (2000).

"Craftsmanship," lyrics by Rich Terfry, reprinted with permission.
"And the band was on fire": *Phantom Power* promotional material, TheHip.com.
"In many ways": Steve Dawson, *Music Makers and Soul Shakers* podcast. April 11, 2017.
"They had developed this pattern": Ibid.
"They rocked so hard": Ibid.
"You could use any small town": HipMuseum.com.
"There isn't really a romantic": Adrian Lee, "Searching for the Tragically Hip's
     mythical Bobcaygeon." Maclean's, July 15, 2016.
"A bit too outside": Dawson, April 11, 2017.
"I thought Don had done": Ibid.
"We had a big balloon drop": *George Stroumboulopoulos Tonight*. CBC-TV,
     Oct. 16, 2012.
"A couple of times": Dawson, April 11, 2017.
"Steven is a wonderful human": Ibid.
"There were times": Vit Wagner, "Tragically Hip greeted with full-swing
     singalong." Toronto Star, June 24, 2000.
"It feels like a whole new band": "The Tragically Hip," *Intimate and Interactive*.
     MuchMusic, June 24, 2000.

     Also referenced:
"A 'Hip' convocation." St. Lawrence College Voyageur, fall 1999.

Bitonti, Daniel. "Remembering Toronto's Christie Pits riot." G&M, Aug. 9, 2013.

Kapoor, Desh. "Racial genocides, Aryan racism and the Aryan invasion theory." Patheos, Oct. 11, 2009.

Levitt, Cyril, and William Shaffir. "The riot at Christie Pits was a turning point." Canadian Jewish News, July 17, 2017.

CHAPTER THIRTEEN: IS IT BETTER FOR US IF YOU DON'T UNDERSTAND?

Author interviews with Kris Abbott, Steve Berlin, Ian Blurton, Chris Brown, Gavin Brown, Dave Clark, José Contreras, Colin Cripps, Steven Drake, Kate Fenner, Jake Gold, Stuart Henderson, Dave Levinson, Ryan McLaren, Rollie Pemberton, Fran Stanhope, Hawksley Workman.

"At full speed": Chris Dafoe, "Whatsit-Palooza has become an ART form." G&M, July 15, 1995. [Dafoe and his headline writer both abbreviated Another Roadside Attraction as ART, for reasons unknown.]

"I've never been so much into": Jim Kelly, "Guitar Summit 2000." Canadian Musician, May 2000.

"He's got a whole pile": Sarah Chauncey, "The Tragically Hip." Canadian Musician, Jan./Feb. 1999.

"Paul is truly one of the": Ibid.

"Definitely one of those brown kids": Chantal Braganza, "We're not Tragically Hip fans—and yes, we're Canadian." TVO.org, Aug. 25, 2016.

"This rigid definition of Canadian-ness": Ibid.

"What's with this fascism": Jesse Brown, "Greasy Jungle." *Canadaland* podcast, Aug. 25, 2016.

Also referenced:

"K-OS covers the Hip. 'I wanted to be ahead by a century.'" Q. CBC Radio, Aug. 17, 2016.

Rabin, Nathan. *You Don't Know Me But You Don't Like Me: Phish, Insane Clown Posse, and My Misadventures with Two of Music's Most Maligned Tribes.* Scribner, 2013.

CHAPTER FOURTEEN: IS THE ACTOR HAPPY?

Author interviews with Chris Brown, Dave Clark, Julie Doiron, Steven Drake, Jake Gold, Kevin Hearn, Dale Morningstar.

"You must experiment": David Mitchinson, *Celebrating Moore: Works from the Collection of the Henry Moore Foundation.* Lund Humphries, 2006.

"When Gord started doing": Jane Stevenson, "The Hip must go on." Toronto Sun, Oct. 21, 2017.

"Maybe Downie wanted": Kerry Gold, CD review of *Coke Machine Glow*. KWS, April 14, 2001.

"How someone so demanding": Robert Everett-Green, "Marriage of words, music not quite made in heaven." G&M, March 22, 2001.

"He was really the first friend": Andrew King, "Gord Downie: Inspiration from everywhere." Canadian Musician, Nov./Dec. 2010.

"They were trashing the place": Trish Crawford, "Musicians praise 'Canada's house band,' Tragically Hip." Toronto Star, Aug. 17, 2016.

Also referenced:

Klaschka, Heidi. "Tragically Hip pack 'em in getting honorary diplomas." KWS, June 19, 1999.

CHAPTER FIFTEEN: A HEART-WARMING MOMENT FOR LITERATURE

Author interviews with Gord Downie (2000), Shadrach Kabango, Hugh Larkin, David O'Meara, Rollie Pemberton, Damian Rogers, John K. Samson, Paul Vermeersch, Andrew Whiteman, Hawksley Workman.

"Like a jazz musician": Lillian Allen, *Women Do This Every Day*. Women's Press, 1993.

"Too many people think it's an elitist pastime": "David Mitchell: 'We cannot change the fact of autism, but we can address ignorance about it.'" G&M, July 21, 2017.

"We gathered around that record": "Gord Downie performs Lou Reed's 'How Do You Think It Feels.'" CBCMusic.ca, May 15, 2014.

"When I first started reading": Sean Flinn, promotional interview for *Coke Machine Glow*. Chapters.Indigo.ca, Sept. 3, 2001.

"I found that the drunk in the bar": Margaret Atwood, foreword to *Beyond Remembering: The Collected Poems of Al Purdy*. Harbour Publishing, 2000.

"Violence will get you nowhere": Al Purdy, "At the Quinte Hotel." *Rooms for Rent in the Outer Planets: Selected Poems 1962–1996*. Harbour Publishing, 1996.

"I don't really know where the songs": Scott Pinkmountain, "The Rumpus interview with Stephen Malkmus." The Rumpus, April 21, 2014.

"There is no direct address in literature": Northrop Frye, *The Educated Imagination: The 1963 Massey Lectures*. House of Anansi, 1993.

"User-friendly": "The Tragically Hip," *Egos & Icons*. MuchMusic, date unknown.

"Comparing this guy as a poet": Stuart Derdeyn, "Plan A flops for the Tragically Hip in Vancouver." Vancouver Sun, Sept. 10, 2013.

"I don't generally read": James Cowan, "The band doesn't get Downie's lyrics either." National Post, June 17, 2002.

"Is Bob Dylan a writer?": Dave Bidini, "Dylan is great but he's no literary Nobel." G&M, Oct. 13, 2016.

"There is a common sense": Craig Morgan Teicher, "Why Bob Dylan's songs are literature." New Republic, Oct. 14, 2016.

"That can be done by just pulling": Flinn, Sept. 3, 2001.

"I really do like collecting words": Ibid.

"I went to bed grumbling": Ibid.

"I use that as words": Dominic Patten, "'Ample and grateful.'" G&M, March 17, 2001.

"Must feel that he is writing": Hugh MacLennan, "Prologue: The writer and his audience." *The Other Side of Hugh MacLennan: Selected Essays Old and New.* MacMillan Company of Canada, 1978.

"Unless I miss my guess": Vit Wagner, "Hip songs, dippy words." Toronto Star, March 21, 2001.

"[Downie's] gentle irony": Kevin Connolly, book review originally in Eye Weekly, quoted on *Coke Machine Glow* page on PenguinRandomHouse.com.

"On the whole": Paul Vermeersch, *"Coke Machine Glow,"* QuillandQuire.com, May 2001.

"I hardly know anyone": Patten, March 17, 2001.

Also referenced:

At the Quinte Hotel. Directed by Douglas Bensadoun, Right Time Productions, 2002.

Charles, Ron. "Does a musician have any right to win the Nobel Prize in Literature?" Washington Post, Oct. 13, 2016.

French, Agatha. "Instapoet Rupi Kaur may be controversial, but fans and book sales are on her side." Los Angeles Times, Oct. 12, 2017.

Wheeler, Brad. "Tale of the tape: Cadence Weapon versus William Shakespeare." G&M, May 30, 2009.

CHAPTER SIXTEEN: AS MAKESHIFT AS WE ARE

Author interviews with Ian Blurton, Dave Clark, Steven Drake, Jake Gold, Allan Gregg, Hugh Padgham.

"Younger Us," lyrics by Brian King, reprinted with permission.

"I saw that there was no": David Hayes, "Song Corpse." Toronto Life, Feb. 2002.

"Song would combine": Ibid.

"We loan artists money": Ibid.

"We'd go out and see their bands": Ibid.

"It was a studied decision": Ibid.

"I had no interest in running": Ibid.

"This was a grand scheme": Larry LeBlanc, "Bankruptcy leaves industry reeling."
    Billboard, May 26, 2001.

"I'd been successful": Hayes, Feb. 2002.

"This is the single worst": LeBlanc, May 26, 2001.

"That's why you get a publishing deal": Derek Raymaker, "Going for a Song."
    G&M, July 7, 2001.

"Alan was the vision guy": Ibid.

"I had to go to summer school": Rod Christie, "The Tragically Hip." Canadian
    Musician, July/Aug. 2002.

"I got up to the mic": Robert Everett-Green, "Into the mystic with Downie."
    G&M, June 7, 2003.

"Took eight months to make": Jordan Zivitz, "Tragically Hip, happily Canuck."
    Montreal Gazette, June 20, 2002.

"I'm not a vintage snob": Christie, July/Aug. 2002.

"Hugh doesn't like to hear": Ibid.

"I would get up at my leisure": Ibid.

"In Violet Light is a solid effort": Vit Wagner, "Hipsters back in groove." Toronto
    Star, June 11, 2002.

"Suffers badly from the hands": Bill Reynolds, "The Hip breaks out the sound and
    fury." G&M, Aug. 3, 2002.

"Gord Downie seems intent": Ben Rayner, review of Battle of the Nudes. Toronto
    Star, June 19, 2003.

"If the Rolling Stones and R.E.M.": In Between Evolution promotional material,
    TheHip.com.

"We wanted to create this": Kevin Young, "The Tragically Hip: capturing the
    essence." Canadian Musician, Sept./Oct. 2004.

"I spent a year": Jordan Zivitz, "Meaningful music can pack a wallop, too."
    Montreal Gazette, Nov. 27, 2004.

"Professionally, it was a difficult": Young, Sept./Oct. 2004.

"It's something that someone": Brad Wheeler, "Thinking outside the box (set)."
    G&M, Nov. 8, 2005.

"Aside," lyrics by John K. Samson, reprinted with permission.

"I'm on my fifth record": Rayner, "Any size fits Tragically Hip." Toronto Star,
June 29, 2004.

Also referenced:
Caswell, Estelle. "How a recording studio mishap shaped '80s music." Vox, Aug.
18, 2017.
Crosbie, Sarah. "Cameron Tomsett's Hip start to a career in art." KWS, April 15,
2004.
Freeborn, Mayan. "Don't tell me what this poet's been doing." Calgary Journal,
Sept. 15, 2010.
LeBlanc, Larry. "Cargo files for bankruptcy." Billboard, Jan. 24, 1998.
LeBlanc, Larry. "Canada's Song Corp. formed." Billboard, July 17, 1999.
LeBlanc, Larry. "Canada's Song Corp. lays off more than a third of its staff."
Billboard, Jan. 20, 2001.
LeBlanc, Larry. "Peermusic/Song Corp. deal welcomed." Billboard, Dec. 7, 2002.
Saxberg, Lynn. "Tragically Hip fully and completely recharged." Ottawa Citizen,
July 10, 2015.
West, David. "Classic drum sounds: 'In the Air Tonight.'" MusicRadar, Feb. 5, 2014.

CHAPTER SEVENTEEN: THE DANCE AND ITS DISAPPEARANCE

Author interviews with Dave Bidini, Chris Brown, Brendan Canning, Shannon
Cooney, Gord Downie (2000), Steven Drake, Kate Fenner, Patrick Finn, Shadrach
Kabango, Hugh Larkin, Mark Mattson, Michelle McAdorey, Rollie Pemberton,
Sam Roberts, Rich Terfry, Bry Webb, Andrew Whiteman.

"Every activity I engage in": Alan Arkin, *An Improvised Life*. Da Capo Press, 2011.
"If you're singing well": Laurie Brown, "Gord Downie: Musician at work." *On the
Arts*. CBC Digital Archives, Feb. 11, 1999.
"I surrender": Joseph Boyden, "'Life's too short for bad coffee.'" Maclean's, April
13, 2009.
"I'd be going on and on": *Q*. CBC Radio, June 4, 2009.
"I feel like I'm playing": Steve Newton, "Hip at Home." Georgia Straight, Oct. 24,
1996.
"We're witnessing the return": Steve Newton, "Gordon Downie says opening for
the Rolling Stones is like being a golf caddy." Georgia Straight, July 2, 1995.

Also referenced:
Citron, Paula. "The wrongs of spring." G&M, June 8, 2001.

CHAPTER EIGHTEEN: ROCK IT FROM THE CRYPT
Author interview with Mark Mattson.

"I get pissed off": Chris Smith, "Bruce Almighty." Vancouver Magazine, March
    2007.
"Hey, listen, the business has changed": Bill Harris, "Bob Rock talks about new
    Hip album." Toronto Sun, Sept. 8, 2006.
"It got to me": World Container promotional material, TheHip.com.
"Was I the metalhead?": Ibid.
"Bob works the room": George Stroumboulopoulos Tonight. CBC-TV, Oct. 22, 2006.
"You begin this dogged pursuit": Ibid.
"I love Tom Petty": Ibid.
"I was probably avoiding it": Ibid.
"I like the band": Joe Bosso, "Production legend Bob Rock on 16 career-defining
    records." MusicRadar, March 1, 2013.
"We wanted to be good for Bob": George Stroumboulopoulos Tonight, Oct. 22, 2006.
"I'm more likely to call myself": Evan Solomon, "Gord Downie's caption: There's
    no dessert, mister!" G&M, June 13, 2009.
"As kids, we spent": Joseph Boyden, "'Life's too short for bad coffee.'" Maclean's,
    April 13, 2009.
"I'd lost contact": Denise Donlon, "Gord Downie uncut interview for Lake
    Ontario Waterkeeper." Lake Ontario Waterkeeper (YouTube), Dec. 20, 2013.
"Cavalier at best": Ibid.
"You can hold up a glass": Solomon, June 13, 2009.
"When we first worked with him": "The Tragically Hip at the Bathouse Pt. 1,"
    The Tragically Hip (YouTube), July 31, 2008.
"It seemed like we were": Ibid.
"'The exact feeling'": Q. CBC Radio, June 4, 2009.
"I've always been a fan": "The Tragically Hip at the Bathouse Pt. 1," July 31, 2008.
"A certain expectation": Q, June 4, 2009.
"Gord Downie and the boys": David J. Goldstein, review of We Are the Same.
    CokeMachineGlow.com, April 10, 2009.

    Also referenced:
"2005 Holiday Jam review." Hipfans.com, Dec. 15, 2005.
Reid, Scott. Review of World Container. CokeMachineGlow.com, Oct. 31, 2006.
Schliesmann, Paul. "Always read to lend a helping hand." KWS, Aug. 20, 2016.

CHAPTER NINETEEN: ARE WE THE SAME?
Author interviews with Gavin Brown, Brendan Canning, Jim Creeggan, Colin Cripps, Jay Ferguson, Michelle McAdorey, Neil Osborne, Sam Roberts, Gord Sinclair (2000).

"Retirement is not something": Q. CBC Radio, June 4, 2009.
"I don't know that a band": Brad Wheeler, "Oh baby I love your live tour." G&M, April 30, 2011.
"What the audience wants": James Keast, "Don't 'play the album.'" Exclaim!, Aug. 16, 2013.
"We made a couple of albums": David Fricke, "Peter Buck on life after R.E.M." Rolling Stone, March 14, 2016.
"Meeting expectations isn't as fun": Q. CBC Radio, Nov. 16, 2012.
"We were on a mission": Q. CBC Radio, April 21, 2017.

Also referenced:
"Episode 22.2," *This Hour Has 22 Minutes*. CBC-TV, Oct. 14, 2014.
Goodwin, Myles. *Just Between You and Me*. HarperCollins, 2016.
"Saddlesore Galactica." *The Simpsons*. Fox, Feb. 6, 2000.
The phrase "gold-watch-and-goodbye phase" is from Rebecca Mead's profile of Margaret Atwood: "The prophet of dystopia." The New Yorker, April 17, 2017.

CHAPTER TWENTY: OH YEAH, *THIS* BAND
Author interviews with Gavin Brown, Dave Clark, Julie Doiron, Sarah Harmer, Dale Morningstar, Mike O'Neill, Amanda Putz.

"Someone asked me": Andrew King, "Gord Downie: Inspiration from everywhere." Canadian Musician, Nov./Dec. 2010.
"In an hour's conversation": Stephanie McKay, "Downie inspired by collaborators in latest project." Saskatoon Star-Phoenix, Sept. 29, 2010.
"What I find interesting": King, Nov./Dec. 2010.
"Happy days collapsed": *The Grand Bounce* promotional material, Universal Records, 2010.
"I am grateful": Ibid.
"That would give me a headache": King, Nov./Dec. 2010.
"Desertion is everywhere": Vish Khanna, *Kreative Kontrol* podcast. May 10, 2010.

"You can film it on your phone": King, Nov./Dec. 2010.

"In full view of everyone": McKay, Sept. 29, 2010.

"The demos were so interesting": *The Tragically Hip: A National Celebration Post-Show*. CBCMusic.ca, Aug. 20, 2016.

"Like a massive torpedo midship": *Q*. CBC Radio, Nov. 16, 2012.

"My jobs were very menial": *George Stroumboulopoulos Tonight*. CBC-TV, Oct. 16, 2012.

"Everything [I wrote]": Ibid.

"Every song doesn't have meaning": Wendy Mesley, *The National*. CBC-TV, Oct. 13, 2012.

"Please, don't make it a cancer album": Mesley, Oct. 13, 2012.

"Where I was trying to help": Ibid.

"We decided that we needed": Joseph Boyden, "North of the 52nd with the Tragically Hip." Maclean's, Feb. 22, 2012.

"We do the Guns N' Roses version": "The members of Northern Revolution on the Great Moon Gathering." Maclean's, Feb. 29, 2012.

"You mean you guys": Gord Downie, "Gord Downie on playing 'Knockin' on Heaven's Door' at the Great Moon Gathering." Maclean's, Feb. 29, 2012.

"I'm trying to paint a picture": *Q*. Nov. 16, 2012.

"The song is about a band": Ibid.

"Kingston City Council voted": Ibid.

"The additional letters": "New sign makes it The Tragically Hip Way." KWS, April 19, 2012.

"Hey, Gilmour!": Patrick Kennedy, "Hockey and the Hip." KWS, Aug. 21, 2016.

"Some of them wanted to try": *The Tragically Hip: A National Celebration Post-Show*. Aug. 20, 2016.

"I asked her which of her talents": Alan Arkin, *An Improvised Life*. Da Capo Press, 2011.

"Wow, we're in it": Andrea Warner, "Weird genius." CBC Music, Aug. 12, 2016.

"Verging on caricature": Stuart Derdeyn, "Plan A flops for the Tragically Hip in Vancouver." Vancouver Sun, Sept. 10, 2013.

"Generation," lyrics by Mike Haliechuk, reprinted with permission.

Also referenced:

Boyden, Joseph and Amanda. "Joseph Boyden's seven love songs for Gord Downie." Maclean's, Aug. 23, 2016.

Cuthbert, Glen. "Tragically Hip plays Hamilton backyard birthday bash." Hamilton Spectator, July 13, 2015.

Morris, Paul. "Interview with Paul Langlois." 97.7 HTZ-FM (Soundcloud), date unknown.

Parpart, Lee. "Rockin' with art." KWS, Sept. 13, 1997.

Saxberg, Lynn. "Strippers Union takes wraps off musical partnership." Ottawa Citizen, June 22, 2005.

Schliesmann, Paul. "Tragically Hip Way it is." KWS, Feb. 21, 2012.

Simpson, Peter. "Hip guitarist switches to Plan B." Winnipeg Free Press, Nov. 18, 2013.

CHAPTER TWENTY-ONE: THE INEVITABILITY OF DEATH

Author interviews with Steve Berlin, Brendan Canning, Chris Brown, José Contreras, Jim Creeggan, Stephen Dame, Kate Fenner, Patrick Finn, Emma Godmere, Sarah Harmer, Mark Mattson, Sam Roberts, Nick Taylor-Vaisey, Rich Terfry.

"It takes the greatest": Northrop Frye, "I, Romeo and Juliet." *Northrop Frye's Writings on Shakespeare and the Renaissance*. University of Toronto Press, 2010.

"All of my patients": News conference on Gord Downie's terminal brain cancer diagnosis. Global TV, May 24, 2016.

"Can't speak for Canada": Ibid.

"They are two guys": Lynn Saxberg, "Tragically Hip fully and completely recharged." Ottawa Citizen, July 10, 2015.

"I think [Downie] trusted us": George Stroumboulopoulos *The Strombo Show*. CBC-Radio, Dec. 18, 2016.

"I just really want": Ibid.

"They play all your songs": Ibid.

"When you're a 25-year-old kid": Jeff Leake, *The Verge*. SiriusXM, June 17, 2016.

"There's lots of room": Ibid.

"I would just sit and listen": *The Strombo Show*, Dec. 18, 2016.

"Dave and Kevin were very funny": Leake, June 17, 2016.

"It seemed like a natural leadoff": Ibid.

"Hand with fingers": Sarah Liss, *Army of Lovers: A Community History of Will Munro*. Coach House Books, 2013.

"We were supposed to tour, right?": LTR.

"The resale factor was so bad": Francois Marchand, "Tragically Hip's penultimate Vancouver show possessed by the human mind." Vancouver Province, July 25, 2016.

"We would finish a song": LTR.

"Don't tell Gord": Ibid.

"I never thought it was going to happen": Ibid.

"It was the rare thing": Ibid.

"There are a whole bunch of people": Jon Dekel, "'It's unbelievable.'" CBCMusic
.ca, Aug. 18, 2016.

"Breathe easy": Mike Devlin and Katherine Dednya, "For Tragically Hip fans, a
sign of relief." Victoria Times-Colonist, July 22, 2016.

"He'd had all this weight": LTR.

"It's unbelievable": Dekel, Aug. 18, 2016.

"When I wondered": Sheryl Ubelacker, "Gord Downie's lead oncologist, longtime
Tragically Hip fan, a mainstay on tour." Canadian Press, Aug. 11, 2016.

"It was pretty intense": George Stroumboulopoulos *The Strombo Show*. CBC-
Radio, Feb. 5, 2017.

"I was really worried": Mark Hebscher and Liz West, *No Fun Intended* podcast.
July 3, 2017.

"It just goes to show": "Winnipeg woman with terminal brain cancer
overwhelmed by Tragically Hip ticket offers." CBC News Manitoba,
June 7, 2016.

"I'm not counting Gord down and out": "Winnipeg Tragically Hip cover band
singer battles terminal cancer." CBC News Manitoba, Aug. 3, 2016.

"At the last night in Kingston": Hebscher and West, July 3, 2017.

Also referenced:

Berman, Stuart. *This Book Is Broken: A Broken Social Scene Story*. House of Anansi, 2013.

Butterfield, Yaron Sidney. "Cancer survivor and Hip fan shares his love and hope
with Gord Downie." Toronto Star, Aug. 26, 2016.

Chen, Dalson. "Former Windsorite engineers sound for historic Tragically Hip
concerts." Windsor Star, Aug. 18, 2016.

Common, David. "'The whole system is rigged.'" CBCNews.ca, Oct. 22, 2016.

Dysart, Pat. "In conversation with Mark Vreeken." HHB Canada, Jan. 16, 2015.

Gibson, Victoria. "No distance too far to watch Hip concert." KWS, Aug. 20, 2016.

King, Andrew. "A fond farewell." Professional Sound, October 2016.

Kirkey, Sharon. "Dreaded diagnosis: Gord Downie's tumour one of the worst
known to medicine." National Post, May 24, 2016.

Lau, Melody. "Canadian designer Izzy Camilleri reveals process behind Gord
Downie's dazzling suits." CBC Music, Aug. 3, 2016.

"Sad but joyful." CBC News Sudbury, Sept. 5, 2016.

"Tragically Hip fan Joanne Schiewe dead of same brain cancer Gord Downie has."
CBC News Manitoba, Aug. 30, 2016.

Weldon, Tori. "Hip concert 'etched on my heart,' says fan with same cancer as
Gord Downie." CBCNews.ca, Aug. 22, 2016.

CHAPTER TWENTY-TWO: EXIT, STAGE 5

Author interviews with Jim Cuddy, Jay Ferguson, Don Harrison, Teva Harrison, Kevin Hearn, Dave Hodge, Geoffrey Kelly, Sarah Liss, Michelle McAdorey, Gabe Roth.

The Sharon Jones section was adapted from the author's story in the Globe and Mail, Nov. 13, 2017, "The life and death of Sharon Jones's new album." Courtesy Barry Hertz.

"I believe that the purpose": Laurie Anderson, "Laurie Anderson's farewell to Lou Reed." Rolling Stone, Nov. 6, 2013.

"Little did I know": TWTETN.

"I woke up in pain": Paul Kalanithi, *When Breath Becomes Air*. Random House, 2016.

"I want to go out with a bang": *Spirit Unforgettable*. Directed by Pete McCormack, Little Kingdom Productions, 2016.

"It's not an unknown phenomenon": Laura Fraser, "Despite Alzheimer's, Spirit of the West's John Mann still 'has a memory for melody.'" CBC News, June 2, 2016.

"I know there are people": *Glen Campbell: I'll Be Me*. Directed by James Keach, PCH Films, 2014.

"It's almost as if by thrusting himself": Stuart Berman, review of *Skeleton Tree*. Pitchfork, Sept. 14, 2016.

"After a time": *One More Time with Feeling*. Directed by Andrew Dominik, Iconoclast, 2017.

"The big problem with a film like this": Caitlin White, "Nick Cave's gripping *One More Time with Feeling* documentary bridges grief's chasm." Uproxx, Dec. 12, 2016.

"Nobody has ever described": TWTETN.

"Doctors to communicate a cancer diagnosis": Susan Sontag, *Illness as Metaphor*. Farrar, Straus & Giroux, 1978.

"People know it's a cancer": "Layton's family still mum on his cause of death." Canadian Press, Aug. 21, 2012.

"We're encouraged to slip away": Teva Harrison, *In Between Days*. House of Anansi, 2016.

"More hunger for life": Ibid.

"If need be": TWTETN.

"That whole chapter in Will's life": Sarah Liss, *Army of Lovers: A Community History of Will Munro*. Coach House Books, 2013.

"He was being such an asshole": Liss, 2013.

"He just came fresh": Brian Hiatt, "David Bowie planned post-*Blackstar* album, 'thought he had a few more months.'" Rolling Stone, Jan. 13, 2016.

"People are so desperate": Hannah Ellis-Petersen, "David Bowie did not know he was dying until final few months." The Guardian, Jan. 6, 2017.

"For now, I'm in remission": Hiatt, Jan. 13, 2016.

"I immediately said": Ellis-Petersen, Jan. 6, 2017.

"I hadn't seen Phife": Touré, "Loss haunts A Tribe Called Quest's first album in 18 years." The New York Times, Nov. 2, 2016.

"Doing this album": Ibid.

"Not specifically": Brian D. Johnson, "Leonard Cohen's third act." Maclean's, Sept. 21, 2016.

"There were only a few": Ibid.

"I'm not much of an optimist": Ibid.

"I know he wanted": Lydia Hutchinson, "Rick Rubin." Performing Songwriter, March 9, 2011.

"So am I supposed to die": Crystal Zevon, *I'll Sleep When I'm Dead*. Ecco, 2007.

"My job is music": Ibid.

"We have to go into showbiz mode": Ibid.

"Excuse me, I have terminal cancer": David Fricke, "Warren Zevon and the art of dying." Rolling Stone, Nov. 28, 2002.

"Do they still make EPs?" Zevon, 2007.

"If I can let someone know": "Warren Zevon," *Inside Out*. VH1, 2004.

"Playing your own wake": Ibid.

"More cancer in him": Hua Hsu, "Stir it up." The New Yorker, July 24, 2017.

"To really think of what energy": Steve Appleford, "Lemmy's last days." Rolling Stone, Dec. 29, 2015.

"Here's the shocker": Ibid.

Also referenced:

Carney, Kat. "Musician fights leukemia, and wins." CNN.com, Sept. 16, 2003.

Greene, Andy. "The inside story of David Bowie's stunning new album, Blackstar." Rolling Stone, Nov. 23, 2015.

Rosen, Jody. "Johnny Cash, cornball." Slate, Aug. 15, 2006.

CHAPTER TWENTY-THREE: THE STRANGER

Author interviews with Mitch Champagne, Jeremy Hoyle, Hayden King, Mark Mattson.

All Mike Downie quotes from episode 88 of *Welcome! with Karim Kanji*, July 26, 2017.

"The Art of Patrons," lyrics by Damian Abraham, reprinted with permission.

"Charlie had more than half": Ian Adams, "The lonely death of Charlie Wenjack." Maclean's, Feb. 1967.

"An Indian kid who had been found": Jody Porter, "Meet the journalist who inspired Gord Downie and Joseph Boyden to write about Chanie Wenjack." CBC News, Oct. 21, 2016.

"He didn't think that my kind of writing": Ibid.

"At least 33 students died": TRC.

"Parental requests to have": Ibid.

"The parents were crying": "The road to reconciliation transcript." CBC Arts, Nov. 6, 2016.

"Kids were abducted": Ibid.

"Down south, none of us": *Gord Downie's Secret Path*. Directed by Mike Downie, CBC Arts, Oct. 23, 2016.

"When I came to take my place": TRC.

"To undertake a healing process": "Phil Fontaine's shocking testimony of sexual abuse." *The Journal*, CBC Archives, Oct. 30, 1990.

"Were based on the assumption": "Statement of apology to former students of Indian Residential Schools." Aadnc-aandc.gc.ca, June 11, 2008.

"Stripped white supremacy": TRC.

"Ongoing public education": Ibid.

"To be a white Canadian": Lee Maracle, *My Conversations with Canadians*. Book Thug, 2017.

"Sometimes—perhaps at the tentative fall": Douglas LePan, "A country without mythology." Quoted in Margaret Atwood's *Survival*. House of Anansi Press, 1972.

"Do you just sit in the basement": Paul Tukker, "'Heartbreaking.'" CBC News, Oct. 20, 2017.

"Look around this room": Video accompanying Ian Brown's "What happens next." Globeandmail.com, Oct. 21, 2016.

"Before the performance started": Hayden King, "The Secret Path, reconciliation and not-reconciliation." Biidwewidam.com, Oct. 19, 2016.

"He is the right person": *Gord Downie's Secret Path*, Oct. 23, 2016.

"Wasted his life telling people": Porter, Oct. 21, 2016.

"We can talk all we want": "The road to reconciliation transcript." Nov. 6, 2016.

"He knows what it's like": *Gord Downie's Secret Path*, Oct. 23, 2016.

"Personal fame counts for nothing": Rebecca Newberger Goldstein, "Making
    Athens great again." The Atlantic, April 2017.
"All I can do is say": Jennie Punter, "The luxury of gradual evolution." Impact,
    Jan./Feb. 1995.
"We're here to honour Gord": Aaron Brophy, "Gord Downie honoured by
    Assembly of First Nations in emotional ceremony." Samaritan Mag,
    Dec. 6, 2016.
"This is the first day of forever": Ibid.
"Here we have a highly recognized": Austin Josephson, "AFN conference explored
    ways of advancing reconciliation." Treaty 4 News, Dec. 14, 2016.
"I don't think being non-Native": Joshua Kloke, "Indigenous artists tell us how
    they feel about Gord Downie's activism." Vice, Oct. 13, 2016.
"Given Gord's cancer diagnosis": Candy Palmater, "Gord Downie was celebrated
    for championing Indigenous rights. Now that he's gone, do people still care?"
    Chatelaine, Dec. 4, 2017.
"At the Governor-General's ceremony": Clayton Thomas-Müller, "Gord Downie,
    when it comes to collective Indigenous resilience, let us speak for ourselves."
    CBC Opinion, June 28, 2017.
"The white man will only listen": Brown, Oct. 21, 2016.
"Whether it be the CBC": Joseph Boyden, "My name is Joseph Boyden."
    Maclean's, Aug. 2, 2017.
"Had to trust that voice": Eric Andrew-Gee, "The making of Joseph Boyden."
    G&M, Aug. 4, 2017.
"Talented outsider": "Indigenous identity and the case of Joseph Boyden," The
    Current. CBC Radio, Jan. 5, 2017.
"A small part of me": Boyden, Aug. 2, 2017.
"I've never claimed": Mark Medley, "The all-star." G&M, April 21, 2017.
"I don't know if I should have": "Jeff Lemire wants to expand beyond the
    'idealized Canada' in his stories," Q. CBC Radio, April 17, 2017.
"In no way do I mean to disrespect": Palmater, Dec. 4, 2017.

Also referenced:
Barrera, Jorge. "Author Joseph Boyden's shape-shifting Indigenous identity."
    APTNnews.ca, Dec. 23, 2016.
Brown, Laurie. "If you could read my mind: Gordon Lightfoot and Gord
    Downie." Presented by Canadian Songwriters Hall of Fame (Soundcloud
    .com/gord-downie), Feb. 4, 2010.
Elliott, Alicia. "The year in reconciliation." Hazlitt, Dec. 13, 2017.

Friesen, Eric. "Joseph Boyden: A spirited voice." Nuvo, May 28, 2011.

Friscolanti, Michael. "The other residential school runaways." Maclean's, Oct. 20, 2016.

Macdonald, Nancy. "Canada's prisons are the 'new residential schools.'" Maclean's, Feb. 18, 2016.

Metatawabin, Edmund, and Alexandra Shimo. *Up Ghost River: A Chief's Journey Through the Turbulent Waters of Native History*. Vintage Canada, 2014.

Ohayon, Albert. "Cold Journey: a feature on residential schools." Blog.nfb.ca, June 9, 2017.

"Public Opinion on Aboriginal Peoples in Canada: Final Report June 2016." Environics Institute, June 30, 2016.

Snow, Rachel A. "Improper educational materials distort history." Two Row Times, June 26, 2017.

Talaga, Tanya. *Seven Fallen Feathers: Racism, Death and Hard Truths in a Northern City*. House of Anansi, 2017.

Vowel, Chelsea. *Indigenous Writes: A Guide to First Nations, Métis and Inuit Issues in Canada*. Portage & Main Press, 2017.

Wherry, Aaron. "The Hip rocks on with their 10th studio record." National Post, June 23, 2004.

CHAPTER TWENTY-FOUR: THAT NIGHT IN KINGSTON

Author interviews with Kris Abbott, Sam Baijal, Ian Blurton, Brendan Canning, Dave Clark, Virginia Clark, José Contreras, Shannon Cooney, Jim Creeggan, Colin Cripps, Stephen Dame, Bruce Dickinson, Vince Ditrich, Julie Doiron, Steven Drake, Kate Fenner, Patrick Finn, Jake Gold, Allan Gregg, Mark Hebscher, Dave Hodge, Tony Ingram, Jeff Johnson, Jerome Johnson, Keith Johnson, Steve Jordan, Shadrach Kabango, Hayden King, Hugh Larkin, Michelle McAdorey, Dale Morningstar, Lucas Murray, Mike O'Neill, Neil Osborne, Rollie Pemberton, Dee Peters, Moe Peters, Jennie Punter, Keeley Renwick, Sam Roberts, Bob Stanhope, Fran Stanhope, Jason Stanton, Steve from Toronto, Chris Tsangarides, Dave Ullrich, William Walton, Bry Webb, Andrew Whiteman.

"If I'm lucky": Raymond Carver, *All of Us: The Collected Poems*. Alfred A. Knopf, 1998.

"Your country seems to be": Elizabeth Renzetti, "What's not to love about the Tragically Hip?" G&M, Nov. 20, 1992.

"The idea of 'remembering'": Alan Cross, liner notes to *Fully Completely* super deluxe edition. Universal Records, 2014.

"An insistence on living": Robert Morrison, "Remembering Gord Downie through his lyrics." The Conversation, Aug. 17, 2017.

"I was quite literally crying the whole summer": Steve Dawson, *Music Makers and Soul Shakers* podcast. April 11, 2017.

"I watched the concert on TV": Chantal Braganza, "We're not Tragically Hip fans—and yes, we're Canadian." TVO.org, Aug. 25, 2016.

CHAPTER TWENTY-FIVE: THE LUXURY

Author interviews with Dave Bielanko, Kevin Hearn.

"It was almost a law": Tess Gallagher, introduction to *A New Path to the Waterfall*, by Raymond Carver. Atlantic Monthly Press, 1989.

"Because I don't know": *The National*. CBC.ca, Oct. 13, 2016.

"I want my kids to be good:" Ibid.

"I mentioned it a lot in lyrics": Ibid.

"If this is the last thing": Ian Brown, "What happens next." G&M, Oct. 21, 2016.

"What are we doing here?": Simon Vozick-Levinson, "Gord Downie, a Canadian rock legend, sings goodbye." The New York Times, Oct. 18, 2017.

"We were documenting": Ibid.

"It means everything": *Metro Morning*. CBC Radio Toronto, Nov. 22, 2017.

"It made it special": Mark Hebscher and Liz West, *No Fun Intended* podcast, July 3, 2017.

"Make the film I've never seen": "Gord Downie's direction to Jennifer Baichwal." TIFF.net, Sept. 14, 2017.

"That kind of crumbled": Hebscher and West, July 3, 2017.

"I received a letter": LTR.

"I was going to go see": *Metro Morning*. Nov. 22, 2017.

"That could be my sensation": Brown, Oct. 21, 2016.

"They were a hockey team": "'He was our Shakespeare:' Ron MacLean remembers Gord Downie." CityNews.ca, Oct. 18, 2017.

Also referenced:

"Power restored to most customers after heavy winds hit Toronto on Sunday." CityNews.ca, Oct. 15, 2017.

INDEX

ACKNOWLEDGEMENTS

I owe an enormous debt to my co-authors on *Have Not Been the Same*, Jason Schneider and Ian A.D. Jack, without whom this book would not ever have seemed possible or come to fruition. It was Jason's encouragement in particular that first made me envision bigger pictures when we both worked at *Id Magazine*, when his Hip fandom fuelled mine when it was about to go dormant. It was with Jason that I first interviewed Gord Downie in a Syracuse hotel room in 2000, and then Gord Sinclair on the band's tour bus later that day. It was Jason who wrote the Hip chapter in *Have Not Been the Same*, and who deserves all the credit for writing the first serious biographical work about the band. I highly recommend his follow-up book, *Whispering Pines*—every fan of Canadian music should own a copy. It's available from ECW Press.

This project exists because ECW editor Michael Holmes said yes. It wasn't the first time. In 2000, he and Jen Hale took a chance on a massive project by three unpublished writers. In 2017, his faith and support allowed this project to be what it is: thorough, unrushed and more than just a straight-up biography. And though I spent years as a professional copy editor myself, the eyes and wisdom of Laura Pastore and Crissy Calhoun were badly needed and deeply appreciated.

Thank you all who shared their time and memories with me for this book, both on and off the record; this story would not have been possible without you—because this story is as much about you as it is the Tragically Hip. Thank you to those who agreed to talk but to whom I didn't have time to respond. And thanks to those who declined to be interviewed but agreed to answer some fact-checking questions and/or provide invaluable guidance. Thank you as well to all those who respectfully declined my requests, for at least getting back to me. To everyone else in this story: I hope this book reflects your own memories and experiences. Chris Tsangarides: rest in power (chords).

The help of these six lovely people was indispensible to this project, and I cannot thank them enough for their eyes, their ears, their advice and their valuable time: Stephen Dame, Colton Eddy, Steve Jordan, Krista Muir, Tanis Rideout, Dianna Symonds.

I had the immense pleasure of working at *Maclean's* for eight years, 2008–16. Thanks to Jen Cutts for her friendship, her intelligence and for making that happen. I worked with brilliant writers there from whom I learned firsthand the art of masterful storytelling: Paul Wells, Anne Kingston, Nicholas Köhler, Nancy Macdonald, Michael Friscolanti, Ken McQueen, Allen Abel and many, many more—but especially Brian D. Johnson, whose writing, support and musical gifts have been an inspiration (be sure to see his film, *Al Purdy Was Here*). Thanks also to the brilliant editors for, among other things, believing in their copy editor: Mark Stevenson, Sarmishta Subramanian, Sue Allan, Alison Uncles, Kim Honey. Thanks to Adrian Lee for the depth of his talent and his support. Thanks especially to Patricia Treble, one of the smartest people I'm ever likely to meet, who has taught me so much about skill and determination. Peeter Kopvillem R.I.P.

In 2000, Patti Schmidt cold-called me one day and offered me a dream job at CBC Radio's *Brave New Waves*, writing for the radio show that changed my life, more than once, in almost every way. Why she wanted a conservative Canuckophile to work on such an innovative show still baffles me. Writing scripts for her made me a better writer and a more curious person. I'm 100 percent positive she hates the Tragically Hip, as do my fiercely talented former co-workers there, Yuani Fragata and Gordon Krieger, and yet this book owes a debt to my experience working beside them. And thank you to Grant Lawrence for abandoning me on several overnight occasions in the CBC Vancouver studios, trusting me to program, host and engineer eight hours of national radio all by my lonesome. I hope I "still got it."

Thank you to the outlets where I started out: *The Ontarion*, *Id* magazine, *Exclaim!*, *Eye Weekly*, CFRU, the *Waterloo Region Record*. Philip Bast R.I.P. Thank you to the broadcasters who inspired me as a teenage music geek, especially Brent Bambury, Laurie Brown, Brian Linehan, Daniel Richler, Bob Mackowycz Sr., David Wisdom.

Thank you to my dear friend Paul Mora, with whom I saw my first Tragically Hip gigs in 1988–91. He also gave me my first accordion. He has a lot to answer for. Thank you also to my dear old friend William Hare, who is 10 times the musician I could ever hope to be.

Thank you to all the musicians I've had the immense pleasure to play with in my life. Every rehearsal, every gig, means the world to me. There is no thrill greater than making music with such talented and beautiful people.

Thank you to my fellow Polaris Music Prize jury members, past and present, for caring about new Canadian music every day.

Thank you to Dave Bidini for his support from the very beginning of my career—even when I wrote things he didn't like—and for nurturing new generations of writers and musicians in this country.

This book would not have been come together so quickly without the endless resources of the Toronto Public Library, the fan community at HipBase.com and HipMuseum.com, and those who share their audio archives online.

Thank you to Stuart Berman and Caryn Ganz for getting me into the Kingston show, and to Virginia Clark and Chris Brown for their hospitality, company and conversation.

Thank you as well—for pro tips, interview leads, life hacks and peace of mind—to: The 507 in the 705, Eric Alper, Ian Brown, Cam Carpenter, Ro Cemm, Judith Coombe, Mary Dickie, Tim Falconer, Paul Faulkner, Cori Ferguson, Emma Godmere, Megan Griffith-Greene, Jeff Harris, Tom Harrison, David Hayes, Stuart Henderson, Peter Hendra, Barry Hertz, Kevin Howes a.k.a. Sipreano, Joanne Huffa, Nicholas Jennings, Stew Jones, John Kendle, Atsuko Kobasigawa, Jeff Leake, David Leyes, Biserka Livaja, Maggie MacDonald, Nancy Macdonald, Mark Mattson, Jason McBride, Paul McEwan, Stephen McGrath, Colin Medley, Shawn Micallef, Lindsay

Michael, Sean Michaels, Josh O'Kane, Angie Pajek and Karl Kannstadter, Tim Powis, Amanda Putz, Don Pyle, Anicka Quin, Simon Racioppa, Marko Shark, Tabassum Siddiqui, Bozena and Jan Spitzer, Jane Stevenson, Liz Sullivan, Kurt Swinghammer, Andrew Tolson, Graham Walsh, Jessica Whyte, Carl Wilson, Michael Philip Wojewoda, Barb Yamazaki.

Finally: the love, faith, support, wit, wisdom, pride and—most important—the patience of Helen Spitzer was essential to *The Never-Ending Present*, a title she chose and I'm thankful for it. In 2009, *We Are the Same* rekindled her own relationship with the Hip's music, which reminded me, yet again, that I should never take this band—or anything or anybody I love—for granted. That includes Judy, Walter, Patrick and especially Leonard.

Thanks to all involved in making the Toronto book launch so unforgettable: Lana Gay, Ian Blurton, Aaron Goldstein, Ryan Gassi, Caitlin Dacey, Sean Dean, Owen Pallett, Michelle McAdorey, Nirmala Basnayake, Mike O'Neill, Tom Wilson, Tony Dekker, Sate. Also Terra Lightfoot, Bob Ciolfi, Ian Daffern, Debby de Groot.

Thanks to all not mentioned earlier who helped make the national book tour such a success, on-stage and off: Wilma Aalbers, Mary Barlow, Darlene Barss, Jessy Bell-Smith, Moe Berg, Michael Brown, Melanie Buddle, Mike Campbell, Nick Craine, Tawny Darbyshire, Douglas Davey, Cynthia Dennis, Brent DeNure, Julie Doiron, Chris Eaton, Dennis Ellsworth and the Fabulously Rich, Francella Fiallos, Patrick Finn, Steven Foord, Colin Fowlie, Fish Griwkowsky, Sheila Gruner, Steve Haley, John Wort Hannam, Amber Healy, Tanya Hobbs, Jeremy Hoyle and Strictly Hip, Dylan Hudecki, Michael Hunter, Rob Jenkins, Danko Jones, Stewart Jones, John Kendle, Vish Khanna, Rolf Klausener, Hanita Koblents, Tyler Kyte, Steve Lambke, Mark Mattson and the National Water Centre, Chris Mazenc, Bob Mersereau, Dan McDonald, Will McGuirk, Jamieson McKay, Stephanie McKay, Jon Mckiel, Ryan McNutt, David McPherson, Claude Munson, Ken Murray, Joe Nolan, Trevor Norris, Steve Packer, Richard Reed Parry, Sandra Patrick, Julie Penner, Wayne Petti, Stéfanie Power, Courtney Pyrke, Ian Reid, Dustin Ritter and his entire Regina crew, Alessandro Rotondi, Matias Rozenberg, Mark Sasso, Lisa Savard-Quong, Sideshow, Mike Spencer, Laurel Sprengelmeyer, Luka Symons, Mike Tutt, Heather Valley, Klarka Weinwurm, Paul Wells, Stewart Whitehead, Jill Wilson, Jan Wong, and everyone else who helped along the way. Thank you for your belief in me, in this project, and in this story. Thank you for creating such a vibrant culture in this small world inside a big country.

MICHAEL BARCLAY sings "whoa-oh" backing vocals on an internationally successful Canadian song, and plays accordion somewhat adequately. He is a co-author of *Have Not Been the Same: The CanRock Renaissance 1985–95* (ECW Press).